The foundations of artificial intelligence

The foundations of artificial intelligence
A sourcebook

Edited by

Derek Partridge
Department of Computer Science, University of Exeter
and

Yorick Wilks
Computing Research Laboratory, New Mexico
State University

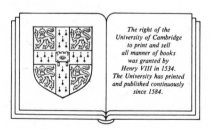

The right of the
University of Cambridge
to print and sell
all manner of books
was granted by
Henry VIII in 1534.
The University has printed
and published continuously
since 1584.

CAMBRIDGE UNIVERSITY PRESS
Cambridge
New York   Port Chester   Melbourne   Sydney

Published by the Press Syndicate of the University of Cambridge
The Pitt Building, Trumpington Street, Cambridge CB2 1RP
40 West 20th Street, New York, NY 10011, USA
10 Stamford Road, Oakleigh, Melbourne 3166, Australia

First published 1990

Printed in Great Britain at the University Press, Cambridge

British Library cataloguing in publication data
The foundations of artificial intelligence: a sourcebook.
1. Artificial intelligence
I. Partidge, D. (Derek), *1945–*
II. Wilks, Yorick Alexander
006.3

Library of Congress cataloguing in publication data
The foundations of artificial intelligence: a sourcebook /
    edited by Derek Partridge and Yorick Wilks.
        p.   cm.
"Selected papers and subsequent discussion from a NSF-supported
    workshop on the foundations of AI held in Las Cruces,
    New Mexico, in 1986" – Pref.
Bibliography.
Includes index.
ISBN 0–521–35103–0. – ISBN 0–521–35944–9 (paperback)
1. Artificial intelligence.
I. Partridge, D. (Derek), 1945– .
II. Wilks, Yorick, 1939– .
0335.F68   1989
006.3 – dc20   89–7321 CIP

ISBN 0 521 35103 0 hard covers
ISBN 0 521 35944 9 paperback

Contents

Contributors

Imre Balogh, Computing Research Laboratory, New Mexico State University

Ranan Banerji, Saint Joseph's University, Philadelphia

Margaret A. Boden, School of Social Sciences, University of Sussex

Alan Bundy, Department of Artificial Intelligence, University of Edinburgh

J. A. Campbell, Department of Computer Science, University College London

B. Chandrasekaran, Laboratory for AI Research, Department of Computer and Information Science, The Ohio State University

Paul M. Churchland, Department of Philosophy, University of California, San Diego

Daniel C. Dennett, Center for Cognitive Studies, Tufts University

Eric Dietrich, State University of New York, Binghamton

Hubert L. Dreyfus, Department of Philosophy, University of California, Berkeley

Stuart E. Dreyfus, Department of Industrial Engineering and Operations Research, University of California, Berkeley

Jerry A. Fodor, Department of Philosophy, City University of New York

F. K. Hanna, Electronics Laboratories, University of Kent

Carl Hewitt, Artificial Intelligence Laboratory, Cambridge, Massachusetts

John McCarthy, Department of Computer Science, Stanford University

The late David Marr

Donald Michie, Machine Intelligence Research Unit, University of Edinburgh

Roger Needham, Computer Laboratory, University of Cambridge

Stellan Ohlsson, Learning Research and Development Center, University of Pittsburgh

Derek Partridge, Department of Computer Science, University of Exeter

Teodor C. Przymusinski, Department of Mathematical Sciences, University of Texas, El Paso

G. D. Ritchie, Department of Computer Science, Heriot-Watt University

Roger C. Schank, Department of Computer Science, Yale University

Thomas W. Simon, Department of Philosophy, University of Florida

Brian Slator, Computer Science Department, North Dakota State University

Paul Smolensky, Department of Computer Science and Institute of Cognitive Science, University of Colorado, Boulder

Karen Sparck Jones, Computer Laboratory, University of Cambridge

Richard W. Weyhrauch, Department of Computer Science, Stanford University

Yorick Wilks, Computing Research Laboratory, New Mexico State University

Terry Winograd, Department of Computer Science, Stanford University

Preface

This book collects together a group of fundamental papers on the foundations of artificial intelligence, with selected papers and subsequent discussion from a workshop on the foundations of AI held in Las Cruces, New Mexico, in 1986. The liveliness of the workshop papers and discussions is intended to complement the older, classic papers.

To give the book a structure that will make it accessible to students of the field, we have added a full annotated bibliography, as well as binding explanatory material between the contributions.

At the Las Cruces workshop one of the first questions confronted was the role played by philosophy in the foundations of AI, since philosophy is a subject that comes running whenever foundational or methodological issues arise. The question is important and inevitable but it must always be remembered that there is still an unreformed core of AI practitioners who believe that such assistance – not only from philosophers but from psychologists and linguists as well – can only detract from serious methodological discussions that should take place only between practitioners in private. (A distinguished AI figure said this during the planning period for the workshop.) We need to ask whether that attitude is normal in the sciences, or would-be sciences. For, if it is, then AI is in no way special in these matters, and we can draw benefit from study of the methodologies of other sciences. If not, then we have to ask again whether AI is yet fit to conduct its own methodological discussion. What are the (well-known) precedents and prognoses? Many early methodologists of science were scientists as well as philosophers (Aristotle, Whewell, Kant, Descartes), but many were not (Mill, Pierce). Most in this century were not (Carnap, Popper, Feyerabend, Kuhn, etc.). The more theoretically oriented scientists in this century were not philosophers in any technical sense (e.g. Einstein, Bohr, Planck, Fermi), though some (like Bohm, Feynman, and von Weizsäcker) had a weakness for philosophical expression of what they had to say. They were clearly methodologists of their field, however, but then physics is a very mature and theoretically developed subject.

Perhaps sciences, and even engineering if AI is that, can and should run their own methodologies, but only when in that mature state. Until then, they should take all the help, positive or negative, they can get, though this should not be accepted uncritically. A distinguished AI researcher once tried to stop one of the editors from critically questioning a well-known philosopher with the words "You idiot, he's on our side!"

"Poets have no special insight into what they do or mean" said T. S. Eliot, and there may be some corresponding and essential inadequacy in doing one's own methodology, wholly autonomously. Perhaps methodologists are a little like accountants, you have to call them in from outside the company to keep straight, at least at intervals. It is this belief that keeps at least a part of philosophy in business, of course.

The fear of the cynic referred to earlier (the one who assumed that discussions might just be wasted if not between AI practitioners) was that the questions the others would want to discuss would not be relevant to the foundations or practice of AI, however much the protagonists might believe them to be: they would always be problem solving in other areas, e.g. clarifying what an "intention" or "mental state" might be, or whether what AI produces are REALLY theories or experiments, in any general sense. Is this fair or true?

The cynic may be right in that no solutions (if there could be any) to such philosophical questions could conceivably affect the agenda of pressing methodological ones that AI has, as seen from the inside. He is unfair in that even partial solutions to such questions (about mental states, intentionality etc.) are important to how AI can describe, present, and interpret what it does, to others and to itself. It has proved almost impossible for AI to describe the function of its programs without drawing on some part of that anthropomorphic vocabulary, and it is the very vocabulary for which AI (and computer science generally) is competing to control, not only with philosophers and psychologists, but poets, novelists, and plain men in the street. It is not because of any particular success of computer science or AI that ordinary people say things like "I think I'm losing core this morning" to mean that their memory is bad.

A serious issue for AI to consider is what its results might be like if purged of all such interpretations: the inverse of the Turing test, as it were, yielding not programs like humans, but successful and useful programs, achieving distinctively human tasks of a high order, but which are described in wholly non-anthropomorphic terms. If that can be done then AI is, at a bound, free, free from discussion by "outsiders" of many of its pretensions and claims. But suppose that cannot be done, and that the chief fault of McDermott's wonderful squib (D. McDermott, 1981) is that he never saw that.

It is one of the interests of the current connectionist movement in AI, much discussed in this volume, that it is in part an attempt to purge AI of the anthropomorphic imagery that inevitably comes with much of the "symbolic baggage" that it opposes so fiercely. This is not in general a conscious aim of connectionists, it simply comes with the history: in this case the long association between connectionism, cybernetics, associationism in psychology back to behaviorism and its antipathy to mental talk.

To return: what is this "pressing agenda of internal concerns" of AI referred to above? It contains, and this volume reflects this, such issues as:

> are AI programs distinct from other parts of computer science?
> can there be experiments in AI, as in science, or is their lack evidence that AI is "really engineering"?
> are programs theories, and if not why not?
> is there a special AI form of advance called "throwaway programs"?
> can we isolate parts of computational modeling problems in any determinate way and work on them one at a time?
> why are some levels of program interpretation so obviously to be preferred to others (machine code)?
> why are so few AI "results" repeatable and does it matter?
> why are there no effective statistically significant results in AI and should there be?
> why is it not possible to tell from many AI papers whether a program exists or not?
> why are programs so poorly described?
> is the activity of "rational reconstruction" of the programs of others a defensible and useful one?
> can an AI researcher succeed without having to claim that his program is really intended to model some aspect of human processing?
> are these really pressing methodological issues or just a bunch of family housekeeping worries?
> how does AI combat the claim from computer scientists that it has not contributed anything not already well-known there under other terms?
> is connectionism, as its proponents claim, more experimental/scientific than normal AI, or is the experimentation it offers more social science than science, i.e. producing repeatable results with only that kind of statistical likelihood?

Almost any AI practitioner considers most of those questions important, whether or not they are classified as foundational, philosophical, methodological, or whatever. Compare the concerns of the modern theoretical physicists named above, and how their work is not considered truly methodological by most philosophers of science, but just the scribblings of hopelessly naïve realists.

Why discussion of these issues, whatever they are, is important is that it helps build a critical and reflective tradition in AI, which is perhaps its most striking lack. Having such a tradition may be a necessary precondition for any mature, autonomous, methodology. AI has virtually no tradition of the careful criticism and comparison of ideas, of sifting them for their antecedents or their coherence in a standard scholarly way, so as to extract general principles. Programs and researchers simply come and go endlessly, with no predecessors or successors: techniques are regularly discovered every few years (Bundy has documented some of this). Few people seem to mind or notice: after all, creativity and novelty are highly prized in AI and having no memory is one way of ensuring they are always present. All this may be a disbenefit of (the otherwise enormous benefit of) having AI centered in the U.S.: the willingness to try anything once, and not to be hampered by constricting theories and searches for *Anfangspünkte*, and the desire to be positive and uncritical at all costs (except of course when reviewing the grant applications of colleagues: brutal honesty and critical frankness are so important there, particularly because one never has to put one's name to anything).

The aim of this volume, then, is to contribute in a small way towards the establishment of that critical and reflective tradition within AI, and to it, and its saints and martyrs, the book is dedicated.

We would like to thank Jeanine Sandefur for her patience, persistence and sheer hard work when she transformed the various submissions from the contributing authors into a homogeneous and machine-readable whole.

Acknowledgments

The publisher and the editors gratefully acknowledge permission to reproduce the following copyright material:

Daniel Dennett, "Evolution, error and intentionality." Reprinted with permission, in slightly revised form, from Daniel Dennett: *The Intentional Stance* (MIT Press/Bradford Books 1987).

Jerry A. Fodor, "Why there still has to be a language of thought." Reprinted with permission from Jerry A. Fodor: *Psychosemantics* (MIT Press/Bradford Books 1987).

Carl Hewitt, "The challenge of open systems." Reprinted with permission from BYTE magazine (April 1985), pp. 223–42. Copyright © by McGraw-Hill, Inc., New York 10020. All rights reserved.

Alan Bundy and Stellan Ohlsson, "The nature of AI principles." Reprinted with permission from DAI Research Paper no. 226. The articles on which this research paper was based appeared in the *AISB Quarterly*, nos. 47, 48, 49, and 50.

David Marr, "Artificial intelligence: a personal view." Reprinted with kind permission of the author's widow, Lucia Vaina. First published in *Artificial Intelligence*, vol. 9 (1977), pp. 37–48.

Donald Michie, "The superarticulacy phenomenon in the context of software manufacture." Reprinted with permission from *Proceedings of the Royal Society, London*, A, vol. 405, pp. 185–212.

Derek Partridge and Yorick Wilks, "Does AI have a methodology which is different from software engineering." Reprinted with permission from *AI Review*, vol. 1, no. 2 (1987), pp. 111–20. Copyright © Intellect Ltd.

xiv   *Acknowledgments*

Graeme Ritchie and F. K. Hanna, "AM: a case study in AI methodology." Reprinted with permission from *AI Journal*, vol. 23, no. 3 (1984), pp. 249–63. Copyright © Elsevier Science Publishers BV.

Paul Smolensky, "On the proper treatment of connectionism." Reprinted with permission, in shortened form, from *Behavioral and Brain Sciences*, vol. 11, no. 1, March 1988. Copyright © Cambridge University Press.

Richard W. Weyhrauch, "Prolegomena to a theory of mechanized formal reasoning." Reprinted with permission, in shortened and revised form, from *AI Journal*, vol. 12, no. 1–2 (1980), pp. 133–70. Copyright © Elsevier Science Publishers BV.

Terry Winograd, "Thinking machines: Can there be? Are we?" Reprinted with permission of the Stanford Humanities Center, Stanford University.

1 Introduction

The opening section presents two very different types of attempt to provide a general characterization of AI. For Schank, AI is a distributed phenomenon: 'potentially . . . the algorithmic study of processes in every field of enquiry.' In the absence of a definition, he characterizes AI in terms of a list of features that he considers to be critical. He argues that the the bifurcation of AI into a scientific and an applications track is so decisive that 'the two routes have nothing to do with each other.' Finally, he lists and briefly discusses ten problem areas in AI that will not admit of solutions in the foreseeable future.

Chandrasekaran's paper lays out in historical perspective the methodological paradigms within which AI projects and explorations have at different times, and in different places, been pursued.

He takes the opening shots at connectionism and the echoes continue throughout this book culminating in the papers of section 9. He also introduces the 'symbolic' paradigm (another recurring theme) and attempts to clarify the issue of 'symbolic' and 'non-symbolic' representations. He offers the 'information processing level of abstraction' as a unifying paradigm.

He presents and discusses, with the aid of representative examples, three classes of theories in AI: architectural theories, logical abstraction theories, and general functional theories of intelligence. The paper concludes with a clear preference for the last class of theories and offers a specific functional-theory-type proposal about the nature of intelligence.

Within the discussion of the class of logic-based theories in AI, Chandrasekaran provides an overview and introduction to this important facet of the foundations of AI – the one that we deal with explicitly in the next chapter.

1

What is AI, anyway?

Roger C. Schank

Artificial intelligence is a subject that, due to the massive, often quite unintelligible, publicity that it gets, is nearly completely misunderstood by people outside the field. Even AI's practitioners are somewhat confused with respect to what AI is really about.

Is AI mathematics? A great many AI researchers believe strongly that knowledge representations used in AI programs must conform to previously established formalisms and logics or else the field will be unprincipled and *ad hoc*. Many AI researchers believe that they *know* how the answer will turn out before they have figured out what exactly the questions are. They *know* that some mathematical formalism or other must be the best way to express the contents of the knowledge that people have. Thus, to them, AI is an exercise in the search for the proper formalisms to use in representing knowledge.

Is AI software engineering? A great many AI practitioners seem to think so. If you can put knowledge into a program, then that program must be an AI program. This conception of AI, derived as it is from much of the work going on in industry in expert systems, has served to confuse AI people tremendously about what the correct focus of AI ought to be, and about what the fundamental issues in AI are. If AI is just so much software engineering, if building an AI program means primarily the addition of domain knowledge such that a program "knows about" insurance or geology, for example, then what is to differentiate an AI program in insurance from any other computer program that works within the field of insurance? Under this conception, it is very difficult to determine where software engineering leaves off and where AI begins.

Is AI linguistics? A great many AI researchers seem to think that building grammars of English and putting those grammars on a machine is AI. Of course, linguists have never thought of their field as having very much to do with AI at all. But, as money for linguistics has begun to disappear, while money for AI has increased, it has become increasingly convenient to claim that work on language that had nothing to do with computers at all, has some computational relevance. Suddenly theories of language that were never considered by their creators to be process models at all, are now proposed as AI models.

Is AI psychology? Would building a complete model of human thought processes and putting it on a computer be considered a contribution to AI? Many AI researchers couldn't care less about the human mind. Yet, the human mind is the only kind of intelligence that we can reasonably hope to study. We have an existence proof. We know the human mind works. But, in adopting this view, one still has to worry about computer models that display intelligence but yet are clearly in no way related to how humans function. Are such models intelligent? Such issues inevitably force one to focus on the issue of the nature of intelligence apart from its particular physical embodiment.

In the end, the question of what AI is all about probably does not have only one answer. What AI is depends heavily upon the goals of the researchers involved. And any definition of AI is very dependent upon the methods that are being employed in building AI models. Last, of course, it is a question of results. These issues about what AI is exist precisely because AI has not yet been completed. They will disappear entirely when a machine begins to really be the way writers of science fiction have imagined it.

There are two main goals in AI that most practitioners would agree upon. First and foremost, the goal is to build an intelligent machine. And, second, the goal is to find out about the nature of intelligence. Both of these goals have at their heart a need to define intelligence. AI people are fond of talking about intelligent machines, but when it comes down to it, there is very little agreement on exactly what constitutes intelligence. And, it thus follows, there is very little agreement in AI about exactly what AI is and what it should be. We all agree that we would like to endow machines with an attribute that we really can't define. Needless to say, AI suffers from this lack of definition of its scope.

One way to attack this problem is to attempt to list some features that we would expect an intelligent entity to have. None of these features would define intelligence – indeed a being could lack any one of them and still be considered to be intelligent. Nevertheless each is an integral part of intelligence in its way.

Let me list the features I consider to be critical and then I shall briefly discuss them. They are: communication, internal knowledge, world knowledge, goal and plans, and creativity.

Communication: An intelligent entity can be communicated with. We can't talk to rocks or tell trees what we want, no matter how hard we try. With dogs and cats we cannot express many of our feelings, but we can let them know when we are angry. Communication is possible with them. If it is very difficult to communicate with someone, we might consider him to be unintelligent. If the communication lines are very narrow with a person, if he can only understand a few things, we might consider him to be unintelligent. No matter how smart your dog is, he can't understand when you discuss physics with him. This does not mean that he doesn't understand something about physics. You can't discuss physics with your pet rock either, but it doesn't understand physics at all. Your small child may know some physics, but discussions of that subject with him will have to be put in terms he can understand. In other words, the easier it is to communicate with an entity, the more intelligent the entity seems. Obviously there are many exceptions to this general feature of intelligence. There are people who are considered to be very intelligent who are impossible to talk to, for example. Nevertheless, this feature of intelligence is still significant, even if it is not absolutely essential.

Internal knowledge: We expect intelligent entities to have some knowledge about themselves. They should know when they need something; they should know what they think about something; and, they should know that they know it. Presently, probably only humans can do all this – we cannot really know what dogs know about what they know. We could program computers to seem as if they know what they know, but it would be hard to tell if they really did. To put this another way, we really cannot examine the insides of an intelligent entity in such a way as to establish what it actually knows. Our only choice is to ask and observe. If we get an answer that seems satisfying then we tend to believe that the entity we are examining has some degree of intelligence. Of course, this is another subjective criterion, a feature that when it is absent may signify nothing.

World knowledge: Intelligence also involves being aware of the outside world and being able to find and utilize the information that one has about the outside world. It also implies having a memory in which past experience is encoded and which can be used as a guide for processing new experiences. You cannot understand and operate in the outside world if you treat every experience as if it were brand new. Thus, intelligent entities must have an ability to see new experiences in terms of old ones. This implies an ability to retrieve old experiences which would have had to have been codified in such a way as make them available in a variety of different circumstances. Entities that do not have this ability can be momentarily intelligent but not globally intelligent. There are cases of people who are brain-damaged who perform adequately in a given moment, but forget what they have done soon after. The same is true of simple machines that can do a given job but do not know that they have done it, and have no ability to draw on that or other experiences to guide them in future jobs.

Goals and plans: Goal-driven behavior means knowing when one wants something and knowing a plan to get what one wants. There is usually a

presumed correspondence between the complexity of the goals that an
entity has and the sheer number of plans that an entity has available for
accomplishing those goals. So, a tree has none or next to none of these, a
dog has somewhat more, and a person has quite a few; very intelligent
people probably have more. Of course, sheer number of recorded plans
would probably not be a terrific measure of intelligence. If it were, machines
could easily be constructed that met that criterion. The real criterion with
respect to plans has to do with interrelatedness of plans and their storage in
an abstract enough way as to allow a plan constructed for situation A to be
adapted and used in situation B.

Creativity: Finally, every intelligent entity is assumed to have some
degree of creativity. Creativity can be defined very weakly, including for
example, the ability to find a new route to one's food source when the old
one is blocked. But, of course, creativity can also mean finding a new way to
look at something that changes one's world in some significant way. And, it
certainly means being able to adapt to changes in one's environment and
being able to learn from experience. Thus, an entity that doesn't learn is
probably not intelligent, except momentarily.

   Now, as I said, one needn't have all of these things to be intelligent, but
each is an important part of intelligence. That having been said, where do
current AI programs fit in? It seems clear that no AI model is very creative
as of yet, although various ideas have been proposed in this regard lately. It
also seems clear that no AI models have a great deal of internal knowledge.
In general, AI programs don't know what they know, nor are they aware of
what they can do. They may be able to summarize a news wire, but they
don't know that they are summarizing it.

   On the other hand, programs that have goals and plans to accomplish
those goals have been around since the inception of AI. Work on such
programs has spawned a variety of ideas on how planning can be accomplished, particularly within the domain of problem solving. Programs that
have external knowledge usually have not been considered to be part of AI
at all. Database retrieval is not in any way connected with AI, although it
has seemed clear to AI researchers that they must eventually concern
themselves with how knowledge is best organized in order to have really
intelligent machines. Nevertheless, many programs for organizing and
retrieving knowledge do, of course, exist.

   Programs that communicate with computers have been around as long as
there have been computers, of course. But this communication has been
less than satisfactory. Most non-computer professionals complain bitterly
about the difficulty in getting a computer to do what is wanted, and of
course, the computer industry has been responsive to this, producing better
and better interfaces. But, in the end, computers will not really be easy to
use until they can see, hear, read, and generally understand what we say to
them and what we want them to do.

In AI, these subjects have always been considered to be important parts of the field and much research has been done on them.

As AI has become more commercialized, the parts of AI research that have been the most advanced in terms of engineering would, one might have imagined, become those areas where the commercial action would begin. But, as often happens, salesmanship and market readiness often determine what gets sold. So AI entered the world through the creation of so-called expert systems, which were engineering attempts to take some of the problem solving and planning models that had been proposed in AI and give them real world relevance. The problem was that these experts lacked what I have termed internal knowledge and creativity. And, it is very difficult to have an expert who doesn't know what he knows, how he came to know it, or how to adapt if circumstances are somewhat different than they were supposed to be. Most of all, experts with no memories are no experts at all.

Partly as a result of the commercialization of expert systems, equating AI with expert systems in the public eye, and partly as a result of the usual battles AI has always faced with older fields of inquiry that relate to it, AI is in a serious state of disruption.

Most AI people seem to have chosen one of two routes, to get them out of their state of confusion. The first of these routes I will call the *applications route*. In this view of AI, the job is to build real working systems. Whether these systems are AI or not loses its import as one begins to work on them. The problem is make them work at all, not to be a purist about what is or is not AI. As anyone who has ever worked on a large software engineering program knows, this task is so complex as to make all other problems pale by comparison. Making big programs work is hard. And when they are finished are they AI? Does it matter?

The second route is what I will call the *scientific route*. This route sounds good in principle and it has as its premise a desire to avoid the commercialization of AI and work only on impossible problems like the brain, or neat problems like logic. Let the applications route people do as they will, the scientific route people have chosen simply to ignore them and bolt the door.

Thus, without actually deciding to do so, AI has made a decision. Either one defines AI as a modern methodological tool now being used in the ancient enterprise of the study of mind, the *scientific answer*, or, one's definition of AI is, in essence, the *applications answer*, namely an attempt to create certain new computer technology that relates to some behaviors previously done only by humans.

This seems fine in principle – many fields have a scientific, theoretical group and an applications group that derives its work from the scientific work. And, this would be nice in AI too, if it were the case. What actually is the case is that the scientific workers are, for the most part, concerned with issues that are very far away from potential applications, and the applications folk have been busy applying results from earlier days which are known to be seriously inadequate. This does not mean that they are not building useful applications, sometimes they are. But, it does mean that, for all intents and purposes, the two routes have nothing to do with each other.

One problem with the applications answer is that it is very imprecise. Is all new computer technology to be labeled AI? Certainly, if one reads the advertisements in the computer magazines, it is easy to believe that AI is anything anyone says it is, that there is no definition. But, to an AI researcher (as opposed to an AI businessman), only a small fraction of advances in computer software and hardware would seem to qualify as advances in AI. The technology that AI people want to create usually involves solving some fundamental problem, and the solution itself involves decisions on the nature of what kinds of things are part of a computer program. Further, AI usually means getting a machine to do what previously only humans have done before (rather than simply improving existing techniques). The problem with this definition has been obvious to AI people for some time. As soon as something radically new has been accomplished, then, since computers have at that point done it, it is thus no longer uniquely human, and thus no longer AI. So, one question that needs to be answered on the technological side is, "Can some definition as to the nature of AI software be made such that, under all circumstances, it will be seen as uniquely part of or derivative from AI?"

What is really the case is that it is not possible to define very clearly which pieces of new software are AI and which are not. In actuality, AI must have an issues-related definition. In other words, people do arithmetic and so do computers. The fact is, however, that no one considers a program that calculates to be an AI program, nor would they, even if that program calculated in exactly the way that people do. The reason that this is so is that calculation is not seen as a fundamental problem of intelligent behavior and also that computers are already better at calculation than people are. This two-sided definition, based upon the perception of the fundamental centrality of an issue with respect to its role in human intelligence, and the practical viewpoint of how good current computers are at accomplishing such a task already, constitutes how one defines whether a given problem is legitimately an AI problem. For this reason, much of the good work in AI has been just answering the question of what the issues are.

Or, to put this another way, what is AI is defined not by the methodologies used in AI, but by the problems attacked by those methodologies. A program is not an AI program because it uses LISP or PROLOG certainly. By the same token, a program is not an AI program because it uses some form of logic or if-then rules. Expert systems are only AI programs if they attack some AI issue. A rule-based system is not an AI program just because it uses rules or was written with an expert system shell. It is an AI program if it addresses an AI issue.

One thing about AI issues though, is that they change. What was an issue yesterday may not be one today. Similarly, the issues that I believe to be critical today may disappear ten years from now. Given that that is the case, defining AI by issues can make AI a rather odd field, with a constantly changing definition. But, there are some problems that will endure, that tend to define AI. I will discuss some of these below:

1 Representation
2 Decoding
3 Inference
4 Control of combinatorial explosion
5 Indexing
6 Prediction and recovery
7 Dynamic modification
8 Generalization
9 Curiosity
10 Creativity

1. **Representation**   Probably the most significant issue in AI is the old problem of the representation of knowledge. *What do we know?*, and *how do we get a machine to know it?* is the central issue in AI. An AI program or theory that makes a statement about how knowledge that is of a generality greater than the range of knowledge covered by the program itself ought to be represented is a contribution to AI.

2. **Decoding**   It is of no use to have a very nice knowledge representation if there is no way to translate from the real world into that representation. In natural language, or vision systems, for example, decoding is often the central problem in constructing an AI program. Sometimes, of course, the decoding work is so difficult that the programmers forget to concern themselves with what they are decoding into, that is, what the ideal representation ought to be, so that they make the work harder for themselves. Deciding that the representation is a given fact, that it is predicate calculus, or syntactic phrase markers, for example, can complicate the problem, relegating the decoding work to some other, often non-existent, program.

3. **Inference**   Information is usually more than the sum of its parts. Once we have decoded a message (visual, verbal, symbolic, or whatever) we must begin to attempt to extract the content of that message. Usually the content is much more than has been expressed directly. We don't say every nuance of what we mean. We expect our hearer to be smart enough to figure some of it out for himself. Similarly, we must attempt to figure out the significance of what we have seen, making assumptions about what it all means. This is the problem of inference.

Human memory is highly inferential, even about prior experiences, and retrieval of information. People are capable of answering questions from very incomplete data. They can figure out if they should know something and whether they might be able to figure it out. Such self-awareness depends strongly upon an ability to know how the world works in general, or, the representation problem again. Building a program that knows if it would know a thing is a very important task.

4. **Control of combinatorial explosion**   Once you allow a program to make assumptions about what may be true beyond what it has been told, the possibility that it could go on forever doing this, becomes quite real. At what point do you turn off your mind and decide that you have thought enough about a problem? Arbitrary limits are just that, arbitrary. It seems a safe assumption that it is the structure of our knowledge that guides the inference process. Knowing what particular knowledge structure we are in while processing can help us to determine how much we want to know about a given event. Or, to put this another way, contexts help narrow the inference process. There are many possible ways to control the combinatorics of the inference process – deciding among them and implementing them is a serious AI problem if the combinatorial explosion was started by an AI process in the first place.

5. **Indexing**   It is all well and good to know a great deal, but the more you know, the harder it should get to find what you know. The most knowledgeable man on earth should also be the slowest to say anything, by that reasoning. This is called the paradox of the expert in psychology. It is a paradox precisely because it is untrue. Obviously, people must have ways of organizing their knowledge so that they can find what they need when they need it. Originally this problem was called the search problem in AI. But, viewed as a search problem, the implication was that faster search methods were what was needed. This would imply that experts were people who searched their data bases quickly and that seems quite absurd. It is the organization and labeling of memory and episodes in memory that is the key issue here. For any massive system, that is for any real AI system, indexing is a central, and possibly the central problem. AI programs are not usually large enough to make their answers to the indexing question meaningful, but the construction of programs of the appropriate size should become more important in the years ahead.

6. **Prediction and recovery**   Any serious AI program should be able to make predictions about how events in its domain will turn out. This is what understanding really means, that is, knowing to some extent what is coming. When these predictions fail, which they certainly must in any realistic system, an intelligent program should not only recover from the failure, but it must also explain the failure. That is, programs must understand their own workings well enough to know what an error looks like, and be able to correct the rule that caused that error in addition to being able to recognize that situation when it occurs again. As an example

of the kind of thing I am talking about, a computer should be able, by use of the same basic scientific theory, to do an adequate job of forecasting stocks or weather, or playing a game of chess, or coaching a football team. What I mean by *the same basic theory* is that the theory of prediction, recovery from error, error explanation, and new theory creation should be identical in principle, regardless of domain.

7. Dynamic modification   AI went through a long period of trying to find out how to represent knowledge. We needed to find out what was learned before we could even consider working on learning itself. But, most of us have always wanted to work on learning. Learning is, after all, the quintessential AI issue. What makes people interesting, what makes them intelligent, is that they learn. People change with experience. The trouble with almost all the programs that we have written is that they are not modified by their experiences. No matter how sophisticated a story under-stander may seem, it loses all credibility as an intelligent system when it reads the same story three times in a row and it fails to get mad, bored, or even to notice. Programs must change as a result of their experiences or else they will not do anything very interesting.

Similarly, any knowledge structures, or representations of knowledge that AI researchers create, no matter how adequately formulated initially, must change over time. Understanding how they are changed by actual use during the course of processing information is one of the major problems in representation itself. Deciding when to create a new structure or abandon an old one is a formidable problem. Thus, new AI programs should be called upon to assimilate information and change the nature of the program in the course of that assimilation. Clearly such programs are necessary before the knowledge acquisition problem can be adequately attacked. It should also be clear that an AI program that cannot build itself up gradually, without requiring all its knowledge stuffed in at the beginning, is not really intelligent.

I will now give a definition of AI that most of our programs will fail. AI is the science of endowing programs with the ability to change themselves for the better as a result of their own experiences. The technology of AI is derived from the science of AI and is, at least for now, unlikely to be very intelligent. But, it should be the aim of every current AI *researcher* to endow his programs with that kind of *dynamic* intelligence.

8. Generalization   A program that can form a generalization from experi-ence that can be tested would be of great significance. This program would have to be able to draw conclusions from disparate data. The key aspect of a good generalization maker is his ability to connect together experiences that are not obviously connectable. This is the essence of creativity. A key AI problem, therefore is to understand new events and make predictions about future events by generalizing from prior events. These generalizations would likely be inadequate at first, but eventually new theories that fit the data should emerge. Ultimately human expertise is embodied not in rules but in cases. People can abstract rules about what they do of course, but the essence of their expertise, that part which is used in the most complex cases, is derived from particular and rather singular cases that stand out in their minds. The job of the expert is to find the most relevant case to reason from in any given instance. Phenomena such as reminding enhance this ability to generalize by providing more data to consider. The very consideration of seemingly irrelevant data makes for a good generalizer. In other words, AI programs should be able to come up with ideas on their own, so to speak.

9. **Curiosity**   Cats, small children, and some adults, are curious. They ask questions about what they see, wonder about what they hear, and object to what they are told. This curiosity is not so wondrous when we realize that once a system makes predictions, those predictions may fail, and the system should wonder why. The ability to wonder why, to generate a good question about what is going on, and the ability to invent an answer, to explain what has gone on to oneself, is at the heart of intelligence. We would accept no human who failed to wonder or failed to explain, as being very intelligent. In the end, we shall have to judge AI programs by the same criteria.

10. **Creativity**   Scientists and technologists would both agree that what is most fascinating of all is the possibility that computers will someday surpass human beings. They are most likely to do this by being creative in some way. Principles of creativity, combined with the other powers of the computer, are likely to create this ultimate fantasy. To this end, I believe it to be necessary for AI people to become familiar with work in other fields that bears upon this issue. Other issues such as consciousness and development relate here also. Thus, another issue is relating ideas in AI to those in allied fields with the purpose of coming to some new scientific conclusions.

Which problems are most important?

All of them are important, of course. But there is one thing above all: an AI program that does not learn is no AI program. Now, I understand that this maxim would not have made much sense in the past. But, one of the problems of defining AI is, as I have said, that AI could, by past definitions, be nearly anything. We have reached a new stage. We have a much better idea of what is learned, therefore it is time to demand learning of our programs. AI programs have always been a promise for the future, a claim about what we could build someday. Each thesis has been the prototype of what we might build if only we would. Well, from the technological perspective, the time to build is now. From the scientific perspective, after the issue of what is learned is taken care of, the issue for AI is learning, although we probably do not have to wait for the former to be finished in order to start.

AI should, in principle, be a contribution to a great many fields of study. AI has already made contributions to psychology, linguistics, and philosophy as well as other fields. In reality, AI is, potentially, the algorithmic study of processes in every field of inquiry. As such, the future should produce AI/anthropologists, AI/doctors, AI/political scientists and so on. There might also be some AI/computer scientists, but on the whole, I believe, AI has less to say, in principle, to computer science than to any other discipline. The reason that this has not been so heretofore is an accident of birth. AI people have been computer scientists, therefore they have tended to contribute to computer science. Computer science has needed tools, as has AI, and, on occasion, these tools have coincided. AI is actually a methodology applicable to many fields. It is just a matter of time until AI becomes part of other fields, and the issue of what constitutes a contribution to AI will be reduced to the question of what constitutes a contribution in the allied field. At that time what will remain of AI will be precisely the issues that transcend these allied fields, whatever they may turn out to be. In fact, that may be the best available working definition of what constitutes a successful contribution in AI today, namely a program whose inner workings apply to similar problems in areas completely different from the one that was tackled originally.

In some sense, all subjects are really AI. All fields discuss the nature of man. AI tries to do something about it. From a technological point of view AI matters to the extent that its technology matters, and the significance of a specific technology is always hard to justify. But from a scientific point of view, we are trying to answer the only questions that really do matter.

What kind of information processing is intelligence?
A perspective on AI paradigms and a proposal

B. Chandrasekaran

1 AI as science of intelligence

Paradigmatic confusion in AI. In spite of what I regard as AI's significant achievements in beginning to provide a computational language to talk about the nature of intelligence, the not so well-kept secret is that AI is internally in a paradigmatic mess. There is really no broad agreement on the essential nature or formal basis of intelligence and the proper theoretical framework for it.

1.1 Intelligence as information processing on representations

Let us first seek some unities. There is something that is shared almost universally among workers in AI: "Significant (all?) aspects of cognition and perception are best understood/modeled as *information processing activities on representations.*" The dominant tradition within AI has been the symbolic paradigm.[1] On the other hand, modern connectionists (and the earlier perceptron theorists) offer largely analog processes implemented by weights of connections in a network. Stronger versions of the symbolic paradigm have been proposed by Newell as the physical symbol system hypothesis (Newell, 1980), and elaborated by Pylyshyn (1984) in his thesis that computation is not simply a metaphorical language to talk about cognition, but that cognition is literally computation over symbol systems. It is important to emphasize that this thesis does not imply a belief in the practical sufficiency of current von Neuman computers for the task, or a restriction to serial computation. Often, disagreements with the symbolic paradigm turn out to be arguments for parallel computers of some type, rather than arguments against computations on discrete symbolic representations.

Is there something that can be recognized as the *essential* nature of intelligence that can be used to characterize all its manifestations – human, alpha-centaurian, and artificial – but which will also distinguish it from other types of computations? It is possible that intelligence is merely a somewhat random collection of information processing transformations acquired over aeons of evolution, but in that case there can hardly be an interesting science of it. It is also possible that there need not be anything that particularly restricts attempts to make intelligent machines, i.e., while there may well be characterizations of human intellectual processes, they need not be taken to apply to other forms of intelligence. While in some sense this seems right – human intellectual processes do not bound the possibilities for intelligence – nevertheless I believe that there is an internal conceptual coherence to the class of information processing activities characterizing intelligence. The oft-stated dichotomy between the simulation of human cognition versus making machines smart is a temporarily useful distinction, but its implication that we are talking about two very different phenomena is, I believe, incorrect. In any case, a task of AI as a science is to explain human intelligence. The underlying unity that we are seeking can be further characterized by asking, "What is it that unites Einstein, the man on the street in a western culture, and a tribesman in a primitive culture, as information processing agents?"

I am only concerned with what AI has had to say about the question "What kind of information processing is intelligence?" I will offer a view of how the field really works as a discipline, and how some disagreements can be understood only by tracing them to the root of the problem: disagreements about the nature of the science.

2 AI theories from the 1940s to the 1960s
2.1 Pre- and quasi-representational theories

The earliest of the modern attempts to come to grips with the nature of intelligence was the *cybernetics* stream, associated with the work of Wiener (1948) who laid some of the foundations of modern feedback control.[2] The importance of cybernetics was that it suggested that *teleology could be consistent with mechanism*. The hallmark of intelligence was said to be adaptation, and since cybernetics seemed to provide an answer to how this *adaptation* could be accounted for with feedback of *information*, and also account for teleology (e.g., "The *purpose* of the governor is to keep the steam engine speed constant"), it was a great source of early excitement for people attempting to model biological information processing. However, cybernetics never really became the language of AI, because it did not have the richness of ontology to talk about cognition and perception: while it had the notion of information processing in some sense, i.e., it had goals and mechanisms to achieve them, it lacked the notion of computation, not to mention representations.

Modeling the brain as automata (in the sense of automata theory) was another attempt to provide a mathematical foundation for intelligence. For example, the finite automata model of nerve nets that McCulloch and Pitts (1943) proposed was among the first concrete postulations about the brain as a computational mechanism. Automata models were computational, i.e., they had states and state transition functions, and the general theory dealt with what kinds of automata can do what kinds of things. However, what AI needed was not theories *about* computation but theories which were descriptions of particular computations, i.e., programs that embody theories of cognition. Naturally enough, automata theory evolved into the formal foundation for some aspects of computer science, but its role in AI *per se* tapered off.

Another strain, which was much more explicit in its commitment to seeking intelligence by modeling its seat, the brain, looked at neurons and neural networks as the units of information processing out of which thought and intelligence can be explained and produced. Neural net simulation and the work on perceptrons (Rosenblatt, 1962) are two major examples of this class of work. Its lineage can be traced to Hebb's work (Hebb, 1949) on cell assemblies which had a strong effect on psychological theorizing. Hebb proposed a dynamic model of how neural structures could sustain thought, how simple learning mechanisms at the neural level could be the agents of higher level learning at the level of thought.

In retrospect, there were really two rather distinct kinds of aims that this line of work pursued. In one, an attempt was made to account for the information processing of neurons and collections of them. In the other line of work in neural models – prefiguring the claims of latter day connectionism – the attempt is to explain intelligence directly in terms of neural computations. Since in AI explanation of intelligence takes the form of constructing artifacts which are intelligent, this is a tall order – the burden of producing programs which simulate neural-like mechanisms on one hand, and at the same time do what intelligent agents do (solve problems, perceive, explain the world, speak in a natural language, etc.) is a heavy one. There is a problem with the level of description here – the terms of neural computation seem far removed from the complex content of thought – and bridging it without hypothesizing levels of abstraction between neuronal information processing and highly symbolic forms of thought is difficult. The general temptation in this area has been to sidestep the difficulties by assuming that appropriate learning mechanisms at the neural level can result in sufficiently complex high-level intelligence. But theorizing and system construction, at the neural level, in AI has not been pursued seriously because of the difficulty of getting the necessary learning to take place in less than evolutionary time (but see section 3).

A large body of work, mainly statistical in character, developed under the rubric of pattern recognition (see a text such as Duda and Hart, 1973). It identified the problem of recognition with classification and developed a number of statistical algorithms for classification. While it had a number of representational elements (the object in question was represented as a vector in a multidimensional space) and shared some of the concerns with the perceptron work (linear or nonlinear separability of patterns in N-dimensional spaces), it developed into a mathematical discipline of its own without making a significant impact on the overall concerns of AI. In Chandrasekaran (1986b), I discuss how more flexible representations are increasingly needed for even the classification problem as the complexity of specific examples increases.

A number of reasons can be cited for the failure of all this class of work – namely, perceptrons, neural nets, and statistical classification – to hold center stage in AI. The loss of interest in perceptrons is often attributed to the demonstration by Minsky and Papert (1969) of their inadequacies. Their demonstration was in fact limited to single layer perceptrons, and was not, in my view, the real reason for perceptrons' disappearance from the scene. The real reason, I believe, is that powerful representational and representation manipulation tools were missing. The alternative of discrete symbolic representations quickly filled this need, and provided an experimental medium of great flexibililty.

2.2 Early AI work based on symbolic representations

The final transition to discrete symbolic representations was rather quick. In addition, the mathematics of computability made some investigations along this line attractive and productive. The end of the period saw not only a decisive shift towards representational approaches, but the preferred form of representation was discrete symbolic.

Early work in this computationalist spirit took on two major forms:

1 It showed mathematically that certain functions thought to be characteristic of intelligence were *computable* (e.g., induction machines of Solomonoff [1957], Gold's work on learning of grammars [1967]).[3]

2 It demonstrated the possibility of AI by building computer programs that solve problems requiring intelligence. Game-playing programs, the Analogy program of Evans, the scene-analysis program of Guzman, and the Logic Theorist and the heuristic compiler of Newell and Simon, etc., etc., showed that the underlying features of intelligence of which they were meant to be demonstrations were in fact capable of artifactual embodiment.

In general, the net result of most (not all) of this work was socio-psychological: it made the idea of AI plausible, and blunted the first round objections, such as, "Ah, but machines cannot learn," and "Ah, but machines cannot create." These early programs were also the means by which psychologists and philosophers became aware of the new kid on *their* block. The attention that AI gained at that time has continued to this day.

3 On the nature of representations: connectionism versus the symbolic paradigm

Let me restate some of the terminology here. I have called the hypothesis that intelligence can be accounted for by algorithmic processes which interpret discrete symbol systems the *symbolic paradigm* or *symbolic approaches*. Let us call the alternative to this the *non-symbolic paradigm or approaches*, for lack of better terminology. Connectionism is an example of this alternative, though not the only one.

3.1 The roots of the debate

The connectionism-symbolic computationalism debate in AI today is but the latest version of a fairly classic contention between two sets of intuitions each leading to a *weltanschauung* about how to study the phenomena of current interest. The debate can be traced at least as far back as Descartes in modern times (and to Plato if one wants to go further back) and the mind-brain dualism that goes by the name of Cartesianism. In the Cartesian world-view, the phenomena of mind are exemplified by language and thought. These phenomena may be implemented by the brain, but are seen to have a constituent structure in their own terms and can be studied abstractly. Logic and symbolic representations have often been advanced as the appropriate tools for studying them.

Functionalism in philosophy, information processing theories in psychology, and the symbolic paradigm in AI all share these assumptions. While most of the intuitions that drive this point of view arise from a study of cognitive phenomena, the thesis is often extended to include perception, as for example, in Bruner's thesis (1957) that *perception is inference*. In its modern versions, this viewpoint appeals to Turing's Hypothesis as a justification for limiting attention to symbolic computational models. These models ought to suffice, the argument goes, since even continuous functions can be computed to arbitrary precision by a Turing machine.

The opposition to this view springs from anti-Cartesian intuitions. My reading of the philosophical impulse behind anti-Cartesianism is that it is a reluctance to assign any kind of ontological independence to mind, a reluctance arising from the feeling that mind-talk is but an invitation to all kinds of further mysticisms, such as soul-talk. Thus anti-Cartesians tend to be materialists with a vengeance, and are skeptical of the separation of the mental from the brain-level phenomena. Additionally, the brain is seen to be nothing like the symbolic processor needed to support the symbolic paradigm. Instead of what is seen as the sequential and combinational perspective of the symbolic paradigm, some of the theories in this school embrace parallel, "holistic," nonsymbol-processing alternatives, while others do not even subscribe to any kind of information processing or representational language in talking about mental phenomena. Those who think information processing of some type is still needed nevertheless reject processing of labeled symbols, and look to analog or continuous processes as the natural medium for modeling the relevant phenomena. In contrast to Cartesian theories, most of the concrete work in these schools deals with perceptual (or even motor) phenomena, but the framework is meant to cover complex cognitive phenomena as well. (Symbolic theories of thought are generally viewed as explanatory and approximate descriptions, rather than accounts of real phenomena.) Eliminative materialism in philosophy, Gibsonian theories in psychology, connectionism in psychology and AI, all these can be grouped as more or less sharing this perspective, even though they differ among each other in a number of issues. For example, the Gibsonian direct-perception theory is anti-representational. Perception, in this view, is neither inference nor a product of any kind of information processing, but a one-step mapping from stimuli to categories of perception, made possible by the inherent properties of the perceptual architecture. All the needed distinctions are already there directly in the architecture, and no processing over representations is needed. To put it simply, the brain is all there is and it isn't a computer either.

Note that the proponents of the symbolic paradigm can be happy with the proposition that mental phenomena are implemented by the brain, which may or may not itself have a computationalist account. However, the anti-Cartesian cannot accept this duality. He is out to show the mind as epiphenomenal.

I need to caution the reader that each of the positions that I have described above is really a composite. Few people in either camp subscribe to all the features described. Most of them may not even be aware of themselves as participating in such a classic debate. In particular, many connectionists may bristle at my inclusion of them on the side of the debate that I did, since their accounts are laced with talk of "connectionist inference" and algorithms for the units. The algorithmic accounts in my view are incidental (I discuss this further in section 3.3). But my account, painted with a broad brush as it is, is helpful to understand the rather diverse collection of bedfellows that connectionism has attracted.

Many connectionists do not have a commitment to brain-level theory making. It is also explicitly representational, its only argument being about the medium of representation. I will try to show that connectionism is a corrective to some of the basic assumptions in the symbolic paradigm, but for most of the central issues of intelligence, connectionism is only marginally relevant.

As a preliminary to the discussion, I want to try to pin down, in the next subsection, some essential distinctions between the symbolic and nonsymbolic approaches to information processing.

3.2 Symbolic and nonsymbolic representations

Consider the problem of multiplying two integers. We are all familiar with algorithms to perform this task. We also know how the traditional slide-rule can be used to do this multiplication. The multiplicands are represented by their logarithms on a linear scale, which are then "added" by being set next to each other, and the result is obtained by reading off the sum's anti-logarithm. While both the algorithmic and slide-rule solutions are *representational*, in no sense can either of them be thought of as an "implementation" of the other. They make very different commitments about what is represented. There are also striking differences between them in practical terms. As the size of the multiplicands increases, the algorithmic solution suffers in the amount of time it takes to complete the solution, while the slide-rule solution suffers in the amount of *precision* it can deliver.

Let us call the algorithmic and slide-rule solutions C1 and C2. There is yet another solution, C3, which is the simulation of C2 by an algorithm. C3 can simulate C2 to any desired accuracy. But C3 has radically different properties from C1 in terms of the information that it represents. C3 is closer to C2 representationally. Its symbol manipulation character is at a lower level of abstraction altogether. Given a blackbox multiplier, ascription of C1 or C2 (among others) as what is *really* going on makes for different theories about the process. Each theory makes different ontological commitments. Further, while C2 is "analog" or continuous, the existence of C3 implies that the essential characteristic of C2 is not continuity *per se*, but a radically different sense of representation and processing than C1.

An adequate discussion of what is a symbol, in the sense used in computation over symbol systems, requires a much larger space and time than I have at present (see Pylyshyn, 1984, for a thorough and illuminating discussion of this topic), but the following points seem useful. There is a type-token distinction that seems relevant: symbols are types about which abstract rules of behavior are known and can be brought into play. This leads to symbols being labels which are "interpreted" during the process, while there are no such interpretations in the process of slide-rule multiplication (except for input and output). The symbol system can thus represent *abstract forms*, while C2 above performs its addition or multiplication not by instantiating an abstract form, but by having, in some sense, all the additions and multiplications directly in its architecture.

While I keep using the word "process" to describe both C1 and C2, strictly speaking there is no process in the sense of a temporally evolving behavior in C2. The architecture directly produces the solution. This is the intuition behind the Gibsonian direct perception in contrast to the Bruner alternative of perception as inference:[4] the process of inference implies a temporal sequentiality. Connectionist theories have a temporal evolution, but at each cycle, the information process does not have a step-by-step character like algorithms do. Thus the alternatives in the nonsymbolic paradigm are generally presented as "holistic." The main point of this section is that there exists functions for which symbol and nonsymbol system accounts differ fundamentally in terms of representational commitments.

3.3 Connectionism and its main features

While connectionism as an AI theory comes in many different forms, they all seem to share the idea that the *representation* of information is based on weights of connections between processing units in a network, and information processing consists of (i) the units transforming their input into some output, which is then (ii) modulated by the weights of connections as inputs to other units. Connectionist theories especially emphasize a form of learning in which continuous functions adjust the weights in the network. In some connectionist theories the above "pure" form is mixed with symbol manipulation processes. My description is based on the abstraction of connectionist architectures as described by Smolensky (1988). Smolensky's description captures the essential aspects of the connectionist architecture.

A few additional comments on what constitutes the essential aspects of connectionism may be useful, especially since connectionist theories come in so many forms. My description above is couched in non-algorithmic terms. In fact, many connectionist theorists describe the units in their systems in terms of algorithms which map their inputs into discrete states. My view is that the discrete-state description of the units' output as well as the algorithmic specification of the units' behavior is not substantially relevant. Smolensky's statement that differential equations are the appropriate language to use to describe the behavior of connectionist systems lends credence to my summary of connectionist systems.

While my description is couched in the form of continuous functions, the arguments in section 3.2 indicate that it is not in the property of continuity *per se* that the essential aspect of the architecture lies, but in the fact that the connectionist medium has no internal labels which are interpreted and no abstract forms which are instantiated during processing. Thus connectionist models stand in the same relationship to the symbolic models that C2 does to C1 in my discussion in section 3.2.

There are a number of properties of such connectionist networks that are worthy of note and that explain why connectionism is viewed as an alternative paradigm to the symbolic theories.

> Parallelism: While theories in the symbolic paradigm are not restricted to serial algorithms, connectionist models are intrinsically parallel, in most implementations massively parallel.
> Distributedness: Representation of information is *distributed* over the network in a very specialized sense, i.e., the state vector of the weights in the network is the representation. The two properties of parallelism

and distribution have attracted adherents who feel that human memory has a "holistic" character – much like a hologram – and consequently have reacted negatively to discrete symbol-processing theories, since these compute the needed information from parts and their relations. Dreyfus (1979), for example, has argued that human recognition does not proceed by combining evidence about constituent features of the pattern, but rather uses a holistic process. Thus Dreyfus looks to connectionism as a vindication of his long-standing criticism of AI. Connectionism is said to perform "direct" recognition, while symbolic AI performs recognition by sequentially computing intermediate representations.

Softness of constraints (Smolensky, 1988):   Because of the continuous space over which the weights take values, the behavior of the network, while not necessarily unimodal, tends to be more or less smooth over the input space.

The above characteristics are especially attractive to those who believe that AI must be based on brain-like architectures, even though within the connectionist camp there is a wide divergence about the degree to which directly modeling the brain is considered appropriate. While some of the theories explicitly attempt to produce neural-level computational structures, some others (see, e.g., Smolensky, 1988) propose a "subsymbolic level" intermediate between symbolic and neural-level theories, and yet others offer connectionism as a computational method that operates in the symbolic-level representation itself. The essential idea uniting them all is that the totality of connections defines the information content, rather than representing information as a symbol structure.

3.4 Is connectionism merely an implementation theory?

Two kinds of arguments have been made that connectionism can at best provide possible implementations for algorithmic AI theories. The traditional one, namely that symbolic computationalism is adequate, takes two forms. In one, continuous functions are thought to be the alternative, and the fact that they can be approximated to an arbitrary degree of approximation is used to argue that only algorithmic solutions need to be considered. In the other, connectionist architectures are thought to be the implementation medium for symbolic theories, much as the computer hardware is the implementation medium for software. In section 3.2, I have considered and rejected these arguments. I showed that in principle the symbolic and nonsymbolic solutions may be alternative theories in the sense that they may make different representational commitments.

The other argument is based on a consideration of the properties of high-level thought, in particular language and problem-solving behavior. Connectionism by itself does not have the constructs, so the argument runs, for capturing these properties, so at best it can only be a way to implement the higher level functions. I will discuss this and related points in section 3.8.

Having granted that connectionism (actually, nonsymbolic theories in general) can make a theoretical difference, I now want to argue that the difference connectionism makes is relatively small to the practice of most of AI. This is the task of the rest of section 3.

3.5 Need for compositionality

Proponents of connectionism sometimes claim that solutions in the symbolic paradigm are composed from constituents, while connectionist solutions are holistic, i.e., they cannot be explained as compositions of parts. Composition, in this argument, is taken to be intrinsically an algorithmic process.

Certainly, for some simple problems there exist connectionist solutions with this holistic character. For example, there are connectionist solutions to character recognition which directly map from pixels to characters and which cannot be explained as composing evidence about the features such as closed curves, lines, and their relations. Character recognition by template matching, though not a connectionist solution, is another example whose information processing cannot be explained as feature composition. But as problems get more complex, the advantages of modularization and composition are as important for connectionist approaches as they are for house-building or algorithmic AI. A key point is that composition may be done connectionistically, i.e., it does not always require algorithmic methods.

To see this, let us consider word recognition, a problem area which has attracted significant connectionist attention (McClelland, Rumelhart, and Hinton, 1986). Let us take the word "QUEEN".[5] A "featureless" connectionist solution similar to the one for individual characters can be imagined, but a more natural one would be one which in some sense composes the evidence about individual characters into a recognition of the word. In fact, the connectionist solution in McClelland, Rumelhart, and Hinton (1986) has a natural interpretation in these terms. The fact that the word recognition is done by composition does not mean either that each of the characters is explicitly recognized as part of the procedure, or that the evidence is added together in a step-by-step, temporal sequence.

Why is such a compositional solution more natural? Reusability of parts, reduction in learning complexity as well as greater robustness due to intermediate evidence are the major computational advantages of modularization. If the reader doesn't see the power of modularization for word recognition, he can consider sentence recognition and see that if one were to go directly from pixels to sentences without in some sense going through words, the number of recognizers and their complexity would have to be very large even for sentences of bounded length.

These examples also raise questions about the claims of distributedness of connectionist representations. For complex tasks, information is in fact localized into portions of the network. Again, in McClelland, Rumelhart, and Hinton's network for word recognition, physically local subnets can be identified, each corresponding to one of the characters. Thus the hopes of some proponents for almost holographic distributedness of representation are bound to be unrealistic.

3.6 Information processing level abstractions

Marr (1982) originated the method of information processing analysis as a way of separating the essential elements of a theory from implementation level commitments. First, identify an information-processing function with a clear specification about what kind of information is available for the function as input and what kind of information needs to be made available as output by the function. Then specify a particular information-processing (IP) theory for achieving this function by stating what kinds of information the theory proposes need to be represented at various stages in the processing. Actual algorithms can then be proposed to carry out the IP theory. These algorithms will make additional representational commitments. Even though Marr talked of algorithms as the way to realize the IP theory, there is in principle no reason why portions of the implementation cannot be done connectionistically.

Thus IP level abstractions constitute the top-level content of much AI theory making. In the example about recognition of the word "QUEEN" in section 3.5, the IP-level abstractions in terms of which the theory of word recognition was couched were the evidences about the presence of individual characters. The difference between schemes in the symbolic and connectionist paradigms is that these evidences are labeled symbols in the former, which permit abstract rules of compositions to be invoked and instantiated, while in the latter they are represented more directly and affect the processing without undergoing any interpretive process. Interpretation of a piece of a network as evidence about a character is a design and explanatory stance, and is not part of the actual information processing.

As connectionist structures evolve (or are built) to handle increasingly complex phenomena, they will end up having to incorporate their own versions of *modularity* and *composition*. We have already seen this in the only moderately complex word recognition example. When and if we finally have connectionist implementations solving a variety of high-level cognitive problems (say natural-language understanding or planning or diagnosis), the design of such systems will have an enormous amount in common with the corresponding symbolic theories. This commonness will be at the level of information processing abstractions that both classes of theories would need to embody. In fact, the *content* contributions of many of the nominally symbolic theories in AI are really at the level of the IP abstractions to which they make a commitment, and not to the fact that they were implemented in a symbolic structure. Symbols have often merely stood in for *abstractions* that need to be captured one way or another, and have often been used as such. The hard work of theory-making in AI will always remain at the level of proposing the right IP level of abstractions, since they provide the content of the representations. Once the IP level specification of the theory has been given, decisions about partitioning the implementation between connectionist networks and symbolic algorithms can properly follow. Thus, connectionist (and symbolic) approaches are both *realizations* of a more abstract level of description, namely the *information processing (IP) level.*[6]

Rumelhart and McClelland (Rumelhart and McClelland, 1986a) comment that symbolic theories that are common in AI are really explanatory approximations of a theory which is connectionist at a deeper level. To take the "QUEEN" example again, saying that the word is recognized by combining evidences about individual characters in a certain way may appear to be giving an algorithmic account, but this description is really neutral regarding whether the combination is to be done connectionistically or algorithmically. It is not that connectionist structures are the reality and symbolic accounts provide an explanation, it is that the IP abstractions contained in AI theories account for a large portion of the explanatory power.

I argued, in section 3.2, that given a function, the approaches in the symbolic and nonsymbolic paradigms may make rather different representational commitments; in compositional terms, they may be composing rather different subfunctions. In this section I am arguing, seemingly paradoxically, that for complex functions the two theories converge in their representational commitments. A way to clarify this is to think of two stages in the decomposition: an architecture-independent and an architecture-dependent one. The former is an IP theory that will be realized by particular architectures for which additional decompositions will need to be made. Simple functions such as multiplication are so close to the architecture level that we only saw the differences between the representational commitments of the algorithmic and slide-rule solutions. The word recognition problem is sufficiently removed from the architectural level to enable us to see macrosimilarities between computationalist and connectionist solutions. The final performance will, of course, have micro-features that are characteristic of the architecture (such as the "softness of constraints" for connectionist architectures).

Where the architecture-independent theory stops and the architecture-dependent starts does not have a clear line of demarcation. It is an empirical issue, partly related to the primitive functions that can be computed in a particular architecture. The farther away a problem is from the architecture's primitive functions, the more architecture-independent decomposition needs to be done at design time. I believe that certain kinds of retrieval and matching operations, and parameter learning by searching in local regions of space are especially appropriate primitive operations for connectionist architectures.

3.7 Learning to the rescue?

What if connectionism can provide learning mechanisms such that one starts without any such abstractions represented, and the system learns to perform the task in a reasonable amount of time? In that case, connectionism can sidestep nearly all the representational problems and dismiss them as the bane of the symbolic paradigm. The fundamental problem of complex learning is the *credit assignment problem*, i.e, the problem of deciding what part of the system is responsible for either the correct or the incorrect performance in a case, so that the learner knows how to change the structure of the system. Abstractly, the range of variation of the structure in a system can be represented as a multi-dimensional space of parameters, and the process of learning as a search process in that space for a region that corresponds to the right structure of the systems. The more complex the system, the more vast the space to be searched. Thus learning the correct set of parameters by search methods which do not have a powerful notion of credit assignment would work in small search spaces, but would be computationally prohibitive for realistic problems. Does connectionism have a solution to this problem?

If one looks at particular connectionist schemes that have been proposed for some tasks, such as learning tense endings (Rumelhart and McClelland, 1986b), a significant part of the abstractions needed is built into the architecture in the choice of inputs, feedback directions, allocation of subnetworks, and the semantics that underlie the choice of layers for the connectionist schemes. That is, the inputs and the initial configuration incorporate a sufficiently large part of the abstractions needed that what is left to be discovered by the learning algorithms, while nontrivial, is proportionately small. The initial configuration decomposes the search space for learning in such a way that the search problem is much smaller in size. In fact the space is sufficiently small that statistical associations can do the trick.

The recognition scheme for "QUEEN" again provides a good example for illustrating this point. In the McClelland, Rumelhart, and Hinton scheme that I cited earlier, essentially the decisions about which subnet is going to be largely responsible for "Q," which for "U," etc., as well as how the feedback is going to be directed are all made by the experimenter before learning starts. The underlying IP theory is that evidence about individual characters is going to be formed directly from the pixel level, but recognition of "QU" will be done by combining information about the presence of "Q" and "U," as well as their joint likelihood. The degree to which the evidence about them will be combined is determined by the learning algorithm and the examples. In setting up the initial configuration, the designer is actually programming the architecture to reflect the above IP theory of recognizing the word. An alternate theory for word recognition, say one that is more holistic than the above theory (i.e., one that learns the entire word directly from the pixels) will have a different initial configuration. (Of course, because of lack of guidance from the architecture about localizing search during learning, such a network will take a much longer time to learn the word. But that is the point: the designer recognized this and set up the configuration so that learning can occur in a reasonable time.) Thus while the connectionist scheme for word recognition still makes the useful *performance* point about connectionist architectures for problems that have been assumed to require a symbolic implementation, a significant part of the leverage still comes from the IP abstractions that the designer started out with, or have been made possible by an earlier learning phase working with highly-structured configurations.

Thus, connectionism is one way to map from one set of abstractions to a more structured set of abstractions. Most of the representational issues remain, whether or not one adopts connectionism for such mappings.

3.8 The domains for connectionism and symbolic computations

For this discussion, a distinction between "micro" and "macro" phenomena of intelligence is useful. Rumelhart, McClelland, *et al.* (1986) use the former term in the subtitle of their book to indicate that the connectionist theories that they are concerned with deal with the fine details of processes. A duration of 50–100 milliseconds has often been suggested as the size of the temporal "grain" for processes at the micro level. Macro phenomena take place over seconds if not minutes in the case of a human. These evolve over time in such a way that there is a clear temporal ordering of some major behavioral states. For example, take the problem-solving behavior represented by the General Problem Solver (GPS) system. The agent is seen to have a goal at a certain instant, to set up a subgoal at another instant, and so on. Within this problem-solving behavior, the selection of an appropriate operator, which is typically modeled in GPS implementations as a retrieval algorithm from a Table of Connection, could be a "micro" behavior. Many of the phenomena of language and reasoning have a large macro component. Thus this domain includes, but is not restricted to, phenomena whose markings are left in consciousness as a temporal evolution of beliefs, hypotheses, goals, subgoals, etc.

Neither traditional symbolic computationalism nor radical connectionism has much use for this distinction, since all the phenomena of intelligence, micro and macro, are meant to come under their particular purview. I would like to present the case for a division of responsibility between connectionism and symbolic computationalism in accounting for the phenomena of interest. Simply put, the architectures in the connectionist mold offer some elementary functions which are rather different from those assumed in the traditional symbolic paradigm. By the same token, the body of macro phenomena seems to me to have a large symbolic and algorithmic content. A proper integration of these two modes of information processing can be a source of powerful explanations of the total range of the phenomena of intelligence.

I am assuming it as a given that much of high-level thought has a symbolic content to it (see Pylyshyn [1984] for arguments that make this conclusion inescapable). *How much* of language and other aspects of thought require symbolic content can be matter of debate, but certainly logical reasoning should provide at least one example of such behavior. I am aware that a number of philosophical hurdles stand in the way of asserting the symbolic content of conscious thought. Saying that all that passes between people when they converse is airpressure exchanges on the eardrum has its charms, but I will forego them in this discussion.

Asserting the symbolic content of macro phenomena is not the same as asserting that the internal language and representation of the processor that generates them has to be in the same formal system as that of its external behavior. The traditional symbolic paradigm has made this assumption as a working hypothesis, which connectionism challenges. Even if this challenge is granted there is still the problem of figuring out how to get the macro behavior out of the connectionist structure.

Fodor and Pylyshyn (1988) have argued that much of thought has the properties of *productivity* and *systematicity*. Productivity refers to a potentially unbounded recursive combination of thought that is possible in human intelligence. Systematicity refers to the capability of combining thoughts in ways that require abstract representation of underlying forms. Connectionism, according to Fodor and Pylyshyn, may provide some of the architectural primitives for performing parts of what is needed to achieve these characteristics, but cannot be an adequate account in its own terms. We need computations over symbol systems, with their capacity for abstract forms and algorithms, to realize these properties.

In order to account for the highly symbolic content of conscious thought and to place connectionism in a proper relation to it, Smolensky (1988) proposes that connectionism operates at a lower level than the *symbolic*, a level he calls *subsymbolic*. He also posits the existence of a *conscious processor* and an *intuitive processor*. The connectionist proposals are meant to apply directly to the latter. The conscious processor may have algorithmic properties, according to Smolensky, but still a very large part of the information processing activities that have been traditionally attributed to algorithmic architectures really belong in the intuitive processor.

A complete connectionist account, in my view, needs to account for how subsymbolic or nonsymbolic structure integrates smoothly with higher-level process that is heavily symbolic. There is an additional problem that an integrated theory has to face. Thought could be epiphenomenal. However, we know that the phenomena of consciousness have a causal interaction with the behavior of the intuitive processor. What we consciously learn and discuss and think affects our unconscious behavior slowly but surely, and vice versa. What is conscious and willful today becomes unconscious tomorrow. All this raises a more complex constraint for connectionism: it now needs to provide some sort of continuity of representation and process so that this interaction can take place smoothly.

Connectionist and symbolic computationalist phenomena, in my view, have different but overlapping domains. The basic functions that the connectionist architecture delivers are of a very different kind than have been assumed so far in AI, and thus computationalist theories need to take this into account in their formulations. A number of investigators in AI who do theories at this higher level correctly feel the attraction of connectionist-style theories for some parts of their theory-making. I have acknowledged the power of the connectionist claims that for some information-processing phenomena, there exist nonalgorithmic schemes which make fewer (and different) commitments in terms of representational content. Where the impact of connectionism is being felt is in identifying some of the component processes of overall algorithmic theories as places where a connectionist account seems to accord better with intuitions. Thus, while memory retrieval may have interesting connectionist components to it, the basic problem will still remain the principles by which episodes are indexed and stored, except that now one might be open to these encodings being represented connectionistically. For example, I am in complete sympathy with the suggestion by Rumelhart, Smolensky, McClelland, and Hinton (1986) that a schema or a frame is not explicitly represented as such, but is constructed as needed from more general connectionist representations. This does not mean to me that schema theory is only a macro approximation. A schema, in the sense of being IP abstractions needed for certain macro phenomena, is a legitimate conceptual construct. Connectionist architectures offer a particularly interesting way to encode such constructs.

With regard to general AI and connectionism's impact on it, I would like to say, as H. L. Mencken is alleged to have said in a different context, "There is something to what you say, but not much." Much of AI (except where micro phenomena dominate and computationalist AI is simply too hard-edged in its performance) will and should remain largely unaffected by connectionism. I have given two reasons for this. One is that most of the work is in coming up with the information-processing theory of a phenomenon in the first place. The more complex the task is, the more common are the representational issues between connectionism and the symbolic paradigm. The second reason is that none of the connectionist arguments or empirical results show that the symbolic, algorithmic character of thought is either a mistaken hypothesis, purely epiphenomenal or simply irrelevant.

But, in fairness, these architectures (connectionist and all sorts of analog computers) ought to be viewed as exploratory, and in that sense they are contributing to our understanding of the capabilities and limitations of alternatives to the symbolic paradigm.

It seems to me that we need to find a *modus vivendi* between three significant insights about mental architectures:

   (i) A large part of the relevant content theory in AI has to do with the what of mental representations. I have called them IP abstractions.
  (ii) Whatever one's position on the nature of representations below conscious processes, it is clear that processes at or close to that level are intimately connected to language and knowledge, and thus have a large discrete symbolic content.
 (iii) The connectionist ideas on representation suggest how nonsymbolic representations and processes may provide the medium in which thought resides.

4 Current styles of theory-making in AI

I shall now review AI theories of the 1970s and 1980s and see if a view of what makes intelligence a coherent computational phenomenon can be constructed. My discussion will deal with the macro phenomena of intelligence within the context of the symbolic tradition.

From the viewpoint of the paradigms of intelligence that characterize the current work in AI, at the end of the 1960s the computationalist paradigm emerged as the preferred one for much theory-making. I see the research in this paradigm in the next two decades until the contemporary period as belonging to one of three broad groups of stances towards what a computational account of intelligence should look like. The characterization, in terms of three types of theories, that I am about to give is a personal one, and not (yet) part of the field's own self-consciousness; that is, it is really in the form of a thesis about what has been going on in the field from the perspective of a science of intelligence, and where people have been looking for answers, and what sorts of (often unconscious) assumptions about the nature of intelligence are implicit in these theories. Another caveat is that these theories are not mutually exclusive (i.e., some important ideas appear in more than one approach, but with a flavor relevant to the approach), but constitute different ways to talk about the stuff of intelligence, and different answers to its nature. The three classes of theory are:

1 Architectural theories;
2 Abstract logical characterization of an agent's knowledge, and inference mechanisms that operate on this representation;
3 Theories that emphasize generic functional processes in intelligence. Each of these processes generates efficient inferences for a type of information processing task, and gives importance to organizational issues as a major source of this efficiency.

In the next several sections, I consider each class of theories and examine their assumptions about the nature of intelligence.

4.1 Architectural theories

Architectural theories attempt to locate the source of the power of intelligence in the properties of the underlying information processing engine. An architecture is an information processing mechanism that can operate on information represented in a form that is specific to the architecture. In symbolic architectures, the form is specified by a programming language. For example, rule-based architectures accept information in rule languages, and the mechanism is some form of chaining of rules.

The first question about architectural proposals is whether they can in fact support the range of behaviors that intelligence has to generate. For example, Fodor and Pylyshyn (1988) have argued that connectionist architectures cannot support linguistic behavior of the kind associated with humans. But within the symbolic paradigm, this question of sufficiency quickly loses interest since most of the proposed architectures are Turing-universal.

An architecture A is able to perform a task T by virtue both of its *mechanism* as well the *information content* (or just *content*) on which the mechanism operates. The following possibilities describe the role of an architecture in the performance of a task:

(i) A provides the right mechanism for performing T, i.e., A provides a direct explanatory account.

(ii) A is merely one of many architectures with the power to implement A', which is the one with the appropriate mechanism to solve T. If A is Turing universal[7], then of course it can implement any A'. In this case A has no significant explanatory role. The content of A in this case can be split into two parts: that which actually implements the mechanism for the higher level method A', and that which is the information for A' to work on. If one were not aware of the fact that it is really A' that is explanatorily related to task T, but merely observes A performing T, one would come up with an inadequate explanation of how T is being performed.

(iii) A' still is the right mechanism for T, but A has the right mechanisms for evolving or learning A' under the right conditions. So now A' still has the major explanatory role in the performance of T. However, if A can evolve or learn the relevant architectures for a large variety of tasks $\{Ti\}$, then A has a significant role to play in explaining the sources of power for performance of $\{Ti\}$ as a whole. The role of A in the evolution or learning has to go beyond its Turing universality. One way in which A can be especially effective in helping to learn A' is if their mechanisms are very similar, differing largely in the level of the abstraction of the content on which they operate.

(iv) A provides the right mechanisms for a *part of* T, while other architectures are appropriate for other parts of T. Different parts of T are being performed by different architectures.

Possibilities (iii) and (iv) look similar: both of them seem to make commitments to multiple mechanisms, but there are important differences. In (iv), I am talking about a "horizontal" form of multiplicity, where the architectures involved have the relationship of co-operation, while in (iii) the relationship is a "vertical" one, where A' is being implemented by A.

Architectural theories in AI have been particularly vulnerable to the confusions of levels suggested in (ii) above: often, architectures at too low a level of abstraction are pushed too hard to provide explanatory accounts of high level phenomena. I want to call this the *unitary architecture* assumption to refer to the implication that the source of the power of intelligence is one mechanism or method. This is a form of reductionism, the impulse toward which is very strong as a result of our scientific traditions.

Let me use some concrete illustrations of the level of confusion that I just mentioned. Consider general representation schemes such as production rules, logical clauses, frames, or semantic networks. For each, a corresponding inference scheme is defined: forward or backward chaining in production systems, truth maintenance (Doyle, 1979) or resolution processes for logical sentences, various kinds of interpreters for frames or semantic networks, and so on. Then any particular problem, say diagnosis or design, is solved by attempting to program a solution using the underlying architecture. For example, diagnosis would be treated as particular example of truth maintenance, backward chaining, propagation of values in a network, or whatever processes the underlying architectures directly support. Thus the diagnostic problem is reduced to programming in a given architecture. The inference machinery at the level of the architecture, which is incidental, is given much more importance than the inference processes that are appropriate for diagnosis as a class of problem.

The case of metarules in production systems can be used to illustrate several points I have made abstractly in previous paragraphs. In spite of the rhetoric that accompanied the birth of rule-based expert systems, which spoke of a domain-specific knowledge base and a general, all-purpose inference engine, the inference processes and control at the rule level were inadequate to perform a wide variety of tasks. The knowledge base, which contained supposedly only domain-specific factual or heuristic knowledge, increasingly acquired rules whose role was to provide strategic knowledge of a domain-independent nature. That is, it was seen that *there were phenomena essential to intelligent behavior that were above the rule level of architecture, but were not merely a collection of agent-specific world facts.* At this point, the idea of *metarules* was introduced, where each metarule was a domain-independent[8] control rule that helped organize the knowledge base for a particular type of problem-solving activity. However, the control versus domain-knowledge distinction is a high level statement about the content or role of knowledge and not a syntactic statement about a particular architecture. If the desired problem solving behavior did come about as the result of the metarule, the rule architecture was not *a priori* responsible; instead, the credit should go to the particular control knowledge represented by the metarule. While metarules had the germ of the idea that interesting control issues were being given short shrift in rule-based approaches, it is interesting that until Clancey's work (Clancey and Letsinger, 1984), the syntactic aspect of metarules, not their content, dominated the discussion on control in rule-based system discussions. Similarly, conflict resolution in rule-based systems was approached in a mainly syntactic manner.

My view is that a satisfactory architectural account of intelligence will need to handle two different kinds of multiplicity of architectures as hinted at in (iii) and (iv). On the one hand, in (iii), a description of the sources of power of intelligence will involve not only an account of the general architecture, but also of the methods and strategies that characterize intelligence and how they relate to the general architecture. On the other hand, the architecture needed for deliberation – the reasoning- or search-based paradigms of problem solving – may well be different from the architecture for memory. The proposals on connectionism, frames and semantic networks are motivated by intuitions about the parallel and associational properties of memory. Hence, these architectures have properties that make them attractive for knowledge storage, organization, and retrieval. The rule-based architectures are motivated by what is needed for sequential reasoning or problem solving by exploration of search spaces. What is needed is an integration of these two sets of intuitions as collaborating architectures, as suggested in (iv) above.

The arguments of this section should not be construed as against the idea of general cognitive architectures. In fact, I believe that the SOAR architecture proposal of Newell, Laird and Rosenbloom (1987) is an attractive general architecture for intelligence in the deliberative mode. SOAR has properties that make it an appropriate implementation vehicle for a variety of higher level methods and strategies, and its learning mechanisms can potentially learn these strategies. My argument in this section is really against architectural reductionism as a point of view, and not than against specific architectural proposals. This reductionism has often restricted the search for the sources of power to the general architecture, and has failed to pay sufficient attention to the reperoire of generic information processing methods and strategies that underlie intelligent behavior. Even when they are implemented using the general architecture, these strategies remain independent sources of power both for scientific explanation and for engineering of knowledge systems.

What are the generic information processing strategies that comprise intelligence and what are their properties? What role do they play in giving intelligence its power? These issues are the subject of sections 4.3 and 5.

4.2 Theories of intelligence based on abstract logical characterization of agents

In many circles some version of logic is thought to be the proper language of characterizing all computation, and by extension, intelligence. By logic is meant a variant of first-order predicate calculus, or at least a system where the notion of truth-based semantics is central and inference-making is characterized by truth-preserving transformations.[9] The way logic has actually been used in AI, however, combines a number of the distinct roles that logic can play. We can begin by noting two broad roles for logic:

1 logic for abstractly characterizing and analyzing what an agent knows, versus
2 logic as a representation for knowledge, and logical deduction as the basic information processing activity in intelligence.

First of all, there seems to be a general tendency, even among those who do not adopt the logic paradigm for knowledge representation and inference, to concede to logic the status as the appropriate language for the abstract characterization of an agent, i.e., for meta-AI analysis. While this seems like one good possibility, it does not seem to me the only or even a compelling possibility. Standing outside an intelligent agent, one can take two distinct abstract stances toward it: the agent as a performer of functions, or the agent as a knower of propositions. There are AI proposals and work that correspond to both these viewpoints. In Marr's work on vision (see section 3.6), for example, the agent is characterized *functionally*, i.e., by an information-processing task that transforms information of one kind into that of another kind. On the other hand, the tradition in logic-based AI is one of attributing a body of knowledge to the agent. It is certainly not obvious why the knowledge view should necessarily dominate even at the level of abstract characterization. I will hold later in this chapter that the functional view has superior capabilities for abstract specification of an intelligent agent.

The idea of abstract characterization of an intelligent agent through logic was first detailed by McCarthy and Hayes (1969) where they proposed the now-famous *epistemic-heuristic* decomposition of an actual intelligent agent. This distinction has echoes of the Chomskyan competence/performance distinction in language (see Gomez and Chandrasekaran, 1981). The agent as a knower is characterized by the epistemic component. What kinds of knowledge are to go into the epistemic component is not clear, but one would think that it would depend on the theorist's view of what kinds of knowledge *characterize* intelligence. Thus the epistemic component must represent a theory of the ontology of the mental stuff. The heuristic part is that part of the agent which actually makes him an efficient information processor, using the knowledge in the epistemic part to solve problems and do whatever intelligent agents do. An analogy would be that a calculator's epistemic part would be the axioms of number theory, while its heuristic part would be the particular representations and algorithms. This example also makes clear the relationship of the epistemic/heuristic distinction to the competence/performance distinction of Chomsky. McCarthy and Hayes proposed that the epistemic part be represented by a logical calculus, and in fact discussed the kind of logic and the kinds of predicates that would be needed for adequacy of representation as they conceived the epistemic part. In this attempt to separate the *what* of intelligence with the *how* of implementation, the McCarthy-Hayes proposal follows a more general idea in computer science, but identifies the *what* with the propositional knowledge of the agent. This is not, however, neutral with respect to consequences.

The epistemic/heuristic distinction as a means of separating the essential content of an agent from the implementation details and "mere" efficiency considerations is independent of logic as a representation. All that the epistemic/heuristic distinction demands is that the essential characterization of an information processor be kept separate from the implementation details. Logical representation of the epistemic part is only one alternative for doing this. As I mentioned, within AI, an alternative to McCarthy and Hayes' suggestion is Marr's proposal that this distinction be carried out by separating the information-processing task (the input-output specification), the algorithm carrying out the task, and the mechanism by which the algorithm is implemented.

Even more important is that there is no self-evident way of deciding, in a theory-neutral fashion, exactly what is epistemic, and what is merely heuristic. In fact, in some logical theories in AI, some important control phenomena have been moving from the heuristic component to the epistemic component, as a consensus builds in AI that a certain phenomenon is *really* not simply heuristic, but part of the stuff of intelligence. A good example of this is the development within the logic camp of families of *default or nonmonotonic logics*.

In his paper on frames, Minsky (1975) argued that if frames could stand for stereotypes of concepts, it was possible to do a form of default reasoning where, in the absence of specific information to the contrary, a reasoning system would assume default values associated with the features of a frame, thus allowing missing information to be plausibly inferred, greatly decreasing storage requirements (only nondefault values, i.e., exceptions, need to be stored), and increasing retrieval speed. At first blush, all these useful properties were "heuristic" aspects, i.e., how to get the computation done faster. However, theorists then started hypothesizing the existence of something called "default reasoning" or "nonmonotonic logic" in order to account for this phenomenon in a rigorous way. It is almost as if the lowly "heuristic" component is in fact what the action in AI is often about, while the epistemic part appropriates the nuggets of organizational wisdom that research in the heuristic component identifies.

Now of course there is nothing wrong with this as a way of making scientific progress: let the system builders discover phenomena experimentally and let the theoreticians follow up with formalization. However, the eventual success of this kind of formalization is questionable. Is there in fact a set of inference rules that compactly characterize all and only default inferences? I propose that terms such as "nonmonotonic logic" are reifications: a complete account would require specification of a much larger set of rules than what is normally thought of as inference rules, so large as to be virtually coextensive with the entire set of distinct types of functions in which frames get used: scripts, plans, etc.

We next discuss how the distinct notions of abstractly characterizing an intelligent agent, namely, the epistemic/heuristic distinction, and logic as a representation for the epistemic component, are often conflated.

4.2.1 Logic for representation

The proposal to use logic for representation of knowledge could be in the service of two rather different purposes: one, in order to reason *about* the agent, and two, to model the reasoning *of* the agent. The former is in the spirit of certain ideas in computer science where a program may be in any appropriate language, but reasoning about the program, for example, to establish its correctness, is often done using logic. However, in practice, almost all use of logic as knowledge representation in AI has been in the service of the latter, i.e., to actually create reasoning agents.

Logic as knowledge representation makes a serious commitment to knowledge as propositions, and to True/False judgements as the basic *use* of knowledge. It is also closely connected to the belief that the aim of intelligence is to draw *correct* conclusions. In this view, what human beings often do (for example, draw plausible, useful, but strictly speaking, logically-incorrect conclusions), is interesting as psychology, but that only shows up humans as approximations to the ideal intelligent agent, whose aim is to be correct.

Now, is "truth" in fact the right kind of basic interpretive framework for knowledge? Or are notions of functional adequacy, i.e., knowledge that helps to get certain kinds of tasks done, or the related notions of plausibility, relevance, etc. more effective in capturing the way agents in fact use knowledge? My 16-month old daughter, when shown a pear, said, "apple!" Is it more than mere parental pride that makes me attribute a certain measure of intelligence to that remark, when, viewed strictly as an utterer of propositions, she told an untruth? What kind of a theory of intelligence can explain that her conclusion was adequate for the occasion: she could get away with that error for most purposes – she could eat the pear and get nourishment, for example – while an equally false proposition, "It's a chair," would not give her similar advantages?

A number of theoretical advantages have been claimed for logic in AI, including *precision* and the *existence of a semantics*. The problem is that the semantics are not at the most appropriate level for the problem at hand, and logic is neither a unique nor a privileged way to be precise.

4.2.2 Intelligence has other functions than correctness

Laws of justification are not identical to laws of thought, Boole notwithstanding. While it would be useful for an intelligent agent to have the former laws and apply them appropriately, those laws alone cannot account for the power of intelligence as a process. It seems highly plausible to me that much of the power of intelligence arises not in its ability to lead to correct conclusions, but in its ability to direct explorations, retrieve plausible ideas, and focus the more computationally expensive justification processes where they are absolutely required. Thus a significant part of the power of intelligence really resides in what has been called the heuristic part, and theories of intelligence will also need to be theories of that part of the decomposition, the part that is most concerned with computational feasibility. Abstraction in the manner proposed by logic advocates *separates knowledge from its function*, and this leads to missing important aspects of the form and content of knowledge.

It is often argued that the epistemic/heuristic distinction is tactical: get the terms needed right, before worrying about how to actually use them in reasoning. For example, before building, say, common-sense reasoners, let us get all ontology of common-sense reasoning right: "know," "cause," etc. The thrust of my argument is that, as a rule, a use-independent study of such terms is likely to make distinctions that are not needed by the processing part and miss some that are.

This is not to say that logic, as a set of ideas about *justification*, is not important to intelligence. How intelligent agents discover justifications, how they integrate them with discovery procedures for a final answer that is plausibly correct, and how this is done in such a way that the total computational process is controlled in complexity are indeed questions for AI as an information-processing theory of intelligence. In this view, logic is a brick intelligence builds, rather than the brick out of which intelligence is built.

In my opinion, the laudable goal of separating the knowledge necessary for intelligence from the implementation details needs to be achieved by concentrating on the functional characteristics of intelligence. This brings me to the third set of theories.

4.3 Generic functional theories of intelligence

The theories that I have in mind in this category identify a generic, functional property of intelligence which is used to solve a "natural kind" of cognitive problem. Examples of such theories are: the GPS means-ends theory of problem solving (Newell and Simon, 1972), the Frame theory of knowledge organization (Minsky, 1975), Schank's Conceptual Dependency theory (CD), scripts (Schank and Abelson, 1977) and memory theories (Schank, 1982a), my own work at Ohio State on generic types of problem solving (Chandrasekaran, 1983; 1986a; 1987). These theories typically emphasize some *organizational* aspect, which facilitates some particular *class of inferences*, or *computations*, or *constructions* in a computationally efficient way. An abstract description of these processes would be replete with terms that carry an information-processing strategy connotation, such as *default, goals, subgoals, expectations, plans,* and *classification.* Knowledge of an agent is encoded using such terms, i.e., these strategy-connoting terms in fact contribute to the epistemic part. Each of these processes constitutes a generic, i.e., domain-independent,[10] information-processing strategy and is a functional unit of intelligence as a process. Each is associated with characteristic types of knowledge and inference.

4.3.1 Generic information-processing strategies in diagnostic reasoning

In my own work on knowledge-based problem solving, I have proposed a number of such generic information processing strategies. In this section, I would like to show how these strategies help in solving a computationally-complex problem such as diagnosis, and thus suggest how strategies of this kind characterize intelligence.

Formally, the diagnostic problem can be defined as follows: find a mapping from the set of all subsets of observations of a system, to the set of all subsets of possible malfunctions, such that the malfunctions in the subset best explain the observations.

A mathematician's interest in the problem would be satisfied once it can be shown that under certain assumptions this task is *computable*, i.e., an algorithm exists to perform this mapping. He might even further wish to derive the computational complexity of this task for various assumptions about the domain and the range of this mapping. This directly leads to AI algorithms of a set-covering variety for diagnosis (Reggia, *et al.*, 1985).

A logician would consider the solution epistemically complete if he can provide a formalism to list the relevant medical facts and formulate the decision problem as deducing a correct conclusion. Some diagnostic formalisms, such as the ones based on truth maintenance systems, view the diagnostic problem as one more version of truth-maintenance activity (Reiter, 1987).

Now, each of these methods is computationally quite complex, and without extensive addition of knowledge as "heuristics," the problem cannot be solved in anything resembling real time. It is clear, however, that the abstract problem is one that faces intelligent agents on a regular basis: *how to map from states of the world to their explanations?* From the tribesman on a hunt who needs to construct an explanation of observations on the jungle ground to a scientist constructing theories, this basic problem recurs in many forms. Of course, not all versions of the problem are in fact solved by humans, but many versions of the problem, such as medical diagnosis, are solved quite routinely. Presumably something about the agent as an intelligent information processor directly plays a role in this solution process.

Because of our concern in this paper with the structure of intelligence, instead of looking for solutions to this problem in particular domains (such as simple devices, where perhaps tractable algorithms – e.g., direct-mapping tables that go from symptoms to diagnoses – might exist and be programmed), let us ask the following question: *What is an intelligence that it can perform this task?* That is, we are interested in the relation between mental structures and the performance of the diagnostic task. The distinction that we are seeking can be made clearer by considering multiplication. Multiplication viewed as a computational task has been sufficiently studied that very fast and efficient algorithms are available, and are routinely used by today's computers. On the other hand if we were to ask, "How does a person (e.g., an arithmetic prodigy) actually perform multiplication in the head?", the answer will be different from the multiplication algorithms just mentioned. The answer would need to be given in terms of how the particular problem is solved by using more generic mental structures. Now, of course, the answer would differ depending upon one's theory of what those mental structures are.

I have already indicated what kinds of answers to this question would be fostered by unitary architectures: in rule-based architectures, the problem solver will simply need to have a sufficient number of rules about malfunctions and observations, and frame-theorists would propose that diagnostic knowledge is represented as frames representing domain concepts such as malfunctions, etc. The inference methods that are applicable to each of the above are fixed at the level of the functional architecture: some form of forward or backward chaining for rule systems, and some form of inheritance mechanisms as embedded procedures for frame systems. I have argued elsewhere how this level of abstraction for control is too low to perspicuously encode the inference processes that apply at the level of the task, i.e., diagnosis.

In my work on knowledge-based reasoning, I have identified several generic strategies, each with a well-defined information processing function. Each of them uses knowledge in certain forms, organized in certain ways, and employs inference strategies that are appropriate to the task. I have described, in a series of papers, how these strategies can be used in different combinations to put together diagnostic or design systems. In the rest of this section, I want to describe briefly how three strategies of the above-described type can come together to solve a number of real world versions of the diagnostic task.

In many domains, knowledge is available in the form of malfunction hierarchies (e.g., disease hierarchies in medicine), and for each malfunction hypothesis in the hierarchy, a mapping from observations to the degree of plausibility of hypothesis can be done using a strategy of concept matching. In concept matching, a concept is matched to data by a hierarchy of abstractions, each of which produces a degree of local match. In such domains, the diagnostic problem can be decomposed into three sub-problems (Chandrasekaran, 1986a; Josephson, *et al.*, 1987):

1 Hierarchical classification: a classification process on the diagnostic hierarchy is invoked. At the end of the classification process a set of tip nodes of the diagnostic hierarchy are "established" to some degree of plausibility, each explaining a set of observations. In the medical domain, these tip nodes will correspond to specific diseases or in the case of mechanical systems, they may be malfunctions of specific components.

2 Concept-matching: each of the hypotheses in the classification process is evaluated by appealing to the appropriate concept-matching structures which map from relevant data to symbolic confidence value for that hypothesis.

3 Abductive assembly: the classification process (in conjunction with the concept matchers) terminates in a small number of highly plausible hypotheses, each explaining a subset of observations. An *abductive assembly* strategy, which uses knowledge about interaction among malfunctions, can be used to assemble a subset of them into a composite hypothesis that best explains all the data.

Under the right conditions of knowledge availability, each of the above strategies is computationally tractable. In hierarchical classification, entire subtrees can be pruned if a node is rejected. The mapping from data to concept matching can be done by hierarchical abstractions giving concept matching a similar computational advantage. Abductive assembly can be computationally expensive, but if some other process can prune the space and generate only a small number of hypotheses to begin with, then its computational demand can be kept under control. This is precisely what hierarchical classification does in the above scheme.

The original intractable problem has been converted, by a series of information-processing strategies and by appropriate types of knowledge and control, into a tractable one *for those versions where knowledge of the required form is available.*

Classification as a strategy is ubiquitous in human reasoning because of the computational advantages of indexing action knowledge over equivalence classes of states, instead of the states themselves. How classification hierarchies are created – from examples, from other types of knowledge structures, etc. – requires an additional set of answers. I have discussed elsewhere (Sembugamorthy and Chandrasekaran, 1986) how knowledge of the relationships between structure and the functions of components, i.e., how the devices work, can often be used to derive such malfunction hierarchies. These processes in turn are generic, requiring knowledge in specific forms and using appropriate but characteristic inference strategies.

Let me make something quite clear at this point. The claim is not that diagnosis is *logically* a classification problem, or even that all human diagnostic reasoning uses classification as one of the strategies. What I have attempted to show is that many versions of the diagnostic problem can be, and often are, solved by having knowledge in forms that this and other generic strategies can use. If that knowledge is not available, either other strategies that can generate knowledge in that form are invoked, or other strategies that can help solve the diagnostic problem without classification hierarchies are attempted. In particular, strategies such as *reasoning by analogy* to an earlier case, or merely retrieval of similar cases and explaining the differences by adding, deleting or modifying diagnostic hypotheses are tried. In fact, as mentioned earlier, the whole collection of retrieval strategies (Schank, 1982a) are themselves information-processing strategies of the functional kind that I have been talking about.

4.3.2 Functional theories: heuristic becomes epistemic
What I have so far called functional theories within AI – GPS, frames as stereotypes, conceptual dependency theory, scripts, and generic tasks in problem solving – all have this in common: they all typically emphasize some organizational aspect and facilitate some particular kind of inference or construction in a computationally efficient way. In other words, computational feasibility – the so-called heuristic component – is built into this kind of theory-making. Organization serves directly in securing computational feasibility. A direct epistemic analysis of the underlying problem would typically miss these constructs. Once you discover them you can go back and start doing epistemic analysis on them, but basically the way of discovering them is not by simply taking an epistemic stance toward them (here I use "epistemic" in the McCarthy and Hayes sense of the term).

Another important thing with respect to knowledge is that each of these approaches provides primitive terms for encoding the relevant knowledge. GPS proposes that some of the knowledge ought to be encoded in the form of goals and subgoals. The conceptual dependency primitives are provided from the CD theory. Our work on generic tasks has resulted in a family of languages, each of which provides primitives to capture the knowledge needed for that one of the generic strategies. In my view, these primitives constitute part of the vocabulary of the language of thought.

The search for such strategies as the basic task of research in AI in fact defines a new view of epistemics: it is the abstract characterization of such strategies and the corresponding types of knowledge. Such an abstract description of these processes would be replete with terms that carry an information processing strategy connotation, such as *default*, *goals*, *sub-goals*, *expectations*, *plans*, and *classification*.

5. A proposal on the nature of intelligent information processing

I have given an overview of the three kinds of theories that have been advanced about the nature of intelligence:[11]

architectural theories
logical abstraction theories, and
functional theories

and indicated a clear preference for functional theories. I would now like to generalize this preference into a proposal about the nature of intelligence.

The Proposal

Intelligence is a coherent repertoire of generic information-processing strategies, each of which solves a type of problem in a computationally efficient way, using knowledge of certain types, organized in a specific way, and using specific and locally appropriate control strategies.

What is common, as intelligent agents, between Einstein, the man-on-the street, the tribesman on a hunt, and, probably, intelligent alpha-centaurians (if such things exist) is that they all face very similar computational problems, and the *kinds* of solutions that they adopt for these problem have an essential similarity. They all use plans, indexed by goals, as an efficient means of synthesizing actions, they all use some version of scripts and conceptual dependency primitives to organize their inferences, they all use classification strategies to match actions to world states, etc., etc. Of course, the strategies that we may discover by *studying human information processing* may not be – and in all likelihood are not – coextensive with the general class of such strategies. That would be too anthropomorphic a view of intelligence. The task of AI as the science of intelligence is to identify these strategies concretely, and understand how they integrate into coherent wholes.

In a sense this approach can be called *abstract psychology* because it doesn't discuss a particular human being or even the class of human beings. What it says is that the description of cognitive strategies provides a language in which to describe intelligent agents. And also, I think, it is consistent with the view of intelligence as a biological, evolvable collection of coherent "kluges" that work together. So intelligence is not really defined as one thing – architecture or function – it is really a collection of strategies. The fact that the strategies all contribute to computational feasibility distinguishes them as a characterizable class of information processes.

Some qualifying remarks about the scope of my discussion are perhaps necessary. Almost all my discussion has emphasized cognitive phenomena in contradistinction to perceptual phenomena. Obviously the role of knowledge and control in perception is not the same issue as its role in cognition. In general, I have not included in my discussion what Fodor (1983b) calls *input modules* (as opposed to central processes): his modules include some aspects of parsing in language, for example. The spirit of what I say in this paper can be extended to these other phenomena, I believe. But that is a task for another day.

6. Concluding remarks

In this final section, I would like to make some remarks about the relationship of functional theories to architectural and abstract characterization theories.

Some of the intuitions behind the architectural theories and abstract characterization theories are in fact valid and useful, but theory-making of these kinds can be enhanced by asking questions of the functional kind first. In particular, considering architectural theories first, it is probably true that there *does* exist an architecture within which mental phenomena can be particularly appropriately implemented. Certainly, in the case of human intelligence there *is* some level to which the information-processing architecture question can be reduced: if needed, to the neuronal information-processing level; possibly to what connectionists call the subsymbolic level; preferably to the level of something like the SOAR architecture. I don't intend to argue against the existence of that level of the architecture and its properties. However, the content phenomena of intelligence as a computation are not expressed at that level, and require an analysis at the functional level as I have indicated.

There is another aspect to the architectural issue. To the extent that each of the strategies uses knowledge primitives, and comes with its own inference methods, a local architecture can be associated with it. For example, we have developed a family of high-level architectures (or, it comes to the same thing, languages) for the generic information-processing strategies that we have identified: a language called CSRL (Bylander and Mittal, 1986) supports hierarchical classification and structured concept matching, PEIRCE (Punch, *et al.*, 1986) supports abductive assembly, and so on. These task-specific architectures are "emergent" from the underlying more general cognitive architecture, but the knowledge and inference terms associated with them provide part of the content of the general architecture, as discussed in section 4.1.

The functional theories suggest a new approach to epistemics. They do not argue against the importance of characterizing intelligence independent of incidental implementation considerations (neurons versus transistors, for example), or of agent-specific heuristic knowledge (such as the knowledge that a particular agent might have – for example, "When considering malfunctions in an electronic circuit, always check the power source first"). It is just that this approach proposes an alternative basis on which to make the abstract characterization. I propose that we ask, "What kinds of processes do intelligent agents perform?", rather than, "What kinds of things do they know?" as the starting point. The claim is that what they *need* to know in order to do the tasks in fact provides a new way of doing the epistemic analysis of an agent in the abstract. At the very least, functional theories provide the content information about intelligence as computation that needs to be specified abstractly.

Intelligence, as we know it, is (so far) a biological phenomenon, rather than a logical or mathematical phenomenon. A comparison is often made between intelligence and flight, and people who would build flying machines by basing them on birds usually come off looking less good in this comparison. The problem with this analogy is that flying is one (rather well-defined) function, while intelligence is not characterized by one function. A better analogy would be with understanding life: all we know about life is that it is what biological phenomena pertain to. Any particular aspect of life, for example, self-reproduction, can be studied mathematically, but there has been precious little so far to show for such studies from the viewpoint of understanding biology. Intelligence is not only analogous to biology, but is also, as a phenomenon in nature, so far only exhibited in biological organisms of a certain complexity. The actual content of information-processing phenomena of intelligence is bound to be rather complex. What is biological about the proposal in this paper is that intelligence is explained as part evolutionary, part cultural, part life-time interaction and integration of a number of elementary strategies into more and more complex strategies, but all of them are united by this basic concern with computational feasibility for the generation of plausible solutions, rather than with deductive correctness. To see biological intelligence as a mere approximate attempt to achieve logical correctness is to miss the point of intelligence completely. Of course, there are processes in intelligence that over a long period of time and collectively over humankind help to produce increasingly higher-fidelity internal representations, but that is just one part of being intelligent, and in any case such processes are themselves subject to computational feasibility constraints. Once highly plausible candidates for hypotheses about the world are put together by such processes (such as abductive assembly that might be used in producing an explanation in science), then explicit justification processes may be used to verify them.

Notes

Support under US Defense Research Projects Agency through RADC Contract F30602–85–C–0010 and by the Air Force Office of Scientific Research, grant 87–0090 during the preparation of this paper is gratefully acknowledged. I would like to thank Dean Allemang, Larry Birnbaum, Tom Bylander, Ashok Goel, Vinod Goel, John and Susan Josephson, Allen Newell, Derek Partridge, Bill Punch, N. Sridharan, and Jon Sticklen for commenting on early drafts. I *know* that few of them agree with all the things that I say here, so the usual qualification that the author takes responsibility for what is said is particularly relevant.

1 I am unhappy with this term to describe the commitment to computation over discrete symbolic systems, since I think that all representations are symbolic, otherwise they wouldn't be representations. There is really no satisfactory, generally-agreed brief term for this. Fodor and Pylyshyn (1988) use the term "classical" models, Dennett (1986) uses the term, "High Church Computationalism" and so on. I will stick with the terms "symbolic paradigm," "symbolic approaches," and "symbolic computationalism" to refer to computation over discrete symbol systems.

2 Cybernetics as a movement had broader concerns than the issues surrounding feedback control, as applied by Wiener to understanding control and communication in animals and machines. Information and automata theories and neural nets as automata were all part of the cybernetic milieu of bringing certain biological phenomena under the rigor of formalisms. I discuss automata and neural nets shortly.

3 It is an open question whether our understanding of induction, for example, was in fact genuinely advanced from the viewpoint of building machines to perform induction machines.

4 Whether perception, if it is an inferential process, necessarily has to be continuous with cognitive processes (i.e., they all have access to one knowledge base of an agent), is a completely different issue (Fodor, 1983b). I am mentioning it here because the perception as inference thesis does not necessarily mean one monolithic process for all the phenomena of intelligence.

5 My description of word recognition is modeled after the example given in McClelland, Rumelhart, and Hinton cited above. The word that they discuss is "TAKE."

6 I am indebted to Dean Allemang and Ashok Goel, who noted that at this level of abstraction, the distinctions between the two approaches to complex problems become small relative to their commonalities.

7 There is nothing in this argument that turns on whether or not intelligence can be accounted for by Turing-computable functions only.

8 The word "domain" is a possible source of confusion. In AI, the term has come to refer almost exclusively to what one might call specific subject matter – or a collection of facts about a miniworld – such as medicine, whereas in many philosophical discussions about mind, I have seen the term refer to any generic

faculty, such as visual perception, or even tasks such as natural-language understanding or diagnostic reasoning. In this paper, I will use the term as it has become familiar in AI. The assumption is that no theory of intelligence need specifically deal with medical facts *per se*, but it will need to deal with phenomena such as diagnostic problem solving or natural-language understanding.

9 I am sure this characterization is not accurate in details. I am told that there are things such as "imperative logics," where some of the above characterization might not hold good. Within AI, nonmonotonic logic relaxes the truth-preserving requirement in transformations. I believe that the thrust of my arguments nevertheless remain valid.

10 Please see the earlier note 8 on the word "domain" here.

11 Specifically, "about the nature of 'macro' phenomena in intelligence," since I have acknowledged that connectionist-like theories may have something useful to say about the microstructure.

2 The formal foundations of AI

In addition to the various edited collections and single-author volumes that concentrate on the philosophical foundations of AI, there is a recent collected volume that is devoted to the formal foundations of AI (Genesereth and Nilsson, 1987). The existence of this specific work relieves us of the necessity of devoting a large number of pages in the present collection to this important foundational aspect of AI. Nevertheless, for the sake of completeness and in order to provide a natural focus for the papers that do consider formal foundational issues, we decided to include the current chapter.

In the previous section Chandrasekaran introduced and discussed the role and flavour of logical abstraction theories in AI. Logical formalisms have always been favored as the best candidates with which to construct a science of AI, and notable successes can be found: McCarthy's LISP, the basic language of AI, based on the lambda calculus, and PROLOG, a language now inextricably intertwined with expert systems' technology. The latter became a practical possibility with the discovery of linear-time algorithms based on Robinson's resolution principle for mechanical proof. Another AI sub-area in which formal results have been obtained is heuristic and non-heuristic search: efficient searching of a large space of possibilities is seen by many to be a paradigm with general applicability in AI, and definite progress has been made with the formal characterization of the problem.

Nevertheless, the search for formal foundations for AI, as most of its advocates would admit, has not been a resounding success. Some of the more well-defined sub-areas of AI can be based on well-understood logics, but others have so far proved beyond the scope of logical schemes. The responses of the formalists are varied: some are exploring more powerful logics, such as non-monotonic systems, others believe that research should remain within well-understood first-order logics and try to restate the intractable problems in that formalism.

In the next section Marr argues for concentrating on phenomena that have simple, abstract theories. In section 4 Wilks will put this class of theory in the context of a number of other important interpretations of the word 'theory.' Banerji then advocates (in section 10) the application to AI of the logic-based program verification techniques favoured in the formal approach to computer science. And in section 11 Hewitt presents the case against the use of logical inference mechanisms to implement intelligent decision-making.

In the following paper, Przymusinski describes a new model-theoretic-based approach to the declarative semantics of logic programs. He then shows its close relationship to four major formalizations of non-monotonic reasoning: circumscription, closed world assumption, autoepistemic logic, and default theory.

In the second paper Weyhrauch describes a working computer program, FOL, which converses in the language of first-order logic. In addition, the system is reflexive, i.e. it can reason about its own operations.

Non-monotonic reasoning versus logic programming: a new perspective

Teodor C. Przymusinski

1 Introduction

The area of *non-monotonic reasoning* and the area of *logic programming* are of crucial and growing significance to artificial intelligence and to the whole field of computer science. It is therefore important to achieve a better understanding of the relationship existing between these two fields.

The major goal in the area of non-monotonic reasoning is to find adequate and sufficiently powerful formalizations of various types of non-monotonic reasoning – including common-sense reasoning – and to develop efficient ways of their implementation. Most of the currently existing formalizations are based on mathematical logic.

Logic programming introduced to computer science the important concept of declarative – as opposed to procedural – programming, based on mathematical logic. Logic programs, however, do not use logical negation, but instead rely on a non-monotonic operator – often referred to as *negation as failure* – which represents a procedural form of negation.

Non-monotonic reasoning and logic programming are closely related. The importance of logic programming to the area of non-monotontic reasoning follows from the fact that, as observed by several researchers (see e.g. Reiter, [to appear]) the non-monotonic character of procedural negation used in logic programming often makes it possible to efficiently implement other non-monotonic formalisms in Prolog or in other logic programming languages. Logic programming can also be used to provide formalizations for special forms of non-monotonic reasoning. For example, Kowalski and Sergot's calculus of events (1986) uses Prolog's negation-as-failure operator to formalize the temporal persistence problem in AI.

The importance of the field of non-monotonic reasoning to logic programming is even more apparent. One of the most important and difficult problems in the area of logic programming is that of finding a suitable declarative semantics for logic programming. The importance of this problem stems from the declarative character of logic programming,

49

whereas its difficulty can be largely attributed to the non-monotonic character of the negation operator used in logic programs. This problem can be viewed as the problem of finding a suitable formalization of the type of non-monotonic reasoning used in logic programming.

In spite of this close relationship, the two research areas have progressed largely independently of each other, or at least without as much interaction as one would expect. Recently, however, several researchers proposed a new approach to the problem of declarative semantics of logic programs and developed an elegant and easily intelligible semantics for such programs. They have shown that the proposed semantics is equivalent to suitable forms of four major non-monotonic formalisms: McCarthy's circumscription, Reiter's closed world assumption, Moore's autoepistemic logic, and Reiter's default logic.

These results shed a new light on the semantics of logic programming and the relationship between logic programming and non-monotonic reasoning. They may also contribute to a better understanding of relations existing between various forms of non-monotonic reasoning and to the eventual discovery of deeper underlying principles of non-monotonic reasoning. The aim of this paper is to present an account of these recent developments.

The paper is organized as follows. In sections 2, 3, and 4 we briefly discuss declarative knowledge, non-monotonic reasoning, and logic programming, respectively. In section 5 we describe the proposed semantics of logic programming, and in section 6 we show its equivalence to the four above-mentioned formalizations of non-monotonic reasoning. Section 7 contains concluding remarks.

2 Declarative knowledge

Since the purpose of this paper is to describe a new approach to the *declarative semantics* of logic programs and to show its close relationship to four major formalizations of *non-monotonic reasoning*, we devote this section to a brief discussion of the role of declarative knowledge in AI and the next section to a short discussion of non-monotonic reasoning.

The idea behind the concept of declarative knowledge is to provide intelligent machines with a mathematically precise definition of the knowledge that they possess, in a manner which is independent of procedural considerations, context-free, and easy to manipulate, exchange and reason about.

The importance of declarative representation of knowledge in AI has been stressed by many researchers. In their fundamental paper, McCarthy and Hayes (1969) wrote:

> A computer program capable of acting intelligently in the world must have a general representation of the world in terms of which its inputs are interpreted.

and in his later paper (1987), McCarthy adds:

> Expressing information in declarative sentences is far more modular than expressing it in segments of computer program or in tables. Sentences can be true in much wider contexts than specific programs can be used. The supplier of a fact does not have to understand much how the receiver functions or how or whether the receiver will use it. The same fact can be used for many purposes, because the logical consequences of collections of facts can be available.

Nilsson made a similar point of view a central thesis of his recent paper (to appear):

> Thus my thesis: "General intelligence depends on context-free, c :clarative knowledge and on the means to manipulate it"... The sharpest boundary exists between us and the "proceduralists" who claim that intelligence consists of having numerous special procedures for dealing with all of the situations that might confront an agent. We admit that these procedures may in fact be said to possess knowledge, but such knowledge is tied to the special situations for which the procedures are designed; it is not portable. In our view, an agent built in this way is a collection of niche intelligencies. Such agents may in fact function well in many situations, but we fail to see how they will be able to transport knowledge from one situation to another.

Even some of the researchers who advocate a largely procedural approach to knowledge representation, still see an important role for declarative semantics. McDermott writes:

> One can accept my conclusions about the futility of formalizing knowledge without a program, and yet still, as I do, have a strong intuition that it is better for a notation to have a denotational semantics than not to. One reason for this might be that at least a sound semantics helps ensure that the deductive inferences done by a program will be right... *(1987)*

2.1 Logic in artificial intelligence

In order to provide intelligent machines with declarative knowledge, a language has to be chosen in which this knowledge can be represented. McCarthy (1960) first proposed to use logic as a language for knowledge representation in AI. Later these ideas were amplified and put to work in his joint paper with Hayes (1969). Presently, the so-called "logical approach" to knowledge representation plays an increasingly important role in artificial intelligence. To quote Reiter (to appear):

> Because an agent must reason about something (its knowledge, its beliefs) any consideration of the nature of reasoning requires a concom-

52 *Teodor C. Przymusinski*

mitant concern with how the agent represents its beliefs. The stance adopted by AI research on non-monotonic reasoning is in agreement with the dominant view in AI on knowledge representation; the "knowledge content" of a reasoning program ought to be represented by data structures interpretable as logical formulas of some kind.

3 Non-monotonic reasoning

In the middle of the 1970s, Minsky (1975) and McCarthy (1977b) pointed out that pure classical logic is inadequate to represent the common-sense nature of human reasoning. This difficulty is caused primarily by the non-monotonic nature of human reasoning. Using McCarthy's words (1987):

> While much human reasoning corresponds to that of traditional logic, some important human common sense reasoning seems not to be monotonic. We reach conclusions from certain premises that we would not reach if certain other sentences were included in our premises. For example, learning that I own a car, you conclude that it is appropriate on a certain occasion to ask me for a ride, but when you learn a further fact that the car is in the garage being fixed you no longer draw this conclusion.

Non-monotonicity of human reasoning is caused by the fact that our knowledge about the world is almost always incomplete and therefore we are forced to reason in the absence of complete information. As a result, we often have to revise our conclusions, when new information becomes available.

3.1 Formalizations of non-monotonic reasoning

Once the need for non-monotonic reasoning in AI had been recognized, work began on finding formal foundations of non-monotonic reasoning. Several formalizations of non-monotonic reasoning have been proposed, among which the best known are McCarthy's circumscription (1980; 1986), Reiter's default theory (1980), Moore's autoepistemic logic (1985) (reconstruction of non-monotonic logics of McDermott and Doyle (McDermott and Doyle, 1980; McDermott, 1982)), and Reiter's closed world assumption (1978) (and its extensions).

All of these formalizations are obtained by augmenting a classical first-order logic with some mechanism, which – by allowing defeasible conclusions – permits us to reason in the absence of complete knowledge. In spite of the fact that none of the proposed formalisms as yet can be considered as a completely satisfactory answer to the problem of formalizing non-monotonic reasoning, and that many open problems remain and many controversies surround this area of research (see Hanks and McDermott, 1986; McDermott, 1987), the results obtained so far are encouraging. To quote Reiter again (to appear):

> Nonmonotonicity appears to be the rule, rather than the exception, in much of what passes for human common sense reasoning. The formal study of such reasoning patterns and their applications has made impressive, and rapidly accelerating progress. Nevertheless, much remains to be done . . . The ultimate quest, of course, is to discover a single theory embracing all the seemingly disparate settings in AI where non-monotonic reasoning arises.

There is no doubt that the area of non-monotonic reasoning is of crucial and growing importance to the whole field of artificial intelligence.

3.2 Model-theoretic approach

There are various ways in which non-monotonicity can be formalized and one of them is model-theoretic. The model-theoretic approach to the problem of formalizing non-monotonicity is to treat as theorems of a logical theory T exactly those sentences that are true in all suitably distinguished models of T. In other words, a suitable set M(T) of models of a given theory T is chosen to represent the declarative semantics of T and a sentence F is declared true if and only if it is satisfied in all models from M(T). When new information is added to T, resulting in a new theory T', the set $M(T')$ may contain new models and therefore some of the conclusions previously derived from T may have to be withdrawn.

The model-theoretic approach is often very intuitive and provides significant flexibility. It has been successfully applied by a number of researchers (see e.g. Etherington, 1986; T.C. Przymusinski, 1986; 1987a; Shoham, 1988) and it has been shown that e.g. circumscription has a simple and intuitive model-theoretic characterization in terms of suitable minimal models of T (see Lifschitz, 1986).

When defining the declarative semantics of logic programs in section 5, we will use the model-theoretic approach.

4 Logic programming

One of the unquestionable successes of a logical approach in computer science was the introduction of logic programming and the rapid proliferation of logic programming languages – especially Prolog. Logic programming was introduced in the early 1970s by Kowalski (1974) and Colmerauer *et al.* (1973), and the first Prolog interpreter was implemented by Roussel in 1972 (Roussel, 1975). The emergence of logic programming was made possible by the earlier fundamental discovery by Robinson of the resolution principle (1965) and subsequent development of efficient resolution refutation strategies, that could serve as inference engines for logic programming systems.

Logic programming is based on the idea of declarative programming stemming from Kowalski's principle of separation of logic and control (1974; 1979). Ideally, a programmer should be concerned only with the declarative meaning of his program, while the procedural aspects of program's execution are handled automatically. Unfortunately, this ideal has not yet been fulfilled. One of the reasons is the lack of clarity as to what should be the proper declarative semantics of logic programs and, in particular, what should be the meaning of negation in logic programming. Without proper declarative semantics the user needs an intimate knowledge of procedural aspects in order to write correct programs.

4.1 Relationship to non-monotonic reasoning

Logic programming systems currently in existence implement negation using the so-called negation-as-failure mechanism, which occurs as an explicit operator in logic programming languages. The non-monotonic character of this operator closely relates logic programming to non-monotonic reasoning. Conversly, because of its non-monotonic character, procedural negation can often be used to implement other forms of non-monotonic reasoning (Reiter, to appear).

In spite of this close relationship between non-monotonic reasoning and logic programming, the two research areas are developing largely in parallel rather than in tandem and there is not as much interaction between the two fields as one would expect. One possible explanation of this phenomenon is the fact that, traditionally, the declarative semantics of logic programming has been based on the non-monotonic formalism, developed by Clark (1978), and called Clark's completion (see Lloyd, 1984). Clark's formalism is based on a very intuitive and useful idea of constructing the completion of a program P by essentially replacing the "if" statements in P by suitable "iff" statements. Unfortunately, Clark's formalism is not sufficiently general to be applied beyond the realm of logic programming and therefore does not play a major role in formalizing general non-monotonic reasoning in AI. In addition, Clark's approach has some other serious drawbacks often discussed in the literature (see e.g. Shepherdson, 1984, 1985, and 1986).

4.2 Calculus of events

Kowalski and Sergot introduced a temporal calculus of events (Kowalski and Sergot, 1986; Kowalski, 1986) which proposes a solution to the non-monotonic character of the temporal persistence problem in AI, based on logic programming and Prolog's negation-as-failure mechanism.

Their approach seems promising and offers another example of a close relationship between logic programming and non-monotonic reasoning in AI. According to Reiter (to appear), calculus of events suffers, however, "from its reliance on negation as failure, whose semantics is far from clear, so it is somewhat closer to an implementation than a specification."

It might be interesting to reconsider Kowalski and Sergot's work in the light of the declarative semantics of logic programs and negation discussed in this paper (cf. Sadri, 1986).

5 Perfect model semantics for logic programs

In this section we define the so-called *perfect model semantics* for logic programs. The results presented here are an outgrowth of recent work of several researchers. Apt, Blair, and Walker (1986) and independently Van Gelder (1986) (see also Naqvi, 1986) introduced the important class of *stratified logic programs* (see also earlier work by Chandra and Harel, 1985), they defined a unique "natural" minimal Herbrand model M_p of a stratified logic program and argued that this model may be taken to represent the declarative semantics of such programs.

T.C. Przymusinski (1987; 1987a) introduced the class of *perfect models* of a logic program and showed that every stratified logic program has exactly one perfect *Herbrand* model, which coincides with the model M_p defined by Apt *et al.* He defined the *perfect model semantics* of logic programs as the semantics determined by the class PERF(P) of all (not necessarily Herbrand) perfect models of a program P. He also extended the notions of stratification and perfect model onto the class of disjunctive deductive databases.

We recall that a *logic program* P is a finite set of universally quantified clauses of the form

$$A \leftarrow L_1, ..., L_m$$

where $m \geq 0$, A is an atom and L_i are positive or negative literals (see Lloyd, 1984). If all literals in all clauses are positive, then we say that the program P is *positive*. Function symbols are allowed and – as is customary in logic programming – commas are used instead of the $\wedge$ connective. A universally quantified headless clause of the form

$$\leftarrow L_1, ..., L_m$$

where $m \geq 0$ and L_is are literals, is called a *goal*. If all literals are positive then the goal is called *positive*. We assume that P satisfies the frequently used set of equality and unique names axioms (see Lloyd, 1984, p.70), called *Clark's Equational Theory* (Kunen, 1986).

If M and N are two distinct models of P with the same universe and the same interpretation of functions (and constants) then we say that $M < N$, if the extension of every predicate in M is contained in its extension in N. A model N of P is called *minimal* if there is no model M of P such that $M < N$.

5.1 Priority relation between predicate symbols

5.1.1. **Example**   Suppose that we know that a typical businessman tends to avoid using advanced mathematics in his work, unless he happens to be a good mathematician, and that Iacocca is a businessman and that Einstein is a physicist. We can express these facts using a logic program as follows:

$$avoids\_math(X) \leftarrow businessman(X),$$
$$\neg \, good\_mathematician(X) \tag{1}$$
$$businessman(iacocca)$$
$$physicist(einstein).$$

This program P has two minimal (Herbrand) models, M_1 and M_2. In both of them Iacocca is the only businessman and Einstein is the only physicist, but in M_1 Iacocca avoids advanced mathematics and in M_2 he is a good mathematician, instead. Do both of these models capture the intended meaning of P? Clearly not. By placing negated predicate good_mathematician(X) among the premises of the rule, we most likely intended to say that businessmen, in general, avoid advanced mathematics *unless* they happen to be good mathematicians. Since we have no information indicating that Iacocca is a good mathematician we are inclined to infer that he does not use advanced mathematics. Therefore, only the first minimal model M_1 seems to correspond to the intended meaning of P.

The reason for this asymmetry is easy to explain. The first clause (1) of P is logically equivalent to clause

$$good\_mathematician(X) \lor avoids\_math(X) \leftarrow \tag{2}$$
$$businessman(X)$$

and models M_1 and M_2 are therefore also minimal models of the theory T, obtained from P by replacing (1) with (2). The clause (2) does not assign distinct *priorities* to predicates good_mathematician and avoids_math, treating them as equally plausible. The program P, on the other hand, gives a *higher priority* to the predicate good_mathematician than to the predicate avoids_math, where by higher priority we mean higher priority for *minimization* of its extension.

We can easily imagine the above priorities reversed. This is for instance the case in the following program:

$$good\_mathematician(X) \leftarrow physicist(X), \neg \, avoids\_math(X)$$
$$businessman(iacocca)$$
$$physicist(einstein)$$

which says that if X is a physicist and if we have no specific evidence showing that he avoids mathematics then we are allowed to assume that he is a good mathematician. Here, the predicate avoids_math has a higher priority for minimization than the predicate good_mathematician.

The above example leads us to the conclusion that the syntax of program clauses determines relative *priorities* between predicate symbols according to the following rules:

> I   negative premises have higher priority than the heads
>
> II   positive premises have priority no less than that of the heads (indeed, if $B \leftarrow A$, decreasing the extension of B immediately results in decreasing the extension of A).

To formalize conditions I and II, we introduce the *dependency graph* G of the program P (see Apt, *et al.*, 1986) and Van Gelder, 1986), whose vertices are predicate symbols occurring in P. If A and B are predicate symbols, then there is a directed edge in G from B to A if and only if there is a clause in P such that A occurs in its head and B in one of its premises. If this premise is negative, then the edge is called *negative*. For any two predicate symbols in P we say that *B has higher priority than A* (briefly, $A < B$) if there is a directed path in G leading from B to A and passing through at least one negative edge. We call the above-defined relation the *priority relation* (T.C. Przymusinski, 1987; 1987a).

5.2 Preference relation and perfect models

Having defined the priority relation, we are prepared to define the notion of a perfect model. Since our goal is to *minimize extensions of high priority predicates as much as possible*, we are willing to do that even at the cost of enlarging extensions of predicates of lower priority. It follows, that if M is a model of P and if a new model N is obtained from M by changing extensions of some predicates in M, then we should consider the new model N to be *preferable* to M if and only if addition of some new element(s) to the extension of a lower priority predicate A is always *justified* by the removal of some elements from the extension of a higher priority predicate B, i.e. such that $A < B$. A model M will be considered perfect, if there are no models preferable to it. More formally:

5.2.1. Definition   (T.C. Przymusinski 1987; 1987a) Suppose that M and N are two distinct models of a general program P, with the same universe and the same interpretation of functions (and constants) and denote by $E_M(A)$ and $E_N(A)$ the extensions in M and N, respectively, of a predicate A. We say that N is *preferable* to M (briefly, $N < M$), if for every predicate A for which the set $E_N(A)-E_M(A)$ is non-empty there is a predicate symbol $B > A$ such that the set $E_M(B)-E_N(B)$ is non-empty. We say that a model M of P is *perfect* if there are no models preferable to M. We call the relation $<$ the preference relation between models and we write $M \leqslant N$, if $M = N$ or $M < N$.

It is easy to prove:

5.2.2. **Theorem** (T.C. Przymusinski, 1987 and 1987a) Every perfect model is minimal.

5.2.3. **Example** Model M_1 in example 5.1.1 is perfect. Indeed:

$$M_1 = \{businessman(i), physicist(e), avoids\_math(i)\},$$
$$M_2 = \{businessman(i), physicist(e), good\_mathematician(i)\},$$

and we know that *good_mathematician* > *avoids_math* and therefore $M_1 < M_2$. Consequently, M_1 is perfect, but M_2 is not.

5.2.4. **Example** Not every logic program has a perfect model. The program:

$$p \leftarrow \neg q, \ q \leftarrow \neg p$$

has only two minimal Herbrand models $M_1 = \{p\}$ and $M_2 = \{q\}$ and since $p < q$ and $q < p$ we have $M_1 < M_2$ and $M_2 < M_1$, thus none of these models is perfect.

The cause of this peculiarity is quite clear: our semantics is based on relative priorities between predicate symbols and therefore we have to be consistent when assigning those priorities to avoid *priority conflicts*, which – in the dependency graph G – correspond to cycles passing through negative edges. This reflects the idea underlying the approach taken by Apt, *et al.* (1966) and by Van Gelder (1986), that *when using negation we should be referring to an already defined relation* to avoid circular definitions.

5.2.5. **Definition** (Apt, *et al.*,1986; Van Gelder, 1986; see also Chandra and Harel, 1985; Naqvi, 1986) A logic program P is *stratified* if its dependency graph does not contain cycles passing through negative edges. Equivalently, a logic program P is stratified if and only if it is possible to decompose the set S of all predicates of P into disjoint sets $S_1, ..., S_r$, called *strata*, so that for every clause

$$C \leftarrow A_1, ..., A_m, \neg B_1, ..., \neg B_n$$

in P, where As, Bs and C are atoms, we have that:

   (i) for every i, stratum(A_i) $\leq$ stratum (C)
   (ii) for every j, stratum(B_j) < stratum(C),

where stratum(A) = i, if the predicate symbol of A belongs to S_i. Any particular decomposition $\{S_1, ..., S_r\}$ of S satisfying the above conditions is called a *stratification of P*.

In the above definition, stratification determines priority levels (strata) of S, with lower level (stratum) denoting higher priority for minimization. For example, the program from example 5.1.1 is stratified and one of its stratifications is $S_1 = \{\text{good\_mathematician}\}$, $S_2 = \{\text{businessman, physicist, avoids\_math}\}$.

The following basic result states that every model of a stratified program P is "subsumed" by a perfect model. This property is exactly analogous to the well-known property of minimal models (Bossu and Siegel, 1985), stating that for every model M of a universal theory T there is a minimal model N such that $N \leqslant M$. Moreover, it shows that P has exactly one perfect *Herbrand* model, which coincides with the "natural" model M_P defined in Apt, *et al.* (1986) and Van Gelder (1986).

5.2.6. Theorem   (T.C. Przymusinski, 1987 and 1987a) For every model N of a stratified program P there exists a perfect model M such that $M \leqslant N$. Moreover, every stratified program has a unique perfect Herbrand model, which coincides with the model M_P.

Now we define the perfect model semantics of a logic program.

5.2.7. Definition   (T.C. Przymusinski, 1987a) Let P be a logic program and let PERF(P) be the set of all perfect models of P. By the *perfect model semantics* of P we mean the semantics induced by the set PERF(P). Under this semantics a sentence F is considered to be true iff F is satisfied in all perfect models of P. In this case we write *PERF(P)* ⊨ *F*. If P does not have any perfect models, then its semantics is undefined.

5.2.8. Remark   It can be shown (T.C. Przymusinski, 1987a), that the *perfect model semantics is stronger than the semantics defined by Clark's completion* comp(P) of the program P, i.e. for any sentence F, if *comp(P)* ⊨ *F*, then *PERF(P)* ⊨ *F* (Apt *et al.*, [1966] showed that Clark's completion is always consistent for stratified programs). In view of the fact that SLDNF-resolution (see Lloyd, 1984), a standard inference procedure used in Prolog, is sound with respect to Clark's semantics, this implies that *SLDNF-resolution is also sound with respect to the perfect model semantics.*

As the following example indicates, the perfect model semantics eliminates some of the unintuitive features of Clark's semantics.

5.2.9. Example   (Van Gelder, 1986) Suppose that we wanted to describe which vertices in a graph are reachable from a given vertex a. We could write

$$edge(a,b)$$
$$edge(c,d)$$
$$edge(d,c)$$
$$reachable(a)$$
$$reachable(X) \leftarrow reachable(Y), edge(Y,X)$$
$$unreachable(X) \leftarrow \neg reachable(X).$$

This seems to be a very reasonable program and we certainly can expect vertices c and d to be unreachable from a. However, Clark's completion of P lacks the power to derive these conclusions (see T.C. Przymusinski, 1987a). On the other hand, it is easy to verify that the program is stratified by a stratification $S_1 = \{$reachable, edge$\}$ and $S_2 = \{$unreachable$\}$ and that the perfect model semantics provides the correct answers.

5.3 Positive logic programs: minimal model semantics

Throughout this section we assume that P is a positive logic program. We know already that every perfect model is minimal. For positive logic programs the converse is true.

5.3.1. Theorem (T.C. Przymusinski, 1987; 1987a) If M is a model of a positive logic program then M is minimal if and only if M is perfect.

This implies that for positive logic programs, the perfect model semantics is in fact equivalent to the *minimal model semantics*, i.e. to the semantics induced by the class MIN(P) of all – not necessarily Herbrand – minimal models of P. It is well-known that every positive logic program has exactly one minimal *Herbrand* model M_P, called the *least Herbrand model of P* (Van Emden and Kowalski, 1976; Apt and Van Emden, 1982), which is therefore the unique *Herbrand* perfect model of P.

According to the next result, the minimal model semantics does not introduce any new positive sentences, where by a positive sentence we mean a sentence, whose normal disjunctive form does not contain any negative literals.

5.3.2. Theorem (Etherington, *et al.*, 1985; Lifschitz, 1985a) For any positive sentence F we have:

$$MIN(P) \vDash F \Leftrightarrow P \vDash F.$$

The above result will help us explain why the definition of the perfect model semantics *should not be limited to Herbrand models of P*.

5.3.3. Example Suppose that our program is simply p(a). Its only perfect *Herbrand* model is the least Herbrand model $M_P = \{p(a)\}$, and therefore the semantics of P based on perfect Herbrand models only or – equivalently – the least Herbrand model semantics of P implies the sentence $F = \forall X\, p(X)$, i.e.

$$M_P \vDash \forall X\, p(X)$$

Clearly, P is a positive program, F is a positive sentence and P itself does not imply F. This choice of semantics would lead to two serious problems:

(a) It would make it difficult – if not entirely impractical – for unification-based computational mechanisms to give expected answers to *universal queries*. Indeed, when we ask the query p(X) in logic programming, we not only want to have an answer to the question "is there an X for which p(X)?", but in fact we are interested in obtaining all bindings (or substitutions) θ for which our semantics implies p(X)θ. Therefore, in this case, if our semantics is determined by the unique Herbrand model M_P and if we ask *p(X)* we would simply expect the answer "yes," indicating that p(X) is satisfied for all X's or – in other words – signifying that the empty substitution is a correct answer substitution. Unfortunately, standard unification-based computational mechanisms will be only capable of returning the special case substitution, namely $\theta = \{X \mid a\}$. In order to verify that p(X) is satisfied for all elements X in the Herbrand universe, the statement p(X) would have to be shown true for all ground terms X, which in most cases would be rather impractical. The absence of such verification, however, would automatically result in serious – almost *built-in* – incompleteness of the used mechanism, with respect to all universal queries.

(b) It would also contradict the principle that *no new positive information should be introduced by the semantics of positive programs*, which – as shown in theorem 5.3.3 – is satisfied for the perfect model semantics. This principle is also satisfied by the semantics based on Clark's completion of P (see Lloyd, 1984) and it appears to reflect a very natural and important property of positive programs. We refer the reader to (T.C. Przymusinski, 1987a) for a more detailed discussion.

The final result shows, however, *as far as ground or existential queries are concerned, using all minimal models or just the unique minimal Herbrand model produces exactly the same results*, so that the addition of non-Herbrand models influences only answers to universal queries.

5.3.4. Theorem (T.C. Przymusinski, 1987a; Gelfond, H. Przymusinska and T.C. Przymusinski, 1987) Suppose that F is an existential sentence or – in particular – a ground one. Then:

$$MIN(P) \vDash F \Leftrightarrow M_P \vDash F.$$

5.4 Procedural semantics: SLS-resolution

In T.C. Przymusinski (1987a), the so-called *SLS-resolution (Linear resolution with Selection function for Stratified programs)* was defined and Przymusinski showed that SLS-resolution is sound and complete (for non-floundering queries) with respect to the perfect model semantics and therefore provides a procedural mechanism for the proposed semantics. SLS-resolution is a natural *generalization* of SLD-resolution (Linear resolution with Selection function for Definite programs) from the class of positive (definite) programs onto the class of stratified programs.

SLS-resolution differs from SLDNF-resolution primarily by not relying on finite failure trees.

Due to the lack of space, below we only quote the two basic results concerning the soundness and completeness of SLS-resolution with respect to the perfect model semantics PERF(P) and we refer the reader to (Przymusinski, 1987a) for the details.

5.4.1. Theorem (Soundness of SLS-resolution)   Suppose that P is a stratified program and $G = \leftarrow W$ is a goal. Then

(i)i If θ is any SLS-answer-substitution, then $PERF(P) \vDash W\,\theta$
(ii) If SLS-tree for G is failed, then $PERF(P) \vDash \neg W$.

5.4.2. Theorem (Completeness of SLS-resolution)   Suppose that P is a stratified program, $G = \leftarrow W$ is a non-floundered goal[1] and θ is a substitution. Then

(i) $PERF(P) \vDash W\,\theta$ iff there exists an SLS-answer-substitution more general than θ;
(ii) $PERF(P) \vDash \neg W$ iff SLS-tree for G is failed.

In the special case when P is a positive program, SLS-resolution reduces to the standard SLD-resolution. Theorem 5.4.2 therefore implies an important result, showing that for positive goals *SLD-resolution is sound and complete with respect to the minimal model semantics*.

5.4.3. Theorem   (Soundness   and   completeness   of   SLD-resolution) Suppose that P is a positive program, $G = \leftarrow W$ is a positive goal and θ is a substitution. Then

(i) $MIN(P) \vDash W\theta$ iff there exists an SLD-answer-substitution more general than θ;
(ii) $MIN(P) \vDash \neg W\theta$ iff SLD-tree for G is failed.[2]

6 Equivalence to non-monotonic formalisms

In this section we show that the perfect model semantics for logic programs described in the previous section is (semantically) equivalent to suitable forms of four major non-monotonic formalisms: (1) circumscription, (2) closed world assumption, (3) autoepistemic logic, and (4) default logic.

These results provide a further argument in favor of the perfect model semantics and underscore the relationship between logic programming and non-monotonic reasoning. They should also contribute to a better understanding of the relation existing between various forms of non-monotonic reasoning.

For a more detailed description of the discussed formalisms, the reader is referred to the literature cited, to Reiter's survey article (to appear) and to Genesereth and Nilsson's book (1987).

6.1 Circumscription

One of the most powerful formalizations of non-monotonic reasoning called circumscription, was introduced by McCarthy (1980; 1986). In describing this notion we follow the approach suggested by Lifschitz (1985a; 1986). Suppose that P is a theory, S is the set of all predicate symbols, $R = \{R_1, ..., R_m\}$ and $Z = \{Z_1, ..., Z_n\}$ are disjoint subsets of S and $Q = S - (R \cup Z)$. The predicate symbols from Z are called *variables*. The process of circumscription transforms P into a stronger second-order sentence CIRC(P;R;Z):

6.1.1. Definition (McCarthy, 1980 and 1986) The *parallel circumscription* of R in P with variables Z is the following sentence CIRC(P;R;Z):

$$P(R,Z) \wedge \forall R',Z' \, [(P(R',Z') \wedge R' \to R) \to R' = R],$$

where $R' = \{R'_1, ..., R'_m$ and $Z' = \{Z'_1, ..., Z'_n$ are lists of predicate variables similar to lists R and Z and $R' \to R$ stands for: $\forall_i, \forall_x R_i(x) \to R(x)$.

This formula states that predicates from R have a minimal possible extension under the assumption that P(R,Z) holds and extensions of predicates from Z are allowed to vary in the process of minimization. Notice that extensions of predicate symbols from Q remain unchanged. To further clarify the notion of circumscription, we reformulate it in model-theoretic terms.

6.1.2. Definition (Lifschitz, 1985a; Etherington, 1986) If M and N are two models of P with the same universe and the same interpretation of functions (and constants) and the same interpretation of predicates from Q, then we say that $M \leq N$ modulo (R,Z), if the extension of every predicate from R in M is contained in its extension in N. A model M of P is (R,Z)-minimal if there is no model N such that: $N \leq M$, but not $M \leq N$. The following result describes the semantics of circumscription:

6.1.3. Theorem (McCarthy, 1980; Lifschitz, 1985a; Etherington, 1986) A model M of P is a model of CIRC(P;R;Z) if and only if M is (R,Z)-minimal. In other words, for any formula F we have $CIRC(P;R;Z) \vDash F$ if and only if $M \vDash F$ for every (R,Z)-minimal model M of P.

Notice that, in particular, if R = S, then the notion of an (R,Z)-minimal model coincides with the notion of a minimal model of P and therefore CIRC(P;R;Z) describes the minimal model semantics (cf. Bossu and Siegel, 1985 and Minker, 1982).

6.1.4. **Example** The following classic example can help to clarify the matter. Let P be defined as follows:

> *bird(tweety)*
> *bird(sam)*
> *abnormal(sam)*
> *fly(X)* ←
> *bird (X)* ∧ ¬ *abnormal(X)*

If we assume that R = {abnormal} and Z = {fly,bird}, then it can be easily shown that

$$CIRC(P;R;Z) \Leftrightarrow P \wedge \forall\, X\ (abnormal(X) \leftrightarrow X = sam)$$

and therefore

$$CIRC(P;R;Z) \vDash fly(tweety).$$

Notice, that P is stratified and one of its stratifications is S_1 = {abnormal} and S_2 = {fly,bird}.

Since predicate "fly" is not minimized, this form of circumscription is not powerful enough to produce a negative answer to a query "Can Sam fly?". To achieve this effect, we have to employ a more powerful version of circumscription, which allows priorities to be assigned to the different predicates from S. Suppose that S is partitioned into disjoint sets $S_1, ..., S_k$.

6.1.5. **Definition** (McCarthy, 1986)   Prioritized circumscription of P with priorities $S_1 > ... > S_k$ is denoted by CIRC(P;$S_1 > ... > S_k$) and defined as follows:

$$CIRC(P;S_1 > ... > S_k) = CIRC(P;S_1;\ \{S_2 \cup ... \cup S_k\}) \wedge$$
$$CIRC(P;S_2\ ;\ \{S_3 \cup ... \cup S_k\}) \wedge ... \wedge)\ CIRC(P;S_k;\ \emptyset).$$

The following result provides semantic counterpart:

6.1.6. **Theorem** (Lifschitz, 1985a)   A model M of P is a model of prioritized circumscription $CIRC(P;S_1 > ... > S_k)$ if and only if M is a model of P such that for every i ≤ k, M is (S$_i$,{$S_{i+1} \cup ... \cup S_k$})-minimal.

If we apply this form of circumscription to the theory P from example 6.1.4 with S_1 = {abnormal} and S_2 = {fly,bird}, then it is easy to show that

$$CIRC(P;S_1 > S_2) \vDash fly(tweety) \wedge \neg fly(sam).$$

The following theorem establishes the equivalence between the perfect model semantics of logic programs and the semantics of prioritized circumscription. A similar result for point-wise circumscription was obtained by Lifschitz (1986) and related results were obtained earlier by Reiter (1982).

6.1.7. **Theorem** (T.C. Przymusinski, 1987 and 1987a)   Suppose that P is a stratified program and {$S_1, ..., S_n$} is a stratification of P. A model of P is perfect if and only if it is a model of prioritized circumscription $CIRC(P; S_1 > ... > S_n)$. Consequently, the perfect model semantics of P coincides with the semantics of prioritized circumscription of P, i.e. for any sentence F

$$PERF(P) \vDash F \Leftrightarrow CIRC(P; S_1 > ... > S_n) \vDash F.$$

For instance, in example 6.1.4, the perfect model semantics of P is equivalent to the semantics of $CIRC(P; S_1 > S_2)$.

6.1.8. Corollary (T.C. Przymusinski, 1987 and 1987a) Suppose that $\{S_1, ..., S_n\}$ and $\{T_1, ..., T_m\}$ are two stratifications of the same program P. Then M is a model of $CIRC(P, S_1 > ... > S_n)$ if and only if it is a model of $CIRC(P, T_1 > ... > T_m)$.

This shows that prioritized circumscription does not depend on the choice of stratification for P. The above theorem has two interesting consequences:

1 Since SLDNF-resolution used in Prolog is sound with respect to the perfect model semantics (see remark 5.2.8) it is also sound with respect to to the semantics of prioritized circumscription. This means that SLDNF-resolution can be used as a sound inference engine for some types of circumscription.[3] This formally confirms Reiter's comment that "partly because it is a nonmonotonic operator, procedural negation can often be used to implement other forms of nonmonotonic reasoning" (Reiter, to appear).

2 In general, it is not clear how to instantiate the circumscription axiom in order to derive the desired consequences of a circumscribed theory. The equivalence between the perfect model semantics and prioritized circumscription shows that in the case of stratified logic programs such an instantiation can be generated automatically based on the syntactic form of the program.

6.2 Closed world assumption

An alternative way to formalize non-monotonic reasoning is to use some form of the closed world assumption. The first step in this direction was made by Reiter, who defined the so-called *naive closure* CWA(P) of theory P (this terminology is due to Etherington [1986]):

6.2.1. Definition (Reiter, 1978) The *naive closure* CWA(P) of P is defined as follows:

$$CWA(P) = P \cup \{\neg p : \text{where p is a ground atom such that } P \nvDash p\}.$$

In his original paper Reiter also assumed that P does not involve function symbols and that the domain closure axiom

$$(DCA) \; \forall X \, X = c_1 \vee ... \vee X = c_n,$$

is satisfied, where $\{c_1, ..., c_n\}$ is the list of all constants in the language of P. He pointed out later that these assumptions are not necessary (see e.g.

Reiter, to appear), but *we will assume* DCA throughout this section to simplify the exposition and to enable us to present stronger results.

Reiter's CWA(P), although suitable for positive programs, is usually inconsistent for programs with negative premises. For example, if P is $p \leftarrow \neg q$, then CWA(P) implies $\neg p$ and $\neg q$ and is inconsistent.

Stimulated by Reiter's work, several researchers proposed more sophisticated forms of the closed world assumption. Minker (1982) defined the so-called Generalized Closed World Assumption (GCWA) that was subsequently improved and extended by Gelfond, H. Przymusinska and T.C. Przymusinski (1986a, 1986b; see also Yahya and Henschen, 1985, and Gelfond and H. Przymusinska, 1986) resulting in the so-called Extended Closed World Assumption (ECWA), which was shown to be consistent and equivalent to parallel circumscription for any disjunctive deductive database.

In order to obtain a syntactic equivalent of prioritized circumscription, Gelfond, H. Przymusinska and T.C. Przymusinski (1986b) generalized ECWA by introducing the so-called Iterated Closed World Assumption (ICWA) and showed its equivalence to prioritized circumscription for disjunctive deductive databases. In view of Theorem 6.1.8, this result implies that for stratified logic programs a suitable form of ICWA is equivalent to the perfect model semantics. Below, we give a simplified definition of ICWA, which is adequate for logic programs.

Let P be a stratified logic program with a stratification $\{S_1, ..., S_k\}$. For every n, let $Q_n = \cup\{S_j : j < n+1\}$ and let P_n be the logic program consisting of all clauses from P whose heads involve predicates from Q_n. Clearly, $P = P_k$.

6.2.2. Definition (Gelfond, H. Przymusinska and T.C. Przymusinski, 1986b) The Iterated Closed World Assumption applied to P is defined as the closure ICWA(P; $S_1 > ... > S_k$) of P obtained by iteration of the appropriate CWA's:

$$ICWA(P_1;S_1) = CWA(P_1);$$
$$ICWA(P_{n+1}; S_1 > ... > S_{n+1})$$
$$= CWA(P_{n+1} + ICWA(P_n; S_1 > ... > S_n)), \text{ for } n > 0,$$
$$ICWA(P; S_1 > ... > S_k) = ICWA(P_k; S_1 > ... > S_k).$$

The following theorem shows that the semantics of ICWA(P;$S_1 > ... > S_k$) is equivalent to the perfect model semantics of P:

6.2.3. Theorem (Gelfond, H. Przymusinska and T.C. Przymusinski, 1986b) Suppose that P is a stratified logic program and $\{S_1, ..., S_k\}$ is a stratification of P. The theory ICWA(P;$S_1 > ... > S_k$) has exactly one model and this model is the unique perfect model of P.

6.2.4. **Example**   The program P in example 6.1.4 is stratified and one of its stratifications is $S_1 = \{abnormal\}$ and $S_2 = \{fly, bird\}$. Consequently, assuming DCA, the only model of ICWA(P;$S_1 > S_2$) is the unique perfect model of P. One easily checks that ICWA(P;$S_1 > S_2$) = P $\cup$ $\{fly(tweety), \neg fly(sam), \neg abnormal(tweety)\}$.

The above theorem provides – assuming the domain closure axiom – a syntactic description of the perfect model semantics in the form of a first-order theory. It generalizes an earlier result of Lifschitz obtained for positive programs and minimal models (1985b). It is easy to see that the unique model of ICWA(P; $S_1 ... S_k$) is in fact the Herbrand model M_P of P introduced in Apt, *et al.* (1986) and Van Gelder (1986). This is not surprising in view of the similarity of iterative constructions used.

6.3 Autoepistemic logic

Autoepistemic logic (AEL) proposed by Moore (1985) as a reconstruction of non-monotonic logics of McDermott and Doyle (McDermott and Doyle, 1980; McDermott, 1982) provides another interesting formalization of non-monotonic reasoning. Moore uses modal logic to formalize an agent's reasoning about his knowledge or beliefs. We will follow Moore and consider here propositional theories only (extensions of Moore's logic to the first-order case were proposed by Levesque [1987] and Marek [1986]).

By an autoepistemic theory T we mean a set of formulae in the language of propositional calculus augmented by a belief operator L, where, for any formula F, LF is interpreted as "F is believed". The set of all propositional consequences of T will be denoted by Th(T).

The central role in Moore's formalization is played by the notion of a stable autoepistemic expansion of T which intuitively represents a possible set of beliefs of an ideally rational agent. The agent is ideally rational in the sense that he believes in all and only those facts which he can conclude from T and from his other beliefs. If this expansion is unique then it can be viewed as the set of theorems which follow from T in the autoepistemic logic.

6.3.1. **Definition**   (Moore, 1985) A set of formulae E(T) is a stable autoepistemic expansion of T if it satisfies the following fixed point condition:

$$E(T) = Th(T \cup \{Lp: p \text{ is in } E(T)\} \cup \{\neg Lp : p \text{ is not in } E(T)\}),$$

where p is a propositional formula.

To establish a relationship between perfect model semantics and autoepistemic logic we have to define an interpretation of propositional formulae in terms of autoepistemic beliefs.

6.3.2. **Definition**   (Gelfond, 1987) For any propositional formula F the interpretation I(F) of F is obtained by replacing every ocurrence of a negative literal ¬ *p* in F by the negative autoepistemic literal ¬ L_p. For a logic program P, by I(P) we denote the set of all autoepistemic formulae I(F), where F is a clause from P.

The following theorem, due to Gelfond and H. Przymusinska, shows that – under the above interpretation – autoepistemic logic is semantically equivalent to the perfect model semantics precisely for the class of stratified logic programs. We assume that all formulae F are in conjunctive normal form.

6.3.3. Theorem   (Gelfond, 1987; H. Przymusinska, 1987a)

(a) If P is a stratified logic program, then autoepistemic logic and perfect model semantics are I-equivalent. More precisely, the theory I(P) has a unique stable autoepistemic expansion E(I(P)) and for every formula F, we have: *PERF(P)* ⊨ *F* iff *E(I(T))* ⊨ *I(F)*.

(b) Let T be a stratified disjunctive database and let C(T) be a consistent extension of T. Then, the autoepistemic expansion E(I(T)) is I-equivalent to C(T) iff T is a logic program and for every formula F, we have: *PERF(T)* ⊨ *F* iff *C(T)* ⊨ *F*.

6.3.4. Example   Let P be the propositional version of the program from example 6.1.4:

> *bird(tweety)*
> *bird(sam)*
> *abnormal(sam)*
> *fly(tweety)* ← *bird(tweety)* ∧ ¬ *abnormal(tweety)*
> *fly(sam)* ← *bird (sam)* ∧ ¬ *abnormal (sam)*

Therefore, the autoepistemic theory I(P):

> *bird(tweety)*
> *bird(sam)*
> *abnormal(sam)*
> *fly(tweety)* ← *bird (tweety)* ∧ ¬ *Labnormal (tweety)*
> *fly(sam)* ← *bird (sam)* ∧ ¬ *Labnormal (sam)*

has exactly one stable autoepistemic expansion E(I(P)), which includes *fly(tweety)*, ¬ *Labnormal(tweety)* and ¬ *Lfly(sam)*.

An interesting feature of the above theorem is the fact that in order to obtain equivalence with the perfect model semantics, it was not necessary to introduce the concept of prioritization into autoepistemic logic, as was the case with circumscription and the closed world assumption. In a sense, prioritization is already "built-in" into autoepistemic logic.

As was the case for circumscription, the above theorem implies that SLDNF-resolution can be used as a sound deductive mechanism for a class of autoepistemic theories. This can be useful in view of the fact that autoepistemic logic was presented non-constructively and no procedural mechanism was provided to derive its theorems.

6.4 Default logic

Another promising approach to the formalization of non-monotonic reasoning was proposed by Reiter (1980) and called default logic. Its distinguishing feature is the introduction of default statements, which function as additional rules of inference rather than formulae in some theory.

A (closed) *default rule* R is a rule of the form

$$\frac{a : Mb_1, \ldots, Mb_n}{c}$$

where a, b_is and c are closed first-order formulae and the intuitive meaning of R is that "if a holds and if each one of b_is can be consistently assumed, then c can be inferred."

A *default theory* is a pair $< D, T >$, where D is a set of default rules and T is a set of closed first-order formulae. T describes facts which are known to be true and the default rules enable us to derive from them additional information, which together with T itself constitutes a more complete extension of the theory. The extensions are defined using the fixed point construction:

6.4.1. Definition (Reiter, 1980) Suppose that $<D,T>$ is a default theory. For any set S of first-order sentences, define G(S) to be the smallest set (it always exists!) with the following properties:

(i) T is contained in G(S);
(ii) G(S) is closed under logical consequence;
(iii) if R is a rule from D (of the above described form) and if a is in G(S) and, for every i, $\neg b_i$ is not in S, then c is in G(S).

Any set of first-order sentences E satisfying E = G(E) is called an *extension* of $<D,T>$, i.e. extensions are fixed points of the operator G.

A default theory $<D,T >$ may have none, one or more than one extension. Any such extension is a possible set of beliefs for an agent. If the theory has exactly one extension E, then E can be considered as the set of theorems of $<D,T>$.

Bidoit and Froidevaux (1986) showed that the perfect model semantics of a stratified logic program P is equivalent to a suitable default theory generated by P. In order to obtain the desired equivalence, Bidoit and Froidevaux in effect introduced the concept of "prioritized default theory" and proved that, as in the case of circumscription, prioritized default theory is equivalent to the perfect model semantics.

Recently, H. Przymusinska (1987b) proposed a simpler, although slightly weaker, approach, which – as in the case of autoepistemic logic – does not require the notion of prioritization. Below we present her approach, limiting it – for the sake of simplicity – to the propositional case, although it can be easily generalized.

Suppose that P is a logic program. Denote by T the set of all positive clauses of P and by D the set of defaults obtained as follows (see Bidoit and Froidevaux, 1986): for any clause

$$C \leftarrow A_1, ..., A_m, \neg B_1, ..., \neg B_n,$$

in P such that $n > 0$, include in D the default rule:

$$\frac{A_1 \wedge ... \wedge A_m : M \neg B_1, ..., M \neg B_n}{C}.$$

and call the resulting default theory $<D,T>$ the *default theory associated with the program P*.

6.4.2. Theorem (H. Przymusinska, 1987b) Suppose that P is a stratified logic program and $<D,T>$ is the associated default theory. The theory $<D,T>$ has exactly one extension E and the unique minimal model of E is the unique perfect model of P.

6.4.3. Example Let P be the program from example 6.3.4. The associated default theory is $<D,T>$, where

$$T = \{bird(tweety), bird(sam), abnormal(sam)\}$$

$$D = \left\{ \frac{bird(tweety) : M \neg abnormal(tweety)}{fly(tweety)}, \frac{bird(sam) : M \neg abnormal(sam)}{fly(sam)} \right\}$$

Therefore, the default theory $<D,T>$ has exactly one extension E, namely E is the set of all propositional consequences of $P \cup fly(tweety)$, and the unique minimal model of E is the unique perfect model of P.

The above approach is similar to that used in the case of autoepistemic logic, which is not surprising in view of the close relationship existing between default and autoepistemic logics (see Konolige, 1987).

7 Conclusion

In this paper we used a model-theoretic approach to describe a new declarative semantics for logic programs. We have shown that the proposed semantics has a number of desirable features and is equivalent to suitable forms of four major formalizations of non-monotonic reasoning:

circumscription, closed world assumption, autoepistemic logic and default theory. We also discussed a new resolution-based procedural mechanism, called SLS-resolution, which generalizes the standard SLD-resolution and is sound and essentially complete with respect to the discussed semantics for stratified programs.

The presented results are an outgrowth of recent work in this area by several researchers and lead to a new perspective in viewing the semantics of logic programming and its relationship to non-monotonic reasoning.

The area of non-monotonic reasoning is of crucial and growing importance to the whole field of artificial intelligence; a better understanding of the relationship between various forms of non-monotonic reasoning, including logic programming, should contribute to a better understanding of deeper underlying principles of non-monotonic reasoning.

Notes

The author is grateful to Derek Partridge and Yorick Wilks for the invitation to write the paper and to Krzysztof Apt, Howard Blair, Michael Gelfond, Jean-Louis Lassez, Vladimir Lifschitz, Jack Minker, Halina Przymusinska, Rodney Topor, and Allen Van Gelder for helpful discussions and comments.

1 See Lloyd, 1984.
2 But not necessarily finitely failed.
3 A query answering algorithm for general circumscriptive theories has been described in T.C. Przymusinski, 1987b.

Prolegomena to a theory of mechanized formal reasoning

Richard W. Weyhrauch

1 Introduction

The title of this paper contains both the words "mechanized" and "theory." I want to make the point that the ideas presented here are not only of interest to theoreticians. I believe that any theory of interest to artificial intelligence must be realizable on a computer.

I am going to describe a working computer program, FOL, that embodies the mechanization of the ideas of logicians about theories of reasoning. This system converses with users in some first-order language. I will also explain how to build a new structure in which theory and metatheory interact in a particularly natural way. This structure has the additional property that it can be designed to reason about itself. This kind of self-reflexive logical structure is new and discussion of the full extent of its power will appear in another paper.

The purpose of this paper is to set down the main ideas underlying the system. Each example in this paper was chosen to illustrate an idea and each idea is developed by showing how the corresponding FOL feature works. I will not present difficult examples. More extensive examples and discussions of the limits of these features will be described in other places. The real power of this theory (and FOL) comes from an understanding of the interaction of these separate features. This means that after this paper is read it still requires some work to see how all of these features can be used. Complex examples will only confuse the issues at this point. Before these can be explained, the logical system must be fully understood. The FOL project can be thought of in several different ways:

1. Most importantly, FOL is an environment for studying epistemological questions. I look on logic as an empirical, applied science. It is like physics. The data we have is the actual reasoning activity of people. We try to build a theory of what that's like. I try to look at the traditional work on logic from this point of view. The important question is: in what way does logic adequately represent the actual practice of reasoning? In addition, its usefulness to artificial intelligence requires a stronger form of adequacy.

Such a theory must be *mechanizable*. My notion of mechanizable is informal. I hope by the end of this note it will be clearer. Below, I outline the mechanizable analogues of the usual notions of model, interpretation, satisfaction, theory, and reflection principle.

2. FOL is a conversational machine. We use it by having a conversation with it. The importance of this idea cannot be overestimated. One of the recurring themes of this paper is the question: what is the nature of the conversation we wish to have with an expert in reasoning? In AI we talk about *expert systems*. FOL can be thought of as a system whose expertise is reasoning. We have tried to explore the question: what properties does an expert conversational reasoning machine have to have, independent of its domain of expertise? I believe that we will begin to call machines intelligent when we can have the kinds of discussions with them that we have with our friends. Let me elaborate on this a little. Humans are not ever likely to come to depend on the advice of a computer which has a simplistic one bit output. Imagine that you are asking it to make decisions about what stocks you should buy. Suppose it says "I have reviewed all the data you gave me. Sell everything you own and buy stock in FOL Incorporated." Most reasonable people would like to ask some additional questions! Why did you make that choice? What theory of price behavior did you use? Why is that better than using a dartboard? And so forth. These questions require a system that knows about more things than the stock market. For example, it needs to know how to reason about its *theories* of price movement. In FOL we have begged the question of *natural* language. The only important thing is having a sufficiently rich language for carrying out the above kinds of conversations. This paper should be looked at from this point of view. This work has direct application in the areas of AI, mathematical theory of computation (MTC), and logic. A discussion of this is found in the original paper.

As I reread this introduction it seems to contain a lot of promises. If they seem exaggerated to you then image me as a hopeless romantic, but at least read the rest of this paper. The things I describe here already exist.

2 FOL as a conversational program

FOL has previously been advertised as a proof-checker. This sometimes brings to mind the idea that the way to use it is to type out a complicated formal proof, then FOL reads it and says yes or no. This picture is all wrong, and is founded on the theorem-proving idea that simply stating a problem is all that a reasoning system should need to know. What FOL actually does is to have a dialogue with a user about some object. The first step in this conversation is to establish what language will be spoken by establishing what words will be used for what parts of speech. In FOL the establishment of this agreement about language is done by making declarations (this will be described below). We can then discuss (in the agreed-upon language) what facts (axioms) are to be considered true, and then finally we can chat about the consequences of these facts.

Let me illustrate this by giving a simple FOL proof. We will begin where logic began, with Aristotle. Even a person who has never had a course in formal logic understands the syllogism:

Socrates is a man
    and
All men are mortal
    thus
Socrates is mortal

Before we actually give a dialogue with FOL we need to think informally about how we express these assertions as well-formed formulas (WFFs) of first-order logic. For this purpose we need an individual constant (IND-CONST), Socrates, two predicate constants (PREDCONSTs), MAN and MORTAL, each of one argument, and an individual variable (INDVAR), x, to express the *all men* part of the second line. The usual rules for forming WFFs apply (see Kleene, 1967, pp.7,78). The three statements above are represented as

MAN (Socrates)
$\forall x.(\text{MAN}(x) \supset \text{MORTAL}(x))$
MORTAL(Socrates)

Our goal is to prove

$(\text{MAN(Socrates)} \land \forall x.(\text{MAN}(x) \supset \text{MORTAL}(x)))$
$$\supset \text{MORTAL(Socrates)}$$

As explained above, the first thing we do when initiating a discussion with FOL is to make an agreement about the language we will use. We do this by making declarations. These have the form

*****DECLARE INDCONST Socrates;
*****DECLARE PREDCONST MORTAL MAN 1;
*****DECLARE INDVAR x;

The FOL program types out five asterisks when it expects input. The above lines are exactly what one would type to the FOL system.

FOL knows all of the natural deduction rules of inference (Prawitz, 1965) and many more. In the usual natural-deduction style, proofs are trees and the leaves of these trees are called assumptions. The assume command looks like

*****ASSUME MAN(Socrates) $\land \forall x.(\text{MAN}(x) \supset \text{MORTAL}(x))$;
1 MAN(Socrates) $\land \forall x.(\text{MAN}(x) \supset \text{MORTAL}(x))$ (1)

The first line above is typed by the user the second is typed by FOL. For each node in the proof tree there is a set of open assumptions. These are printed in parentheses after the proofstep. Notice that assumptions depend on themselves. We want to instantiate the second half of line 1 to the particular MAN, Socrates. First we must get this WFF onto a line of its own. FOL can be used to decide tautologies. We type TAUT followed by the WFF we want, and then the line numbers of those lines from which we think it follows.

*****TAUT $\forall x.(MAN(x) \supset MORTAL(x))$ 1;
2 $\forall x.(MAN(x) \supset MORTAL(x))$ (1)

This line also has the open assumption of line 1. We then use the $\forall$-elimination rule to conclude

*****$\forall$E 2 Socrates;
3 MAN(Socrates) $\supset$ MORTAL(Socrates) (1)

It now follows, tautologically, from lines 1 and 3, that Socrates must be MORTAL. Using the TAUT command again gets this result. More than one line can be given in the reason part of the TAUT command.
rates)

*****TAUT MORTAL(Socrates) 1,3;
4 MORTAL(Socrates) (1)

This is almost the desired result, but we are not finished yet; this line still depends upon the original assumption. We close this assumption by creating an implication of the first line implying the fourth. This is done using the deduction theorem. In the natural deduction terminology this is called *implication* ($\supset$) *introduction*.

*****$\supset$I 1 $\supset$ 4;
5 (MAN(Socrates) $\forall x.(MAN(x) \supset MORTAL(x))$) $\supset$ MORTAL(Socrates)

This is the WFF we wanted to prove. Since it has no dependencies, it is a theorem. It is roughly equivalent to the English sentence "If Socrates is a man, and for all x if x is a man, then x is mortal, then Socrates is mortal."

This example was also used in Filman and Weyhrauch (1976), and illustrates the sense in which FOL is an interactive proof constructor, not simply a proof-checker.

3 The logic used by FOL

The logic used by FOL is an extension of the system of first-order predicate calculus described in (Prawitz, 1965). The details appear in the original paper (Weyhrauch, 1980).

4 Simulation structure and semantic attachment

Here I introduce one of the most important ideas in this paper: simulation structures. Simulation structures are intended to be the mechanizable analog of the notion of model. We can intuitively understand them as the computable part of some model. It has been suggested that I call them effective partial interpretations, but I have reserved that slogan for a somewhat more general notion. A full mathematical description of these ideas is beyond the scope of this paper but appears in Weyhrauch (The logic of FOL, Informal Note 15, unpublished). Here I will give an operational description, mostly by means of some examples.

Consider the first-order language L, and a model M.

$$L = (P,F,C)$$
$$M = (D,P,F,C)$$

As usual, L is determined by a collection, P, of predicate symbols, a collection, F, of function symbols, and a collection, C, of constant symbols (Kleene, 1952, pp. 83–93). M is a structure which contains a domain, D, and the predicates, functions and objects which correspond to the symbols in L.

$$S = (D,P,F,C)$$

Loosely speaking, a simulation structure, S, also has a domain, D, a set of "predicates," P, a set of "functions," F, and a distinguished subset, C, of its domain. However, they have strong restrictions. Since we are imagining simulation structures as the mechanizable analogs of models we want to be able to actually implement them on a computer. To facilitate this we imagine that we intend to use a computer language in which there is some reasonable collection of data structures. In FOL we use LISP. The domain of a simulation structure is presented as an algorithm that acts as the characteristics function of some subset of the data structures. For example, if we want to construct a simulation structure for Peano arithmetic the domain is specified by a LISP function which returns T (for true) on natural numbers and NIL (for false) on all other s-expressions. Each "predicate" is represented by an algorithm that decides for each collection of arguments if the predicate is true or false or if it doesn't know. This algorithm is also total. Notice that it can tell you what is false as well as what is true. Each "function" is an algorithm that computes for each set of arguments either a value or returns the fact that it doesn't know the answer. It too is total. The distinguished subset of the domain must also be given by its characteristic function.

These restrictions are best illustrated by an example. A possible simulation structure for Peano arithmetic together with a relation symbol for "less than" is

S = (natural numbers, ⟨{2 < 3, ¬ 5 < 2}⟩, ⟨plus⟩, {2,3})

I have not presented this simulation structure by actually giving algorithms but they can easily be supplied. This simulation structure contains only two facts about "less than" – two is less than three, and it's false that five is less than two. As mentioned above, since this discussion is informal {2 < 3, ¬ 5 < 2} should be taken as the description of an algorithm that answers correctly the two questions it knows about and in all other cases returns the fact that it cannot decide "plus" is the name of an algorithm that computes the sum of two natural numbers. The only numerals that have interpretations are two and three. These have their usual meaning.

Intuitively, if we ask is "2 < 3" (where here "2" and "3" are numerals in L) we get the answer "yes". If we ask is "5 < 2" it says, "I don't know"! This is because there is no interpretation in the simulation structure of the numeral "5". Curiously, if you ask is "2 + 3 < 2" it will say false. The reason is that the simulation structure has an interpretation of " + " as the algorithm "plus," and 5 is in the domain even though it is not known to be the interpretation of any numeral in L. A more reasonable simulation structure for Peano arithmetic might be

S = ⟨natural numbers, <lessthan>, <suc,pred,plus,times>, natural numbers⟩

Simulation structures are not models. One difference is that there are no closure conditions required of the function fragments. Thus we could know that three times two is six without knowing about the multiplicative properties of two and six. Just as in the case of a model, we get a natural interpretation of a language with respect to a simulation structure. This allows us to introduce the idea of a sentence of L being satisfiable with respect to a simulation structure. Because of the lack of closure conditions and the partialness of the "predicates," etc. (unlike ordinary satisfaction) this routine will sometimes return "I don't know." There are several reasons for this. Our mechanized satisfaction cannot compute the truth or falsity of quantified formulas. This in general requires an infinite amount of computing. It should be remarked that this is exactly why we have logic at all. It facilitates our reasoning about the result of an infinite amount of computation with a single sentence. It is also important to understand that we are not introducing a three-valued logic or partial functions. We simply acknowledge that, with respect to some simulation structures, we don't have any information about certain expressions in our language.

Below is an example of the FOL commands that would define this language, assert some axioms and build this simulation structure. As mentioned above, in the FOL system one of the few defaults is that numerals automatically come declared as individual constants and are attached to the expected integers. Thus the following axiomization includes the numerals and their attachments by default.

The first group of commands creates the language. The second group are Robinson's axioms Q without the equality axioms (Robinson, 1950). The next is the induction axiom. The fourth group makes the semantic attachments that build the simulation structure. The expressions containing the word "LAMBDA" are LISP programs. I will not explain the REPRESENT command as it is unimportant here. The parts of the declarations in square brackets specify binding power information to the FOL parser.

DECLARE INDVAR $n\ m\ p\ q \in$ NATNUM;
DECLARE OPCONST suc pred (NATNUM) = NATNUM;
DECLARE OPCONST + (NATNUM, NATNUM) = NATNUM [R ← 458, L ← 455];
DECLARE OPCONST * (NATNUM, NATNUM) = NATNUM [R ← 558, L ← 555];
DECLARE PREDCOSN ↔ (NATNUM, NATNUM) [INF];
DECLARE PREDPAR P (NATNUM);

AXIOM   Q;
AXIOM   ONEONE: $\forall n\ m.(\text{suc}(n) = \text{suc}(m) \supset n = m)$;
        SUCCI: $\forall n, \neg (\emptyset = \text{suc}(n))$;
        SUCC2: $\forall n. \neg (\emptyset = n \supset \exists m.(n = \text{suc}(m)))$;
        PLUS: $\forall n.n + \emptyset = n$
                  $\forall n\ m.n + \text{suc}(m) = \text{suc}(n+m)$;
        TIMES: $\forall n.n * \emptyset = \emptyset$
                  $\forall n.m.n * \text{suc}(m) = (n*m) + m$;;;

AXIOM   INDUCT: $P(\emptyset) \wedge \forall n.(P(n) \supset P(\text{suc}(n))) \supset \forall n.P(n)$;;

REPRESENT {NATNUM} AS NATNUMREP;
ATTACH suc   ↔ (LAMBDA (X) (ADD1 X));
ATTACH pred ↔ (LAMBDA (X) (COND ((GREATERP $X\ \emptyset$) (SUB1 X)) (T $\emptyset$)));
ATTACH +   ↔ (LAMBDA $(X\ Y)$ (PLUS $X\ Y$));
ATTACH *   ↔ (LAMBDA $(X\ Y)$ (TIMES $X\ Y$));
ATTACH <   ↔ (LAMBDA $(X\ Y)$ (LESSP $X\ Y$));

Using these commands we can ask questions like:

*****SIMPLIFY 2 + 3 < pred(7);
*****SIMPLIFY 4*suc(2) + pred(3) < pred(pred(8));

Of course semantic simplification only works on ground terms, i.e. only on those quantifier free expressions whose only individual symbols are individual constants. Furthermore, such an expression will not evaluate unless all the constants have attachments, and there is a constant in the language for a value of the expression. Thus a command like

*****SIMPLIFY $n*\emptyset$ < 3;

where n is a variable, will not simplify. This facility may seem weak as we usually don't have ground expressions to evaluate. Below I will show that when we use the metatheory and the meta-metatheory we frequently do have ground terms to evaluate, thus making this a very useful tool.

5 Syntactic simplifier

FOL also contains a syntactic simplifier, called REWRITE. This facility allows a user to specify a particular set of universally quantified equations or equivalences as rewriting rules. We call such a collection a *simplification set*. The simplifier uses them by replacing the left hand side of an equation by its right hand side after making the appropriate substitutions for the universal variables.

For example, $\forall x \, y.\mathrm{car}(\mathrm{cons}(x,y)) = x$ will rewrite any expressions of the form $\mathrm{car}(\mathrm{cons}(t_1,t_2))$ to t_1, where t_1 and t_2 are arbitrary terms.

When given an expression to simplify, REWRITE uses its entire collection of rewrite rules over and over again until it is no longer possible to apply any. Unfortunately, if you give it a rule like

$$\forall x \, y.x + y = y + x$$

it will simply go on switching the two arguments to "+" forever. This is because the rewritten term again matches the rule. This is actually a desired property of this system. First, it is impossible in general to decide if a given collection of rewrite rules will lead to a non-terminating sequence of replacements. Second, any simple way of guaranteeing termination will exclude many things that you really want to use. For example, suppose you had the restriction that no sub-expression of the right hand side should match the left hand side of a rewrite rule. Then you could not include the definition of a recursive function even if you know that it will not rewrite itself forever in the particular case you are considering. This case occurs quite frequently.

This simplifier is quite complicated and I will not describe its details here. There are three distinct sub-parts.

1 *A matching part*. This determines when a left hand side matches a particular formula.
2 *An action part*. This determines what action to take when a match is found. At present the only thing that the simplifier can do under the control of a user is the replacement of the matched expression by its right hand side.
3 *The threading part*. That is, given an expression in what order should the sub-expression be matched.

The details of these parts are found in Weyhrauch (FOL: reasoning system, Informal Note 6, unpublished). This simplifier behaves much like a PROLOG interpreter (Warren, 1977), but treats a more extensive collection of sentences. I will say more about first-order logic as a programming language (Kowalski, 1974) below. (See Appendix E in Weyhrauch [1980] for a detailed example which illustrates the control structure of the simplifier.)

6 A general first-order logic expression evaluator

Unfortunately, neither of the above simplifiers will do enough for our purposes. This section describes an evaluator for arbitrary first-order expressions which is adequate for our needs. I believe that the evaluator presented below is the only natural way of considering first-order logic as a programming language.

Consider adding the definition of the factorial function to the axioms above.

DECLARE OPCONST fact(NATNUM) = NATNUM;
AXIOM FACT: $\forall n$.fact(n) = IF $n = 0$ THEN 1 ELSE n—fact(pred(n));;

Suppose we ask the semantic simplifier to

*****SIMPLIFY fact(3);

Quite justifiably it will say, "no simplifications." There is no semantic attachment to fact. Now consider what the syntactic simplifier will do to fact(3) just given the definition of factorial.

fact (3) = IF 3 = 0 THEN 1 ELSE 3*fact(pred(3))
       = IF 3 = 0 THEN 1
              ELSE 3*(IF pred(3) = 0 THEN 1 ELSE pred(3)*fact-
       (pred(pred(3)))))

The rewriting will never terminate because the syntactic simplifier doesn't know anything about 3 = 0 or pred (3) = 0, etc. Thus it will kindly replace fact by its definition forever. The above computation could be made to stop in several ways. For example, it would stop if

(3 = 0) ≡ FALSE
$\forall X Y$.(IF FALSE THEN X ELSE Y) = Y
pred(3) = 2
fact(2 = 2
3*2 = 6

were all in the simplification set. Or if we stopped after the first step and the semantic attachment mechanism knew about = on integers and pred then we would get

syn   fact(3) = IF 3 = 0 THEN 1 ELSE 3*fact(pred(3))
sem   = 3*fact(2)
syn   = 3*(IF 2 = 0 THEN ELSE 2*fact(pred(2)))
sem   = 3*(2*fact(1))
syn   = 3*(2(IF 1 = 0 THEN 1 ELSE 1*fact(pred(1))))
sem   = 3*(2*(1*fact(0)))
syn   = 3*(2*(1*(IF 0 = 0 THEN 1 ELSE 0*fact(pred(0)))))))

sem $= 3*(2*(1*1))$
        halt

This "looks better." The interesting thing to note is that if we had a semantic attachment to * this would have computed fully. On the other hand, if we had added the definition of * in terms of + then it would have reduced to some expression in terms of addition. In this case, if we didn't have a semantic attachment to * but only to + this expression would have also "computed" 6.

Notice that this combination of semantic plus syntactic simplification acts very much like an ordinary interpreter. We have implemented such an interpreter and it has the following properties.

1   It will compute any function whose definition is hereditarily built up, in a quantifier free way, out of functions that have attachments, on domains that have attachments.

2   Every step is a logical consequence of the function definitions and the semantic attachments. This implies that, as a programming system this evaluator cannot produce an incorrect result. Thus correctness of the expression as a "program" is free. This evaluator will be used extensively below.

7 Systems of language and simulations structures

As mentioned in the introduction, one of the important things about the FOL system is its ability to deal with metatheory. In order to do this effectively we need to conceptualize on what *objects* FOL is manipulating. As I have described it above, FOL can be thought of as always having its attention directed at an object consisting of a language, L, a simulation structure, SS, attachments between the two, and a set of facts, F, i.e. the finite set of facts that have been asserted or proved. We can view this as shown in figure 1. Below I will sometimes represent these 3-tuples schematically as

$\langle$ L,SS,FF $\rangle$

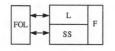

Figure 1 A view of FOL as a metatheory

I will abuse language in two ways. Most of the time I will call these structures "LS pairs," to emphasize the importance of having explicit representations as data structures for languages, the objects mentioned and the correspondence between the two. At other times I will call this kind of structure a "theory."

The importance of LS pairs cannot be overestimated. I believe they fill a gap in the kinds of structures that have previously been used to formalize reasoning. Informally their introduction corresponds to the recognition that we reason about objects, and that our reasoning makes use of our understanding of the things we reason about.

Let me give a mathematical example and a more traditional AI example. Consider the following theorem of real analysis (Royden, 1963).

Theorem.
Let $\langle F_n \rangle$ *be a sequence of nonempty closed intervals on the real line with* $F_{n+1} \subset F_n$, *then if one of the* F_n *is bounded, the intersection of the* F_n *is nonempty.*

The goal I would like you to consider is: give an example to show that this conclusion may be false if we do not require one of these sets to be bounded.

The usual counterexample expected is the set of closed intervals $[n, \infty]$ of real numbers. Clearly none of these are bounded and their intersection is empty. The idea of describing a counterexample simply cannot be made sense of if we do not have some knowledge of the models of our theories. That is, we need some idea of what objects we are reasoning about. The actualization of objects in the form of simulation structures is aimed in part at this kind of question.

As an AI example I will have to use the missionaries and cannibals puzzle. As the problem is usually posed we are asked to imagine three missionaries, three cannibals, a river, its two banks, and a boat. We then build a theory about those objects. The point here is that we have explicitly distinguished between the objects mentioned and our theory of these objects. That is, we have (in our minds, so to speak) an explicit image of the objects we are reasoning about. This is a simulation structure as defined above.

One could argue that simulation structures are just linguistic objects anyway and we should think of them as part of the theory. I believe this is fundamentally wrong. In the examples below we make essential use of this distinction between an object and the words we use to mention it.

In addition to the practical usefulness that simulation structures have, they allow us, in a mechanized way, to make sense out of the traditional philosophic questions of sense and denotation. That is, they allow us to mention in a completely formal and natural way the relation between the objects we are reasoning about and the words we are using to mention them. This basic distinction is exactly what we have realized by making models of a language into explicit data structures.

One way of describing what we have done is to say that we have built a data structure that embodies the idea that when we reason we need a language to carry out our discussions, some information about the object this language talks about, and some facts about the objects expressed in the language. This structure can be thought of as a mechanizable analog of a theory. Since it is a data structure like any other, we can reason about this theory by considering it as an object described by some other theory. Thus we give up the idea of a "universal" language about all objects to gain the ability to formally discuss our various theories of these objects.

Currently, FOL has the facility to simultaneously handle as many LS pairs as one wants. It also provides a facility for changing one's attention from one pair to another. We use this feature for changing attention from theory to metatheory as explained below.

8 Metatheory

I have already used the word "metatheory" many times and since it is an important part of what follows I want to be a little more careful about what I mean by it. Here I am not concerned with the philosophical questions logicians raise in discussions of consistency, etc. I am interested in how metatheory can be used to facilitate reasoning using computers. One of the main features of my argument is the way in which I use *reflection principles* (Feferman, 1962) to connect theories and metatheories. Reflection principles are described in the next section.

In this section I do not want to justify the use of metatheory. In ordinary reasoning it is used all the time. Some common examples of metatheory are presented in the next section. Here I will present examples taken from logic itself, as they require no additional explanation.

In its simplest form metatheory is used in the following way. Imagine that you want to prove some theorem of the theory, i.e. to extend the facts part, f, of some LS to F. One way of doing this is to use FOL in the ordinary theorem-constructing way to generate a new fact about the objects mentioned by the theory. An alternative way of doing it may be to use some metatheorem which "shortens" the proof by stating that the result of some complicated theorem generation scheme is valid. Such shortcuts are sometimes called *subsidiary deduction rules* (Kleene, 1952, p.86). We represent

Figure 2 The use of a metatheorem to shorten a proof

this schematically by the diagram shown in figure 2. Consider the metatheorem: if you have a propositional WFF whose only sentential connective is the equivalence sign, then the WFF is a theorem if each sentential symbol occurs an even number of times. In FOL this could be expressed by the metatheory sentence

$$\forall w.(\text{PROPWFF}(w) \wedge \text{CONTAINS\_ONLY\_EQUIVALENCES}(w)$$
$$\supset (\forall s. (\text{SENTSYM}(s) \wedge \text{OCCURS}(s,w) \supset \text{EVEN}(\text{count}(s,w)))$$
$$\supset \text{THEOREM}(w)))$$

The idea of this theorem is that since it is easier to count than to construct the proofs of complicated theorems, this metatheorem can save you the work of generating a proof. In FOL's metatheory this theorem can either be proved or simply asserted as axiom.

We use this theorem by directing our attention to the metatheory and instantiating it to some WFF and proving that THEOREM(w). Since we are assuming that our axiomatization of the metatheory is sound, we are then justified in asserting w in the theory. The reflection principles stated below should be looked at as the reason that we are justified in asserting w. More detailed examples will be given in the next section.

In FOL we introduce a special LS pair, META. It is intended that META is a general theory of LS pairs. When we start, it contains facts about only those things that are common to all LS pairs. Since META behaves like any other first-order LS pair, additional axioms, etc., can be added to it. This allows a user to assert many other things about a particular theory. The extent of META isn't critical and this paper is not an appropriate place to discuss its details as implemented in FOL. Of course, in addition to the descriptions of the objects contained in the LS pair, it also has axioms about what it means to be a "theorem," etc. Thus META contains the proof theory and some of the model theory of an LS pair. As with any first-order theory its language is built up of predicate constants, function symbols, and individual constant symbols. What are these? There are constants for WFFs, TERMs, derivations, simulation structures, models, etc. It contains functions for doing "and introductions", for substituting TERMs into WFFs, constructors and selectors on data structures. It has predicates "is a well formed formula," "is a term," "equality of expressions except for change of bound variables," "is a model," "is a simulation structure," "is a proof," etc.

Suppose that we are considering the metatheory of some particular LS pair, LSO = $\langle L,SS,F \rangle$. At this point we need to ask a critical question:

What is the *natural* simulation structure for META?

The answer is: firstly, we actually have in hand the object we are trying to axiomatize, LSO, and secondly, the code of FOL itself contains algorithms for the predicates and functions mentioned above.

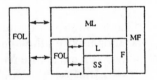

Figure 3 Use of FOL as a metatheory

This leads to the picture of figure 3. It is this picture that leads to the first hint of how to construct a system of logic that can *look* at itself. The trick is that when we carry out the above construction on a computer, the two boxes labeled FOL are physically the same object. I will expand on this in the section on self-reflection.

9 Reflection

A *reflection principle* is a statement of a relation between a theory and its metatheory. Although logicians use considerably stronger principles (see Feferman, 1962), we will only use some simple examples, i.e. statements of the soundness of the axiomatization in the metatheory of the theory. An example of a reflection principle is

(in T)
$$\frac{\backslash | /}{w}$$

(in MT) $\overline{\mathrm{Prf}(\text{``}\backslash | /\text{''}, \text{``}w\text{''})}$

In natural-deduction formulations of logic, proofs are represented as trees. In the above diagram let "$\backslash | /$" be a proof and "w" be the well-formed formula which it proves. Let Prf be a predicate constant in the metatheory, with Prf(p,x) true if and only if p is a proof, x is a WFF, and p is a proof of x. Also, let "$\backslash | /$" and "w" be the individual constants in the metatheory that are the names of "$\backslash | /$" and "w", respectively. Then the above reflection principle can be read as: if "$\backslash | /$" is a proof of "w" in the theory we are allowed to assert Prf("$\backslash | /$", "w") in the metatheory and vice versa.

A special case of this rule is "w" has no dependencies, i.e. it is a theorem.

(in T) $\dfrac{w}{}$ with no dependencies

(in META) $\overline{\mathrm{THEOREM}(\text{``}w\text{''})}$

A simpler example is

(in T) $\dfrac{\text{an individual variable } x}{}$

(in META) $\overline{\mathrm{INDVAR}(\text{``}x\text{''})}$

Suppose we have the metatheorem

ANDI: $\forall$thm1 thm2. THEOREM (mkand(wffof(thm1),wffof(thm2)))

This (meta)theorem says that if we have any two theorems of the theory, then we get a theorem by taking the conjunction of the two WFFs associated with these theorems. I need to remark about what I mean by the WFF associated with a theorem. Theorems should be thought of as particular kinds of facts. Facts are more complicated objects than only sentences. They also contain other information. For example, they include the reason we are willing to assert them and what other facts their assertion depends on. Facts also have names. Thus the above line is an incomplete representation of the metatheoretic fact whose name is ANDI. The WFF associated with this fact is just

∀thm1 thm2.THEOREM(mkand(wffof(thm1),wffof(thm2)))

Remember the reflection principle associated with THEOREM is

(in T) $\dfrac{w}{\text{THEOREM}(\text{"}w\text{"})}$ with no dependencies
(in META)

Thus we can imagine the following scenario. Suppose we have two theorems called T1 and T2 in the theory. These facts are represented as FOL data structures. Now suppose we want to assert the conjunction of these two in the theory. One way to do this is to use the *and introduction* rule of FOL. This example, however, is going to do it the hard way: first we switch to the metatheory, carrying with us the data structures for T1 and T2. We then declare some individual constants t1 and t2 to be of some theorem in the metatheory, and use the semantic attachment mechanism at the metatheory level to attach the data structures for T1 and T2 to the individual constants t1 and t2 respectively. We then instantiate the meta-theorem ANDI to t1 and t2. Note that the resulting formula is a ground instance of a sentence without quantifiers. This means that if we have attachments to all the symbols in the formula we can evaluate this formula. In this theorem we have the predicate constant THEOREM. In META it is the only constant in this sentence that is not likely to have an attachment. This is because being a theorem is not in general decidable. Fortunately, we can still use the reflection principle, because we understand the intended interpretation of the metatheory. So if we use the evaluator on

mkand(wffof(t1),wffof(t2)),

we can pick up the data structure computed in the model, instead of the term. Then, since we know that it is a theorem, we can make it into one in the theory.

This idea has been implemented in a very nice way. In FOL we have the following command.

*****REFLECT ANDI T1,T2;

The reflect command understands some fixed list of reflection principles, which includes those above. When FOL sees the word "REFLECT," it expects the next thing in the input stream to be the name of a fact in the metatheory of the current theory. So it switches to the metatheory and scans for a fact. It then finds that this fact is universally quantified with two variables ranging over facts in the theory. It holds on to the data structures that it gets in that way and switches back to the metatheory. Once there, it makes the attachments of these structures to newly-created individual constants, first checking whether or not it already has an attachment for either of these structures. We then instantiate the theorem to the relevant constants and evaluate the result. When we look at the result we notice that it will probably simply evaluate to

THEOREM(mkand(wffof(t1),wffof(t2))).

This is because we don't have an attachment to THEOREM and we also don't have an individual constant which names mkand(wffof(t1),wffof(t2)). But what we do notice is that we have reduced the theorem to the form THEOREM(–), and we know about reflection principles involving THEOREM. Thus we go back and evaluate its argument, mkand-(wffof(t1),wffof(t2)), and see if it has a value in the model. In this case, since it does, we can reflect it back into the theory, by returning to the theory and constructing the appropriate theorem.

This example is a particularly simple one, but the feature described is very general. I will give some more examples below. One thing I want to emphasize here is that what we have done is to change theorem-proving in the theory into evaluation in the metatheory. I claim that this idea of using reflection with evaluation is the most general case of this, and that this feature is not only an extremely useful operation but a fundamental one as well. It is the correct technical realization of how we can use declarative information. That is, the only thing you expect a sentence to do is to take its intended interpretation seriously.

The metatheorem we use in reflection does not need to be of the form THEOREM(–). This is the reason for needing the evaluator rather than simply either the syntactic or the semantic simplification mechanisms alone. Consider the following general metatheorems about the theory of natural numbers. If you find it hard to read it is explained in detail in the next subsection.

$\forall vl\ x.(\text{LINEAREQ}(\text{wffof}(v1),x)$
$$\supset \text{THEOREM}(\text{mkequal}(x,\text{solve}(\text{wffof}(v1,x)))));$$
$\forall w\ x.(\text{LINEAREQ}(w,x) \equiv$
   $\text{mainsym}(w) = \text{Equal} \land$
   $(\text{mainsym}(\text{lhs}(w)) = \text{Sum} \lor \text{mainsym}(\text{lhs}(w)) = \text{Diff}) \land$
   $\text{larg}(\text{lhs}(w)) = x \land$
   $\text{NUMERAL}(\text{rarg}(\text{lhs}(w))) \land$
   $\text{NUMERAL}(\text{rhs}(w))) \land$
   $(\text{mainsym}(\text{lhs}(w)) = \text{Sum} \supset \text{mknum}(\text{rhs}(w)) <$
$$\text{mknum}(\text{rarg}(\text{lhs}(w)))));$$
$\forall w\ x.(\text{solve}(w,x) = \text{IF mainsym}(\text{lhs}(w)) = \text{SUM}$
      $\text{THEN mknumeral}(\text{mknum}(\text{rhs}(w)) -$
$$\text{mknum}(\text{rarg}(\text{lhs}(w))))$$
      $\text{ELSE mknumeral}(\text{mknum}(\text{rhs}(w)) +$
$$\text{mknum}(\text{rarg}(\text{lhs}(w))))\ );;$$

These axioms together with the reflection mechanism extend FOL, so that it can solve equations of the form $x + a = b$ or $x - a = b$, when there is a solution in natural numbers. We could have given a solution in integers or for n simultaneous equations in n unknowns. Each of these requires a different collection of theorems in the metatheory.

This axiomatization may look inefficient but let me point out that solve is exactly the same amount of writing that you would need to write code to solve the same equation. The definition of LINEAREQ is divided into two parts. The first five conjunctions are to do type checking, the sixth conjunct checks for the existence of a solution before you try to use solve to find it. The above example actually does a lot. It type checks the argument, guarantees a solution and then finds it.

9.1 Can a program learn?

Here I want to digress from the stated intent of the paper and speak a little more generally about AI. It is my feeling that it is the task of AI to explain how it might be possible to build a computer individual that we can interact with as a partner in some problem-solving area. This leads to the question of what kinds of conversations we want to have with such an individual and what the nature of our interactions with him should be.

Below I describe a conversation with FOL about solving linear equations. As an example it has two purposes. The first is to illustrate the sense in which FOL is a conversational machine that can have rich discussions (even if not in natural language), and the second is to explore my ideas of what kinds of dialogues we can have with machines that might be constructed as the computer individual learning. I believe that after the discussion presented below we could reasonably say that FOL had learned to solve linear equations. That is, by having this conversation with FOL we have taught FOL some elementary algebra.

Imagine that we have told FOL about Peano arithmetic (see Appendix B of Weyhrauch [1980] for the necessary axioms). We can then have a discussion about numbers. For example, we might say

*****ASSUME $n + 2 = 7$;
1 $(n + 2) = 7$ (1)

and we might want to know what is the value of n. Since we are talking about numbers in the language of Peano arithmetic, the only way we have of discussing this problem is by using facts about numbers. Suppose that we already know the theorems

THM1: $\forall p\ q\ m.(p = q \supset p - m = q - m)$
THM2: $\forall p\ q\ m.(p + q) - r = p + (q - r)$
THM3: $\forall p.(p + 0) = p$

then we can prove that $n = 5$

*****∀E THM1 n + 2,7,2;
2 $(n + 2) = 7 \supset ((n + 2) - 2) = (7 - 2)$
*****EVAL BY {THM2,THM3};
3 $(n + 2) = 7 \supset n = 5$
***** $\supset$ E 1,3;
4 $n = 5$ (1)

In this case what we have done is proved that $n = 5$ by using facts about *arithmetic*. To put this in the perspective of *conversation*, we are having a discussion about numbers.

If we were expecting to discuss with FOL many such facts, rather than repeating the above conversation many times we might choose to have a single discussion about *algebra*. This would be carried out by introducing the notion of *equations* and a description of how to *solve* them. What is an equation? Well, it simply turns out to be a special kind of *atomic formula* of theory of arithmetic. That is, we can discuss the solution to equations by using metatheory.

In FOL we switch to the metatheory. We make some declarations and then define what it means to be a linear equation with a solution by stating the axiom

$\forall w\ x.(\text{LINEARQ}(w,x) \equiv$
  $\text{mainsym}(w) = \text{Equal} \wedge$
      $(\text{mainsym}(\text{lhs}(w)) = \text{Sum} \vee \text{mainsym}(\text{lhs}(w)) = \text{Diff}) \wedge$
  $\text{larg}(\text{lhs}(w)) = x \wedge$
  $\text{NUMERAL}(\text{rarg}(\text{lhs}(w))) \wedge$
  $\text{NUMERAL}(\text{rhs}(w)) \wedge$
  $(\text{mainsym}(\text{lhs}(w)) = \text{Sum} \supset \text{mknum}(\text{rhs}(w)) >$
                          $\text{mknum}(\text{rarg}(\text{lhs}(w)))))$

Here w is a (meta) variable ranging over WFFs, and x is a (meta)variable ranging over individual variables. Spelled out in English, this sentence says that a well-formed formula is a linear equation if and only if:

  (i)   it is an equality,
  (ii) its left hand side is either a sum or a difference,
  (iii) the left hand argument of the left hand side of the equality is x,
  (iv) the right hand argument of the left hand side of the equality is a numeral,
  (v)   the right hand side of the equality is a numeral and
  (vi) if the left hand side is a sum then the number denoted by the numeral on the right hand side is greater than the number denoted by the numeral appearing in the left hand side.

In more mathematical terminology it is: that the well-formed formula must be either of the form $x + a = b$ or $x - a = b$ where a and b are numeral and x is an individual variable. Since here we are only interested in the natural numbers, the last restriction in the definition of LINEAREQ is needed to guarantee the existence of a solution.

We also describe how to find out what is the *solution* to an equation.

$\forall w\, x.$(solve(w,x) = IF mainsym(lhs(w)) = Sum
        THEN mknumeral(mknum(rhs(w)) −
                            mknum(rarg(lhs(w))))
        ELSE mknumeral(mknum(rhs(w)) +
                            mknum(rarg(lhs(w)))));;

This is a function definition in the metatheory. Finally, we assert that if we have an equation in the theory then the numeral constructed by the solver can be asserted to be the answer.

$\forall$v1 $x.$(LINEAREQ(wffof(v1),x) $\supset$
            THEOREM(mkequal(x,solve(wffof(v1),x)))));

We then tell FOL to remember these facts in a way that is convenient to be used by FOL's evaluator.

This then is the conversation we have with FOL about equations. Now we are ready to see how FOL can use that information, so we switch FOL's attention back to the theory. Now, whenever we want to solve a linear equation, we simply remark, using the reflect command, that he should remember our discussion about solving equations.

We can now get the effect of the small proof above by saying

*****REFLECT SOLVE 1;
5 $n = 5$ (1)

In effect FOL has learned to solve simple linear equations.

We could go on to ask FOL to prove that the function solve actually provides a solution to the equation, rather than our just telling FOL that it does, but this is simply a matter of sophistication. It has to do with the question of what you are willing to accept as a justification.

One reasonable justification is that the teacher told me. This is exactly the state we are in above. On the other hand, if that is not satisfactory then it is possible to discuss with FOL the justification of the solution. This could be accomplished by explaining to FOL (in the metatheory) not to assert the solution of the equations in the theory, but rather to construct a proof of the correctness of the solution as we did when we started. Clearly this can be done using the same machinery that was used here. This is important because it means that our reasoning system does not need to be expanded. We only have to tell it more information.

A much more reasonable alternative is to tell FOL (again in the metatheory) two things: firstly, what we have above, i.e. we need to assert the solution of the equation; secondly, if asked to justify the solution, then that proof has to be produced. This combines the advantages each of the above possibilities. I want to point out that this is very close to the kinds of discussions that you want to be able to have with people about simple algebra.

Informally we always speak about solving equations. That is, we think of them as syntactic and learn how to manipulate them. This is not thinking about them as relations, which is their usual first-order interpretation. In this sense going to the metatheory and treating the equations as syntactic objects is very close to our informal use of these notions.

I believe that this is exactly what we want in an AI system dealing with the question of *teaching*. Notice that we have the best of both worlds. On the one hand, at the theory level, we can "execute" this learning, i.e. use it, and on the other hand, at the metatheory level, we can reason about what we have learned about manipulating equations. In addition, the correct distinction between equations as facts and equations as syntactic objects has been maintained. The division between theory and metatheory has allowed us to view the same object in both these ways without contradiction or the possibility of confusion.

As is evident from the above description, one of the things we have here is a very general-purpose programming system. In addition it is extendable. Above we have shown how to introduce any new subsidiary deduction rule that one chooses, "simply" by telling FOL what one would like it to do. This satisfies the desires of Davis and Schwartz (1977), but in a setting not restricted to the theory of hereditarily finite sets. As I said above: we are using first-order logic in what I believe is its most general and natural setting.

There are hundreds of examples of this kind where their natural description is in the metatheory. Much of the intent of natural language can only be understood if you realize that a lot of what we say is about our use of language, not about objects in the world. This kind of conversation is most naturally carried out in the metatheory with the use of the kind of self-reflective structures hinted about below.

10 Self-reflection

In the traditional view of metatheory we start with a theory and we axiomatize that theory. This gives us metatheory. Later we may axiomatize that theory. That gives us meta-metatheory. If you believe that most reasoning is at some level (as I do) then this view of towers of metatheories leads to many questions. For example, how is it that human memory space doesn't overflow. Each theory in the tower seems to contain a complete description of the theory below thus exponentiating the amount of space needed!

In the section on metatheory, I introduced the LS pair, META. Since it is a first-order theory just like any other, FOL can deal with it just like any other. Since META is the general theory of LS pairs and META is an LS pair, this might suggest that META is also a theory that contains facts about itself. That is, by introducing the individual constant Meta into the theory META and by using semantic attachment to attach the theory (i.e. the actual machine data structure) META to Meta we can give META its own name.

The rest of this section is composed of more general notions which have consequences that we have just begun to work out.

FOL handles many LS pairs simultaneously. I have shown how, given any LS pair, we can direct FOL's attention to META using reflection. Once META has an individual constant which is a name for itself and we have attached META to this constant, then META is FOL's theory of itself. Notice two things:

1. If META has names for all of the LS pairs known to FOL then it has the entire FOL system as its simulation structure:
2. Since META is a theory about any LS pair, we can use it to reason about itself.

We can illustrate this in FOL by switching to META and executing the following command.

*****REFLECT ANDI ANDI ANDI;
1∀thm1 thm2.THEOREM(mkand(wffof(thm1),wffof(thm2))) ∧
    ∀thm1 thm2.THEOREM(mkand(wffof(thm1),wffof(thm2)))

The effect we have achieved is that when FOL's attention is directed at itself, then when we reflect into its own metatheory we have a system that is capable of reasoning about itself.

When looking at human reasoning I am struck by two facts. First, we seem to be able to apply the Meta facts that we know to any problems that we are trying to solve, and second, even though it is possible to construct simple examples of use/mention conflicts, most people arrive at correct answers to questions without even knowing there is a problem. In other words, although natural language is filled with apparent puns that arise out of use/mention confusions, the people speaking do not confuse the names of things with the things. That is, the meaning is clear to them.

The above command suggests one possible technical way in which both of these problems can be addressed. The structure of FOL knew that the first occurrence of ANDI in the above command was a "use" and that the second and third were "mentions." Furthermore, the same routines that dealt effectively with the ordinary nonself-reflective way of looking at theory/metatheory relations also dealt with this case of self-reflection without difficulty.

Notice that I said, "this case." It is possible with the structure that I have described above to ask META embarrassing questions. For example, if you ask META twice in a row what the largest step number in its proof is you will get two different answers. This would seem to lead to a contradiction.

The source of this problem is in what I believe is our traditional idea of what it means to be a rule of inference. Self-reflective systems have properties that are different from ordinary systems. In particular, whenever you "apply a rule of inference" to the facts of this system, you change the structure of META itself, and as a result you change the attachment to Meta. This process of having a rule of inference that changes the models of a theory as well as the already proven facts simply does not happen in traditional logics. This change of point of view requires a new idea of what is a valid rule of inference for such systems.

11 Conclusion

I want to review what I consider to be the important features of this paper. One is the observation that, when we reason, we use representations of the objects we are reasoning about as well as a representation of the facts about these objects. This is technically realized by FOL's manipulation of LS pairs using semantic attachment. It is incorrect to view this as a procedural representation of facts. Instead, we should look at it as an ability to explicitly represent procedures. That is, simulation structures give us an opportunity to have a machine representation of the objects we want to reason about as well as the sentences we use to mention them.

Second, the evaluator I described above is an important object. When used by itself it represents a mathematical way of describing algorithms together with the assurance that they are correctly implemented. This is a consequence of the fact that the evaluator only performs logically valid transformations on the function definitions. In this way, we could use the evaluator to actually generate proof that the computed answer is correct. In these cases, evaluation and deduction become the same thing. This is similar in spirit to the work of Kowalski (1974), but does not rely on any normalization of formulas. It considers the usual logical function definitions and takes their intended interpretation seriously. This evaluator works on any expression with respect to any LS pair, and its implementation has proved to be only two to three times slower than a LISP interpreter.

Third is the observation that the FOL proof-checker is itself the natural simulation structure for the theory META of LS pairs. This gives us a clean way of saying what the intended interpretation of META is. This observation makes evaluation in META a very powerful tool. It is also the seed of a theory of self-reflective logic structures which, like humans, can reason about themselves.

Fourth is the use of reflection principles to connect an LS pair with META. This, together with the REFLECT command, is a technical explanation of what has been called the declarative/procedural controversy. Consider the META theorem ANDI described above. When we use the REFLECT command to point at it from some LS pair, ANDI is viewed procedurally. We want it to do an *and introduction*. On the other hand, when we are reasoning in META, it is a sentence like any other. Whether a sentence is looked at declaratively or procedurally depends on your point of view, i.e. it depends where you are standing when you look at it.

I have presented here a general description of a working reasoning system that includes not only theories but also metatheories of arbitrarily high level. I have given several examples of how these features, together with reflection, can be used to dynamically extend the reasoning power of the working FOL system. I have made some references to the way in which one can use the self-reflective parts of this system. I have given examples of how heuristics for using subsidiary deduction rules can be described using these structures. In addition, since everything you type to FOL refers to some LS pair, all of the above things can be reasoned about using the same machinery.

3   Levels of theory

One of the important complexities that confounds many discussions of AI is its claims to be a science, and the significance of AI programs is that the constituent phenomena can be represented, explored, refuted, and supported, etc. at many different, but not obviously separable, levels. Is theorizing in AI carried forward primarily by building and observing the behavior of models, or should we have a complete, formal specification prior to modeling, with the model providing merely an existence proof of practical viability? Advocates can be found for both sides of this methodological argument, which is taken up again, from other viewpoints, in subsequent sections.

Marr's paper argues for caution in "explaining" phenomena in terms of a working program (a Type 2 theory in Marr's terminology). This level of theory, embodying as it does a "mound of small administrative decisions that are inevitable whenever a concrete program is designed," can all too easily obscure and hide some simple, abstract theory (a Type 1 theory) that may underlie it. He concludes that exploration at the program level should continue, but we must be careful not to overvalue results at this methodological level: "in the present state of the art [in AI], it seems wiser to concentrate on problems that probably have Type 1 solutions, rather than on those that are almost certainly of Type 2." Marr, like Hoare and Dijkstra (see Partridge and Wilks paper in section 10), is suggesting that we limit AI research, initially at least.

Boden sees AI as having provided psychologists with a new level of theorizing: "it has provided a standard of rigor and completeness to which theoretical explanations should aspire." And, although she accepts the cautions of Marr, she argues for the benefits of a level of theorizing that allows detailed questioning of not only WHAT the mind does, but HOW it does what it does.

Partridge presents a methodology for relating theories to programs in AI. It is suggested that a process of stepwise abstraction is used to build a bridge between these two objects, and that this bridge can then serve as an explicit basis for claims that the program embodies (in some sense) the theory. The sequence of abstractions generated is not in itself a justification of the program-theory relationship; it is merely an explicit basis for argument about the validity of such a claim. The sequence is comprised of restatements of the principles or theory at successively more abstract levels. The implicit claim is that there is no correct or 'best' level of theorising but that different levels of statement are appropriate for different purposes, and that a sequence of restatements is necessary to support reasoned argument.

Artificial intelligence: a personal view

David Marr

Artificial intelligence is the study of complex information-processing problems that often have their roots in some aspect of biological information processing. The goal of the subject is to identify interesting and solvable information-processing problems, and solve them.

The solution to an information-processing problem divides naturally into two parts. In the first, the underlying nature of a particular computation is characterized, and its basis in the physical world is understood. One can think of this part as an abstract formulation of what is being computed and why, and I shall refer to it as the "theory" of a computation. The second part consists of particular algorithms for implementing a computation, and so it specifies how. The choice of algorithm usually depends upon the hardware in which the process is to run, and there may be many algorithms that implement the same computation. The theory of a computation, on the other hand, depends only on the nature of the problem to which it is a solution. Jardine and Sibson (1971) decomposed the subject of cluster analysis in precisely this way, using the term "method" to denote what I call the theory of a computation.

To make the distinction clear, let us take the case of Fourier analysis. The (computational) theory of the Fourier transform is well understood, and is expressed independently of the particular way in which it is computed. There are, however, several algorithms for implementing a Fourier transform – the Fast Fourier transform (Cooley and Tukey, 1965), which is a serial algorithm, and the parallel "spatial" algorithms that are based on the mechanisms of coherent optics. All these algorithms carry out the same computation, and the choice of which one to use depends upon the available hardware. In passing, we also note that the distinction between serial and parallel resides at the algorithm level and is not a deep property of a computation.

Strictly speaking then, a result in AI consists of the isolation of a particular information-processing problem, the formulation of a computational theory for it, the construction of an algorithm that implements it, and a practical demonstration that the algorithm is successful. The important point here, and it is what makes progress possible, is that once a computational theory has been established for a particular problem, it never has to be done again, and in this respect a result in AI behaves like a result in mathematics or any of the hard natural sciences. Some judgment has to be applied when deciding whether the computational theory for a problem has been formulated adequately: the statement "take the opponent's king" defines the goal of chess, but it is hardly an adequate characterization of the computational problem of doing it.[1] The kind of judgment that is needed seems to be similar to that which decides whether a result in mathematics amounts to a substantial new theorem, and I do not feel uncomfortable about having to leave the basis of such judgments unspecified.[2]

This view of what constitutes a result in AI is probably acceptable to most scientists. Chomsky's (1965) notion of a "competence" theory for English syntax is precisely what I mean by a computational theory for that problem. Both have the quality of being little concerned with the gory details of algorithms that must be run to express the competence (i.e. to implement the computation). That is not to say that devising suitable algorithms will be easy, but it is to say that before one can devise them, one has to know what exactly they are supposed to be doing, and this information is captured by the computational theory. When a problem decomposes in this way, I shall refer to it as having a Type 1 theory.

The fly in the ointment is that while many problems of biological information processing have a Type 1 theory, there is no reason why they should all have. This can happen when a problem is solved by the simultaneous action of a considerable number of processes, whose interaction is its own simplest description, and I shall refer to such a situation as a Type 2 theory.[3] One promising candidate for a Type 2 theory is the problem of predicting how a protein will fold. A large number of influences act on a large polypeptide chain as it flaps and flails in a medium. At each moment only a few of the possible interactions will be important, but the importance of those few is decisive. Attempts to construct a simplified theory must ignore some interactions; but if most interactions are crucial at some stage during the folding, a simplified theory will prove inadequate. Interestingly, the most promising studies of protein folding are currently those that take a brute force approach, setting up a rather detailed model of the amino acids, the geometry associated with their sequence, hydrophobic interactions with the circumambient fluid, random thermal perturbations, etc., and letting the whole set of processes run until a stable configuration is achieved (Levitt and Warshel, 1975).

The principal difficulty in AI is that one can never be sure whether a problem has a Type I theory. If one is found, well and good; but failure to find one does not mean that it does not exist. Most AI programs have hitherto amounted to Type 2 theories, and the danger with such theories is that they can bury crucial decisions, which in the end provide the key to the correct Type 1 decomposition of the problem, beneath the mound of small administrative decisions that are inevitable whenever a concrete program is designed. This phenomenon makes research in AI difficult to pursue and difficult to judge. If one shows that a given information-processing problem is solved by a particular, neatly circumscribed computational theory, then that is a secure result. If, on the other hand, one produces a large and clumsy set of processes that solves a problem, one cannot always be sure that there is not a simple underlying computational theory for one or more related problems whose formulation has somehow been lost in the fog. With any candidate for Type 2 theory, much greater importance is attached to the performance of the program. Since its only possible virtue might be that it works, it is interesting only if it does. Often, a piece of AI research has resulted in a large program without much of a theory, which commits it to a Type 2 result, but that program either performs too poorly to be impressive or (worse still) has not even been implemented. Such pieces of research have to be judged very harshly, because their lasting contribution is negligible.

Thus we see that as AI pursues its study of information-processing problems, two types of solution are likely to emerge. In one there is a clean underlying theory in the traditional sense. Examples of this from vision are Horn's (Horn, 1975) method for obtaining shape from shading; the notion of the primal sketch as a representation of the intensity changes and local geometry of an image (Marr, 1976); Ullman's (Ullman, 1976) method for detecting light sources; Binford's (Binford, 1971) generalized cylinder representation, on which Marr and Nishihara's (Marr and Nishihara, 1977) theory of the internal representation and manipulation of 3-D structures was based; a recent theory of stereo vision (Marr, 1974; Marr and Poggio, 1976);[4] and Poggio and Reichardt's (Poggio and Reichardt, 1976) analysis of the visual orienting behavior of the housefly. One characteristic of these results is that they often lie at a relatively low level in the overall canvas of intellectual functions, a level often dismissed with contempt by those who purport to study "higher, more central" problems of intelligence. Our reply to such criticisms is that low-level problems probably do represent the easier kind, but that is precisely the reason for studying them first. When we have solved a few more, the questions that arise in studying the deeper ones will be clearer to us.

But even relatively clean Type 1 theories such as these involve Type 2 theories as well. For example, Marr and Nishihara's 3-D representation theory asserts that the deep underlying structure is based on a distributed, object-centered coordinate system that can be thought of as a stick figure, and that this representation is explicitly manipulated during the analysis of an image. Such a theory would be little more than speculation unless it could also be shown that such a description may be computed from an image and be manipulated in the required way. To do so involves several intermediate theories, for some of which there is hope of eventual Type 1 status, but others look intractably to be of Type 2. For example, a Type 1 theory now exists for part of the problem of determining the appropriate local coordinate system from the contours formed in an object's image (Marr, 1977b), but it may be impossible to derive a Type 1 theory for the basic grouping processes that operate on the primal sketch to help separate figure from ground. The figure-ground "problem" may not be a single problem, being instead a mixture of several subproblems which combine to achieve figural separation, just as the different molecular interactions combine to cause a protein to fold. There is, in fact, no reason why a solution to the figure-ground problem should be derivable from a single underlying theory. The reason is that it needs to contain a procedural representation of many facts about images that derive ultimately via evolution from the cohesion and continuity of matter in the physical world. Many kinds of knowledge and different techniques are involved; one just has to sort them out one by one. As each is added, the performance of the whole improves, and the complexity of the images that can be handled increases.

We have already seen that to search for a Type 2 theory for a problem may be dangerous if in fact it has a Type 1 theory. This danger is most acute in premature assaults on a high-level problem, for which few or none of the concepts that underlie its eventual Type 1 theory have yet been developed, and the consequence is a complete failure to formulate correctly the problems that are, in fact, involved. But it is equally important to realize that the opposite danger exists lower down. For example, in our current theory of visual processing, the notion of the primal sketch seems respectable enough, but one might have doubts about the aesthetics of the grouping processes that decode it. There are many of them; their details are somewhat messy; and seemingly arbitrary preferences occur (e.g., for vertical or horizontal organizations). A clear example of a Type 2 theory is our assertion that texture-vision discriminations rest on these grouping processes and first-order discriminations applied to the information held in the primal sketch of the image (Marr, 1976). As such, it is less attractive than Julesz's (Julesz, 1975) clean (Type 1) theory that textured regions are discriminable only if there is a difference in the first- or second-order statistics of their intensity arrays. But as Julesz himself found, there exist patterns with different second-order statistics that are nevertheless indiscriminable; and one can in fact view our own work as attempting to define precisely what characteristics of the second-order statistical structure cause discriminability.

This inevitably forces us to relinquish the beauty of Julesz's concise theory, but I feel that one should not be too distressed by the need at this level of investigation to explore rather messy and untidy details. We already know that separate modules must exist for computing other aspects of visual information – motion, stereoscopy, fluorescence, color – and there is no reason why they should all be based on a single theory. Indeed, one would a priori expect the opposite: as evolution progressed, new modules came into existence that could cope with yet more aspects of the data, and as a result kept the animal alive in ever more widely ranging circumstances. The only important constraint is that the system as a whole should be roughly modular, so that new facilities can be added easily.

So, especially at the more peripheral stages of sensory information processing, and perhaps also more centrally, one should not give up if one fails to find a Type 1 theory – there may not be one. More importantly, even if there were, there would be no reason why that theory should bear much relation to the theory of more central phenomena. In vision, for example, the theory that says 3-D representations are based on stick-figure coordinate systems and shows how to manipulate them is independent of the theory of the primal sketch, or for that matter of most other stages *en route* from the image to that representation. In particular, it is especially dangerous to suppose that an approximate theory of a peripheral process has any significance for higher-level operations. For example, because Julesz's second-order statistics idea is so clean and so neatly fits much data, one might be tempted to ask whether the idea of second-order interactions is in some way central to higher processes. In doing so, one should bear in mind that the true explanation of visual-texture discrimination may be quite different in nature even if the theory is very often a correct predictor of performance.

The reason for making this point at such length is that it bears upon another issue, namely the type of theory that the grammar of natural language might have. The purpose of human language is presumably to transform a data structure that is not inherently one-dimensional into one-dimensional form for transmission as a sequential utterance, thereafter to be retranslated into some rough copy of the original in the head of the listener. Viewed in this light, it becomes entirely possible that there may exist no Type 1 theory of English syntax of the type that transformational grammar attempts to define – that its constraints resemble wired-in conventions about useful ways of executing this tedious but vital operation, rather than deep principles about the nature of intelligence. An abstract theory of syntax may be an illusion, approximating what really happens only in the sense that Julesz's second-order statistics theory approximates the behavior of the set of processes that implement texture vision and which, in the final analysis, are all the theory there is. In other words, the grammar of natural language may have a theory of Type 2 rather than of Type 1.

Even if a biological information-processing problem has only a Type 2 theory, it may be possible to infer more from a solution to it than the solution itself. This comes about because at some point in the implementation of a set of processes, design constraints attached to the machine in which they will run start to affect the structure of the implementation. This observation adds a different perspective to the two types of research carried out by linguists and by members of the artificial intelligence community. If the theory of syntax is really of Type 2, any important implications about the CNS are likely to come from details of the way in which its constituent processes are implemented, and these are often explorable only by implementing them.

Implications of this view

If one accepts this view of AI research, one is led to judge its achievements according to rather clear criteria. What information-processing problem has been isolated? Has a clean theory been developed for solving it, and if so how good are the arguments that support it? If no clean theory has been given, what is the evidence that favors set-of-processes solution or suggests that no single clean theory exists for it, and how well does the proposed set of mechanisms work? For very advanced problems like story-understanding, current research is often purely exploratory. That is to say, in these areas our knowledge is so poor that we cannot even begin to formulate the appropriate questions, let alone solve them. It is important to realize that this is an inevitable phase of any human endeavor, personally risky (almost surely no exploring pioneer will himself succeed in finding a useful question), but a necessary precursor of eventual success.

Most of the history of AI (now fully 16 years old) has consisted of exploratory studies. Some of the best-known are Slagle's (1963) symbolic integration program, Weizenbaum's (1965) Eliza program, Evans' (1968) analogy program, Raphael's (1968) SIR, Quillian's (1968) semantic nets, and Winograd's (1972) SHRDLU. All these programs have (in retrospect) the property that they are either too simple to be interesting Type 1 theories, or very complex yet performed too poorly to be taken seriously as a Type 2 theory. Perhaps the only really successful Type 2 theory to emerge in the early phase of AI was Waltz's 1972 program (Waltz, 1975). Yet many things have been learned from these experiences – mostly negative things (the first twenty obvious ideas about how intelligence might work are too simple or wrong) but including several positive things. The MACSYMA algebraic manipulation system (Moses, 1974) is undeniably successful and useful, and it had its roots in programs like Slagle's. The mistake made in the field lay not in having carried out such studies – they formed an essential part of its development – but mainly in failures of judgment about their value, since it is now clear that few of the early studies themselves formulated any solvable problems. Part of the reason for these internal failures of judgment lay in external pressures for early results from the field, but this is not the place to discuss what in the end are political matters.

Yet, I submit, one would err to judge these failures of judgment harshly. They are merely the inevitable consequence of necessary enthusiasm, based on a view of the long-term importance of the field that seems to me correct. All important fields of human endeavor start with a personal commitment based on faith rather than on results. AI is just one more example. Only a crabbed and unadventurous spirit will hold it against us.

Current trends

Exploratory studies are important. Many people in the field expect that, deep in the heart of our understanding of intelligence, there will lie at least one and probably several important principles about how to organize and represent knowledge that in some sense captures what is important about the general nature of our intellectual abilities. An optimist might see the glimmer of such principles in programs like those of Sussman and Stallman (1975), of Marr and Nishihara (1977), in the overall attitudes to central problems set out by Minsky (1975), and possibly in some of Schank's (1973, 1975a) work, although I sometimes feel that he failed to draw out the important points. Although still somewhat cloudy, the ideas that seem to be emerging (and which owe much to the early exploratory studies) are:

1 That the "chunks of reasoning, language, memory, and perception ought to be larger than most recent theories in psychology have allowed (Minsky, 1975). They must also be very flexible – at least as flexible as Marr and Nishihara's (1977) stick-figure 3-D models, and probably more. Straightforward mechanisms that are suggested by the terms "frame" and "terminal" are certainly too inflexible.
2 That the perception of an event or of an object must include the simultaneous computation of several different descriptions of it, which capture diverse aspects of the use, purpose, or circumstances of the event or object.
3 That the various descriptions described in (2) include coarse versions as well as fine ones. These coarse descriptions are a vital link in choosing the appropriate overall scenarios demanded by (1), and in establishing correctly the roles played by the objects and actions that caused those scenarios to be chosen.

An example will help to make these points clear. If one reads

A The fly buzzed irritatingly on the window-pane
B John picked up the newspaper

the immediate inference is that John's intentions toward the fly are fundamentally malicious. If he had picked up the telephone, the inference would be less secure. It is generally agreed that an "insect-damaging" scenario is somehow deployed during the reading of these sentences, being suggested in its coarsest form by the fly buzzing irritatingly. Such a scenario will contain a reference to something that can squash an insect on a brittle surface – a description that fits a newspaper but not a telephone. We might therefore conclude that when the newspaper is mentioned (or, in the case of vision, seen) it is described not only internally as a newspaper and some rough 3-D description of its shape and axes set up, but also as a light, flexible object with area. Because sentence (B) might have continued "and sat down to read," the newspaper may also be being described as reading matter similarly, as a combustible article, and so forth. Since one does not usually know in advance what aspect of an object or action is important, it follows that most of the time a given object will give rise to several different coarse internal descriptions. Similarly for actions. It may be important to note that the description of fly-swatting or reading or fire-lighting does not have to be attached to the newspaper; merely that a description of the newspaper is available that will match its role in each scenario.

The important thing about Schank's "primitive actions" seems to me not the fact that there happens to be a certain small number of them, nor the idea that every act is expressed solely by reduction to them (which I cannot believe at all), nor even the idea that the scenarios to which they are attached contain all the answers for the present situation (that is where the missing flexibility comes in). The importance of a primitive, coarse catalogue of events and objects lies in the role such coarse descriptions play in the ultimate access and construction of perhaps exquisitely tailored specific scenarios, rather in the way that a general 3-D animal model in Marr and Nishihara's theory can finish up as a very specific Cheshire Cat, after due interaction between the image and information stored in the primitive model. What after sentence (A) existed as little more than a malicious intent toward the innocent fly becomes, with the additional information about the newspaper, a very specific case of fly-squashing.

Marr and Nishihara have labeled the problem of providing multiple-descriptions for the newspaper its "reference-window problem." Exactly how it is best done, and exactly what descriptions should accompany different words or perceived objects, is not yet known. These insights are the result of exploratory studies, and the problems to which they lead have yet to be precisely formulated, let alone satisfactorily solved. But it is now certain that some problems of this kind do exist and are important; and it seems likely that a fairly respectable theory of them will eventually emerge.

Mimicry versus exploration

Finally, I would like to draw one more distinction that seems to be important when choosing a research problem, or when judging the value of completed work. The problem is that studies – particularly of natural-language understanding, problem-solving, or the structure of memory – can easily degenerate into the writing of programs that do no more than mimic in an unenlightening way some small aspect of human performance. Weizenbaum (1976) now judges his program Eliza to belong to this category, and I have never seen any reason to disagree. More controversially, I would also criticize on the same grounds Newell and Simon's (e.g. Newell and Simon, 1972) work on production systems, and some of Norman and Rumelhart's (Norman and Rumelhart, 1974) work on long-term memory.

The reason is this. If one believes that the aim of information-processing studies is to formulate and understand particular information-processing problems, then it is the structure of those problems that is central, not the mechanisms through which they are implemented. Therefore, the first thing to do is to find problems that we can solve well, find out how to solve them, and examine our performance in the light of that understanding. The most fruitful source of such problems is operations that we perform well and fluently (and hence unconsciously), since it is difficult to see how reliability could be achieved if there were no sound underlying method. On the other hand, problem-solving research has tended to concentrate on problems that we understand well intellectually but perform poorly on, like mental arithmetic and criptarithmetic or on problems like geometry theorem-proving, or games like chess, in which human skills seem to rest on a huge base of knowledge and expertise. I argue that these are exceptionally good grounds for *not* studying how we carry out such tasks yet. I have no doubt that when we do mental arithmetic we are doing *something* well, but it is not arithmetic, and we seem far from understanding even one component of what that something is. Let us therefore concentrate on the simpler problems first, for there we have some hope of genuine advancement.

If one ignores this stricture, one is left in the end with unlikely looking mechanisms whose only recommendation is that they cannot do something we cannot do. Production systems seem to me to fit this description quite well. Even taken on their own terms as mechanisms, they leave a lot to be desired. As a programming language they are poorly designed and hard to use, and I cannot believe that the human brain could possibly be burdened with such poor implementation decisions at so basic a level.

A parallel may perhaps be drawn between production systems for students of problem-solving and Fourier analysis for visual neurophysiologists. Simple operations on a spatial frequency representation of an image can mimic several interesting visual phenomena that seem to be exhibited by our visual systems. These include the detection of repetition, certain visual illusions, the notion of separate linearly adding channels, separation of overall shape from fine local detail, and a simple expression of size invariance. The reason why the spatial frequency domain is ignored by image analysts is that it is virtually useless for the main job of vision – building up a description of what is there from the intensity array. The intuition that visual physiologists lack, and which is so important, is for how this may be done. A production system exhibits several interesting ideas – the absence of explicit subroutine calls, a blackboard communication channel, and some notion of a short-term memory. But just because production systems display these side effects (as Fourier analysis "displays" some visual illusions) does not mean that they have anything to do with what is really going on. My own guess would be, for example, that the fact that short-term memory can act as a storage register is probably the least important of its functions. I expect that there are several "intellectual reflexes" that operate on items held there, about which nothing is yet known and which will eventually be held to be the crucial things about it because they perform central functions like opening up an item's reference window. Studying our performance in close relation to production systems seems to me a waste of time, because it amounts to studying a mechanism, not a problem, and can therefore lead to no Type 1 results. The mechanisms that such research is trying to penetrate will be unraveled by studying problems, just as vision research is progressing because it is the problem of vision that is being attacked, not neural visual mechanisms.

A reflection of the same criticism can be made of Norman and Rumelhart's work, where they studied the way information seems to be organized in long-term memory. Again, the danger is that questions are not asked in relation to a clear information-processing problem. Instead, they are asked and answers proposed in terms of a mechanism – in this case, it is called an "active structural network," and it is so simple and general as to be devoid of theoretical substance. They may be able to say that such and such an "association" seems to exist, but they cannot say of what the association consists, nor that it has to be so because to solve problem X (which we can solve) you need a memory organized in such-and-such a way; and that if one has it, certain apparent "associations" occur as side effects. Experimental psychology can do a valuable job in discovering facts that need explaining, including those about long-term memory, and the work of Shepard (1975), Rosch (1976), and Warrington (1975), for example, seems to me very successful at this; but like experimental neurophysiology, experimental psychology will not be able to explain those facts unless information-processing research has identified and solved the appropriate problems X.[5] It seems to me that finding such problems X, and solving them, is what AI should be trying to do.

Notes

Although I take full responsibility for the purely personal views set out here, any virtues that they may have are due in part to many conversations with Drew McDermott. This report describes work done at the Artificial Intelligence Laboratory of the Massachusetts Institute of Technology. Support for the Laboratory's artificial intelligence research is provided in part by the Advanced Research Projects Agency of the U.S. Department of Defense under Office of Naval Research contract number N00014–75–C–0643.

1 One computational theory that in principle can solve chess is exhaustive search.
   The real interest lies, however, in formulating the pieces of computation that we

apply to the game. One presumably wants a computational theory that has a general application, together with a demonstration that it happens to be applicable to some class of games of chess, and evidence that we play games in this class.

2 New algorithms for implementing a known computational theory may subsequently be devised without throwing substantial new light upon the theory, just as S. Winograd's (Winograd, 1976) Very Fast Fourier Transform sheds no new light on the nature of Fourier analysis.

3 The underlying point here is that there is often a natural modularity in physics (e.g., under normal conditions, electrical interactions are independent of gravitational interactions), but some processes involve several at the same time and with roughly equal importance, like protein folding. Thus the Type 1-Type 2 distinction is not a pure dichotomy, and there is a spectrum of possibilities between them.

4 The notion of cooperative computation, or relaxation-labeling (Zucker, 1976), is a notion at the algorithm level. It suggests a way of implementing certain computations but does not address the problem of what should be implemented which seems to be the real issue for vision no less than elsewhere.

5 In the present state of the art, it seems wisest to concentrate on problems that probably have Type 1 solutions, rather than on those that are almost certainly of Type 2.

Has AI helped psychology?

Margaret A. Boden

A psychologist of my acquaintance, neither unaware of nor unsympathetic to work influenced by AI, recently referred to computational psychology as 'very specialized'. Is this a fair assessment? Is AI-based psychology a mere hidden backwater, separated from the psychological mainstream? Sociologically, it must be admitted that it is. But theoretically? Perhaps the backwater is where the action is (and so much the worse for those who cannot see it)? Could it become the mainstream itself? In short, has AI helped psychology, or has it failed to live up to its early promise?

AI has undoubtedly helped psychology in some, very general, ways. It has provided a standard of rigour and completeness to which theoretical explanations should aspire (which is not to say that a program is in itself a theory). It has highlighted the importance of asking detailed questions about mental *processes* – about not just *what* the mind does, but *how*. It has alerted theoretical psychologists to the enormous richness and computational power of the mind. And it has furthered our understanding of how psychological, intentional, phenomena are possible in a basically material universe. If only for these reasons, AI has already been of lasting benefit to psychology. Certain sorts of theoretical inadequacies should be less common in the future than in the past.

But has it given us any more than this? Granted that it tells us something in general terms about what good psychological theories should look like, and how complex they are likely to be, has it helped us to find any? Has it even suggested what specific questions psychologists should ask in particular areas?

In some domains, it has indeed provided specific questions – and even some specific answers. Broadly, those (largely peripheral) aspects of mental processes which Fodor (1983b) calls 'modules' appear to respond to computational analysis and modelling. Here, there has been some specific scientific advance. The prime example is low-level vision, wherein the basic nature and psychological processes of various visual abilities, such as stereopsis, have been greatly clarified. A second example is low-level natural-language understanding. Questions about on-line parsing, and the relation between syntactic and semantic interpretation, have been sharpened by way of the AI approach.

But what of 'the higher mental processes'? Most work in AI (including that which was motivated by broadly psychological interests) concerns phenomena like problem-solving, planning, theorem-proving, interpretation of natural-language texts, belief-fixation, and semantic or episodic memory: all higher mental processes *par excellence*. Does the large amount of such research give us cause to hope that adequate psychological theories of these matters will be developed with AI's help?

One need not be an opponent of AI and computer modelling to be sceptical about this question. Some people *within* the computationalist camp deny that AI has – or perhaps ever could – help provide us with psychological theories about central thought-processes.

Thus Marr (1982) argued that scientific theorizing in psychology presupposes the identification of some abstractly definable information-processing task underlying the domain in question. As regards the majority of what have traditionally been regarded as 'psychological domains', these tasks have not yet been identified – and perhaps never can be. Moreover, they would not necessarily map neatly on to what we (mistakenly) take to be 'natural kinds' in psychology. Marr dismissed even Newell and Simon's (Newell and Simon, 1972) work as psychologically irrelevant, doubting whether 'problem-solving' or even 'mental arithmetic' are genuine psychological categories. (According to him, their careful 'task-analysis' does not qualify because – unlike mental arithmetic – the theoretically crucial information-processing tasks are almost certainly unconscious.) He would have given still shorter shrift to studies of 'attitudes', 'learning', 'belief', or 'personality'. For Marr, no psychological study that is not based on prior abstract task-analysis can be more than mere anecdotal reportage or idle speculation.

Similarly, Fodor rejects much AI work on language and problem-solving as psychologically trivial. He goes so far as to deny that any scientific theories of central cognitive phenomena are in principle possible. His main reason is that the mind's contents are so diverse, and its inferencing-associative powers so flexible, that its generative capacity is virtually unconstrained. If 'anything goes', then scientific prediction is impossible, and cognitive psychology is impossible too.

Both Marr's view and Fodor's are overly pessimistic, and too narrow in their conception of the aims of 'science'.

Marr is right to point out that we are on strong ground if we can define an underlying task (and associated computational constraints) in terms abstracted from procedural details, for we can then hope to justify hypothetical procedures by proving them competent to perform these tasks. But his three-level account of psychological explanation is rational reconstruction of scientific method, not a description of how science is – or even should be – done. Work in scene-analysis, for instance, showed the need for rigorous knowledge of 2-D to 3-D mapping, and eventually led (via Mackworth, 1973) to the theory of 'gradient-space' which Marr himself used in his own theory of vision. To reject it as 'unscientific' because (at least in the early phases) it was not based on firm understanding of these matters is to mistake the ideal for the actuality. It is true, also, that many domains which psychologists take to be 'natural kinds' may not be so. The AI approach has already shown the inappropriateness, for example, of dividing 'perception' from 'problem-solving' and 'memory'. Marr's question – What is or are the basic computational tasks underlying everyday psychological phenomena? – is well-taken. But he was perhaps over-quick to dismiss the possibility of finding any answers.

Likewise, we *need* not accept Fodor's persuasive definition of 'scientific psychology'. *Pace* Fodor, science does not seek only to predict, only to show how *this event and no other* was possible. Science aims also to explain (*post hoc*) how something is possible, by showing that it – and many other events which might have occurred, but did not – lies in a class of phenomena which can be generated in such-and-such sorts of ways. With respect to thought-processes, AI offers a number of suggestions as to how certain sorts of inference might take place. Admittedly, many of these are unsurprising, since they lie close to commonsense and/or previous psychological theories – for example, frames, schemata, scripts, TAUs (thematic apperception units) and *semantic nets* in general. But we can reasonably expect to arrive at a deeper understanding of 'high-level processes' if we undertake not only to program them, but also to try to identify common computational principles underlying our programs (as Bundy and Silver, (1982) have done for learning).

Whether the familiar ways of approaching computer modelling are the best, is another question. The 'dogma' of traditional AI – that hardware, and specifically the brain, can be ignored – is under attack. Current work on 'connectionism' has suggested some intriguing possibilities for computation in various sorts of (brainlike) parallel-processing systems. Hinton (Hinton, 1981; Hinton and Sejnowski, 1983a), for instance, has produced some surprising theoretical results about the computational powers of connectionist models. Practical exploration awaits the requisite hardware.

It may very likely turn out that only 'non-von' machines can provide adequate models of psychological processes. Some critics of AI take this to mean that AI has failed. They point out that traditional AI relied on serial general-purpose von Neuman machines, assuming that such machines could model human thinking in practice as well as in theory. And/or they point out that 'computation' was traditionally defined in terms of syntactic operations on symbolic structures (and is still so defined by many people), from which they conclude that recent advances in AI suggest that many mental processes are not computational after all.

Such distinctions are important (Boden, 1984), but they do not give us reason to accuse AI of failure. To define 'AI', or 'computational psychology', in a way which freezes them in a particular historical period would be as unreasonable as to define 'physics' by strict reference to Galileo or Newton. Like other sciences, AI must be allowed to change – and computational psychology will change too. As a latter-day Mark Twain might put it: 'The reports of AI's death are premature'.

What's in an AI program?
A concept-learning cognitive language understander by any other name will behave the same

Derek Partridge

Artificial Intelligence is a methodological mess: a surfeit of programs and a dearth of justified theories and principles. Typically we have a large and complex program that exhibits some interesting behaviours. The underlying principles are anybody's guess.

In addition, if principles are presented, the gulf between program and principle is sufficient to preclude any systematic discussion of the program-principle relationship. We must do more than just present a principle.

A methodology for abstracting and justifying the principles that underlie an AI program is explained and demonstrated. The viewpoint taken is that we cannot prove that a program embodies a given principle; we can only make a claim to this effect with an explicit supporting argument, and thereby provide a concrete basis for discussion of the credibility of the putative principle.

Introduction

AI is largely a behavioural science: a science that is founded upon the behaviour of programs. The working program embodies the theory or set of principles.

Computer programs are very persuasive arguments for the theory that they model. They are also largely incomprehensible to anyone but (or including?) their author. Hence whilst the credibility of the theory is founded on the program the theory, presented perhaps in terms of principles, is necessarily couched in the vagaries and generalizations of the English language; the relationship between the working program and the comprehensible principles can only be founded on faith. We need something better than this.

Any long-term AI watcher can only applaud the recent Bundy-Ohlsson (Bundy and Ohlsson, 1988) debate that finally settled on the three types (or stages) of AI research:

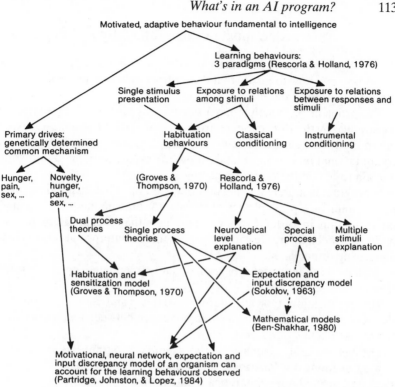

Figure 1   A summary of the theoretical framework for the program that explores basic learning behaviours

1 The AI program development cycle in which the primary result is an AI program with at least some interesting behaviours.
2 The abstraction of program-independent principles that underlie the input-output (I-O) adequate program developed in (1).
3 Investigation of the scope and limitations of the principles (or techniques) abstracted in (2).

The vast majority of AI work is of type 1 whilst types 2 and 3 are more fundamental to scientific progress in this domain.

Earlier examples of the call for abstracting or extracting underlying principles from AI programs can be found in Wielinga (1978) and Pylyshyn (1978).

I will first indicate what I believe to be a basic problem of type 2 research and then describe and illustrate a methodology for supporting type 2 research.

Abstraction must be constrained by justifications

Anyone can abstract any principle from any program, almost. The problem is how to justify that the abstraction is in some sense valid, and is not just wishful thinking.

The problem of exactly what principles to abstract is to some extent constrained by the I-O adequate program in that the program's behaviour is interpreted by means of a semantic mapping. That is to say, the formal computational objects input and output are typically mapped into another domain to obtain the desired meaning.

A program is merely a collection of coded machine instructions, it does not contain any principles in isolation. A human theorizer applies an interpretation in order to make the claim that the program has some interesting behaviour. He can then apply further interpretations to abstract underlying principles.

Each of these interpretations, or semantic mappings, must be justified, they cannot be proven.

The justification typically derives from a combination of the larger theoretical context and from a correspondence between empirical data and the model's behaviour.

The behavioural adequacy of the example program has been demonstrated in Johnston, Partridge, and Lopez (1983) and figure 1 provides a summary of the larger theoretical context of the program. There are two points to note. First, justifications cannot be expected to be complete or proven. They are the bones of an argument and by being explicitly given they provide a firm basis for discussion of their validity of the principles abstracted. Second, the use of suggestive names in a program clearly facilitates perception of the correspondences between the code and abstractions derived from it. But the use of overly suggestive names is a pernicious AI trend that D. McDermott (1981) drew attention to some years ago. Again, empirical data and theoretical context are an explicit attempt to justify the suggestive naming of objects both within the program and within the principles abstracted. This attempt to explicitly justify important re lations (between formal objects in the model and concepts within the domain of the principles abstracted) should help to achieve a balance between helpful and meaningful names, and overly suggestive, misleading names.

Bridging the gulf with stepwise abstraction

A program is just a pile of code and AI programs have an unfortunate tendency to be large piles. The underlying principles are usually dispersed and well hidden by the idiosyncrasies of both the programming language and its particular implementation.

The inevitable result is that a yawning chasm separates the behaviourally interesting program from any succinct and comprehensible principle that is abstracted from it. The presence of this chasm has two unfortunate consequences:

1 The AI researcher, after many iterations through the run-debug-edit cycle, loses track of his original principles and must reassure himself of exactly what principles underlie the behaviour of his program. After a series of modifications, does the program still embody the original principles or have the principles also been modified?
2 The interested observer of this program has no basis upon which to question the validity of an abstracted principle nor any means of examining the relationships between the principle and the program.

In short, the AI researcher does not know if his programmed model's support for his principles is based on anything more reliable than wishful thinking, and the interested observer must accept (or reject) the proffered principles largely on faith.

Thus the gulf between a succinct and comprehensible principle and the program from which it purportedly derives is bridged by a sequence of intermediate abstractions – a chain of stepping stones that will support the weight of reasoned argument.

The sequence of abstractions is derived stepwise starting with the behaviourally adequate program. It is true that the programmer has a good idea of what principles he expects to abstract, but the actual principles abstracted are the outcome of a step-by-step process, each step constrained by explicit justifications and the previous abstraction; the result is an informal 'proof' sequence to support the credibility of the final principles.

An example of stepwise abstraction

As an example of the above arguments, a basic learning principle was abstracted from the above referenced program (i.e. the program in Johnston, Partridge and Lopez, 1983); a program which exhibited a wide range of basic learning behaviours.

The principle abstracted is:

Humans are genetically predisposed to learn only significant events.

A question that might then arise is: what is meant by the term 'significant'? By recourse to lower levels the question can be answered. Within the next more detailed level of abstraction it will be found that 'significant' was derived from:

. . . primary drive reducing.

This might give rise to two questions: what are the primary drives and how are they reduced? Within the next level down we find some of the answers.

> . . . f(food when hungry, pain when sensitive, novel events when bored . . .)

The above abstraction shows that the model employed three primary drives and that the significance of an event is claimed to be some function of all three individual drives. But novelty drive was the primary drive under investigation, so for the results presented, the term 'significant' in the highest level abstraction of the theory was, in effect, derived from:

> . . . novel events when bored . . .

A number of questions might arise from this statement. How is the novelty of an event measured? How is 'bored' computed? What, if any, is the relationship between novel events and boredom?

Reference to the next level of detail will reveal that the novelty of an event is the discrepancy between the input stimulus pattern received by the animal and the pattern that it expected.

> novelty is f(input-expectation discrepancy)

There are many ways to compute such a discrepancy, the next level of detail shows that the function used was computed with measures of both the qualitative and quantitative differences between the two patterns.

> novelty is f(quantitative difference, qualitative difference)

Clearly this statement could be traced down through further levels of detail to determine how each of these differences was computed and exactly what function was used to combine them. Instead we will return to examine more detail for the broader questions of novelty, boredom and their interrelationship.

The abstraction given above, namely

> novel events when bored

was derived from:

> boredom is increased by expected stimuli and decreased by novel stimuli, and significance is the lesser of, novelty or boredom level

which was abstracted from:

> boredom level increased by f(1/novelty);
> **IF** novelty of input stimulus < boredom level
>   THEN significance is f(novelty) and boredom level is reduced
>   by f(novelty)

ELSE significance is f(boredom level) and boredom level is
a minimum;

This last abstraction gives more detail to the computation of significance as a function of the novelty value of an event and the boredom
level of the animal.

The final level of detail is the Pascal program code itself, and it is as
follows:

```
boredomlevel : = boredomlevel + stimulusexpectedness;
IF novelty < boredom level
     THEN
          BEGIN
               significance : = novelty;
               boredomlevel : = boredomlevel - novelty
          END
     ELSE
          BEGIN
               significance : = boredomlevel;
               boredomlevel : = 0
          END
```

So the above section of program code is the implementation of the
concept 'significant' within the principle abstracted.

We have a complete sequence of successively more specific principles
down to the abstraction at which the theorizer feels that further details
cannot be adequately justified.

Stepwise abstraction of principles is clearly akin to the well-known
program design technique of stepwise refinement; but it is not just
program documentation: stepwise refinement in reverse. The goals are
different and the objects abstracted are different (this issue is dealt with
at length in Partridge, 1986).

Summary

In conclusion I'll list a few disclaimers before summarizing the
significance of the proposed methodology. No claim is made that all
principles can or should be abstracted from programs. No claim is made
that a program as such embodies any particular principles. There is no
claim that the process of abstracting underlying principles is either quick,
easy or straightforward.

The basic claim is that the purported significance of an AI program is
typically not open to any systematic criticism or discussion. Couple this
with the fact that programmed implementations are the major research

medium in AI and we have the fundamental problem with the methodology of AI research.

An existence proof of the practical viability of stepwise abstraction for communicating principles from a large AI program can be found in Partridge, Johnston, and Lopez (1984).

4   Programs and theories

A continuing AI debate is the relationship of programs to theories. Some clarification of this issue would do much to put AI on firmer foundations.

Wilks attempts to clarify some basic issues concerning the relationships between theories and models by laying out a taxonomy for these two variously-used terms. Using the example of AI programs for language processing, he argues that such programs are not so much theories in the more classical senses, but can usefully be considered to be theories of computational processes.

We have reprinted the Bundy and Ohlsson debate from the AISB Quarterly (1984). In this interchange of ideas as to what one has a right to expect from AI research, and, in particular, what the relationship between programs and theories ought ideally to be, we see apparently very different opinions move surprisingly close together once certain terms (such as 'principle') have been clarified. Nevertheless, Bundy remains committed to the significance of mechanisms or techniques as the essential principles in an AI program; and Ohlsson stands by his demand for validating behavioral principles as the important product of AI programming. These two viewpoints correspond to the representations at the two ends of the sequence of abstractions discussed by Partridge in the previous chapter. And, interestingly, Bundy's analysis of Ohlsson's principle bogs down at several points just because the meaning of seemingly straightforward terms in the principle are in fact open to several interpretations and there are no more-precise restatements to fall back on (as there would be if the principle existed in the context of a sequence of abstractions).

Finally, in this section, Simon discusses the program-theory issue. He argues that there are three phases of theory construction: pre-program, program, and post-program stages. He concludes that "Programs are not theories, but programs constitute aspects of theories. Theories are not programs, but computer simulation aids in analysis of theories."

One small head: models and theories

Yorick Wilks

I

And still they gazed, and still the wonder grew, That one small head could carry all he knew.

Goldsmith's rustics were quite right about the village schoolmaster, of course, well in advance of their time and, apparently, of Goldsmith. But perhaps the time has come for less of such gazing, by AI researchers in particular, and more attention to their proper business. I am sure, for reasons I shall try to make clear, that the present situation, where much new work in AI is immediately proposed as new 'model of the human brain or behaviour', is an undesirable one.

This is a philosophical discussion about AI rather than a practical one; and intended to remind some AI researchers of standard uses of the words 'model' and 'theory' that they may have forgotten, and to explore some of the terminological consequences of a less liberal approach to these words than is the current fashion within AI.

Since it is a philosophical discussion, it is not intended to criticize any form of *activity*, or to suggest that it should not be carried out. It is concerned with how such work should be described, in the sense of what its ultimate subject matter is, and that such descriptions should be both revealing and consistent, and above all not misleading. I take it for granted in what follows that such questions are not "mere matters of words" or convention, and that it is no defence at any point to say that one can use the words 'theory' and 'model' to mean whatever one chooses. The use of these two key terms is particularly important to AI in its present early stage of scientific development. At the end of the paper, I shall depart in one particular from this neutrality, in order to advocate a different type of theory, one suggested by the usage of 'theory' I advocate in the body of the paper.

121

II

It is not hard to see, in a sympathetic way, how AI got into a situation that I claim is an over-use of 'model'. I will illustrate my point from natural-language processing, the area of AI I know best, but it could be made with respect to virtually any claims about computing and mental functions. The chief cause, I would argue, is the inadequacy of what might be called the standard descriptions of AI activity, such as "providing structural descriptions of sentences" or, for the more linguistically motivated, "describing sentences in such a way as to predict correctly native speakers' judgements of grammaticality, meaningfulness and so forth".

It is not at all easy to be clear about the *status* of such conclusions as 'x1 is a correct structural description for sentence X, but x2 is not', since deciding the truth of such a conclusion is not at all like deciding whether a sentence X in one natural language is or is not a proper translation of a sentence Y in another. The latter is a question about which large numbers of untrained people would willingly decide because its statement is objective, in the sense that it does not use or mention any of the internal formalisms or terms of the craft. Nor has it been merely lack of the appropriate training that has impeded the understanding of non-AI researchers, for the experts themselves seemed to have no way of deciding the truth of conclusions like the first in a manner consistent with the normal standards of rational argument.

I have not dismissed the above explanations of AI activity, but am merely pointing out that their disputability may explain the overuse of 'model', in that the presentation of research work as being ultimately no less than a 'brain model' may have come to seem a natural, and worthier, description of the aims of modern AI. I shall argue here, though against a background of standard uses of the term, that much of the present widespread use of 'model' in AI is unfortunate because an element essential to the proper use of the term is lacking in the present state of our knowledge of the brain, and to continue to use the term, that being so, can lead to a certain resignation about our almost total ignorance of how the brain actually works.

III

Several years ago, Chao (1962) surveyed the contemporary usage of 'model', and Suppes (1960) carried out a more rigorous and wide-ranging study. Chao adopted a Websterian, or 'hundred flowers', approach to the diverse uses of the word in the research of that time. He would, I think, have accepted an opening remark in a paper by Mey (1970) that I shall return to for illustrative purposes:

> An important notion in the behavioral sciences is that of a model as a set of hypotheses and empirical assumptions leading to certain testable conclusions called predictions (on this cf. Braithwaite) . . .

Now, of course, that is precisely the kind of entity that Braithwaite wrote should be called not a model but a theory, though he did admit (Suppes, 1960) that confusion need not *necessarily* result if 'model' is used in this way. Braithwaite claims that there will only be confusion if 'model' is used at one and the same time to cover both the standard sense of 'theory' (as Mey does above), and the standard sense of 'model'. I shall argue that this confused situation does obtain in modern AI. But first, what is the standard sense of 'model'? Briefly stated, Braithwaite's view is that a model is an alternative, second, interpretation of the calculus expressing a theory (Braithwaite, 1962, p. 225). That is to say, a theory and a model for it are both theories, and have the same deductive structure, in some defined sense of that phrase.

To take Braithwaite's own example, and one closer to our concerns here, of a computer modelling a theory of the brain; this, he says could be proposed in two senses. Firstly, there is a weak one, in which the computer is used as a 'black box', considered only as a system of inputs and outputs. "Here", he writes,

> if the deductive apparatus of the theory is already incorporated in the working of the machine, the machine will in fact be operating the calculus representing the theory ... So the working of the machine should be regarded as equivalent more properly to the calculus itself than to an interpretation of the calculus as a theory. (*Suppes, 1960, p. 226*)

This mode of explanation, then is not really modelling, for in the second sense, the strong one,

> the switching operations of the computer are taken as corresponding to the 'firings' of synapses in the brain. Strictly speaking the computer as a piece of hardware will be a model of a brain in the vulgar sense of, e.g., a clockwork model locomotive: what in my sense is a model for a theory of cerebral functioning will be the theory of the internal functioning of the computer, which will include propositions relating what happens in it at one time to what happens at a later time, corresponding to hypotheses about the temporal relationships of events in the brain. (*Suppes, 1960, p. 226*)

Admittedly Braithwaite's is the most conservative view of how 'model' should be used, and I am not *advocating* it here. He tried to assimilate the use of the word in empirical science to its use in mathematics, where it is normally used to mean a *second interpretation* of a calculus yielding an understood branch of the subject. The fact that a model, in this sense, exists shows that the first interpretation of the calculus (which is the theory in question, the one being 'modelled') is a consistent interpretation. So, in Tarski's words, "a possible realization in which all valid sentences of a theory are satisfied is called a model of the theory" (Tarski, 1965). Let us call Tarski's view MATH. It is this (MATH) sense of 'model' that is familiar in formal AI proper and, in my view, it is the coexistence of the two senses of 'model' within AI: MATH, and Mey's use of the word to mean just 'theory', that does constitute exactly the confusion that Braithwaite diagnosed as harmful. Braithwaite's view (BRAITH) has been widely discussed, and criticized on the ground that it puts too much emphasis on the calculus, and on the theory as an interpretation of the calculus, in a way that is untrue to the actual psychological processes of scientists. Opponents of that view argue (Hesse (1965), Achinstein (1965)) that the interpreted, concrete, model comes first, and that working scientists import features *metaphorically* or *analogically*, from their chosen model 'backwards' into the theory under construction. This view I shall call SIMPLESCI. It may subsequently turn out, as Braithwaite argues, that model and theory can be shown to be interpretations of a single calculus, but that is all formal tidying up, such opponents would say, after the real work is over.

However, this difference, between the views that I have called BRAITH and SIMPLESCI respectively, is more a difference of emphasis than might appear. Braithwaite, for example, has discussed how, within his view of matters, one can talk of a (SIMPLESCI) 'modelist' moving from model to theory by 'disinterpreting' his model's calculus in order to reinterpret it in the terms of the theory proper. Braithwaite contrasts that with his own 'contextualist' view that the theory is an interpretation of an originally uninterpreted calculus, with the model entering the picture only afterwards.

For my purpose here it is important to emphasize Braithwaite's point that both the BRAITH and SIMPLESCI views of models see the *theoretical terms* of the theory as gaining their interpretations from the bottommost, empirical, level of the theory upwards. Braithwaite refers to this important process as a 'semantic ascent'.

IV

Mey is, of course, correct when he says (Mey, 1970) that, in the behavioural sciences' 'model' is used in a sense different from these three, MATH, BRAITH and SIMPLESCI. The interesting question is why is it used differently and is there any need to do so, unless by so doing something previously unclear is made clear. Let us call the view quoted at the beginning MEY: namely, that of a model as a set of hypotheses, etc., leading to testable conclusions called predictions. That is to say that a model (MEY) is what is conventionally called a theory on what I take here to be the standard view (see further Carnap, 1936).

Let us now imagine a MEY model for natural-language processing by computer. It doesn't much matter what it is, but presumably it will, at some point, generate word strings, which many will want also to be meaningful strings. And that need not just mean sentence strings, in the typesetter's sense, but could mean utterances of any length, including dialogue, that were meaningful and coherent. The distinction between 'grammatical' and 'meaningful' need not disturb us at this point.

The central point of this part of the paper is concerned with the process of interpretation of theoretical terms that I referred to earlier, by Braithwaite's phrase 'semantic ascent': the terms of a theory are given meaning by reference to lower levels of the theory, that is to say, the empirical base. At the highest levels of a scientific theory there may be entities with no *direct* interpretation in terms of the observational base. These, like 'neutrinos' in quantum physics, are sometimes referred to as *occult entities*, and philosophers go about asking of them 'do neutrinos really exist?' Nonetheless such entities usually have a firm place in a theory provided they occur only at the topmost levels: in other words, provided that the process of interpretation can get some reasonable way up from the observational base.

But in the case of a theory, proffered as a MEY model of the brain, the situation is quite different. At the bottom level, as it were, we can observe what people actually say and write; or, if one prefers, what they ought to say and write, it doesn't matter which for the moment. But, in the present state of neurophysiological investigations, the matter ends there. There is no possibility of interpreting further, of identifying any item of structure in the brain corresponding to any item of structure, at any 'level' of the theory. And that situation is quite different from that of the empirical 'unreachability' of neutrinos, for the brain items or structures are not so much unreachable as unreached. Nor is this 'unreachedness' in any way the result of a 'black box' situation, where constraints must be put on the form of a theory because the experimental situation is such that the box's contents cannot be inspected without being themselves physically altered by the inspection.

It is these points, I think, that Chomsky missed when he compared (Chomsky, 1957) the role of unreachable occult entities such as grammars innate in the mind, with the positive role or occult entities like gravitation in Newton's theory. Gravitation features as a topmost item of a theory that admits a paradigmatic semantic ascent from an observational base. But in the case of the brain there is as yet no agreement at all on how the brain stores and processes information of the type under discussion, and so there can be no question of a semantic ascent up an AI theory of the brain, and so no *model* of the brain until that is known.

It should be clear here that what are unavailable in the case of the brain are items to function in a theory to be interpreted. We cannot just blithely say that the synapses are the items because they happen to be identifiable objects in the brain.

The situation here is different from even such crude situations in the physical sciences as the Ptolemaic model of the universe. That was a model, potentially at least, because the items of the theory, the gross heavenly bodies, were at least *available*, then as now.

It remains the case, though, that the SIMPLESCI notion is an important one, perhaps closer to most people's intuitions than BRAITH or MATH. Nonetheless, it is only appropriate to sciences like physics, where modelling *is possible*, in a full sense. It is, I have argued, a wrong paradigm for other disciplines like AI, where it can be no more than what Putnam called a 'psychological crutch'.

V

Having distinguished the principal senses of 'model', let us now take a look at the distinction among models (MEY) that Mey actually proposes (Mey, 1970). The (BRAITH) theory, or (MEY) model, Mey proposes to call a *descriptive model* (MEYD). He cautions us that

> it need not be (and should not be) considered a faithful reproduction of reality, in the sense that to each part of the model there corresponds, by some kind of isomorphic mapping a particular chunk of 'real life'. In other words, this descriptive kind of model does not attempt to imitate the behavior of the description.   (*Mey, 1970, p. 2*)

Mey goes on, "The other kind of model I propose to call the simulative one . . . a conscious effort to picture, point by point, the activities that we want to describe" (ibid., pp. 2–3). His elucidation of the distinction, between MEYD and what I shall call MEYS, is wholly in terms of Chomsky's competence-performance distinction, which may seem to some remote from AI concerns, but has in fact been very influential.

If these two entities, the human and the MEYD, give the same result, then as I have argued above, the one does not explain the other *in the sense that a model, or interpreted theory,* explains what it is a model of. Mey writes in the last quoted passage as if there are other similarities, between grammar and human, other than output identity. But what could they be?

Again, the quoted passage makes clear that MEYSs describe by definition, just as do MEYDs. According to the definition given, the distinguishing feature of MEYSs is that they picture 'point by point' the human language activity. But, as I have argued above in connection with the general notions of model and theory, that is just what they cannot conceivably do, at least not at the moment while there is no hint available as to what the 'points' to be pictured are. In the case of human beings, as of machines, output is output, so what distinction could Mey offer between MEYDs and MEYSs since ultimately all they both have to 'model' is human output?

It is not my intention to discuss Chomsky's competence-performance distinction in detail here – it has been done by many besides myself (Wilks, 1972a) and it is peripheral to the main issue here. But two points about the distinction are relevant. Firstly, Chomsky has been more wary than many of his followers about his use of 'theory' and 'model'. He has concentrated on the more liberal 'theory', relegating 'model' to the area of performance where he does not recommend its construction, so he can hardly be accused of the confusions detailed here. One formulation of this familiar point of Chomsky's is: "A generative grammar is not a model for a speaker or a hearer" (Chomsky, 1965, p. 9). An extreme example of his caution about 'model' is his paper (Chomsky, 1962) titled 'Explanatory Models in Linguistics', which does not actually mention the notion of model at all. Secondly, it should be noticed that Chomsky, although generally scrupulous over his use of 'model', has occasional peculiar lapses. The best example I know is where he writes:

> *Obviously*, every speaker of a language has mastered and internal-ized a generative grammar that expresses his knowledge of his lan-guage. This is not to say that he is aware of the rules of grammar or even that he can become aware of them, or that his statements about his intuitive knowledge of his language are necessarily accurate. (*Chomsky, 1965, p. 8, my italics.*)

What is interesting about this quotation, in the context of the arguments of this paper, is that if that fact IS indeed obvious, then of course AI has no need of models at all, but for the very odd reason that the theory (the grammar, or competence theory in Chomsky's terms) and what the theory is a theory of (the brain in this case) *are the same* and can be seen to be so. The grammar is simply there in the head, *and* there in the text books, and that is that.

Now of course Chomsky would reply that he did not mean to be taken in this way. He can see as well as anyone that, if an explicans and explicandum are identical, then nothing at all is explained. But I think the slip, and it is a slip, is interesting and important for the following reason: it exemplifies a tendency to superrationalism in AI, as in linguistics, of *knowing in advance how things must be*; an attitude that contrasts with the resigned attitude to models I described earlier, as well as with the experimental approach to AI that I advocate, and which, I argue below, is best stimulated within computational AI, where theories can be tested in some sense.

VI

I have argued so far that AI cannot, and should not, provide 'models of the brain', or, rather, that what AI researchers actually do is best presented in some other way. I now want to look at, and criticize, some ways of presenting AI as a *theory* of something; after which I shall go on, in a more positive vein, to argue for a particular presentation of theory, one in which the standard uses of 'model' and 'theory' are preserved for, naturally enough, I am not suggesting that AI goes into some state of academic hibernation to await further discoveries in brain physiology.

The first thing to be clear about is that 'theory' is at least as liberal a term as 'model', even though both have central, or standard, senses. Theories do not *have* to predict (think of mathematical theories), so there is no reason why an AI theory cannot be a theory of the brain if one desires to so present it.

Again, there is no reason why an AI theory cannot be a theory of several things at once; just as several theories can at the same time be theories of the same subject. Einstein pointed out that the person moving in an elevator could not know whether his motion was due to acceleration or gravitation. Both theories explain his movement and are, in a sense, precisely equivalent yet, incidentally, have quite different models, if the difference between theory and model still needs pointing up. So, then, an AI theory could at the same time be a theory of the brain, and of behaviour, and of a language.

We come now to our central question: *what is an AI theory best considered a theory of?* We have seen that there can be a number of simultaneous answers to this by no means trivial question; and also that we need not, perhaps, be as restrictive about this concept as about that of model, since the long-term 'theory', though often vague, does not have the vicious ambiguity of 'model', which, as we saw, can be used to cover radically different things: those both more (as in MATH) real *and* less real (SIMPLESCI) than the subject matter of the corresponding theory. All we need for a set of statements to be a theory is that they stand in some reasonable logical relation to each other and to a given subject matter.

It must be noted, though, that we can retain 'theory' without promising predictions, but we cannot then claim to have a *scientific* theory, in any general sense of the last word. It is important to make this point clear, and to do so, I will refer to Chomsky's well-known view that linguistic theory is a theory of language, L, and that such a theory *is* scientific in the normal sense:

> A grammar of the language L is essentially a theory of L. Any scientific theory is based on a finite number of observations, and it seeks to relate the observed phenomena and to predict new phenomena by constructing general laws in terms of hypothetical constructs ... Similarly a grammar of English is based on a finite corpus of utterances (observations), and it will contain certain grammatical rules (laws) stated in terms of the particular phonemes, phrases, etc., of English (hypothetical constructs). These rules express structural relations among the sentences of the corpus and the indefinite number of sentences generated by the grammar beyond the corpus (predictions). (*Chomsky, 1957, p. 49*)

Fairly straightforward considerations tell against this way of looking at transformational grammars. For, in the case of scientific theories cast in standard hypothetico-deductive form, there is a fairly clear notion of what it is to disconfirm a particular theory. There are difficulties about making the notion of disconfirmation (or falsification) precise: nonetheless there is general agreement about both its form and its importance. But Chomsky has formulated the theory of transformational grammar so as to rule out the possibility of disconfirmation. For when describing what it is to be an 'utterance' for the purpose of inclusion in a 'corpus', Chomsky makes it quite clear that he is not going to include what appear to be utterances, but which are sayings containing 'grammatical mistakes' (Chomsky, 1964). And the notion of 'grammatical mistake' is defined with respect to the grammar in question, so that there can never be a rejected grammar.

What have been shown non-predictive here are only what Chomsky called 'competence theories', so the question still arises of what a competence theory is a theory of, given that it cannot, by definition for Chomsky, be brought into contact with human behavior, and is not intended to be a brain model either ("the deeper absurdity of regarding the system of generative rules as a *point-by-point* model for the actual construction of a sentence by a speaker" (Chomsky, 1965, p. 139, my italics)), where I am taking the '*point-by-point*' phrase to mean something that could be no other than a brain model. I shall return to this point below by pressing further Chomsky's quoted remark that "A grammar of the language L is essentially a theory of L." But for the moment let us stay with the question of whether an AI theory can be scientific in the strong sense of making predictions.

I touched earlier on the possibility that an AI theory might be considered a theory (rather than a model) of the brain, given a liberal view of 'being a theory of'. There is no doubt that when a strong (physiological) theory of brain emerges, it will be a predictive theory, but no existing (or likely) AI theory could fill such a role, because it lacks the bottom-level object terms: there are no terms in an AI theory that could conceivably name brain items and so no such predictions could be stated in such a theory. The gap between the techniques of AI and the organic subject matter of physiology is simply too large for this to be a serious possibility.

The remaining possibility for a predictive, and hence scientific, AI theory is as a theory of human behaviour, even though Chomsky has dismissed this as a possible role for a serious linguistic theory, and virtually no central AI researcher has ever made such a claim either (though, unsurprisingly, computationally orientated psychologists often do so). By central AI researcher, I mean attitudes such as those that McCarthy has expressed many times that AI is the exploration of intelligence-as-such, independently of its implementation in humans, animals or machines. This is a sentiment very close to Chomsky's, and hence the concentration on Chomsky and language processing in this paper is not misleading as an account of this point in AI in general.

This remaining possibility I shall call the *psychological approach*. AI in this role would not be a *behavioural theory*, in any sense of that phrase that dismisses putative mechanisms in favour of observed behaviour. Indeed, in the sense of 'theory' used in this paper, 'behavioural theories' are not theories at all. I think that an AI theory cannot be usefully cast in this role, though for a reason unconnected with the difficulties Chomsky raises about 'performance'.

My reason is that, unlike many areas of behaviour, language behaviour cannot be circumscribed in the way that almost all AI researchers seem to assume.

I have set out my argument in considerable detail elsewhere (Wilks, 1971, and Wilks, 1972a). I cannot do justice to the argument itself here by summary, but its substance is that any view of language as a set of sentences requiring production, *in the sense* that a mathematical theory explains, by producing, a set of theorems, must rest upon a false analogy, because natural-language sentences do not constitute a set in the required sense. This is to say that there is not an intuitively acceptable bound to the set of 'meaningful sentences of English', or even of the more dubious 'grammatical sentences' of English, in the same way that there is agreement about, say, the set of theorems provable in group theory or in the propositional calculus.

I shall call this, undemonstrated, argument the circumscription argument, and refer to it again below. At this point it only serves against any form of the psychological approach that requires prediction, since I do not think anyone would entertain a predictive theory of behaviour in the absence of a demarcated set of permissible utterances.

None of this implies for a moment that we should try to eliminate mention of human behaviour from the formulation and discussion of AI theories, for that would be absurd. It means only that such theories cannot be primarily scientific-predictive theories in the way that some AI researchers believe, and we might do well to look elsewhere for the answer to the question as to what an AI theory is a theory of. My claim is that AI cannot be forced into another paradigm of science, such as that of the hypothetic-deductive theory, at the present time. At the end of this paper I shall argue that AI is essentially a form of engineering, albeit theory based, and that recognizing the fact would be a great relief all round, and relieve a continuing source of tension among AI researchers, that of continually trying to prove how scientific the subject is.

VII

There remain, it seems to me, at least three other possible views, of what natural-language theories in AI are theories of, that result from pressing further Chomsky's definition of a *grammar* as a 'theory of a language, L'. The following are possible explanations of the opaque phrase 'theory of a language, L'. An AI theory is a theory of:

1 a set of sentences in the sense that a mathematical theory is *a theory of* a set of theorem sentences;
2 a set of sentences in the *empiricist* scientific sense;
3 a particular class of algorithms, a view I shall argue for and loosely identify with part of the province of computational linguistics.

It might seem that the first of the above formulations of theory, as a set of sentences in the mathematical sense, would be the most suitable explanandum of the notion of an AI theory in natural-language processing as a theory of a language, L. However, if there is any validity at all in what I called the circumscription argument, then this is not so, for a natural language cannot be viewed usefully as a set of sentences in any sense of those words. The reason for this, stated briefly and without the detailed treatment given in Wilks (1971 and 1972a), is that for no sequence of words can we know of it that it cannot be included in the supposed set of meaningful sentences that make up a natural language.

This fact, if it is a fact as I claim, has disastrous consequences for the metamathematical view of natural language as a whole, for it follows that what one might call an understanding system, an operating system of rules that was prepared, in principle, to analyse and interpret any input, could only be represented in metamathematical terms by a self-contradictory system of rules. This is because, in any conventional Tarskian axiomatization, from a self-contradictory set of axioms anything whatever can be deduced (Tarski, 1965), and any set of 'axioms' from which any randomly chosen sentence can be deduced/produced must be itself a self-contradictory system of 'axioms'.

However, given that human beings do operate with their languages in the way described, in that their main effort is to understand and interpret *whatever* superficially unpromising input they receive, rather than to reject it, it seems clear that the proper deduction from the last paragraph is that it is the metamathematical analogy for language that must give way, rather than the facts of language-use. The point at issue here serves to mark a clear distinction between natural languages and artificial languages, such as programming languages LISP, ALGOL, FORTRAN and so on, where it is perfectly proper to speak of a programming language as a model (MATH) of, say, the phrase-structure calculus.

Even if 'sentences' is taken in a wide sense, so as to include whole discourses of any reasonable length, there seem strong and traditional objections to the second of the three suggested explications. For the proposal would be little more than a resurrection of the form of logical empiricism in the philosophy of science most closely associated with Neurath (1959). For Neurath, a scientific theory was no more or less than a production system for the *basic sentences*, or Protokolsaetze, of a science. Beyond that, all theory was wholly dispensable, and there was no place in his views for models of any sort, or 'semantic ascents' up the levels of theory.

There are well-known objections to such a view of theories in general. From the standpoint of the present argument, the view is unacceptable because an AI theory that was merely a theory of a set of sentences with no added qualification, would also, on the Neurathian view of theories, be *trivially* a theory of anything at all producing such a set of sentences. Among these things could be human beings, their brains, machines, sets of rules, this view of theories is essentially, and intentionally, content-free and would not, I think be defended by any participants in disputes about the central questions of this paper. I shall therefore pass on to the last and, for my purposes, the most important, of the three explanations.

I would myself suggest a serious reconsideration of the last of the above views: namely that AI theories are best viewed as the production of sentences by algorithms or programs. There is an implicit restriction included there, naturally enough, to non-trivial methods that would exclude the printing out of any prestored list of sentences. That formulation may sound like no more than an analytic definition of the phrase 'computational natural-language processing', if we exclude concordance-making activities, and indeed, philosophical proposals are usually no more than the announcement of a platitude. But in the present state of the use of 'model' and 'theory' in AI, any single way of speaking of theories would be an advantage if it replaced the current Babel in a generally acceptable manner. Anyone who still doubts that there is such a problem should consult Chao's survey of the usage of 'model' that I referred to earlier. Indeed, one of the oddities of the present situation in AI is that a number of mutually incompatible views (of what an AI theory is a theory of) coexist in some strange way, often within the writings of a single author. Each view is known to be inadequate in itself, as the behaviour view and the metama-thematical view are demonstrably inadequate, yet together they appear to be felt to support, rather than contradict, each other, and there seems little pressure to set out an adequate single view of the matter.

On the proposed view, then, the items of an AI theory could, without too much difficulty, be identified with subparts of the algorithm, in the way that cannot be done for the brain. More importantly, this view could be related in a coherent fashion to current notions of theory and model, and in that sense would have an obvious advantage over the loose talk of 'psychological modelling' that I have described. For example, it would be possible for such a theory of natural-language processing to have a model (BRAITH and MATH), in the sense of an area of logic or mathematics with suitably related properties. These models almost certainly exist for a number of natural-language processing theories – those using phrase-structure algo-rithms, for example.

On the proposed view of theories there is no reason why what people say about their language structure, and what facts psychological experiment can elicit about the associations between speech items, should not lead to suggestive models (SIMPLESCI) for proper theories of natural-language processing. Indeed, those who, like Hesse (1965), adopt an 'interaction' view of the role of (SIMPLESCI) models would say that this possibility was to be expected.

Again, there is no reason why, on this view, AI theories should not be suggestive for brain researchers (see Pribram, 1971), or, more strongly, why they should not indicate limits on possible theories, or models, of the brain. To adapt an old example: if a man goes from London to Edinburgh we cannot know from that alone that he must have gone through Carlisle. Analogously, a theory adequate to describe behaviour does not allow us to draw conclusions about real underlying mechanisms. However, if further constraints can be brought in from outside, such as that he did make the journey overland, then indeed we can know that he must have passed between, say, Newcastle and Glasgow at some point. Hence, we can impose a clear limitation on any subsequently found description, or explanation, of his journey. AI might, at some future stage of development, be able to impose analogous restrictions on possible brain theories.

It may be objected finally that the view proposed is too particular. Given the flourishing state of automata theory proper, and the theory of algorithms, whether viewed as a part of mathematics, logic, or mathematical AI, it might seem as absurd to suggest this view of natural-language processing as to seek to propagate the 'Chemistry of the Apple' as an independent subject. However, there need be no conflict here, and on the view under discussion it would be quite reasonable to conceive of natural-language processing within either formal AI or automata theory as their implemented aspect, one which might be expected *ipso facto* to be less mathematically interesting than the general theory of algorithms or the theory of abstract machines.

A last point of some importance is appropriate here. The proposal above, for viewing an AI theory of natural-language processing at least as a theory of algorithms for the production of particular sets of sentences, is consistent with my original promise that relabelling theory-building activity in this way was a merely philosophical enterprise, one that would not in any way affect the actual work being done, but only its theoretical status.

However, that proposal can now be seen to be inconsistent with my central point about the non-circumscription of well-formed language strings. It will be remembered that my main argument against viewing AI theories as theories of behaviour (on what I called the psychological approach) was that the notion of human language as a closed set of sentences for explication was untrue to actual behaviour, in that human speakers are prepared to interpret/understand virtually any combination of words whatever. So then the question arises as to what would be said, on the view of AI theories proposed here, about an algorithmic system that was, in principle, prepared to interpret/translate/understand, in some adequately defined sense, virtually any sentence whatever, and did not reject 'asterisked anomalies' in a way that any system based on the single derivational algorithm of modern AI must do.

But, as those familiar with the details of AI research will know, much work has been done on the cónstruction of such systems, (under such labels as Preference Semantics, Conceptual Dependency, Flexible Parsing, Metaphor and so on). The arguments of this paper suggest that natural-language processing is a foundation stone, and has no need of a mere niche, in modern AI.

The nature of AI principles: a debate in the AISB Quarterly

Alan Bundy and Stellan Ohlsson

1 Tell me your problems: a psychologist visits AAAI 82
Stellan Ohlsson

Introduction

Following the advice of the philosopher Karl Popper to remember that science is about problems and their solutions I expected each paper on the American Association for AI's 1982 conference (AAAI 82) held in Pittsburgh to contain two main parts: (a) the problem attacked, and (b) its proposed solution. In fact, almost no speaker stated an information-processing problem, and even fewer proposed solutions to one. The problems I want to address here are "What is an information processing problem?" and "If AI speakers do not present solutions to such problems, what do they, in fact, do?" The proposed solutions are presented forthwith.

Information processing problems

What kind of problems does AI research solve? The answer may seem self-evident: "How to program a computer to do X?", where X is medical diagnosis, natural-language understanding, etc. But such questions will soon be of very little interest. In a few decades' time, any school teacher will be able to make a computer do amazing things, without any knowledge of computer science. If you doubt this, then you have not imagined an instructable production system with a sophisticated natural-language interface, running on a descendant of the Cray supercomputer. In fact, the schoolteacher is likely to find it easier to instruct the computer.

Besides, we have good reasons to believe that a program which can do X exists (human performance of X as proof of computability plus Church's conjecture plus universality of our computers). Thus, that someone who has gone off on a search through the space of all possible programs is able

135

to report that he found one that can do X should surprise nobody. Judging from the many bored faces at AAAI 82, it doesn't.

The sophisticated AI person thinks the above criticism old hat. He already knows that a pile of code is not a contribution to a science of information processing; he points to the principles according to which the pile was put together, i.e. he proposes that AI is an attempt to solve the problem "What are the principles of information processing?"

But the claim that AI researchers worry about principles is rather unconvincing when one observes their practice. Most AI contributions do not seem to propose, prove, criticize, refute, extend, generalize, relate or apply any principles. At a recent European conference, I heard the head of an American AI laboratory begin his talk by saying that programs must work according to principles to be interesting, and then continue with the details of an analogy-using program he had written. Full stop.

There are deeper problems here than bad practice, however. Even when people try to elucidate the principles 'behind' their programs, as several speakers at AAAI 82 did, to me the principles look like a schematic description of how the program works. This raises the question of what counts as a principle. If the full description of the program, the pile of code, is not a principle, why is the schematic description of it a principle? At what point along the abstraction variable does mere code turn into a principled result?

Further, if the schematic description of a program is a principle, on what evidence is it based? How does one go about collecting more evidence to back up a principle that one believes in? What counts as a counter-evidence? When is a principle refuted?

Even more puzzling, what are such principles about? If they are to be more interesting than the code, they must refer to something besides the program they are abstracted from. What?

Also, even if the overall goal of AI could be conceived of as finding the principles of information processing, we would still have to ask what the specific research problems are that people work on and for which the proposed principles are offered as solutions. For instance, if "unified data-directed and goal-directed control" is a principle, what particular intellectual puzzlement is dispelled by it?

Finally, there is something peculiar about regarding the principles according to which programs are constructed as the *outputs* of an AI research project. They are *inputs*, aren't they?

To resolve the puzzlement caused by these reflections, I want to suggest that an *Information processing problem* can be stated through the following three steps:

(a) Defining a type of mechanism to be explored. Searching the space of all mechanisms is useless. The first trick in setting up a fruitful problem is to delimit a subspace. This must be done by stating constraints on the mechanism. The power of the research problem will depend on whether those constraints affect the performance of the mechanism in interesting ways. Rather than always shooting for the most intelligent program one is able to invent, the present suggestion implies that one should begin by putting limits on it.

Once the subspace is defined, one should find the dimensions which can be used to characterize the individual mechanisms in it. (If there aren't any, you defined the wrong subspace.)

(b) Defining a *task type* by stating the abstract properties of the kind of task to which the mechanism is going to be applied. The goal should be that for any concrete problem, it should be decidable whether it belongs to the task type or not. I found it very frustrating to listen to lecture after lecture, being unable to decide whether the research presented was relevant to my own work or not. Clearly, every program reacts to some properties only of the tasks presented to it. Nevertheless, speakers generally refer to tasks either through conventional names (e.g. "medical diagnosis") or through concrete examples ("This slide shows a cute thing I gave to my program..."). What one needs is an abstract description which shows those features or aspects of a problem which the program is capable of reacting to.

(c) Defining a performance description by listing those aspects of the behaviour of the mechanism which are going to be investigated. Today, the performance of programs is most often described in terms of what it can and cannot do. Among psychologists, this concept is known as '% correct'. It is the most primitive performance description there is. In cognitive psychology, it is now almost universally discarded in favour of richer descriptions like solution time curves, Guttman Scales, eye-movement patterns, problem behaviour graphs, etc. Research in AI would do well to move in the same direction.

Given (a), (b) and (c), an information-processing problem can be stated in the general form "How do the properties of a mechanism of the described type relate to the properties of its performance, when applied to a task of the relevant type?" The problem is answered by exploring variants of the mechanism, investigating how the properties of the mechanism affect the performance. The goal is to understand on what the properties of the performance depends. For instance, if a learning system exhibits gradual learning, will any mechanism of the same type show gradual learning, or can the system be made to exhibit all-or-none learning through trivial changes? The emphasis is on the relation between properties of the mechanism and properties of its performance (with respect to some task).

If information-processing problems are conceived in this way, we can see that their solutions are not just descriptions of how programs work. What counts as a principle is a law-like statement relating mechanisms to their behaviours. A principle is about a type of mechanism, i.e. it should be true of all programs implementing that mechanism. Evidence for such a principle can be collected either by mathematical investigations or by constructing actual systems. Counter-evidence is given by a system of the relevant type with a different behaviour than that specified by the principle. Particular research problems are generated by delimiting different mechanisms (different subspaces) and different task types for exploration. Finally, descriptions of how programs work, are assigned their intuitively correct role as one of the 'inputs' or 'givens' of a research project.

Looking around for famous projects which one could recruit as plausible examples of the approach advocated here, one finds the work on the General Problem Solver (GPS) and the Perceptron project, and the nice contrast between them. In both cases, a type of mechanism was extensively explored. In the case of GPS (Ernst and Newell, 1967; Ernst and Newell, 1969; Newell and Simon, 1972; Newell, 1969), implemented versions of its various variants played a major role, while mathematics of a more traditional type was used extensively in the case of Perceptrons (Minsky and Papert, 1969; Newell, 1977).

The fields of search theory and the theory of computational complexity deserve special mention here. Both of them relate mechanisms to their behaviours, and both employ richer performance descriptions than merely '% correct'. The fact that these two fields have come further towards developing a body of theory than other areas might very well depend on the fact that they are asking the right kind of questions.

Pat Langley's BACON project can serve as an example as well (Langley, 1980). With some simplification, the BACON project asks how a purely data-driven, domain-independent induction system (type of mechanism) can find equations to account for relatively noise-free numerical data (task type). Different variants of the program are constructed, and their performance investigated. My criticism would be that this project does not yet employ very interesting performance descriptions. BACON's performance is almost solely reported in terms of its successes and f. . . well successes, anyway.

As a final example, I mention a modest project of my own with the admittedly immodest name "Universal Puzzle Learner" (UPL). The task type is heuristics learning. The system starts with a problem space, but without any heuristics for how to search it other than some general weak search method; it is to construct heuristics which allows it to solve problems in that (kind of) problem space without any search. The mechanism is constrained by having incomplete search-control (it can only back up to the initial state, not to any state in between), limited memory (it can only 'see' one state at a time), and by being able to form context-free heuristics only (the condition of the heuristics can only refer to the current state and to the goal-tree). An initial version of such a system is up and running, and it does learn in a few simple domains (Ohlsson, 1982a; Ohlsson, 1982b). But what I hope to be able to report eventually is not that I have a program that can learn whatever, but what the effects of such constraints are on the shape of learning curves, and on the ability to transfer learning results to new problems.

What AI speakers do

If AI researchers do not, in fact, state and solve information-processing problems, what do they do when they give a talk? I offer three observations.

AI speakers talk about the *activities* they are engaged in, rather than about concepts. ("My pals and I have been hacking away at the WIZARD system these past few years . . .") They tell about the origins of the project, and about how it meanders along.

AI speakers expound on their *hopes* for their projects, both in terms of what they would like their system to be able to achieve ultimately, and also in terms of what other systems cannot do. ("Systems A and B could not do X, therefore we want our WIZARD system to do just that.")

AI speakers talk about the *difficulties* they have encountered. ("The *n* th version of WIZARD could not do X, so now we have . . . ")

The last point is particularly important. I believe that most AI researchers experience their task as one of overcoming the difficulties encountered in constructing whatever system they happen to be working on. But difficulties are not problems. A problem is a question about how a mechanism of a certain type performs on some task. A difficulty is an obstacle to the construction of a mechanism of the specified type. The two should not be confused.

Obviously, a technology of system implementation, as a prescription for how to generate a system with particular properties, is not unimportant (witness the importance of laboratory technology, e.g. CERN, for physics). But such a technology should not be confused with a science of information processing.

2 The nature of AI: a reply to Ohlsson
Alan Bundy

AI is certainly a methodological mess, and as we have seen above Stellan Ohlsson makes a valiant attempt to clean it up. Unfortunately, the attempt fails, because Ohlsson has a fundamental misconception of the nature of AI. AI is not an empirical science like psychology or physics, i.e. it is not a study of everyday natural phenomenon. It requires a methodology of its own and cannot be tidied up by the imposition of the methodology of psychology.

The best analogy I have found for AI, among the existing disciplines, is applied mathematics, with psychology playing the role of physics and computer science the role of pure mathematics. The remit of applied maths is to investigate mathematical techniques with potential for modelling physical phenomena. The remit of AI is to investigate computational techniques with potential for exhibiting intelligent behaviour. Investigating techniques means discovering new ones and exploring their properties and interrelations. It is a moot point whether one regards applied maths, pure maths, computer science or AI as sciences, but these questions need not detain us.

One possible reason for confusion about the nature of AI is its close association with computational psychology, which is an empirical science. It is often difficult to separate the practitioners or the researches of each. Similar confusions arise between applied maths and theoretical physics.

The analogy should not be pressed too far. For instance, no one claims that planets make arithmetic calculations before deciding on what gravitational attraction to exert, but computational psychologists do claim that human mental processes can be regarded as computational "calculations". So AI techniques do not have the same relation to psychological processes as mathematical techniques have to physical ones. However, the analogy is useful as a guide to explicating AI methodology and to evaluating Ohlsson's proposals.

Ohlsson asks "what counts as a principle", and seems reluctant to accept that a mere "schematic description" might count. Presumably he is expecting some physics-like laws; AI will not produce such laws. It will produce *techniques*, and these are its principles. For communication and to aid extendability, these are best presented in a code-free, schematic way, but there is not magic point at which "piles of code" suddenly turn into "principles". AI techniques are not generalizations of experimental data. (What is the experimental data for differential calculus?) Nor are they, a priori, "about" anything, but they can be used to model various things.

There is nothing peculiar about regarding AI techniques as the *output* of research. AI researchers have discovered that one fruitful method for exploring the potential of computational techniques, extending such techniques, and discovering new ones, is to build computer programs to do particular tasks. They start building the program in various stages of vagueness about the details of the techniques to be explored. The run/debug/edit cycle they are then involved in is an exploratory process which exposes the limitations of their ideas and offers a framework for having new ideas. The difficulties they encounter in making the program work are the stimuli for these new ideas, and both difficulties and solutions are rightly given prominence in their presentations. AI researchers rightly aim their programs at examples that cannot be done by existing techniques, because this is a good method of producing new techniques.

Ohlsson's implication that fully formed techniques are the *input* to AI program building, reduces this central AI creative activity to routine drudgery, and displays a gross misunderstanding of AI methodology. His suggestion that program building could be made more interesting by artificially constraining the potential techniques is inimical to this creative activity. His request for a decision procedure to delimit the applicability of a technique is preposterous. The discovery of unexpected applications of an existing technique is a major part of the creative process in AI, as it is in applied maths.

The essence of a computational technique may be communicated by a schematic description and worked examples, but its power and limitations are harder to convey. The usual method is to quote problems which the program can and cannot solve, and to explain why with worked examples. The crucial questions concern the ability of the mechanism to cope with noise, ambiguity and unexpected situations and to avoid irrelevant steps, and the reasons for its ultimate breakdown. Recitation of examples solved, may sound like "% correct" to Ohlsson, but to the practitioner with experience of the special problems of these examples, more is conveyed. Some examples are shared, state of the art, "tough nuts". Ohlsson's suggestion that AI should adopt the cognitive psychology "richer descriptions" of "solution time curves, frequence distributions of error type, accuracy-speed tradeoffs", etc. will not help. These are all descriptions of *behaviour*. They do nothing to reveal the underlying mechanism, and it is this that the AI researcher wants to convey.

The implication of Ohlsson's opening paragraphs is that if this is all there is to AI then it is pretty trivial and boring stuff; we already know that a computer program can be built to do anything a human can do and in a few decades any school teacher will be able to do better. I can only assume that Ohlsson has not done much AI programming himself, or he would know that it is neither trivial or boring. If school teachers are building intelligent programs in a few decades then this will be because of breakthroughs in AI, not despite them.

3 Mathematics, behaviour and creativity: reply to Bundy
Stellan Ohlsson

Listening to the speakers of the AAAI 82 conference, I found it difficult to identify the problems being worked on, as well as to see what solutions were proposed. In "Tell me your problems: a psychologist visits AAAI 82", I offered an opinion about the concept of a "problem" in information-processing research. In brief, my comments called for more precise problem formulations, and for efforts to encode results in the form of law-like principles. Alan Bundy disagrees completely with my views. What follows are some reflections prompted by his criticisms.

Bundy makes an analogy between (applied) mathematics and physics, on the one hand, and AI and psychology on the other. This is precisely the analogy I have been using for years to explain to psychologists in my country why AI is relevant to them.

But Bundy states, as an objection to my views, that AI will not discover law-like principles; instead, it will find computational techniques. The first thing to notice about mathematics, pure or applied, is that it is a body of theories consisting of principles. The principles refer to certain mathematical objects, and they are interesting because they are true of those objects. To picture mathematics as a collection of computational techniques would meet with resistance from mathematicians, pure and applied. Computational techniques are based on, or derived from, theories and principles, rather than serving in their stead.

We have two historical examples of where concern with computational techniques might lead: in ancient Babylon, it did not lead to the theory of arithmetic; in ancient Egypt, it did not lead to the theory of geometry.

Analogies do not prove anything. All Bundy has to do to rebut the above comments is to say that he does not want to push the analogy that far. The question then remains why he pushed it at all. How could *any* analogy with mathematics – of all enterprises – be used to object to a concern with principles?

Bundy also objects to my suggestion that AI should develop richer descriptions of program behaviour than those used today by saying that AI is concerned with understanding underlying mechanisms rather than behaviour. But to my mind, being able to explain its behaviour is part of what we *mean* by "understanding a mechanism". To re-state my suggestion: Since a mechanism reveals itself in its behaviour, it might be helpful to have an informative description of the behaviour when trying to understand the mechanism. There is no contradiction between being interested in the mechanism and being interested in the behaviour.

Bundy is upset because he believes that my suggestion that AI study constrained classes of mechanisms is inimical to the run/debug/edit cycle which he sees as the bridge between a vague initial hunch and a fully implemented advance on existing techniques. I have a feeling that Bundy is sticking his neck out quite far here. I suspect that many people in AI would not agree that hacking away on the basis of a foggy idea should be dignified as the "central creative AI activity"; they'd rather call it "kludging".

Be that as it may, my own answer to this criticism is that there is no opposition between constraining the phenomenon to be studied and creativity. On the contrary, deep results often come about precisely because someone has found an interesting constraint on a more general concept. For example, the set of all functions is not a very seminal concept, but the set of *continuous functions* is; the set of all polyhedrons is less interesting than the set of *regular* polyhedrons; etc. The investigation of such a constrained class of objects might require considerable creativity.

Similarly, there might not be many AI results waiting to be discovered about the set of all programs. However, "purely data-driven generalization mechanisms" or "heuristic learners with severe memory limitations" might turn out to be interesting concepts. The exploration of such a concept will involve many applications of the run/debug/edit cycle.

(Incidentally, the pattern of first circumscribing an area and then exploring it extends outside science. A composer who decides to write a fugue or a symphony accepts several constraints on the form of the music to be explored. Nobody has suggested that this limits the creativity involved in composing. Similarly, the French painter Herbin sometimes sets himself the task of making a picture using only certain forms and colours selected in advance.)

In short, Bundy's comments build on three different polar pairs: computational techniques versus law-like principles, underlying mechanisms versus behavioural descriptions, and creativity versus precise delimitation of problem areas. Since all three oppositions are unwarranted, his criticisms have no force.

Finally, let me comment on the rather amusing circumstance that Bundy believes that I am an experimental psychologist who wants to impose the methodology of experimental psychology on AI. He is wrong on both points, and I want to . . . but wait! Maybe I have been influenced by experimental psychology: I keep having images of white rats running around in a large maze of possibilities, computer printouts clasped under their forepaws, with nothing but vague ideas to guide them towards the cheese.

4 Principled behaviour
Alan Bundy

Methodological malaise

I now have a better appreciation of what led Ohlsson to write his first critique of AI; he is as disturbed as I am by what we both see as a methodological malaise in AI. The symptoms of this malaise are:

> differences among referees and critics as to the criteria for judging AI research;
> the fragility of AI programs;
> the difficulty of rebuilding AI programs from published descriptions.

The last symptom has become particularly acute with the advent of expert systems. Papers 'describing' such systems often restrict themselves to a summary of *what* the program does, e.g. "write articles for AISBQ", with an explanation of *how* it does it. In a gesture to 'principles', the paper may end with a tribute to some vague or debased term like, 'production rules', 'frames' or 'multiple representations of knowledge'. It is not possible to reconstruct the program from such a 'description', and as Drew McDermott has chronicled (1981), the application area becomes classified as 'done' and further (perhaps more principles) work on it is blocked.

Ohlsson's proposed solutions to these problems would make them worse. By urging AI researchers to use the terminology of psychology to give sophisticated, behavioural descriptions of their programs, Ohlsson is legitimizing the practice of omitting mechanistic descriptions. Of course, including better behavioural descriptions does not exclude mechanistic descriptions, and in an ideal world, with no page allowances for conference papers, it would be nice to have both. However, encouraging behavioural descriptions focuses attention on the wrong problem.

By urging AI researchers to employ more abstract, law-like principles when describing their work, Ohlsson is legitimizing the practice of drawing vague and meaningless conclusions about the import of a program, e.g. describing it as a triumph for production rules *et al*.

What principles?

To reject principles in AI would be like rejecting motherhood or apple pie, and I was careful not to do so in my article. What I rejected was "physics-like laws". AI is not a science like physics, and to search for such laws can only lead to confusion and misrepresentation. The question to ask is: what kind of principles *can* we expect to find in AI?

The analogy of AI to applied maths, advanced in my reply, suggests an answer. AI has discovered a variety of computational techniques and investigated the behaviour that these techniques are capable of. The principles of AI are: these techniques, the relationships between them, and the relationships of these techniques to their behaviours. On this last point Ohlsson and I at least seem to agree. He says "What counts as a principle is a law-like statement relating mechanisms to their behaviours."

Research methodology to discover such principles can take several forms:

1 To discover totally new techniques, take some task known to be beyond current techniques, and try to build a program to do it. The principle (technique) is the *output* of the program, although some half-baked version of it might also be *input*. The run/debug/edit cycle is used to firm up this idea by subjecting it to the uncompromising logic of the computer.

2 To refine and extend the scruffy techniques (to use Schank's term) that emerge from type 1 research they must be abstracted from the program by analysis and rational reconstruction, and subjected to theoretical analysis.

3 To discover the limits of the neat techniques that emerge from type 2 research and the tradeoffs between related techniques, and to suggest improvements, apply them to new problems. In such work the mechanism to be used *is* determined in advance and is *input* to the program. The original content is to adapt this mechanism to some unexpected task.

Type 1 research is the dominant AI methodology. It was the one I had in mind when rejecting Ohlsson's idea of restricting the type of mechanism in advance. This kind of restriction is anathema to AI researchers because the point of type 1 research is to encourage the ·creation of new types of mechanism. It explains why they react so strongly against the restrictions that Chomskian linguists try to impose on grammars. Such restrictions are, of course, appropriate to type 3 research. Type 1 AI research is not completely unconstrained; the behaviour required of the program is determined in advance and this directs the creative process.

Type 2 and type 3 research are sadly neglected, perhaps because too few people understand the nature of AI. Researchers are satisfied with a scruffy, but working, program, not appreciating that the goal of type 1 research is not met until the techniques have been abstracted. Referees reject type 2 and 3 research variously: as too mathematical, as unoriginal, and as having failed. If Ohlsson's purpose, in proposing the input of principles to programs and the restriction of the type of mechanism employed, was to encourage type 3 research, then he is to be applauded.

How can mechanisms be described?

How can we cure the methodological malaise mentioned above?

As a builder of a complex system, I am aware of the other side of the problem. AI systems are often too big and complex to describe, in the limits set by journals and conferences, in sufficient detail to allow other researchers to reproduce them. If you break off a small piece and describe it in detail then referees are liable to reject it in favour of the 'whole story'.

We lack the vocabulary to describe AI mechanisms precisely in a few words. What vocabulary we do have is flawed; we have several words for each term and several terms for each word. To put our house in order we must build up a vocabulary of precise words for neat techniques. This should be a natural by-product of type 2 AI research, but there is not a lot of it around.

Coda

There seems to be a severe danger of Ohlsson and I coming to an agreement, thus depriving readers of some innocent amusement and Ohlsson and I of the opportunity to compose more titles of the form "X:Y". I think we now agree on the problem we are trying to solve, and on at least some of the solutions.

He took all the pleasure out of it for me by claiming not to be a psychologist. His title was "A psychologist visits etc.," and he suggested using psychological terminology, so I naturally assumed . . . I never did trust this plausible inference stuff.

5 Mechanisms, behaviours, principles: a time for examples
Stellan Ohlsson

In his latest contribution to our debate about AI Alan Bundy divides AI research into three types, which I will take the liberty to re-christen as stages. Stage 1: Construct a working program. Stage 2: State the computational technique embedded in the program in an abstract (implementation-independent) way. Stage 3: Investigate the properties of the technique (e.g. its limitations). Bundy recognizes the similarity between stage 3 research and my original proposal that AI researchers try to state their results in the form of principles.

Furthermore, I now suspect that Bundy's use of the term "computational technique" is very similar to my use of the term "information-processing mechanism". As examples, consider *a problem solver using means-ends analysis*, and *a heuristics learner using version spaces*. Presumably, Bundy regards means-ends analysis and version spaces as "techniques". If so, stage 2 activities correspond closely to my original proposal that AI researchers define precisely what type of mechanism they are investigating.

In short, Bundy's description of stages 2 and 3 constitutes a reformulation of my original proposal, or is at least very similar to it. (I will ignore for the time being that Bundy probably dislikes my inclusion of the task – problem solving, heuristics learning – in the very definition of the mechanism.)

So far, so good.

I see three remaining issues of general interest. First, there is the question of the *status of stage 1 research*. The motivation for "Tell me your problems: a psychologist visits AAAI 82" was my experience that reports of stage 1 activities tend to leave me uniformed, the fact that so much research in AI is in stage 1, and my belief that outputs from stage 1 activities are not yet scientific results. In essence, I wish that AI would raise its standards so that results are not deemed publishable until they reach stage 3, or at least stage 2. Bundy agrees that we should have more stage 2 and stage 3 research, but it is unclear to me what he wants to do about getting it.

Second, there is the matter of *rich behaviour descriptions*. Bundy now states that they would be nice to have, but that mechanistic descriptions should be given priority when page allowances prevent both from being included. Perhaps so (shrug). But that is taking the problem too lightly. I doubt that lack of space is the main reason why AI research is weak on behavioural descriptions. Let me give an example. Focusing on the area of machine learning, I think that reports on rule-learning programs would do well to describe at least the following aspects of the program's behaviour:

Q1 How much of what there is to learn in the relevant task domain does the program pick up? Does it exhibit perfect performance, in some sense, after learning or not?

Q2 How many rules did the program need to acquire to reach a certain level of performance?

Q3 What is the rate of learning (in terms of rules acquired per unit effort)? How does the rate of learning vary with the number of already acquired rules?

Q4 Does the program create only useful rules, or does it generate harmful rules as well? If so, how are they handled?

Q5 How useful are the rules learned? More specifically, if the program is applied to a random sample of N tasks from its domain, on what proportion of the N trials does a particular acquired rule contribute to the solution?

Q6 Do the acquired rules transfer to other problems? To simpler problems? To more complex problems?

I see no signs that AI researchers spend time thinking about aspects such as Q1–Q6 above. As the International Joint Conference on AI, 1983, recently held in Karlsruhe showed, even people who are given one hour for their lecture (and 500 dollars, too) do not consider it worthwhile to spend one minute on aspects such as the above. Indeed, these aspects are not even certain to be discussed in depth in journal articles. I find this quite disturbing.

Third, there is the topic of principles. Bundy now states that he loves principles as he loves motherhood and apple pie, he just objects to "physics-like" principles. As an objection to my views, this is rather confusing, since my original proposal did not call for physics-like principles; in fact, the term "physics-like principle" has been introduced into the debate by Bundy, not by me. Again, we should consider an example to see what the issue is. Here, I suggest, is a tentative law of AI:

> A generalization-based rule-learner will arrive at the correct form of a complex rule before arriving at the correct form of a simple rule; for a discrimination-based rule-learner the opposite is the case; for a rule-learner using version spaces, the rate of arriving at the correct form of a rule is independent of the complexity of the rule.

(The first two clauses of the law are due to Langley (1982), while the third clause is a conjecture by me.) I would expect Bundy to agree that the above principle is interesting and useful, and that it exemplifies at least one kind of principle that we can expect AI to produce. The debate could end there. Whether or not such principles are "physics-like" is immaterial to the practice of AI.

However, from the point of view of the philosophy of science, the question of whether AI principles are "physics-like" or not has some interest, because it touches on the problem of the unity between the various sciences. For this reason, let me briefly outline a view in which the above principle is "physics-like". Physical laws are usually quantitative, and expressed in the form of equations. These are superficial aspects (one could argue). The deep-structure of physical knowledge is that the physical world is divided into a family of *types of systems*: mechanical systems, ideal gases, electric circuits, heat sources/sinks, communicating vessels, etc. For each type of system, there is a collection of laws which link the properties of such systems to each other. The laws are assumed to hold for some real object if there is evidence that the object in question is an instance of the type of system which the law is about.

Given this view of physical knowledge, we can see that the above principle has the same deep-structure. It mentions a type of system – a rule-learner – and states a link between the "direction" in which it learns (specific-to-general, general-to-specific, both-at-once) and its rate of learning. Clearly, whether AI principles are "physics-like" or not depends upon one's analysis of physical knowledge. Any reader who hasn't yet studied the role of principles in physics and mathematics might enjoy the general analysis by Feynman (1965), and the case study by Lakatos (1976).

Summary and suggestion

The discussion has yielded three reasonably well-defined issues. What is a proper balance between stage 1, 2, and 3 activities, and how can we go about achieving it? What kind of behavioural descriptions is it reasonable to ask AI reports to provide? What kind of principles can we expect AI to produce? Each of these issues is certainly "a significant open problem of great interest" (to use the currently fashionable AI terminology for problems that one has failed to solve).

Of these three, the last one seems most fundamental.

Finally

I really must clear up the question of what I am. I have Bundy all confused because I call myself a psychologist, while denying being an experimental psychologist. The solution is that I am a computational (or theoretical) psychologist. This, incidentally, illustrates another law of (A)I: plausible inference works, but only when the right conceptual distinctions are attended to.

6 Superficial principles: an analysis of a behavioural law
Alan Bundy

The story so far

Stellan Ohlsson and myself have been arguing about AI methodology. The debate has concerned the standards of AI research, the role of behavioural descriptions, and the nature of AI principles. After some initial misunderstanding, we now seem to have reached some kind of agreement, to wit:

> We both agree that there is not enough abstraction and generalization of the techniques embedded in AI programs, nor enough investigation of the properties of these techniques.
> We both see some role for behavioural descriptions, but whereas Ohlsson would like to give them a central role, I would relegate them to a minor one, and would give more importance to mechanistic descriptions.
> I define principles in AI to consist of these techniques, their properties, the relations between them, and the relationship of these techniques to their behaviours. Ohlsson wants only the last of these to count as principles.

In his latest contribution, Ohlsson suggested a principle drawn from machine learning. I want to comment on this example and use it to explain my preference for mechanistic over behavioural descriptions.

A candidate principle – the Langley/Ohlsson Law

Ohlsson's "tentative law of AI" is:

> A generalization-based rule-learner will arrive at the correct form of a complex rule before arriving at the correct form of a simple rule; for a discrimination-based rule-learner the opposite is the case; for a rule-learner using version spaces, the rate of arriving at the correct form of a rule is independent of the complexity of the rule.

I assume that rate of arrival is measured in numbers of examples or non-examples required to learn the rule. The first two clauses of this 'law' are from Langley (1982) and the last clause is a conjecture of Ohlsson's. I will call it the Langley/Ohlsson Law.

The Langley/Ohlsson Law describes the relationship of three AI learning techniques to their behaviour. Hence, I agree with Ohlsson that it counts as a principle. However, its behavioural nature makes it both superficial and misleading, as I will demonstrate.

How version spaces work

To substantiate these criticisms it is necessary to explain how the learning techniques of generalization, discrimination and version spaces have the behaviour claimed by the Langley/Ohlsson Law.

Mitchell's version space technique is roughly a combination of generalization and Langley's discrimination. The relationship between these three learning techniques is explored in more detail in Bundy *et al.* (1984). For the

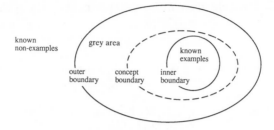

Figure 1   The space of situations

purposes of this debate, version spaces can be visualized as working on the set of situations diagrammed in figure 1. The hypothesis of the rule to be learnt describes a subset of these situations, labelled the *concept boundary* in figure 1. Its location is discovered by version spaces. At any stage of the learning process, some objects are known to be examples of the concept – these are the ones lying inside the *inner boundary*. Other situations are known to be non-examples – these are the ones lying outside the *outer boundary*. Between these boundaries lies the *grey area* of unsettled cases. Hence, the concept boundary lies between the inner boundary and the outer boundary.

Generalization moves the inner boundary outwards to meet the concept boundary. Discrimination moves the outer boundary inwards to meet the concept boundary. The inner boundary is initialized to be the first example of the concept, and the outer boundary is initialized to be the whole space. When generalization and discrimination have combined to make the inner and outer boundaries coincide then the version space learning technique terminates and outputs the concept boundary.

Learning programs based only on either generalization or discrimination are incomplete because these techniques are not guaranteed to terminate. Another example, in the case of discrimination, may cause the boundary to be moved again. The user of such an incomplete learning technique must choose some arbitrary criteria for terminating the learning process and declaring the boundary found so far to be the concept boundary.

Why the Langley/Ohlsson Law is true

Concepts near the inner boundary tend to be more complex than those near the outer boundary. This is because all the techniques outlined above are used mainly on *conjunctive concepts*, i.e. those composed of conjunctions of propositions. The description of a situation consists of the conjunction of all those properties and relations which hold in that situation, for example:

brick(a) & wedge(b) & supports (a,b) & blue(a)
or
brick(a) & brick(b) & supports(a,b) & red(a)

Initially, the inner boundary consists of the description of a single situation, and may contain a number of relations which are irrelevant to the concept being learnt. The initial outer boundary is the empty conjunction, because this encompasses the whole space.

The effect of generalization is to remove some prepositions as irrelevant, e.g. blue(a), and generalize some relations, e.g. wedge(b) ⇒ parallelepiped(b), in order to include a new example. Since we are dealing only with conjunctive concepts, generalization never complicates a concept by replacing a proposition by a disjunction, e.g. wedge(b) ⇒ wedge(b)∨ brick(b). Thus generalization never makes concepts more complex and sometimes makes them simpler.

The effect of discrimination is to add a new proposition or specialize an existing proposition in order to rule out a non-example. Thus discrimination never makes concepts simpler and sometimes makes them more complex.

Thus a complex concept will be closer to the inner boundary than a simple concept will be. Remember that rate of arrival is measured in numbers of examples or non-examples required to move the inner or outer boundary to the concept boundary. Hence a generalization-based concept-learner will arrive at the complex concept first and a discrimination-based concept-learner will arrive at the simple concept first. A version space concept-learner must wait for discrimination and generalization to arrive at the same place, so its rate of arrival is independent of the concept's complexity.

These observations prove the Langley/Ohlsson Law, with the following caveats.

> The learning techniques involved are all concept-learners rather than rule-learners. They can be made to learn rules by treating the hypothesis of the rule as a concept.
>
> Generalization- and discrimination-based concept-learners may arrive at the 'correct form' of a concept, but their incompleteness will prevent them from asserting that this is the correct form in the strong sense that a version spaces concept-learner could assert it.
>
> The truth of the Law depends on the concepts in question being conjunctive.
>
> The truth of the Law depends on there being fewer (non-)examples needed to move the inner (outer) boundary to one closer to it than one further away. However, the rate of travel of the boundary depends on the (non-)examples used. For instance, an example which is very different from the current inner boundary will move it much further than one that is very close. To make the Law true, 'rate of arrival' needs to be defined in some average or probabilistic sense, which it is difficult to make precise.

These caveats considerably diminish the force of the 'Law'. The Langley/Ohlsson Law is misleading because:

It contrasts two incomplete techniques with their combination, but this
is not apparent in its statement;

it refers to arriving at the "correct form" of the rule, even though two of
the techniques in question cannot guarantee this;

it depends on an unstated assumption about the concepts being conjunctive;

it is not strictly true if the obvious sense of 'rate of arrival' is used.

The Langley/Ohlsson Law is superficial because nothing in its statement
suggests why it might be true or false. The mechanistic account we have
given above justifies the Law and describes circumstances in which it would
be true and others in which it would be false. It also gives a more interesting
relationship between generalization, discrimination and version spaces,
namely that the last is a rough combination of the other two.

Better principles

In his AISBQ 48 article, Ohlsson asks for reader's suggestions of
principles and expresses moderate interest in what my suggestions would
be.

Note above that I include techniques and relations between them among
my principles. Hence, as an AI principle, I would suggest generalization,
discrimination and versions spaces, together with the relationship that the
last is a rough combination of the other two. The 'rough' has to stay because
techniques of generalization and discrimination described by Langley have
minor difference to those in Mitchell's version spaces, although the equation is true in spirit (see Bundy et al., 1984, for details).

A further problem is that the term 'generalization' is used in many
different senses within AI. For instance, Mitchell and Winston use it in a
wider sense than that used here: a sense which includes discrimination.
Plotkin (1969) uses generalization to mean a dual of unification, which is
different again. This illustrates the point I made earlier about the need to
clean up our ambiguous technical vocabulary in AI.

Conclusion

This debate between Ohlsson and myself has clarified my
thoughts on AI methodology and on the nature of AI principles.

It was interesting that Ohlsson and I were motivated by a commonly
perceived problem (poor standards in AI) to suggest radically different
solutions; he to call for *more* behavioural descriptions and behavioural
laws; me to call for *less*. However, we do now seem to have reached a
limited agreement about the need for more theoretical analysis of techniques in AI.

By my analysis above, I hope to have demonstrated how superficial and misleading behavioural descriptions of AI programs and techniques can be. I hope that more people will be encouraged to extract, rationally reconstruct, compare and extend the techniques that lie hidden in AI programs. This will not only give us a better theoretical understanding of AI, but also make AI easier to teach and easier to apply. In fact, such theoretical work is vital if we are not to disappoint the people who are currently placing so much faith (and money) in AI.

7 AI principles: the functions of scientific laws
Stellan Ohlsson

In his latest contribution to our ongoing debate about the methodology of AI, Alan Bundy makes an in-depth analysis of a tentative law of AI which I proposed. The law, which Bundy calls the Ohlsson/ Langley Law and which I will modestly rename the Rule Learning Law, goes as follows:

> A generalization-based rule-learner will arrive at the correct form of a complex rule before arriving at the correct form of a simple rule; for a discrimination-based rule-learner the opposite is the case; for a rule-learner using version spaces, the rate of arriving at the correct form of a rule is independent of the complexity of the rule.

The Rule Learning Law was offered as an example of a *type* of law which I believe AI would do well to look for: it mentions a type of mechanism (a rule-learner), and it relates the way it works to its behaviour. Bundy explains in detail why the Rule Learning Law is true. In so doing, he discovers various things about it: the terms "arrive at the correct form" and "rate of arriving" need to be defined in technical ways for the Law to be true; the Law is only applicable if we are talking about conjunctive concepts, etc.

From this Bundy concludes that the Law is superficial and misleading, and therefore, one is led to infer, unnecessary. Furthermore, Bundy implies that the law is unnecessary *because* it relates mechanisms to their behaviours. We can do without this Law (and others like it), Bundy says; all we need is his explanation of why it is true.

But Bundy's investigation into the grounds for the Rule Learning Law does not establish either that this particular law is unnecessary nor that the type of law it was meant to exemplify is useless. In order to see this, we need to consider the *functions* of laws in scientific practice. A full-scale treatise on the philosophy of science cannot be inserted here. A few simple assertions will have to suffice.

Laws are *not* eternal, unchanging outputs of research, to be formulated only at a time when a particular theory seems to be congealing into its "final" form. Laws have important heuristic, organizational and practical functions. As a minor detail, consider the fact that laws have names or labels. This makes it easy to refer to specific pieces of a subject matter or a theory, thus facilitating discussion of it. More importantly, the fact that some laws can be derived from others imposes a partial ordering on a subject matter. As we know from the history of physics, this partial ordering is very useful in the extension, application, presentation and acquisition of physical knowledge.

Most relevant for the present discussion is the fact that *laws serve as foci for debate*. A proposed law stimulates debate by inviting criticism, counter-examples and alternative formulations. A proposed law stimulates debate by separating a statement from its justification, thus inviting its supporters to find alternative justifications, should the initial justification prove insufficient. A proposed law stimulates theoretical work by structuring it into distinct tasks: to inquire into the grounds for the law to define the terms used in formulating that law clearly, to circumscribe its domain of applicability, to derive its predictions or consequences, to find its relations to other laws, to apply the law to problems which have failed to yield other methods, etc. As this continues, a law may be reformulated, constrained, split into different cases, generalized, transferred into a different formalism, etc. Such activities do not imply that the law which stimulated them is unnecessary.

Applying these comments to the case in hand, we see that the Rule Learning Law stimulated Bundy to investigate its justification, thereby discovering several facts about its applicability, etc. If Bundy had not been strongly committed by his stand in the current debate to reject this *kind* of law, he would naturally have ended his investigation, not by concluding that the law is unnecessary, but by *proposing a better formulation of it*. The fact that an inquiry into the foundations for a law reveals that it needs to be reformulated implies neither that laws of that type are useless, nor that it was unnecessary to propose that law in the first place.

In summary, investigations like the one presented by Bundy here are what we need in order to extract, rationally reconstruct, compare and extend AI techniques, and one of the functions of principles like the Law of Rule Learning is to stimulate people to undertake such investigations. Thus, although Bundy's *principles* still contradict my view of AI methodology, his actual *behaviour* is now in accordance with it. With this I am content to let the current debate come to an end.

Artificial methodology meets philosophy

Thomas W. Simon

Introduction

Philosophers constantly debate the nature of their discipline. These interminable debates frustrate even the most patient observer. Workers in AI also disagree, although not so frequently, about how to conduct their research. To equate programs with theories may offer a simple unifying tool to achieve agreement about the proper AI methodology. To construct a program becomes a way to construct a theory. When AI researchers need to justify their product as scientific, they can simply point to their successful programs. Unfortunately, methodological agreement does not come so easily in AI.

For a number of reasons, theorists in any discipline do not relish washing their proverbially dirty laundry in public. Methodology creates a great deal of that dirt, and philosophy of science supposedly supplies the soap to cleanse the discipline's methodology. Scientists often appeal to philosophers of science to develop methodological canons. It certainly does not instill confidence in a discipline if its practitioners cannot even agree on how to evaluate each other's work. Despite public images to the contrary, disagreements over how to approach a subject matter predominate in most scientific disciplines. Can philosophy of science come to the rescue of AI methodology? Yes and no.

Before describing the middle ground occupied by philosophy of science in its relationship to AI, we need to examine how some dismiss the AI research project altogether. In a previous article I argued against the various philosophical obstacles to the program/theory equation (Simon, 1979). I considered three types of objections to AI research: impossibility, ethical, and implausibility. If any of these positions hold, then the programs-as-theories debate cannot even get off the ground. Except in a very restricted range of proofs within the exact sciences, impossibility arguments do not withstand criticism. Furthermore, many ethical darts thrown at AI, curiously enough, depend upon some version of the impossibility arguments. The implausibility arguments remain

155

troublesome, but I want to examine these from a slightly different angle.

Two foundational issues underlie the program-as-theories debate: (1) what constitutes a scientific methodology, and (2) what is understanding, scientific and otherwise. These issues closely connect. In order to show this I will consider an updated version of the impossibility argument as set forth by Dreyfus and Dreyfus (1986). In contrast to my previous analysis, I am now more concerned with the methodological implications than the philosophical status of their claims. While Dreyfus and Dreyfus fail to stymie AI research, they do show the limitations to exactly specifying methodological dictates for a discipline. Within these limitations, helpful methodological heuristics or guidelines make sense. In order to construct those heuristics a critical dialogue between AI and philosophy of science is needed. This paper is intended to take us in that direction.

Theories as institutions

Dreyfus and Dreyfus see the AI research program as doomed. They claim their indictment of AI goes even further than Hubert Dreyfus's very controversial attack entitled What Computers Can't Do.

> In What Computers Can't Do, written in 1969 (2nd edition, 1972), the main objection to AI was the impossibility of using rules to select only those facts about the real world that were relevant in a given situation. The "Introduction" to the paperback edition of the book, published by Harper & Row in 1979, pointed out further that no one had the slightest idea how to represent the common sense understanding possessed even by a four-year-old. (*Dreyfus and Dreyfus, 1986, p. 102*)

They now think that the situation has deteriorated even further. Not only does theoretical AI lead us down a fruitless road but even the much-touted expert systems' feats in AI, or what they call "knowledge engineering", will never deliver on its promises.

Rather than evaluate these global claims about the current and future state of AI progress, I want to look at the Dreyfuses' position in the context of AI methodology. For H. Dreyfus, a program consists of a fairly rigid set of rules which does not explain the human mind because the human mind does not follow rules. We can only speculate on how Dreyfus knows how the human mind works, but here I want to compare the Dreyfus and AI versions of psychology.

Dreyfus and Dreyfus seem to want to replace AI conjecture with a mystery. Humans just somehow intuit things. They claim that "human decision making [is] an inscrutable business, a mysterious blending of careful analysis, intuition, and the wisdom and judgment distilled from experience" (Dreyfus and Dreyfus, 1986, p. 8). To know how to ride a bicycle cannot reduce to a knowing-that sequence of rules ("lean to the right until . . ."). I simply mysteriously know how to do it. The analysis stops at the exact point where things get interesting.

The fact that AI does not give a complete explanation does not imply that the mystery remains and that no understanding is gained. At least AI tries to present something far less mysterious than intuition. The AI account may not satisfy everyone, and the AI analysis may even take us down the wrong path. Nevertheless, at a very minimum, the AI conjectures attain some degree of plausibility in that they help make sense of mental functioning. As discussed more fully later, to make sense of something like mental functions is no small feat.

Dreyfus and Dreyfus criticize Schank (see Schank, 1982b) for not going far enough in his script analysis. Schank proposes that "we understand something like restaurant behavior in terms of scripts, which set the context for analysis".

> We define a script as a predetermined causal chain on conceptualizations that describe the normal sequence of things in a familiar situation. Thus there is a restaurant script, a birthday-party script, a football game script, a classroom script, and so on. (*Schank, 1975b, p. 131*)

Dreyfus and Dreyfus complain that Schank does not provide an analysis of how frames change and interact. Nonetheless, Schank at least provides some analysis. For Dreyfus and Dreyfus, resignation prevails; complexity implies mystery. I exaggerate slightly, since Dreyfus and Dreyfus propose their own analyses such as a classification of skill attainment levels. Their own brand of psychological theory, however, does not move far beyond common sense.

We need to recognize the value of small steps along the ladder of understanding. Dreyfus and Dreyfus justifiably deflate the more grandiose claims and pretensions of AI workers. The merits of that attack, however, should not mislead anyone to reject the entire AI project. In fact, many AI researchers welcome challenges which claim that a computer cannot simulate a particular mental activity. The Dreyfus and Dreyfus analysis, however, may present a different kind of challenge to the programs-as-theories debate.

Part of the Dreyfus and Dreyfus case against AI rests on the difference between "knowing how" and "knowing that." By their analysis AI proponents mistakenly reduce knowing-how to knowing-that activities. The know-how needed for expertise does not break down into a set of rules. Does understanding, scientific or otherwise, of other humans fit more into the knowing-how than into the knowing-that category? If so, do the attempts to construct methodological rules for scientific theories about humans fail because scientific understanding is not rule-governed?

Both the AI and the Dreyfuses' positions have merit when applied to scientific understanding. On the other hand, something mysterious remains. We can break down scientific understanding into component parts. Yet, that does not mean a complete and exhaustive analysis exists. Scientists and philosophers can provide explicit details that govern scientific understanding, even if the analysis is incomplete. "A mysterious blending of careful analysis, intuition, and the wisdom and judgment distilled from experience" sounds vague, but that does describe the elements missed by the analysis. In the next section, some of the more explicit aspects of scientific understanding begin to come into focus.

Programs as theories

A leading AI theorist, Roger Schank, has bemoaned that "AI would have a fairly difficult time justifying itself as a scientific discipline" (Schank, 1982b). Some AI theorists disagree and try to spell out the ingredients for a methodology. Let us turn to these.

Hayes advocates a strong link between theory and program:

> AI's criterion is not experimental corroboration, but implementability. An acceptable explanation of a piece of behavior must be, in the last analysis, a program which can actually be implemented and run. And such an explanation is a good explanation just to the extent that the program, when run, does exhibit the behavior which was to be explained. (*Hayes, 1979b, p. 158*)

This makes the tie between theory and program too tight.

To link programs to theories makes AI vulnerable to Searle's attack. Searle distinguishes between two brands of AI:

> According to weak AI, the principle value of the computer in the study of the mind is that it gives us a very powerful tool. For example, it enables us to formulate and test hypotheses in a more rigorous and precise fashion than before. But according to strong AI the computer is not merely a tool in the study of the mind; rather the appropriately programmed computer really is a mind in the sense that computers given the right programs can be literally said to understand and have other cognitive states. And according to strong AI, because the programmed computer has cognitive states, the programs are not mere tools that enable us to test psychological explanations rather, the programs are themselves the explanations. (*1980, pp. 417–418*)

By Searle's account, strong AI makes the strong claim that once a program successfully runs, then the simulated activity is explained.

Not all AI programmers make or could make this claim. More importantly, they need not make that claim. To simulate an activity is not to duplicate it. A computer programmed to simulate goal directed behavior does not thereby exhibit goal directedness.

AI fascinates and boggles the mind because of the excitement generated over philosophical questions such as "DO MACHINES THINK?" Whatever the merits of these debates, when it comes to formulating a methodology for AI, philosophy of mind may prove more of a hindrance than a help. Within the context of philosophy of mind the thesis forging a strong link between programs and theories reads as follows:

> Programs are theories because machines have human attributes.

However, from the standpoint of methodology, to ascribe human mental properties to machines begins the problem and does not supply the grounds for the programs-as-theories thesis. Why complicate matters with the strong version of AI when, for methodological purposes, the weak version will do?

Problems still confront the programs-as-theories thesis. As Partridge *et al.* persuasively argue, "the main drawback of programs as theories is that the theory is typically dispersed and hidden under a mass of detail that is irrelevant to the theory" (1984, p. 541). They then encourage abstracting from this massive pile of code in order to construct a theory. The program itself does not equal a theory, but the abstracted claims from the program plus the program do equal a theory.

Despite their concessions to these abstractions, Partridge *et al.* still retain the program as the foundation stone of the theory since "the program is the only reliable statement of the theory" (1984, p. 558). While I recognize the value of programs, I am not as convinced that programs always need to occupy a central place in the theory. The statements abstracted from the program could, in some situations, enhance our understanding more than the program.

To analyze a complex behavioral capacity into relatively less problematic capacities at the program level does, in some sense, provide a series of explanations (Cummins, 1977). Yet, decomposing to the program level does not necessarily increase the level of understanding. To explain a person building a model airplane, I might decompose the overall set of instructions she follows into sub-routines. To further divide the sub-routines to the level of synapses firing will not necessarily enhance our understanding of the activity one iota.

Abstraction has its pitfalls as well. Certainly, not every abstraction suffices. From a pile of program code the theorist can construct an infinite variety of flow diagrams. How much creative license should we allow in labeling those little boxes? Ah, let's call that box "understanding." A magic flick of the pen labels, simulates, and explains mental processes.

Can philosophers of science devise methodological maxims to restrict the wilder flights of imagination? Again, yes and no. Success at rule construction confronts limits. In the last analysis, we are left with good old-fashioned criticism. I criticize the label "understanding" because you gave little justification for it.

So, programs play a role in theories, but they do not constitute theories. From programs as problems we turn to theories as problems.

Theories as programs

Many incorrectly assume that scientists and philosophers basically agree on the meaning of critical terms such as model, explanation, theory, and understanding. Debates over the status of programs as theories assume a relatively clear sense of theory. Unfortunately, or perhaps fortunately, 'theory' lacks a clear and unambiguous definition.

AI researchers rigorously formulate vague intuitions and hunches in terms of programs. Perhaps the intuitions as to what constitutes a theory can benefit from computer simulation. To give a theoretical account of something is to provide a type of understanding. Although Roger Schank in his *Explanation Patterns: Understanding Mechanically and Creatively* (1986) has some very different purposes in mind, his simulation of understanding shows the possibility of a fruitful interaction between AI and philosophy of science. AI studies could profit from and, in turn, illuminate philosophy of science.

Schank begins his study with a much looser sense of understanding than one would find in the philosophy of science literature. But perhaps Schank's analysis of understanding could prove useful in philosophy of science. Schank breaks down understanding into the following types:

making sense – cognitive understanding – complete empathy

Schank, in a roundabout way, agrees with Searle that computers will never achieve empathic understanding. Other AI projects fall to the elementary end of the understanding spectrum.

> SHRDLU (Winograd, 1972), MYCIN (Shortliffe *et al.*, 1973) and other programs in AI, therefore, can be said to understand at the level of making sense since they can explain why they did what they did to the extent of being able to describe the steps that they went through in performing their respective tasks. (*Schank, 1986, p. 14*)

Similarly, the suitably abstracted theory from the SHRDLU program explains in the weak but noteworthy sense that it makes sense of a narrow range of behavior. Given our limited knowledge of mental processes, this making-sense level represents a perfectly legitimate step along the path of scientific understanding.

Schank thinks of his most recent simulations as cognitive understandings, in the middle of the understanding spectrum.

> The task is to get computers to explàin things to themselves, to ask questions about their experiences so as to cause those explanations to be forthcoming, and to be creative in coming up with explanations that have not been previously available. (*Schank, 1986, p. 19*)

Although this formulation has problems, Schank's emphasis on the questioning and creative components of theory places his analysis above many found in philosophy of science – for example, those where theory is explicated in terms of universal laws and deductive structure. Such rigid conceptions of theories have little applicability in the social sciences.

Now, how can AI benefit from philosophy of science? It is one thing to start off with intuitions in AI work, but we want those intuitions as clear and precise as possible. Schank's intuitions about understanding and explanation set the boundary conditions for his entire project. The overall success of his study rests, in part, on his initial intuitions. The following illustration from the philosophy of science shows how to sharpen the intuitions in AI.

Peter Achinstein's *Concepts of Science* (1968) does not exactly dovetail with Schank's work. Achinstein provides an analysis of what it is for a person, most likely a scientist, to have a theory, whereas Schank wants to simulate any person's understanding. The two projects overlap by more than is revealed by a surface glance, as the following analysis should demonstrate.

Achinstein proposes these semantically relevant conditions for *x* having a theory:

1 Conjectural or speculative
2 Plausibility
3 Potentially explanatory
4 Propositional
5 Relatively fundamental
6 Somewhat integrated.

He summarizes these as:

> T is a theory to a context, if and only if T is a set of propositions that (depending on the context) is (was, might have been, and so forth) not known to be true or to be false but believed to be somewhat plausible, potentially explanatory, relatively fundamental, and somewhat integrated. (*1968, p. 129*)

Achinstein's and Schank's analyses come closer together when we realize that when someone understands something, she or he has a theory about that. Given this similar territory, which analysis wins?

To set the stage for this debate, I propose that theory construction takes place at a very early, pre-programming phase. To program and to abstract from the program constitute only two aspects of theory construction. The

AI programmer needs to decide on a fairly detailed analysis of, in this case, cognitive understanding prior to the program phase. I do not have the space to carry out the debate between Schank and Achinstein. I hypothesize that out of this and similar debates a much more robust theory would emerge from both camps.

Achinstein's analysis helps illuminate the programs-as-theories problem in other ways. Achinstein proposes a much broader sense of theory than AI proponents seem to want in the programs-as-theories debate. One strong reason to refocus that search in Achinstein's direction lies in the fact that Achinstein's analysis more closely captures the wide variety of theories actually found in scientific practice. In accepting a theory, scientists do not meet some unified set of stringent conditions. Theories come in many different forms. As Wittgenstein might say, theories resemble each other like family members resemble each other. Seldom do we find exact duplicates with the same features. More likely we find some shared features, at least enough to recognize each as a member of the family.

According to Achinstein, condition 2 differentiates "having a theory" from "having a theoretical model." Someone may propose a theoretical model knowing full well "that it is applicable only within a very limited range and not very accurate even within that range" (Achinstein, 1968, p. 123). This implies for AI that programs more closely resemble theoretical models than theories. In other words, AI proponents could readily admit that computers did not think, understand, possess intelligence, etc., and still claim that computer simulation is a valuable way of doing science since programs are, in part, theoretical models.

Achinstein lists the characteristics of theoretical models. A theoretical model is:

1 A set of assumptions about some object or system.
2 A description of a type of object or system which attributes to it what might be called an inner structure, composition, or mechanism, reference to which is intended to explain various properties exhibited by that object or system.
3 Treated as a simplified approximation useful for certain purposes.
4 Proposed within the broader framework of some more basic theory or theories.
5 Often formulated, developed, and even named, on the basis of an analogy between the object or system described in the model and some different object or system. (*Achinstein, 1968, pp. 212–216*)

So, computer simulations do qualify as theoretical models just as the Bohr model of the atom qualifies. Characteristic 4 may present some problems. The Bohr model lies within the framework of classical electrodynamics and classical mechanics. What sets the broader framework for AI? As an example of a theoretical model from psychology Achinstein proposes models of learning behavior, which presumably fall within the broader framework of learning theory. If Achinstein includes these as theoretical models, then computer simulations certainly qualify. Partridge *et al.* (1984), for example, show very clearly how their simulations fit into the overall framework of learning theories.

Thus, philosophers have something to learn from the simulationists and vice versa.

Conclusion

The various threads of the discussion can now be woven together in the following diagram:

Intuition	Making-Sense	Cognitive-Understanding1	Cognitive-Understanding2	Empathy
(1)	(2)	(3)	(4)	(5)
Dreyfus	Winograd	Schank	Achinstein	Searle

From the discussion the following conclusions can be drawn: first of all, in terms of providing some understanding (2), (3), and (4) generally surpass (1). People like Dreyfus and Dreyfus do want to keep the human mind a mystery. Yet, (1) does show limitations to our ability to give not any set but to give a complete set of explicit rules that govern understanding. Secondly, (3) and (4) as respective representatives of AI and philosophy of science could mutually benefit from each other's analyses and criticisms. Thirdly, in terms of scientific methodology philosophy of mind questions such as those raised in the context of (5) should be avoided. Finally, with respect to (2), given our scanty understanding of the human mind, those theories which at least make sense of some aspects of mental functions warrant serious consideration.

What meta-methodological points follow from this analysis? For one thing, at this stage of development the prospects for a rigid list of methodological criteria look dim. Despite this, to employ and debate various criteria remains critical. Instead of indicating an unhealthy state, methodological debates signal the robustness and vitality of a discipline. Philosophy of science will not come to the rescue of AI, but the two can play mutually supportive roles. Nothing can replace sound criticism and debate in either area.

Finally, we turn to the main topic at hand, the debate over programs as theories. Theories in AI operate at three levels. Even before the program runs, AI researchers start to articulate their theory. Contrary to Hayes, programs do not link so closely with theories, even though programs are ingredients in AI theories. After the program successfully runs, the theoretical work continues, for the program needs interpretation and integration into a theoretical framework. So, we have three phases of theory construction: pre-program, program, and post-program stages.

Theories are not intuitions, but intuitive elements enter into theories. Programs are not theories, but programs constitute aspects of theories. Theories are not programs, but computer simulation aids an analysis of theories. And finally, debate and disagreement over methodology lie at the very heart of a healthy, vibrant discipline.

5   The role of representations

This section is the least concerned with concrete methodological issues, but there is, we believe, a need to explore some of the arguments concerning the abstract representations that underlie programs and theories in AI. Several other collections of philosophically-oriented AI papers address these issues quite well, and these are covered in the annotated bibliography. Nevertheless, there are a number of arguments that are either new, or will contribute significantly to the unity of this particular collection.

Winograd addresses, at a very general level, the promises and problems of AI: he is no longer as optimistic as he used to be. He briefly reviews the physical symbol system hypothesis (PSSH, see Newell, 1980) which is typically taken as one of the foundation stones of AI. Winograd then singles out for attack the essential sub-component, representation – "complete and systematic representation is crucial to the paradigm."

He claims that an underlying philosophy of "patchwork rationalism" is responsible for the unwarranted optimism that pervades much of AI. And he briefly introduces an alternative basis – "hermeneutic constructivism."

He examines three types of problem that arise from the misguided foundations of AI: gaps of anticipation, blindness of representation, and restriction of the domain. He sees the PSSH as leading AI into the necessity for decontextualized meaning – i.e. AI systems are constructed with rules that "deal only with the symbols, not their interpretation." We are forced to deal with the representation as an object "stripped of open-ended ambiguities and shadings." Only a very limited form of AI can be constructed on this basis, Winograd claims.

Dennett presents an interesting argument that we humans are not so special as some anti-AI people would claim; he undermines one well-known reason for claiming that AI will always be limited to something less than human intelligence. He attacks the claim that humans possess original intentionality whilst that of an artifact is necessarily derived intentionality – a derivation from the real (i.e., human) thing.

Dennett imports and reuses a provocative argument from biology: Dawkins' theory of selfish genes accounting for why we are just what we are.

165

Thinking machines: Can there be? Are we?

Terry Winograd

1 Introduction

Futurologists have proclaimed the birth of a new species, *machina sapiens*, that will share (perhaps usurp) our place as the intelligent sovereigns of our earthly domain. These "thinking machines" will take over our burdensome mental chores, just as their mechanical predecessors were intended to eliminate physical drudgery. Eventually they will apply their "ultra-intelligence" to solving all of our problems. Any thoughts of resisting this inevitable evolution is just a form of "speciesism," born from a romantic and irrational attachment to the peculiarities of the human organism.

Critics have argued with equal fervor that "thinking machine" is an oxymoron – a contradiction in terms. Computers, with their foundations of cold logic, can never be creative or insightful or possess real judgment. No matter how competent they appear, they do not have the genuine intentionality that is at the heart of human understanding. The vain pretensions of those who seek to understand mind as computation can be dismissed as yet another demonstration of the arrogance of modern science.

Although my own understanding developed through active participation in artificial intelligence research, I have now come to recognize a larger grain of truth in the criticisms than in the enthusiastic predictions. But the story is more complex. The issues need not (perhaps cannot) be debated as fundamental questions concerning the place of humanity in the universe. Indeed, artificial intelligence has not achieved creativity, insight, and judgment. But its shortcomings are far more mundane: we have not yet been able to construct a machine with even a modicum of common sense or one that can converse on everyday topics in ordinary language.

The source of the difficulties will not be found in the details of silicon micro-circuits or of Boolean logic. The basic philosophy that has guided the research is shallow and inadequate, and has not received sufficient scrutiny. It is drawn from the traditions of rationalism and logical empiricism but has taken a novel turn away from its predecessors. This new "patchwork rationalism" will be our subject of examination.

First, we will review the guiding principles of artificial intelligence and see how they are embodied in current research. Then we will look at the fruits of that research. I will argue that "artificial intelligence" as now conceived is limited to a very particular kind of intelligence: one that can usefully be likened to bureaucracy in its rigidity, obtuseness, and inability to adapt to changing circumstances. The weakness comes not from insufficient development of the technology, but from the inadequacy of the basic tenets.

But, as with bureaucracy, weaknesses go hand in hand with unique strengths. Through a re-interpretation and re-formulation of the techniques that have been developed, we can anticipate and design appropriate and valuable uses. In conclusion I will briefly introduce an orientation I call hermeneutic constructivism and illustrate how it can lead down this alternative path of design.

2 The mechanization of rationality

In their quest for mechanical explanations of (or substitutes for) human reason, researchers in artificial intelligence are heirs to a long tradition. In his "Discourse on the method of properly guiding the reason in the search of truth in the sciences" (1637), Descartes initiated the quest for a systematic method of rationality. Although Descartes himself did not believe that reason could be achieved through mechanical devices, his understanding laid the groundwork for the symbol-processing machines of the modern age.

In 1651, Hobbes described reason as symbolic calculation:

> When a man reasoneth, he does nothing else but conceive a sum total, from addition of parcels; or conceive a remainder . . . These operations are not incident to numbers only, but to all manner of things that can be added together, and taken one out of another . . . the logicians teach the same in consequences of words; adding together two names to make an affirmation, and two affirmations to make a syllogism; and many syllogisms to make a demonstration.   (*Quoted in Haugeland, 1985*)

Leibniz[1] cherished through his life the hope of discovering a kind of generalized mathematics, which he called *Characteristica Universalis*, by means of which thinking could be replaced by calculation. "If we had it," he says "we should be able to reason in metaphysics and morals in much the same way as in geometry and analysis. If controversies were to arise, there would be no more need of disputation between two philosophers than between two accountants. For it would suffice to take their pencils in their hands, to sit down to their slates, and to say to each other . . . 'Let us calculate'."

Behind this program of mechanical reason was a faith in a rational and ultimately understandable universe. The model of "Let us calculate" is that of Euclidean geometry, in which a small set of clear and self-evident postulates provides a basis for generating the right answers (given sufficient diligence) to the most complex and vexing problems. Reasonable men could be relied upon to agree on the postulates and the methods, and therefore dispute could only arise from mistaken calculation.

The empiricists turned to physical experience and experiment as the true basis of knowledge. But in rejecting the a priori status of the propositions on which reasoning was based, they did not abandon the vision of rigorous (potentially mechanizable) logical procedures. For our purposes here, it will suffice to adopt a broader characterization, in which much of both rationalism and empiricism fall within a common "rationalistic tradition." (Winograd and Flores, 1986). This label subsumes the varied (and at times hotly opposed) inheritors of Descartes' legacy – those who seek to achieve rational reason through a precise method of symbolic calculation.

The electronic computer gave new embodiment to mechanical rationality, making it possible to derive the consequences of precisely specified rules, even when huge amounts of calculation are required. The first decades of computing emphasized the application of numerical techniques. Researchers in operations research and decision theory addressed policy questions by developing complex mathematical models of social and political systems and calculating the results of proposed alternatives.[2] Although these techniques work well in specialized cases (such as scheduling delivery vehicles or controlling the operations in a refinery), they proved inadequate for the broader problems to which they were applied. The "mathematization" of experience required simplifications that made the computer results – accurate as they might be with respect to the models – meaningless in the world.

Although there are still attempts to quantify matters of social import (for example in applying mathematical risk analysis to decisions about nuclear power), there is an overall disillusionment with the potential for adequately reducing human concerns to a precise set of numbers and equations (see for example, Davis and Hersh, 1986). The developers of artificial intelligence have rejected traditional mathematical modeling in favor of an emphasis on symbolic – rather than numerical – formalisms. Leibniz's "Let us calculate" is taken in Hobbes' broader sense to include not just numbers but also "affirmations" and "syllogisms."

3 The promise of artificial intelligence

Attempts to duplicate formal non-numerical reasoning on a machine date back to the earliest computers, but the endeavor began in earnest with the AI projects of the mid 1950s (see Gardner, 1985, for an overview of the historical perspective). The goals were ambitious: to fully duplicate the human capacities of thought and language on a digital computer. Early claims that a complete theory of intelligence would be achieved within a few decades have long since been abandoned, but the research has not diminished. For example, a recent book by Minsky (one of the founders of AI) offers computational models for phenomena as diverse as conflict, pain and pleasure, the self, the soul, consciousness, confusion, genius, infant emotion, foreign accents, and freedom of will (these are among the section headings in Minsky, 1986).

In building models of mind, there are two distinct but complementary goals. On the one hand is the quest to explain human mental processes as thoroughly and unambiguously as physics explains the functioning of ordinary mechanical devices. On the other hand is the drive to create intelligent tools – machines that apply intelligence to serve some purpose, regardless of how closely they mimic the details of human intelligence. At times these two enterprises have gone hand in hand, at others they have led down separate paths.

Researchers such as Newell and Simon (two other founding fathers of artificial intelligence) have sought precise and scientifically testable theories of more modest scope than Minsky suggests. In reducing the study of mind to the formulation of rule-governed operations on symbol systems, they focus on detailed aspects of cognitive functioning, using empirical measures such as memory capacity and reaction time. They hypothesize specific "mental architectures" and compare their detailed performance with human experimental results (e.g., Newell and Simon, 1972; Laird *et al.*, 1986). It is difficult to measure the success of this enterprise. The tasks that have been examined (such as puzzle-solving and the ability to remember abbreviations for computer commands) do not even begin to approach a representative sample of human cognitive abilities, for reasons we will examine below.

On the other side lies the goal of practical system building. In the late 1970s, the field of artificial intelligence was drastically affected by the continuing precipitous drop in computing costs. Techniques that previously demanded highly specialized and costly equipment came within the reach of commercial users. A new term, "knowledge engineering," was coined to indicate a shift to the pragmatic interests of the engineer, rather than the scientist's search for theoretical knowledge.

"Expert systems," as the new programs were called, incorporate "knowledge bases" made up of simple facts and "if . . . then" rules, as illustrated in figure 1.

FACTS:

Tank no. 23 contains sulfuric acid.

The plaintiff was injured by a portable power saw.

RULES:

If the sulfate ion test is positive, the spill material is sulfuric acid.

If the plaintiff was negligent in the use of the product,

the theory of contributory negligence applies.

Figure 1   Rules for an expert system (from D. Waterman, 1986, p. 16)

These systems do not attempt to explain human intelligence in detail, but are justified in terms of their practical applications, for which extravagant claims have been made.

> Humans need expert systems, but the problem is they don't often believe it. . . At least one high-performance medical diagnosis program sits unused because the physicians it was designed to assist didn't perceive that they needed such assistance; they were wrong, but that doesn't matter . . . There's a manifest destiny in information processing, in knowledge systems, a continent we shall all spread out upon sooner or later (*Feigenbaum and McCorduck, 1983*).

The high hopes and ambitious aspirations of knowledge engineering are well-documented, and the claims are often taken at face value, even in serious intellectual discussions. In fact, although a few widely-known systems illustrate specific potentials, the successes are still isolated pinnacles in a landscape of research prototypes, feasibility studies, and preliminary versions. It is difficult to get a clear picture of what has been accomplished and to make a realistic assessment of what is yet to come. We need to begin by examining the difficulties with the fundamental methods these programs employ.

4 The foundations of artificial intelligence

Artificial intelligence draws its appeal from the same ideas of mechanized reasoning that attracted Descartes, Leibniz, and Hobbes, but it differs from the more classical forms of rationalism in a critical way. Descartes wanted his method to stand on a bedrock of clear and self-evident truths. Logical empiricism sought truth through observation and the refinement of formal theories that predicted experimental results. Artificial intelligence has abandoned the quest for certainty and truth. The new patchwork rationalism is built upon mounds of "micro-truths" gleaned through common sense introspection, *ad hoc* programming and so-called "knowledge acquisition" techniques for interviewing experts. The grounding on this shifting sand is pragmatic in the crude sense – "If it seems to be working, it's right."

The resulting patchwork defies logic. Minsky observes:

> For generations, scientists and philosophers have tried to explain ordinary reasoning in terms of logical principles – with virtually no success. I suspect this enterprise failed because it was looking in the wrong direction: common sense works so well not because it is an approximation of logic; logic is only a small part of our great accumulation of different, useful ways to chain things together. (*Minsky, 1986*)

In the days before computing, "ways to chain things together" would have remained a vague metaphor. But the computer can perform arbitrary symbol manipulations that we interpret as having logical import. It is easy to build a program to which we enter "Most birds can fly" and "Tweety is a bird" and which then produces "Tweety can fly" according to a regular (although logically questionable) rule. The artificial intelligence methodology does not demand a logically correct answer, but one that works sufficiently often to be "heuristically adequate."

In a way, this approach is very attractive. Everyday human thought does not follow the rigid strictures of formal deduction. Perhaps we can devise some more flexible (and even fallible) system that operates according to mechanical principles, but more accurately mirrors the mind.

But this appeal is subtly deceptive. Minsky places the blame for lack of success in explaining ordinary reasoning on the rigidity of logic, and does not raise the more fundamental questions about the nature of all symbolic representations and of formal (though possibly "non-logical") systems of rules for manipulating them. There are basic limits to what can be done with symbol manipulation, regardless of how many "different, useful ways to chain things together" one invents. The reduction of mind to the interactive sum of decontextualized fragments is ultimately impossible and misleading. But before elaborating on the problems, let us first review some assumptions on which this work proceeds:

1 Intelligence is exhibited by "physical symbol systems."
2 These systems carry out symbol manipulations that correspond to some kind of "problem solving."
3 Intelligence is embodied as a large collection of fragments of "knowledge."

4.1 The physical symbol system hypothesis

The fundamental principle is the identification of intelligence with the functioning of a rule-governed symbol-manipulating device. It has been most explicitly stated by Newell and Simon:

> A physical symbol system has the necessary and sufficient means for general intelligent action . . . By "general intelligent action" we wish to indicate the same scope of intelligence we see in human action: that in any real situation behavior appropriate to the ends of the system and adaptive to the demands of the environment can occur, within some limits of speed and complexity. (*Newell and Simon, 1976*)

This "physical symbol system hypothesis" presupposes materialism: the claim that all of the observed properties of intelligent beings can ultimately be explained in terms of lawful physical processes. It adds the claim that these processes can be described at a level of abstraction in which all relevant aspects of physical state can be understood as the encoding of symbol structures and that the activities can be adequately characterized as systematic application of symbol manipulation rules.

The essential link is *representation* – the encoding of the relevant aspects of the world. Newell lays this out explicitly:

> An intelligent agent is embedded in a *task environment*; a *task statement* enters via a *perceptual* component and is encoded in an initial *representation*. Whence starts a cycle of activity in which a *recognition* occurs . . . of a method to use to attempt the problem. The method draws upon a memory of *general world knowledge* . . . It is clear to us all what *representation* is in this picture. It is the data structures that hold the problem and will be processed into a form that makes the solution available. Additionally, it is the data structures that hold the world knowledge and will be processed to acquire parts of the solution or to obtain guidance in constructing it. [emphasis in original] (*Newell, 1982*)

Complete and systematic symbolic representation is crucial to the paradigm. The rules followed by the machine can deal only with the symbols, not their interpretation.

4.2 Problem-solving, inference, and search

Newell's and Simon's physical symbol systems aspire not to an idealized rationality, but to "behavior appropriate to the ends of the system and adaptive to the demands of the environment." This shift reflects the formulation that won Simon a Nobel prize in economics. He supplanted decision theories based on optimization with a theory of "satisficing" – effectively using finite decision-making resources to come up with adequate, but not necessarily optimal plans of action.

As artificial intelligence developed in the 1950s and 1960s, this methodology was formalized in the techniques of "heuristic search."

The task that a symbol system is faced with, then, when it is presented with a problem and a problem space, is to use its limited processing resources to generate possible solutions, one after another, until it finds one that satisfies the problem-defining test (Newell and Simon, 1976).

The "problem space" is a formal structure that can be thought of as enumerating the results of all possible sequences of actions that might be taken by the program. In a program for playing chess, for example, the problem space is generated by the possible sequences of moves. The number of possibilities grows exponentially with the number of moves, and is beyond practical reach after a small number. However, one can limit search in this space by following heuristics that operate on the basis of local cues ("If one of your pieces could be taken on the opponent's next move, try moving it . . ."). There have been a number of variations on this basic theme, all of which are based on explicit representations of the problem space and the heuristics for operating within it.

Figure 1 illustrated some rules and facts from expert systems. These are not represented in the computer as sentences in English, but as symbols intended to correspond to the natural language terms. As these examples indicate, the domains are naturally far richer and more complex than can be captured by such simple rules. A lawyer will have many questions about whether a plaintiff was "negligent," but for the program it is a simple matter of whether a certain symbolic expression of the form "Negligent(x)" appears in the store of representations, or whether there is a rule of the form "If . . . then Negligent(x)," whose conditions can be satisfied.

There has been a great deal of technical debate over the detailed form of rules, but two principles are taken for granted in essentially all of the work:

1 Each rule is true in a limited (situation-dependent), not absolute sense.
2 The overall result derives from the synergistic combination of rules, in a pattern that need not (in fact could not in general) be anticipated in writing them.

For example, there may be cases in which the "sulfate ion test is positive" even though the spill is not sulfuric acid. The overall architecture of the rule-manipulating system may lead to a conclusion being drawn that violates one of these rules (on the basis of other rules). The question is not whether each of the rules is true, but whether the output of the program as a whole is "appropriate." The knowledge engineers hope that by devising and tuning such rules they can capture more than the deductive logic of the domain.

> "While conventional programs deal with facts, expert systems handle "lore" . . . the rules of thumb, the hunches, the intuition and capacity for judgement that are seldom explicitly laid down but which form the basis of an expert's skill, acquired over a lifetime's experience." (*Michie and Johnston, 1984*)

This *ad hoc* nature of the logic applies equally to the cognitive models of Newell and Simon, in which a large collection of separate "production rules" operates on a symbolic store or "working memory." Each production rule specifies a step to be carried out on the symbols in the store, and the overall architecture determines which will be carried out in what order. The symbols don't stand for chemical spills and law, but for hypothesized psychological features, such as the symbolic contents of short-term memory. Individual rules do things like moving an element to the front of the memory or erasing it. The cognitive modeler does not build an overall model of the system's performance on a task, but designs the individual rules in hopes that appropriate behavior will emerge from their interaction.

Minsky makes explicit this assumption that intelligence will emerge from computational interactions among a plethora of small pieces.

> I'll call 'Society of Mind' this scheme in which each mind is made of many smaller processes. The smaller processes we'll call agents. Each mental agent by itself can only do some simple thing that needs no mind or thought at all. Yet when we join these agents in societies – in certain very special ways – this leads to true intelligence. (*Minsky, 1986*)

Minsky's theory is quite different from Newell's cognitive architectures. In place of finely-tuned clockworks of precise production rules we find an impressionistic pastiche of metaphors. Minsky illustrates his view in a simple 'micro-world' of toy blocks, populated by agents such as BUILDER (which stacks up the blocks), ADD (which adds a single block to a stack), and the like:

> for example, BUILDER's agents require no sense of meaning to do their work; ADD merely has to turn on GET and PUT. Then GET and PUT do not need any subtle sense of what those turn-on signals "mean" – because they're wired up to do only what they're wired up to do. (*Minsky, 1986*)

These agents seem like simple computer subroutines – program fragments that perform a single well-defined task. But a subsequent chapter describes an interaction between the BUILDER agent and the WRECKER agent, which are parts of a PLAY-WITH-BLOCKS agent:

> inside an actual child, the agencies responsible for BUILDING and WRECKING might indeed become versatile enough to negotiate by offering support for one another's goals. "Please, WRECKER, wait a moment more till BUILDER adds just one more block: it's worth it for louder crash!". (*Minsky, 1986*).

With a simple "might indeed become versatile . . .," we have slipped from a technically feasible but limited notion of agents as subroutines, to an impressionistic description of a society of *homunculi*, conversing with each other in ordinary language. This sleight of hand is at the center of the theory. It takes an almost childish leap of faith to assume that the modes of explanation that work for the details of block manipulation will be adequate for understanding conflict, consciousness, genius, and freedom of will.

One cannot dismiss this as an isolated fantasy. Minsky is one of the major figures in artificial intelligence and he is only stating in a simplistic form a view that permeates the field.

In looking at the development of computer technology, one cannot help but be struck by the successes at reducing complex and varied tasks to systematic combinations of elementary operations. Why not, then, make the jump to the mind. If we are no more than protoplasm-based physical symbol systems, the reduction must be possible and only our current lack of knowledge prevents us from explicating it in detail, all the way from BUILDER's clever ploy down to the logical circuitry.

4.3 Knowledge as a commodity

All of the approaches described above depend on interactions among large numbers of individual elements: rules, productions, or agents. No one of these elements can be taken as representing a substantial understandable truth, but this doesn't matter since somehow the conglomeration will come out all right. But how can we have any confidence that it will? The proposed answer is a typical one of our modern society: "More is better!" "Knowledge is power, and more knowledge is more power."

A widely-used expert systems text declares:

> It wasn't until the late 1970s that AI scientists began to realize something quite important: The problem-solving power of a program comes from the knowledge it possesses, not just from the formalisms and inference schemes it employs. The conceptual breakthrough was made and can be quite simply stated. *To make a program intelligent, provide it with lots of high-quality, specific knowledge about some problem area.* [emphasis in the original] (*Waterman, 1986*)

This statement is typical of much writing on expert systems, both in the parochial perspective that inflates homily into "conceptual breakthrough" and in its use of slogans like "high-quality knowledge." Michie (the doyen of artificial intelligence in Britain) predicts:

> [Expert systems] . . . can actually help to codify and improve expert human knowledge, taking what was fragmentary, inconsistent and error-infested and turning it into knowledge that is more precise, reliable and comprehensive. This new process, with its enormous potential for the future, we call "knowledge refining." (*Michie and Johnston, 1984*)

Feigenbaum proclaims:

The miracle product is knowledge, and the Japanese are planning to package and sell it the way other nations package and sell energy, food, or manufactured goods . . . The essence of the computer revolution is that the burden of producing the future knowledge of the world will be transferred from human heads to machine artifacts. (*Feigenbaum and McCorduck, 1983*)

Knowledge is a kind of commodity – to be produced, refined, and packaged. The knowledge engineers are not concerned with the age-old epistemological problems of what constitutes knowledge or understanding. They are hard at work on techniques of "knowledge acquisition" and see it as just a matter of sufficient money and effort:

> We have the opportunity at this moment to do a new version of Diderot's *Encyclopedia*, a gathering up of all knowledge – not just the academic kind, but the informal, experiential, heuristic kind – to be fused, amplified, and distributed, all at orders of magnitude difference in cost, speed, volume, and *usefulness* over what we have now. [emphasis in the original] (*Feigenbaum and McCorduck, 1983*)

Lenat has embarked on this task of "encod[ing] all the world's knowledge down to some level of detail." The plan projects an initial entry of about 400 articles from a desk encyclopedia (leading to 10,000 paragraphs worth of material), followed by hiring a large number of "knowledge enterers" to add "the last 99 percent." There is little concern that foundational problems might get in the way. Lenat *et al.* (1986) asserts that "AI has for many years understood enough about representation and inference to tackle this project, but no one has sat down and done it."

5 The fundamental problems

The optimistic claims for artificial intelligence have far out-stripped the achievements, both in the theoretical enterprise of cognitive modeling and in the practical application of expert systems.

In cognitive modeling we seek to fit a model's performance with measured human behavior but the enterprise is fraught with methodological difficulty, as it straddles the wide chasm between the engineering bravado of computer science and the careful empiricism of experimental psychology. When a computer program duplicates to some degree some carefully restricted aspect of human behavior, what have we learned? It is all too easy to write a program that would produce that particular behavior, and all too hard to build one that covers a sufficiently general range to inspire confidence. As Pylyshyn (an enthusiastic participant in cognitive science) observes:

> Most current computational models of cognition are vastly under-constrained and *ad hoc*; they are contrivances assembled to mimic

arbitrary pieces of behavior, with insufficient concern for explicating the principles in virtue of which such behavior is exhibited and with little regard for a precise understanding. (*Pylyshyn, 1984*)

Newell and his colleagues' painstaking attention to detailed architecture of production systems is an attempt to better constrain the computational model, in hopes that experiments can then test detailed hypotheses. As with much of experimental psychology, a highly artificial experimental situation is required to get results that can be sensibly interpreted at all. Proponents argue that the methods and theoretical foundations that are being applied to micro-behavior will eventually be extended and generalized to cover the full range of cognitive phenomena. As with Minsky, this leap from the micro-structure to the whole human is one of faith.

In the case of expert systems, there is a more immediate concern. Applied AI is widely seen as a means of managing processes that have grown too complex or too rapid for unassisted humans. Major industrial and governmental organizations are mounting serious efforts to build expert systems for tasks such as air traffic control, nuclear power plant operation, and – most distressingly – the control of weapons systems. These projects are justified with claims of generality and flexibility for AI programs. They ignore or downplay the difficulties that will make the programs almost certain to fail in just those cases where their success is most critical.

It is commonplace in the field to describe expert systems as "brittle" – able to operate only within a narrow range of situations. The problem here is not just one of insufficient engineering, but is a direct consequence of the nature of rule-based systems. We will examine three manifestations of the problem: gaps of anticipation; blindness of representation; and restriction of the domain.

5.1 Gaps of anticipation

In creating a program or knowledge base, one takes into account as many factors and connections as feasible. But in any realistically complex domain, this gives at best a spotty coverage. The person designing a system for dealing with acid spills may not consider the possibility of rain leaking into the building, or of a power failure, or that a labeled bottle does not contain what it purports to. A human expert faced with a problem in such a circumstance falls back on common sense and a general background of knowledge.

The hope of patchwork rationalism is that with a sufficiently large body of rules, the thought-through spots will successfully interpolate to the wastelands in between. Having written rule A with one circumstance in mind and rule B with another, the two rules in combination will succeed in yet a third. This strategy is the justification for the claim that AI systems are more flexible than conventional programs. There is a grain of truth in the comparison, but it is deceptive. The program applies the rules blindly with erratic results. In many cases, the price of flexibility (the ability to operate in combinations of contingencies not considered by the programmer) is irreparable and inscrutable failure.

In attempting to overcome this brittleness, expert systems are built with many thousands of rules, trying to cover all of the relevant situations and to provide representations for all potentially relevant aspects of context. One system for medical diagnosis, called CADUCEUS (originally INTER-NIST) has 500 disease profiles, 350 disease variations, several thousand symptoms, and 6,500 rules describing relations among symptoms. After fifteen years of development, the system is still not on the market. According to one report, it gave a correct diagnosis in only 75 per cent of its carefully selected test cases. Nevertheless, Myers, the medical expert who developed it, "believes that the addition of another 50 [diseases] will make the system workable and, more importantly, practical" (Newquist, 1987).

Human experts develop their skills through observing and acting in many thousands of cases. AI researchers argue that this results in their remembering a huge repertoire of specialized "patterns" (complex symbolic rules) that allows them to discriminate situations with expert finesse and to recognize appropriate actions. But it is far from obvious whether the result of experience can be adequately formalized as a repertoire of discrete patterns (see discussion in Dreyfus and Dreyfus, 1986). To say that "all of the world's knowledge" could be explicitly articulated in any symbolic form (computational or not) we must assume the possibility of reducing all forms of tacit knowledge (skills, intuition, and the like) to explicit facts and rules. Heidegger and other phenomenologists have challenged this, and many of the strongest criticisms of artificial intelligence are based on the phenomenological analysis of human understanding as a "readiness-at-hand" of action in the world, rather than as the manipulation of "present-at-hand" representations (see, for example Dreyfus, 1979; Winograd and Flores, 1986).

Be that as it may, it is clear that the corresponding task in building expert systems is extremely difficult, if not theoretically impossible. The knowledge engineer attempts to provide the program with rules that correspond to the expert's experience. The rules are modified through analyzing examples in which the original rules break down. But the patchwork nature of the rules makes this extremely difficult. Failure in a particular case may not be attributable to a particular rule, but rather to a chance combination of rules that are in other circumstances quite useful. The breakdown may not even provide sharp criteria for knowing what to change, as with a chess program that is just failing to come up with good moves. The problem here is not simply one of scale or computational complexity. Computers are perfectly capable of operating on millions of elements. The problem is one of human understanding – the ability of a person to understand how a new situation experienced in the world is related to an existing set of representations, and to possible modifications of those representations.

In trying to remove the potentially unreliable "human element," expert systems conceal it. The power plant will no longer fail because a reactor-operator falls asleep, but because a knowledge engineer didn't think of putting in a rule specifying how to handle a particular failure when the emergency system is undergoing its periodic test, and the backup system is out of order. No amount of refinement and articulation can guarantee the absence of such breakdowns. The hope that a system based on patchwork rationalism will respond "appropriately" in such cases is just that: a hope, and one that can engender dangerous illusions of safety and security.

5.2 The blindness of representation

The second problem lies in the symbol system hypothesis itself. In order to characterize a situation in symbolic form, one uses a system of basic distinctions, or terms. Rules deal with the interrelations among the terms, not with their interpretations in the world.

Consider ordinary words as an analogy. Imagine that a doctor asks a nurse "Is the patient eating?" If they are deciding whether to perform an examination, the request might be paraphrased "Is she eating at this moment?" If the patient is in the hospital for anorexia and the doctor is checking the efficacy of the treatment, it might be more like "Has the patient eaten some minimal amount in the past day?" If the patient has recently undergone surgery, it might mean "Has the patient taken any nutrition by mouth," and so on. In responding, a person interprets the sentence as having relevance in the current situation, and will typically respond appropriately without conscious choosing among meanings.

In order to build a successful symbol system, decontextualized meaning is necessary – terms must be stripped of open-ended ambiguities and shadings. A medical expert system might have a rule of the form: "IF Eating(x) THEN . . .", which is to be applied only if the patient is eating, along with others of the form "IF . . . THEN Eating (x)" which determine when that condition holds. Unless everyone who writes or reads a rule interprets the primitive term "Eating" in the same way, the rules have no consistent interpretation and the results are unpredictable.

In response to this, one can try to refine the vocabulary. "Currently-Dining" and "Taking-Solids" could replace the more generic term, or we could add construal rules, such as "in a context of immediate action, take 'Eating' to mean 'Currently-Dining'." Such approaches work for the cases that programmers anticipate, but of course are subject to the infinite regress of trying to decontextualize context. The new terms or rules themselves depend on interpretation that is not represented in the system.

5.3 Restriction of the domain

A consequence of decontextualized representation is the difficulty of creating AI programs in any but the most carefully restricted domains, where almost all of the knowledge required to perform the task is special to that domain (i.e., little common-sense knowledge is required). One can find specialized tasks for which appropriate limitations can be achieved, but these do not include the majority of work in commerce, medicine, law, or the other professions demanding expertise.

Holt characterized the situation: "A brilliant chess move while the room is filling with smoke because the house is burning down does not show intelligence. If the capacity for brilliant chess moves without regard to life circumstances deserves a name, I would naturally call it 'artificial intelligence.'"[3]

The brilliance of a move is with respect to a well-defined domain: the rules of chess. But acting as an expert doctor, attorney, or engineer takes the other kind of intelligence: knowing what makes sense in a situation. The most successful artificial intelligence programs have operated in the detached puzzle-like domains of board games and technical analysis, not those demanding understanding of human lives, motivations, and social interaction. Attempts to cross into these difficult territories, such as a program said to "understand tales involving friendship and adultery" (see discussion of BORIS program in Winograd and Flores, 1986), proceed by replacing the real situation with a cartoon-like caricature, governed by simplistic rules whose inadequacy is immediately obvious (even to the creators, who argue that they simply need further elaboration).

This reformulation of a domain to a narrower, more precise one can lead to systems that give correct answers to irrelevant problems. This is of concern not only when actions are based directly on the output of the computer system (as in one controlling weapons systems), but also when, for example, medical expert systems are used to evaluate the work of physicians (Athanasiou, 1987). Since the system is based on a reduced representation of the situation, it systematically (if invisibly) values some aspects of care while remaining blind to others. Doctors whose salaries, promotions, or accreditations depend on the review of their actions by such a program will find their practice being subtly shaped to its mold. The attempt to encode "the world's knowledge" inevitably leads to this kind of simplification. Every explicit representation of knowledge bears within it a background of cultural orientation that does not appear as explicit claims, but is manifest in the very terms in which the 'facts' are expressed and in the judgment of what constitutes a fact. An encyclopedia is not a compendium of "refined knowledge," but a statement within a tradition and a culture. By calling an electronic encyclopedia a 'knowledge base' we mystify its source and its grounding in a tradition and background.

6 The bureaucracy of mind

Many observers have noted the natural affinity between computers and bureaucracy. Lee argues that "bureaucracies are the most ubiquitous form of artificial intelligence . . . Just as scientific management found its idealization in automation and programmable production robots, one might consider an artificially intelligent knowledge-based system as the ideal bureaucrat" (Lee, 1985). Lee's stated goal is "improved bureaucratic software engineering," but his analogy suggests more.

Stated simply, *the techniques of artificial intelligence are to the mind what bureaucracy is to human social interaction.*

In today's popular discussion, bureaucracy is seen as an evil – a pathology of large organizations and repressive governments. But in his classic work on bureaucracy, Weber argued its great advantages over earlier, less formalized systems, calling it the "unambiguous yardstick for the modernization of the state." He notes that "bureaucracy has a 'rational' character, with rules, means-ends calculus, and matter-of-factness predominating," (Weber, 1968), and that it succeeds in "eliminating from official business love, hatred, and all purely personal, irrational, and emotional elements which escape calculation" (Weber, 1968).

> The decisive reason for the advance of bureaucratic organization has always been its purely *technical* superiority over any other form of organization. The fully developed bureaucratic apparatus compares with other organizations exactly as does the machine with the non-mechanical modes of production. Precision, speed, unambiguity, knowledge of the files, continuity, discretion, unity, strict subordination, reduction of friction and of material and personal costs – these are raised to the optimum point in the strictly bureaucratic administration. [emphasis in original]   (*Weber, 1968*)

The benefits of bureaucracy follow from the reduction of judgment to the systematic application of explicitly articulated rules. Bureaucracy achieves a predictability and manageability that is missing in earlier forms of organization. There are striking similarities here with the arguments given for the benefits of expert systems, and equally striking analogies with the shortcomings as pointed out, for example, by March and Simon:

> The reduction in personalized relationships, the increased internalization of rules, and the decreased search for alternatives combine to make the behavior of members of the organization highly predictable; i.e., they result in an increase in the *rigidity of behavior* of participants [which] increases the *amount of difficulty with clients* of the organization and complicates the achievement of client satisfaction. [emphasis in original]   (*March and Simon, 1958*)

Given Simon's role in artificial intelligence, it is ironic that he notes these weaknesses of human-embodied rule systems, but sees the behavior of rule-based physical symbol systems as "adaptive to the demands of the environment." Indeed, systems based on symbol manipulation exhibit the rigidities of bureaucracies, and are most problematic in dealing with "client satisfaction" – the mismatch between the decontextualized application of rules and the human interpretation of the symbols that appear in them. Bureaucracy is most successful in a world that is stable and repetitive – where the rules can be followed without interpretive judgments. Expert systems are best in just the same situations. Their successes have been in stable and precise technical areas, where exceptions are not the rule.

Michie's claim that expert systems can encode "the rules of thumb, the hunches, the intuition and capacity for judgement . . ." is wrong in the same way that it is wrong to seek a full account of an organization in its formal rules and procedures. Modern sociologists have gone beyond Weber's analysis, pointing to the informal organization and tacit knowledge that make organizations work effectively. This closely parallels the importance of tacit knowledge in individual expertise. Without it we get rigidity and occasional but irreparable failure.

The depersonalization of knowledge in expert systems also has obvious parallels with bureaucracy. When a person views his or her job as the correct application of a set of rules (whether human-invoked or computer-based), there is a loss of personal responsibility or commitment. The "I just follow the rules" of the bureaucratic clerk has its direct analog in "That's what the knowledge base says." The individual is not committed to appropriate results (as judged in some larger human context), but to faithful application of the procedures. This forgetfulness of individual commitment is perhaps the most subtle and dangerous consequence of patchwork rationality. The person who puts rules into a knowledge base cannot be committed to the consequences of applying them in a situation he or she cannot foresee. The person who applies them cannot be committed to their formulation or to the mechanics by which they produce an answer. The result belongs to no-one. When we speak here of "commitment," we mean something more general than the kind of accountability that is argued in court. There is a deep sense in which every use of language is a reflection of commitment, as we will see in the following section.

7 Alternatives

We began with the question of thinking machines – devices that mechanically reproduce human capacities of thought and language. We have seen how this question has been reformulated in the pursuit of artificial intelligence, to reflect a particular design based on patchwork rationalism. We have argued that the current direction will be inadequate to explain or construct real intelligence.

But, one might ask, does that mean that no machine could exhibit intelligence? Is artificial intelligence inherently impossible, or is it just fiendishly difficult? To answer sensibly we must first ask what we mean by "machine." There is a simple a priori proof that machines can be intelligent if we accept that our own brains are (in Minsky's provocative words) nothing but "meat machines." If we take "machine" to stand for any physically constituted device subject to the causal laws of nature, then the question reduces to one of materialism, and is not to be resolved through computer research. If, on the other hand, we take machine to mean "physical symbol system" then there is ground for a strong skepticism. This skepticism has become visible among practitioners of artificial intelligence as well as the critics.

7.1 Emergent intelligence

The innovative ideas of cybernetics a few decades ago led to two contrasting research programmes. One, which we have examined here, took the course of symbol processing. The other was based on modelling neural activity and led to the work on "perceptrons," a research line that was discounted for many years as fruitless and is now being rehabilitated in "connectionist" theories, based on "massively parallel distributed processing." In this work, each computing element (analogous to a neuron) operates on simple general principles, and intelligence emerges from the evolving patterns of interaction.[4]

Connectionism is one manifestation of what Turkle calls "emergent AI" (Turkle, 1987). The fundamental intuition guiding this work is that cognitive structure in organisms emerges through learning and experience, not through explicit representation and programming. The problems of blindness and domain limitation described above need not apply to a system that has developed through situated experience.

It is not yet clear whether we will see a turn back towards the heritage of cybernetics or simply a "massively parallel" variant of current cognitive theory and symbol processing design. Although the new connectionism may breathe new life into cognitive modeling research, it suffers an uneasy balance between symbolic and physiological description. Its spirit harks back to the cybernetic concern with real biological systems, but the detailed models typically assume a simplistic representational base much closer to traditional artificial intelligence. Connectionism, like its parent cognitive theory, must be placed in the category of brash unproved hypotheses, which have not really begun to deal with the complexities of mind, and whose current explanatory power is extremely limited.

In one of the earliest critiques of artificial intelligence, Dreyfus compared it to alchemy (Dreyfus, 1965). Seekers after the glitter of intelligence are misguided in trying to cast it from the base metal of computing. There is an amusing epilogue to this analogy: in fact, the alchemists were right. Lead can be converted into gold by a particle accelerator hurling appropriate beams at lead targets. The AI visionaries may be right in the same way, and they are likely to be wrong in the same way. There is no reason but hubris to believe that we are any closer to understanding intelligence than the alchemists were to the secrets of nuclear physics. The ability to create a glistening simulacrum should not fool us either into thinking the rest is "just a matter of encoding a sufficient part of the world's knowledge" or into a quest for the philosopher's stone of "massively parallel processing."

7.2 Hermeneutic constructivism

Discussions of the problems and dangers of computers often leave the impression that on the whole we would be better-off if we could return to the pre-computer era. In a similar vein one might decry the advent of written language, which created many new problems. For example, Weber attributes the emergence of bureaucracy to the spread of writing and literacy, which made it possible to create and maintain systems of rules. Indeed, the written word made bureaucracy possible, but that is far from a full account of its relevance to human society.

The computer is a physical embodiment of the symbolic calculations envisaged by Hobbes and Leibniz. As such, it is not really a thinking machine, but a language machine. The very notion of "symbol system" is inherently linguistic and what we duplicate in our programs with their rules and propositions is really a form of verbal argument, not the workings of mind. It is tempting – but ultimately misleading – to project the image of rational discourse (and its reflection in conscious introspection) onto the design of embodied intelligence. In taking inner discourse as a model for the activity of Minsky's tiny agents, or of productions that determine what token to process next, artificial intelligence has operated with the faith that mind is linguistic down to the microscopic level.

But the utility of the technology need not depend on this faith. The computer, like writing, is fundamentally a communication medium – one that is unique in its ability to perform complex manipulations on the linguistic objects it stores and transmits. We can reinterpret the technology of artificial intelligence in a new background, with new consequences. In doing so we draw on an alternative philosophical grounding, which I will call hermeneutic constructivism.

We begin with some fundamental questions about what language is and how it works. In this we draw on work in hermeneutics (the study of interpretation) and phenomenology, as developed by Heidegger and Gadamer, along with the concepts of language action developed from the later works of Wittgenstein and through the speech act philosophy of Austin, Searle, and Habermas (see chapter 5 of Winograd and Flores, 1986).

Two guiding principles emerge:

1 People create their world through language.
2 Language is always interpreted in a tacitly understood background.

Austin pointed out that "performative" sentences do not convey information about the world, but act to change that world. "You're hired," when uttered in appropriate conditions, creates – not describes – a situation of employment. Searle applied this insight to mundane language actions such as asking questions and agreeing to do something. Habermas extended it further, showing how sentences we would naively consider statements of fact have force by virtue of an act of commitment by the speaker.

> The essential presupposition for the success of [a language] act consists in the speaker's entering into a specific engagement, so that the hearer can rely on him. An utterance can count as a promise, assertion, request, question, or avowal, if and only if the speaker makes an offer that he is ready to make good insofar as it is accepted by the hearer. The speaker must engage himself, that is, indicate that in certain situations he will draw certain consequences for action. (*Habermas, 1979*)

Descartes' descendants in the rationalistic tradition take the language of mathematics as their ideal. Terms are either primitive or can be fully defined; the grammar is unambiguous; and precise truth conditions can be established through formal techniques. But even in apparently simple and straightforward situations, human language is metaphorical, ambiguous and undefinable. What we can take as fundamental is the engagement – the commitment to make good what cannot be fully made precise.

This grounding is especially evident for statements of the kind that Roszak characterizes as "ideas rather than information" (Roszak, 1986). "All men are created equal" cannot be judged as a true or false description of the objective world. Its force resides in the commitments it carries for further characterization and further action. But it is critical to recognize that this social grounding of language applies equally to the mundane statements of everyday life. "The patient is eating" cannot be held up to any specific set of truth conditions across situations in which it may be uttered. The speaker is not reporting an objectively delineated state of affairs, but indicating the "engagement" to enter sincerely into a dialogue of articulation of the relevant background.

This unavoidable dependence of interpretation on unspoken background is the fundamental insight of the hermeneutic phenomenologists, such as Gadamer. It applies not just to ordinary language, but to every symbolic representation as well. We all recognize that in "reducing things to numbers" we lose the potential for interpretation in a background. But this is equally true of "reducing them to symbol structures."

Whenever a computer program is intended to guide or take action in a human domain, it inevitably imports basic values and assumptions. The basic nature of patchwork rationalism obscures the underlying constitutive "ideas" with a mosaic of fragmentary bits of "information." The social and political agenda concealed behind these patches of decontextualized and depersonalized belief is dangerous in its invisibility.

7.3 Language machines

Symbol structures are ultimately created by people and interpreted by people. The computer, as a language machine, manipulates symbols without respect to their interpretation. To the extent that relations among the meanings can be adequately reflected in precise rules, the computational manipulations make sense. The error is in assuming that these manipulations capture, rather than augment or reify parts of the meaning. If an expert system prints out "Give the patient penicillin" or "Fire the missiles now," room for interpretation is limited and meaning is lost. But instead we can see the computer as a way of organizing, searching, and manipulating texts that are created by people, in a context, and ultimately intended for human interpretation.

We are already beginning to see a movement away from the early vision of computers replacing human experts. For example, the medical diagnostic system described above is being converted from "Internist" (a doctor specializing in internal medicine) to an "advisory system" called "QMR" (for "Quick Medical Reference") (Newquist, 1987). The rules can be thought of as constituting an automated textbook, which can access and logically combine entries that are relevant to a particular case. The goal is to suggest and justify possibilities a doctor might not otherwise have considered. The program need not respond with an evaluation or plan for action, but is successful through providing relevant material for interpretation by an expert. Similarly, in areas of real-time control (like a nuclear power plant), an advisory system can monitor conditions and provide warnings, reports, and summaries for human review. In a similar vein, an interactive computer-based encyclopedia need not cover all of human knowledge or provide general purpose deduction in order to take advantage of the obvious computer capacities of speed, volume, and sophisticated inferential indexing.

Another opportunity for design is in the regularities of the structure of language use. As a simple example, a request is normally followed in coherent conversation by an acceptance, a rejection, or a request to modify the conditions. These in turn are followed by other language acts in a logic of "conversation for action" oriented towards completion (a state in which neither party is awaiting further action by the other). The theory of such conversations has been developed as the basis for a computer program called The Coordinator which is used for facilitating and organizing computer-message conversations in an organization (see Flores, 1982; Winograd and Flores, 1986; Winograd, 1987/88). It emphasizes the role of commitment by the speaker in each speech act and provides the basis for timely and effective action.

Howard has studied the use of computer systems by professionals evaluating loan applications for the World Bank. He argues that their use of computers while on field missions increases the "transparency" of their decision-making process, hence increasing their accountability and enhancing opportunities for meaningful negotiation. The computer serves as a medium of discourse in which different commitments and their consequences can be jointly explored.

> As a result, the dialogue between them [the bankers and their clients] suddenly becomes less about the final results – "the numbers" – and more about the assumptions behind the numbers, the criteria on which decisions are themselves based . . .[quoting a bank professional] "Instead of just saying, 'I don't believe you, my opinion is X,' we explore it. We say, 'let's see what the consequences of that are.' And, sometimes, we end up changing our assumptions." (*Howard, 1986*)

Current expert systems methodologies are not well suited to this kind of dialogue. They separate the construction of the knowledge base from the use of its "expertise."

The experts (with the help of knowledge engineers) enter the knowledge in the laboratory, and the users apply it in the field to get results. But we might instead use the computer to support the discourse that creates the reality – as a tool for the cooperative articulation of the characterizations and rules that will be applied. Rather than seeing the computer as working with objectified refined knowledge, it can serve as a way of keeping track of how the representations emerge from interpretations: who created them in what context, and where to look for clarification.

8 Conclusion

The question of our title demands interpretation in a context. As developed in the paper, it might be formulated more precisely "Are we machines of the kind that researchers are building as 'thinking machines'?" In asking this kind of question we engage in a kind of projection – understanding humanity by projecting an image of ourself onto the machine and the image of the machine back onto ourselves. In the tradition of artificial intelligence, we project an image of our language activity onto the symbolic manipulations of the machine, then project that back onto the full human mind.

But these projections are like the geometric projection of a three-dimensional world onto a two-dimensional plane. We systematically eliminate dimensions, thereby both simplifying and distorting. The particular dimensions we eliminate or preserve in this exercise are not idiosyncratic accidents. They reflect a philosophy that precedes them and which they serve to amplify and extend. In projecting language as a rule-governed manipulation of symbols, we all too easily dismiss the concerns of human meaning that make up the humanities, and indeed of any socially grounded understanding of human language and action. In projecting language back as the model for thought, we lose sight of the tacit embodied understanding that undergirds our intelligence. Through a broader understanding, we can recapture our view of these lost dimensions, and in the process better understand both ourselves and our machines.

Notes

I thank Gary Chapman, Brad Hartfield and especially Carol Winograd for insightful critical readings of early drafts. I am also grateful for my continuing conversation with Fernando Flores, in which my understanding has been generated.

1 As described by Russell (1952) in *A History of Western Philosophy*.
2 One large-scale and quite controversial example was the Massachusetts Institute of Technology/Club of Rome simulation of the world social and economic future (The Limits of Growth).
3 Remarks made by Anatol Holt at the Advanced Research Project's Agency Principal Investigator's Conference, Los Angeles, February 6–8, 1974 (unpublished manuscript).
4 For a historical account and analysis of the current debates, see H. Dreyfus and S. Dreyfus, *Making a Mind vs. Modeling the Brain* (1988). For a technical view, see Rumelhart and McClelland (1986a), *Parallel Distributed Processing*. Maturana and Varela, in *The Tree of Knowledge* (1987), offer a broad philosophy of cognition on this base.

Evolution, error, and intentionality

Daniel C. Dennett

The foundational problem of the semantics of mental representation has been perhaps the primary topic of philosophical research in cognitive science in recent years, but progress has been negligible, largely because the philosophers have failed to acknowledge a major but entirely tacit difference of outlook that separates them into two schools of thought. My task here is to bring this central issue into the light.

The Great Divide I want to display resists a simple, straightforward formulation, not surprisingly, but we can locate it by retracing the steps of my exploration, which began with a discovery about some theorists' attitudes towards the interpretation of artifacts. The scales fell from my eyes during a discussion with Jerry Fodor and some other philosophers about a draft of a chapter of Fodor's *Psychosemantics* (Fodor, 1987). The chapter in question, "Meaning and the World Order," concerns Fred Dretske's attempts (1981, especially chapter 8; 1985; 1986) to solve the problem of misrepresentation. As an aid to understanding the issue, I had proposed to Fodor and the other participants in the discussion that we first discuss a dead simple case of misrepresentation: a coin-slot testing apparatus on a vending machine accepting a slug. "That sort of case is irrelevant," Fodor retorted instantly, "because after all, John Searle is right about one thing; he's right about artifacts like that. They don't have any intrinsic or original intentionality – only derived intentionality."

The doctrine of original intentionality is the claim that whereas some of our artifacts may have intentionality derived from us, we have original (or intrinsic) intentionality, utterly underived. Aristotle said that God is the Unmoved Mover, and this doctrine announces that we are Unmeant Meaners. I have never believed in it, and have often argued against it. As Searle has noted, "Dennett ... believes that *nothing* literally has any *intrinsic intentional* mental states" (1982, p.57), and in the long-running debate between us (Searle, 1980, 1982, 1984a, 1984b; Dennett, 1980; Hofstadter and Dennett, 1981; Dennett, 1982, 1984b) I had assumed that Fodor was on my side on this particular point.

Did Fodor really believe that Searle is right about this? He said so.

190

Dretske (1985) goes further, citing Searle's attack on artificial intelligence (Searle, 1980) with approval, and drawing a sharp contrast between people and computers:

> I lack specialized skills, knowledge and understanding, but nothing that is essential to membership in the society of rational agents. With machines, though, and this includes the most sophisticated modern computers, it is different. They do lack something that is essential. (*p.23*)

Others who have recently struggled with the problem of misrepresentation or error also seemed to me to fall on Searle's side of the fence: in particular, Tyler Burge (1986) and Saul Kripke (1982, especially pp. 34ff.). In fact, as we shall see, the problem of error impales all and only those who believe in original or intrinsic intentionality.

Are *original intentionality* and *intrinsic intentionality* the same thing? We will have to approach this question indirectly, by pursuing various attempts to draw a sharp distinction between the way our minds (or mental states) have meaning, and the way other things do. We can begin with a familiar and intuitive distinction discussed by Haugeland. Our artifacts

> only have meaning because we give it to them; their intentionality, like that of smoke signals and writing, is essentially borrowed, hence *derivative*. To put it bluntly: computers themselves don't mean anything by their tokens (any more than books do) – they only mean what we say they do. Genuine understanding, on the other hand, is intentional "in its own right" and not derivatively from something else. (*1981, pp. 32–33*)

Consider an encyclopedia. It has derived intentionality. It contains information about thousands of things in the world, but only insofar as it is a device designed and intended for our use. Suppose we "automate" our encyclopedia, putting all its data into a computer, and turning its index into the basis for an elaborate question-answering system. No longer do we have to look up material in the volumes; we simply type in questions and receive answers. It might seem to naïve users as if they were communicating with another person, another entity endowed with original intentionality, but we would know better. A question-answering system is still just a tool, and whatever meaning or aboutness we vest in it is just a byproduct of our practices in using the device to serve our own goals. It has no goals of its own, except for the artificial and derived goal of "understanding" and "answering" our questions correctly.

But suppose we endow our computer with somewhat more autonomous, somewhat less slavish goals. For instance, a chess playing computer has the (artificial, derived) goal of defeating its human opponent, of concealing what it "knows" from us, of tricking us perhaps. But still, surely, it is only our tool or toy, and although many of its internal states have a sort of aboutness or intentionality – e.g., there are states that represent (and hence are about) the current board positions, and processes that investigate (and hence are about) various possible continuations of the game – this is just derived intentionality, not original intentionality.

This persuasive theme (it is not really an argument) has convinced more than a few thinkers that no artifact could have the sort of intentionality we have. No computer program, no robot we might design and build, no matter how strong the illusion we may create that it has become a genuine agent, could ever be a truly autonomous thinker with the same sort of original intentionality we enjoy. For the time being, let us suppose that this is the doctrine of original intentionality, and see where it leads.

The case of the wandering two-bitser

I will now press my vending machine example – the example Fodor insisted was irrelevant – explicitly, for it makes vivid exactly the points of disagreement, and casts several recent controversies (about "individualistic psychology" and "narrow content," about error, about function) in a useful light. Consider a standard soft-drink vending machine, designed and built in the United States, and equipped with a transducer device for accepting and rejecting US quarters.[1]

Let's call such a device a two-bitser. Normally, when a quarter is inserted into a two-bitser, the two-bitser goes into a state, call it Q, which "means" (note the scare-quotes) "I perceive/accept a genuine US quarter now." Such two-bitsers are quite clever and sophisticated, but hardly foolproof. They do "make mistakes" (more scare-quotes). That is, unmetaphorically, sometimes they go into state Q when a slug or other foreign object is inserted in them, and sometimes they reject perfectly legal quarters – they fail to go into state Q when they are *supposed to*. No doubt there are detectable patterns in the cases of "misperception." No doubt at least some of the cases of "misidentification" could be predicted by someone with enough knowledge of the relevant laws of physics and design parameters of the two-bitser's transducing machinery, so that it would be just as much a matter of physical law that objects of kind K would put the device into state Q as that quarters would. Objects of kind K would be good "slugs" – reliably "fooling" the transducer.

If objects of kind K became more common in the two-bitser's normal environment, we could expect the owners and designers of two-bitsers to develop more advanced and sensitive transducers that would reliably discriminate between genuine US quarters and slugs of kind K. Of course trickier counterfeits might then make their appearance, requiring further advances in the detecting transducers, and at some point such escalation of engineering would reach diminishing returns, for there is no such thing as a *foolproof* mechanism. In the meantime, the engineers and users are wise to make do with standard, rudimentary two-bitsers, since it is not cost-effective to protect oneself against negligible abuses.

The only thing that makes the device a quarter-detector rather than a slug-detector or a quarter-*or*-slug-detector is the shared intention of the device's designers, builders, owners, users. It is only in the environment or context of those users and their intentions that we can single out some of the occasions of state Q as "veridical" and others as "mistaken." It is only relative to that context of intentions that we could justify calling the device a two-bitser in the first place.

I take it that so far I have Fodor, Searle, Dretske, Burge, Kripke, *et al.* nodding their agreement: that's just how it is with such artifacts; this is a textbook case of derived intentionality, laid bare. And so of course it embarrasses no one to admit that a particular two-bitser, straight from the American factory and with "Model A Two-Bitser" stamped right on it, might be installed on a Panamanian soft-drink machine, where it proceeded to earn its keep as an accepter and rejecter of quarter-balboas, legal tender in Panama, and easily distinguished from US quarters by the design and writing stamped on them, but not by their weight, thickness, diameter, or material composition. (I'm not making this up. I have it on excellent authority – Albert Erler of the Flying Eagle Shoppe, Rare Coins – that Panamanian quarter-balboas minted between 1966 and 1984 are indistinguishable from US quarters by standard vending machines. Small wonder, since they are struck from US quarter stock in American mints. And – to satisfy the curious, although it is strictly irrelevant to the example – the current official exchange rate for the quarter-balboa is indeed $.25!)

Such a two-bitser, whisked off to Panama (the poor man's Twin-Earth), would still normally go into a certain physical state – the state with the physical features by which we used to identify state Q – whenever a US quarter or an object of kind K or a Panamanian quarter-balboa is inserted in it, but now a different set of such occasions count as the mistakes. In the new environment, US quarters count as slugs, as inducers of error, misperception, misrepresentation, just as much as objects of kind K do. After all, back in the US a Panamanian quarter-balboa is a kind of slug.

Once our two-bitser is resident in Panama, should we say that the state we used to call Q still occurs? The physical state in which the device "accepts" coins still occurs, but should we now say that we should identify it as "realizing" a new state, QB, instead? Well, there is considerable freedom – not to say boredom – about what we should say, since after all a two-bitser is just an artifact, and talking about its perceptions and misperceptions, its veridical and non-veridical states – its intentionality, in short – is "just metaphor." The two-bitser's internal state, call it what you like, doesn't *really* (originally, intrinsically) mean either "US quarter here now" or "Panamanian quarter-balboa here now." It doesn't *really* mean anything. So Fodor, Searle, Dretske, Burge, and Kripke (*inter alia*) would insist.

The two-bitser was originally designed to be a detector of US quarters. That was its "proper function" (Millikan, 1984), and, quite literally, its *raison d'être*. No one would have bothered bringing it into existence had not this purpose occurred to them. And given that this historical fact about its origin licences a certain way of speaking, such a device may be primarily or originally characterized as a two-bitser, a thing whose function is to detect quarters, so that *relative to that function* we can identify both its veridical states and its errors.

We can assure ourselves that nothing *intrinsic* about the two-bitser considered narrowly all by itself and independently of its prior history would distinguish it from a genuine q-balber, made to order on commission from the Panamanian government. Still, given its ancestry, is there not a problem about its function, its purpose, its meaning, on this first occasion when it goes into the state we are tempted to call Q? Is this a case of going into state Q (meaning "US quarter here now") or state QB (meaning "Panamanian quarter-balboa here now")? I would say, along with Millikan (1984), that whether its Panamanian début counts as going into state Q or state QB depends on whether, in its new niche, it was *selected for* its capacity to detect quarter-balboas – literally selected, e.g., by the holder of the Panamanian Pepsi-Cola franchise. If it was so selected, then even though its new proprietors might have forgotten to reset its counter, its first "perceptual" act would count as the correct identification of a quarter-balboa, for that is what it would *now* be *for*. (It would have acquired quarter-balboa detection as its proper function.) If, on the other hand, the two-bitser was sent to Panama by mistake, or if it arrived by sheer co-incidence, its debut would mean nothing, though its utility might soon – immediately – be recognized and esteemed by the relevant authorities (those who could press it into service in a new role), and thereupon its *subsequent* states would count as tokens of QB.

Presumably Fodor *et al.* would be content to let me say this, since, after all, the two-bitser is just an artifact. It has no intrinsic, original intention-ality, so there is no "deeper" fact of the matter we might try to uncover. This is just a pragmatic matter of how best to talk, when talking metaphor-ically and anthropomorphically about the states of the device.

But we part company when I claim to apply precisely the same morals, the same pragmatic rules of interpretation, to the human case. In the case of human beings (at least), Fodor and company are sure that such *deeper facts* do exist – even if we cannot always find them. That is, they suppose that, independently of the power of any observer or interpreter to discover it, there is always a fact of the matter about what a person (or a person's mental state) *really means*. Now we might call their shared belief a belief in *intrinsic* intentionality, or perhaps even *objective* or *real* intentionality. There are differences among them about how to characterize, and name, this property of human minds, which I will continue to call *original intentionality*, but they all agree that minds are unlike the two-bitser in this regard, and this is what I now take to be the most fundamental point of disagreement between Fodor and me, between Searle and me, between Dretske and me, between Burge and me, etc. Once it was out in the open, many things that had been puzzling me fell into place. At last I understood (and will shortly explain) why Fodor dislikes evolutionary hypotheses almost as much as he dislikes artificial intelligence (see, e.g. "Tom Swift and his Procedural Grand-mother" in Fodor, 1981 and the last chapter of Fodor 1983b); why Dretske must go to such desperate lengths to give an account of error; why Burge's "anti-individualism" and Kripke's ruminations on rule-following, which strike some philosophers as deep and disturbing challenges to their com-placency, have always struck me as great labors wasted in trying to break down an unlocked door.

I part company with these others, because although they might agree with me (and Millikan) about what one should say in the case of the transported two-bitser, they say that we human beings are not just fancier, more sophisticated two-bitsers. When we say that we go into the state of believing that we are perceiving a US quarter (or some genuine water as opposed to XYZ, or a genuine twinge of arthritis) this is no metaphor, no mere manner of speaking. The following parallel example will sharpen the disagreement.

Suppose some human being, Jones, looks out the window and thereupon goes into the state of thinking he sees a horse. There may or may not be a horse out there for him to see, but the fact that he is in the mental state of thinking he sees a horse is not just a matter of interpretation (these others say). Suppose the planet Twin-Earth were just like Earth, save for having schmorses where we have horses. (Schmorses look for all the world like horses, and are well-nigh indistinguishable from horses by all but trained biologists with special apparatus, but they aren't horses, any more than dolphins are fish.) If we whisk Jones off to Twin-Earth, land of the schmorses, and confront him in the relevant way with a schmorse, then either he really is, still, provoked into the state of believing he sees a horse (a mistaken, non-veridical belief) or he is provoked by that schmorse into believing, for the first time (and veridically), that he is seeing a schmorse. (For the sake of the example, let us suppose that Twin-Earthians call schmorses, *horses* (*chevaux*, *Pferde*, etc.) so that what Jones or a native Twin-Earthian *says to himself* – or others – counts for nothing.) However hard it may be to determine exactly which state he is in, he is really in one or the other (or perhaps he really is in neither, so violently have we assaulted his cognitive system). Anyone who finds this intuition irresistible believes in original intentionality, and has some distinguished company: Fodor, Searle, Dretske, Burge, and Kripke, but also Chisholm and Sellars, 1956; Chisholm, 1957; Nagel, 1986; and Popper and Eccles, 1977). Anyone who finds this intuition dubious if not downright dismissible can join me, the Churchlands, Davidson, Haugeland, Millikan, Rorty, Stalnaker, and our distinguished predecessor, Quine, in the other corner (along with Hof-stadter, Minsky and almost everyone else in AI).

There, then, is a fairly major disagreement. Who is right? I cannot hope to refute the opposing tradition in the short compass of a chapter, but I will provide two different persuasions on behalf of my side: I will show what perplexities Fodor, Dretske, *et al.* entangle themselves in by clinging to their intuition, and I will provide a little thought experiment to motivate, if not substantiate, my rival view. First the thought experiment.

Designing a robot

Suppose you decided, for whatever reasons, that you wanted to experience life in the twenty-fifth century, and suppose that the only known way of keeping your body alive that long required it to be placed in a hibernation device of sorts, where it would rest, slowed down and comatose, for as long as you liked. You could arrange to climb into the support capsule, be put to sleep, and then automatically be awakened and released in 2401. This is a time-honored science fiction theme, of course.

Designing the capsule itself is not your only engineering problem, for the capsule must be protected and supplied with the requisite energy (for refrigeration or whatever) for over 400 years. You will not be able to count on your children and grandchildren for this stewardship, of course, for they will be long dead before the year 2401, and you cannot presume that your more distant descendants, if any, will take a lively interest in your well-being. So you must design a supersystem to protect your capsule, and to provide the energy it needs for 400 years.

Here there are two basic strategies you might follow. On one, you should find the ideal location, as best you can foresee, for a fixed installation that will be well supplied with water, sunlight, and whatever else your capsule (and the supersystem itself) will need for the duration. The main drawback to such an installation or "plant" is that it cannot be moved if harm comes its way – if, say, someone decides to build a freeway right where it is located. The second alternative is much more sophisticated, but avoids this drawback: design a mobile facility to house your capsule, and the requisite early-warning devices so that it can move out of harm's way, and seek out new energy sources as it needs them. In short, build a giant robot and install the capsule (with you inside) in it.

These two basic strategies are obviously copied from nature: they correspond roughly to the division between plants and animals. Since the latter, more sophisticated strategy better fits my purposes, we shall suppose that you decide to build a robot to house your capsule. You should try to design it so that above all else it "chooses" actions designed to further your best interests, of course. "Bad" moves and "wrong" turns are those that will tend to incapacitate it for the role of protecting you until 2401 – which is its sole *raison d'être*. This is clearly a profoundly difficult engineering problem, calling for the highest level of expertise in designing a "vision" system to guide its locomotion, and other "sensory" and locomotory systems. And since you will be comatose throughout and thus cannot stay awake to guide and plan its strategies, you will have to design it to generate its own plans in response to changing circumstances. It must "know" how to "seek out" and "recognize" and then exploit energy sources, how to move to safer territory, how to "anticipate" and then avoid dangers. With so much to be done, and done fast, you had best rely whenever you can on economies: give your robot no more discriminatory prowess than it will probably need in order to distinguish what needs distinguishing in its world.

Your task will be made much more difficult by the fact that you cannot count on your robot being the only such robot around with such a mission. If your whim catches on, your robot may find itself competing with others (and with your human descendants) for limited supplies of energy, fresh water, lubricants, and the like. It would no doubt be wise to design it with enough sophistication in its control system to permit it to calculate the benefits and risks of cooperating with other robots, or of forming alliances for mutual benefit. (Any such calculation must be a "quick and dirty" approximation, arbitrarily truncated. See Dennett, 1987.)

The result of this design project would be a robot capable of exhibiting self-control, since you must cede fine-grained real-time control to your artifact once you put yourself to sleep). (For more on control and self-control, see Dennett, 1984a and 1987.) As such it will be capable of deriving its own subsidiary goals from its assessment of its current state and the import of that state for its ultimate goal (which is to preserve you). These secondary goals may take it far afield on century-long projects, some of which may be ill-advised, in spite of your best efforts. Your robot may embark on actions antithetical to your purposes, even suicidal, having been convinced by another robot, perhaps, to subordinate its own life mission to some other.

But still, according to Fodor *et al.*, this robot would have no original intentionality at all, but only the intentionality it derives from its artifactual role as your protector. Its simulacrum of mental states would be just that – not *real* deciding and seeing and wondering and planning, but only *as if* deciding and seeing and wondering and planning.

We should pause, for a moment, to make sure we understand what this claim encompasses. The imagined robot is certainly vastly more sophisticated than the humble two-bitser, and perhaps along the path to greater sophistication we have smuggled in some crucial new capacity that would vouchsafe the robot our kind of original intentionality. Note, for instance, that our imagined robot, to which we have granted the power to "plan" new courses of actions, to "learn" from past errors, to form allegiances, and to "communicate" with its competitors, would probably perform very creditably in any Turing Test to which we subjected it. Moreover, in order to do all this "planning" and "learning" and "communicating" it will almost certainly have to be provided with control structures that are rich in self-reflective, self-monitoring power, so that it will have human-like access to its own internal states, and be capable of reporting, avowing, and commenting upon what it "takes" to be the import of its own internal states. It will have "opinions" about what those states mean, and we should no doubt take those opinions seriously as very good evidence – probably the best evidence we can easily get – about what those states "mean" *metaphorically speaking* (remember: it's only an artifact). The two-bitser was given no such capacity to sway our interpretive judgments by issuing apparently confident "avowals."

There are several ways one might respond to this thought experiment, and we will explore the most promising in due course, but first I want to draw out the most striking implication of standing firm with our first intuition: no artifact, no matter how much AI wizardry is designed into it, has anything but derived intentionality. If we cling to this view, the conclusion forced upon us is that our own intentionality is exactly like that of the robot, for the science fiction tale I have told is not new; it is just a variation on Dawkins' (1976) vision of us (and all other biological species) as "survival machines" designed to prolong the futures of our selfish genes. We are artifacts, in effect, designed over the aeons as survival machines for genes that cannot act swiftly and informedly in their own interests. Our interests as we conceive them and the interests of our genes may well diverge – even though were it not for our genes' interests, we would not exist: their preservation is our original *raison d'être*, even if we can learn to ignore that goal and devise our own *summum bonum*, thanks to the intelligence our genes have installed in us. So our intentionality is derived from the intentionality of our "selfish" genes! They are the Unmeant Meaners, not us!

Reading Mother Nature's mind

This vision of things, while it provides a satisfying answer to the question of whence came our own intentionality, does seem to leave us with an embarrassment, for it derives our own intentionality from entities – genes – whose intentionality is surely a paradigm case of mere *as if* intentionality. How could the literal depend on the metaphorical? Moreover, there is surely this much disanalogy between my science-fiction tale and Dawkins' story: in my tale I supposed that there was conscious, deliberate, foresighted engineering involved in the creation of the robot, whereas even if we are, as Dawkins says, the product of a design process that has our genes as the primary beneficiary, that is a design process that utterly lacks a conscious, deliberate, foresighted engineer.

The chief beauty of the theory of natural selection is that it shows us how to eliminate this intelligent Artificer from our account of origins. And yet the process of natural selection is responsible for designs of great cunning. It is a bit outrageous to conceive of genes as *clever* designers; genes themselves could not be more stupid; *they* cannot reason or represent or figure out anything. They do not do the designing themselves; they are merely the beneficiaries of the design process. But then who or what does the designing? Mother Nature, of course, or more literally, the long slow process of evolution by natural selection.

To me the most fascinating property of the process of evolution is its uncanny capacity to mirror *some* properties of the human mind (the intelligent Artificer) while being bereft of others. While it can never be stressed enough that natural selection operates with no foresight and no purpose, we should not lose sight of the fact that the process of natural selection has proven itself to be exquisitely sensitive to rationales, making myriads of discriminating "choices," and "recognizing" and "appreciating" many subtle relationships. To put it even more provocatively, when natural selection selects, it can "choose" a particular design *for one reason rather than another* – without ever consciously (or unconsciously!) – "representing" either the choice or the reasons. (Hearts were chosen for their excellence as blood circulators, not for the captivating rhythm of their beating – though that *might* have been the reason something was "chosen" by natural selection.)

There is, I take it, *no representation at all* in the process of natural selection. And yet it certainly seems that we can give principled explanations of evolved design features that invoke, in effect, "what Mother Nature had in mind" when that feature was designed.[2]

Just as the Panamanian Pepsi-Cola franchise-holder can select the two-bitser *for* its talent at recognizing quarter-balboas, can adopt it *as* a quarter-balboa-detector, so evolution can select an organ *for* its capacity to oxygenate blood, can establish it as a lung. And it is only relative to just such design "choices" or evolution-"endorsed" purposes – *raisons d'être* – that we can identify behaviors, actions, perceptions, beliefs, or any of the other categories of folk psychology. (See Millikan, 1984, 1986, for a forceful expression of this view.)

The idea that we are artifacts designed by natural selection is both compelling and – today – familiar; some would go so far as to say that it is quite beyond serious controversy. Why, then, is it resisted not just by Creationists, but also (rather subliminally) by the likes of Fodor, Searle, Dretske, Burge and Kripke? My hunch is because it has two rather unobvious implications that some find terribly unpalatable. First, if we are (just) artifacts, then what our innermost thoughts mean – and whether they mean anything at all – is something about which we, the very thinkers of those thoughts, have no special authority. The two-bitser turns into a q-balber without ever changing its inner nature; the state that used to mean one thing now means another. The same thing could in principle happen to us, if we are just artifacts, if our own intentionality is thus not original but derived. Those – such as Dretske and Burge – who have already renounced this traditional doctrine of privileged access can shrug off, or even welcome, that implication; it is the second implication that they resist: if we are such artifacts, not only have we no guaranteed privileged access to the deeper facts that fix the meanings of our thoughts, but *there are no such deeper facts*. Sometimes, functional interpretation is obvious, but when it is not, when we go to read Mother Nature's mind, there is no text to be interpreted. When "the fact of the matter" about proper function is controversial – when more than one interpretation is well supported – there is no fact of the matter.

The tactic of treating evolution itself from the intentional stance needs further discussion and defense, but I want to approach the task indirectly. The issues will come into better focus, I think, if first we diagnose the resistance to this tactic – and its Siamese twin, the tactic of treating ourselves as artifacts – in recent work in philosophy of mind and language.

Error, disjunction, and inflated interpretion

Dretske's attempt (1981, 1985, 1986) to deal with these issues invokes a distinction between what he calls *natural meaning* and *functional meaning*. Natural meaning (*meaning$_n$*) is defined in such a way as to rule out misrepresentation; what a particular ringing of the doorbell means$_n$ depends on the integrity of the circuit that causes the ringing. "When there is a short-circuit, the ring of the doorbell (regardless of what it was designed to indicate, regardless of what it normally indicates) does not indicate that the door-button is being depressed." "This is what is it *supposed* to mean-ing$_n$, what it was *designed* to meaning$_n$, what (perhaps) tokens of that type *normally* meaning$_n$, but not what it *does* meaning$_n$." (1986, p. 21)

It then falls to Dretske to define *functional meaning*, what it is for something to *meaning$_f$* that such-and-such, in such a way as to explain how a sign or state or event in some system can, on occasion, misrepresent something or "say" something false. But "if these functions are (what I shall call) *assigned* functions, then meaning$_f$ is tainted with the purposes, intentions and beliefs of those who assign the function from which meaning$_f$ derives its misrepresentational powers." (p. 22) Clearly, the meaning of the two-bitser's acceptance state Q is just such an assigned functional meaning, and Dretske would say of it: "That is the function we assign it, the reason it was built and the explanation for why it was built the way it was. Had our purposes been otherwise, it might have meant$_f$ something else." (p. 23)

Since merely *assigned* functional meaning is "tainted," Dretske must seek a further distinction. What he must characterize is the *natural* functions of the counterpart states of organisms, "functions a thing has which are independent of *our* interpretive intentions and purposes" (p. 25) so that he can then define natural functional meaning in terms of those functions.

... we are looking for what a sign is *supposed* to mean$_n$ where the "supposed to" is cashed out in terms of the function of that sign (or sign system) in the organism's own cognitive economy. (*p. 25*)

The obvious way to go, as we saw in the last section, is to substitute for our interpretive intentions and purposes the intentions and purposes of the organism's designer, Mother Nature – the process of natural selection – and ask ourselves what, in *that* scheme, any particular type of signal or state is designed to signal, supposed to mean. Just as we would ultimately appeal to the engineers' rationales when deciding on the best account of representation and misrepresentation in our imagined survival machine robot, so we can appeal to the discernible design rationales of natural selection in assigning content, and hence the power of *mis*representation, to event types in natural artifacts – organisms, ourselves included.

But although Dretske pays homage to those who have pursued that evolutionary path, and warily follows it some distance himself, he sees a problem. The problem is none other than the biological version of our question about what principled way there is to tell whether the state of the two-bitser (in some particular environment) means "quarter here now" or "quarter-balboa here now" or "thing of kind F or kind G or kind K here now." We must find an interpretation principle that assigns content, Dretske says, "without doing so by artificially *inflating* the natural functions of these systems" – while at the same time avoiding the too-deflationary principle which resolves all functional meaning into brute natural meaning, where misrepresentation is impossible.

Consider the classic case of what the frog's eye tells the frog's brain (Lettvin, *et al.*, 1959). Suppose we provoke a frog into catching and swallowing a lead pellet we toss at it (cf. Millikan, 1986). If we interpret the signal coming from the eye as "telling" the frog that there is a fly flying towards it, then it is the eye that is passing mistaken information to the frog, whereas if we interpret that signal as merely signalling a dark moving patch on the retina, it is "telling the truth" and the error must be assigned to some later portion of the brain's processing. (See Dennett, 1969, p. 83.) If we are strenuously minimal in our interpretations, the frog never makes a mistake, for every event in the relevant pathway in its nervous system can always be *de-interpreted* by adding disjunctions (the signal means something less demanding: fly *or* pellet *or* dark moving spot *or* slug of kind K *or* . . .) until we arrive back at the brute meaning$_n$ of the signal type, where misrepresentation is impossible. No matter how many layers of transducers contribute to a signal's specificity, there will always be a deflationary interpretation of its meaning as meaning$_n$ unless we relativize our account to some assumption of the normal (Normal, in Millikan's sense) function. (See Dennett, 1969, section 9, "Function and Content.")

Dretske is worried about over-endowing event-types with content, attributing a more specific or sophisticated meaning to them than the facts dictate. But given the stinginess of Mother Nature the engineer, this otherwise laudable hermeneutical abstemiousness puts one at risk of failing to appreciate the "point," the real genius, of her inventions. A particularly instructive instance of the virtues of "inflationary" functional interpretation is Braitenberg's (1984) speculative answer to the question of why so many creatures – from fish to human beings – are equipped with special purpose hardware that is wonderfully sensitive to visual patterns exhibiting symmetry around a vertical axis. There can be little doubt about what the deflationary description of the content of these intricate transducers is: they signal "instance of symmetry around vertical axis on the retina." But why? What is this *for*? The provision is so common that it must have a very general utility. Braitenberg asks what, in the natural world (before there were church façades and suspension bridges) presents a vertically symmetrical view? Nothing in the plant world, and nothing in the terrain. Only this: other animals, *but only when they are facing the viewer!* (Rear views are often vertically symmetrical, but generally less strikingly so.) In other words, what a vertical symmetry transducer tells one is (roughly) "someone is looking at you." Needless to say, this is typically a datum well worth an animal's attention, for the other creature, in whose cross-hairs the animal currently sits, may well be a predator – or a rival or a mate. And so it is not surprising that the normal effect of the symmetry detector's being turned ON is an immediate orientation reaction, and (in the case of fish, for instance) preparation for flight. Is it inflationary to call this transducer a predator-detector? Or a predator-or-mate-or-rival-detector? If you were hired to design a fish's predator-detector, would you go for a more foolproof (but cumbersome, slow) transducer, or argue that this is really the very best sort of predator-detector to have, in which the false alarms are a small price to pay for its speed and its power to recognize relatively well hidden predators?

We saw in the case of human-designed artifacts that we could use our appreciation of the costs and benefits of various design choices to upgrade our interpretation of the two-bitser's discriminatory talent from mere disk-of-weight-w-and-thickness-t-and-diameter-d-and-material-m detection to quarter detection (or quarter-balboa detection, depending on the user's intentions). This is, if you like, the *fundamental tactic* of artifact-hermeneutics. Why should Dretske resist the same interpretive principle in the case of natural functional meaning? Because it is not "principled" enough, in his view. It would fail to satisfy our yearning for an account of what the natural event *really* means, what it means under the aspect of "original" or "intrinsic" intentionality.[3]

In "Machines and the Mental," (1985) Dretske claims that the fundamental difference between current computers and us is that while computers may process information by manipulating internal symbols of some sort, they have "no access, so to speak, to the *meaning* of these symbols, to the things the representations represent" (p.26.). This way of putting it

suggests that Dretske is conflating two points: something's meaning something *to* or *for* a system or organism, and that system or organism's being in a
position to know or recognize or intuit or introspect that fact from the
inside.

> Unless these symbols have what we might call an *intrinsic* [my empha-
> sis] meaning, a meaning they possess which is independent of our
> communicative intentions and purposes, then this meaning *must* be
> irrelevant to assessing what the machine is doing when it manipulates
> them. (*p.28*)

Dretske quite correctly insists that the meaning he is seeking for mental
states must *make a real difference* in, and to, the life of the organism, but
what he fails to see is that the meaning he seeks, while it is, in the case of an
organism, independent of *our* intentions and purposes, is not independent
of the intentions and purposes of Mother Nature, and hence is, in the end,
just as derived, and hence just as subject to indeterminacy of interpretation,
as the meaning in our two-bitser.

Dretske attempts to escape this conclusion, and achieve "functional
determination" in the face of threatened "functional indeterminacy," by
devising a complicated story of how *learning* could make the crucial
difference. According to Dretske, a learning organism can, through the
process of repeated exposures to a variety of stimuli and the mechanism of
associative learning, come to establish an internal state type that has a
definite, *unique* function, and hence functional meaning.

Confronted with our imagined robotic survival machine, Dretske's
reaction is to suppose that in all likelihood some of its states do have natural
(as opposed to merely assigned) functional meaning, in virtue of the
learning history of the survival machine's first days or years of service. "I
think we could (logically) create an artifact that *acquired* original intentionality, but not one that (at the moment of creation, as it were) *had* it"
(personal correspondence). The functions dreamt of, and provided for, by
its engineers are only assigned functions – however brilliantly the engineers
anticipated the environment the machine ends up inhabiting – but once the
machine has a chance to respond to the environment in a training or
learning cycle, its states have at least the opportunity of acquiring natural
(definite, unique) functional meaning – and not just the natural meaning in
which misrepresentation is ruled out.

I will not present the details of this ingenious attempt, because, for all its
ingenuity, it won't work. Fodor (1987), in the chapter with which we began,
shows why. First, it depends, as Fodor notes, on drawing a sharp line
between the organism's learning period, when the internal state is *developing* its meaning, and the subsequent period when its meaning is held to be
fixed. Misrepresentation is possible, on Dretske's view, only in the second
phase, but any line we draw must be arbitrary. (Does a whistle blow, Fodor
wonders, signaling the end of the practice session and the beginning of

playing for keeps?) Moreover, Fodor notes (not surprisingly), Dretske's account cannot provide for the fixed natural functional meaning of any innate, unlearned representative states.

Dretske does not view this as a shortcoming. So much the worse for innate concepts, he says. "I don't think there are, or can be, innate concepts or beliefs . . . Beliefs and desires, *reasons* in general (the sort of thing covered by the intentional stance), are (or so I would like to argue) invoked to explain patterns of behavior that are acquired during the life history of the organism exhibiting the behavior (i.e., learned)" (personal correspondence).

The motivation for this stand can be brought out by considering an example. The first thing a baby cuckoo does when it hatches is to look around the nest for other eggs, its potential competitors for its adoptive parents' attention, and attempt to roll them over the edge. It surely has no inkling of the functional meaning of its activity, but that meaning is nevertheless there – *for* the organism, and to the organism – unless we suppose by the latter phrase that the organism has to "have access" to that meaning, has to be in a position to reflect on it, or avow it, for instance. The rationale of the cuckoo's chillingly purposive activity is not in question; what remains to be investigated is *to what extent* the rationale is the fledgling's rationale, and to what extent it is free-floating – merely what Mother Nature had in mind. For Dretske, however, this is an all-or-nothing question, and it is tied to his intuition that there must be unique and unequivocal (natural functional) meanings for mental states.

Dretske seems to be trying to do two things at one stroke: first, he wants to draw a principled (and all-or-nothing) distinction between free-floating and – shall we say? – "fully appreciated" rationales; and second, he wants to remove all interpretive slack in the specification of the "actual" or "real" meaning of any such appreciated meaning-states. After all, if we appeal to our introspective intuitions, that is just how it seems: not only is there something we mean by our thoughts – something utterly determinate even if sometimes publicly ineffable – but it is our recognition or appreciation of *that meaning* that explains what we thereupon do. There certainly is a vast difference between the extremes represented by the fledgling cuckoo and, say, the cool-headed and cold-blooded human murderer who "knows just what he is doing, and why," but Dretske wants to turn it into the wrong sort of difference. Echoing Searle, Dretske would sharply distinguish between syntax and semantics: in the human murderer, he would say, "it is the structure's having this meaning (its semantics), not just the structure that has this meaning (the syntax), which is relevant to explaining behavior" (personal correspondence – cf. Dretske, 1985, p.31.). Even supposing Dretske could motivate the placement of such a threshold, dividing the spectrum of increasingly sophisticated cases into those where syntax does all the work and those where semantics comes inexorably into play, it is out of the question that the rigors of a learning history could break through *that* barrier, and somehow *show* an organism what its internal states "really meant."

Furthermore, *if* Dretske's learning-history move worked for learned representations, the very same move could work for innate representations "learned" by the organism's ancestors via natural selection over the aeons. That is, after all, how we explain the advent of innate mechanisms – as arising out of a trial-and-error selection process over time. If, as Dretske supposes, "soft"-wiring can acquire natural functional meaning during a organism's lifetime, thanks to its relations to environmental events, "hard"-wiring could acquire the same natural functional meaning over the lifetime of the species.

And again, when do we blow the whistle and freeze, for all future time, the meaning of such a designed item? What started out as a two-bitser can become a q-balber; what started out as a wrist bone can become a panda's thumb (Gould, 1980), and what started out as an innate representation meaning one thing to an organism can come, over time in a new environment, to mean something else to that organism's progeny. (There are further problems with Dretske's account, some well addressed by Fodor, but I will pass over them.)

What, then, does Fodor propose in place of Dretske's account? He too is exercised by the need for an account of how we can *pin an error* on an organism. ("No representation without misrepresentation" would be a good Fodorian motto.) And like Dretske, he draws the distinction between derivative and original intentionality:

> I'm prepared that it should turn out that smoke and tree rings represent only relative to our interests in predicting fires and ascertaining the ages of trees, that thermostats represent only relative to our interest in keeping the room warm, and that English words represent only relative to our intention to use them to communicate our thoughts. I'm prepared, that is, that it should turn out that only mental states (hence, according to the Representational Theory of Mind, only mental representations) should have semantic properties *in the first instance*; and hence that a naturalized semantics should apply, strictu dictu, to mental representations only. (*p. 99*)

And then, like Dretske, he faces what he calls the disjunction problem. What principled or objective grounds can we have for saying the state means "quarter here now" (and hence is an error, when it occurs in perceptual response to a slug) instead of meaning "quarter or quarter-balboa or slug of kind K or . . . " (and hence, invariably, is not an error at all)? Fodor is no more immune than Dretske (or anyone else) to the fatal lure of teleology, of discovering what the relevant mechanism is "supposed to do," but he manfully resists:

> I'm not sure that this teleology/optimality story is false, but I do find it thoroughly unsatisfying . . . I think maybe we can get a theory of error

without relying on notions of optimality and teleology, and if we can, we should. All else being equal, the less Pop-Darwinism the better, surely.   (*pp. 105–106*)

I appreciate the candor with which Fodor expresses his discomfort with appeals to evolutionary hypotheses. (Elsewhere he finds he must help himself to a bit of "vulgar Darwinism" to buttress an account he needs of the functions of transducers.) Why, though, should he be so unwilling to follow down the path? Because he sees (I gather) that the most one can ever get from any such story, however well buttressed by scrupulously gathered facts from the fossil record, etc., is a story with all the potential for indeterminacy that we found in the tale of the transported two-bitser. And Fodor wants real, original, intrinsic meaning – not for the states of artifacts, heaven knows, for Searle is right about them! – but about our own mental representations.

Does Fodor have an account that will work better than Dretske's? No. His is equally ingenious, and equally forlorn. Suppose, Fodor says, "I see a cow which, stupidly, I misidentify. I take it, say, to be a horse. So taking it causes me to effect the tokening of a symbol; viz., I say 'horse'." There is an asymmetry, Fodor argues, between the causal relations that hold between horses and "horse"-tokenings on the one hand and between cows and "horse"-tokenings on the other:

> In particular, misidentifying a cow as a horse wouldn't have led me to say "horse" *except that there was independently a semantic relation between "horse" tokenings and horses.* But for the fact that the word "horse" expresses the property of *being a horse* (i.e., but for the fact that one calls *horses* "horses", it would not have been *that* word that taking a cow to be a horse would have caused me to utter. Whereas, by contrast, since "horse" does mean *horse*, whether horses cause me to say "horse" does not depend upon there being any semantic – or, indeed, any – connection between "horse" tokenings and cows.   (*pp. 107–108*)

This doctrine of Fodor's then gets spelled out in terms of counterfactuals that hold under various circumstances. Again, without going into the details (for which see Akins, 1988), let me just say that the trouble is that our nagging problem arises all over again. How does Fodor establish that, in his mental idiolect, "horse" means *horse* – and not *horse-or-other-quadruped-resembling-a-horse* (or something like that)? Either Fodor must go Searle's introspective route and declare that this is something he can just tell, from the inside, or he must appeal to the very sorts of design considerations and the "teleology/optimality story" that he wants to resist. Those of us who have always loved to tell that story can only hope that he will come to acquire a taste for it, especially when he realizes how unpalatable and hard to swallow the alternatives are.

This brings me to Burge, who has also constructed a series of intuition pumps designed to reveal the truth to us about error. Burge has been arguing in a series of papers against a doctrine he calls *individualism*, a thesis about what facts settle questions about the content or meaning of an organism's mental states. According to individualism,

> An individual's intentional states and events (types and tokens) could not be different from what they are, given the individual's physical, chemical, neural, or functional histories, where these histories are specified non-intentionally and in a way that is independent of physical or social conditions outside the individual's body. (*1986, p.4*)

Or in other words:

> The meaning or content of an individual's internal states could not be different from what it is, given the individual's *internal* history and constitution (considered independent of conditions outside its "body").

The falsehood of this thesis should not surprise us. After all, individualism is false of such simple items as two-bitsers. We changed the meaning of the two-bitser's internal state by simply moving it to Panama and giving it a new job to perform. Nothing structural or physical inside it changed, but the meaning of one of its states changed from Q to QB in virtue of its changed embedding in the world. In order to attribute meaning to functional states of an artifact, you have to depend on assumptions about what it is supposed to do, and in order to get any leverage about that, you have to look to the wider world of purposes and prowesses. Burge's anti-individualistic thesis is then simply a special case of a very familiar observation: functional characterizations are relative not only to the embedding environment, but to assumptions about optimality of design. (See, e.g., Wimsatt, 1974. Burge, 1986, seems to appreciate this in footnote 18 on p.35.)

Moreover, Burge supports his anti-individualism with arguments that appeal to just the considerations that motivated our treatment of the two-bitser. For instance, he offers an extended argument, pp.41ff., about a "person P who normally correctly perceives instances of a particular objective visible property O" by going into state O', and it turns out that in some circumstances, a different visible property, C, puts P into state O'. We can substitute "two-bitser" for "P," "Q" for "O'," "quarter" for "O," and "quarter-balboa" for "C," and notice that his argument is our old friend, without addition or omission.

But something is different: Burge leaves no room for indeterminacy of content; his formulations always presume that there is a fact of the matter about what something *precisely* means. And he makes it clear that he means to disassociate himself from the "stance-dependent" school of functional interpretation. He chooses to "ignore generalized arguments that mentalistic ascriptions are deeply indeterminate" (1986, p. 6), and announces his realism by noting that psychology seems to presuppose the reality of beliefs and desires, and it seems to work. That is, psychology makes use of interpreted that-clauses "or what we might loosely call 'intentional content.' I have seen no sound reason to believe that this use is merely heuristic, instrumentalistic, or second class in any other sense" (p. 8.). That is why his thesis of anti-individualism seems so striking; he seems to be arguing for the remarkable view that *intrinsic* intentionality, *original* intentionality, is just as context-sensitive as derived intentionality.

Although Burge, like Dretske and Fodor, is drawn inexorably to evolutionary considerations, he fails to see that his reliance on those very considerations must force him to give up his uncomplicated realism about content. For instance, he champions Marr's (1982) theory of vision as a properly anti-individualistic instance of successful psychology without noticing that Marr's account is, like "engineering" accounts generally, dependent on strong (indeed too strong – see Ramachandran, 1985a, 1985b) optimality assumptions that depend on making sense of *what Mother Nature had in mind* for various subcomponents of the visual system. Without the tactic I have been calling artifact hermeneutics, Marr would be bereft of any principle for assigning content. Burge himself enunciates the upshot of the tactic:

> The methods of individuation and explanation are governed by the assumption that the subject has adapted to his or her environment sufficiently to obtain veridical information from it under certain normal conditions. If the properties and relations that normally caused visual impressions were regularly different from what they are, the individual would obtain different information and have visual experiences with different intentional content.   (*p.35*)

When we attribute content to some state or structure in Marr's model of vision, we must defend our attribution by claiming (in a paraphrase of Dretske on assigned functional meaning) that that is the function Mother Nature assigned this structure, the reason why it was built and the explanation for why it was built the way it was. Had her purposes been otherwise, it might have meant$_f$ something else.

The method Burge endorses, then, must make the *methodological* assumption that the subject has adapted to his or her environment sufficiently so that when we come to assigning contents to the subject's states – when we adopt the intentional stance – the dictated attributions are those that come out veridical – *and useful*. Without the latter condition, Burge will be stuck with Fodor's and Dretske's problem of disjunctive dissipation of content, because you can always get veridicality at the expense of utility by adding disjuncts. Utility, however, is not an objective, determinate property, as the example of the two-bitser made clear. So contrary to what Burge assumes, he must relinquish the very feature that makes his conclusion initially so intriguing: his realism about "intentional content," or in other words his belief that there is a variety of intrinsic or original intentionality that is not captured by our strategies for dealing with merely derived intentionality like that of the two-bitser.

The realism about intentional content that Burge assumes, along with Fodor and the others, is also presupposed by Putnam, whose Twin-Earth thought experiments (Putnam, 1975) set the agenda for much recent work on these issues. We can see this clearly, now, by contrasting our two-bitser with a Putnamian example. In the case of the two-bitser, the laws of nature do not suffice to single out what its internal state *really means* – except on pain of making misrepresentation impossible. Relative to one rival interpretation or another various of its moves count as errors, various of its states count as misrepresentations, but beyond the resources of artifact hermeneutics there are no deeper facts to settle disagreements.

Consider then the members of a Putnamian tribe who have a word, "*glug*," let us say, for the invisible, explosive gas they encounter in their marshes now and then. When we confront them with some acetylene, and they call it glug, are they making a mistake or not? All the gaseous hydrocarbon they have ever heretofore encountered, we can suppose, was methane, but they are unsophisticated about chemistry, so there is no ground to be discovered in their past behavior or current dispositions that would licence a description of their glug-state as methane-detection rather than the more inclusive gaseous-hydrocarbon-detection. Presumably, gaseous hydrocarbon is a "natural kind" and so are its subspecies, acetylene, methane, propane and their cousins. So the laws of nature will not suffice to favor one reading over the other. Is there a deeper fact of the matter, however, about what they *really mean* by "glug"? Of course once we educate them, they will have to *come* to mean one thing or the other by "glug," but in advance of these rather sweeping changes in their cognitive states, will there already be a fact about whether they believe the proposition that *there is methane present* or the proposition that *there is gaseous hydrocarbon present* when they express themselves by saying "Glug!"?

If, as seems likely, no answer can be wrung from exploitation of the intentional stance in their case, I would claim (along with Quine and the others on my side) that the meaning of their belief is simply indeterminate in this regard. It is not just that I can't tell, and they can't tell; there is nothing to tell. But Putnam and the other realists about intentional content would hold that there is a further fact, however inaccessible to us interpreters, that settles the questions about which cases of glug-identification don't merely *count* as but *really are* errors – given what "glug" really means. Is this deeper fact any more accessible to the natives than to us outsiders? Realists divide on that question.

Burge and Dretske argue against the traditional doctrine of privileged access, and Searle and Fodor are at least extremely reluctant to acknowledge that their thinking ever rests on any appeal to such an outmoded idea. Kripke, however, is still willing to bring this skeleton out of the closet. In

Kripke's (1982) resurrection of Wittgenstein's puzzle about rule-following, we find all our themes returning once more: a resistance to the machine analogy on grounds that meaning in machines is relative to "the intentions of the designer" (p.34), and the immediately attendant problem of error:

> How is it determined when a malfunction occurs? . . . Depending on the intent of the designer, any particular phenomenon may or may not count as a machine malfunction . . . Whether a machine ever malfunctions and, if so, when, is not a property of the machine itself as a physical object but is well defined only in terms of its program, as stipulated by its designer. (*pp. 34–35*)

This familiar declaration about the relativity and derivativeness of machine meaning is coupled with a frank unwillingness on Kripke's part to offer the same analysis in the case of human "malfunction." Why? Because it suggests that our own meaning would be as derivative, as inaccessible to us directly, as to any artifact:

> The idea that we lack "direct" access to the facts whether we mean plus or quus [Q or QB, in the two-bitser's case] is bizarre in any case. Do I not know, directly, and with a fair degree of certainty, that I mean plus? . . . There may be some facts about me to which my access is indirect, and about which I must form tentative hypotheses: but surely the fact as to what I mean by "plus" is not one of them! (*p.40.*)

This declaration is not necessarily Kripke speaking *in propria persona*, for it occurs in the midst of a dialectical response Kripke thinks Wittgenstein would make to a particular skeptical challenge, but he neglects to put any rebuttal in the mouth of the skeptic, and is willing to acknowledge his sympathy for the position expressed.

And why not? Here, I think, we find as powerful and direct an expression as could be of the intuition that lies behind the belief in original intentionality. This is the doctrine Ruth Millikan calls *meaning rationalism*, and it is one of the central burdens of her important book, *Language, Thought, and Other Biological Categories*, to topple it from its traditional pedestal (Millikan, 1984. See also Millikan, forthcoming) Something has to give. Either you must abandon meaning rationalism – the idea that you are unlike the fledgling cuckoo not only in having access, but in having privileged access to your meanings – or you must abandon the naturalism that insists that you are, after all, just a product of natural selection, whose intentionality is thus derivative and hence potentially indeterminate.

Notes

A longer version of this paper appears in my book, (Dennett, 1987) *The Intentional Stance.*

1 This tactic is hardly novel. Among earlier discussions of intentionality drawing on such examples of simple discriminating mechanisms are MacKenzie unpublished (1978) and Ackermann (1972).
2 "There must, after all, be a finite number of general principles that govern the activities of our various cognitive-state-making and cognitive-state-using mechanisms and there must be explanations of why these principles have historically worked to aid our survival. To suppose otherwise is to suppose that our cognitive life is an accidental epiphenomenal cloud hovering over mechanisms that *evolution devised with other things in mind* [my emphasis]" (Millikan, 1986, p.55).
3 Dretske happens to discuss the problem of predator-detection in a passage that brings out this problem with his view: "If [certain] bacteria did not have something inside that meant that that was the direction of magnetic north, they could not orient themselves so as to avoid toxic surface water. They would perish. If, in other words, an animal's internal sensory states were not rich in information, intrinsic natural meaning, about the presence of prey, predators, cliffs, obstacles, water and heat, it could not survive" (1985, p.29). The trouble is that, given Dretske's conservative demands on information, the symmetry-detector wouldn't count as sending a signal with information (intrinsic natural meaning) about predators but only about patterns of vertical symmetry on the retina, and while no doubt it could be, and normally would be, supplemented by further transducers designed to make finer-grained distinctions between predators, prey, mates, rivals, and members of ignorable species, these could be similarly crude in their actual discriminatory powers. If, as Dretske suggests, some bacteria can survive with only north-detectors (they don't need toxic-water-detectors, as it happens), other creatures can get by with mere symmetry-detectors, so the last sentence quoted above is just false: most animals survive and reproduce just fine without the benefit of states that are rich enough in (Dretskean) information to inform their owners about prey, predators, cliffs, and the like.

6   The role of programs in AI

If there are defining characteristics of AI, one must be the centrality of programs. Computer science or software engineering might be considered to have a better claim to this characteristic, but closer inspection of the role of programs within those fields reveals that not to be so. Formal specifications and means of realizing them in machine-executable representations dominate these fields; individual programs are relatively secondary in importance. But in AI implementations (programs) have always played the central role.

Bundy offers a three-fold division of AI, and claims that the role of a program is dependent upon which subdivision some particular AI work falls within. His three categories of AI are "applied AI," "cognitive science," and "basic AI." It is important to sort out these issues (he claims) if we are to cure the "methodological malaise" in AI.

Dietrich then argues that a keystone in the foundations of modern AI is that intelligent thought is symbol manipulation, and, moreover, symbol manipulation of the type manifest in Turing-von-Neumann computers. Hence, the search for AI is reduced to finding the right program, but with no guide as to how to find it.

The role of programs in AI (according to Dietrich) is little better than random attempts to hit upon this program (or class of algorithms) whose existence (but little else) is promised by the foundational theory. Dietrich questions the legitimacy of treating such unconstrained assumptions as a theoretical basis for a science. In particular, he claims that the physical symbol system hypothesis (PSSH) (Newell, 1980) is not a hypothesis at all but a dogma, and that one way to get AI back onto a proper foundation would be to treat the PSSH as merely a hypothesis.

What kind of field is AI?

Alan Bundy

I want to ask 'What kind of field is artificial intelligence?' and to give an answer. Why is this an important question? Because there is evidence within AI of a methodological malaise, and part of the reason for this malaise is that there is not a generally agreed answer to the question.

As an illustration, several papers in this volume draw a number of different analogies between artificial intelligence and other fields. AI is compared to physics, to chemical engineering, to thermodynamics and to psychology; in fact it is said to *be* psychology. Each of these is a very different kind of field with different kinds of methodology, criteria for assessing research and so on. Depending on which of these you think artificial intelligence is really like, you would decide what to do, how to do it, and how to assess other people's work.

1 Evidence of malaise

One of the symptoms of this malaise is a difference amongst referees of papers as to the standard which is expected for conferences, journals, etc. When I was programme chairman of a major AI conference, I noted that for more than 50 percent of the papers the referees disagreed as to whether the papers should be accepted or rejected. And this wasn't just a question of having different thresholds of acceptability, because the opinions would reverse on other kinds of papers. So clearly the referees were applying very different criteria when deciding which papers were worth accepting.

A second symptom of this malaise, which has been noted for instance by D. McDermott (1981), is the fragility of programs. Typically they run on the example in the thesis or paper, and in the words of Bobrow *et al.* (1977), on other examples they simulate total aphasia or death.

A third symptom is the poverty of published accounts. Some people have alluded to this in their criticism of papers about expert systems, where it is particularly prevalent. For instance, a paper describing an expert system for diagnosing bee diseases, might concentrate on the nature and importance of bee diseases. At the end of the paper you might find the statement 'I built a rule based system' or 'I built a blackboard architecture', but that is all you learn about how the program actually worked. It is very difficult to build on and extend such work.

That leads me to my fourth symptom: that there is often a lack of continuity in AI research. There are in AI traditions of building on a sequence of programs, or a sequence of techniques, and these are honourable exceptions, but often one gets a one-off program which is then not continued in any way.

Part of the solution to this malaise is to identify what kind of field AI is. It is not the only answer, there are other aspects of the problem, but I don't want to dwell on these here.

2 Kinds of AI

One difficulty is that there are a number of different kinds of AI, each one of which has its own criteria and methodology. These tend to get confused together, so that different people have different conceptions of what kind of a field AI is. I want to disentangle the confusion by separating out the different kinds of AI.

The different kinds of AI correspond to different motivations for doing AI. The first kind, which has become very popular in the past five to ten years, is *applied AI*,[1] where we use existing AI for commercial techniques, military or industrial applications, i.e. to build products. Another kind of AI is to model human or animal intelligence using AI techniques. This is called *cognitive science*, or *computational psychology*. Those two kinds of AI have often been identified in the past, but there is a third kind on which I want to concentrate most of my attention. I call it *basic AI*.[2]

The aim of basic AI is to explore computational techniques which have the potential for simulating intelligent behaviour.

3 What is an AI technique?

All these definitions rely on a notion of AI technique so it is necessary for me to say something about what an AI technique is. I will be fairly catholic about this. The obvious candidate for an AI technique is an algorithm. An example would be the circumscription technique that John McCarthy has developed for non-monotonic reasoning. An older example would be means-ends analysis. The boundaries between AI algorithms and other more conventional kinds of algorithms in computer science is obviously very fuzzy. One should not expect or attempt to draw a hard and fast boundary, but it is something to do with the potential of these techniques for simulating intelligent behaviour in a wide sense.

There are other kinds of techniques in AI, for instance, techniques for representing knowledge (e.g. situation calculus, frame systems, semantic nets). Even the new work on connectionism may be thought of as the development of new AI knowledge representation techniques.

On a wider front there are architectures for AI systems. The best example I can think of here is the blackboard architecture, but this is not a very precisely defined technique. Getting precise notions of architecture is an area of weakness in AI. There are probably some good ideas around which need tightening up and given more precise form.

Lastly, there are a collection of techniques for knowledge elicitation, for instance, protocol analysis. Notice that protocol analysis is not just a cognitive science technique; it has found application in expert systems. Knowledge elicitation techniques are also used in basic AI as a source of inspiration when developing new ideas.

4 An analogy with mathematics and physics

In order to sharpen up this three-fold division of AI I want to draw an analogy with other kinds of science. I also want to show that AI is not essentially different from other kinds of science. My analogy is drawn from mathematics and physics because they are classic sciences with which most of us are familiar, although one could draw analogies with other areas of science. In my analogy, computer science is similar to mathematics, basic AI is similar to applied mathematics and also to pure engineering, applied AI is similar to engineering, cognitive science is similar to theoretical physics, and psychology is similar to physics.

The idea is that physics and psychology are natural sciences, i.e. psychologists and physicists both try to study and model real world phenomena. Mathematics and computer science provide an armoury of techniques for building theories and/or models for these natural sciences. In applied mathematics and basic AI, people study those techniques of mathematics and computer science which are particularly useful for modelling in these natural sciences. So, in applied mathematics, one might study those partial differential equations which have proved useful for modelling hydrodynamics. In basic AI, one might study inference techniques like circumscription, frames, blackboard architectures, etc., which have been found to be useful for modelling intelligence. Then one can take those techniques and build commercial products with them. That is what is done in engineering and in applied AI.

Somewhere between the natural science of physics and applied mathematics is the area of theoretical physics, where scientists are concerned with applying the modelling techniques of applied mathematics to account for the observations of physical phenomena. Similarly, cognitive scientists are concerned to apply the modelling techniques of basic AI to account for observations of intelligent behaviour.

It is also possible to draw an analogy between AI and engineering. Sometimes engineers are concerned with building particular houses or particular bridges or synthesizing particular chemicals, but they are also interested in developing new, general-purpose engineering techniques. I will call this activity *pure engineering*. An example is a study of new structures for building bridges without an attempt to build a particular bridge. Another example is a study of reinforced concrete in which the engineer develops various methods of doing the reinforcing and then subjects each method to a batch of tests to discover its ageing and strength characteristics. Similarly, in basic AI, researchers develop new techniques, test them and find out their interrelationships. These techniques can then be used in applied AI or in cognitive science.

The reason that it is possible to have this analogy both with applied mathematics and with pure engineering is that computer programs are strange beasts; they are both mathematical entities and artifacts. They are formal abstract objects, which can be investigated symbolically as if they were statements in some branch of mathematics. But they are also artifacts, in that they can do things, e.g. run a chemical plant. They are machines, but they are not physical machines, they are *mental machines* (Bundy, 1981). I think it is interesting that applied mathematics and pure engineering should turn out to be similar kinds of fields.

5 Is AI a science?

Whether AI is a science depends on the kind of AI and what is meant by science. We can identify two kinds of science: natural science and engineering science. In a natural science, we study some phenomena in the world and try to discover theories about them. Examples of natural sciences are physics, chemistry, biology and psychology. In an engineering science, we develop techniques and discover their properties and relations. Examples of engineering sciences are pure engineering and mathematics.

Cognitive science is a natural science. It is the study of the mind and the attempt to build theories of the mind with the aid of computational tools. Part of this study is the building of computer programs to model aspects of mental behaviour, and the comparison of the behaviour of the program with that of real minds.

Basic AI is an engineering science. It consists of the development of computational techniques and the discovery of their properties and inter-relations. Part of this study is the building of computer programs that embody these techniques to: extend them, explore their properties, and generally discover more about them.

It makes sense to ask whether the theories of cognitive science are true, i.e. whether they accurately describe real minds. It does not make sense to ask whether the techniques of basic AI are true, any more than it would make sense to ask whether differentiation, group theory or internal combustion were true. It does make sense to ask whether properties of and relationships between techniques are true, e.g. whether negation as failure is a special case of circumscription, whether resolution is complete.

6 Criteria for assessing basic AI research

If you accept the analogy to physics and mathematics and the three-fold division of AI into basic AI, applied AI and cognitive science, what is the payoff? The analogy suggests criteria for assessing research in each kind of AI. It suggests how to identify what constitutes an advance in the subject and it suggests what kind of methodology AI researchers might adopt.

In demonstrating this I will concentrate on basic AI. It is also important to do this kind of exercise for applied AI and for cognitive science, but it is less urgent for these two because people have already thought about criteria for assessing research aimed at applications and psychological modelling. There has not been so much thought about criteria for assessing research in which AI techniques are developed for their own sake. In the case of applied AI there is a major criterion that what you build is in fact a successful commercial product which fills a need. In the case of cognitive science there are acid tests about doing experiments to see if the model exhibits all and only the behaviour that has been observed in humans or animals. In basic AI it is not so obvious what the criteria are.

Here are some criteria. I drew up this list by starting with particular criticisms of existing AI research and then generalizing and negating them. Although I have asserted that there is widespread disagreement about the virtues of AI research illustrated by the disagreements among referees about research papers, there is, in fact, considerable agreement about the shortcomings. People will often agree what is wrong with a piece of work without agreeing what is right. So this methodology of negating criticisms is a productive one.

The criteria discovered in this way are similar to the criteria used to assess the techniques of any engineering science. This corroboration lends support to the criteria themselves and to the classification of basic AI as an engineering science.

My first criterion is *clarity*. The technique should be describable in a precise way, independent of any program that implements it, so that it is simple to understand. Logical calculi are often useful as a language of description. They are not the only language; diagrams are another. Consider the way in which minimax is usually explained: in terms of backing up scores in a game tree. Counter-examples can be found in papers that explain what a program does, but say nothing about how it does it, or in papers that describe a program only by describing how each Lisp function works. I have put clarity first because it is a necessary first step before one can go on to investigate the properties of the technique.

My second criterion is the *power* of the technique. A technique is judged to be more valuable if it has a wide range of application and if it is efficient in its operation. A typical counter-example is the Ph.D. program that works on the toy example in the thesis, but which either does not work at all or runs out of resources on other examples. If that is wrong then what is right is that the program should work on lots of examples and the more the better, and that it should work fast and use little space.

My third criterion is *parsimony*. Other things being equal, the technique which is simpler to describe should get more credit. This is often neglected in AI, but Occam's Razor ought to apply to AI techniques as much as it applies to other sciences. A counter-example would be an excessively complex program for some task where no principled attempt had been made to build a simple program for the same task.

My fourth criterion is *completeness*, i.e. that the work should be finished in some sense. For instance, a computer program should be finished and should work. We can all think of counter-examples to that. Similarly, a knowledge-representation formalism should be capable of representing the kinds of knowledge that it was intended to represent. Were it not for the counter-examples, this criterion might be thought too obvious to be worth stating.

My fifth, and last, criterion is *correctness*, i.e. that the program should behave as required, that the proofs of any theorems about the technique should be correct, etc.

7 Advances in basic AI

Given that basic AI consists of the invention and development of techniques, we can identify what constitutes an advance in the field. An obvious advance would be the invention of a new technique. Its merits can be judged according to the criteria listed in the last section. Of course, it is also an advance if a technique is improved along one of the dimensions defined by these criteria, i.e. if it is made more clear, powerful, parsimonious, complete or correct.

In assessing the merit of an advance, one must also take into account how different a new technique is from previous techniques, how surprising it is that it can be stated so clearly, parsimoniously or completely or correctly, or that it turns out to be so powerful. We can summarize this as the *novelty* of the advance.

But advances can also come from an improved understanding of the properties of, or relationships between techniques. For instance,

> a proof that a technique obeys some specification, e.g. the soundness and completeness proofs for resolution;
> the discovery of the complexity of a technique;
> a demonstration that one technique is a special case of another technique;
> a demonstration that what appears to be one technique in the literature, turns out, under closer examination, to be two or three slightly different techniques which deserve different names;
> or, vice versa, that two or more apparently different techniques are essentially the same;
> a demonstration that a technique applies to a new domain;
> an exploration of the behaviour of a technique on a range of standard examples.

Again we want to use the novelty of the advance as one measure of its merit.

8 A methodology for basic AI

What methodology does this suggest for basic AI? To answer this question we have to take a partly descriptive and a partly normative stance, that is, we need to see what methodology is actually followed in AI and then see what modifications to this methodology are suggested by our analysis. The major methodology in AI is *exploratory programming*; one chooses some task which has not been modelled before, and then, by a process of trial and error programming, develops a program for doing this task. Suppose you want to build a program which can suggest new Chinese recipes, then you might set to work developing such a program. You will dream up a scenario of how a particular recipe might be generated, implement the procedure this suggests, and then test it on further examples. This testing will show up inadequacies and suggest ways of modifying and improving the program. This trial and error cycle will continue until you are satisfied with the program.

At this stage there ought to be an *analysis* of the program in order to try to tease out in a more precise way the techniques which underlie it. Suppose that the Chinese recipe program works by matching some set of ingredients against an existing list of recipes and trying to get a close match. Somewhere in the program there must be some kind of analogical matching routine. Careful analysis of the program will reveal what form it takes.

It is quite likely that this analogical matching technique will be *ad hoc* and domain specific. So the next step is to *generalize* and to formulate a *rationally reconstructed* algorithm which does the same thing but is more robust. We then need to explore the properties of this rationally reconstructed technique according to the list given in the last section, i.e. construct a specification and verify the technique, discover its complexity, explore its relationship to other techniques, apply it to new domains and test it on standard examples. This exploration will suggest further generalizations and improvements.

Analysis should also help identify the weaknesses of existing techniques and hence suggest what problems we should focus on in the future. Where the weaknesses cannot readily be met by the extension of existing techniques then they might be addressed by exploratory programming. A task must be identified for which the existing techniques are inadequate because of these weaknesses, and where there is some prospect that progress might be made. An attempt should then be made to build a program for this task. Thus the methodology cycles.

These latter steps in the methodology of AI – of analysis, generalization, rational reconstruction and exploration of properties – are not generally recognized or practised. It follows from my analysis of basic AI that they are very important and that they deserve a lot more attention.

9 Conclusion

To sum up: the malaise which I have identified in AI can be cured, in part, by careful definition and sub-division of the field into basic AI, applied AI and cognitive science. For each kind of AI we can identify different sets of criteria for assessing research, different notions of what constitutes an advance and different methodologies for conducting research. I have identified these for basic AI. If we do not subdivide the field then these criteria and methodologies become entangled, leading to a confusion in the way that AI research is conducted and judged.

This is not to suggest that there are not researchers with multiple motives who would like to contribute to more than one kind of AI, and that there are not pieces of work which do contribute to more than one kind of AI. Judging such work is difficult, but it can be done by separating out the work's contributions to basic AI, applied AI and cognitive science.

Notes

1 Elsewhere (Bundy, 1983) I have called it *technological AI*.
2 Elsewhere (Bundy, 1983) I have called it *mainstream AI*.

Programs in the search for intelligent machines: the mistaken foundations of AI

Eric Dietrich

Of course, unless one has a theory, one cannot expect much help from a computer (unless *it* has a theory). *Marvin Minsky*

1 Introduction

Computer programs play no single role in artificial intelligence. To some, programs are an end; to others, they are a means. These two groups might be thought to contain those who think AI is an engineering discipline, and those who think AI is a science. This is only partially true; the real situation is more complicated.

The first group is by far the largest and contains many of the most prominent AI researchers. For example, in his book *Problem Solving Methods in Artificial Intelligence*, Nils Nilsson states that

> Future progress in [artificial intelligence] will depend on the development of both practical and theoretical knowledge ... As regards theoretical knowledge, some have sought a unified theory of artificial intelligence. My view is that artificial intelligence is (or soon will be) an engineering discipline since its primary goal is to *build* things. (*1971, pp. vii-viii, his emphasis*)

Barr and Feigenbaum (taking a slightly more cautious position) also claim that "whether or not [AI leads] to a better understanding of the mind, there is every evidence that [AI] will lead to a new *intelligent technology*" (1981/1982, p. 3, their emphasis).

Many researchers who see themselves as theorists or scientists also belong in this group because they think that the ultimate goal of their work on theory is to produce a computer program that does something useful, whereas in other disciplines, the goal of theorists and scientists is to produce a *theory*. Roger Schank, for example, in the preface to *Conceptual Information Processing* (1975a) states

> We discuss here a theory of natural language and the implementation of that theory on a computer. We have taken what is basically an [a]rtificial [i]ntelligence approach to linguistics. That is, it was our objective to write computer programs that could understand and generate sentences. The work is intended to be a first step towards the long range goal of a computer that can communicate with people in natural language.

Finally, many AI researchers who see themselves as scientists primarily concerned with producing theories belong to the first group because they think their programs *are* theories (see Winston, 1977)!

The second group is composed of those who use computer programs to test ideas or hypotheses. Terry Winograd's SHRDLU can be construed as such a test (1972). SHRDLU affirmatively settled the issue of whether or not it was possible to represent data (specifically, knowledge of the meaning of a word) procedurally (i.e. as a mini-program). Other possible members of this group include Lenat, for AM (1982), and Langley, Bradshaw, and Simon, for the BACON series of programs (1983).[1]

For some reason, the ambiguous status of computer programs in AI goes largely unnoticed within the AI community. There is, for example, little discussion within the community of what it could mean for a program to be a theory (but see Partridge *et al.*, 1984; for a discussion from outside the community, see Simon, 1979). Of course, it is rare for any discipline to concern itself with what are essentially meta-theoretical issues. This is true for physics, chemistry, psychology, linguistics, etc. AI is no exception; the status of computer programs is a meta-theoretical issue, and there are plenty of theoretical and engineering issues to be concerned about. However, to someone who steps back for a wider perspective, the confusion over the role of computer programs in AI is disturbing; it may indicate a deep theoretical confusion.[2] In this paper, I will argue that this is in fact the case. I will attempt to explain the confusion about computer programs in AI in terms of the community's commitment to the wrong theoretical foundation. I will develop my argument historically. Then, I will suggest a new theoretical foundation, and argue that adopting it would provide a clear, unequivocal role for programs: they would be controlled experiments, and AI would become a science.

2 The theoretical foundations of artificial intelligence

The roots of artificial intelligence are often said to lie in the work of Turing and Church on the theory of computation (see for example, Barr and Feigenbaum, 1981/1982; Haugeland, 1981). However, the relevance to AI of the theory of computation was established after AI had already emerged. The primary influence on the early AI researchers like Newell and Simon was the work of cyberneticists and neurophysiologists such as

McCulloch, Shannon, and Wiener, who were working on information theory, information processing, neural models, and computers (cf. McCorduck, 1979; Fields, 1987; and see Ashby, 1956; McCulloch and Pitts 1943; Wiener, 1948).

Two central ideas developed by the cyberneticists and neurophysiologists influenced Newell, Simon, and their colleagues. The first was that the computer was not just a number cruncher, but was rather a general symbol manipulator (cf. Shannon, 1950). That is, the computer could manipulate symbols that represented much more than numbers; the symbols manipulated by a computer could represent anything: words, propositions, concepts, dogs, cats, and rocks. In the 1940s and 1950s, this idea was revolutionary. For example ENIAC, one of the first computers, was intended solely for numerical calculations.[3]

From the work of neurophysiologists like McCulloch came the second idea that at least some neural activity was information processing, and hence that some kinds of thought could be explained in terms of information theory and information processing. This was the first time a mechanistic view of the mind and intelligence could plausibly be sustained. Earlier mechanistic views, relying as they did on metaphors with steam engines and pulleys, were too simple, and were always undone by the complexity of human behavior and human mental activity.

Late in 1955, Newell and Simon brought these two ideas together. Their synthesis was this: computers manipulate information by processing or manipulating symbols; since intelligent thought was also (hypothesized to be) information processing via symbol manipulation, computers could be intelligent. The important next step which Newell and Simon took was to implement a program that would replicate intelligent behavior to some extent. In the summer of 1956, at the first AI conference, they introduced their seminal attempt to build a thinking machine: Logic Theorist (Newell, Shaw, and Simon, 1963). Logic Theorist was a program that could prove some theorems in propositional logic derived from Whitehead and Russell's *Principia Mathematica*.[4]

Newell and Simon aimed at nothing less than uncovering the mysteries of creative, intelligent thought. They say:

> we wish to understand how a mathematician, for example, is able to prove a theorem even though he does not know when he starts how, or if, he is going to succeed.   (*Newell, Shaw, and Simon, 1963, p. 109*)

With such a goal and such a heady hypothesis – computers can think – any success with Logic Theorist was bound to be interpreted at least somewhat positively. Logic Theorist was able to prove *some* theorems from the *Principia* (e.g., $((p \Rightarrow \sim p) \Rightarrow \sim p)$). However, Logic Theorist could not prove many simple theorems; for example it could not prove (p or $\sim\sim\sim$ p). This of course meant that Newell and Simon failed to achieve their goal. And the failure continues to this day: we have virtually no idea of how mathematicians prove new theorems, and in general we have no acceptable theory of human problem solving.[5] Moreover, the failure of Logic Theorist meant that their hypothesis was unsupported.

In the face of the obvious failures of Logic Theorist (and its successor, General Problem Solver) Newell, Simon, and their colleagues needed a stronger theoretical foundation for their hypothesis that a computer could think. It was at this point that Turing's work first became important.

The work of Frege and Russell had provided mathematical systems for deduction, i.e. they had formalized one aspect of reasoning. This in turn meant that certain aspects of intelligent thought could be formalized. What Turing and Church (and others) showed was that formalized deduction was a certain kind of computation, and that computation could be described as the formal manipulation of symbols (see Turing, 1936; Church, 1936). These two results, the formalization of deductive reasoning, and the demonstration in principle of the automation of that formalization, formed the basis of Turing's fundamental insight: in theory, machines could think. He argued for this claim in his famous paper "Computing Machinery and Intelligence" (1950). Today, many mark this date as the beginning of AI (see Barr and Feigenbaum, 1981/1982, chapter 1; Haugeland, 1981, and Charniak and McDermott, 1985, chapter 1). The formal, mathematical results were what Newell, Simon, and the rest thought they needed to place their work on solid foundations. Their hypothesis *had* to be correct: Turing machines could think, and computers were Turing machines. The problem was not the theory; it was rather that Logic Theorist and General Problem Solver (and a host of other programs since) simply embodied the wrong computer program. Hence the goal was to find the right program . . . and AI has been searching for the right program ever since.

In summary, the situation that emerged in the late 1950s and early 1960s (and continues today) was this: early AI researchers were convinced that a digital computer, the standard von Neumann machine which computes using data structures and algorithms, could be programmed to think; this they got from the cyberneticists and neurophysiologists. For a theoretical foundation, they pointed to the theory of computation developed by Turing and others. Finally, they explained their failures as merely not having the correct program.

3 The mistaken foundation of AI

The preceding account of the history of AI explains both the central place programs have in artificial intelligence, and the diversity of views about programs within the AI community. Having "theoretically" delimited the search for an intelligent machine to standard, serially processing computers, the next step was to find the right program by trying out programs of different types. There is no theory delimiting this search and no theory about how to conduct it, so the best one can do is proceed on one's hunches, being as systematic as possible. To put this another way, if the theoretical foundation of AI has already been established, there remains only the matter of developing detailed, theoretical extensions and ultimately the "correct" programs. The best strategy at this stage is to add to the "loosely structured but growing body of computational techniques" comprising AI (Nilsson, 1980) until finally intelligent machines are developed (see Nilsson, 1980, Barr and Feigenbaum, 1981/1982, and Rich, 1983).[6]

However, there are two serious errors in the reasoning I am attributing to the early AI researchers: they mistakenly assumed they knew what kind of computing thinking is, and they assumed that the theory of computation is the theoretical foundation of AI.

Turing's conclusion in 1950 that a computer could think is subtly but crucially different from Newell and Simon's synthesis of the ideas of the cyberneticists and neurophysiologists. Turing's conclusion is simply that intelligent thought can be captured in a recipe, that is, that thinking is executing some effective procedure or computable function.

Turing based his argument on the notion of a *general* computational engine – a *general* symbol manipulator. He left unspecified what kind of symbol manipulating intelligent thought is. The abstract nature of the Turing machine guaranteed this. Its abstractness and generality provided no clues as to which of the infinite number of functions it can compute constitutes intelligent thought. Furthermore, Turing offered no guidance for how to find the right function. His claim was that presented with a computable function the execution of which would be intelligent thought, a computer could be programmed to execute that function. Finding the function and determining that it is the function for intelligent thought is another matter.

Newell and Simon, however, had a very different view. They thought they knew how to find the "intelligent thought function." They thought that the symbolic processing performed by standard computers provided the essential clue to the nature of intelligence. Evidence for this claim is that the standard computer model of processing information (i.e. using data structures and algorithms) has been enshrined by Newell and Simon (and AI, in general) as the central hypothesis of artificial intelligence. It is called the *physical symbol system hypothesis* (Newell and Simon, 1976, Newell, 1980, see also Rich, 1983, chapter 1). It states simply that "a physical symbol system has the necessary and sufficient means for general intelligent action" (1976, p. 116). A physical symbol system is a system of physically realized symbols and physically realized processes for transforming them (1976, p. 116), i.e. a system containing data structures and executing algorithms defined over those data structures – a computer, in short.

It is true that if Turing's argument is correct, then on the assumption that ordinary computers are equivalent to Turing machines (up to the size of memory), correctly programmed computers can think (assuming enough memory). But this fact is useless in helping us *find* the correct program, which is where all the action is. Assuming that this fact *is* useful is the first error. Consider an analogous case: we know now that the brain is the organ responsible for thinking, but this does not tell us what thinking is, except quite generally.

The second error is related to the first one. Though it may be true that (intelligent) thinking is computing some recursive function, it does not follow that the theory of computation is a theory of intelligent thought, nor the foundation of such a theory. The theory of computation cannot be an adequate foundation for AI because it does not help us discover what kind of computation thinking is.

All of the foregoing would have been recognized years ago if the physical symbol system hypothesis were indeed a hypothesis. However, it is not a hypothesis at all. It is dogma. There is no other explanation for the unquestioned allegiance it enjoys. For example, there is evidence that a physical symbol system does *not* have the sufficient means for general intelligent action. The famous AI programs such as Logic Theorist, GPS, AM, EURISKO, and BACON are physical symbol systems. Yet the gap between what these programs could do and what was claimed for them was wide enough that were the physical symbol system hypothesis a genuine hypothesis, it would by now be subjected to close scrutiny.[7] There are also arguments to the effect that physical symbol systems do not have the necessary means for general intelligent action. These are the arguments propounded by the subsymbolic connectionists. They argue that systems that are not symbol systems (at least not explicitly) can nevertheless be intelligent (e.g. see Smolensky, 1986a). Whether these arguments are correct or not is yet to be determined. Nevertheless, such arguments do mount an important attack on Newell and Simon's hypothesis. Yet the only researchers questioning the hypothesis are those making the arguments: the subsymbolic connectionists. Within AI, the hypothesis remains unchallenged (an exception to this is Partridge, 1987).[8]

It will be instructive at this point to compare artificial intelligence to astrology of a few centuries back. Astrology at that time was intellectually reputable, and indeed had internal integrity (see Kuhn, 1970). Practicing astrologers were well aware of many predictions that categorically failed (Thorndike, 1923), and they were completely open about such failures. Moreover, astrologers had perfectly reasonable explanations of such failures: forecasting an individual's future was immensely complex and sensitive to the slightest errors, the relevant heavenly bodies were constantly in motion and the astronomical tables used to compute their configuration at the moment of an individual's birth were known to be inaccurate, and no one knew the precise instant of the birth, though this was required for accurate predictions. At the time they were used, such explanations of failure did not beg the question; they were perfectly reasonable. It is only from our twentieth-century perspective, now that we have eschewed astrology, that such explanations appear to be question-begging (see Kuhn, 1970).

During its heyday, astrology was based on a theory about the relationship between the propensities of individuals and heavenly bodies, and this theory defined the practices which astrologers followed in their everyday work. As mentioned above, astrologers knew these practices were faulty and frequently resulted in predications that failed. Because of this, practitioners wanted a stronger, more detailed theory. Yet even without a new, stronger theory, practitioners did not abandon astrology. After all, the discipline was plausible, badly needed, and had had a few successes (seemingly).

Artificial intelligence today is much like astrology was then. As I argued above, AI is based on a mistaken theoretical assumption: the idea that we now know what kind of computing thinking is, which in turn mistakenly draws support from the theory of computation. AI researchers have seemingly reasonable explanations for the shortcomings of their programs: an insufficient number of rules, the wrong heuristics, or not enough processing speed. Moreover, though there are some AI researchers concerned with the problematical foundations of AI (e.g. Chandrasekaran, this volume, and Winograd and Flores, 1986), and though many researchers want a stronger more detailed theory of intelligence, none seem willing to question AI's basic principles: the physical symbol system hypothesis, the claim that heuristic search is the basic problem-solving strategy, and the belief that the theory of computation supports the current AI methodology of merely looking for the correct intelligent program. The attitude within AI remains optimistic; after all, it is plausible that artifacts will one day think, such artifacts would be very useful, and AI has achieved some success in building such artifacts, notably expert systems.

It is possible, of course, that AI is just in its infancy and will one day mature into a science (or possibly an engineering discipline provided that the requisite science has also emerged). Other disciplines which can reasonably be called sciences today have resembled ancient astrology in their infancy, for example medicine before about 1850, and early meteorology.[9] Since there is no way to prove that AI is like astrology, the matter can ultimately only be settled by waiting to see what happens. But given AI's confusion about what computer programs are for, its confusion about its theoretical foundations, and its dogmatic refusal to take its failures seriously, it is time that we at least considered the possibility that current AI is incapable of sustaining an inquiry into the nature of intelligence and intelligent thought.

4 The science of intelligent systems

Some early disciplines were based on fundamentally wrong ideas about the nature of the universe. Astrology, for example, assumed that there was some relationship between what happened to an individual and the positions of stars and planets. Disciplines such as these simply died. Others, like early physics and chemistry, though initially based on wrong notions, eventually evolved into robust sciences. Though they now bear little relation to their ancestors, modern sciences carry the influences of the disciplines they evolved from. I believe that one day there will be a robust science of intelligent systems, whether they are biological or not, but it will not evolve from current AI and current computer science as it is used in AI. Following is my sketch of how such a science will look.[10]

The science of intelligent systems would begin with the idea that we *do not* know what kind of computing thinking is. Indeed, it would not assume that thinking is computing at all. It is the *goal* of such a science to tell us what thinking is, and if it is computing, to tell us what kind of computing it is. Such a science would contrast sharply with current AI: instead of assuming that inquiry into the nature of intelligence is by and large finished, it would assume that we are just beginning.

Though it is impossible to say what the ultimate foundation of a science of intelligent systems might be, it is reasonably clear what it should be in the beginning: neuroscience and systems theory. Neuroscience constitutes our current best theory of the processes underlying thought. From it we have learned two fundamental facts. First, the patterns of neural activity which we describe as cognition and perception are very complex, vastly more complex than the activities in electrical components in computers. This complexity is different in kind, too. That is, one cannot achieve the complexity in structure and function in the brain merely by making more and more complex computers. The complexity in the brain depends directly on the *plasticity* of its individual neurons: individual neurons can perform a wide variety of distinct functions depending on their input, and they develop the capacity for performing the particular functions they do on the basis of the input they receive.[11]

The second fact learned is that the neural systems do not record and store information from the external world. Rather, "knowledge" of its environment is actively constructed by the perceptual and other cognitive systems of the organism. In the case of humans, for example, the colors we see are not "out there," but rather derived from input and current neural activity. This means that brains do not have data structures in the conventional sense at all; hence intelligent thought, at least at the neural level of description, cannot be a matter of processes defined over data structures. (Therefore, at the neural level of description the physical symbol system hypothesis is false: brains do not function like digital computers.)[12]

This is where systems theory makes its entrance. Though neuroscientists do study intelligence to some extent, it is not their primary concern. Furthermore, they are necessarily limited to a neural perspective on intelligence. Neuroscientists cannot develop a theory of intelligence wide enough to cover other types of systems which exhibit intelligence, such as computers, organizations, and societies. However, systems theorists could produce such a theory.

Systems theory is the discipline that studies systems in the abstract. Its goal is to describe features common to all systems, such as the processing of information, the ability to interact with environments, and the ability to adaptively respond to environmental changes. Typically, systems are thought of either as functions together with function operations such as composition, or as abstract data types, i.e. as collections of objects operated on so as to produce input-output pairs. The interesting capacities of systems are described in terms of the interactions of their defining functions. I claim that systems theory would provide the framework and requisite theoretical language for developing a theory of intelligence. For example, systems theory provides us with mathematical tools needed to precisely state a general definition of intelligence based on the well-known observation that intelligence is the ability to act appropriately in a situation even when the system is ignorant of most of the information relevant to the situation (see Dietrich and Fields, 1987, Fields and Dietrich, 1987). Moreover, with its abstract view of systems, systems theory is ideal for incorporating the work of neuroscience, including the two ideas mentioned above, as well as results from operations research, control theory, cybernetics, and social biology.

Now, finally, we can return to programs. The science of intelligent systems that I have sketched above will be an experimental science, as all sciences are to some extent. It will enable researchers to perform experiments on natural systems such as neurosystems, and some populations (e.g. ant colonies). However, not all of the systems that fall under its purview will be open to experimentation (e.g. human populations). Furthermore, some of its hypotheses might not initially map onto any existing natural system (they might, for example, simply be wrong hypotheses, or we might not be able to recognize their instantiation in natural systems). In these cases, computer programs could be used to model the systems with respect to the given hypotheses. In the science of intelligent systems, therefore, computer programs would have a definite role: they would allow scientists to experiment with hypotheses about the nature of intelligence.[13]

Notes

1 Researchers change group membership depending on their current interests and views, and a researcher may be in both groups at the same time.

2 The ambiguous status of programs is disturbing for another reason. Research in AI is typically not taken seriously unless a program accompanies it. But with their status so ambiguous, it is not clear why programs legitimize research, or even that they should.

3 See Randell (1982) and Ceruzzi (1986). Howard Aiken, who built the first electromechanical computer in the United States once said " if it should ever turn out that the basic logics of a machine designed for the numerical solution of differential equations coincide with the logics of a machine intended to make bills for a department store, I would regard this as the most amazing coincidence that I have ever encountered." (1956)

4 For an explanation of Logic Theorist, see also Barr and Feigenbaum (1981). For a good presentation of the history surrounding the development of Logic Theorist, see McCorduck (1979).

5 Heuristic search is often touted as the basic problem-solving strategy used by, for example, creative mathematicians (see, e.g., Newell, Shaw, and Simon, 1963; and Barr and Feigenbaum, 1981). It seems clear, however, that heuristic search is not powerful enough, and that some other strategy is needed (see Dietrich and Fields, 1987 and 1986).

6 This situation somewhat resembles filling out the existing theory, in what Kuhn has called *normal science* (1962).

7 I have already discussed the failure of Logic Theorist, above. When work was halted on GPS, it could only solve a handful of small puzzles. For a discussion of the performance of GPS, see Ernst and Newell (1969), and Barr and Feigenbaum (1981). A discussion of the failures of AM, Eurisko, and Bacon are beyond the scope of this paper. These programs didn't fail, exactly, rather their (limited) success appears to have crucially depended on massaging the input data so that solutions were easily discovered, and liberally interpreting the output and behavior of the programs. For AM, see Lenat (1982), and Lenat and Brown (1984). For EURISKO, see Lenat (1983). For BACON, see Langley, *et al.* (1983); Grabiner (1986) gives a clear, detailed account of its failure. For another example, see Winston (1978) who discusses the possibility of the failure of his learning program, but, typically, does not pursue such a possibility. There is a class of AI programs that do perform well in their proper, limited environments. This is the class of expert systems that are used in industry, e.g. MACSYMA (MACSYMA group, 1977), DENDRAL (Buchanan and Feigenbaum, 1978), and R1 (J. McDermott, 1981). It is well-known that these expert systems perform as well or better than their human counterparts for the specific problems they were designed for. However, expert systems are *tools*, just like word-processors and hand-held calculators; they are not attempts to build generally intelligent machines (see Stefik, *et al.*, 1982; Hayes-Roth, *et al.*, 1983; Barr and Feigenbaum, 1982; and Fields, 1987).

8 In some circles, the physical symbol system hypothesis is losing all of its scientific status, and becoming a methodology. And, AI is becoming the discipline consisting only of adherents to this methodology. Thus, AI is becoming the discipline which just *assumes* that thinking is symbol manipulation. Of course, such a position is very dangerous: if it should turn out that this assumption is false, AI will disappear.

9 Modern psychoanalysis has also been likened to early astrology. (For more on this point see Kuhn, 1970.)

10 Certainly, one way for AI to become a science is to begin to treat the physical symbol system hypothesis as a hypothesis, and to *explore* whether or not digital computers can actually be intelligent. Of course, it has been my thesis that were AI to do this, it would immediately have to come to terms with the fact that its large class of significant failures seriously jeopardizes this hypothesis.

11 See for example, Hubel and Wiesel (1970), and Delbruck (1986).

12 See for example, Maturana (1970). For work on color vision, see Land (1977).

13 My thinking on the subject of intelligence and intelligent systems has been greatly influenced by my colleague Chris Fields. I have greatly benefited also from discussions with Dan Fass, Robin Hill, Derek Partridge, Tony Plate, Liz Rachele, and Yorick Wilks.

7 Rational reconstruction as an AI methodology

Rational reconstruction (reproducing the essence of the program's significant behavior with another program constructed from descriptions of the purportedly important aspects of the original program) has been one approach to assessing the value of published claims about programs.

Campbell attempts to account for why the status of AI vis-a-vis the conventional sciences is a problematic issue. He outlines three classes of theories, the distinguishing elements of which are: equations; entities, operations and a set of axioms; and general principles capable of particularization in different forms. Models in AI, he claims, tend to fall in the last class of theory.

He argues for the methodology of rational reconstruction as an important component of a science of AI, even though the few attempts so far have not been particularly successful, if success is measured in terms of the similarity of behavior between the original AI system and the subsequent rational reconstruction. But, as Campbell points out, it is analysis and exploration of exactly these discrepancies that is likely to lead to significant progress in AI.

The second paper in this section is a reprint of one of the more celebrated attempts to analyse a famous AI program. In addition, to an analysis of the published descriptions of how the program works with respect to the program's behaviour (Lenat's 'creative rediscovery' system AM), Richie and Hanna discuss more general considerations of the rational-reconstruction methodology.

Three novelties of AI: theories, programs and rational reconstructions

J. A. Campbell

Most of the difficulty of including AI in the standard collection of sciences is that there are recurring features of the best or most-publicized work in AI that are hard to fit into the conventional observation-hypothesis-deduction-observation pattern of those sciences. Some parts of the difficulty can be clarified and resolved by showing that certain details of what is involved in AI have underlying similarities with corresponding steps in other sciences, despite their superficial differences. The treatment of 'theories' and 'programs' below is intended as a commentary on that remark. A further part of the difficulty is that AI still lacks some scientific credibility because it does not yet seem to have the standard of reproducibility and communicability of results that is built into other sciences. The difficulty is illuminated by activities in AI research that have come to be known as 'rational reconstructions'. While the earliest attempts at rational reconstruction have generally been less than successful, the idea itself is potentially useful as a means of generating new knowledge or mapping out new territory in AI.

On theories, models and representations

Sciences are supposed to have underlying theories, and technologies rely on theories through the help of their supporting sciences. The first hesitation among outside observers to give AI full credit for being a science or technology comes from the difficulty of identifying AI's theory or theories. It is common for people inside AI to say in response that such a theory may seem unconventional to others merely because it is contained within a program or because it *is* a program – but this statement has never converted an outsider in my experience. Instead, it reinforces the hesitation. An alternative way to tackle this problem of persuasion or education is to ask what are the possible structures of theories, and then to see how AI (among other subjects) can claim to respect them.

Broadly speaking, there are three types of theories in scientific subjects. One is expressed through equations; quantum mechanics and special and

237

general theories of relativity are of this type. A second variety, common in mathematics, is stated in terms of basic entities and operations, plus sets of axioms. Anything that can be done with the operations and that respects the axioms is a legal consequence of the theory. Here, the axioms act as constraints, helping to specify boundaries and internal structure of the space of possible results or behaviours, but not having much to say about the relative importance of different parts of that space. The third variety starts from a statement of a general principle or principles, and is capable of particularization in many different forms when the more specific details are filled in. The general statement is often taken to *be* the theory, especially by people who can find uses for it without having to supply any more specific details. What is popularly meant by the Darwinian 'theory' of evolution is probably the best-known example.

All three types of theory are explored routinely through the medium of computer programs when their expected consequences are too complex to generate otherwise. The question of complexity, in the particular case of AI, is discussed further in the next section. Explorations of theories do not divide into three sharply-defined classes; there are grey areas on their mutual boundaries. For equation-based theories, the programs are normally entirely algorithmic and solve the relevant equations, but there are nevertheless instances of heuristic search for solutions where no algorithm is known. Campbell (1979) gives one such example. In the case of theories relying on axioms or constraints, which are usually mathematical, heuristics that are appropriate for control of the exploration of the space of possible results can be very subtle and reflect such things as a mathematician's sense of aesthetics. In most of these situations the user and the program act as partners, with the user supplying the subjective evaluations, but it is possible to leave significant aspects of the choice of direction to the program if relatively simple criteria of purpose or optimization are added. Some exercises in automatic theorem-proving and symbolic mathematical simplifications are of this kind.

For the third class of theory to appear inside a program, it is necessary for its generalities to be backed up by enough specific details to allow the program to compute something of interest. The combination of general and specific information is often described as a model. In some cases, e.g. in cognitive science, models do not evolve to a finished state on paper before they are written into a program; particularly if some of the specifics are axiomatic or declarative, the model may be developed through interactive changes to the program until the developer regards the resulting computations as sufficiently interesting or relevant. It is then not unreasonable to speak of the program as the model, particularly if there is no obvious way to summarize the effects of the control mechanisms that have arisen during the development process short of running the programs on numerous test problems. Where this picture illustrates a piece of work in AI, the program/model is in fact a fleshed-out basic theory of the third type mentioned above.

Models in AI often fit this last form of description in the details but seem to be open to criticism for lacking the 'general principles' that are either its backbone or its scaffolding. However, the description gives an equally good account of scientists' experiments with (and tuning of) theoretical constructs of the second or 'axiomatic' kind, where there is no need for the broad organizing principles to exist. It is rather unlikely that a programmable theoretical construct in AI will be of the first (equational) kind, but the second and third kinds of description together cover typical activities in AI research rather well. Moreover, they cover typical activities in other fields of scientific research equally well. In terms of adjectives that are now quite popular in discussions of method in AI, these descriptions refer to scruffy theories while equational theories are neat. Reluctance to regard theory-making or model-making work in AI as respectable can be traced frequently to the mistaken view that the only respectable scientific theories are neat theories.

No example of any of these classes of theories has much claim to being scientifically interesting unless its essence is a representation which associates information and definitions in a compressed form that is capable of yielding much more information economically and reproducibly. Representations in successful sciences get much of their power of compression by using as building-blocks abstractions which are not-necessarily-intuitive transformations of terms that are themselves accessible to (say) lower-division undergraduates studying those sciences. The Hamiltonian formulation of classical mechanics is a good instance.

Similar instances have begun to be recognized in AI. Representational schemes like first-order logics, semantic nets, version spaces, frames and scripts have already demonstrated their value by providing good service that is not problem-specific, and much activity in AI research involves either explicit or implicit evaluation of the possible usefulness of other schemes. If there is any recurring element in criticism of AI at the level of representations, it is that the stock of representations in AI is not as large or static as in the established sciences and technologies. But this view is merely another way of saying that the established sciences and technologies are older than AI. Moreover, representations in any science can change when the science is passing through a lively stage of development. In that respect, older subjects like elementary-particle physics (especially where it touches on general relativity) are just as lively as AI, or vice versa.

A theory is not convincing unless it is accompanied by a set of methods that cause it to yield up its information readily. Normally, a theory and its methods are considered as one entity, but this is likely to be unjust to other subjects besides AI (where the separation is the rule rather than the exception). For example, quantum electrodynamics (QED) in 1948 looked very different from QED in, say 1955, because of the post–1948 acceptance of Feynman rules and diagrams as methods that changed the way in which a basically unchanged information-carrying representation (a classical Hamiltonian formalism extended by quantum-mechanical features which were already in place and well appreciated by 1948) could be understood. One way to see the difference is to compare the coverage of the same general topic by Eliezer (1946) and Feynman (1962).

While AI has not yet shown any equally dramatic shifts of view, the search for methods and techniques is now a recognized part of AI research. The details of such methods as pattern-directed invocation, propagation of constraints and inheritance of properties are influencing the details of generally-useful representation schemes, and are being influenced by them in turn.

On these interpretations of theory, method and representation, AI needs no extra help to justify membership in the league of sciences. The primary element of an AI 'theory' is just a *representation* of information from which substantial consequences can be derived by prescribed methods or operations. To establish the soundness of a theory in principle, the methods' feasibility need be demonstrated just in principle. In practice, a representation is only useful in AI when it is joined with methods that can extract the consequences in acceptable times and with acceptable demands on computing resources. The best illustration that this last point is not trivial is that the large-scale use of one class of representations (first-order logics), whose importance was first asserted early in the history of AI, was nevertheless delayed for some time – until the arrival of the computing interpretations and techniques of Prolog, to be exact.

On programs

The usual way of testing a theory or model is to extract its consequences or predictions for a chosen situation that has few enough controlled variables to allow trustworthy and repeated observations, make observations of the phenomena that have been predicted, and then compare the predictions with what is observed. In this two-stage picture, any step which is not part of the process of observation is part of the process of prediction. Where typical sciences use computer programs, the programs are auxiliary supports for their pen-and-paper theories rather than independently-interesting objects in the exercise. (Simulation programs fit the same description if we replace 'theories' by 'experiments'.)

Given the typical scientific and technological attitudes to programs, what special features of AI justify the opinion that an AI program can be an object with its own scientific importance? The answer seems to be the same as the answer to the question of why a puppet is uninteresting while Frankenstein's[1] monster is interesting. The puppet is a purely algorithmic object (apart from any seemingly random bugs in the implementation), performing functions that its operator can perform equally well but finds it convenient not to. Frankenstein's monster is capable of behaviour that is autonomous and not always predictable or imitatable by the builder or by the experts on the design-standards committee of his professional association. This behaviour may occur because the methods of extracting *qualitatively* new results from the underlying theory are so complex that not all of their consequences can be identified or visualized before the program-execution stage. (The italicized word is used to distinguish this situation from most large conventional programming exercises, but the distinction is not sharp enough to exclude some of the most adventurous large FORTRAN exercises, such as the 'experimental mathematics' of dynamical systems and cellular automata. A probable lesson for AI is that we should try to accommodate them rather than to exclude them, e.g. by lending them tools for backtracking and heuristic search.) It may also occur because the collection of relevant methods is incomplete and because the only way to identify acceptable results is 'generate and test'. Or, as a member of the US Supreme Court is reported to have said about pornography: 'I can't define it, but I know it when I see it.' Whichever of these explanations is responsible for the Frankenstein's-monster effect in any particular case, the interest of an AI program as such lies in the non-algorithmic complexity of the interaction of components that are not necessarily complex in themselves.

This last description can also be applied to simulation programs, which suggests (correctly, in my opinion) that there is some genuine and not merely incidental overlap between content and technique for AI and for simulation, e.g. in object-oriented programming and in dealing efficiently with inheritance of properties. However, there are two further comments about complexity of program behaviour which distinguish AI from topics like simulation. The first is that simulation is a means of dealing with complexity where a sufficient scaling-down of the problem allows 'finding the exact answer' to take over. For example, simulations are common in computational physics to determine the behaviour of systems of 100 or more molecules (a model for a gas) in motion in an enclosed volume, but a reduction of 100+ to 2 would make it possible just to solve the appropriate equations of motion. While something of the same kind may be possible for some AI problems, this is obviously not the rule. Interesting AI problems may remain interesting simply because there is no significant scaling-down which does not change their character. The effect is present in many families of non-linear equations where individual equations may be solved, or the equations characterized, by the use of fixed-point theorems or similar mathematical tools. The same theorems show that the typical simplifications of the equations that can be justified by the desire to scale down a problem or to discard its smallest inputs change the character of the solutions completely, i.e. the simplified conditions describe qualitatively different problems. In general only linear systems escape this difficulty. And whatever else AI is, it is a safe bet that it is not a linear science.

The second comment is that, while the first AI programs written to help solve a given problem usually rely heavily on a non-algorithmic approach, as evidenced by emphasis on heuristics, search and backtracking, further progress on that problem commonly means a shift towards fixing contexts, defining frames or scripts, or even devising algorithms, to be built into better programs. This development can be seen in the chart-parsing schemes for natural language and in the fact that the Waltz filtering procedure and the Hough transform have both been regarded as highlights of progress in parts of AI. The best example of the development is so good that it is invisible to most AI workers: the conversion of symbolic integration from the heuristic subject of Slagle's (1963) program SAINT and the mainly-heuristic subject of Moses' program SIN (usually quoted as a part of the MACSYMA system) in 1966–67 (Moses, 1967) to the algorithmic subject of Davenport's (1981) book (which describes the majority of the current properties of symbolic integration as used in MACSYMA and other systems, though some AI authorities seem to believe that nothing has changed there since 1966). An indication of the success of the development is that AI researchers do not now consider symbolic integration as a part of AI, despite the past contributions that AI has made to the success.

A considerable justification for the concentration on programs in AI is that programs are the natural vehicles for the study of evolution of the problem-solving behaviour that is characteristic of intelligence. The evolution starts from pure or general heuristics, and can proceed through stages of 'generate and test' and the recognition of successful tools, macros, scripts etc. to the assembly of successful components into models and sometimes later into algorithms. However, this evolution can involve cycles as well as limit points, i.e. it may be premature for AI specialists to abandon a line of research or turn it over to somebody else when an algorithmic solution is in sight. For example, the current integration algorithm contains a term-generating procedure that can be frightened into generating large numbers of spurious terms (whose coefficients are found to be zero by later stages of the algorithm) by integrands containing products of moderately high powers of elementary trigonometric functions. The procedure can be replaced for these cases by heuristics, which generally work better. Why? And what does 'generally' mean? AI is just as likely as mathematics to produce answers to these questions if it is prepared to readmit integration to its list of respectable problems.

An incidental bonus of the description in the last two paragraphs is that it illustrates almost exactly the standard observation-hypothesis-deduction-observation cycle of scientific development. Here, mathematical results that are apparently obtained through a mixture of techniques play the part of the initial unstructured field of observations, and the mixture of behaviours in the term-generating procedure for symbolic integration is an example of the new and unsuspected problems that turn up at the end of any cycle mediated by a good theory. (I am assuming that 'good' is not the word for any theory or hypothesis that solves problems without raising new ones.) Heuristics have been essential in this case to allow better understanding of the questions of integration and to speed up progress towards a sound general hypothesis. Heuristics have the same job in other sciences, but they are not often acknowledged as essential to progress. Therefore AI may have a contribution to make to the better understanding of the scientific process as a whole, through stressing the importance of heuristics and heuristic reasoning.

On rational reconstructions

To a non-American observer, it seems surprising that US AI groups in certain areas do not report more often that they have received and further developed the *programs* embodying the work of other groups that have announced significant advances in performance capabilities in those areas. To a general observer brought up in the traditions of the physical or biological sciences, progress in AI looks more like the result of a random walk than the focused progress that is achieved by defining short-term to medium-term landmark problems, identifying the consequent defects in theories or needs for crucial experiments, and acting on the identifications. To an American observer, probably the most curious trend (even though it has not been a large one so far) in European AI is the rise of the rational-reconstruction industry, in which European researchers start from the published information about an American project or program and try to reconstruct or reproduce (usually unsuccessfully) the performance of the corresponding program or method. Examples are the work of Knapman (1978) on analogy-formation as reported in Winston's Ph.D. thesis, Ritchie and Hanna (1984a and reprinted in this volume) on Lenat's AM program, and Bramer and Cendrowska (1984) on MYCIN and expert systems.

The first conclusion that can be drawn from the fact that anyone has any significant problems with a rational reconstruction is that AI as a subject may need some internal repairs, to improve the standard of reproducibility and communicability of results. In the better-established sciences (where, incidentally, the idea of a rational reconstruction does not exist), such problems are either absent or are relatively short-lived and have a special status that is mentioned below. Apart from this latter special case, which does not seem to be relevant to past experiments in rational reconstruction in AI, there are arguments in favour of looking for and correcting any internal qualitative or quantitative defects in the subject that may make it easier for witch-doctors to practise than in normative sciences like physics and biology.

Some of AI's difficulties of communication can be cured administratively. Any widely-acceptable means of reducing the average percentage of citations of unpublished or unrefereed works in AI papers to the average found in papers in other experimental sciences will do. This can reduce the risk, for example, of persistence of misunderstandings of what an unpublished and hard-to-find reference X actually says or means when claims about its contents are made or repeated too uncritically in published reference Y1, then repeated in published reference Y2 that cites both X and Y1 but takes the information about X only from Y1, then repeated in Y3 . . . and so on. Thanks to the commercial attractiveness of AI to publishers in the present and foreseeable future, the past unavailability of enough avenues of publication to give a fair chance for circulation of X as well as Y1, Y2, etc. is unlikely to be an impediment.

Where the entity of scientific interest is not a method but a theory or a program, conventional publication may be impractical. However, because of the special status of programs in AI as discussed above, 'unconventional publication' is a better answer than unofficial announcement in a research report. A program-and-documentation registry with agreed and publicized submission standards and standards for acceptance (though obviously more relaxed than the kinds of standards that would apply for, say, a journal or for a library of numerical-algorithm packages in FORTRAN), free access, and facilities for accumulating case-study and commentary information on the program material that it holds, is a possible answer[2] to the needs of reproducibility and communicability where AI achievements are intrinsic to programs or programmed models. This is not a proposal for collecting commercial knowledge-based systems; the material of interest is likely to be limited to products of Ph.D. thesis projects and the work of research groups that are specifically concerned with AI basics rather than applications. Similar schemes with some of these features are in operation on a small scale for other subjects already, usually as one of a larger number of activities in a substantial centre of research, and with running costs covered by income from agencies that offer research contracts or grants.

Although the previous discussion suggests that the existence of rational-reconstruction activity shows that a subject is in some methodological trouble, this is by no means the only conclusion that can be drawn. Happier conclusions are also possible. For example, some of the particular difficulties that have been seen in AI during attempts at rational reconstruction have also been noted in other subjects. In the case of AI, these difficulties have included inability to reproduce some behaviour from an agreed toolkit of components or methods, and inability to achieve an agreed behaviour with the same toolkit that has been used by another group. In other scientific subjects these are known but short-lived phenomena which are perceived as important problems in themselves when they arise, requiring early attention or (re)definition of terms or both. Historically this treatment has often been a key to progress, e.g. by setting up new conceptual units or bases, or by showing equivalence of supposedly incompatible approaches. Hence there is a case for giving more exposure to examples of rational-reconstruction problems when they occur in AI, and for thorough discussion of their details, rather than for regarding them as embarrassments which should be quietly buried.

In addition, experiments in rational reconstruction are worth active encouragement because of their potential for exploration of dependence of the behaviour of programs or models on 'inessential' details. Given adequate communication of specifications and results, it is unlikely that a rational reconstruction will produce surprising behaviour (or a surprising lack of behaviour) because of misunderstandings about major and basic features of a design. However, lesser features or aspects of design that are taken for granted or covered only in outline in an original description may be misunderstood, and therefore not reproduced, in a reconstruction. In a space of conceivable programs or models, the reconstruction will then be a point fairly close to the point representing the original work. In scientific terms, the behaviour of the reconstruction should then also be fairly close to the behaviour of the original: discontinuities in such spaces are not very common. But if the behaviours fail to correspond closely, then the reconstructors will have discovered something new and presumably unexpected about the properties of that part of the space, which will be of importance for (and give impetus to) further work on improving the understanding of the relevant issues or assumptions in AI. Even semi-accidental progress is still progress: the fact that Columbus operated with approximate sailing directions for China and found Cuba instead is generally regarded as a positive event in the evolution of geography.

Summary

The main arguments that have been made above are:

> that AI fits the normal paradigm for scientific development where 'theory' or 'hypothesis' is replaced by 'representation' and 'means of extracting information from a representation'. (These alternative labels are well adapted to describing the theoretical stage of the development cycle in other sciences too, but their meanings are probably never so well separated as in AI.)

> that programs in AI are legitimate objects of scientific interest where a conventional 'theory' is too static or insufficiently expressive to describe phenomena for which the essential issue is the non-algorithmic complexity of the interaction of components that are not necessarily complex in themselves. This is particularly so when the phenomena are destroyed by any significant scaling-down.

> that AI emphasizes the status of heuristics in the step between observations and the formulation of theories or hypotheses, and that this emphasis may also lead to improvements in the understanding of the character of other sciences.

> that AI would be improved as a science if more effort were devoted to improvements in reproducibility and communicability of research results, particularly where these results are inseparable from the operation of programs.

that rational-reconstruction difficulties deserve inspection rather than minimization, because they may be AI's example of 'representational-incompatibility' or 'discontinuity-finding' problems whose study in other sciences has often led to significant progress.

Notes

1 The original version of this paper was written when I was based at the University of Exeter, which tends to miss out on the currents of intellectual history for reasons of geography and climate. It is therefore a pleasure to note here one particular exception to that rule: Dr Frankenstein was in fact a local boy. His model in real life, Andrew Crosse, was a West Somerset landowner in the late eighteenth century. Crosse's resulting income allowed him some leisure to carry out scientific experiments in the style of a West Country Benjamin Franklin (Haining, 1979).

2 There have been some trends in this direction since the paper was first written. For example, a periodical *Artificial Intelligence Abstracts*, which has abstracted both published papers and less formal material, has appeared (although it has now disappeared again because of production difficulties). A similar and more extensive abstracting service is provided by the Turing Institute in Glasgow. More recently, Carnegie-Mellon University and the On-Line Computer Library Center have started a project called Mercury for the American Association for Artificial Intelligence, "to provide electronic access to materials in Artificial Intelligence". Potential users can obtain further information by sending a message to the electronic mail address AM77@vma.cc.cmu.edu with HELP as the first word of its text, and potential contributors are also being invited (at the address KG18@andrew.cmu.edu in the first instance). It is likely that the special needs and features of AI, mentioned above, will lead to further developments of this kind.

AM: a case study in AI methodology

G.D. Ritchie and F.K. Hanna

1 Introduction

Artificial intelligence is still a relatively young science, in which there are still various influences from different parent disciplines (psychology, philosophy, computer science, etc.). One symptom of this situation is the lack of any clearly defined way of carrying out research in the field (see D. McDermott, 1981, for some pertinent comments on this topic). There used to be a tendency for workers (particularly Ph.D. students) to indulge in what McCarthy has called the "look-ma-no-hands" approach (Hayes, 1975b), in which the worker writes a large, complex program, produces one or two impressive printouts and then writes papers stating that he has done this. The deficiency of this style of "research" is that it is theoretically sterile – it does not develop principles and does not clarify or define the real research problems. What has happened over recent years is that some attempt is now made to outline the principles which a program is supposed to implement. That is, the worker still constructs a complex program with impressive behaviour, but he also provides a statement of how it achieves this performance. Unfortunately, in some cases, the written "theory" may not correspond to the program in detail, but the writer avoids emphasizing (or sometimes even conceals) this discrepancy, resulting in methodological confusion. The "theory" is supposedly justified, or given empirical credibility, by the presence of the program (although the program may have been designed in a totally different way); hence the theory is not subjected to other forms of argument or examination. Anyone trying to repeat or develop the reported work may find that the written accounts are inconsistent or apparently incorrect, despite the fact that they have been presented as tried and tested. In this situation, the unfortunate person who wishes to continue in this field must return to the beginning, since the alleged "state-of-the-art" (i.e. his predecessor's "theory") gives very little guidance. It specifies a performance to be attained, but not how to attain it. What then has the original work achieved, in scientific terms?

We will illustrate this methodological phenomenon using an example of

247

recent research in artificial intelligence. Lenat (1976) has described a program ("AM") which "discovers" concepts and conjectures in elementary mathematics, and he claims that the program progresses from pre-numerical knowledge to that of an undergraduate mathematics student. Since Lenat was invited to give the 1977 *Computers and Thought* lecture (Lenat, 1977b), we assume that this work (hailed in Meltzer, 1977, as a major advance) was held in high esteem by the AI community. Although Lenat makes some interesting proposals which can be assessed on their own merits, the substance of his research is based on the AM program. Close inspection of the written accounts of AM (Lenat, 1976, Lenat, 1977a, Lenat, 1979) suggests that there are some worrying discrepancies between the theoretical claims and the implemented program, and it is this aspect which we wish to consider here. We accept that the AM program was capable of producing the published output. What we wish to argue is that the written accounts (particularly Lenat, 1977a, and the early chapters of Lenat, 1976) give a misleading view of how the program worked, to an extent which obscures the real contribution of the work, and which may confuse others in the field.

Sections 2–4 will contain an examination of the account of the AM program given in Lenat (1976). This will involve a large amount of technical detail, but this is necessary to substantiate our main argument. In section 5 we will return to the issue of research methodology and make some observations based on technical discussion in the body of the paper.

2 The official overview

The behavior of AM is neatly summarized by Lenat:

> AM began its investigations with scanty knowledge of a hundred elementary concepts of finite set theory. Most of the obvious set-theoretic concepts and relationships were quickly found (e.g. de Morgan's laws; singletons), but no sophisticated set theory was ever done (e.g. diagonalization). Rather, AM discovered natural numbers and went off exploring elementary number theory. Arithmetic operations were soon found (as analogs to set-theoretic operations) and AM made rapid progress to divisibility theory. Prime pairs, Diophantine equations, the unique factorization of numbers into primes, Goldbach's conjecture – these were some of the nice discoveries by AM. (*Lenat, 1977a, p. 839*)

The program initially contains data-structures representing about 100 elementary mathematical concepts (e.g. sets, composition of operations) and about 230 "heuristic rules". The data-structures are similar to the "frames" of Minsky (1975) or Bobrow and Winograd (1979), in that they are "concepts" containing a list of "facets" (slots) which can be filled with other data-items. The "heuristic rules" are like "productions" (Newell, 1978), in that each rule has a "test" (a conjoined list of truth-valued expressions) and an "action" (a list of executable statements, with side-effects). AM proceeds by trying to fill in facets of concepts using the rules. The program is controlled by an "agenda" of "tasks", in order of priority. Each task-descriptor on the agenda includes a note of a particular "operation-type" (of which there are only two or three), a particular "facet-name" (of which there are about twenty) and a particular concept-name. That is, a task is always of the form

"Do operation A to facet F of concept C".

The task descriptor has other information (e.g. the amount of time and space allocated to it) but no associated program (that is, it is not like an executable process description, but is more like a specification of a "goal" to be achieved). The scheduler in AM always takes the top (highest priority) task from the agenda, and attempts to carry it out by finding suitable heuristic rules. Every rule has, as the first conjunct of its list of tests, a check to see what the operation-type, facet and concept of the current task are, and so each rule can be stored on exactly the facet to which it is appropriate. That is, every facet of every concept has a few "sub-facets" (one for each of the operation-types), containing lists of rules appropriate to tasks involving that combination of concept, facet and operation-type.

Having found the relevant rules by this indexing mechanism, the AM system applies each one by checking its "tests" and, if all these yield "true", executing its actions. This goes on until the collected group of rules are all applied, or the time/space allocation for the current task is exhausted.

The concepts are organized into a hierarchy of "specializations" and "generalizations", with each concept having a facet to hold a list of known examples. In this way, heuristic rules can be stored only once for a general concept, and more specialized concepts (lower down the hierarchy) can inherit the general rules during the process of retrieving relevant heuristics. In general, any facet of a concept will be "inherited" by that concept's specializations.

Each task has a priority rating, and every facet and concept in the initial data-structure has a "worth", representing how "interesting" it is. These numerical measures, and computations on them, are used to direct the flow of the program in useful directions. Newly created concepts are given "worths" according to various formulae in the rules which create them.

The program prints out various messages to inform the human user of its progress, and the user can interrupt at any point to request further information or to give AM a limited amount of direction.

Starting with the initial base of about 100 concepts and 230 rules, AM "discovers" (i.e. constructs and categorizes as "interesting") various mathematical concepts, including natural numbers, and several conjectures, such as the fact that numbers can be uniquely factorized into primes.

3 Assessing AM

It is extremely hard to evaluate work of this nature. Lenat (1976) discusses AM from various standpoints, but most of his comments are based on the assumption that the program had "discovered" various mathematical concepts using a very simple, uniform, concept-based search procedure. He goes on to discuss further issues, such as the need for "meta-heuristics", (rules about rules) or how AM's perfomance compares with a human's (about "undergraduate math major", he estimates). We would like to discuss the more fundamental question of what it was that AM actually did. To be more specific:

(3.1) Was the control structure simply the uniform regime described in Lenat, 1976, chapters 1–6 and in Lenat, 1977a? This is not a mere implementation detail, since the organization of tasks, concepts and rules (outlined in section 2 above) is Lenat's answer to the crucial question: how does the program choose what to do at any given point in its inferences?

(3.2) Were there procedures and statements in the program (other than the heuristic rules) which embodied important "knowledge" for the operation of the system?

(3.3) What did AM actually discover, and to what extent should it be assessed on its results (as opposed to its internal workings)?

We shall attempt to answer some of these questions in the following sections, using quotations from Lenat, 1976 wherever appropriate, but without listing all the evidence exhaustively. (All page numbers will be from Lenat, 1976 unless otherwise stated.)

4 How does AM work?
4.1 Control structure

The description in Lenat, 1977a and in Lenat, 1976, chapters 1–6 states, quite definitely, that AM has only the simple control structure outlined in section 2 above. The scheduler takes the top priority task, finds the relevant rules via the operation/concept/facet triple, and executes these rules:

> AM repeatedly selects the top task from the agenda and tries to carry it out. This is the whole control structure! (*p. 15*)

> The flow of control is simple: AM picks the task with the highest priority value, and tries to execute it. (*p. 34*)

> What precisely does AM do, in order to execute the task? . . . The answer can be compactly stated as follows: "AM selects relevant heuristics, and executes them." (*p. 35*)

Also, the heuristic rules are claimed to be stored in the relevant concept structures:

> The secret is that each heuristic rule is stored somewhere apropos to its 'domain of applicability'. This 'proper place' is determined by the first conjunct in the left-hand side of the rule. (*p. 54*)

> The key observation is that a heuristic typically applies to *all examples of a particular concept C* . . . This is in fact where the heuristic rule is stored. (*p. 55*)

> Initially, the author identified the proper concept C and facet F for each heuristic H which A possessed, and tacked H onto C.F [C.F is the abbreviation for facet F of concept C]. This was all preparation, completed long before AM started up. Each heuristic was tacked on to the facet which uniquely indicates its domain of applicability. (*p. 55*)

The relevant concept-facet pair for storing each rule is determined thus:

> The first conjunct of the IF-part of each heuristic indicates where it is stored and where it is applicable. (*p. 55*)

> In fact, AM physically attaches each rule to the facet and concept mentioned in its first conjunct. (*p. 37*)

The rules' first conjuncts should specify not only a concept/facet pair, but also an action:

> The first conjunct will always be written out as follows, in this document (where A, F and C are specified explicitly): The current task (the one just selected from the agenda) is of the form 'Do action A to the F facet of concept C'. (*p. 37*)

> . . . each facet of each concept can have two additional 'subfacets' . . . named Fillin and Check. 'Fillin' field of facet F of concept C is abbreviated C.F.Fillin. The format of that subfield is a list of heuristic rules, encoded into LISP functions. Semantically, each rule in C.F.Fillin should be relevant to filling in entries for facet F of any concept which is a C. (*p. 101*)

It must be emphasized that these quotations are not taken misleadingly out of context; the written accounts (e.g. Lenat, 1977a) do give a very definite impression that the principle claim being advanced for the AM program was that a simple, uniform control structure does in fact produce the impressive output already alluded to. Closer inspection of the thesis and (more particularly) the rules in the Appendix 3 reveals that the AM program did not actually function in this way.

There is some confusion about the "sub-facets" on which rules may be entered. Sometimes (for example, p. 101), two sub-facets (Check and Fillin) are listed, whereas other remarks (for example, p. 67) refer to three (Check, Fillin and Suggest). On p. 41, there is the remark (pertaining to task-types):

> Each possible act A (e.g. Fillin, Check, Apply, etc.) . . .

which seems to imply a wider set than just Fillin and Check. ("Apply" is not referred to elsewhere.) The rules in the appendix are categorized under four subheadings – Check, Fillin, Suggest and Interest. Of these, only Check and Fillin fit clearly into the generalization of being actions that define a task (as in the quotations from p. 37 and p. 101 given above). The "Suggest" rules are described (p. 100) as rules to be used when there are no sufficiently interesting tasks on the agenda, but no explanation is given as to why they should, in this case, be attached to concepts or facets. Obviously, it would allow the Suggest rules to be scanned by running through all the concepts in the system, but this could be achieved by having a simple global list of all Suggest heuristics in the system. No details are given of how this search occurs (e.g. from the top of the Concept hierarchy), despite the fact that this is a fairly central question when considering AM's decision process. ("AM may call on all the Suggest facets in the system" (p. 100).) Also, it is still not clear whether "Suggest" is a facet (containing the rules associated with a concept) or a sub-facet (as implied on p. 226).

The "Interest" rules do not seem to fit into the scheme of being a rule "to do A to facet F of C", since they state aspects of a structure which make it "interesting": e.g.

> An operation is interesting if its values are interesting.

On p. 67, a facet is defined thus (for any concept C):

> Interestingness: what special features make C especially interesting?

The casual reader might think that this had something to do with "Interest" rules since all the "Interest" rules given in Lenat, 1976 are under headings like "Operation.Interest", "Composition.Interest". However, pp. 97–99 describe the contents of the "Interest" facet, and these are "Interest features" (not heuristic rules). It is left to the reader to make the following deduction:

> Interest rules compute Interest values for a Concept.
> There is (p. 67), a facet "Worth" which rates how interesting a Concept is.
> Hence, Interest rules can be looked on as filling in (or altering) the "Worth" of Concepts.

Hence, these rules should be stored in the "Fillin" or "Check" subfacets of the "Worth" facet.

(I.e. the many headings in the appendix to Lenat, 1976 of the form "C.Interest" are shorthand for "C.Worth.Fillin".)

Many rules in the appendix are listed against a sub-facet of a *concept*, not of a facet of a concept. (For example, "Insertion.Check", "Coalesce. Fillin", "Canonise.Suggest".) This seems to suggest that a concept may have a group of Check, Fillin and Suggest heuristics which are not associated with any facet in particular. There is also the interpretation that such entries are really rules stored on the Examples facet for that concept; that is, subheadings such as Insertion.Check, Coalesce.Fillin are abbreviations for the Insertion.Examples.Check, Coalesce.Examples.Fillin, respectively. As it happens, almost all the rules given in Lenat, 1976 are under subheadings which do not specify a facet-name. Only the rules associated with "Any-concept" have full subheadings of the form "C.F.A" (e.g. Any-concept.Analogies.Fillin). Hence all the Fillin and Check rules (apart from those on Any-concept) are in fact (if we adopt the convention suggested here) attached to the Example facet of the Concept – other facets have no Check or Fillin rules. Further confusion is introduced on p. 230, where there is a comment about "Any-concept":

> This concept has a huge number of heuristics. For that reason, I have partitioned off – both here and in AM – the heuristics which apply to each kind of facet. Thus the LISP program has a separate concept 'Examples-of-any-concept', another concept called 'Definitions-of-any-concept'. etc.

This renders the concept of a "concept" even less clear.

So far, the arrangement is still fairly systematic. We have to modify the statements (in the quotations above) slightly so that:

(4.1.1) Interest heuristics are stored on the Fillin sub-facets of the "Worth" facet. That is, they are invoked when a task is executed which is trying to Fillin the Worth of a Concept. (Some may also be on the Check sub-facet of the Worth facet.)

(4.1.2) Suggest heuristics are used when AM is trying to generate tasks for the agenda. They are stored on sub-facets and on concepts, but the way of using this attachment, or of choosing which rules to invoke (i.e. the way of scanning the concept hierarchy), is not specified.

(4.1.3) Heuristics described in Lenat, 1976, appendix as being on C.Check or C.Fillin are in fact stored on the corresponding sub-facet of the Examples facet of C.

(In some parts of Lenat, 1976, (for example, p. 178), Concepts are listed with facets called "Fillin", "Check", "Suggest" and "Interest", but this is presumably just an expository convenience, since it does not accord with usage elsewhere.) This still leaves one or two loose ends regarding the way that rules are stored and indexed. Some of the heuristics (section 3.1 of the appendix) are said to be for dealing with "any item X, be it concept, atom, event, etc.". It is not clear here that these could be indexed, since the rule-retrieval routines described elsewhere operate only on the hierarchy of concepts, not "atoms" or "events". (The idea of an "event" is not mentioned anywhere else.) These rules appear to be generalizations that have been included in the written description in order to summarize the effect of *various* sections of the LISP program, rather than statements of actual individual rules which AM contained in the form stated in the thesis.

The whole notion of a "Concept" is confusing. In the descriptions of how the AM program operates (e.g. pp. 14–15, pp. 28–29, pp. 42–45, most of chapter 5), a "Concept" seems to be defined as a particular kind of data-structure, having about twenty "facets" (Generalizations, Specializations, Examples, Algorithms, etc.) and representing a mathematical idea. Most of the written accounts seem to be based round this notion. However, on pp. 105–106 of Lenat, 1976, there is a diagram of "AM's Starting Concepts" which depicts a hierarchy including, at the top level, a universal class called "Anything" which is divided into "Any-concept" and "Non-concepts". The question then arises – what are "Non-concepts", in this sense? Do they have "facets"? If not, how do they fit into the hierarchy? If they do have "facets", in what sense are they not "Concepts" as defined in the earlier chapters? Do they have rules attached to them? If so, how? Are there two definitions of "Concept" in use? If so, what statements apply to which?

There are further confusing aspects concerning the invocation of rules. Many of the written rules do not have first conjuncts of the form "if current task is 'do A to facet F of C'", but have conditions that seem imcompatible with the simple control regime given in the main part of Lenat, 1976. For example, many rules are of the form "After . . .", and some refer to rather ill-defined aspects of the computation:

After verifying a conjecture for concept C . . .   (*Rule 71*)

If operation F has just been applied and has yielded a new concept C as a result . . .   (*Rule 154*)

If the structure is to be accessed sequentially until some condition is met, and if the precise ordering is superfluous . . .   (*Rule 236, listed under "ordered-struc.check"*)

If the current task involves a specific analogy, and the request is to find more conjectures . . .   (*Rule 78, listed under "any-concept.analogies-.fillin"*)

An obvious interpretation is that in the appendix to Lenat, 1976, Lenat has adopted an abbreviatory convention whereby the first conjunct of a rule (i.e. the part which would be of the form "Do A to F of C") is omitted, since the subheading within the list of rules contains that information (e.g. "Any-concept.Defn.Check"). Section 3.4 of the appendix notes such a convention explicitly for the rules in that section, but it is not adhered to throughout the appendix, since some of the rules include a first clause which echoes the subheading. However, this flexibility probably helps to express the rules more fluently. Even if we assume that suitable first conjuncts are to be appended where necessary, the rules cited above (and some others) then have puzzling *second* conjuncts; for example, Rules 71 and 154 need some details of past history, Rule 236 describes a condition that is not, on the face of it, computable, and Rule 78 seems ambiguous between a task to "fill-in" analogies and one to "fill-in" conjectures.

Further evidence that the implemented control structure was not quite that described in the main chapters of Lenat, 1976, comes from some less noticeable areas of that document:

> Unfortunately, AM's heuristics are not all coded as separate LISP entities, which one could then 'trace'. Rather, they are often inter-woven with each other into large program pieces. (*p. 140*)

> Note that although the Fillin and Suggest heuristics are blended into the relevant facets (e.g. into the Algorithms for Compose), the Interest-ingness type heuristics are kept separate, in this facet. (*p. 220*)

The latter quotation is in a footnote to a sample of AM program in which various "rules" appear as directly-called pieces of LISP (including Rule 145 cited above): that is, the "blending in" is not just the attachment of a procedure to a "sub-facet", but involves actually putting the heuristic commands in the body of the facet's entry (the algorithm, in this example).

Many of the "rules" given in (Lenat, 1976) seem to be justifications or summaries of computations that AM does as a result of various pieces of program within it, and which Lenat therefore regards as "knowledge" that AM has. That is, the "knowledge" is not built into actual rules, but is an interpretation which can be placed on various procedures and statements in the LISP implementation. For example:

> If structure S is always to be maintained in alphanumeric order, then AM can actually maintain it as an unordered structure, if desired. (*Rule 237*)

> The user may sometimes indicate 'Conjunction' when he really means 'Repeating'. (*Rule 224*)

The queries raised in this section are not minor organizational matters or implementation details. The whole flow of "reasoning" in AM is embodied in the execution of the rules, and how AM chooses what to do at any given moment depends entirely on the way that the rules are invoked. Otherwise, what claims or proposals does the thesis make about guiding heuristic search? If the implemented version is simply a large LISP program in which various procedures call each other in a partly pre-programmed way, it cannot be said that the control structure given in Lenat, 1977a (or in Lenat, 1976, chapters 1–6) has actually been tested on the subject matter described.

4.2 Use of other information

It would, of course, be impractical for Lenat to publish the full LISP code for the heuristics, and using English summaries of the rules is an obvious alternative. This has the possible weakness of introducing difficulties of interpretation for the reader, so it is important to make allowances for the imprecision of the medium (English) when assessing the published version. However, there are some instances where some work which is significant (and difficult to reconstruct by guess-work) is covered by some brief phrase. For example:

> A nonconstructive existence conjecture is interesting.   (*Rule 74*)

> If two expressions (especially: two conjectures) are structurally similar, and appear to differ by a certain substitution, then if the substitution is permissible we have just arrived at the same expression in various ways, and tag it as such, but if the substitution is not seen to be tautologous, then a new analogy is born. Associate the constituent parts of both expressions. This is made interesting if there are several concepts involved which are assigned new analogues.   (*Rule 218*)

> Concept C is interesting if some normally-inefficient operation F can be efficiently performed on C's   (*Rule 22*)

> ... replace the value obtained by some other (very similar) value ...   (*Rule 129*)

> If AM just referenced X and almost succeeded, but not quite, then look for a very similar entity Y, and retry activity Y in place of X.   (*Rule 4, with the comment "There is a separate precise meaning for 'almost succeed', 'similar entity' and 'retry' for each kind of entity and activity that might be involved."*)

> Formulate a parameterised conjecture, a 'template', which gets slowly specialised or instantiated into a definite conjecture.   (*Rule 69*)

The problem with these obscurities is that they hide what are probably the most crucial parts of the "discovery" process. Given the discussion in section 4.1 above, it seems that the use of a hierarchy of concepts together with heuristic rules indexed to these structures is not the main mechanism of discovery – much non-trivial work occurs in the procedures called by these rules. Ways of computing "non-constructiveness" or "efficiency" or "similarity" are interesting and (presumably) make a significant contribution to the discovery process.

Sometimes the text admits that the procedures involved are "hacks" or "special-purpose":

> ... symbolically instantiate a definition ... (*Rule 31, with the comment "simply says to use some known tricks, some hacks".*)

> ... it's worth creating more boundary examples and boundary non-examples by slowly transforming x and y into each other. (*Rule 39, with comment "The rules for this slow transformation are again special purpose."*)

> ... ensure that every scrap of C.Defn has been used. (*Rule 58, with comment "this rule contains several hacks (tricks) for checking that the definition has been stretched to the fullest."*)

> Examine C for regularities (*Rule 67 in its entirety, with the comment that this contains "... a few special-purpose hacks and a few ultra-general hacks."*)

It is not clear what the reader is to infer from these deprecating comments. Are the rules over-simple, theoretically uninteresting, badly programmed, or unsatisfactory in some other way? Whatever the implication of dismissive epithets such as "hack" and "special purpose", the work which these procedures carry out seems to be fairly substantial, and without further explanation the reader has to accept an essentially subjective judgement (from Lenat) on these points.

Some of the information used by AM is far from obvious. Consider Rule 2:

> If the user has recently referred to X, then boost the priority of any tasks involving X.

Hence, if the user re-names a concept, AM will devote more resources to examining it (as in task 44 on p. 300). This means that re-naming (as shown in all the sample runs) is not a purely notational alteration, but represents advice from the user.

Many of the rules allude to data-structures, markings on structures, or scheduling procedures which are not fully explained and which seem to be additional to those described in the main part of the thesis (e.g. footnote 5, p. 239). Some of these are simple data-management rules (concerning the space occupied by a structure, and guidelines for disposing of neglected concepts, etc.), but others seem to contribute to the substance of the inference:

> This is a slight extra boost given to each new operation, predicate, etc. Thus bonus decays rapidly with time . . . (*comment on Rule 144*)

> After dealing with concept C, slightly temporarily boost the priority value of each existing task which involves an Active concept whose domain or range is C. (*Rule 14*)

> This rule is tagged as explosive, and is not used very often by AM. (*comment on Rule 152*)

> The formula also incorporates a small factor which is based on the overall value of coalescings which A has done so far in the run . . . (*comment on rule 202*)

> . . . the interestingness of F is weakly tied to that of C . . . (*Rule 173, with comment "If the new concept becomes very valuable, then F will rise slightly in interest. If C is so bad it gets forgotten, F will not be regarded so highly"*)

These last few obscurities tend to suggest that the actual mechanism used by the implemented program has not been fully explained (quite apart from the omissions and confusions detailed in section 4.1 above). This is not to suggest that these mechanisms were pernicious or unsatisfactory, but that the amount of detail given is not appropriate to their apparent importance.

4.3 AM's discoveries

It would be possible to carry out AI research in which the value of the research could be assessed quite independently of the results produced by some particular program (see the discussion in section 5 below). However, the impression given by the published accounts of AM is that the program produced significant discoveries, and much of the public impact of the system (particularly outside the AI research community) derived from the claims made (e.g. the quotation at the beginning of section 2 above). For example, Lenat states that AM discovered Goldbach's conjecture (i.e. that every even number is the sum of two primes). Although one of the published runs (pp. 25–26) seems to illustrate this, Bundy (1980, chapter 13) observes that the example on p. 312 (which is also labelled as "Goldbach's conjecture") seems to illustrate a much more trivial conjecture (namely, that every even number is the sum of *some* primes, e.g. 2+2+ ... +2). It may well be that the designer of AM feels that no importance should be attached to what AM actually did, but the published accounts certainly place great emphasis on the program's performance. It is pertinent, therefore, to examine this performance in more detail.

One of AM's more striking discoveries was that of "natural numbers". As can be estimated from the graph on p. 123, and as Lenat comments (p. 144, footnote 22), most of the later "discoveries" depend on this one; if numbers are not found, AM cannot go on to further triumphs (e.g. the Unique Prime Factorization conjecture). Let us look more closely at the steps involved in this particular discovery.

The following is an outline of how AM makes the discovery:

(4.3.1) The concept "object-equality", which is roughly the LISP notion of recursive "equal" (i.e. two lists are equal if all the elements are "equal", with atoms being equal if they are the same atom), can be generalized in two ways. If the recursive checking of each element (each CAR) is omitted, we get "equal-except-cars" (which AM calls "Genl-obj-equal"); if the recursive checking of the tail of the list (each CDR), we get "equally-nested-first element" (which AM calles "Genl-obj-equal–1").

(4.3.2) There is a concept "Canonise" in the initial data for AM, which, when given two predicates P1 and P2, produces a function F mapping elements of the domain of P1 to elements of the domain of P2, with the condition that for all x, y in domain of P1, P1(x,y) iff P2(F(x),F(y)). AM tries to form this function F for P1 = Genl-obj-equal–1, P2 = Obj-equal and also for P1 = Genl-obj-equal, P2 = Obj-equal. (Notice that Genl-obj-equal is effectively the "same-length" test for two lists, so this latter attempt is trying to find an operation which will map lists of the same length to objects which Obj-equal will class as "equal".) The F constructed (to canonise Genl-obj-equal and Obj-equal) maps an object (list or bag) to a bag which contains a copy of the constant atom "T" for each element in the original structure.

(4.3.3) AM constructs an analogy between bag-operations (e.g. bag-union) and operations on these "canonical bags", and explores this (i.e. constructs the analogous operators). The canonical bags (of "T"s) can be regarded as natural numbers, and the operators constructed under the analogy correspond to addition, subtraction, etc.

Let us explore this sequence in more detail. The description given (p. 196) for initial concept "Canonise" is puzzling. One of its definitions is simply a statement (in English) of the definition given above (4.3.2), with no indication of how to execute it (e.g. how to verify the "iff" clause). The other two definitions use "Canonise.Algs" (i.e. the algorithms for Canonise), but Canonise has *no* algorithms – the description merely notes that heuristic rules will produce and fill in canonisations in various ways (that is, there is no recipe for making canonical forms – they are a consequence of the interaction of several rules).

How does Canonise come into the computation? This is extremely obscure. After AM creates the two generalizations of Obj-equal, and fills in some of their examples, there is a lull, since there are no sufficiently "interesting" tasks on the agenda (p. 329). AM therefore invokes "Suggest" heuristics to find something to do. As noted in section 4.1 above, it is never explained what the selection procedure is for knowing what Suggest rules to use. After these deliberations, the agenda has two new tasks at positions 1 and 2; these are "Canonise Genl-obj-equal–1 and Obj-equal" and "Canonise Same-size and Obj-equal" (the user has just renamed Genl-obj-equal as "Same-size"). These have been suggested by Rule 213. AM goes on to construct a canonical connection as requested by the first task, using (presumably) Rules 206 and 207, and produces the set of lists which are either atoms or lists of one atom (apparently – the commentary does not explain this in detail). AM also posits an analogy between Objects and Canonical-Objects, but this does not seem to be followed up. In fact, this whole thread of exploration seems to be neglected, despite the fact that it starts as a wholly symmetrical partner alongside the examination of Gen-obj-equal (Same-size). Why is one followed and not the other, particularly as Gen-obj-equal–1 is actually further developed (e.g. canonised with respect to Obj-equal) first? There is a hint (p. 290) that this has something to do with the lack of variety of lists known to AM (with respect to their behaviour under these comparison operations), but this is not fully explained. (The user does re-name Gen-obj-equal as Same-size, which may boost its interest value, as commented in section 4.2 above.) The process of canonisation is repeated for the other pair (Same-size and Obj-Equal) again using Rules 206 and 207. These rules look distinctly *ad hoc*. Rule 206 contains a "special hand-crafted piece of knowledge" to tell AM how to canonise bags into bags-of-Ts, and Rule 207 is a "special-purpose rule . . . used to guide a series of experiments". The "worth" of the resulting canonisation function is given by Rule 208, for which "in the actual LISP code, an extra small term is added which takes into account the overall value of the Canonisations which AM has recently produced". Once again an analogy is posited between Bag-strucs and Canonical-bag-strucs, using Rule 209 (which says, roughly, that once a canonisation has been constructed, specific analogies should be tried). Analogies are one of the less satisfying parts of AM: "The Analogy facets are not implemented in full generality in the existing LISP version of AM." (p. 82.) The exploration of this analogy leads, by various rules, to operations on Canonical-bag-strucs (the "natural numbers") which correspond to arithmetic manipulations.

None of the sample traces shows exactly what rules are used at what points, so we can only speculate about the details of these runs. However, it is possible to gain the impression that the successful "discovery" was the result of various specially-designed pieces of information, aimed at achieving this effect. That fact alone would not vitiate AM's contribution to AI research. Suppose that someone were to design the relevant heuristics for this chain of discoveries by trying to devise a systematic route from sets, etc. (the initial concepts) to "canonical bags"; that is, by specifically attempting to make explicit a logical sequence of steps from a chosen origin to a definite destination. (There is a hint (p. 3) that this would be one way to design AM.) If this exercise were successful, then that in itself would be interesting, since we would have a detailed, machine-tested, mechanical inferential route from non-numeric concepts to the natural numbers. Such a result is not supposed to be the outcome of the AM project, and the written accounts do not propose this approach. For example, there are few details of rules such as 206, 207, 208 (see above), which would be part of the central body of the research under such a strategy, as the whole value of the work would be in these very details. The written accounts (e.g. Lenat, 1977a) do not seem to be putting forward such a result (i.e. a careful mechanization of one or two chosen paths between concepts), and there is the statement (Lenat, 1976, p. 18) that the knowledge base is not "finely tuned to elicit this one chain of behaviors". It is therefore probably not appropriate to try to assess AM in this light.

The question of "rating" of discoveries is also slightly under-explained, since Lenat's description simply classes the new concepts and conjectures into "winners" and "losers", without giving further details (e.g. the numerical interest ratings).

In a run starting with 115 concepts, AM developed 185 more concepts, which are classed (p. 125) as containing about 25 winners, 100 acceptable concepts, and about 60 losers. A full list of "losers" is not provided, and the list (pp. 224–225) of about 70 acceptable concepts does not show numerical ratings or distinguish the "winners". There are very few comments on the distinction between the two main classes (winners and losers). For example:

> Thus AM did not develop the sixty 'losers' very much: they ended up with an average of only 1.5 tasks relevant to them ever having been chosen. The 'winners' averaged about twice as many tasks which helped to fill them out more. Also, the worth ratings of the losers were far below those of the winners. (*p. 141*)

> Unfortunately, the sixty or seventy concepts which were losers were *real* losers. (*p. 139*)

Another pertinent question is: did AM ever form a concept which a human could regard as a "winner", and yet class it as uninteresting? That is, how many of the lower-rated results were actually valid mathematical concepts? If AM did underrate concepts or conjectures that are actually fairly interesting, this would not in itself be a great failure. However, if such misjudgements were combined with converse errors (i.e. overrating trivial items), then this would suggest that the system of interest-rating was not very accurate on the whole. This question is not fully discussed although it is mentioned (p. 287) that "some concepts were created which were interesting to *us* . . . but which AM never bothered to develop".

This lack of information is not as crucial as that discussed in sections 4.1 and 4.2 above, since the interest-ratings indicate AM's degree of "success" which is perhaps not as fundamental as the question of how AM actually works.

5 Methodological consequences

The AM project is a substantial piece of work in AI, and seems to contain a large amount of originality, creativity and detailed effort. We do not intend to detract from Lenat's interesting demonstration, but we believe that the published accounts of AM exemplify a style of scientific reporting within the AI community which is not conducive to continuity and the gradual development of a theoretical framework. The central point in our criticism is the apparent discrepancy between published claims (about performance and techniques) and implementation details. (The criticism is aimed entirely at the accounts of the AM program, and we are not discussing the question of whether Lenat could repair these deficiencies by writing another program which conforms more closely to his outline.) Our doubts can be summarized thus:

(5.1.1) Is the control structure simply the *uniform*, *minimal* mechanism given in Lenat (1977a), with the current task defining exactly what rules to execute?

(5.1.2) Are the data-structures *uniformly* represented as Concepts, with Facets and Sub-facets as defined?

(5.1.3) Are there no "extra" processing mechanisms which have significant effects?

(5.1.4) How much of the real discovery work is buried in unexplained procedures?

(5.1.5) If the mathematical discoveries really are an important aspect of the work, can they be shown to have resulted *directly* from the search procedure as described?

In view of the pre-scientific nature of AI, it is always hard to assess the exact contribution of a piece of research, and it is necessary to be very careful in deciding what AM has contributed to progress in artificial intelligence. It would be unrealistic to demand that an AI project conform to the (rather idealized) notion of scientific investigation which is sometimes outlined in textbooks on the philosophy of science (e.g. Hempel, 1966, Rudd, 1966). We are still at an early stage in the development of our scientific methodology, and very little of AI research fits into the traditional "experimental paradigm" in which well-defined hypotheses are refuted by empirical investigations. Let us weaken the demands for "scientific method", and try to formulate some realistic guidelines for AI research.

There are various ways in which the typical AI project (e.g. a doctoral thesis) could contribute usefully to our collective knowledge.

(5.2.1) It could introduce, in outline, a novel (or partly novel) idea or set of ideas. For example, ideas such as "consider a semantic structure as a computational procedure" (see Winograd, 1972), or "regard computation as a sequence of messages between autonomous entities" (see Hewitt, 1977) are examples of general approaches which have been influential within AI. This kind of contribution could perhaps be forced into the mould of a scientific hypothesis by appending the predicate ". . . is a useful idea" to each proposed concept, but this would not add much real rigour, since this variety of informal proposal is usually not precise enough to admit definite empirical refutation (nor is the notion of "useful" very precise). The refutation of the "usefulness" would come not from a specific critical experiment, but either from a general feeling that the concept in question had failed to form the basis of other "useful" work (despite various attempts), or from some theoretical argument as to its incoherence (as Fodor attempted for "procedural semantics" (Fodor, 1978)). These may not be very striking or well-defined "refutations", but they are the best we can manage at present.

(5.2.2) It could elaborate the details of some approach. That is, starting from some idea (of the kind discussed in 5.2.1), the research could criticize it, or fill in further details, in order to transform a slogan-like idea or metaphor into a fuller theory. This activity is comparable to theory-construction in a traditional science, but it is not directly tied to some standard means of testing, as will be discussed below.

(5.2.3) It could apply some articulated theory to some actual subject matter or data, and report the consequences. This is the nearest counterpart to traditional "experiment", but it differs in some important respects. Typically, the practical investigation proceeds by writing and running a computer program, and the assessment of the result of this activity is difficult, since AI ideas tend not to be formulated in such a way as to allow specific success/failure judgements.

An empirical AI "experiment" as in 5.2.3 can be scrutinized in various ways:

(5.3.1) Experiment design (static): does the structure of the program reflect the theory it purports to test?

(5.3.2) Experiment design (dynamic): does the internal processing behaviour of the program correspond to the dynamic aspects of the theory (if any)?

(5.3.3) Consistency: has the program been successfully run (repeatedly)?

(5.3.4) Results: what were the consequences, in terms of internal behaviour and in terms of output, of the program's execution?

(5.3.5) Interpretation: what do these results mean in terms of the theoretical constructs?

(5.3.6) Conclusions: what are the consequences for the theory of the interpreted results?

Much AI work contributes under all three categories (5.2.1 – 5.2.3), with most of the effort being expended on 5.2.2 and 5.2.3. We would accept that the AM project has contributed in respect 5.2.1; there is the proposal that mathematical discovery proceeds as a form of inference using domain-specific rules indexed to a hierarchical arrangement of concepts. The substance of the 5.2.2 contribution is less clear, since there is no separate statement of the theory apart from the description of the program, and

Lenat (1977a, p. 834) dismisses many of the program's characteristics as being simply convenient assumptions to enable the project to proceed. However, the main problem arises with the question of empirical testing (5.2.3), since the answers to questions 5.3.1 and 5.3.2 seem to be "no", and this renders the criteria (5.3.3 – 5.3.6) largely irrelevant.

Given the striking nature of Lenat's original claims (constructing a program which made "discoveries" comparable to those of Ramanujan, and which progressed from pre-numerical concepts to mathematics-student knowledge in a few hours), it seems strange that no corroborative work has appeared in the past five years. It is one of the peculiarities of AI that, although replication of practical results is a cornerstone of traditional science, it is rare to see published accounts of repetitions of AI work. It is not clear how to interpret this phenomenon: it may be that few people have ever successfully reimplemented a large AI program, or it may be that those who do manage to repeat a published project (e.g. AM), do not regard this as publishable material. It may also be the case that an *unsuccessful* attempt at re-implementation would not be widely notified, since this might appear as an admission of incompetence. These circumstances impede the establishment of scientific standards within AI.

The positive contribution of the AM project is the proposal that mathematical discovery may be a systematic form of inference, based on a particular kind of knowledge-structure (hierarchically organized frames) and a particular arrangement of rules (indexed to the relevant concepts). What has *not* been achieved is a detailed, programmed test of these ideas since the AM program departs from these original proposals. The negative contribution is that the impression has been given that such a test has been carried out (with impressive results), thus obscuring the real strengths and weaknesses of the scheme, and making it difficult for anyone to follow up this research systematically (see D. McDermott, 1981). We believe that it would be extremely difficult to base further research in this area on AM, since the disparity between the written account and the actual program means that there is not in fact a tested theoretical basis from which to work. That is, we have a piece of work which publicly sets a very high standard of performance as the "current state of the art", but which gives insufficient information as to how one might, in practice, attain that performance.

There is a tendency for impressive AI programs to become part of the established "folklore" of the field, and to appear in introductory textbooks as examples of the achievements of AI. In view of the role of textbooks in passing on scientific knowledge to newcomers to the subject, it seems unfortunate that the picture presented should be based on unrepresentative "samples" of AI work.

Program-construction is the dominant research technique in AI, and this leads to the rather difficult problem of how the rest of the community can check a piece of work. In principle, each interested party could check the actual text of a program and its behaviour when running, and try to check the points (5.3.1 – 5.3.6) (particularly the correspondence to the proposed theory). Since this is rarely feasible for a complex program such as AM, much of this information remains private (i.e. known only by the creator of the program) rather than public and it is not realistic to regard the mere existence of the program as a remedy for this state of affairs. Lenat has attempted more than most other workers in AI to render his program available to public assessment, both by making it available for running and by supplying such detailed appendices in his thesis. The whole discussion in this paper could not have commenced if Lenat had not provided this unusual level of documentation. If all work were as fully described, perhaps higher standards would develop naturally. What would be desirable would be a greater effort to supply theoretical statements (distinct from descriptions of implementations), a clearer (and, if possible, more publicly visible) correspondence between theory and program, and ways of reporting work in a detailed way which will be of direct practical use to successors in the field.

Note

This work was carried out with the support of Science Research Council grant number GR/A/74760. We would like to thank Alan Bundy for his comments on an earlier draft.

8 Is AI special in regard to its methodology?

Needham sets out the view that AI has nothing special about it (except perhaps an unhealthy concern with being special). He compares AI to chemical engineering and finds that there are no real differences, and concludes that we should get on with what is essentially engineering and cease worrying about 'foundations.'

Sparck Jones explores the nature of programs as experiments in AI, and comes to the conclusion that if we view AI programming as an engineering type of enterprise, we obtain an appropriate interpretation of events. In particular, she examines the idea of adequacy of AI programs, which is rather different from the notions of correctness that software engineers normally associate with their programming endeavours.

Finally, we have reprinted McCarthy's Presidential message to the American Association for AI (AAAI). He laments the lack of agreed standards for evaluating AI research. AI is special in the sense that it claims to be a science and yet the research methodology is undefined (or ill-defined) in a number of critical places. In particular, he argues that we need standards for evaluating research results in AI.

Is there anything special about Artificial Intelligence?

Roger M. Needham

From the beginning of computing people have been trying to make computers do more and more difficult things. At first these things were difficult in the sense that people could do them but rather tediously and unreliably, like solving lots of simultaneous equations. Then they were things that for practical purposes people could not do at all, like the calculations of theoretical chemistry. Progress was made by:

> Throwing more cycles and memory at problems, which has been the leading source of progress at all times;
> Algorithmic invention, such as the use of symbolic differentiation in the early fifties to support theoretical chemistry computations;
> Better understanding of what a problem was about – a modern example is to abstract problems of distributedness.

Researchers were slightly surprised to find that, when they wanted computers to do things that people find relatively easy, progress was much more difficult. This should perhaps be rephrased a bit. After all, people do not pick up objects in a three-pronged steel gripper, and they do not translate from French to English starting with the text punched on cards. Nor do they see through television cameras or hear through microphones. It was hard to progress with problems that looked as if they were in all material respects like things that people can do fairly easily. One way of accounting for the difficulty would be to assert that:

> The hard computer problem was an inadequate or misconceived abstraction of something people do easily, and that was why it was hard. There were more and different material respects than had been thought of!

Maybe it was because computers were so small and slow that it was common to leave out what I, being as neutral as possible in my language, will describe as the great number of inputs which people show signs of having met before. Small computers encourage laziness about large collections of facts. In this context I think also of certain kinds of pattern recognition being regarded as an abstraction for general vision, and of the idea of translation via an interlingua. I do not know whether this is a valid diagnosis, but it is at least as plausible as:

> The computer problem was hard because we do not know how people do it. The hackneyed analogy with planes and birds is not wrong for being hackneyed.

It is much more plausible than:

> The computer problem is hard because we are trying to do something intrinsically impossible or even impious.

That is about as much use as the vitalist objections to synthetic organic chemistry 150 or so years ago.

An example

Consider translation of text from French to English. This is something that many people do fairly well fairly easily, and some people do very well, fairly or very easily. The computer problem does not look very much different from the real one in that we don't seem to lose very much by keypunching the text. We quite possibly lose something; a human translator may be helped or at least influenced by beautiful typography. We certainly now know that to abstract the translation process as something done with a matching algorithm, a dictionary, an input, and an output is a gross over-simplification.

We also know, however, that translation can be done by programs to a useful extent using a rather more fancy abstraction of the problem; and, to avoid appearing to commit others, I know that people don't do it in at all the way the programs do.

What is important is that the usefulness of the result is not impaired by its unanthropomorphic generation, and it does not in some strange way lose credibility by being produced unanthropomorphically. If we know more about how people do it we might do better. It isn't obvious that we would.

What is even more important is the irrelevance of comments to the effect that the translation task is so quintessentially human that only people can do it at all. Perhaps the best response to this is that in the specific case of translation it is not uncommon to deny that people can do it right either, which is why we should all learn Greek or eschew Homer.

Of course we lay ourselves open to criticism if we make any one of a few rash statements such as:

> Success at a technological goal of imitating some human activity will afford insight into the way people work, or

Success in the technological task depends on knowing or even on understanding how people do it,

and in my view everyone in AI is well-advised not to say things like that, which includes anything that can be remotely construed as a second cousin of things like that. A basic piece of AI mechanism such as goal-directed search and backtrack does not depend for its usefulness and validity on people working that way. For all I know they do not.

Many years ago I worked in what was then known as automatic classification, namely the definition of a set of classes based on the given properties of a given set of objects, and the assignment of the original and subsequent object to them. Since this was before botanists took a simple version of the problem and called it numerical taxonomy, I undoubtedly believed that I was engaged in a work of AI and was quite certain that the methods I used had nothing conceivably to do with the way people do the job. It is in fact sufficiently rare for people to do that particular job at all that there is unusual difficulty in studying how they proceed. (Linnaeus is no longer with us.) Lest there be any misunderstanding, this does not at all seek to denigrate the operation of trying to find out how people work, which is self-evidently a scientific endeavour of the first importance.

If one accepts the goal as being to get computers to do interesting and difficult tasks then no holds are to be barred. If one is an AI person, presumably the tasks one selects will have an AI element, but success will often depend on all sorts of other skills too.

One must be very careful about adopting an AI approach to a task or a part of a task when a conventional approach will easily deliver. While not an intellectually wrong thing to do as a means of research, there is a serious danger of being the object of the attentions of some latter-day Sir James Lighthill. (Of course if a conventional approach delivers only with great difficulty, that is something else.)

It may perhaps appear that I am adopting a rather anti-intellectual approach to our topic, which I would strenuously deny.

I would like to make some sort of analogy with chemical engineering. This is an activity of substantial importance and difficulty which depends upon all kinds of other disciplines being well-understood in theory, in practice, or in both. They include: chemistry, rheology, pipework design, pumps, materials science, control theory and many others.

Chemical engineering is about how to make things happen, as is all engineering, and the chemical engineer makes use of any body of knowledge that is to hand and appears helpful. I am not sure whether the most significant one is chemistry or not. That chemical engineering depends on an *omnium gatherum* of knowledge does not mean that it is in any way disreputable. Nor does it imply the absence of skill and knowledge that are characteristic to it as a subject. Another important aspect of chemical engineering is that its practitioners often make contributions to the disciplines it depends upon. It would be surprising if it were not so, particularly if the disciplines in question are new and in the process of establishment when their relevance to chemical engineering is perceived.

If a chemical engineer discovers general principles appropriate to many applications he will be happy in the same way as researchers in any other subject. What there absolutely is not is a 'fundamental problem of chemical engineering'.

There may be a problem faced by many chemical engineers that occupies a lot of the research effort of that community until it is solved. That is quite different.

I believe some people have said that there is, or may be, a 'fundamental problem of artificial intelligence' (or perhaps several of them). There is no reason to believe in the existence of such things, or in the existence of some piece of basic theory that underlies all artificial intelligence.

I can only speculate that people who believe the contrary do so because there has been occasional mention of the possibility of making computers behave in all respects like people. It is even said that you have not solved the REAL PROBLEM until you have achieved this, and anything else is just playing with insignificant problems. I cannot comment about this without exceeding my role as a hard-faced engineer, so I shall simply say that this is not in my opinion correct.

I think artificial intelligence is like chemical engineering. It depends upon a variety of other disciplines, some concerned with computers, some concerned with people, some of a mathematical and logical character not concerned with anything. People in artificial intelligence make contributions to these. My own discipline of computer science has gained vastly from the efforts of workers in artificial intelligence. I cannot speak for the others.

I believe that the AI researcher has goals rather similar to those of the researcher in chemical engineering. He wants to make new things happen, or old things happen in new and better ways, and he will draw on whatever knowledge is available to help him.

Some of this will be knowledge about computing. It may be specific to artificial intelligence or it may be part of the general stock of knowledge of the subject. Note that it will often be considered part of the general stock although it was put there for AI purposes at the outset.

Some of this will be knowledge about people. Some will not be exactly that, but will be suggested by general facts about human activities. For example, one can do a decent job of translating *Germinal* without having to read everything Zola ever wrote. One might call it contextual limitation.

Some of it will be knowledge about parts of people. If the eye can recognize an edge without knowing whether it is the edge of a grandfather clock or of a chaise-longue, this may be a hint as to how a successful program could be structured (no more than a hint, mind).

Some of it will be knowledge that in the ordinary way only AI practitioners have.

The purpose of all this is to suggest that there isn't anything special about artificial intelligence. This is a very good thing for those who carry out research in the subject. If there were something special about artificial intelligence then it would presumably consist of some body of propositions that might mean something and be capable of being disagreed with. Worst of all would be the case where the propositions didn't mean anything and were nevertheless disagreed with. That is to say, if there were believed to be logical or philosophical reasons for the goals of researchers in artificial intelligence being unattainable it would be very inexpedient. It might become difficult to get support for perfectly valid research.

Artificial intelligence, like chemical engineering, is justified by what it can do. As time goes on, it can do more. It can do more than it could do twenty years ago – not as much more as might have been hoped, but there have been lots of practical problems that took a long time to sort out, and of course some we give up on.

You must judge the future of AI by what you think it can do and when, and by your opinions or prejudices about how many principles of some degree of general application can be found. You must not judge the future of AI with reference to any ideal, because there isn't one, any more than there is for chemical engineering, and for the same reasons.

Two final remarks: there aren't any workshops on the foundations of chemical engineering. Though there isn't anything special about artificial intelligence, there is something queer. People worry about its foundations in a rather distinctive way, and maybe they shouldn't.

What sort of a thing is an AI experiment?

Karen Sparck Jones

Prolegomenon

My concern is with what an AI experiment is, and hence with what AI is. I shall talk about what experiments are actually like, but suggest that this is what they must be like.

Thus is it reasonable to suppose that AI experiments are, or could be, like the experiments of classical physics? I do not believe it is. This is not because we cannot expect the result of a single critical experiment to validate a theory, as we cannot expect a single translation to validate a translation program, for example: we can presumably extend the classical model to cover the case where validation depends on a set of results, for different data. Nor is it because we have not in practice got anything like an adequate predictive theory. I believe that we cannot in principle have the sort of predictive theory associated with physics, because we are not modelling nature in the classical physics sense. I shall elaborate on what I think we are doing, but claim now that we reach the same conclusion if we consider the suggestion that we are not in the classical physics position, but rather in that of investigative biologists, doing experiments to find out what nature is like (notionally without any theory at all, though perhaps in fact influenced by some half-baked theory). This is because there is nothing natural to discover. What AI is doing is engineering. While we may indeed have ideas about how to build something so it will work, so we have a predictive theory in a sense, this is not the sort of predictive theory, modelling nature, that physics has. Predicting that people will like what they get, say from a translation program, is not making any specific predictions about the way the translation program models 'real' translation. In other words, AI experiments are engineering experiments serving the designs of task systems, i.e. of artefacts. These systems are artefacts as human task systems are also artefacts. In either case, therefore, we evaluate by performance, so we have no interest in whether the human and computer systems in themselves are the same.

In looking at what AI experiments are like, I shall take the natural-language area as my main example. But I shall start from experiments in an area apparently outside AI, because of the light this may throw on AI experiments without supposing one is engaged in something special.

The information retrieval case

I have been led to consider the question of what an experiment is in AI from a very mundane starting point. I have been concerned with trying to build information retrieval (IR) systems, in the sense of document retrieval systems; i.e. my concern has been with how to index documents and requests and to manipulate index descriptions in searching so as to retrieve documents relevant to the user's need. Indexing and searching are not usually thought of as part of natural-language processing, and hence AI, partly through sheer snobbery, and partly because of the techniques involved. The point here is not that indexing does not require significant natural-language understanding, which is false, but that the difficulty of building indexing programs depending on any material understanding of the objects being indexed, i.e. on understanding enough of the contents of scientific papers to pick out and appropriately express the key concepts they embody, has led to the use of statistical information as a surrogate, e.g. to select words with particular distributional properties as index terms. Statistical information about word distributions has a genuine role to play in large-scale text handling, as a contribution to text understanding, but it is not adequate as a surrogate.

However there is some automatic indexing work aimed at natural language understanding, or natural-language processing in a more proper sense, and, more importantly for present purposes, some results, if only modest ones, sufficient to justify the belief that one could have natural-language programs identifying significant concepts in text. For example, we have done work in Cambridge using proper syntactic and semantic analysis to obtain representations of requests from which complex term sources can be extracted and sets of equivalent linguistic expressions generated for searching files of texts. The important question here is then: what is one doing in seeking to build IR systems applying this or some other natural-language processing technology?

Consider what is involved in an indexing and retrieval system. We have the givens, i.e. the data variables. Even without taking into account the properties of users as these determine relevance judgements, and confining ourselves to the more accessible parts of the data, namely documents and requests, as information objects, we have a large number of variables, some with many possible values. For example, for document texts we have more obvious variables like language, subject, length, specialization, type, etc., and similarly for requests. Particularly from the document point of view, these are properties of objects both as individuals and as members of (possibly very large) collections. Some of these properties, like subject, can clearly have many values. We have further to take types of need, e.g. for a few relevant documents or all of them, into account. There are also less obvious properties like the well-formedness of requests. Similarly, for indexing and searching, we have many system parameters, with many possible settings, for instance the indexing language, form, length etc. of index descriptions, searching strategy, matching function as the number of shared terms or some other scoring coefficient and so forth.

As this list shows, an IR system is not a natural entity: it is an artefact. But it is no more, or no more fundamentally, an artefact than many other language-based information systems, whether these are the private systems of individuals or community systems. The important point is that an IR system is a system which is designed to solve a problem, that of describing the content of documents and the nature of users' requests so that a match between descriptions is correctly deemed to indicate a document is relevant to the user's request (or more properly, to his underlying need). Important additional constraints seen most clearly in designing IR systems for community use are that one is unavoidably designing for average use, and coping with the impact of scale on strategy performance, given the normal requirement to select the very few relevant documents from the many non-relevant.

The problem, then, in designing IR systems is fighting one's way to fitting parameter settings to variable values, when the variables themselves may be substitutes for inaccessible system components, e.g. words for ideas, request texts for user needs, and when the variables also interact, as do the parameters, e.g. term specificity and description exhaustivity. There are further daunting problems, in evaluating system designs, of finding appropriate measures of performance, especially average performance, given the differences between requests, and in testing of sampling (one cannot judge the relevance of every document for every request), and of significance testing. Here we are dealing with the second-order parameters of experiments. (For a fuller discussion of these questions see Sparck Jones, 1981.)

None of this is indeed special to IR system design as opposed to other engineering system design. The material point here is that one is dealing with processing information expressed in natural language, supposedly an AI activity, and so with the implications for building AI systems of such engineering design enterprises.

These are, first, that the only way to try to figure out whether one's system is doing what one intended, i.e. that the observed performance is attributable to the interaction between the assigned parameter settings and perceived variable values, is by rigorous, controlled experiment. The complexity of IR systems, and the limitations of our understanding of how they behave, together mean that whatever theory we have of how to build them needs intensive and extensive testing. The number of variables and parameters, and in some cases of their possible values, makes IR experiment a grinding business of systematic variation with not much confidence in the certainty and uniqueness of the value-setting correlations and hence performance-factor attribution. The second, more significant, point is that strictly there are no right answers for the system to deliver: the set of relevant documents for a query is not well-defined. In practice something may be said about it, e.g. that whatever else, this document is relevant to this query, which is sufficient to drive evaluation in an empirical spirit; but relevance is a furry concept, which limits the definition of experiments. One feature of relevance, for example, is that the user's view of what is relevant can change as he proceeds through the system's output. Thus the evaluation problem for the IR system designer is ultimately one of principle: he may be able to approximate the set of relevant documents well enough for useful testing, but he cannot specify his goal sufficiently precisely for it to give him an absolute check on performance.

How does this reality of experiment in IR system design apply to AI in general? First, as suggested earlier, it is not obvious that IR itself is not an AI activity: determining what texts are about, and indicating their essential meaning, implies language understanding. Similarly, relating one text to another, whether that of one document to another, or of a document to a request, i.e. searching for information, implies language-based reasoning. The determination, representation and use of linguistically expressed knowledge is a characteristic activity of AI. This is not, however, to suggest that current automatic indexing and searching practice comes anywhere near this, though some research is closer. So it is useful to consider here another linguistic task for which current research claims natural-language understanding techniques, and also a non-linguistic AI task. Do either of these presuppose experiments of the kind described?

The summarizing case

Consider summarizing as a natural-language processing task. Summarizing is of interest here in that though I have described indexing in a manner which means it merges into summarizing, one is in principle often looking for something altogether richer than an index description (compare the abstract of a scientific paper with an index description, even one in the form of a phrasal subject heading, let alone a simple list of terms), and certainly aiming at something richer than the product of current automatic indexing practice. Producing a worthwhile abstract clearly requires natural-language understanding of a serious sort, i.e. an extremely complex program.

This program will have very many elements, e.g. syntactic category set, semantic feature system, parsing strategy, focus determination mechanism, anaphor resolution procedure, recovery methods for ill-formed input, etc, applicable to text interpretation, with analogous processes for generation, as well as a central summarizer. These elements may take many forms – for example there are many possible semantic feature systems. In such complex systems we have to allow for considerable elaboration of the notion of parameter and setting, but it applies nonetheless. There are also many data variables, with their possible values, to take into account, e.g. language, text type, sentence type etc., again implying a much more extensive structure of data characterization than the IR case, but not one different in principle. Similarly, the function summaries should serve is the system goal analogous to the IR system requirement to deliver relevant documents. A summarizing system is a task system, like an IR system, though what purpose summaries, as opposed to index descriptions, serve is the crux, as the points which follow show.

The many factors involved in a summarizing system mean that, as in the IR case, it may be far from obvious how features of the system's outputs are to be attributed to particular combinations of given variable values and chosen parameter settings (whether the specification of values and settings is supplied or system selected is irrelevant). It is easy to identify manifestations of bugs in natural-language processing programs, for instance incorrect inflections or wrongly resolved pronouns, but as the second example suggests, it may not be so obvious with a complex anaphor resolution procedure involving, say, a linguistic focus mechanism and non-linguistic inference on sentence representations delivered by syntactic and semantic processors, where the source of the trouble is. This is particularly likely in summarizing, where the results of intermediate processing, e.g. focus determination or the extraction of presuppositions from input sentences, are not necessarily carried forward to the output but where failures in them may influence the output. Thus a 'wonky' pronoun in the output summary text could be attributable to a variety of causes including faulty input sentence interpretation, defective summarizing, or an inadequate generator. But this kind of opacity is not special to AI programs, and though practically tiresome is not theoretically interesting.

The more important point is that a summarizing program can apparently fail in a way which is not attributable, crudely, to a bug, i.e. we are talking about performance in a looser sense: a summary can be a good one, or a fair one, or a poor one, and we may find one better than another. It is true we may claim in some instance, for example if we can point to a missing concept, that a summarizer has failed in a fairly straightforward, somewhat buggy sense. But we can talk about a poor summary or say that one summary is less good than another without being able to point to anything comparatively definite like a missing concept. More seriously, we could get two alternative summaries, from different program designs, with, for example, different relative emphases on different concepts, without it being at all obvious which one is better, as indeed one program by itself could deliver a perfectly satisfactory looking summary. What then is right or correct? We can seek to apply the kind of evaluation criteria used for the evaluation of human abstracting, like 'Are the main points covered?'. But these criteria are typically rather high-level or crude ones which are difficult, if not impossible, to correlate with specific components of the system and their parameter settings, for instance the style of lexical entries or even, if individual lexical entries are treated as parameters, the content of a specific entry. Thus the criteria are very general, and can only be used in a very undiscriminating way.

This is unfortunate but inevitable: these vague criteria reflect the fact that there is no such thing as an objectively right or correct summary of a text. We can talk about an acceptable (because useful) summary, but this is a very weak form of program control. With summarizing, therefore, we are up against the fundamental problem that the required form of processing can only be put in vague terms like 'pick out the essentials', with the consequence that we cannot get the precise measure of output quality needed to feed back to program design. The same problem of what makes one summary better than another also appears, for example, in comparing a more summary summary with a less summary one, or even so-called types of abstract, indicative, informative and evaluative, with one another. It may be as unobvious that one length or type is better than another as it is that one alternative of the same length or type is better than another. Thus even if one supposes that an evaluative abstract is superior to an indicative one, say, this belief needs justification in relation to some manifest summarizing purpose.

Candidate formal criteria for abstracting, like requiring proper entail-ment relations between source and abstract text, do not, quite apart from the formal problems this criterion itself involves, do anything to solve the key problem either, which is determining the important items we want to constitute the abstract. Attempts to select these by looking, for instance at the entailment productivity of propositions, in turn get into all the difficul-ties associated with a reduction to counting, where any particular formula seems an arbitrary way of capturing a general concept. The root problem of summarizing is just that summarizing involves selection, or alternatively elimination, so it is difficult to compare source text and abstract, especially when many possible different selections can be made. The only base for evaluation is thus the functional one.

The significant point about a summarizing system, therefore, is not so much that its greater complexity makes it much harder to attribute output phenomena to their program sources, though this is true, but that there are problems about determining the quality of the output. There is a significant difference between IR systems and summarizing systems as I have described them, residing in the way summaries are used. This may only be a matter of degree, but it is a large and so important one. Though I described the core process in the document retrieval case, namely indexing, so as to emphasize its similarity with abstracting, index descriptions in retrieval services are designed for machine searching, which is not true of summaries, certainly in practice, and even in principle. The scale of retrieval services like DIALOG implies machine searching, and is indeed their justification. The point about a summarizer is that its output is for the human reader, in just the same way as any other text is primarily for its human reader; i.e. searching delivers relevant documents to the user; reading delivers nothing so definite. The problem then is what comes of performance measures. We have an independent means of evaluating the quality of indexing in a retrieval system because we can measure the system's ability to deliver all and only relevant documents, even though, as pointed out earlier, our means are necessarily limited. A retrieval system's claim that the documents it deems relevant to a request, because its description matching function is satisfied, are in fact relevant can be tested, if only crudely.

When we look at an abstract on the other hand, and say it is a good one, on some abstracting criteria, as we may also look at index descriptions, this assessment cannot be anything like as exigent as the retrieval test. Of course whether retrieval searching is done mechanically or not is not the essential point, it merely emphasizes it. Thus even if index descriptions are read rather than mechanically searched, this is still to achieve a relatively defined purpose, namely the identification of relevant documents. The problem with summarizing being for the human reader is that this is a manifestation of the fact that there is no well-defined task associated with the reading for measuring the effectiveness of the summary; we have no clear functional basis for evaluation. Exploiting summaries in further mechanical processing, whether in the form of an 'internal' representation of their content or in explicit natural-language text form, does not affect the issue. The summaries are then being used for some purpose which provides a context to evaluate them. The evaluation may be more or less rigorous, according to the system's function, but only if the purpose is unusually narrow will it be possible to have clear evaluation of something as intrinsically complex as a summary.

Thus my argument is that the complexity of natural-language objects (or their representations) is generally correlated with the indefiniteness of their uses. The more indefinite the need the more complex it actually is, and hence the richer and less easy it is to define the object required to satisfy this need. Indeed the problems in the IR case with the notion of relevance are a reflection of the fact that even here the user's need, and hence the system's task, are not very well defined. The point about summarizing is thus primarily that it much more clearly poses the problem of system evaluation without a well-defined task, and therefore a means of establishing whether the system has delivered the right or correct answer. The only form of evaluation that seems possible in cases like this is that the system delivers acceptable output – and this is a fairly weak form of evaluation.

Non-linguistic cases

Similar problems, though with differences of emphasis, apply to other language processing system tasks like translation. However a more serious question is whether the same issues arise in other non-linguistic areas of AI, i.e. whether there are other situations where we have a complex artefact and necessarily no very precise base for performance evaluation, so one has to proceed essentially on a trial and error basis weakly supported by intuitive judgement or socio-economic measures of effectiveness. It is not difficult to see at least some robot applications and even more some expert systems as of this kind. How are we to say whether a robot vehicle wandering round the surface of a planet is performing optimally: what would optimal performance be? We may assert a robot fails if it falls down a hole, but how can we say it has picked up the best set of rock samples? The same goes for an expert system like a holiday advisor (I am concentrating here on the non-linguistic decision-making apparatus of the system). With a medical expert system we may have something like an independent performance measure: its decisions are those of a panel of doctors; or the patient lives. But for a holiday advisor it is not obvious that there is anything like a specific independent measure: even if the advisor performed the same as a clutch of travel agents, how relevant is this to the quality of the advice; and if it is not, how are we to define what satisfactory advice is?

Conclusion

The conclusion is therefore that the role of experiments in AI is to try out designs for engineering artefacts, to see how well some system will meet some need. The detailed methods adopted can vary: one can use customer samples, or simulation, for example. This implies a performance measure related to the system's purpose, which may be more or less easy to find. But it is a measure of acceptability, not of truth. The fact that one is dealing with artefacts, moreover, does not imply that these systems are distinctively different from the human ones being emulated: they too are personal or social artefacts. Thus in the language case, as one characteristic example, we should not overrate the objective reality of human processing as something to measure a program's internal operations against; we can only evaluate systems by their performance, and that very loosely for activities like summarizing. But evaluating by acceptability is perfectly respectable. What humans do is in the real sense *ad hoc*: they build systems to work well enough. There is therefore no reason to require program builders to do anything different.

We need better standards for AI research

John McCarthy

The state of the art in any science includes the criteria for evaluating research. Like every other aspect of science, it has to be developed. The criteria for evaluating AI research are not in very good shape. If we had better standards for evaluating research results in AI the field would progress faster.

One problem we have yet to overcome might be called the "Look, ma, no hands" syndrome. A paper reports that a computer has been programmed to do what no computer program has previously done, and that constitutes the report. How science has been advanced by this work or other people are aided in their research may not be apparent.

Some people put the problem in moral terms and accuse others of trying to fool the funding agencies and the public. However, there is no reason to suppose that people in AI are less motivated than other scientists to do good work. Indeed I have no information that the average quality of work in AI is less than that in other fields. I have grumbled about there being insufficient basic research, but one of the reasons for this is the difficulty of evaluating whether a piece of research has made basic progress.

It seems that evaluation should be based on the kind of advance the research purports to be. I haven't been able to develop a complete set of criteria, but here are some considerations.

1. Suppose the research constitutes making the computer solve a problem that hasn't previously been solved by computer.

Let us suppose that there are no theoretical arguments that the methods are adequate for a class of problems but merely a program that performs impressively on certain sample problems together with some explanation of how the program works.

This is a difficult kind of research to explain adequately. The reader will not easily be able to assure himself that the program is not overly specialized to the particular example problems that have been used in developing the program. It has often turned out that other researchers have not been able to learn much from the paper. Sometimes a topic is so intractable that this is the best that can be done, but maybe this means that the topic is too intractable for the present state of the art.

2. A better result occurs when a previously unidentified intellectual mechanism is described and shown to be either necessary or sufficient for some class of problems.

An example is the alpha-beta heuristic for game playing. Humans use it, but it wasn't identified by the writers of the first chess programs. It doesn't constitute a game playing program, but it seems clearly necessary, because without it, the number of positions that have to be examined is sometimes the square of the number when it is used.

3. Experimental work should be repeatable.

In the older experimental sciences, e.g. physics and biology, it is customary to repeat previous experiments in order to verify that a phenomenon claimed to exist really does, or to verify a claimed value of an experimentally determined constant. The referees are supposed to be sure that papers describing experimental work contain enough of the right details so that this can be done.

Perhaps the most typical problem concerns a piece of experimental AI research, say a Ph.D. thesis. The general class of problems that the researcher would like to attack is described, followed by a description of his program and a description of the results obtained on his sample problems. Often there is only one sample problem. The class of problems which it is claimed the program or the methods embody will solve is often not stated. The reader is free to suspect that the program has been tuned so that it will solve the specific example described in the paper and that the author doesn't even know whether it will solve any others.

If we aspire to testable and repeatable work in AI, then journal authors and referees should require a statement of the generality of the program. The referee should be able to try out the program if language, hardware and communication facilities permit. Moreover, the methods should be described well enough so that someone skilled in the art can embody them in a program of his own and test whether they are adequate for the claimed class of programs.

Repetition of other people's experiments should be as normal in AI as it is in the other experimental sciences. On the whole, it should be easier in AI, because more-or-less standard hardware and programming languages can be used. Perhaps this is a good apprentice task for graduate students beginning work in AI or people coming into the field from the outside. Students and other newcomers will take pleasure in trying to find a simple example that the program is supposed to solve but doesn't.

Stating the generality of a piece of work is likely to be difficult in many cases. It is best done after the program has solved the example problems, because the researcher can then understand what compromises he has had to reach with generality in order to make the program do his examples. He is most likely to make the necessary effort if he knows that some smart student is likely to look for counterexamples to his.

4. We also need criteria for formalizations.

Logic-based approaches to AI require that general facts about the common-sense world be expressed in languages of logic, and that reasoning principles (including non-monotonic principles) be stated that permit determining what a robot should do given its goals (stated in sentences), the general facts, and the facts of the particular situation. The major criteria for judging the success of the formalization of such facts are generality and epistemological adequacy. Generality is partly a property of the language, and in the case of a first-order language, this means the collection of predicate and function symbols. The original set of predicates and functions should not have to be revised when extensions are wanted. Generality is also partly a property of the set of axioms. They too should be extendable rather than having to be changed. The recent development on non-monotonic formalisms should make this easier.

The author of a paper proposing logical formalisms should state, if he can, how general they are. The referee and subsequent critics should try to verify that this is achieved.

Epistemological adequacy refers to the ability to express the facts that a person or robot in that information system is likely to be able to know and need to know.

5. The criteria for evaluating methods that purport to reduce search are perhaps better established than in other fields.

Taking my own experience with game-playing programs in the late 1950s and early 1960s, it was possible to demonstrate how much alpha-beta, the killer heuristic, and various principles for move ordering reduce search.

6. On the other hand, the evaluation of programs that purport to understand natural language is worse off.

People often simply don't believe other people's claims to generality.

In this area I can offer two challenge problems. First, I can provide the vocabulary (sorted alphabetically) of a certain news story and the vocabulary of a set of questions about it. The computational linguistic system-builder can then build into his system the ability to "understand" stories and questions involving this vocabulary. When he is ready, I will further provide the story and the questions. He can take the questions in natural language or he can translate them into suitable input for his system. The limitations of the system should be described in advance. We will then see what questions are successfully answered and to what extent the author of the system understood its limitations.

The second problem involves building a system that can obtain information from databases that purport to interact with their users in English. Again the vocabulary is given in advance, and the system-builder tunes his system for the vocabulary. It is then tested as to whether it can answer the questions by interacting with the database. For example, Lawrence Berkeley Laboratory has (or had) a database of 1970 census data. It would be interesting to know whether a program could be written that could determine the population of Palo Alto interacting with the interface this database presents to naïve human users.

I think both of these problems are quite hard, and whatever groups could perform reasonably on them would deserve a lot of credit. Perhaps this would be a good subject for a prize – either awarded by the American Association for AI or someone else.

However, such challenge problems are no substitute for scientific criteria for evaluating research in natural-language understanding.

7. Likewise the Turing test, while a challenge problem for AI, is not a scientific criterion for AI research.

The Turing test, suitably qualified, would be a sufficient criterion for convincing skeptics that human-level AI had finally been achieved. However, we need criteria for evaluating more modest claims that a particular intellectual mechanism has been identified and found to be necessary or sufficient for some class of problems.

Incidentally, even as a sufficient condition, the Turing test requires qualification. The ability to imitate a human must stand up under challenge from a person advised by someone who knows how the program works. Otherwise, we are in the situation of someone watching a stage magician. We can't figure out the trick, but there must be one. *A fortiori*, looking at dialogs and figuring out which one is with a machine isn't adequate.

9   Does connectionism provide a new paradigm for AI?

Fodor restates his language of thought hypothesis, which presents a serious challenge to the view that the architecture of cognition is network-based. Fodor claims that, whatever the representation underlying thought at the level of semantic interpretation, it must have constituent structure, i.e. a structure such that belief in the truth of (A and B) necessarily involves belief in the truth of both of the constituents, A and B, separately. Such necessity is not, in general, supported by network architecture whereas it is in Turing machine-type representations.

The rest of the papers in this section respond (directly or indirectly) to this challenge to the significance of connectionism in AI. Is connectionism just implementation detail, an essentially Turing machine-type architecture implemented with an activity-passing network? Or are sub-symbolic networks inherently more powerful than the traditional symbolic-level processing representations that have dominated much of AI? Smolensky is firmly on the side of connectionism as a fundamentally new and powerful 'sub-symbolic' paradigm for AI. Wilks discusses and denies the central claims of both Fodor and Smolensky, arguing that, at the moment, benificent agnosticism is the best position on connectionism, awaiting further clarification of its claims and more empirical results.

Churchland supports the connectionist movement but his support is based on the similarities between connectionist principles and the architecture of the brain. He argues for the study of neuroanatomy as a source of system-building constraints in AI. He describes in some detail, and with specific examples, two general functional schema (representation by state-space position, and computation by coordinate transformation) that support basic components of intelligent behavior in a biologically realistic fashion. His general schema clearly fit more comfortably in the connectionist paradigm than in the traditional symbolic-search-space paradigm of AI.

Why there STILL has to be a language of thought

Jerry A. Fodor

"But why," Aunty asked with perceptible asperity, "does it have to be a language?" Aunty speaks with the voice of the Establishment, and her intransigence is something awful. She is, however, prepared to make certain concessions in the present case. First, she concedes that there are beliefs and desires and that there is a matter of fact about their intentional contents; there's a matter of fact, that is to say, about which proposition the intentional object of a belief or a desire is. Second, Aunty accepts the coherence of physicalism. It may be that believing and desiring will prove to be states of the brain, and if they do that's OK with Aunty. Third, she is prepared to concede that beliefs and desires have causal roles, and that overt behavior is typically the effect of complex interactions among these mental causes. (That Aunty was raised as a strict behaviorist goes without saying. But she hasn't been quite the same since the sixties. Which of us has?) In short, Aunty recognizes that psychological explanations need to postulate a network of causally related intentional states. "But why," she asks with perceptible asperity, "does it have to be a language?" Or, to put it more succinctly than Aunty often does, what – over and above mere Intentional Realism – does the Language of Thought Hypothesis buy? That is what this discussion is about.[1]

A prior question: what – over and above mere Intentional Realism – does the Language of Thought Hypothesis (LOT) *claim*? Here, I think, the situation is reasonably clear. To begin with, LOT wants to construe propositional attitude tokens as relations to symbol tokens. According to standard formulations, to believe that P is to bear a certain relation to a token of a symbol which means that P. (It is generally assumed that tokens of the symbols in question are neural objects, but this assumption won't be urgent in the present discussion.) Now, symbols have intentional contents and their tokens are physical in all the known cases. And – *qua* physical – symbol tokens are the right sorts of things to exhibit causal roles. So there doesn't seem to be anything that LOT wants to claim *so far* that Aunty needs to feel up tight about. What, then, exactly is the issue?

Here's a way to put it. Practically everybody thinks that the *objects* of

289

intentional states are in some way complex: for example, that what you believe when you believe that John is late for dinner is something composite whose elements are – as it might be – the concept of John and the concept of being late for dinner (or – as it might be – John himself and the property of being late for dinner). And, similarly, what you believe when you believe that P&Q is also something composite, whose elements are – as it might be – the proposition that P and the proposition that Q.

But the (putative) complexity of the *intentional object* of a mental state does not, of course, entail the complexity of the mental state itself. It's here that LOT ventures beyond mere Intentional Realism, and it's here that Aunty proposes to get off the bus. LOT claims that mental states – and not just their propositional objects – *typically have constituent structure.* So far as I can see, this is the *only* real difference between LOT and the sorts of Intentional Realism that even Aunty admits to be respectable. So a defense of LOT has to be an argument that believing and desiring are typically structured states.

Consider a schematic formulation of LOT that's owing to Steven Schiffer. There is, in your head, a certain mechanism, an INTENTION BOX. To make the exposition easier, I'll assume that every intention is the intention to make some proposition true. So then here's how it goes in your head, according to this version of LOT, when you intend to make it true that P. What you do is, you put into the intention box a token of a mental symbol that MEANS that P. And what the box does is: it churns and gurgles and computes and causes and the outcome is that you behave in a way that (*ceteris paribus*) makes it true that P.

So, for example, suppose I intend to raise my left hand (I intend to make true the proposition that I raise my left hand). Then what I do is, I put in my intention box a token of a mental symbol that means 'I raise my left hand.' And then, after suitable churning and gurgling and computing and causing, my left hand goes up. (Or it doesn't, in which case the *ceteris paribus* condition must somehow not have been satisfied.) Much the same story would go for my intending to become the next King of France, only in that case the gurgling and churning would continue appreciably longer.

Now it's important to see that, although this is going to be a Language of Thought story, it's not a Language of Thought story yet. For, so far, all we have is what Intentional Realists *qua* Intentional Realists (including Aunty *qua* Aunty) are prepared to admit: viz., that there are mental states that have associated intentional objects (like, for example, the state of having a symbol that means 'I raise my left hand' in my intention box), and that these mental states that have associated intentional objects also have causal roles (for example, my being in one of these states causes my left hand to rise). What makes the story a Language of Thought story, and not just an Intentional Realist story, is the idea that these mental states that have content also have syntactic structure – constituent structure in particular – that's appropriate to the content that they have. For example, it's compatible with the story I told above that what I put in the intention box when I intend to raise my left hand is a *rock*; so long as it's a rock that's semantically evaluable. Whereas, according to the LOT story, what I put in the intention box has to be something like a *sentence*; in the present case, it has to be a formula which contains, *inter alia*, an expression that denotes me and an expression that denotes my left hand.

Similarly, on the merely Intentional Realist story, what I put in the intention box when I intend to make it true that I raise my left hand and hop on my right foot might also be a rock (though not, of course, the same rock since the intention to raise one's left hand is not the same as the intention to raise one's left hand and hop on one's right foot). Whereas, according to the LOT story, if I intend to raise my left hand and hop on my right foot, I must put into the intention box a formula which contains, *inter alia*, a subexpression that means *I raise my left hand* and a subexpression that means *I hop on my right foot*.

So then, according to the LOT story, these semantically evaluable formulas that get put into intention boxes typically contain semantically evaluable subformulas as constituents; and, moreover, they can *share* the constituents that they contain since, presumably, the subexpression that denotes 'foot' in 'I raise my left foot' is a token of the same type as the subexpression that denotes 'foot' in 'I raise my right foot.' (Similarly, *mutatis mutandis*, the 'P' that expresses the proposition P in the formula 'P' is a token of the same type as the 'P' that expresses the proposition P in the formula 'P & Q.') If we wanted to be slightly more precise, we could say that the LOT story amounts to the claims that: (1) (some) mental formulas have mental formulas as parts; and (2) the parts are 'transportable': the same parts can appear in lots of mental formulas.

It's important to see – indeed, it generates the issue that this discussion is about – that Intentional Realism doesn't logically require the LOT story; it's no sort of *necessary* truth that only formulas – only things that have syntactic structure – are semantically evaluable. No doubt it's puzzling how a rock (or the state of having a rock in your intention box) could have a propositional object; but then, it's no less puzzling how a formula (or the state of having a formula in your intention box) could have a propositional object. It is, in fact, approximately equally puzzling how *anything* could have a propositional object, which is to say that it's puzzling how Intentional Realism could be true. For better or for worse, however, Aunty and I are both assuming that Intentional Realism *is* true. The question we're arguing about isn't, then, whether mental states have a semantics. Roughly, it's whether they have a syntax. Or, if you prefer, it's whether they have a *combinatorial* semantics; the kind of semantics in which there are (relatively) complex expressions whose content is determined, in some regular way, by the content of their (relatively) simple parts.

So here, to recapitulate, is what the argument is about: everybody thinks that mental states have intentional objects; everybody thinks that the

292   *Jerry A. Fodor*

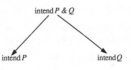

Figure 1

intentional objects of mental states are characteristically complex – in effect, that propositions have parts; everybody thinks that mental states have causal roles; and, for present purposes at least, everybody is a functionalist, which is to say that we all hold that mental states are individuated, at least in part, by reference to their causal powers. (This is, of course, implicit in the talk about 'intention boxes' and the like: to be – metaphorically speaking – in the state of having such and such a rock in your intention box is just to be – literally speaking – in a state that is the normal cause of certain sorts of effects and/or the normal effects of certain sort of causes.) What's at issue, however, is the internal structure of these functionally individuated states. Aunty thinks they have none; only the intentional objects of mental states are complex. I think they constitute a language; roughly, the syntactic structure of mental states mirrors the semantic relations among their intentional objects. If it seems to you that this dispute among Intentional Realists is just a domestic squabble, I agree with you that that is true. But so was the Trojan War.

   In fact, the significance of the issue comes out quite clearly when Aunty turns her hand to cognitive architecture; specifically to the question 'what sorts of relations among mental states should a psychological theory recognize?' It is quite natural, given Aunty's philosophical views, for her to think of the mind as a sort of directed graph; the nodes correspond to semantically evaluable mental states, and the paths correspond to the causal connections among these states. To intend, for example, that P&Q is to be in a state that has a certain pattern of (dispositional) causal relations to the state of intending that P and to the state of intending that Q. (Eg. being in the first state is normally causally sufficient for being in the second and third.) We could diagram this relation in the familiar way shown in figure 1.

   NB, in this sort of architecture, the relation between – as it might be – intending that P&Q and intending that P is a matter of *connectivity* rather than *constituency*. You can see this instantly when you compare what's involved in intending that P&Q on the LOT story. On the LOT story, intending that P&Q requires having a sentence in your intention box – or, if you like, in a register or on a tape – one of whose parts is a token of the very same type that's in the intention box when you intend that P, and another of which is a token of the very same type that's in the intention box when you intend that Q.

   So, it turns out that the philosophical disagreement about whether there's a Language of Thought corresponds quite closely to the disagreement – current among cognitive scientists – about the appropriate architecture for mental models. If propositional attitudes have internal structure, then we need to acknowledge constituency – as well as causal connectivity – as a fundamental relation among mental states. Analogously, arguments that suggest that mental states have constituent structure *ipso facto* favor Turing/Von Neuman architectures – which can compute in a language whose formulas have transportable parts – as against associative networks which, by definition, cannot. It turns out that dear Aunty is, of all things, a New Connectionist Groupie. If she's in trouble, so are they, and for much the same reasons.[2]

In what follows I propose to sketch three reasons for believing that cognitive states – and not just their intentional objects – typically have constituent structure. I don't suppose that these arguments are knock down; but I do think that, taken together, they ought to convince any Aunty who isn't *parti pris*.

Argument 1: a methodological argument

I don't, generally speaking, much like methodological arguments; who wants to win by a technical knockout? But, in the present case, it seems to me that Aunty is being a little unreasonable even by her own lights. Here is a plausible rule of nondemonstrative inference that I take her to be at risk of breaking:

Principle P: Suppose there is a kind of event c1 of which the normal effect is a kind of event e1; and a kind of event c2 of which the normal effect is a kind of event e2; and a kind of event c3 of which the normal effect is a complex event e1 & e2. Viz:

$c1 \rightarrow e1$

$c2 \rightarrow e2$

$c3 \rightarrow e1 \,\&\, e2$

Then, ceteris paribus, *it is reasonable to infer that c3 is a complex event whose constituents include c1 and c2.*

So, for example, suppose there is a kind of event of which the normal effect is a bang and a kind of event of which the normal effect is a stink, and a kind of event of which the normal effect is that kind of a bang and that kind of a stink. Then, according to P, it is *ceteris paribus* reasonable to infer that the third kind of event consists (*inter alia*) of the co-occurrence of events of the first two kinds.

You may think that this rule is arbitrary, but I think that it isn't; P is just a special case of a general principle which untendentiously requires us to prefer theories that *minimize accidents*. For, if the etiology of events that are e1 and e2 does not somehow include the etiology of events that are e1 but not e2, then it must be that there are *two* ways of producing e1 events;

and the covergence of these (*ex hypothesi*) distinct etiologies upon events of type e1 is, thus far, unexplained. (It won't do, of course, to reply that the convergence of two etiologies is only a very *little* accident. For, in principle, the embarrassment *iterates*. Thus, you can imagine a kind of event c4, of which the normal effect is a complex event e1 & e10 & e12 . . . etc. And now, if P is flouted, we'll have to tolerate a *four-way* accident. That is, barring P – and all else being equal – we'll have to allow that theories which postulate four kinds of causal histories for e1 events are just as good as theories which postulate only one kind of causal history for e1 events. It is, to put it mildly, hard to square this with the idea that we value our theories for the generalizations they articulate.)

Well, the moral seems clear enough. Let c1 be intending to raise your left hand, and e1 be raising your left hand; let c2 be intending to hop on your right foot and e2 be hopping on your right foot; let c3 be intending to raise your left hand and hop on your right foot, and e3 be raising your left hand and hopping on your right foot. Then the choices are: *either* we respect P and hold that events of the c3 type are complexes which have events of type c1 as constituents, *or* we flout P and posit two etiologies for e1 events, the convergence of these etiologies being, thus far, accidental. I repeat that what's at issue here is the complexity of mental events and not merely the complexity of the propositions that are their intentional objects. P is a principle that constrains etiological inferences, and I assume that the intentional properties of mental states are not *per se* etiological.

But we're not home yet. There's a way out that Aunty has devised; she is, for all her faults, a devious old dear. Aunty could accept P but deny that (for example) raising your left hand counts as *the same sort of* event on occasions when you *just* raise your left hand as it does on occasions when you raise your left hand while you hop on your right foot. In effect, Aunty can avoid admitting that *intentions* have constituent structure if she's prepared to deny that *behavior* has constituent structure. A principle like P, which governs the assignment of etiologies to complex events, will be vacuously satisfied in psychology if no behaviors are going to count as complex.

But Aunty's back is to the wall; she is, for once constrained by vulgar fact. Behavior does – very often – exhibit constituent structure, and that it does is vital to its explanation, at least as far as anybody knows. Verbal behavior is the paradigm, of course; everything in linguistics, from phonetics to semantics, depends on the fact that verbal forms are put together from recurrent elements; that, for example, [oon] occurs in both 'Moon' and 'June.' But it's not just verbal behavior for whose segmental analysis we have pretty conclusive evidence; indeed, it's not just *human* behavior. It turns out, for one example in a plethora, that bird song is a tidy system of recurrent phrases; we lose 'syntactic' generalizations of some elegance if we refuse to so describe it.

To put the point quite generally, psychologists have a use for the distinction between segmented behaviors and what they call "synergisms."

(Synergisms are cases where what appear to be behavioral elements are in fact 'fused' to one another, so that the whole business functions as a unit; as when a well practiced pianist plays a fluent arpeggio.) Since it's empirically quite clear that not all behavior is synergistic, it follows that Aunty may not, in aid of her philosophical prejudices, simply help herself to the contrary assumption.

Now we *are* home. If, as a matter of fact, behavior is often segmented, then principle P requires us to prefer the theory that the causes of behavior are complex over the theory that they aren't, all else being equal. And all else is equal to the best of my knowledge. For, if Aunty has any *positive* evidence against the LOT story, she has been keeping it very quiet. Which wouldn't be at all like Aunty, I assure you.

Argument 2: psychological processes (why Aunty can't have them for free)

In the cognitive sciences mental symbols are the rage. Psycholinguists, in particular, often talk in ways that make Aunty simply livid. For example, they say things like this: 'When you understand an utterance of a sentence, what you do is construct a *mental representation* [sic; emphasis mine] of the sentence that is being uttered. To a first approximation, such a representation is a parsing tree; and this parsing tree specifies the constituent structure of the sentence you're hearing, together with the categories to which its constituents belong. Parsing trees are constructed left to right, bottom to top, with restricted look ahead . . . ' and so forth, depending on the details of the psycholinguist's story. Much the same sort of examples could be culled from the theory of vision (where mental operations are routinely identified with transformations of structural descriptions of scenes) or, indeed, from any other area of recent perceptual psychology.

Philosophical attention is hereby directed to the logical form of such theories. They certainly look to be quantifying over a specified class of mental objects: in the present case, over parsing trees. The usual apparatus of ontological commitment – existential quantifiers, bound variables and such – is abundantly in evidence. So you might think that Aunty would argue like this: 'When I was a girl ontology was thought to be an a priori science; but now I'm told that view is out of fashion. If, therefore, psychologists say that there are mental representations, then I suppose that there probably are. I therefore subscribe to Language of Thought hypothesis.' That is not, however, the way that Aunty actually does argue. Far from it.

Instead, Aunty regards Cognitive Science in much the same light as Sodom, Gomorrah and Los Angeles. If there is one thing that Aunty believes in in her bones, it is the ontological promiscuity of psychologists.

Figure 2

So, in the present case, although psycholinguists may *talk as though* they were professionally committed to mental representations, Aunty takes that to be *loose* talk. Strictly speaking, she explains, the offending passages can be translated out with no loss to the explanatory/predictive power of psychological theories. Thus, an ontologically profligate psycholinguist may speak of perceptual processes that construct a parsing tree; say one which represents a certain utterance as consisting of a noun phrase followed by a verb phrase, as in figure 2.

But Aunty recognizes no such processes and quantifies over no such trees. What she admits instead are: (1) the utterance under perceptual analysis (the 'distal' utterance, as I'll henceforth call it); and (2) a mental process which eventuates in the distal utterance being HEARD AS consisting of a noun phrase followed by a verb phrase. Notice that this ontologically purified account, though it recognizes mental states with their intentional contents, does *not* recognize mental representations. Indeed, the point of the proposal is precisely to emphasize as live for Intentional Realists the option of postulating representational mental states and then crying halt. If the translations go through, then the facts which psychologists take to argue for mental representations don't actually do so; and if those facts don't, then maybe nothing does.

Well, but *do* the translations go through? On my view, the answer is that some do and others don't, and that the ones that don't make the case for a Language of Thought. This will take some sorting out.

Mental representations do two jobs in theories that employ them. First, they provide a canonical notation for specifying the intentional contents of mental states. But second, mental symbols constitute domains over which *mental processes* are defined. If you think of a mental process – extensionally, as it were – as a sequence of mental states each specified with reference to its intentional content, then mental representations provide a mechanism for the construction of these sequences; they allow you to get, in a mechanical way, from one such state to the next *by performing operations on the representations*.

Suppose, for example, that this is how it goes with English wh-questions: Such sentences have two constituent structures, one in which the questioned phrase is in the OBJECT position as per figure 3, and one in which the questioned phrase is in the SUBJECT position, as per figure 4.

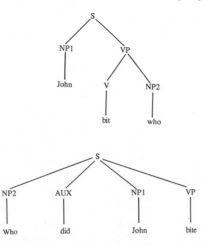

Figure 3

Figure 4

And suppose that the psycholinguistic story is that the perceptual analysis of utterances of such sentences requires the assignment of these constituent structures in, as it might be, reverse order. Well, Aunty can *tell* that story *without* postulating mental representations; a fortiori without postulating mental representations that have constituent structure. She does so by talking about THE INTENTIONAL CONTENTS OF THE HEARER'S MENTAL STATES rather than the mental representations he constructs. "The hearer," Aunty says, "starts out by representing the distal utterance as having 'John' in the subject position and a questioned NP in the object position; and he ends up by representing the distal utterance as having these NPs in the reverse configuration. Thus we see that when it's *properly* construed, claims about 'perceiving as' is all that talk about mental representation ever really comes to." Says Aunty.

But in saying this, it seems to me that Aunty goes too fast. For, what *doesn't* paraphrase out this way is the idea that the hearer gets from one of these representational states to the other *BY MOVING A PIECE OF THE PARSING TREE (e.g. by moving the piece that represents 'who' as a constituent of the type NP2). This untranslated part of the story isn't, notice, about what intentional contents the hearer entertains or the order in which he entertains them. Rather, it's about the mechanisms that mediate the transitions among his intentional states. Roughly, the story says that the mechanism of mental state transitions is computational*; and if the story's true, then (a) there must *be* parsing trees to define the computations over; and (b) these parsing trees need to have a kind of structure that will sustain talk of moving part of a tree while leaving the rest of it alone; in effect, they need to have constituent structure.

I must now report a quirk of Aunty's that I do not fully understand: she refuses to take seriously the ontological commitments of computational theories of mental processes. This is all the more puzzling because Aunty is usually content to play by the following rule: given a well-evidenced empirical theory, either you endorse the entities that it's committed to, or you find a paraphrase that preserves the theory while dispensing with the commitments. Aunty holds that this is simply good deportment for a philosopher; and I, for once, agree with her completely. So, as we've seen, Aunty has a proposal for deontologizing the computational story about which state understanding a sentence is: she proposes to translate talk about trees in the head into talk about hearing utterances under descriptions, and that seems to be all right as far as it goes. But it doesn't go far enough because the ontological commitments of psychological theories are inherited not just from their account of mental states, but also from their account of mental processes; and the computational account of mental processes would appear to be *ineliminably* committed to mental representations construed as structured objects.

The moral, I suppose, is that if Aunty won't bite the bullet, she will have to pay the piper. As things stand now, the cost of not having a Language of Thought is not having a theory of thinking. It's a striking fact about the philosophy of mind that we've indulged for the last fifty years or so that it's been quite content to pony up this price. Thus, while an eighteenth-century Empiricist – like Hume, say – took it for granted that a theory of cognitive *processes* (specifically, Associationism) would have to be the cornerstone of psychology, modern philosophers – like Wittgenstein and Ryle and Gibson and Aunty – *have* no theory of thought to speak of. I do think this is appalling; how can you seriously hope for a good account of belief if you have no account of belief *fixation*? But I don't think it's entirely surprising. Modern philosophers who haven't been overt behaviorists have quite generally been covert behaviorists. And while a behaviorist can recognize mental states – which he identifies with behavioral dispositions – he has literally no use for cognitive processes like causal trains of thought. The last thing a behaviorist wants is mental causes ontologically distinct from their behavioral effects.

It may be that Aunty has not quite outgrown the behaviorist legacy of her early training (it's painfully obvious that Wittgenstein, Ryle, and Gibson never did.) Anyhow, if you ask her what she's prepared to recognize in place of computational mental processes, she unblushingly replies (I quote): "Unknown Neurological Mechanisms." (I think she may have gotten that from John Searle, whose theory of thinking it closely resembles.) If you then ask her whether it's not rather unreasonable to prefer no psychology of thought to a computational psychology of thought, she affects a glacial silence. Ah well, there's nothing can be done with Aunty when she stands upon her dignity and strikes an Anglo-Saxon attitude; except to try a different line of argument.

Argument 3: productivity and systematicity.

The classical argument that mental states are complex reverts to the productivity of the attitudes. There is a (potentially) infinite set of – for example – belief state types, each with its distinctive intentional object and its distinctive causal role. This is immediately explicable on the assumption that belief states have combinatorial structure; that they are somehow built up out of elements and that the intentional object and causal role of each such state depends on what elements it contains and how they are put together. The LOT story is, of course, a paradigm of this sort of explanation since it takes believing to involve a relation to a syntactically structured object for which a compositional semantics is assumed.

There is, however, a notorious problem with productivity arguments. The facts of mortality being what they are, not more than a finite part of any mental capacity ever actually gets exploited. So it requires idealization to secure the crucial premise that mental capacities really *are* productive. It is, for example, quite possible to deny the *productivity* of thought even while admitting that people are forever thinking new things. You can imagine a story – vaguely Gibsonian in spirit – according to which cognitive capacity involves a sort of 'tuning' of the brain. What happens, on this view, is that you have whatever experiences engender such capacities, and the experiences have Unknown Neurological Effects (these Unknown Neurological Effects being mediated, it goes without saying, by the corresponding Unknown Neurological Mechanisms) and the upshot is that you come to have a very large – but finite – number of, as it were, *independent* mental dispositions. For example, the disposition to think that the cat is on the mat on some occasions; and the disposition to think that 3 is prime on other occasions; and the disposition to think that secondary qualities are epiphenomenal on other occasions . . . and so forth. New occasions might thus provoke novel thoughts; and yet the capacity to think wouldn't have to be productive. In principle it could turn out, after a lot of thinking, that your experience catches up with your cognitive capacities so that you actually succeed in thinking everything that you are able to. It's no good saying that you take this consequence to be absurd; I agree with you, but Aunty doesn't.

In short, it needs productivity to establish that thoughts have combinatorial structure, and it needs idealization to establish productivity; so it's open to somebody who doesn't want to admit productivity (because, for example, she doesn't like LOT) simply to refuse to idealize. This is, no doubt, an empirical issue in the very long run. Scientific idealization is demonstrably appropriate if it eventually leads to theories that are independently well confirmed. But vindication in the very long run is a species of cold comfort; perhaps there's a way to get the goodness out of productivity arguments *without* relying on idealizations that are plausibly viewed as tendentious.

Here's how I propose to argue:

(a) There's a certain property that linguistic capacities have in virtue of the fact that natural languages have a combinatorial semantics.
(b) Thought has this property too.
(c) So thought too must have a combinatorial semantics.

Aunty, reading over my shoulder, remarks that this has the form of affirmation of the consequent. So be it; one man's affirmation of the consequent is another man's inference to the best explanation.

The property of linguistic capacities that I have in mind is one that inheres in the ability to understand and produce sentences. That ability is – as I shall say – *systematic*: By which I mean that the *ability to produce/understand some of the sentences is INTRINSICALLY connected to the ability to produce/understand many of the others*. You can see the force of this if you compare learning a language the way we really do learn them with learning a language by memorizing an enormous phrase book. The present point isn't that phrase books are finite and can therefore exhaustively describe only *non*productive languages; that's true, but I've sworn off productivity arguments for the duration of this discussion, as explained above. The point that I'm now pushing is that you can learn *any part* of a phrase book *without learning the rest*. Hence, on the phrase-book model, it would be perfectly possible to learn that uttering the form of words 'Granny's cat is on Uncle Arthur's mat' is the way to say that Granny's cat is on Uncle Arthur's mat, and yet have *no idea* how to say that it's raining (or, for that matter, how to say that Uncle Arthur's cat is on Granny's mat). I pause to rub this point in. I know – to a first approximation – how to say "Who does his mother love very much?" in Korean; viz: "Ki-iy emma-ka nuku-lil newu saranna-ci?" But since I did get this from a phrase book, it helps me not at all with saying anything else in Korean. In fact, I don't know how to say anything else in Korean; I have just shot my bolt.

Perhaps it's self-evident that the phrase-book story must be wrong about language acquisition because a speaker's knowledge of his native language is never like that. You don't, for example, find native speakers who know how to say in English that John loves Mary but don't know how to say in English that Mary loves John. If you did find someone in such a fix, you'd take that as presumptive evidence that he's not a native English speaker but some sort of a tourist. (This is one important reason why it is so misleading to speak of the block/slab game that Wittgenstein describes in paragraph 2 of the *Investigations* as a "complete primitive language"; to think of languages that way is precisely to miss the systematicity of linguistic capacities (to say nothing of their productivity).)

Notice, by the way, that systematicity (again like productivity) is a property of sentences but not of words. The phrase-book model really *does* fit what it's like to learn the *vocabulary* of English since when you learn English vocabulary you acquire a lot of basically *independent* dispositions.

So you might perfectly well learn that using the form of words 'cat' is the way to refer to cats and yet have no idea that using the form of words 'deciduous conifer' is the way to refer to deciduous conifers. My linguist friends tell me that there are languages – unlike English – in which the lexicon, as well as the syntax, is productive. It's candy from babies to predict that a native speaker's mastery of the vocabulary of such a language is always systematic. Productivity and systematicity run together; if you postulate mechanisms adequate to account for the one, then – assuming you're prepared to idealize – you get the other automatically.

What sort of mechanisms? Well, the alternative to the phrase-book story about acquisition depends on the idea, more or less standard in the field since Frege, that the sentences of a natural language have a combinatorial semantics (and, *mutatis mutandis*, that the lexicon does in languages where the lexicon is productive). On this view, learning a language is learning a perfectly general procedure for determining the meaning of a sentence from a specification of its syntactic structure together with the meanings of its lexical elements. Linguistic capacities *can't help* but be systematic on this account because, give or take a bit, the very same combinatorial mechanisms that determine the meaning of any of the sentences determine the meaning of all of the rest.

Notice two things:

First, you can make these points about the systematicity of language without idealizing to astronomical computational capacities. *Productivity* is involved with our ability to understand sentences that are a billion trillion zillion words long. But *systematicity* involves facts that are much nearer home: such facts as the one we mentioned above, that no native speaker comes to understand the form of words 'John loves Mary' except as he *also* comes to understand the form of words 'Mary loves John.' Insofar as there are 'theory neutral' data to constrain our speculations about language, this surely ought to count as one of them.

Second, if the systematicity of linguistic capacities turns on sentences having a combinatorial semantics, the fact that sentences have a combinatorial semantics turns on their having constituent structure. You can't construct the meaning of an object out of the meanings of its constituents unless it has constituents. The sentences of English wouldn't have a combinatorial semantics if they weren't made out of recurrent words and phrases.

OK, so here's the argument: linguistic capacities are systematic, and that's because sentences have constituent structure. But cognitive capacities are systematic too, and that must be because *thoughts* have constituent structure. But if thoughts have constituent structure, then LOT is true. So I win and Aunty looses. Goody!

I take it that what needs defending here is the idea that cognitive capacities are systematic, not the idea that the systematicity of cognitive capacities implies the combinatorial structure of thoughts. I get the second claim for free for want of an alternative account. So then, how do we know that cognitive capacities are systematic?

A fast argument is that cognitive capacities must be *at least* as systematic as linguistic capacities since the function of language is to express thought. To understand a sentence is to grasp the thought that its utterance standardly conveys; so it wouldn't be possible that everyone who understands the sentence 'John loves Mary' also understands the sentence 'Mary loves John' if it weren't that everyone who can think the thought that John loves Mary can also *think the thought* that Mary loves John. You can't have it that language expresses thought *and* that language is systematic unless you also have it that thought is as systematic as language is.

And that is quite sufficiently systematic to embarrass Aunty. For, of course, the systematicity of thought does not follow from what Aunty is prepared to concede: viz. from mere Intentional Realism. If having the thought that John loves Mary is just being in one Unknown But Semantically Evaluable Neurological Condition, and having the thought that Mary loves John is just being in another Unknown But Semantically Evaluable Neurological Condition, then it is – to put it mildly – not obvious why God couldn't have made a creature that's capable of being in one of these semantically Evaluable Neurological Conditions but not in the other, hence a creature that's capable of thinking one of these thoughts but not the other. But if God could have made such a creature, then mere Intentional Realism is exhausted by the claim that there *are* Semantically Evaluable Neurological Conditions.

To put it in a nutshell, what you need to explain the systematicity of thought appears to be Intentional Realism *plus* LOT. LOT says that having a thought is being related to a structured array of representations; and, presumably, to have the thought that John loves Mary is *ipso facto* to have access to the same representations, and the same representational structures, that you need to have the thought that Mary loves John. So *of course* anybody who is in a position to have one of these thoughts is *ipso facto* in a position to have the other. LOT explains the systematicity of thought; mere Intentional Realism doesn't (and neither, for *exactly* the same reasons does connectionism.) Thus I refute Aunty and friends!

Four remarks to tidy up:

First: this argument takes it for granted that systematicity is *at least sometimes* a contingent feature of thought; that there are *at least some cases* in which it is logically possible for a creature to be able to entertain one but not the other of two content-related propositions.

I want to remain neutral, however, on the question of whether systematicity is *always* a contingent feature of thought. For example, a philosopher who is committed to a strong 'inferential role' theory of the individuation of the logical concepts might hold that you can't, in principle, think the thought that (P or Q) unless you are able to think the thought that P. (The argument might be that the ability to infer (P or Q) from P is *constitutive of having* the concept of disjunction.) If this claim is right, then – to that extent – you don't need LOT to explain the systematicity of thoughts which contain the concept OR; it simply *follows from* the fact that you can think that P or Q that you can also think that P.

Aunty is, of course, at liberty to try to explain *all* the facts about the systematicity of thought in this sort of way. I wish her joy of it. It seems to me perfectly clear that there could be creatures whose mental capacities constitute a proper subset of our own; creatures whose mental lives – viewed from our perspective – appear to contain gaps. If inferential role semantics denies this, then so much the worse for inferential role semantics.

Second: it is, as always, essential not to confuse the properties of the attitudes with the properties of their objects. I suppose that it is necessarily true that the *propositions* are 'systematic'; i.e. that if there is the proposition that John loves Mary, then there is also the proposition that Mary loves John. But that necessity is no use to Aunty since it doesn't explain the systematicity of our capacity to *grasp* the propositions. What LOT explains – and, to repeat, mere Intentional Realism does not – is a piece of our empirical psychology: the *de facto*, contingent connection between our ability to think one thought and our ability to think another.

Third: many of Aunty's best friends hold that there is something *very* special about language; that it is *only* when we come to explaining linguistic capacities that we need the theoretical apparatus that LOT provides. But, in fact, we can kick the ladder away: we don't need the systematicity of language to argue for the systematicity of thought. All we need is that it is on the one hand true, and on the other hand not a *necessary* truth, that whoever is able to think that John loves Mary is *ipso facto* able to think that Mary loves John.

Of course, Aunty has the option of arguing the *empirical* hypothesis that thought is systematic only for creatures that speak a language. But think what it would mean for this to be so. It would have to be quite usual to find, for example, animals capable of learning to respond selectively to a situation such that a R b, but quite unable to learn to respond selectively to a situation such that b R a (so that you can teach the beast to choose the picture with the square larger than the triangle, but you can't for the life of you teach it to choose the picture with the triangle larger than the square.) I am not into rats and pigeons, but I once had a course in comparative psychology, and I'm prepared to assure that animal minds aren't in general, like that.

It may be partly a matter of taste whether you take it that the minds of animals are *productive*; but it's about as empirical as anything can be whether they are systematic. And – by and large – they are.

Fourth: just a little systematicity of thought will do to make things hard for Aunty since, as previously remarked, mere Intentional Realism is compatible with there being no systematicity of thought at all. And this is just as well because, although we can be sure that thought is somewhat systematic we can't perhaps be sure of *just how* systematic it is. The point is that if we are unable to think the thought that P, then I suppose we must also be unable to think the thought that we are unable to think the thought that P. So it's at least arguable that, to the extent that our cognitive capacities are *not* systematic, the fact that they aren't is bound to escape our attention. No doubt this opens up some rather spooky epistemic possibilities; but, as I say, it doesn't matter for the polemical purposes at hand. The fact that there are *any* contingent connections between our capacities for entertaining propositions is remarkable when rightly considered. I know of no account of this fact that isn't tantamount to LOT. And neither does Aunty.

So we've found at least three reasons for preferring LOT to mere Intentional Realism, and three reasons ought to be enough for anybody's Aunty. But is there any *general* moral to discern? Maybe there's this one: if you look at the mind from what has recently become the philosopher's favorite point of view, it's the semantic evaluability of mental states that looms large. What's puzzling about the mind is that anything *physical* could have satisfaction conditions, and the polemics that center around Intentional Realism are the ones that this puzzle generates. On the other hand, if you look at the mind from the cognitive psychologist's viewpoint, the main problems are the ones about mental processes. What puzzles psychologists is belief fixation and, more generally, the contingent, causal relations that hold among states of mind. The characteristic doctrines of modern cognitive psychology (including, notably, the idea that mental processes are computational) are thus largely motivated by problems about mental causation. Not surprisingly, given this divergence of main concerns, it looks to philosophers as though the computational theory of mind is mostly responsive to technical worrys about mechanism and implementation; and it looks to psychologists as though Intentional Realism is mostly responsive to metaphysical and ontological worrys about the place of content in the natural order. So, deep down, what philosophers and psychologists really want to say to one another is: 'Why do you care so much about *that*?'

Now as Uncle Hegel used to enjoy pointing out, the trouble with perspectives is that they are, by definition, *partial* points of view; the Real problems are appreciated only when, in the course of the development of the World Spirit, the limits of the perspective come to be transcended. Or, to put it less technically, it helps to be able to see the whole elephant. In the present case, I think the whole elephant looks like this: the key to the nature of cognition is that mental processes preserve semantic properties of mental states; trains of thought, for example, are generally truth preserving, so if you start your thinking with true assumptions you will generally arrive at conclusions that are also true. The central problem about the cognitive mind is to understand how this is so. And my point is that *neither* the metaphysical concerns that motivate Intentional Realists, nor the problems about implementation that motivate cognitive psychologists suffice to frame this issue. To see this issue, you have to look at the problems about content and the problems about process *at the same time*. Thus far has the World Spirit progressed.

If Aunty's said it once, she's said it a hundred times: children should play nicely together and respect each other's points of view. I do think Aunty's right about that.

Notes

1 Aunty's not the only one who'd like to know; much the same question has been raised by Noam Chomsky, John Searle, Brian Loar, David Isreal, Jon Barwise and John Perry, and Tyler Burge to name just a few. Aunty and I are grateful to all of the above for conversations which led to the present reflections. Also to Ned Block for characteristically perceptive comments on an earlier draft.

2 Do *not* be misled by the fact that the *node labels* in associative networks are composed of transportable constituents; the labels play no part in the theory. See Fodor (1966) where this point is made twelve thousand eight hundred and fifteen times.

    By the way, it isn't the *associative* part of 'associative network' that's at issue here. Classical Associationists – Hume, say – held that mental representations have transportable constituents and, I suppose, a combinatorial semantics: the mental image of a house contains, as proper parts, mental images of proper parts of houses. Hume is therefore on my side of the argument as against Aunty and the New Connectionists. The heart of the issue – to repeat the text – is whether you need *both* constituency *and* connectivity as basic relations among the semantically evaluated mental objects, or whether you can make do with connectivity alone.

Connectionism and the foundations of AI

Paul Smolensky

There are few principles on which nearly all practitioners of AI will agree. One of them is that intelligence is the formal manipulations of symbols. This nearly unanimous consensus is being systematically challenged by an approach to AI that models intelligence as the passing of numerical *activation values* within a large network of simple parallel processors. In this *connectionist* approach to AI, intelligence is an *emergent property* of the network's processing: each individual processor has no intelligence, and the messages they exchange – real numbers – participate only in very simple numerical operations. Input to the network is coded as a set of numerical activity values on the input processors, and after this activity has propagated through the connections in the network, a pattern of activity appears on the output processors: this pattern encodes the system's output for the given input. Each connection between processing units has a numerical strength or *weight*; each unit typically computes its activity by using these weights to form the weighted sum of the activity of all the units giving it input, and passing this weighted sum through a non-linear response function such as a threshold or sigmoid curve.

This paper addresses the sense in which intelligence is supposed to "emerge" in these connectionist systems, and the relation that this implies between the connectionist and traditional approaches to AI. The characterization I will formulate for a connectionist approach to AI is controversial in certain respects, and is *not intended as a consensus connectionist view*. A sample of connectionist research that by and large fits with the framework I will describe can be found in the books, *Parallel Distributed Processing: Explorations in the Microstructure of Cognition* (Rumelhart, McClelland, and the PDP Research Group, 1986; McClelland, Rumelhart, and the PDP Research Group, 1986).

A few comments on terminology: I will refer to the traditional approach to AI as the *symbolic paradigm*, intending to emphasize that in this approach, cognitive descriptions are built of entities that are *symbols* both in the semantic sense of referring to external objects and in the syntactic sense of being operated upon by "symbol manipulation." The connectionist

306

approach I will formulate will be called the *subsymbolic paradigm*; the term "subsymbolic" is intended to suggest cognitive descriptions built up of *constituents* of the symbols used in the symbolic paradigm; these fine-grained constituents might be called *subsymbols*. Entities that are typically represented in the symbolic paradigm by symbols are typically represented in the subsymbolic paradigm by a large number of subsymbols. Along with this semantic distinction comes a syntactic distinction. Subsymbols are not operated upon by "symbol manipulation": they participate in numerical – not symbolic – computation. Operations that in the symbolic paradigm consist of a single discrete operation (e.g. a memory fetch) are often achieved in the subsymbolic paradigm as the result of a large number of much finer-grained (numerical) operations.

Most of the foundational issues surrounding the connectionist approach turn, in one way or another, on the *level of analysis* adopted. Since the level of cognitive analysis adopted by the subsymbolic paradigm for formulating connectionist models is lower than the level traditionally adopted by the symbolic paradigm, for the purposes of relating these two paradigms it is often important to analyze connectionist models at a higher level; to amalgamate, so to speak, the subsymbols into symbols. While the symbolic and subsymbolic paradigms each have their preferred level of analysis, the cognitive models they offer can each be described at multiple levels. It is therefore useful to have distinct names for the levels: I will call the preferred level of the symbolic paradigm the *conceptual level* and that of the subsymbolic paradigm the *subconceptual level*. These names are not ideal, but will be further motivated in the course of characterizing these levels. A primary goal of this paper is to articulate a coherent set of hypotheses about the subconceptual level: the kind of cognitive descriptions that are used, the computational principles that apply, and the relations between the sub-conceptual and conceptual levels.

The choice of level greatly constrains the appropriate formalism for analysis. Probably the most striking feature of the connectionist approach is the change in formalism relative to the symbolic paradigm. Since the birth of cognitive science and AI, *language* has provided the dominant theoretical model. Formal cognitive models have taken their structure from the syntax of formal languages, and their content from the semantics of natural language. The mind has been taken to be a machine for formal symbol manipulation, and the symbols manipulated have assumed essentially the same semantics as words of English.

The subsymbolic paradigm challenges both the syntactic and semantic role of language in AI. Section 1 formulates this challenge. Alternative fillers are described for the roles language has traditionally played in AI, and the new role left to language is delimited. The fundamental hypotheses defining the subsymbolic paradigm are formulated, and the question is considered of whether it can offer anything fundamentally new. Section 2 briefly discusses the preferred level of the subsymbolic paradigm, the subconceptual level, and its relation to the neural level. Section 3 elaborates briefly on the computational principles that apply at the subconceptual level. Section 4 discusses how higher, conceptual-level descriptions of subsymbolic models approximate symbolic models (under their conceptual-level descriptions).

There is not space here to consider a number of important issues: the characterization of what makes a system *cognitive* at the subconceptual level; the implications of the subsymbolic paradigm for explanations of cognitive behavior, for semantics, for rationality, and for the constituent structure of mental states; the subsymbolic approach to modeling the conscious use of rules. For treatment of these issues, the reader is referred to Smolensky (1988).

In this paper I have tried to typographically isolate concise formulations of the main points. Most of these numbered points serve to characterize the subsymbolic paradigm, but a few define opposing points of view; to avoid confusion, the latter have been explicitly tagged: *to be rejected*.

1 Formalization of knowledge
1.1. Cultural knowledge and conscious rule interpretation

What is an appropriate formalization of the knowledge cognitive agents possess and the means by which they use that knowledge to perform cognitive tasks? As a starting point, we can look to those knowledge formalizations that predate AI and cognitive science. The most formalized knowledge is found in sciences like physics that rest on mathematical principles. Domain knowledge is formalized in linguistic structures like "energy is conserved" (or an appropriate encryption), and logic formalizes the use of that knowledge to draw conclusions. Knowledge consists of axioms, and drawing conclusions consists of proving theorems.

This method of formulating knowledge and drawing conclusions has extremely valuable properties:

(1) a. *Public access*: the knowledge is accessible to many people.
   b. *Reliability*: different people (or the same person at different times) can reliably check whether conclusions have been validly reached.
   c. *Formality; bootstrapping, universality*: the inference operations require very little experience with the domain to which the symbols refer.

These three properties are important for science because science is a *cultural activity*. It is of limited social value to have knowledge that resides purely in one individual (1a). It is of questionable social value to have knowledge formulated in such a way that different users draw different conclusions (e.g. can't agree that an experiment falsifies a theory) (1b). For cultural propagation of knowledge, it is helpful if novices with little or no experience with a task can be given a means for performing that task, and thereby a means for acquiring experience (1c).

There are other cultural activities besides science with similar requirements. The laws of a nation and the rules of an organization are also linguistically formalized procedures for effecting action which different people can carry out with reasonable reliability. In all these cases, the goal is to create an abstract decision system that resides outside any single person.

Thus *at the cultural level* the goal is to express knowledge in a form that can be executed reliably by different people, even inexperienced ones. We can view the top-level conscious processor of individual people as a *virtual machine* – the *conscious rule interpreter* – and we can view cultural knowledge as a program that runs on that machine. Linguistic formulations of knowledge are perfect for this purpose. The procedures different people can reliably execute are explicit, step-by-step linguistic instructions. This is what has been formalized in the theory of *effective procedures*. Thanks to property (1c), the top-level conscious human processor can be idealized as *universal*: capable of executing any effective procedure. The theory of effective procedures – the classical theory of computation – is physically manifest in the von Neumann computer. One can say that the von Neumann computer is a machine for automatically following the kind of explicit instructions that people can fairly reliably follow – but much faster and with perfect reliability.

Thus we can understand why the production system of computation theory, or more generally the von Neumann computer, has provided a successful model of how people execute instructions (e.g. models of novice physics problem-solving such as Larkin, McDermott, Simon and Simon, 1980). In short, when people (e.g. novices) consciously and sequentially follow rules (e.g. that they have been taught), their cognitive processing is naturally modeled as the sequential interpretation[1] of a linguistically formalized procedure. The rules being followed are expressed in terms of the consciously accessible concepts with which the task domain is conceptualized. In this sense, the rules are formulated at the *conceptual level* of analysis.

To sum up:

(2) a. Rules formulated in natural language can provide an effective formalization of cultural knowledge.

   b. Conscious rule application can be modeled as the sequential interpretation of such rules by a virtual machine called the conscious rule interpreter.

   c. These rules are formulated in terms of the concepts consciously used to describe the task domain – they are formulated at the conceptual level.

1.2. Individual knowledge, skill, and intuition in the symbolic paradigm

But the constraints on *cultural knowledge formalization* are not the same as those on *individual knowledge formalization*. The intuitive knowledge in a physics expert or a native speaker may demand, for a truly accurate description, a formalism that is not a good one for cultural purposes. After all, the individual knowledge in an expert's head does not possess the properties (1) of cultural knowledge: it is not publicly accessible, is not completely reliable, and is completely dependent on ample experience. Individual knowledge is a program that runs on a virtual machine that need not be the same as the top-level conscious processor that runs the cultural knowledge. By definition, conclusions reached by intuition do not come from conscious application of rules, and intuitive processing need not have the same character as conscious rule application.

What kinds of programs are responsible for behavior that is not conscious rule application? I will refer to the virtual machine that runs these programs as the *intuitive processor*. It is (presumably) responsible for all of animal behavior, and a huge portion of human behavior: perception, practiced motor behavior, fluent linguistic behavior, intuition in problem-solving and game-playing – in short, practically all of skilled performance. The transference of responsibility from the conscious rule interpreter to the intuitive processor during the acquisition of skill is one of the most striking and well-studied phenomena in cognitive science (e.g./ Anderson, 1981). An analysis of the formalization of knowledge must consider both the knowledge involved in novices' conscious application of rules and the knowledge resident in experts' intuition, as well as their relationship.

An appealing possibility is this:

(3) a. The programs running on the intuitive processor consist of linguistically formalized rules that are sequentially interpreted. (*To be rejected.*)

This has traditionally been the assumption of cognitive science. Native speakers are unconsciously interpreting rules, as are physics experts when they are intuiting answers to problems. Artificial intelligence systems for natural-language processing and problem-solving are programs written in a formal language for the interpretation of symbolic descriptions of procedures for manipulating symbols.

To the syntactic hypothesis (3a) there corresponds a semantic one:

(3) b. The programs running on the intuitive processor are composed of elements – symbols – referring to essentially the same concepts as are used to consciously conceptualize the task domain. (*To be rejected.*)

This applies to production-system models in which the productions representing expert knowledge are compiled versions of those of the novice (e.g. Anderson, 1983; Lewis, 1978) and to the bulk of AI programs.

Hypotheses (3a) and (3b) together comprise

> (3) **The unconscious rule interpretation hypothesis**: *(To be rejected.)*
> The programs running on the intuitive processor have a syntax and semantics comparable to those running on the conscious rule interpreter.

This hypothesis has provided the foundation for the symbolic paradigm for cognitive modeling. Cognitive models of both conscious rule application and intuitive processing have been programs constructed of entities which are *symbols* both in the syntactic sense of being operated on by "symbol manipulation" and in the semantic sense of (3b). Because these symbols have the conceptual semantics of (3b), I will call the level of analysis at which these programs provide cognitive models the *conceptual level*.

1.3. The subsymbolic paradigm and intuition

The hypothesis of unconscious rule interpretation (3) is an attractive possibility which a connectionist approach to cognitive modeling rejects. Since my purpose here is to formulate rather than argue the scientific merits of a connectionist approach, I will not argue against (3) here. I will point out only that in general, connectionists do not casually reject (3). Several of today's leading connectionist researchers were intimately involved with serious and longstanding attempts to make (3) serve the needs of cognitive science.[2] Connectionists tend to reject (3) because they find the consequences that have actually resulted from its acceptance to be quite unsatisfactory, for a number of quite independent reasons, for example:

> (4) a. Actual AI systems built on hypothesis (3) seem too brittle, too inflexible, to model true human expertise.
> b. The process of articulating expert knowledge in rules seems impractical for many important domains (e.g. common sense).
> c. Hypothesis (3) has contributed essentially no insight into how knowledge is represented in the brain.

What motivates pursuit of connectionist alternatives to (3) are hunches that such alternatives will better serve the goals of cognitive science. Comprehensive empirical assessment of these hunches is probably at least a decade away.

One possible alternative to (3a) is

> (5) **The neural architecture hypothesis:** *(To be rejected.)* The intuitive

processor for a particular task uses the same architecture that the brain employs for that task.

Whatever appeal this hypothesis might have, it seems incapable in practice of supporting the needs of the vast majority of cognitive models. We simply do not know what architecture the brain uses for performing most cognitive tasks. There may be some exceptions (like vision and spatial tasks), but for problem-solving, language, and many others, (5) simply cannot now do the necessary work.

These points and others relating to the neural level will be deferred to section 2. For now the point is simply that viably characterizing the level of analysis of connectionist modeling is not trivially a matter of identifying it with the neural level. While the level of analysis adopted by most connectionist models is not the conceptual level, it is also not the neural level.

The goal now is to formulate a connectionist alternative to (3) that, unlike (5), provides a viable basis for cognitive modeling. A first, crude cut at this hypothesis is:

(6) The intuitive processor possesses a certain kind of connectionist architecture (which abstractly models a few of the most general features of neural networks). *(To be elaborated.)*

Postponing the parenthetical remark to section 2, we now consider the relevant kind of connectionist architecture.

The kind of connectionist model I will consider can be described as a network of very simple processors, *units*, each possessing a numerical *activation value* that is dynamically determined by the values of the other processors in the network. The *activation equation* governing this interaction has numerical parameters which determine the direction and magnitude of the influence of one activation value on another; these parameters are called the *connection strengths* or *weights*. The activation equation is a differential equation (usually approximated by the finite difference equation that arises from discrete time slices; the issue of discrete approximation is taken up in section 3.1). The weights modulate the behavior of the network: they constitute the "program" for this architecture. A network is sometimes programmed by the modeler, but often a network programs itself to perform a task by changing its weights in response to examples of input/output pairs for the task. The *learning rule* is the differential equation governing the weight changes.

The knowledge in a connectionist system lies in its connection strengths. Thus for the first part of our elaboration on (6) we have the following alternative to (3a):

(7) a. **The connectionist dynamical system hypothesis:** The state of the intuitive processor at any moment is precisely defined by a vector of numerical values (one for each unit). The dynamics of the intuitive

processor are governed by a differential equation. The numerical parameters in this equation constitute the processor's program or knowledge. These parameters may change according to a learning equation.

This hypothesis states that the intuitive processor is a certain kind of dynamical system, with the same general character as dynamical systems traditionally studied in physics. The special properties that distinguish this kind of dynamical system – *a connectionist dynamical system* – are only vaguely described in (7a), and a more precise specification is needed. It is premature at this point to commit to such a specification, but one large class of subsymbolic models is that of *quasi-linear dynamical systems*, explicitly discussed in Smolensky (1986b) and Rumelhart, Hinton, and Williams (1986). Each unit in a quasi-linear system computes its value by first calculating the weighted sum of its inputs from other units, and then transforming this sum with a non-linear function. An important goal is to characterize the computational properties of various kinds of connectionist dynamical systems (such as quasi-linear systems) and to thereby determine which kinds provide models of various types of cognitive processes.

The connectionist dynamical system hypothesis (7a) provides a connectionist alternative to the syntactic hypothesis (3a) of the symbolic paradigm. We now need a semantic hypothesis compatible with (7a) to replace (3b). The question is: What does a unit's value *mean*? The most straightforward possibility is that the semantics of each unit is comparable to that of a natural-language word; each unit represents such a concept, and the connection strengths between units reflect the "degree of association" between the concepts.

> (8) **The conceptual unit hypothesis:** (To be rejected.) Individual intuitive processor elements – individual units – have essentially the same semantics as the conscious rule interpreter's elements – words of natural language.

But (7a) and (8) make an infertile couple. Activation of concepts spreading along "degree of association" links may be adequate for modeling simple aspects of cognition – like relative times for naming words in various contexts, or the relative probabilities of perceiving letters in various contexts – but it cannot be adequate for complex tasks like question-answering or grammaticality judgments. The relevant structures cannot even be feasibly represented in such a network, let alone effectively processed.

Great computational power must be present in the intuitive processor to deal with the many cognitive processes that are extremely complex when described at the conceptual level. The symbolic paradigm, based on hypothesis (3), gets its power by allowing highly complex, essentially arbitrary, operations on symbols with conceptual-level semantics: simple semantics, complex operations. If the operations are required to be as simple as those allowed by hypothesis (7a), we cannot get away with a semantics as simple as that of (8).[3] A semantics compatible with (7a) must be more complicated:

> (7) b. **The subconceptual unit hypothesis:** The entities in the intuitive processor with the semantics of conscious concepts of the task domain are *complex patterns of activity over many units*. Each unit participates in many such patterns.

(See Hinton, McClelland, and Rumelhart, 1986, and several of the papers in Hinton and Anderson, 1981; the neural counterpart is associated with Hebb, 1949 and Lashley, 1950, about which see Feldman, 1986.) The interactions between *individual units* are simple, but these units do not have conceptual semantics: they are *subconceptual*. The interactions between the entities with conceptual semantics – interactions between complex patterns of activity – are not at all simple. Interactions at the level of activity patterns are not directly described by the formal definition of a subsymbolic model; they must be computed by the analyst. Typically, these interactions can be computed only approximately. There will generally be no precisely valid, computable formal principles at the conceptual level; such principles exist only at the level of the units – the *subconceptual level*.

> (7) c. **The subconceptual level hypothesis:** Precise, formal descriptions of the intuitive processor are generally tractable not at the conceptual level, but only at the subconceptual level.

Hypotheses (7a-c) can be summarized as

> (7) **The subsymbolic hypothesis:** The intuitive processor is a subconceptual connectionist dynamical system that does not admit a precise formal conceptual-level description.

This hypothesis is the corner-stone of the subsymbolic paradigm.[4]

1.4. The incompatibility of the symbolic and subsymbolic paradigms

I will now show that the symbolic and subsymbolic paradigms, as formulated above, are incompatible – the hypotheses (3) and (7) about the syntax and semantics of the intuitive processor are not mutually consistent. This issue requires care, since it is well known that one virtual machine can often be implemented in another, that a program written for one machine can be translated into a program for the other. The attempt to distinguish subsymbolic and symbolic computation might well be futile if each can simulate the other. After all, a digital computer is in reality some sort of dynamical system simulating a von Neumann automaton, and in turn digital computers are usually used to simulate connectionist models. Thus it seems possible that the symbolic and subsymbolic hypotheses (3) and (7) are *both* correct: that the intuitive processor can be regarded as a virtual machine for sequentially interpreting rules on one level *and* as a connectionist machine on a lower level.

This possibility fits comfortably within the symbolic paradigm, under a formulation such as

(9) Valid connectionist models are merely implementations, for a certain kind of parallel hardware, of symbolic programs that provide exact and complete accounts of behavior at the conceptual level. *(To be rejected.)*

However (9) contradicts hypothesis (7c), and is thus fundamentally incompatible with the subsymbolic paradigm. The symbolic programs that (3) hypothesizes for the intuitive processor could indeed be translated for a connectionist machine, but the translated programs would not be the kind of subsymbolic program that (7) hypothesizes.

What about the reverse relationship, where a symbolic program is used to implement a subsymbolic system? Here it is crucial to realize that the symbols in such programs represent the activation values of units and the strengths of connections. By hypothesis (7b), these do not have conceptual semantics, and thus hypothesis (3b) is violated. The subsymbolic programs that (7) hypothesizes for the intuitive processor can be translated for a von Neumann machine, but the translated programs are *not* the kind of symbolic program that (3) hypothesizes.

These arguments show that unless the hypotheses of the symbolic and subsymbolic paradigms are formulated with some care, the substance of the scientific issue at stake can easily be missed. It is well known that von Neumann machines and connectionist networks can simulate each other. If one cavalierly characterizes the approaches *only syntactically*, using (3a) and (7a) alone, then indeed the issue – connectionist or not connectionist – appears to be "one of AI's wonderful red herrings."[5] It is a mistake to claim that the connectionist approach has nothing new to offer cognitive science. The issue at stake is a central one: *Does a complete formal account of cognition lie at the conceptual level?* The answer offered by the subsymbolic paradigm is: *No – it lies at the subconceptual level.*

2 The subconceptual and neural levels

Hypothesis (7b) leaves open important questions about the semantics of subsymbolic systems. What kind of subconceptual features do the units in the intuitive processor represent? Which activity patterns actually correspond to particular concepts?

Each individual subsymbolic model has adopted particular procedures for relating patterns of activity – activity vectors – to the conceptual-level descriptions of inputs and outputs that define the model's task. The vectors chosen are often vectors of values of fine-grained features of the inputs and outputs, based on some pre-existing theoretical analysis of the domain. For example, for the task studied in Rumelhart and McClelland (1986b), transforming root phonetic forms of English verbs to their past-tense forms, the input and output phonetic strings were represented as vectors of values for context-dependent binary phonetic features. The task description at the conceptual level involves consciously available concepts such as the words "go" and "went," while the subconceptual level employed by the model involved a very large number of fine-grained features such as "roundedness preceded by frontalness and followed by backness." The representation of "go" is a large pattern of activity over these features.

Substantive progress in subsymbolic cognitive science requires that systematic commitments to vectorial representations be made for individual cognitive domains. The vectors chosen to represent inputs and outputs crucially affect a model's predictions, since the generalizations the model makes are largely determined by the similarity structure of the chosen vectors. Unlike symbolic tokens, these vectors lie in a topological space, in which some are close together and others far apart.

It might seem that the mapping between patterns of activity and conceptual-level interpretations ought to be determined by neuroscience. This brings us back to the parenthetical comment in (6) and the general issue of the relation between the subconceptual and neural levels. Space does not permit the investigation of this issue here; in Smolensky (1988), the salient features of neural computation are compared to those of typical connectionist AI models, leading to the following conclusions:

(10) a. Unlike the symbolic architecture, the subsymbolic architecture possesses a number of the most general features of the neural architecture.
   b. However, the subsymbolic architecture lacks a number of the more detailed but still quite general features of the neural architecture; the subconceptual level of analysis is higher than the neural level.
   c. For most cognitive functions, neuroscience cannot now provide the relevant information to specify a cognitive model at the neural level.
   d. The general cognitive principles of the subconceptual level will likely be important contributors to future discoveries of those specifications of neural computations that we now lack.

In other words, the study of subsymbolic computational principles is a research program that is likely to inform and be informed by neuroscience, but its value as exploration of a new computational framework for AI stands quite independently of neuroscience.

3 Computation at the subconceptual level

Hypothesis (7a) offers a brief characterization of the connectionist architecture assumed at the subconceptual level by the subsymbolic paradigm. In this section, I consider the computational principles implicit in that hypothesis.

3.1. Continuity

According to (7a), a connectionist dynamical system has a continuous space of states and changes state continuously in time. I would like first to motivate this continuity condition, reconcile it with some apparent counterexamples, and point out some of its implications. Within the symbolic paradigm, the basic, uncomplicated descriptions of a number of cognitive processes assume a quite discrete nature:

(11) a. Discrete memory locations, in which items are stored without mutual interaction.
   b. Discrete memory storage and retrieval operations, in which an entire item is stored or retrieved in a single, atomic (primitive) operation.
   c. Discrete learning operations, in which new rules become available in an all-or-none fashion.
   d. Discrete inference operations, in which new conclusions become available in an all-or-none fashion.
   e. Discrete categories, to which items either belong or do not.
   f. Discrete production rules, with conditions that are either satisfied or not, and actions that either execute or do not execute.

Cognitive behavior often shows much less discreteness than this. Indeed, cognition seems to be a richly interwoven fabric of continuous and discrete processes. One way to model this interplay is to posit separate discrete and continuous processors in interaction. This approach has a number of theoretical problems: it is difficult to introduce a hard separation between the soft and the hard components of processing. An alternative is to adopt a fundamentally symbolic approach, but to soften various forms of discreteness by hand. For example, the degree of match to conditions of production rules can be given numerical values, productions can be given strengths, interactions between separately stored memory items can be put in by hand, and so on (e.g. see Anderson, 1983).

The subsymbolic paradigm offers another alternative. All the discrete features of (11) are neatly swept aside in one stroke by adopting a fundamentally continuous framework. Then, when the continuous system is analyzed at a higher level, various aspects of discreteness emerge naturally. These aspects of hardness are intrinsically embedded in a fundamentally soft system.

It may appear that the continuous nature of subsymbolic systems is contradicted by the fact that it is easy to find in the literature models that are quite within the spirit of the subsymbolic paradigm but which have neither continuous state spaces nor continuous dynamics: for example, models having units with binary values that jump discretely on the ticks of a discrete clock (e.g. the Boltzman machine, Hinton and Sejnowski, 1983b, Ackley, Hinton and Sejnowski, 1985; harmony theory, Smolensky, 1983, 1986a). I will now argue that these models should be viewed as discrete simulations of an underlying continuous model, considering first discretization of time and then discretization of the units' values.

Dynamical systems evolving in continuous time are nearly always simulated on digital computers by discretizing time. Since subsymbolic models have almost always been simulated on digital computers, it is no surprise that they too have been so simulated. The equations defining the dynamics of the models can be more easily understood by most cognitive scientists if the differential equations of the underlying continuous dynamical system are avoided in favor of the discrete-time approximations that actually get simulated.

When subsymbolic models employ binary-valued units, these values are best viewed not as symbols like T and NIL that are used for conditional branching tests, but as numbers (not numerals!) like 1 and 0 that are used for numerical operations (e.g. multiplication by weights, summation, exponentiation). These models are formulated in such a way that they are perfectly well-defined for continuous values of the units. Discrete numerical unit values is a simplification that is sometimes convenient.

Some dramatic historical evidence for the view that subsymbolic computation should be viewed as fundamentally continuous is a case where switching from discrete to continuous units enabled a revolution in subsymbolic learning theory. In their classic, *Perceptrons*, Minsky and Papert (1969) exploited more or less discrete mathematical methods that were compatible with the choice of binary units. They were incapable of analyzing any but the simplest learning networks. By changing the discrete threshold function of perceptrons to a smooth, differentiable curve, and thereby defining continuously-valued units, Rumelhart, Hinton, and Williams (1986) were able to apply continuous analytic methods to more complex learning networks. The result has been a major advance in the power of subsymbolic learning.

The final point is a foundational one. The theory of discrete computation is quite well understood. If there is any new theory of computation implicit in the subsymbolic approach, it is likely to be a result of a fundamentally different, continuous formulation of computation.

It must be emphasized that the discrete/continuous distinction is not to be clearly understood by looking at simulations. Discrete and continuous machines can of course simulate each other. The claim here is that the most analytically powerful descriptions of subsymbolic models are continuous ones while those of symbolic models are not.

The continuous nature of subsymbolic computation has profound significance because it implies that many of the concepts used to understand cognition in the subsymbolic paradigm come from the category of continuous mathematics, while those used in the symbolic paradigm come nearly exclusively from discrete mathematics. Concepts from physics, from the theory of dynamical systems, are at least as likely to be important as concepts from the theory of digital computation. And analog computers, both electronic and optical, provide natural implementation media for subsymbolic systems (e.g. Anderson, 1986; Cohen, 1986).

3.2. Subsymbolic computation

An important instance of the continuous/discrete mathematics contrast that distinguishes subsymbolic and symbolic computation is found in inference. A natural way to look at the knowledge stored in connections is to view each connection as a *soft constraint*. A positive ("excitatory") connection from unit a to unit b represents a soft constraint to the effect that if a is active, then b should be too. A negative ("inhibitory") connection represents the opposite constraint. The numerical magnitude of a connection represents the strength of the constraint.

Formalizing knowledge in soft constraints rather than hard rules has important consequences. Hard constraints have consequences singly; they are context-independent rules that can be applied separately, sequentially, irrespective of whatever other rules may exist. But *soft constraints have no implications singly*; any one can be overridden by the others. It is only the *entire set* of soft constraints that has any implications. Inference must be a cooperative process, like the parallel relaxation processes typically found in subsymbolic systems. Furthermore, adding additional soft constraints can repeal conclusions that were formerly valid. Subsymbolic inference is fundamentally non-monotonic.

One way of formalizing soft constraint satisfaction is in terms of statistical inference. In certain subsymbolic systems, the soft constraints can be identified as statistical parameters and the activation passing procedures can be identified as statistical inference procedures (Hinton and Sejnowski, 1983a; Geman and Geman, 1984; Smolensky, 1986a; see also Shastri, 1985; Pearl, 1985). This identification is usually rather complex and subtle, and is usually not simply a matter of identifying the strength of the connection between two units with the correlation between their activity. An important goal is to determine how statistical and other formal theories of continuous (as opposed to logical) inference can be employed to mathematically elucidate the inference found in other subsymbolic systems.

To sum up:

(12)　a.　Knowledge in subsymbolic computation is formalized as a large set of soft constraints.

    b. Inference with soft constraints is fundamentally a parallel process.

    c. Inference with soft constraints is fundamentally non-monotonic.

    d. Certain subsymbolic systems can be identified as employing statistical inference.

4 Conceptual-level descriptions of intuition

The previous section concerned computation in subsymbolic systems analyzed at the subconceptual level, the level of units and connections. In this final section I consider analyses of subsymbolic computation at the higher, conceptual level. I focus on subsymbolic models of intuitive processes, and my conclusion will be this: conceptual-level descriptions of aspects of subsymbolic models of intuitive processing roughly approximate symbolic accounts. The picture that emerges is of a symbiosis between the symbolic and subsymbolic paradigms: the symbolic paradigm offers concepts for better understanding subsymbolic models, and those concepts are in turn illuminated with a fresh light by the subsymbolic paradigm.

4.1. The Best Fit Principle

The notion that each connection represents a soft constraint can be formulated at a higher level:

(13) **The Best Fit Principle:** Given an input, a subsymbolic system outputs a set of inferences that, as a whole, give a best fit to the input, in a statistical sense defined by the statistical knowledge stored in the system's connections.

In this vague form, this principle can be regarded as a desideratum of subsymbolic systems. But it is exactly true in a precise sense, at least in an idealized limit, for the class of connectionist dynamical systems that have been studied in harmony theory (Riley and Smolensky, 1984; Smolensky, 1983, 1984a, 1984b, 1986a, 1986c).

To render the Best Fit Principle precise, it is necessary to provide precise definitions of "inferences," "best fit," and "statistical knowledge stored in the system's connections." This is done in harmony theory, where the central object is the harmony function H which measures, for any possible set of inferences, the goodness of fit to the input with respect to the soft constraints stored in the connection strengths. The set of inferences with the largest value of H, i.e. highest harmony, is the best set of inferences, with respect to a well-defined statistical problem.

Harmony theory basically offers three things. It gives a mathematically precise characterization of the prediction-from-examples goal as a statistical inference problem. It tells how the prediction goal can be achieved using a connectionist network with a certain set of connections. And it gives a procedure by which the network can learn the correct connections with experience, thereby satisfying the prediction-from-examples goal.

The units in harmony networks are stochastic units: the differential equations defining the system are stochastic. There is a system parameter called the *computational temperature* that governs the degree of randomness in the units' behavior: it goes to zero as the computation proceeds. (The process is *simulated annealing*, as in the Boltzmann machine: Ackley, Hinton, and Sejnowski, 1985; Hinton and Sejnowski, 1983a, 1983b, 1986. See Rumelhart, McClelland, and the PDP Research Group, 1986, p. 148, and Smolensky, 1986a, for the relations between harmony theory and the Boltzmann machine.)

4.2. Productions, sequential processing, and logical inference

A simple harmony model of expert intuition in qualitative physics was described in Riley and Smolensky (1984) and Smolensky (1986a, 1986c). The model answers questions like "what happens to the voltages in this circuit if I increase this resistor?" Higher-level descriptions of this subsymbolic problem-solving system illustrate several interesting points.

It is possible to identify *macro-decisions* during the system's solution of a problem; these are each the result of many individual micro-decisions by the units of the system, and each amounts to a large-scale commitment to a portion of the solution. These macro-decisions are approximately like the firing of production rules. In fact, these "productions" "fire" in essentially the same order as in a symbolic forward-chaining inference system. One can measure the total amount of order in the system, and see that there is a qualitative change in the system when the first micro-decisions are made: the system changes from a disordered phase to an ordered one.

It's a corollary of the way this network embodies the problem domain constraints, and the general theorems of harmony theory, that the system, when given a well-posed problem, and infinite relaxation time, will always give the correct answer. So under that idealization, the *competence* of the system is described by *hard* constraints: Ohm's Law, Kirchoff's Law. It's as though it had those laws written down inside it. However, as in all subsymbolic systems, the *performance* of the system is achieved by satisfying a large set of *soft* constraints. What this means is that if we go outside of the ideal conditions under which hard constraints seem to be obeyed, the illusion that the system has hard constraints inside is quickly dispelled. The system can violate Ohm's Law if it has to, but if it doesn't have to violate the law, it won't. Thus, *outside the idealized domain of well-posed problems and infinite processing time, the system gives a sensible performance.* It isn't brittle the way that symbolic inference systems are. If the system is given an ill-posed problem, it satisfies as many constraints as possible. If it is given inconsistent information, it doesn't fall flat, and deduce anything. If it is given insufficient information, it doesn't just sit there and deduce nothing. Given finite processing time, the performance degrades gracefully as well. So the competence/performance distinction can be addressed in a sensible way.

We can sum this up neatly using a physics-level analogy, in which subsymbolic theory corresponds to quantum mechanics and symbolic theory corresponds to classical mechanics. The subsymbolic inference system just described is a "quantum" system that appears to be "Newtonian" under the proper conditions. A system that has, at the micro-level, soft constraints, satisfied in parallel, *appears* at the macro-level, under the right circumstances, to have hard constraints, satisfied serially. But it doesn't *really*, and as soon as we step outside the "Newtonian" domain, we see that it's really been a "quantum" system all along.

4.3. Conceptual-level spreading activation

According to the subconceptual unit hypothesis (7b), the concepts we use to consciously represent problem domains correspond in subsymbolic systems to patterns of activity over many network units. A situation in which many concepts occur corresponds to an activity pattern that incorporates the subpatterns corresponding to the relevant concepts, all suitably superimposed in a way not yet fully understood. Using the mathematics of the superposition operation, it is possible to approximately analyze connectionist dynamical systems at the conceptual level. If the connectionist system is purely linear (so that the activity of each unit is precisely a weighted sum of the activities of the units giving it input), it can easily be proved that the higher-level description obeys formal laws of just the same sort as the lower level: the computation of the subconceptual and conceptual levels are *isomorphic*. Linear connectionist systems are, however, of limited computational power, and most interesting connectionist systems are non-linear. However, most of these are in fact *quasi-linear*: each unit combines its inputs linearly even though the effects of this combination on the unit's activity is non-linear. Further, the problem-specific *knowledge* in such systems is in the combination weights, i.e. the *linear part* of the dynamical equations; and in learning systems it is generally only these linear weights that adapt. For these reasons, even though the higher level is not isomorphic to the lower level in non-linear systems, there are senses in which the higher level *approximately* obeys formal laws similar to the lower level. (For details, see Smolensky, 1986b.)

The conclusion here is a rather different one from the preceding section, where we saw how there are senses in which higher-level characterizations of certain subsymbolic systems approximate productions, serial processing, and logical inference. What we see now is that there are also senses in which the laws approximately describing cognition at the conceptual level are *activation-passing laws* like those at the subconceptual level, but operating between units with individual conceptual semantics. Such semantic level descriptions of mental processing (which include *local* connectionist models; see note 3) have been of considerable value in cognitive science. We can now see how these "spreading activation" accounts of mental processing fit into the subsymbolic paradigm.

4.4. Schemata

The final conceptual-level notion I will consider is that of the *schema* (e.g. Rumelhart, 1980). This concept goes back at least to Kant (1787/1963) as a description of mental concepts and mental categories. Schemata appear in many AI systems in the forms of frames, scripts, or similar structures: they are prepackaged bundles of information that support inference in stereotyped situations.

I will very briefly summarize work on schemata in connectionist systems reported in Rumelhart, Smolensky, McClelland, and Hinton (1986; see also Feldman, 1981, and Smolensky, 1986a, 1986c). This work addressed the case of schemata for rooms. Subjects were asked to describe some imagined rooms using a set of 40 features like has-ceiling, has-window, contains-toilet, and so on. Statistics were computed on this data and these were used to construct a network containing one node for each feature, and containing connections computed from the statistical data.

This resulting network can perform inference of the same general kind as that carried out by symbolic systems with schemata for various types of rooms. The network is told that some room contains a ceiling and an oven; the question is, what else is likely to be in the room? The system settles down into a final state, and the inferences contained in that final state are that the room contains a coffee cup but no fireplace, a coffee pot but no computer.

The inference process in this system is simply one of greedily maximizing harmony. To describe the inference of this system on a higher level, we can examine the global states of the system in terms of their harmony values. How internally consistent are the various states in the space? It's a 40-dimensional state space, but various 2-dimensional subspaces can be selected and the harmony values there can be graphically displayed. The harmony landscape has various peaks; looking at the features of the state corresponding to one of the peaks, we find that it corresponds to a prototypical bathroom; others correspond to a prototypical office, and so on for all the kinds of rooms subjects were asked to describe. There are no units in this system for bathrooms or offices: there are just lower-level descriptors. The prototypical bathroom is a pattern of activation, and the system's recognition of its prototypicality is reflected in the harmony peak for that pattern. It is a consistent, "harmonious" combination of features:

better than neighboring points like one representing a bathroom without a bathtub, which has distinctly lower harmony.

During inference, this system climbs directly uphill on the harmony landscape. When the system state is in the vicinity of the harmony peak representing the prototypical bathroom, the inferences it makes are governed by the shape of the harmony landscape there. This shape is like a "schema" that governs inferences about bathrooms. (In fact, harmony theory was created to give a connectionist formalization of the notion of schema; see Smolensky, 1984b, 1986a, 1986c.) Looking closely at the harmony landscape we can see that the terrain around the "bathroom" peak has many of the properties of a bathroom schema: variables and constants, default values, schemata embedded inside of schemata, and even cross-variable dependencies, which are rather difficult to incorporate into symbolic formalizations of schemata. The system behaves as though it had schemata for bathrooms, offices, etc., even though they are not "really there" at the fundamental level: these schemata are strictly properties of a higher-level description. They are informal, approximate descriptions – one might even say they are merely metaphorical descriptions – of an inference process too subtle to admit such high-level descriptions with great precision. Even though these schemata may not be the sort of object on which to base a formal model, nonetheless they are useful descriptions that help us understand a complex inference system.

4.5. Conclusion

The view of symbolic structures that emerges from viewing them as entities of high-level descriptions of dynamical systems is quite different from the view provided by the symbolic paradigm.

(14) a. Macro-inference is not a process of firing a symbolic production but rather of qualitative state change in a dynamical system, such as a phase transition.

b. Schemata are not large symbolic data structures but rather the potentially quite intricate shapes of harmony maxima.

c. Categories (it turns out) are attractors in connectionist dynamical systems: states that "suck in" to a common place many nearby states, like peaks of harmony functions.

d. Categorization is not the execution of a symbolic algorithm but the continuous evolution of the dynamical system, the evolution that drives states into the attractors, to maximal harmony.

e. Learning is not the construction and editing of formulae, but the gradual adjustment of connection strengths with experience, with the effect of slowly shifting harmony landscapes, adapting old and creating new concepts, categories, schemata.

The heterogenous assortment of high-level mental structures that have been embraced in this section suggests that the conceptual level lacks formal unity. This is just what one expects of approximate higher-level descriptions, which, capturing different aspects of global properties, can have quite different characters. According to the subsymbolic paradigm, the unity underlying cognition is to be found not at the conceptual level, but rather at the subconceptual level, where relatively few principles in a single formal framework lead to a rich variety of global behaviors.

Notes

I am indebted to a number of people for very helpful conversations on these issues: Rob Cummins, Denise Dellarosa, Jerry Fodor, Zenon Pylyshyn, and Georges Rey. Dave Rumelhart's ideas have been extremely influential on the view argued for here, although I of course bear full responsibility for the formulation.

This research has been supported by National Science Foundation grant IST–8609599 and by the Department of Computer Science and Institute of Cognitive Science at the University of Colorado, Boulder.

A considerably revised and much expanded version of this paper appeared in *The Behavioral and Brain Sciences*, vol. 11, no. 1, March 1988; I am most grateful to the Editor for permission to reprint portions of that paper here.

1 In this paper, when "interpretation" is used to refer to a process, the sense intended is that of computer science: the process of taking a linguistic description of a procedure and executing that procedure.
2 Consider, for example, the connectionist symposium at the University of Geneva held September 9, 1986. The advertised program featured Feldman, Minsky, Rumelhart, Sejnowski, and Waltz. Of these five researchers, three were major contributors to the symbolic paradigm for many years: consider Minsky, 1975; Rumelhart, 1975, 1980; and Waltz, 1978, for example.
3 This is an issue that divides connectionist approaches. "Local connectionist models" (e.g. Dell, 1985; Feldman, 1985; McClelland and Rumelhart, 1981; Rumelhart and McClelland, 1982; Waltz and Pollack, 1985) accept (8), and often deviate significantly from (7a). This approach has been championed by the Rochester connectionists (see Feldman, Ballard, Brown, and Dell, 1985). Like the symbolic paradigm, this school favors simple semantics and more complex operations. The processors in their networks are usually more powerful than those allowed by (7); they are often rather like digital computers running a few lines of simple code. ("If there is a 1 on this input line then do X else do Y," where X and Y are quite different little procedures; e.g. Shastri, 1985.) This style of connectionism, quite different from the subsymbolic style, has much in common with the branch of traditional computer science that "parallelizes" serial algorithms by decomposing them into routines that can run in parallel, often with certain synchronization points built in. The grain size of the Rochester parallelism, while large compared to the subsymbolic paradigm, is small compared to standard parallel programming: the processors are allowed only a few internal states and allowed to transmit only a few different values (Feldman and Ballard, 1982).

4 As stated in the introduction, a large sample of research that by and large falls under the subsymbolic paradigm can be found in the books, Rumelhart, McClelland and the PDP Research Group (1986), *Parallel Distributed Processing: Explorations in the Microstructure of Cognition*, and McClelland, Rumelhart and the PDP Research Group (1986), *Parallel Distributed Processing: Explorations in the Microstructure of Cognition*. While this work has come to be labelled "connectionist," the term "PDP" was deliberately chosen to distinguish it from the localist approach which had previously adopted the name "connectionist" (Feldman and Ballard, 1982).

5 The phrase is Roger Schank's, in reference to "parallel processing" (Waldrop, 1984). Whether he was referring to connectionist systems I do not know; in any event, I don't mean to imply that the grounds for his comment are addressed here.

Some comments on Smolensky and Fodor

Yorick Wilks

This discussion seeks to compare, in very brief compass, a current radical argument for connectionism and a radical argument against. It is not clear that the very same version of connectionism is defended by Smolensky as is attacked by Fodor, but since I do not bring the two arguments directly in contact, that will not matter. My own inconclusive view is that the jury is still out, and there is no pressing need at the moment to believe what Smolensky says, though one may respect it and be stimulated by it, nor to reject the whole thing on the grounds Fodor gives. One can legitimately be, in a narrow and strict sense, an agnostic, without giving that word the force of active disbelief it is often made to carry.

Smolensky

Smolensky (this volume) declines to base his version of connectionism on the brain: on the supposed analogy of the brain to connectionist networks, and for this all critics must give much thanks. Connectionism for him must stand or fall on its own merits as a model of processing and behavior, and not on gross and randomly drawn similarities with natural phenomena, similarities that cannot be assessed in any scientific manner, but which either appeal or fail to do so, depending on the mood of the audience.

His distinctive contribution is what he calls the Subsymbolic Paradigm (PTC hereafter, his own acronym) by which he intends a thoroughgoing version of connectionism, one opposed not only to the conventional AI paradigm of symbolic processing, but also to weaker versions of connectionism, normally called "localist," which can be considered as no more than a different style of symbolic processing. He explicitly claims that a PTC machine is not a Turing/von Neumann machine but a "dynamical system," speculating that such systems may challenge the "claim that the class of well-defined computations is exhausted by those of Turing machines." This speculation is unsupported and prima facie implausible, given the all-encompassing definition of such machines. In particular, argues Smolensky, there will be nothing at all in a dynamical system corresponding to the atoms that function as semantically interpretable entities in symbolic systems: there will be only and no more than "activity patterns." Similarly the correlate of laws will not be symbolic manipulations but only differential equations.

His PTC paradigm is initially attractive because (a) it claims to offer something totally different, even from localist connectionism, and (b) it has an incomprehensible element about it, which has always been attractive in artificial intelligence: researchers have normally been pleased rather than sorry when their programs do something they do not expect and cannot explain, as parents sometimes are with their children.

It is tempting to exaggerate this element in artificial intelligence but it is perfectly real: programming and debugging are hard and there is a genuine charm in making something such that we do not know how it works. We are close again to real creation and alchemy. Fodor has suggested that not wanting to know how things work in the cognitive domain is no more than "disguised behaviorism." But, and Smolensky would say this too, that tendency must be resisted. One of his claims for the PTC is that it returns AI to a norm in the scientific explanation, that of a dividing line between explanatory levels for phenomena: as between gross body mechanics and quantum phenomena, for example, where on one side of the line phenomena are intrinsically statistical, even though this discontinuity is not seen as an obscurantism in science but a necessary part of it.

Initially Smolensky defines PTC rather in the way the medievals defined God through the Via Negativa by enumerating what He was not. Smolensky (this volume) states that PTC is not:

a. Disguised local-symbolic computation,
b. Digital approximation of analog computation,
c. Language translation or compilation, nor
d. Neural modeling.

Since the PTC is not any of these fairly well-understood things, what then is it? Smolensky offers two positive clues:

1 that the semantics of symbol processing and subsymbolic processing will be "incomparable" across the neural-digital divide, and
2 that, as we noted above, this non-comparability across the divide will allow AI to conform to the "norm in science", where there is also a lack of direct, quantitative, equivalence and prediction.

The first suggestion is to some extent trivial and non-revolutionary, since Scott and Strachey (1971) say the same is true, in a clear sense, for the semantics across a language-level translation. And the second presupposes that this norm is a good thing; but, in AI, one could continue to argue that clarity and comprehensibility across levels of abstraction remain important if they can be had, and are not features to give up lightly. It may not be unreasonable to demand that computing, a human artifact, retains more perspicuity than natural phenomena themselves.

But, whatever is the case about this general objection to wanting barriers to explanation, the fact is that Smolensky's model does not conform to the standard-explanation-in-physics model in one important particular: he believes that only the subsymbolic model gives a precise description of the phenomena. His principle (7c) reads: "Complex, formal and precise descriptions of the intuitive processor are generally tractable not at the conceptual level, but only at the subconceptual level."

Now this is both questionable in itself and tells against the general analogy with physics that Smolensky wishes to draw for the PTC. First, the subsymbolic level may be covered in some sense by the statistical equations that describe the behavior of a subsymbolic system, but such a description is not precise in the Maxwellian (which is also the common-sense) reading of precise and complete as giving the detailed description of the activity of all component parts. It is precisely the intractability of statistical and quantum descriptions which has made them so unattractive. Much more importantly, (7c) shows that Smolensky sees the subconceptual level of description and explanation as incompatible with the conceptual/symbolic level. This, again, is quite different from what obtains in the case of physics, where the Newtonian and quantum levels of description cannot possibly be incompatible, nor is one right and the other wrong, they simply describe different levels and aspects of the world.

A consequence of this is that Smolensky really is taking sides: as he himself puts it, he is against "bland ecumenicism." He is opting for one level of explanation and description of cognitive phenomena as against another, and he is deliberately picking the counter-intuitive one. This is bold but must in some sense necessarily fail: there cannot in principle be an explanation of cognitive phenomena that ignores or is incompatible with the cognitive level of intuitions. As philosophers have enjoyed pointing out for decades, no researches on the eye, nor on light wavelengths in angstroms, can show us we are all wrong about what red is. Such a demonstration could not make empirical sense.

Dietrich and Fields (1988) have made the points that Smolensky's claimed incompatibility between levels sits uneasily with his claimed closeness to explanation in physics; and that he shares with Fodor (to whom he believes himself utterly opposed) the view that one level of explanation is clearly superior to the other: they differ merely about which level to prefer. I think they are wrong about this last point, and that the closeness of Fodor and Smolensky is greater than they think. They are surely right that the Smolensky-Fodor difference is fundamentally about semantics and not at all about architectures and implementations. To see this is to rob the debate of its freshness: much of the Fodor-Smolensky debate is simply a rerun of points made in the Procedural Semantics debate in the last decade about the right level of interpretation of programs that claim to explicate cognitive phenomena. And that debate predates the current revival of connectionism.

But by trying to show that the PTC can deal with the phenomenon of "Conscious Rule Application," Smolensky again tackles the symbolic competition head on: attempting to answer those critics who say that connectionism cannot explain or represent the function of rules in knowledge structures. But, again, we ask what connectionism has to offer besides translation? If an imaginary decompiler from the subsymbolic microrules to the symbolic rules is, almost by definition, an impossible device, then the PTC can never be known to represent rule-based behavior faithfully, for it may always be a different rule that is actually represented; on the other hand, if the decompiler is possible, then why bother with PTC at all?

In the course of that debate between Johnson-Laird (1977) and Fodor (1978) the latter attacked the notion of any kind of "procedural semantics" on the ground that it must in the end be parasitic upon formal model-theoretic semantics because any program, in whatever high-level language, is translated down by its translator or compiler to machine language which has simple denotations in terms of addresses etc.

Johnson-Laird then produced the Scott-Strachey (ibid.) reference to make the point that the semantics of different levels of programming language are independent, even if they are translations or compilations of each other. However, Fodor's point in that earlier discussion dangerously exposes his position in the current, connectionist, debate since his claim against procedural semantics suggests that he would not be able to preserve a semantics for a high-level representation language, like a Language of Thought, independent of its implementation, whether that was connectionist or otherwise. It is clear that Fodor needs exactly this independence even though he did not realise that in the earlier debate, and it is an independence that Smolensky also needs for his "incomparability" point. Thus, Dietrich and Fields' point (b) above is correct but only just.

Whatever is the case there, Smolensky has chosen an unpersuasive example, because the methodology of conscious rule application is a false picture of learning language and most forms of expertise – we do not learn by being offered explicit rules – so Smolensky is submitting to unnecessary gymnastics to accommodate the learning paradigm of his competitors.

Fodor

Let us now turn to some of Fodor's criticism of connectionism (this volume). Fodor's position over the years could be characterized as a subtle and sustained attempt to move the traditional concerns of Chomskyan linguistics into serious discussion of the mind within Cognitive

Science. In that sense Fodor's work (and his Language of Thought hypothesis, 1975, is the best statement) is a distinctive version of the Symbolic Processing hypothesis which connectionism, at least in versions like PTC, seeks to undermine.

This is not to suggest that the Chomskyan version of symbolic processing that Fodor espouses has anything else in common with symbolic AI. In fact the distinctive Chomskyan/Fodorian assumptions about human language processing would be shared by only a minority of AI researchers on language processing. Those assumptions can be summarized as:

i natural language has an infinite productivity, without gaps or discontinuities: a language will not have a sentence like *Mary loves John*, but
refuse to admit *John loves Mary* is a sentence. There are in fact no
languages that are small, constrained, model, or toy-languages of the
sort Wittgenstein constructed to show their inadequacies; languages
and language skills cannot be identified with any kind of phrase-book
mastery.

ii natural languages are systematic, which means something very like
being fully describable by a generative grammar of the type found in
Chomsky's various theories.

iii natural language and mental states have a compositional nature, in the
sense of the compositional principle often attributed to Frege: there
must be identifiable subparts in such structures that contribute in a
non-trivial functional manner to the structure and interpretation of a
larger whole, such as a sentence.

Each of these principles or assumptions is highly questionable taken alone, and has been vigorously questioned in the linguistics and AI literatures. So, for example, gaps, discontinuities, and lack of systematicity can be emphasized as a feature of natural languages by noting that humans appear to be able to process center-embedded sentences only down to some fairly fixed depth. *The man the dog bit died*, is quite comprehensible, but embedding a further clause in its middle, such as *The cat hated*, to yield *The man the dog the cat hated bit died*, renders it incomprehensible. Yet the systematic rule that embeds the second clause, to talk in semi-procedural transformational jargon for a moment, is the same as the one that embedded the first. Yet this is a problem: if there is to be systematicity and no gaps or discontinuities, then that distinction in comprehension should not arise. Chomskyans have traditionally tackled this criticism by arguing that both forms are sentences, however difficult they may be to understand in fact, and that there is no discontinuity, and details of human understanding in actual performance are not part of the subject matter of descriptive linguistics. But this route is not open to one like Fodor who claims he is interested in processing and in cognitive mechanisms.

Again, in the statement of Fregean compositionality above, the non-triviality proviso is important and hard to operate, since any subpart of a sentence, say, could yield a whole structure, while all other subparts yielded nothing, rather as *I really would like you to stop*, could be said to have its whole structure and force given by only the last word in it. Yet, if generalized, this example would lead to a total trivialization of the compositionality principle.

Fodor's criticism of connectionism (this volume) is that it does not, on the face of it, share these assumptions. One form of this is the size issue: that most forms of connectionist system do not "scale up": tackling five-word sentences requires enormously more network structure than five, single-word sentences. It is just such simple size restrictions that rule-based approaches find absurd, since linguistic rules, whether of a Chomskyan or any other type such as phrase-structure, deal with constituents and structures independently of their length. The size issue is of some interest because connectionists, too, have made the ability to deal with large-scale phenomena (as on 64,000 processor machines) a crucial argument for their case, the difference being that the two sides are using "size" in quite different senses.

Fodor's key argument concerns a form of compositionality of structure (assumption iii above): ". . . the mechanism of mental state transitions is computational . . . there must be parsing trees and . . . these need the kind of structure that sustain the task of moving part of a tree while leaving the rest of it alone . . ." (this volume).

This is a very specific claim about the structure of mental representations, and it comes of course, straight from Chomskyan linguistics, where moving tree subparts about was exactly what transformational rules always did.

The link to computational-alias-mental architecture then follows: ". . . arguments that suggest that mental states have constituent structure *ipso facto* favor Turing/von Neumann architecture, which can compute in a language whose formulas have transportable parts as against associative networks which, by definition, cannot." (Fodor, this volume.)

Fodor's point here, whatever its continuity with Chomskyan linguistic structures, is undoubtedly intended to be of wider significance for mental states and their structures: this can be seen clearly from his points (this volume) about the constituent AND structure of INTENDING A AND B, though the force of his point is somewhat weakened by his insistence that the relation between that conjoined proposition and the constituent propositions (INTENDING A and INTENDING B, respectively) is "a matter of *connectivity* rather than *constituency*" (p. 292).

But the main force of Fodor's case against connectionism is clear: constituency is essential to combinatorial syntax and semantics, and connectionism cannot represent such constituency in a general way. For him it is not an accidental consequence of representational choices that such constituency cannot be systematically represented but it is "part of the connectionist theory that there is no combinatorial syntax/semantics for the intentional states it posits (i.e. that nodes have no internal syntactic/semantic structure)."(Fodor, 1987.)

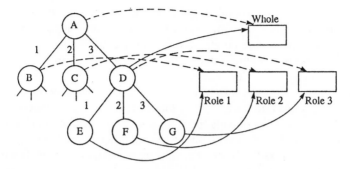

Figure 1   The solid and broken lines show two different ways of mapping a part-whole hierarchy (on the left) into the same connectionist hardware (on the right). Notice that node D in the hierarchy can be represented by two totally different activity patterns that have nothing in common

That then is the general case, but many particular linguistic phenomena could be drawn in to illustrate the case further: gapping phenomena, for example, would do equally well for Fodor's case. How could a connectionist explain why, on hearing "Gate 23" I can and do, in the right (airport) context, access or construct something like "The plane will arrive at gate 23"? We shall return to this kind of example below.

I want to describe some recent unpublished work that I feel should be brought into the debate here: it is wholly tentative but shows how a connectionist reply could be made precisely to Fodor's points about constituency, and in empirical rather than theoretical terms. It also shows that it is certainly not the case, as Fodor's remarks quoted above suggest, that it is part of connectionist theory not to be able to demonstrate "constituency relevant" behavior in systems. Hinton (1988) set out diagramatically how a distributed connectionist system might represent tree structures of unspecified depth on a fixed set of nodes (shown in figure 1).

This work was not implemented, but recent experiments by Pollack (1988) not yet published suggest that a quite general answer to Fodor may be possible within connectionist assumptions. What Pollack has done, in very simple outline, is to develop a coding method, first for stacks and then, more generally, for trees so that a system with a fixed set of nodes is given a training set of complex binary tree structures. The trees are coded, along with the labels on their terminal nodes (the "sentence" to which each tree corresponds) by a numerical compression algorithm, such that every tree results in a set of n digits (where n is the number of nodes in the system).

Then, for the training set, the system is given the "sentence" and returns the tree, independently of its depth. This alone is sufficient to show that Hinton's original suggestion made sense, and that there can be a general algorithm for coding trees of unspecified depth on a fixed node set. It may turn out that there are depth limits to be encountered for the retrieval of trees, but that fact will not support Fodor's case unless the limits found turn out to be essentially different from the known depth-limits on human processing (e.g. in phenomena like center-embedding).

So far there is no more than a proof of principle; a more important matter will be the generativity or systematicity of Pollack's system: how far can the system then produce a tree from a sentence outside the training set. Early results suggest that it can do this, but that its ability will depend on the order in which structures outside the training set are presented. That is, it may be able to structure a new sentence P, but not unless new sentence Q has already been encountered. That fact would be consistent both with what abstract learnability theory (e.g. Gold, 1967) suggests and the known results about children learning their first language.

Nothing yet follows from all this: it only suggests that the a priori claims of Fodor may be too strong, and that connectionists can meet his demands. As throughout this note, that suggests adopting a position of agnosticism about both opposed positions.

It is probably too soon to explore what the "systematicity" of such a device as Pollack's might be and how we would judge it. Much of Chomsky's linguistics was concerned with abstract notions of systematicity in a grammar, but that gave, and was intended to give, little hint as to how to assess the systematicity of the behavior of a performing device, whether a human or a network.

In his contribution to this volume, Fodor sets a very high standard for such systematicity, roughly that a device that can learn aRb should, *ipso facto*, be able to learn bRa (where those forms could be glossed in terms of the ability to learn that "John loves Mary" is a proposition, given that it has learned that "Mary loves John" is one). "What the Connectionists need is a mechanism that insures that if you get one then you do get the other. Whereas what they've got is mechanism which is compatible with getting both if you get either. It's approximately the difference between "Necessarily (if A then B)" and "If A then (possibly B)"; what they need is the first but what they've got is only the second." (Fodor 1987.)

This is a major issue and there is no scope for its examination here, but I suggest that this standard is too high, and that for real language structures there can, and should, be no real demonstrations of such necessity; too many pragmatic factors intervene in real organisms. We would not want a demonstration that an organism-with-systematicity having encountered "Lions eat people" as a sentence then knows *ipso facto* that "People eat lions" is one too. The implausibility of the content often renders people unable to accept (at the simplest crudest level of acceptance) such sentences as sentences, and no amount of reference to performance or pragmatic factors will ease the situation. Any such demonstration of necessary structural relationships between sentence classes would be inapplicable in practice to humans, and should therefore not be lightly imposed on devices. What Pollack's networks can learn, given their previous experience, will be a wholly empirical matter as it is with humans, and I look forward to the results.

The above has been a naïve demonstration by example that a device can, and probably does, exist that Fodor says cannot. However, Smolensky has also (this volume) made some attempt to reply directly to Fodor's arguments about constituency.

His claim is that Fodor's arguments tell only against localist connectionism (the version of connectionism that deals with accessible structures, as opposed to his own subsymbolic version that does not). But this is a most curious argument, one in which the ability to present explicit structures to combat an argument (as I have argued Pollack's structures and processes do against the straightforward version of Fodor's case) becomes a demerit! This is another example of the curious, obscurantist, feature in the arguments of Smolensky and other Parallel Distributed Processing (PDP) connectionists, that takes the inability to give structural, symbolic or even precise accounts of their proposals as a positive advantage: the message to the questioner is then essentially religious, a demand to stop asking certain kinds of awkward questions and to have faith in a certain form of conduct.

It is certainly not true that Fodor's demands tell only against a particular form of connectionism: his demands are on any proposed representational system, and even PDP connectionism is that. Smolensky in fact attempts a reply (this volume) in answer, not to Fodor's constituency demands, but to Pylyshyn's earlier ones concerned with the structure of "coffee" in the context of the associations of coffee with a range of surroundings (cups, spoons, meals, etc.). Smolensky's arguments (this volume) do, in spite of himself, make certain concessions to structural questions (and lead him to a theory of connectionist context as "internal to a representation" whereas symbolic context is "external to a representation," i.e. is other symbols). This claim will no doubt receive extended analysis elsewhere, but it does illustrate how a connectionist response might be constructed to the symbolic representationalist demand above concerning gapping, and the retrieval of "The plane arrives at Gate 23" from the input from the airline employee "Gate 23" (an example type not from Fodor's discussion but from David Farwell).

The symbolicist reply is well known in AI in terms of speech act inference computations or, more plausibly perhaps, matching into known stereotypes of elisions in English. But Smolensky's subsymbolic account has to deal with plausible associated features, while denying, at a fundamental level, any need for discrete identifiable features. Smolensky's account (this volume) of the "coffee" example is laden with symbolic features like "cups," "brown liquid," "porcelain," but yet we must accept that these are dispensable because they can have no real role in a subsymbolic account. His problem is very real: to argue for the dispensability of (language dependent) features in language in which names must be used. This problem was well-known in the medieval mystical literature.

But however much one sympathizes with this expository problem, certain uncomfortable facts remain for Smolensky: the "gap filling" in the airport example comes up against all the classic problems of associationism, well known, if not remembered, since the times of classic associationism. On the plausible assumption that planes arrive and leave gates equally frequently, why should we fill out the representation with the plane arriving rather than it leaving?

These problems are all unresolved at the time of writing. A reasonable intellectual position at this time would be charitable and well-disposed agnosticism: one that combines total distrust of Smolensky and Fodor's demonstrations of the impossibility of each other's positions, with eager anticipation of news of the performances of devices.

Note

I would like to acknowledge the useful discussions with Jordan Pollack, David Farwell, and Dan Fass while writing this paper.

Representation and high-speed computation in neural networks

Paul M. Churchland

1 Introduction

What I want to sell you is some neuroscience. I want to sell you the idea that current neuroscience has become directly relevant to the cognitive/computational issues that have always concerned AI. In what follows I shall outline a highly general scheme for representation and computation, a scheme inspired in part by the microarchitecture of both the cerebral and the cerebellar cortex. We shall also explore some of the interesting properties displayed by computing systems of this general kind.

The basic claim, to be explained as we proceed, is that the brain represents specific states of affairs by implementing specific positions in an appropriate state space, and it performs computations on such representations by means of general coordinate transformations from one state space to another. (There is no suggestion that this is the only mode of information-processing in the brain. But its role does seem to be non-trivial.)

That one can perform computations by this abstract means will be old news to some readers. For them, I hope to occasion surprise with evidence about the implementation of these procedures in the microanatomy of the empirical brain. Also intriguing is the natural way in which problems of sensorimotor coordination can be solved by this approach, since from an evolutionary point of view, sensorimotor coordination is where cognitive activity had its raw beginnings. Of further interest is the very great representational power of such systems, and the truly extraordinary speed with which even biological implementations of such procedures can perform computations of great complexity.

The emerging relevance of neuroscience coincides with what many of us think to be a doldrums in the affairs of traditional ('program writing') AI, and in the affairs of orthodox cognitive psychology, for which macroscopic behavior provides the sole significant constraint on theory. The diagnosis offered here is that traditional AI needs desperately to explore, not new areas within 'program space,' but new areas within the space of possible hardwares. The hardware – or 'wetware' – of the empirical brain represents an existence proof of what can be done with parallel architectures radically different from those found in general-purpose serial machines. It behoves AI to try to learn from that example.

The diagnosis of orthodox cognitive psychology is much the same. Whatever computational activities psychology might ascribe to us, those activities must not only produce the behavior we display, they must be implemented in the wetware we possess. To ignore the nature of that wetware, as the neurosciences are now revealing it, would be to ignore some of the strongest available constraints on the development of cognitive theory.

The basic point here is as follows. So long as we assume that the brain, like a standard serial computer, is truly a general-purpose machine, then of course the nature of the hardware will carry negligible information about the algorithms being executed. For the hardware will be a constant over the infinite range of 'programs' the brain might be running. But if the brain is not a general-purpose machine in the technical sense at issue; if the hardware is highly 'devoted' to relatively narrow areas of computational space; then the nature of that hardware assumes an enormous importance.

Accordingly, I propose to enter this discussion from the hardware end of things. In what follows I shall outline for you some of the well-known but still deeply puzzling structural features of the brain's neural architecture. I shall then outline, as a possible account of the functional significance of those structures, the scheme of representation and computation mentioned above. Bear with me, therefore, while we race through a short rehearsal of the relevant brain microstructure.

2 Laminar cortex, vertical connections, and topographic maps

The outer surface of the brain's great cerebral hemispheres consists of a thin layer, the classical "grey matter," in which most of their neuronal cell bodies are located (see figure 1a). If one examines the internal structure of this wrinkled layer, one finds that it subdivides into further layers (see figure 1b). Human cortex has six of these layers. Other creatures display a different number, but the laminar pattern is standard.

These further layers are distinguished by the type and concentration of cells within each sublayer. Moreover, these distinct layers are further distinguished by their proprietary inputs or outputs. The top several layers tend to have only inputs of one kind or another, from the sensory periphery, from other parts of the cortex, or from other parts of the brain. And the bottom layer seems invariably to be an output layer.

Finally, these distinct layers are systematically connected, in the fashion of nails struck through plywood, by large numbers of vertically-oriented

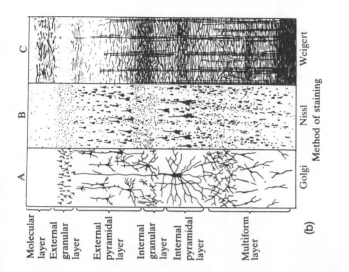

	A	B	C
Molecular layer			
External granular layer			
External pyramidal layer			
Internal granular layer			
Internal pyramidal layer			
Multiform layer			
	Golgi	Nissl	Weigert
		Method of staining	

(b)

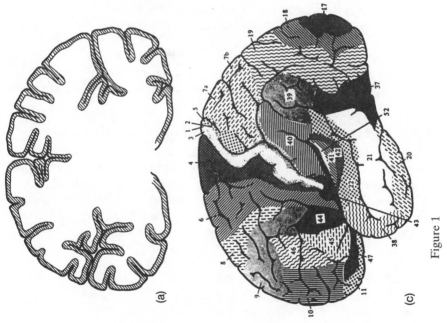

(a)

(c)

Figure 1

cells that permit communication between the several layers. These vertical cells conduct neuronal activity "downwards," from the superficial input layers above to the output layer below.

If we now leave our microscopic edgewise perspective and look down at the cortical sheet from the outside, we find that the cortical surface divides into a patchwork of smaller regions (see figure 1c). These areas are distinguished to some degree by differences in their laminar cytoarchitecture. An initial taxonomy, into what are called Brodmann's areas after their discoverer, is based on this criterion.

These areas, or subareas of them, are of further interest because several of them plainly constitute topographic maps of some aspect of the sensory or motor periphery, or of some other area of the brain. For example, the neighborhood relations holding between the cells in a given layer of the visual cortex at the rear of the brain correspond to the neighborhood relations holding between the cells in the retina from which they receive inputs. The bundle of axonal projections from the retinal cells to the cortical cells preserves the topographic organization of the retinal cells. The surface of the primary visual cortex thus constitutes a topographic map of the retinal surface.

It is termed a 'topographic map,' rather than simply a 'map,' because the distance relations among retinal cells are generally not preserved. Typically, such maps are metrically deformed, as if they were made of rubber and then stretched in some fashion.

Many such maps have been identified. The so-called "visual cortex" (areas 17, 18) has already been mentioned. The upper layer of the somatosensory cortex (area 3) is a topographic map of the body's tactile surface. The lower layer of the motor cortex (area 4) is a topographic map of the body's muscle system. The auditory cortex (areas 41, 42) contains a topographic map of frequency space. And there are many other cortical areas, less well understood as to exactly what they map, but whose topographical representation of distant structure is plain.

This general pattern of neural organization is not confined to the surface of the great cerebral hemispheres. As well, various nuclei of "grey matter" in the more central regions of the brain – for example, the superior colliculus, the hippocampus, and the lateral geniculate nucleus – display this same multilayered, topographically organized, vertically connected structure. Not everything does (the cerebellum, for example, is rather different, of which more later), but the pattern described is one of the major organizational patterns to be found in the brain.

Why this pattern? What is its functional or cognitive significance? What do these structures do, and how do they do it? We can make contact with the representational and computational hypothesis suggested in the introduction if we first address the independently intriguing problem of sensorimotor coordination.

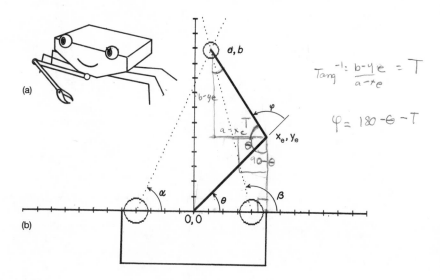

The following handwritten annotations appear in the figure:

$$\mathrm{Tang}^{-1} : \frac{b - y_e}{a - x_e} = T$$

$$\varphi = 180 - \Theta - T$$

Figure 2

3 Sensorimotor coordination

Let me begin by suggesting that vertically connected laminar structures are one of evolution's simplest solutions to a crucial type of problem, one that any sensorimotor system beyond the most rudimentary must somehow solve. In order to appreciate this type of problem, let us consider a schematic creature of a deliberately contrived simplicity.

Figure 2b is a plan view of a crab-like schematic creature (2a) with two rotatable eyes and an extendable arm. If this equipment is to be useful to the crab, the crab must embody some functional relationship between its eye-angle pairs when an edible object is triangulated, and its subsequent shoulder and elbow angles, so that the arm can assume a position that makes contact with the edible target. Crudely, it must be able to grasp what it sees, wherever the seen object lies.

We can characterize the required arm/eye relationship as follows. First of all, let us represent the input (the pair of eye angles) by a point in a two-dimensional sensory-system coordinate space or state space (figure 3a). The output (the pair of arm angles) can also be represented by an appropriate point in a separate two-dimensional motor state space (figure 3b).

We now need a function to take us from any point in the sensory state space to a suitable point in the motor state space, a function that will coordinate arm-position with eye-position in the manner described. (I here sketch the deduction of the relevant function so that its origin will not be a mystery, but the reader may leap past the algebra without any loss of comprehension. The only point to remember is that we are deducing a

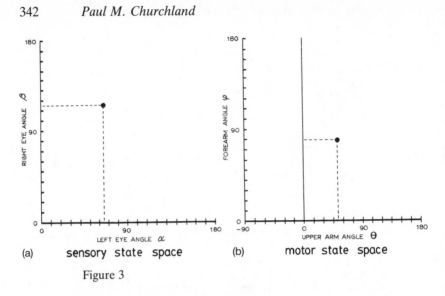

(a)   sensory state space   (b)   motor state space

Figure 3

suitable function to take us from eye configurations to arm configurations.)

The two eye angles (a,b) determine two lines that intersect at the seen object. The coordinates (a,b) of that point (in real) space are given by

$$a = -4(\tan \alpha + \tan \beta)/(\tan \alpha - \tan \beta)$$
$$b = -8(\tan \alpha \cdot \tan \beta)/(\tan \alpha - \tan \beta)$$

The tip of the arm must make contact with this point. Assuming that both the forearm and upper arm have a fixed length of seven units, the elbow will therefore have to lie at the intersection of two circles of radius seven units: one centered at (a,b), and the other centered at $(0,0)$, where the upper arm projects from the crab's body. Solving for the relevant intersection, the real-space elbow coordinates (x_e, y_e) are given by

$$x_e = ((49 - ((a^2 + b^2)^2/4b^2) \cdot (1 - ((a^2/b^2)/$$
$$((a^2/b^2) +))))^{1/2} + (((a/b) \cdot ((a^2 + b^2)/2b))/$$
$$((a^2/b^2) + 1)^{1/2}))/((a^2/b^2) + 1)^{1/2}$$
$$y_e = (49 - x_e^2)^{1/2}$$

The three points in real space, (a,b), (x_e, y_e), $(0,0)$, determine the position of the arm, whose upper arm and forearm angles (θ, ψ) are finally given by

$$\theta = \tan^{-1}(y_e/x_e)$$
$$\psi = 180 - (\theta - \tan^{-1}((b - y_e)/(a - x_e)))$$

These are the desired coordinates of the arm in motor state space. The reader will note that the assembled functions that yield them are rather tangled ones.

Tangled or not, if the crab is drawn on a computer screen, such that its final arm-position (drawn by the computer as output) is the specified

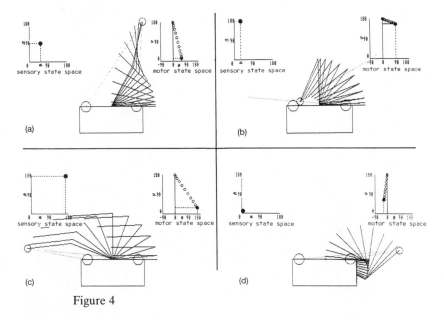

Figure 4

function of its eye-positions (entered by us as input), then it constitutes a very effective and well-behaved sensorimotor system, especially if we write the controlling program as follows.

Let the program hold the crab's arm folded against its chest (at $\theta = 0°, \psi = 180°$), until some suitable stimulus registers on the fovea of both eyes. The arm is then moved from its initial state-space position (0°,180°), along a straight line in motor state space, to its computed target position in motor state space. This is the state-space position at which in real space, the tip of the arm contacts the triangulation point of the eyes. This arrangement produces a superficially realistic system that reaches unerringly for whatever it sees, anywhere within reach of its arm (figure 4a-c).

The algebraic representation of the crab's sensorimotor transformation, as represented in the six equations listed earlier, supplies no intuitive conception of its overall nature. A geometrical presentation is much more revealing. Let us therefore consider the projection of the active portion of the crab's sensory state space (figure 5a) into the orthogonal grid of its motor state space (figure 5b), as imposed by the function under discussion. That is to say, for *every* point in the displayed sensory grid, we have plotted the corresponding arm-position within the motor grid.

Here we can see at a glance the distortion of the vertical and horizontal lines of sensory space, as projected into motor space. The topological features of the sensory space are preserved, but its metrical properties are not. What we see is a systematic transformation of coordinates. (The heavy scored triangle and rectangle are drawn in solely to help the reader locate corresponding positions in the deformed and undeformed grids. Note also

projection of sensory grid
onto motor state space

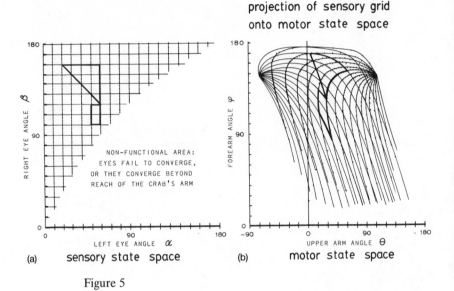

(a)   sensory state space   (b)   motor state space

Figure 5

that the left border or β-axis of figure 5a shrinks to the left radial point in figure 5b, and that the top border of figure 5a shrinks to the right radial point in figure 5b.)

4 Coordinate transformation: its physical implementation

The transformation described above sustains effective and realistic sensorimotor behaviour. But how could a real nervous system possibly compute such a complex coordinate transformation? It is not realistic to expect it to compute this complex trigonometric function step-by-step, as our computer simulation does. Nevertheless, given their sophisticated sensorimotor coordination, biological systems somehow must be computing transformations like these, and others more complex still. How might they do it?

Figure 5 suggests a surprisingly simple means. If we suppose that the crab contains internal representations of both its sensory state space, and its motor state space, then the following arrangement will effect the desired transformation. Let the crab's sensory state space be represented by a physical grid of signal-carrying fibres, a grid that is metrically deformed in real space in just the way displayed in figure 5b. Let its motor state space be represented by a second grid of fibres, in undeformed orthogonal array. Position the first grid over the second, and let them be connected by a large number of short vertical fibres, extending from coordinate intersections in

COORDINATE TRANSFORMATION BY
CONTIGUOUS TOPOGRAPHIC MAPS

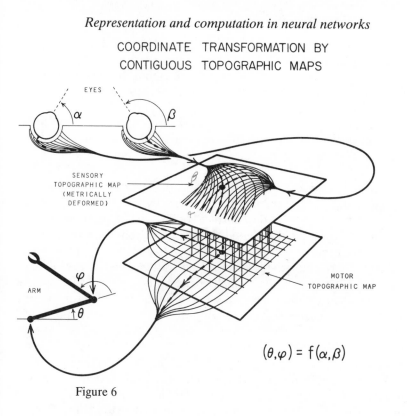

$$(\theta, \varphi) = f(\alpha, \beta)$$

Figure 6

the sensory grid down to the nearest coordinate in the underlying motor grid, as in figure 6.

Suppose that the fibres of the sensory grid receive input from the eyes' proprioceptive system, such that the position of each eye stimulates a unique fibre in the upper (deformed) grid. The left eye activates one fibre from the right radial point, and the right eye activates one from the left. Joint eye-position will thus be represented by a simultaneous stimulation at the appropriate coordinate intersection in the upper grid.

Underneath that point in the upper map lies a unique intersection in the motor grid. Suppose that this intersecting pair of orthogonal motor fibres, when jointly activated, induces the arm to assume the position that is appropriate to the specific motor coordinate intersection where this motor signal originates in the lower map.

Happily, the relative metrical deformations in the maps have placed in correspondence the appropriate points in the upper and lower maps. We need now suppose only that the vertical connections between the sensory grid and the motor grid function as "and-gates" or "threshold switches," so that a signal is sent down the vertical connection to the motor grid exactly if the relevant sensory intersection point is simultaneously stimulated by both of its intersecting sensory fibres. Such a system will compute the desired coordinate transformations to a degree of accuracy limited only by the grain of the two grids, and by the density of their vertical connections. I call such a system a *state-space sandwich*.

Three points are worth noting immediately about the functional properties of such an arrangement. First, it will remain partially functional despite localized damage. A small lesion in either grid will produce only a partial dyskinesia (two permanent "shadows" of fibre inactivity downstream from the lesion), for which a shift of bodily position will usually compensate (by bringing the target's state-space position out of the shadow).

Indeed, if the position of the crab's eyes is coded not by the activation of a single point in the upper grid, but rather by the activation of a large area (set of points) centered around the 'correct' point, and if the arm muscles respond by averaging the distributed output signal from the now multiply-stimulated lower map, then an appropriate motor response will be forthcoming even if the sandwich has suffered the scattered loss of a great many cells. Such a system will be functionally persistent despite widespread cell damage. The quality of the sensorimotor coordination will be progressively degraded under cell damage, but a roughly appropriate motor response will still be forthcoming.

Second, the system will be very, very fast, even with fibres of biological conduction velocities ($10 < v < 100$ m/s). In a creature the size of a crab, in which the total conduction path is less than 10 cm, this system will yield a motor response in well under 10 milliseconds. In the crab-simulation described earlier, my computer (doing its trigonometry within the software) takes 20 times that interval to produce a motor response on-screen, and its conduction velocities are on the order of the speed of light. Evidently, the massively parallel architecture of the state-space sandwich buys it a large advantage in speed, even with vastly slower components.

And third, the quality of the crab's coordination will not be uniform over its field of motor activity, since in the maximally deformed areas of the sensory grid, small errors in sensory registration produce large errors in the motor response (see again figure 5b). Accordingly, the crab is least well coordinated in the area close between its eyes, and to its extreme right and left.

All three of these functional properties are biologically realistic. And the sandwich appears biologically realistic in one further respect: it is relatively easy to imagine such a system being grown. Distinct layers can confine distinct chemical gradients, and can thus guide distinct morphogenetic processes. Accordingly, distinct topographical maps can appear in closely adjacent layers. But given that the maps are so closely contiguous, and assuming that they are appropriately deformed, the problem of connecting them up so as to produce a functional system becomes a trivial one: the solution is just to grow conductive elements that are roughly orthogonal to the layers.

Different creatures will have different means of locating objects, and different motor systems to effect contact with them, but all of them will face the same problem of coordinating positions in their sensory state space with positions in their motor state space, and the style of solution here outlined is evidently quite general in nature. The point to be emphasized is that a state-space sandwich constitutes a simple and biologically realistic means for effecting any two-dimensional to two-dimensional coordinate transformation, whatever its mathematical complexity, and whatever features – external or internal, abstract or concrete – that the coordinate axes may represent to the brain. If the transformation can be graphed at all, a sandwich can compute it. The sensorimotor problem solved above is merely a transparent example of the general technique at work.

Switching now from functional to structural considerations, I hope it is apparent that, beyond the issue of functional realism, the system of interconnected maps in figure 6 is suggestively similar to the known physical structure of typical laminar cortex, including the many topographic maps distributed across the cerebral surface. In all of these areas, inputs address a given layer of cells, which layer frequently embodies a metrically deformed topographic map of something-or-other. And outputs leave the area from a different layer, with which the first layer enjoys massive vertical connections.

I therefore propose the hypothesis that the scattered maps within the cerebral cortex, and many subcerebral laminar structures as well, are all engaged in the coordinate transformation of points in one neural state space into points in another, by the direct interaction of metrically deformed, vertically connected topographic maps. Their mode of representation is state-space position; their mode of computation is coordinate transformation; and both functions are simultaneously implemented in a state-space sandwich.

I can cite not a single cerebral area for which this functional hypothesis is known to be true. To decide the issue would require knowing in some detail both the topical and the metrical character of the topographic maps in each of the contiguous laminae that constitute a given area of cerebral cortex. In general, we still lack such information. However, there is a phylogenetically older and simpler laminar structure located on the dorsal midbrain whose upper and lower maps have both been decoded, and it does display both the structural and the functional pattern portrayed in figure 6.

The superior colliculus (figure 7) sustains the familiar reflex whereby the eye makes an involuntary saccade so as to foveate or look directly at any sudden change or movement that registers on the retina away from its central high-resolution area of fovea. We have all had the experience of being in a darkened movie theater when someone down in the front row left suddenly ignites a match or lighter to light a cigarette. Every eye in the house makes a ballistic saccade to fixate this brief stimulus, before returning to the screen. This reflex is the work of the superior colliculus. Appropriately enough, this is sometimes called the 'visual grasp reflex.'

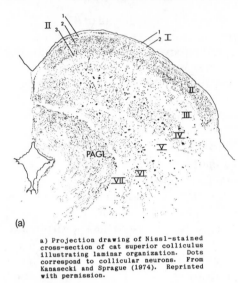

(a)

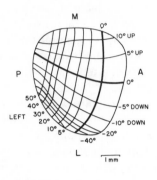

(b)

a) Projection drawing of Nissl-stained
cross-section of cat superior colliculus
illustrating laminar organization. Dots
correspond to collicular neurons. From
Kanasecki and Sprague (1974). Reprinted
with permission.

b) Retinotopic map: a metrically deformed
topographic map of the visual hemifield,
in rectangular coordinates, on the superficial layer of the right colliculus of
the cat. M = medial; L = lateral; A =
anterior; P = posterior. Adapted from
Schiller (1984).

Figure 7

In humans and the higher mammals the superior colliculus is a visual
center secondary to the more important striate cortex (areas 17 and 18 on
the Brodmann map) located at the rear of the cerebral hemispheres, but in
lower animals such the frog or snake, which lack any significant cortex, the
superior colliculus (or optic tectum, as it is called in them) is their principal
visual center. It is an important center even for mammals, however, and it
works roughly as follows.

The top-most layer of the superior colliculus (hereafter, SC) receives
projections directly from the retina, and it constitutes a metrically-
deformed topographic map of the retinal surface (figure 7b) (Schiller, 1984;
Goldberg and Robinson, 1978; Cynader and Berman, 1972; Gordon, 1973).
Vertical elements connect this layer to the deepest layer of the SC. These
vertical connections appear to consist of a chain of two or three short
interneurons descending stepwise through two intervening layers (Schiller,
1984, pp. 460, 466), of which more later. Also, the dendrites of some of the
deep-layer neurons appear to ascend directly into the visual layer, to make
synaptic connections with visual cells (Mooney, et al., 1984, p. 185). The
neurons of the deepest layer project their output axons via two distinct
nervous pathways, one of which leads eventually to the pair of extra-ocular
muscles responsible for vertical eye movements, and the other to the pair
responsible for horizontal eye movements (Huerta and Harting, 1984,
p. 287).

Intriguingly, this underlying motor layer also embodies a topographic
map, a map of a state space that represents changes in the contractile
position of the ocular muscles, the muscles that make the eye jump

(Robinson, 1972, p. 1800). Microstimulation by an electrode at any given point in this deepest layer causes the eyes to execute a saccade of a size and direction characteristic for that point, a saccade which moves the eye's fovea into the position originally occupied by that retinal cell which projects to the immediately overlying cell in the top-most layer of the colliculus (Robinson, 1972; Schiller and Stryker, 1972). In other words, the relative metrical deformations in the two maps have placed into correspondence the appropriate points in the upper and lower maps. (This means that the "deformation" seen in figure 7b should not of itself be taken as evidence for the state-space sandwich hypothesis. What is crucial is the deformation of the maps relative to each other.)

Finally, any sufficiently strong retinally produced stimulation in that top-most visual map is conveyed downwards to the motor map by the appropriate vertical elements, where it produces a saccade of just the size and direction appropriate for the foveation of the external stimulus that provoked it. The SC thus appears to be an instance of both the structural and the functional pattern displayed in figure 6. It foveates on changing or moving visual targets by essentially the same means whereby the schematic cortex of the crab reaches out for triangulated objects.

A word of caution is in order here, since the account just offered does not do justice to the full complexity of the superior colliculus. In mammals, especially the higher mammals, the SC is a tightly integrated part of a larger modulating system that includes inputs from the visual cortex and the frontal eye fields, and output to the neck muscles. The functional properties of the entire system are more varied and more subtle than the preceding suggests, and the job of sorting them out is still underway (Mays and Sparks, 1980; Schiller and Sandell, 1983). The preceding is submitted as an account of the central or more primitive functions of the SC, at best.

With these examples in mind – the crab's "cortex," and the superior colliculus – it is appropriate to focus on the many other topographically-organized multilayered cortical areas scattered throughout the brain, and ask what coordinate transformations they might be effecting. Here it is very important to appreciate that the topographic maps we seek to decode need not be, and generally will not be, maps of something anatomically obvious, such as the surface of the retina, or the surface of the skin. More often they will be maps of some abstract state space, whose dimensional significance is likely to be opaque to the casual observer, though of great functional importance to the brain. Two pretty examples of such abstract maps are the map of echo delays in the bat's auditory cortex, and the map of binaural disparities in the owl's inferior colliculus (Konishi, 1986).

All of this suggests that the brain may boast many more topographic maps than have so far been identified, or even suspected. Certainly the brain has a teeming abundance of topographically organized areas, and recent work has expanded the number of known sensory-related maps considerably (Merzenich and Kaas, 1980; Allman *et al.*, 1982). All of this further suggests that we will make better progress in trying to understand the significance of the many topographically-organized cortical areas when we approach them as maps of abstract but functionally relevant state spaces.

5 Cortex with more than two layers

While we are discussing the biological reality of the laminar mechanism proposed, consider the objection that our model cortex has only two layers, whereas the typical human cortex has six layers, and, counting fine subdivisions, perhaps eight or nine in some areas. What are they for?

There is no difficulty in perceiving a function for such additional layers. Let us return again to the superior colliculus, which illustrates one of many possibilities here. Between the visual and motor maps of the SC there are, in some creatures, one or two intermediate layers (see again figure 7). These appear to constitute an auditory map and/or a somatosensory map (a facial or whisker map), whose function is again to orient the eye's fovea, this time toward the source of sudden auditory and/or somatosensory stimulation (Goldberg and Robinson, 1978). Not surprisingly, these intervening maps are each metrically deformed in such a fashion as to be in rough coordinate "register" with the motor map, and hence with each other. Altogether, this elegant three- or four-layer topographic sandwich constitutes a multimodal sensorimotor coordinate transformer.

Multilayered structures have further virtues. It is plain that maps of several distinct modalities, suitably deformed and placed in collective register within a "club sandwich," provide a most effective means of cross-modal integration and comparison. In the SC, for example, this multimodal arrangement is appropriate to the production of a motor response to the joint receipt of faint but spatiotemporally coincident auditory and visual stimuli, stimuli which, in isolation, would have been subthreshold for a motor response. For example, a faint sound from a certain compass point may be too faint to prompt the eyes into a foveating saccade, and a tiny movement from a certain compass point may be similarly impotent; but if both the sound and the movement come from the same compass point (and are thus coded in the SC along the same vertical axis), then their simultaneous conjunction will indeed be sufficient to make the motor layer direct the eyes appropriately. This prediction is strongly corroborated by the recent results of Meredith and Stein (1985).

Further exploration reveals that multilayered sandwiches can subserve decidedly sophisticated cognitive functions. In an earlier publication (Churchland, 1986a), I have shown how a three-layer state-space sandwich can code, and project, the path of a *moving* object in such a fashion as to position the crab's arm to catch the moving target on the fly. Evidently, a multilayered cortex can offer considerable advantages.

6 Beyond state-space sandwiches

The examples studied above are uniform in having an input state space of only two dimensions, and an output state space of only two dimensions. It is because of this fact that the required coordinate transformation can be achieved by a contiguous pair of sheet-like maps. But what of cases where the subsystems involved each have more than two parameters? What of cases where the coordinate transformations are from an input space of *n* to an output space of *m* dimensions, where *n* and *m* are different, and both greater than 2? Consider, for example, the problem of coordinating the joint angles of a limb with three or more joints, and the problem of coordinating several such limbs with each other. Or consider the problem of coordinating the even larger number of muscles that collectively control such limbs. As soon as one examines the problems routinely faced, and solved, by real creatures, one appreciates that many of them are far more complex than can be represented by a simple two-dimensions to two-dimensions transformation.

Perhaps some of these more complex problems might be solved by dividing them into a set of smaller ones, problems that can be managed after all by a set of distinct two-dimensional state-space sandwiches, each addressing some slice or aspect of the larger problem (for some specific suggestions in this vein, see Ballard, 1986). The predominance of laminar cortex in the brain certainly encourages speculation along these lines. But such solutions, even approximate ones, cannot in general be guaranteed. The brain badly needs some mechanism beyond the state-space sandwich if it is routinely to handle these higher dimensional problems.

Andras Pellionisz and Rodolfo Llinas (1979, 1982, 1984, 1985) have already outlined a mechanism adequate to the task, and have found impressive evidence of its implementation within the cerebellum. The cerebellum is the large structure at the rear of the brain, just underneath the cerebral hemispheres. Its principal function, divined initially from lesion studies, is the coordination of complex bodily movements, such as would be displayed in preparing a dinner or in playing basketball. It displays a neural organization quite different from that of the cerebral hemispheres, an organization whose significance may be rendered transparent by the Pellionisz/Llinas account.

To illustrate this more general mechanism for coordinate transformation, let us consider an input system of four dimensions whose inputs a, b, c, d, are transformed into the values x, y, z, of a three-dimensional output system. As before, the inputs and outputs can each be regarded as points in a suitable state space. Since they are the *n*-tuples, each can also be regarded as a vector (whose base lies at the origin of the relevant state space, and whose arrowhead lies at the point specified by the *n*-tuple).

352   Paul M. Churchland

$$\langle a, b, c, d \rangle \cdot \begin{bmatrix} p_1 & q_1 & r_1 \\ p_2 & q_2 & r_2 \\ p_3 & q_3 & r_3 \\ p_4 & q_4 & r_4 \end{bmatrix}$$

$$= \langle x, y, z \rangle$$

Figure 8

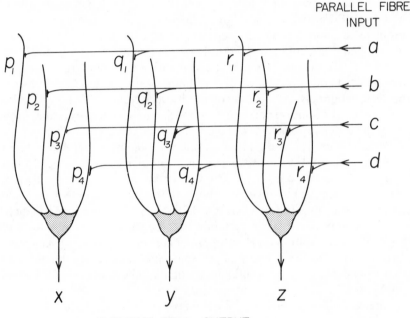

PARALLEL FIBRE
INPUT

PURKINJE CELL OUTPUT

Figure 9

A standard mathematical operation for the systematic transformation of vectors into vectors is matrix multiplication. Here it is the matrix that embodies or effects the desired coordinate transformation. To see how this works, consider the matrix of figure 8, which has four rows and three columns. To multiply the input vector $\langle a, b, c, d \rangle$ by this matrix we multiply a times p_1, b times p_2, c times p_3, d times p_4, and then sum the four results to yield x. We then repeat the process with the second column to yield y, and again with the third column to yield z. Thus results the output vector $\langle x,y,z \rangle$.

This algebraic operation can be physically realized quite simply by the neural array of figure 9. The parallel input fibres at the right each send a train of electrochemical "spikes" towards the waiting dendritic trees. The numbers a, b, c, d represent the amount by which the momentary spiking

SCHEMATIC SECTION: CEREBELLUM

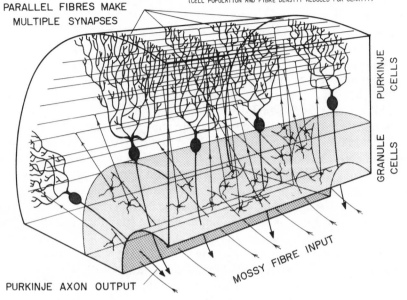

Figure 10

frequency of each of the four fibres is above (positive number) or below (negative number) a certain baseline spiking frequency. The top-most input fibre, for example, synapses onto each of the three output cells, making a stimulatory connection in each case, one that tends to depolarize the cell body and make it send a spike down its vertical output axon. The output frequency of spike emissions for each cell is determined first by the simple *frequency* of the input stimulations it receives from all incoming synaptic connections, and second, by the *weight* or strength of each synaptic connection, which is determined by the placement of the synapses and by their cross-sectional areas. These strength values are individually represented by the coefficients of the matrix of figure 8. The neural interconnectivity thus implements the matrix. Each of the three cells of figure 9 "sums" the stimulation it receives, and emits an appropriate train of spikes down its output axon. Those three output frequencies differ from the background or baseline frequencies of the three output cells by positive or negative amounts, and these amounts correspond to the output vector $\langle x,y,z \rangle$.

Note that with state-space sandwiches, the coding of information is a matter of the spatial location of neural events. By contrast, with the matrix-multiplication style of computation under discussion, input and output variables are coded by sets of spiking frequencies in the relevant pathways. The former system uses "spatial coding"; the later system used "frequency coding." But both systems are engaged in the coordinate transformation of state-space positions.

The example of figure 9 concerns a three-by-four matrix. But it is evident that neither the mathematical operation nor its physical realization suffers any dimensional limitations. In principle, a Pellionisz/Llinas connectivity matrix can effect transformations on state spaces of a dimensionality into the thousands and beyond.

The schematic architecture of figure 9 corresponds very closely to the style of microorganization found in the cerebellum (figure 10). (For an accessible summary of cerebellar architecture, see Llinas, 1975). The horizontal fibres are called parallel fibres, and they input from the higher motor centers. The bushy vertical cells are called Purkinje cells, and they output through the cerebellar nucleus to the motor periphery. In fact, it was from the observation of the cerebellum's beautifully regular architecture, and from the attempt to recreate its functional properties by modeling its large-scale physical connectivity within a computer, that Pellionisz and Llinas were originally led to the view that the cerebellum's job is the systematic transformation of vectors in one neural hyperspace into vectors in another neural hyperspace (Pellionisz and Llinas, 1979).

Given that view of the problem, the tensor calculus emerges as the natural framework with which to address such matters, especially since we cannot expect the brain to limit itself to Cartesian coordinates. In the examples discussed so far, variation in position along any axis of the relevant state space is independent of variation along any of the other axes, but this independence will not characterize state spaces with non-orthogonal axes. Indeed this generalization of the approach, to include non-Cartesian hyperspaces, is regarded by Pellionisz and Llinas as one of the most important features of their account, a feature that is essential to understanding all but the simplest coordination problems. I cannot pursue this feature here.

Four final points about the neural matrix of figure 9. First, it need not be limited to computing linear transformations. The individual synaptic connections might represent any of a broad range of functional properties. They need not be simple multipliers. In concert then, they are capable of computing a large variety of non-linear transformations. Second, a neural matrix will have the same extraordinary speed displayed by a state-space sandwich. And third, given a great many components, such matrices will also display a fierce functional persistence despite the scattered loss of their cellular components.

Finally, such systems can be plastic in the transformations they effect: changes in the weights and/or numbers of the synaptic connections are all that is required. What is problematic is how a useful set of weights, i.e. a set that effects a transformation useful to the organism, gets established in the first place. How does the matrix 'learn' to implement the right transformation?

This problem is certainly solvable in principle. The 'back-propagation' learning algorithm of Rumelhart, Hinton, and Williams (1986) has shown that distributed processors of this general type can learn with extraordinary efficiency, given a suitable regime for propagating discovered error back through the elements of the system. And it may be solvable in fact, since the cerebellar network does contain a second input system: the climbing fibres (not shown in figures 9 and 10 for reasons of clarity). These ascend from below each Purkinje cell and wrap themselves like vines around the branches of its dendritic tree. They are thus in a position to have a direct effect on the nature of the synapses made by the parallel fibres onto the Purkinje dendrites. According to a recent model by Pellionisz and Llinas (1985), the cerebellum can indeed become 'coordinated' by essentially this method.

These brief remarks do not do justice to the very extensive work of Pellionisz and Llinas, nor have I explored any criticisms. (For the latter, see Arbib and Amari, 1985. For a reply, see the closing sections of Pellionisz and Llinas, 1985.) The reader must turn to the literature for deeper instruction. The principal lesson of this section is that the general functional schema being advanced here – the schema of representation by state-space position, and computation by coordinate transformation – does not encounter implementational difficulties when the representational and computational task exceeds the case of two dimensions. On the contrary, the brain boasts neural machinery that is ideally suited to cases of very high dimensionality. We have then at least two known brain mechanisms for performing coordinate transformations: the state-space sandwich specifically for two-dimensional cases, and the neural matrix for cases of any dimensionality whatever.

7 The representational power of state spaces

Discussion so far has been concentrated on the impressive computational power of coordinate transformations of state spaces, and on the possible neural implementation of such activity. But it is important to appreciate fully the equally powerful representational capacity of neural state spaces. A global circumstance comprised of n distinct variables can be economically represented by a single point in an abstract n-dimensional state space. And such a state-space point can be neurally implemented, in the simplest case, by a specific distribution of n spiking frequencies in a system of only n distinct fibres. Moreover, a state-space representation embodies the metrical relations between distinct possible positions within it, and thus embodies the representation of *similarity* relations between distinct items thus represented. These claims can be illustrated by the outputs of several of our sensory organs.

Consider first a simple case: the human gustatory system has a four-channel output, with each of the four pathways representing the level of stimulation at one of the four sets of taste sensors in the mouth, the so-called sweet, sour, salty, and bitter receptors. Any humanly possible taste sensation, it is therefore conjectured, is a point somewhere within a four-dimensional gustatory state space. Or more literally, it is a quadruple of spiking frequencies in the four proprietary pathways carrying information from the gustatory receptors for distribution to the rest of the brain.

A sweet taste, for example, is coded as a specific set of activity levels across the four pathways (a high value on one, and a low value on each of the other three). Other combinations of activity levels yield all of the taste sensations possible for humans. The qualitative or subjective similarity of sensations emerges, both theoretically and experimentally, as the proximity of the relevant codings within gustatory state-space.

Such a coding system also gives us an enormous range of discrimination at a very low price. Just to illustrate the point, suppose our discrimination of distinct positions (activity levels) along each of the four axes of gustatory state space is limited to just ten positions. This gives us an overall four-dimensional space with fully 10^4 discriminable points. This state-space approach to gustatory sensations appears in the neuroscience literature as the *across-fibre pattern* theory (Bartoshuk, 1978; Smith, 1983; Pfaff, 1985).

An account of this same general kind may hold for our olfactory system, which has six or more distinct types of receptor. A six-dimensional space, at 10-unit axial discrimination, will permit the discrimination of 10^6 odors. And if we imagine only a seven-dimensional olfactory space, with only three times the human axial discrimination, which space a dog almost certainly possesses, then we are contemplating a state space with 30^7, or 22 billion, discriminable positions! Given this, the canines' ability to distinguish, by smell, any one of the 3.5 billion people on the planet no longer presents itself as a mystery.

Consider also the human 'module' for facial recognition. We apparently have one, since the specific ability to recognize faces can be destroyed by specific right parietal lesions. Here it is plausible to suggest an internal state-space representation of perhaps twenty dimensions, each coding some salient facial feature such as nose length, facial width, and so on. (Police 'Identikits' attempt to exploit such a system, with some success.) Even if discrimination along each axis were limited to only five distinct positions, such a high-dimensional space would still have an enormous volume ($= 5^{20}$ positions), and it would permit the discrimination and recognition of billions of distinct faces. It would also embody similarity relations, so that close relatives could be successfully grouped, and so that the same person could be reidentified in photos taken at different ages. Consider two photos of the young and the old Einstein. What makes them similar? They occupy proximate positions in one's facial state space.

Finally, let us turn to a motor example, and let us consider one's "body image": one's continuously updated sense of one's overall bodily configura-

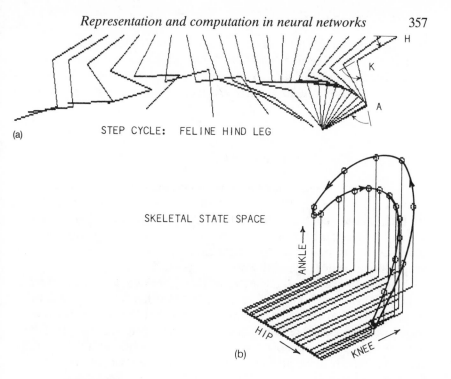

(a)   STEP CYCLE: FELINE HIND LEG

SKELETAL STATE SPACE

(b)

Figure 11

tion in space. That configuration is constituted by the simultaneous position and tension of several hundreds of muscles, and one monitors it all quite successfully, to judge from the smooth coordination of most of one's movements. How does one do it? With a high-dimensional state space, according to the theories of Pellionisz and Llinas, who ascribe to the cerebellum the job of computing appropriate transformations among high-dimensional codings of actual and intended motor circumstances, codings lodged in the input parallel fibers and the output Purkinje axons.

Some of the possibilities here can be evoked by a very simple example. Consider a highly complex and critically orchestrated periodic motion, such as occurs in feline locomotor activity (figure 11a). Consider now a three-dimensional joint-angle motor state space for the cat's hind limb, a space in which every possible configuration of that limb is represented by a point, and every possible movement is represented by a continuous path. The graceful step cycle of the galloping cat will be very economically represented by a closed loop in that joint-angle state space (figure 11b). If the relevant loop is specified or "marked" in some way, then the awesome task of coordinated locomotion reduces to a clear-cut tracking problem: make your motor state-space position follow the path of that loop.

Once we have taken the step beyond the cognitive significance of points in two-dimensional state space, to the cognitive significance of lines and closed loops in n-dimensional state spaces, it seems possible that we will also find cognitive significance in surfaces, and hypersurfaces, and intersections of hypersurfaces, and so forth. What we have opening before us is a "geometrical," as opposed to a narrowly syntactic, conception of cognitive activity.

8 Concluding remarks

We have seen how a representational scheme of this kind can account, in a biologically realistic fashion, for a number of important features of motor control, sensory discrimination, and sensorimotor coordination. But has it the resources to account for the so-called higher cognitive activities, as represented by language use, for example, and by our propositional knowledge of the world in general?

Conceivably, yes. One might try to find, for example, a way of representing "anglophone linguistic hyperspace" so that all grammatical sentences turn out to reside on a proprietary hypersurface within that hyperspace, with the logical relations between them reflected as spatial relations of some kind. I do not know how to do this, of course, but it holds out the possibility of an alternative to, or potential reduction of, the familiar Chomskyan picture.

As for the "set of beliefs" that is commonly supposed to constitute a person's knowledge, it may be that a geometrical representation of sentences will allow us to solve the severe problem of "tacit belief" (Dennett, 1975; Lycan, 1985). Just as a hologram does not "contain" a large number of distinct three-dimensional images, curiously arranged so as to present a smoothly changing picture of a real object as the hologram is viewed from different positions, so may humans not "contain" a large number of distinct beliefs, curiously arranged so as collectively to present a coherent account of the world.

Perhaps the truth is rather that, in both cases, a specific image or belief is just an arbitrary projection or "slice" of a deeper set of data structures, and the collective coherence of such sample slices is a simple consequence of the manner in which the global information is stored at the deeper level. It is not a consequence of, for example, the busywork of some fussy inductive machine applying inductive rules for the acceptance or rejection of discrete slices taken singly. Which means that, to understand learning, we may have to understand the forces that dictate directly the evolution of the global data structures at the deeper level. The learning algorithm of Rumelhart, Hinton, and Williams comes to mind again here, for in a network of that sort no symbols of any kind are being manipulated. Rather, in the course of a training session a function is progressively approximated, and the information the network acquires is stored in nothing more contentful than a distributed set of synapse-like weights.

These highly speculative remarks illustrate one direction of research suggested by the theory outlined in this paper: just what are the abstract representational and computational capacities of a system of state spaces interacting by coordinate transformations? Can we use a system of state spaces to articulate models for the "higher" forms of cognitive activity? The theory also begs research in the opposite direction, toward the neurophysiology of the brain. Given that the brain is definitely not a "general purpose" machine in the way that a digital computer is, it may often turn out that, once we are primed to see them, the brain's localized computational tactics can simply be read off its microstructure. There is point, therefore, to studying that microstructure. (For an accessible review of cognitive neurobiology, see Patricia Churchland, 1986.)

Taken jointly, the prodigious representational and computational capacities of a system of state spaces interacting by coordinate transformations suggest a powerful and highly general means of understanding the cognitive activities of the nervous system, especially since the physical mechanisms appropriate to implement such a system are widespread throughout the brain.

Notes

Thanks to Patricia Churchland, Jeff Foss, Larry Jordan, Rodolfo Llinas, Andras Pellionisz, Bruce Bolster, Montgomery Furth, Michael Arbib, Francis Crick, David Zipser, and Dave Rumelhart. This research was supported by a grant from the Institute for Advanced Study, Princeton; by the Social Sciences and Humanities Research Council of Canada, grant no. 451–83–3050; by a sabbatical leave from the University of Manitoba; and by the University of California, San Diego. Much of this paper is drawn from an earlier presentation (Churchland 1986b) aimed at philosophers. My thanks to the editors of *Mind* for permission to use some of that material here.

10   The role of correctness in AI

There is a continuing concern in AI that proof and correctness, the touchstones of the theory of programming, are being abandoned to the detriment of AI as a whole. On the other hand, we can find arguments to support just the opposite view, that attempts to fit AI programming into the specify-and-prove (or at least, specify-and-test correctness) paradigm of conventional software engineering, is contrary to the role of programming in AI research.

Similarly, the move to establish conventional logic as the foundational calculus of AI (currently seen in the logic programming approach and in knowledge-based decision-making implemented as a proof procedure) is another aspect of correctness in AI; and one whose validity is questioned (for example, Chandrasekaran's paper in section 1 opened the general discussion of such issues when it examined logic-based theories in AI, and Hewitt, in the section 11, takes up the more specific question of the role of logic in expert systems). Both sides of this correctness question are presented below.

Does AI have a methodology different from software engineering?

Derek Partridge and Yorick Wilks

Introduction: Kuhnian paradigms in AI

Is it helpful or revealing to see the state of AI in, perhaps over-fashionable, Kuhnian (Kuhn, 1962) terms? In the Kuhnian view of things, scientific progress comes from social crisis: there are pre-paradigm sciences struggling to develop to the state of "normal science" in which routine experiments are done within an overarching theory that satisfies its adherents, and without daily worry about the adequacy of the theory.

At the same time, there will be other scientific theories under threat, whose theory is under pressure from either disconfirming instances or fundamental doubts about its foundations. In these situations, normal science can continue if the minds of adherents to the theory are closed to possible falsification until some irresistible falsifying circumstances arise, by accretion or by the discovery of a phenomenon that can no longer be ignored.

There is much that is circular in this (the notion of "irresistible," for example) and there may be doubts as to whether AI is fundamentally science or engineering (we return to this below). But we may assume, for simplicity, that even if AI were engineering, similar social descriptions of its progress might apply (see Duffy, 1984).

Does AI show any of the signs of normality or crisis that would put it under one of those Kuhnian descriptions, and what would follow if that were so? It is easy to find normality: the production of certain kinds of elementary expert system (ES) within commercial software houses and other companies. These work well enough for straightforward applications, yet doubts about their extensibility are widespread.

Crisis and pathology are even easier to find, and our diagnosis in brief is this: normal AI is impeded by the fact that, whether they are aware of it or not, a wide range of AI's academic practitioners are struggling to conform to another paradigm because they suspect their own is inadequate. On our view, the natural normal paradigm of AI is RUDE (Run-Understand-Debug-Edit). But pressure and crisis come from the SPIV (Specify-Prove-

363

Implement-Verify) methodology, and its weaker version SAT (complete Specification-And-Testability of program behavior). The nature of this crisis is not one of disconfirming *instances* – for how could that be (and this absence of disconfirming instances is itself a factor which adds to the strong evidence that we should be talking in terms of engineering not scientific practice) – but from pressure concerning foundations.

The basic pressure is coming from the methodology of software engineering (SE) and its unlikely allies, and their belief that software development must proceed by a certain path: that of SPIV. Some work in expert systems, at least of the more simple-minded variety, is a leading edge of this pressure on AI, because it shares the central SPIV assumption that applications are, or should be, to areas of phenomena that are completely specifiable as to their behaviors, and specifiable in advance, not during the process of programming. We shall discuss this issue in detail below; here we just want to note a key ally of SPIV, and one that might be thought historically unlikely: Chomskyan linguistics and its current phrase-structure grammar successors (e.g. Gazdar, 1983).

The natural-language case is a central and relevant one, for it is the area of human phenomena modeled by AI where the strongest case can be made that the data are not of a type that allows complete pre-specification, in the sense that that would be the case if the set of sentences of, say, English were a decidable set. Yet, Chomsky's intention was always to show that his grammars did cover such a set, and even though that enterprise failed, his successors have made it a central feature of their claims about grammar that the set to be covered should be recursively decidable (Gazdar, 1984). In the sense under discussion, therefore, some recent work in AI and natural-language processing (NLP) has been an example of SPIV methodology and in an area where it is, to some at least, the most counter-intuitive. We shall expand on this point below.

Our claim, then, is that AI methodology is under threat from an opposing paradigm, one not appropriate to AI's subject matter, and one that encompasses conventional SE plus much of current ES and areas of NLP. As we shall discuss below, the SPIV paradigm is not a viable one for practical software development, and it is a matter of some contention as to whether the current lack of practical utility is a logical necessity, or just a puzzle to be eventually solved in the course of normal science or engineering.

Nevertheless, what we do see in the methodology of practical software engineering is a firm adherence to both prior specification of the problem and clear testability of program behavior, in that any given instance of program behavior is decidably correct or incorrect. We shall call this methodological variant on SPIV, which lacks the stronger requirement of the proof of the software's correctness, SAT.

The advocates of SPIV

Dijkstra (1972) laments the state of programming and predicts a revolution that will enable us "well before the seventies have run to completion . . . to design and implement the kind of systems that . . . will be virtually free of bugs." Two key arguments that he uses are:

1 "the programmer only needs to consider intellectually manageable problems"
2 "The only effective way to raise the confidence level of a program significantly is to give a convincing proof of its correctness . . . correctness proof and program grow hand in hand."

Almost ten years on, in his preface to Gries (1981), Dijkstra says: "the 'program' we wrote ten years ago and the 'program' we can write today can both be executed by a computer, that is about all they have in common . . . The difference between the 'old program' and the 'new program' is as profound as the difference between a conjecture and a proven theorem, between pre-scientific knowledge of mathematical facts and consequences rigorously deduced from a body of postulates."

Gries himself is more cautious. He admits the truth of the charge that the formal approach to reasoning about programs has only been successfully applied to small (and we might add) abstract, problems. Nevertheless, he writes "I believe the next ten years will see it extended to and practiced on large programs." Gries sees himself as taking "a middle view" on proving program correctness: "one *should* develop a proof and program hand-in-hand, but the proof should be a mixture of formality and common sense" (our emphasis).

Clearly this is a weakened view of the proof notion in software engineering, but still it takes for granted that there is some crucial essence of the program (i.e., the underlying algorithm) to be proven correct with respect to the problem specification, and further that this is the sort of process that admits the possibility of classical proof.

Hoare (1981) in his Turing Lecture states that "A lack of clarity in specification is one of the surest signs of a deficiency in the program it describes, and the two faults must be removed simultaneously before the project is embarked upon." Hoare also believes in the necessity of proving programs correct, and his axiomatic semantics is a formalism designed to do just that.

A "sad remark" in Dijkstra's (1976) book is: "we have witnessed the proliferation of baroque, ill-defined and, therefore, unstable software systems. Instead of working with a formal tool, which their task requires, many programmers now live in a limbo of folklore, in a vague and slippery world, in which they are never quite sure what the system will do to their programs. Under such regretful circumstances the whole notion of a correct program – let alone a program that has been proven correct – becomes void.

What the proliferation of such systems has done to the morale of the computing community is more than I can describe."

These are not clear statements of what we have called SPIV, but they all take it for granted: (a) that a formal specification of the problem is a necessary prerequisite of serious software engineering; and (b) that formal proof of correctness of a program is, at least in principle if not in practice, possible. They admit no alternative in software engineering science. They hold SPIV as the single exemplar to which they should aspire.

We can draw two possible implications from this hardline SPIV viewpoint:

> either (i) implementation of certain problems should never be attempted because they are not formally circumscribable problems; hence AI software is a fundamentally misguided notion.
> or (ii) the absence of formal specifications in some areas is only a reflection of our current ignorance, and eventually problems such as NLP will yield to formal circumscription and thus the SPIV methodology. The present task is to develop the requisite formalisms first, rather than hack at implementations.

We argue that the truth of (i) is an open question but would be widely resisted by workers in AI presumably, and that (ii) is false. Certain problems are not formally circumscribable, even in principle, but nevertheless there are possibilities quite outside the SPIV paradigm for producing robust and reliable software products. But only if this possibility is accepted can we expect sufficient work on the alternative RUDE methodology to generate a discipline of incremental program development.

Dijkstra (1972) states "an article of faith . . . viz., that the only problems we can really solve in a satisfactory manner are those that admit a nicely factored solution." He further expects that living with this limitation "will repeatedly lead to the discovery that an initially intractable problem can be factored after all." Thus Dijkstra seems to favor implication (ii) above – the one that appears to be more promising for the practical applications of AI, but also the one that we believe is quite demonstrably wrong.

Practical SE is still SPIVish

It can be argued that SPIV is just a straw man, and is just not a practical methodology. It might be said that programming realists know that iteration, incremental development, and testing for correctness are essential components of practical software development. We maintain that this is true but that the general SPIV paradigm under which they operate only permits exploration of alternatives that are consistent with the two key assumptions of SPIV given earlier. In fact, assumption (b) is weakened to correct/incorrect testability of specific program behaviors: from proof of correctness of an algorithm to clear testability of specific instances of behavior. And this is what we are calling SAT (complete Specification and Testability), and we will maintain that it is still quite distinct from RUDE.

First, we can see the crucial role of specification (and this is the key assumption that to some extent implies the clear testability of program behavior). Thus, we find this assertion in Liskov and Guttag (1986), "The principal tenet of the book is that abstraction and specification are the linchpins of any effective approach to programming."

Yourdon (1975), an important figure in practical, large-scale software engineering, makes the general point about the feasibility of top-down design (the most popular strategy) being critically reliant upon the prior existence of a complete and rigorous specification. He says: "It is extremely difficult to develop an organized top-down design from incoherent, incomplete, disorganized specifications." None of those qualities is desirable, of course, but although we can eliminate the first and third from AI, we must learn to live with the second.

From the largely unquestioned assertion about the centrality of SAT in conventional software engineering, we can briefly examine some recent, AI-related, attempts to propose more realistic practical program-development methodologies – attempts that seem to recognize the crucial role of incremental program development in some problem areas. At first sight these "new paradigms" appear to be attempts to develop the RUDE methodology, but on closer inspection we can see that they are actually SAT proposals.

Balzer, Cheatham, and Green (1983) call their scheme "a new paradigm" for "software technology in the 1990's." Essentially what they propose is that the iteration and incremental development is restricted to a formal specification which can be more or less automatically transformed into an implementation. This proposal clearly hinges on the prior and continued availability of a formal specification, and this being the case it is a SAT scheme that does not solve our problem. This approach has been suggested as a solution to the problem of incremental program development in AI (Mostow, 1985), and some of the problems with it have been pointed out elsewhere (Partridge, 1986a briefly, and at length in Partridge, 1986b).

Kowalski's (1984) presentation of a "new technology" for software design describes an iterative, trial-and-error process for "analysing the knowledge that lies behind the user requirement." But once we have a formal specification the situation is different: "Good programmers start with rigid, or at least formal, software specifications and then implement them correctly first time round – never get it wrong." Clearly, formal specification is still the key assumption, and the notion of a correct implementation is there also. This is a scheme that is at least SAT, if not something a lot closer to true SPIV.

Rapid prototyping is a key idea in the methodology of expert systems development: build a quick, small-scale version in order to generate an understanding of the problem such that the real system can then be specified and implemented. We accept the value of exploring the application domain using a working program, but the implication is that one preliminary venture into the field will be sufficient to support a full-scale specification of the problem. It is almost as if one iteration of SPIV followed by SPIV is expected to take care of the performance-mode specification aspects of AI problems; and this seems unlikely to us.

Much more akin to the spirit of the RUDE methodology are some of the general schemes that are being abstracted from the practice of constructing expert systems.

The "stages in the evolution of an expert system" described by Hayes-Roth, Waterman, and Lenat (1983) are:

> identification – determining problem characteristics
> conceptualization – finding concepts to represent knowledge
> formalization – designing structures to organize knowledge
> implementation – formulating rules that embody knowledge
> testing – validating rules that embody knowledge.

Clearly, there is still a belief in the desirability of formalization, and this is quite consistent with RUDE, for it is not a complete a priori formalization of the problem. Testing is also a feature of the above design scheme, but it is not the testability of SAT: in general it is a judgment of adequacy of system output. We begin to see a significant departure from the SPIV paradigm, and this will eventually lead us into the RUDE paradigm.

Circumscribability and decidability as needed for SPIV

Let us then stand back and look at why SPIV cannot be applied to certain areas of phenomena. That applicability requires both:

(a) circumscribability of behavior, in that the data must form a recursive, decidable set
(b) in its strongest form SPIV requires openness to proofs of the program.

Natural language at least is the clearest example of a phenomenon where this is not possible: the set of meaningful sentences, however described, will be confronted with meaningful utterances outside it. We could all perform this operation if called upon to do so – it is not so much a matter of ingenuity as part of the processes of everyday life. This case is set out in detail in Wilks (1971). If that case is correct, all current post-Chomskyan attempts to introduce what is essentially SPIV methodology into AI work on natural-language processing drag that part of AI in the direction of the SPIV/SAT methodology; all such attempts are, therefore, misguided, and should be abandoned. Natural language will be understood by machines in terms of complex pattern-matching and motivated relaxation of rules, or the accommodation of new data to existing representations.

The second requirement, involving the nature of proof, is more complex, and applies only to the stronger forms of SPIV. This again can be reduced to proof by example: there are no useful striking examples of basic AI programs proved correct, ones where trust in them in any way depends on that proof. We agree with De Millo *et al.* (1979) that the history of mathematics suggests that program proof could never be more reliable in principle than proof in mathematics, and that has shown itself to be a shifting ideal, utterly dependent on time-dependent social standards.

The conclusion from this, for us, is not at all the advocacy of a new methodology for AI but a call to return to RUDE, which is the classic methodology of AI. Its distinctive feature in both areas (of behaviors and proof) is that traditionally associated with the term "heuristic": that which does not admit of formal proof. What is needed is proper foundations for RUDE, and not a drift towards a neighboring paradigm.

An introduction to RUDE methodology

If all problems are not subsumable under SPIV or SAT, and we do not wish to abandon the possibility of implementing those problems, what methodology could we use? Can we forgo the comfort of complete, prior, formal specification, the notion of program correctness, and even the clear testability of program behavior, and yet still generate useable software? It seems to us that the (almost) unanimous response to this question from computer science and AI researchers alike is, NO. We believe that this negative position is both premature and entails severe limitations on the future of AI software if true. Thus we would like to see a thorough exploration of alternatives which reject the key assumptions of SPIV and SAT, and in this regard we shall offer some remarks on what the necessary methodology might look like. Essentially what we shall propose is a disciplined development of the 'hacking' methodology of classical AI. We believe that the basic idea is correct but that the paradigm is in need of substantial development before it will yield robust and reliable AI software.

It would seem that any development of RUDE must yield programs that are inferior to those of pure SPIV (with its guarantees of correctness), if only SPIV can be applied to the problems of AI. So one of the prerequisites for a serious consideration of RUDE must be to demonstrate that SPIV is an impossible ideal. SAT adherents have regretfully waived the requirement of proof. They work with SAT as an inferior stopgap that future puzzle-solving will transform into something more closely approaching SPIV; the RUDE methodology has no such pretensions.

We propose that adequate implementations of, say, the NLP problem can be generated by incremental development of a machine-executable specification. In place of the correctness notion of SPIV or the clear testability of SAT, we argue for a notion of adequacy. Intelligence is not typically associated with the notion of correctness in some absolute sense. The criteria of intelligence are adequacy and flexibility. It is misguided to impose absolute binary decisions on say, the meaning of a sentence, or even on its grammaticality. More realistically there is likely to be a set of more or less adequate meanings given certain contextual constraints.

Rather than implementation of an abstract specification, we propose exploration of the problem space in a quest for an adequate approximation to the NLP problem. The key developments that are needed are methodological constituents that can guide the exploration – since a random search is unlikely to succeed. We can list some of the puzzles (we would claim) of the RUDE paradigm – puzzles which, if they are indeed solvable as such, are *en route* to a disciplined version of the RUDE methodology.

decompiling – deriving consequences for the 'form' from observations of the 'function'

stepwise abstraction – a sequence of decompiling operations

structured growth – techniques for reversing the usual entropy increase that accompanies incremental development

adequacy validation – adequacy usefully considered as a lack of major performance inadequacies, etc.

controlled modification – a strategy of incremental change through analysis of program abstractions, subsuming both decompiling and structured growth.

A RUDE-based methodology that also yields programs with the desiderata of practical software – reliability, robustness, comprehensibility, and hence maintainability – is not close at hand. But if the alternative to developing such a methodology is the nonexistence of AI software then the search is well motivated.

Further sociological complexity

Let us expand for a moment on this notion of the paradigms SPIV and SAT that are neighbors to RUDE. An illustrative table might be the following ordered list of methodologies:

1 Only properly proved programs are OK.
2 Only programs conforming to the standards of SE are OK.
3 Only programs founded upon adequate logical or linguistic theories are OK.
4 Expert systems as a form of SE are OK.

5 AI programs that exist as practical/commercial software are OK.
6 Working AI demonstration programs of the standard type in AAAI
   papers are OK.

OK is a hopelessly weak term here, and readers may prefer to substitute
"acceptable" or "intellectually defensible" or any term they prefer. The
point of the table is its order and not the predicates attached to lines. For
each level, its adherents believe that those below it are NOT OK! Readers
may also enjoy the exercise of attaching names of individuals or companies
to each line: it is easily done, and provides an easy check on the table via the
transitivity-of-scorn rule. The upwards direction in the table is not simply
interpretable, but a close approximation is: anything above this line cannot
be seriously performed, but might be OK if it were. By our classification 5
and 6 are RUDE, 2, 3, and 4 are SAT, and 1 is SPIV.

Putting RUDE on a better intellectual foundation

Where should we seek for this, for it must not be simply a matter
of sociological issues but intellectual ones? It is a familiar argument that
computer projects, particularly large-scale ones (see Bennett, 1982; or the
classic, Brooks, 1975) fail for an extraordinary range of social and organizational reasons, and that would continue to be the case even if, per
impossible, realistic proofs of programs were to become available. Conversely, the problems that AI seems to have in getting out into the world, in
convincing itself and others that there is or has been at least one piece of real
red-blooded useful and workable AI, is not a matter of social constraints
and inhibitions as Schank seemed to claim (in Schank, 1983). The fact is
that the only saleable parts of real AI at the moment (apart from chess
games, perhaps) seem to be toolkits for building other bits (which might
seem to confirm Bundy's view, expressed in his reply to Schank [Bundy
1983] that AI is really a toolkit set, but not in a way that he would like).

Even if RUDE is, in some sense, the basic, classical, method of advance
in AI, would it be sufficient to simply declare that and carry on as before?
Almost certainly not, and even if AI were deemed to be at some level
engineering, there too the search for proper defensible foundations cannot
be avoided.

One natural place to look is where there is a claim that programs
themselves can be theories: this has been defended before (e.g. Wilks,
1974); declared to be not impossible (e.g. Simon, 1979); supported,
indirectly at least, but in terms that no AI practitioner could accept (e.g.
Sampson, 1975, which requires that the area under study be a closed form
like that of a dead language – this would be a drastic return to the very
Chomskyan assumptions that RUDE advocates would reject); and even
demonstrated by example (Partridge, Johnston, and Lopez, 1984).

Note that it might be a *reductio ad absurdum* to have programs as theories, but this is just the kind of *reductio* that AI has willingly embraced in the past: consider, for example, the position that seems natural to many AI researchers in which every truth in a world is considered an axiom, a *reductio* Tarski foresaw.

Finally, we note that these issues of methodological validity may not be a purely parochial concern of the AI community. It has been suggested (e.g. Giddings, 1984) that the SPIV/SAT paradigm may be inappropriate for much of SE as well. It may be that RUDE should be the *major* paradigm instead of SPIV/SAT.

AI, computer science and education: a position paper

Ranan Banerji

Introduction

I am writing this paper only for those people who will agree with me that research in AI very often lacks a disciplined approach and that this situation should be changed. Trying to establish this fact for those who disagree with me and to do so in a way acceptable to a normal scientific community will need much more work than I can afford and, if what I say is true, would be a futile thing to do anyway.

Of course, even though one may agree with me in my above view, one may not agree with me about how the situation should be changed. My fear is that the situation will be hard to change: it will not happen till a number of years have elapsed after there is a change in our approach to the field of computer science.

Even to argue that point I will have to assume that AI depends heavily on computers and on programming. I think that it is safe to believe that we have agreement on that. If there are any proponents of "disembodied AI," I might be one among them: and I am quite prepared to keep that view in abeyance.

Programs are written for different purposes in AI. I can think of three: to study human psychological processes through simulation, to produce or to experiment with programs which exhibit intelligent behavior irrespective of their relationship with the human mind, and to produce a commercial product which interacts with a human in an intelligent way to help him in a complex activity. Success in all three activities depends heavily on the quality of the program involved and – equally importantly – on the scientific communities understanding of the properties of that program. So what I want to say is irrespective of subfield.

Programming and computer science

In recent years, the major thrust in computer science has shifted from the art of writing programs to the science of understanding programs. The reason for this has been the growing conviction that the art can be significantly strengthened by the science: perhaps even that the art is now at a plateau and will continue to stay there without input from the science. Computer programming has evolved from a trade into a discipline.

Now my point is that this need for understanding a program remains important even if that program is written for AI purposes. Even if the program "works," we have need to know what "works" means (i.e what the specification of the program is) and how to change the program if we want to change its behavior in a specific way. Such knowledge has to be more than intuitive: it has to be verbaliseable, in the interest of dissemination of the knowledge and for scientific cooperation. And, at the risk of offending some, I have to admit that mere intuitive knowledge unbacked by disciplined argument, even if held by an extremely intelligent person, can be erroneous.

Education in computer science

People outside the field of AI who have the need to write large and complex programs seem to have come to the conclusion that such programs cannot be written, improved, updated, and maintained without the development of rather involved techniques. To master these techniques, one has to have facility and training in areas of knowledge older than, and often seemingly independent of, the art of programming. By this I do not mean that these older disciplines already hold solutions to the problems of computer science. I merely say that the chances of developing viable techniques *de nouveau* without dependence on any previous discipline does not seem to be high.

Even today this realization has not been entirely translated into curricular considerations in our teaching institutions. Although efforts are made to expose students of computer science to these disciplines, such students are often incapable of seeing the relation between these and the programs they write. Even worse, they have scant practice in using these techniques during their training. As an example, there are lots of people in the field who may know the term "NP-complete" and its general significance, can identify a problem class as NP-complete by name but cannot explain why, and therefore, even if they wanted, could not go about establishing that the class may have a polynomial or even a linear subclass. Their discovery of a strong algorithm which may be very efficient for such a subclass would then be explained by the vague concept of "difference between theory and practice!"

I have watched young students wanting to establish the correctness of an algorithm or the precise definition of a concept they are developing. They often have great difficulty in distinguishing between a precise definition and a motivating explanation. And this is true across the field of computer science and independent of the quality of the school where they received their undergraduate education.

The reason is not far to seek. Till recently, although the importance of precise arguments and formal reasoning was recognized in computer science, there was no clear idea as to how the techniques for these were to be taught and illustrated. Good books for teaching them were not available. People realized that most major innovations in the field were coming from mathematicians (and this was true even in the early days of AI) but also knew that one could not make every computer professional to go through an entire mathematics curriculum: there was not time. Moreover, significant innovations were being made by competent and intelligent people outside the field of mathematics. So for a while (and in many schools even today) the mathematics requirements for the students were carelessly designed and often apologetically taught. There were difficulties in the way of fitting a mathematics curriculum geared to computer science into a curriculum designed for mathematics and physical-science majors.

Bachelors of computer science entered graduate school under the handicaps engendered by these difficulties. On top of these, graduate programs in computer science, especially in the early days, had no undergraduate schools to feed them and accepted students with all undergraduate backgrounds: it really was not clear that there was any undergraduate training specially suitable for the development of proficiency in computer science. Often the term meant proficiency in code writing rather than in algorithm development – indeed it was not clear in the early days that there was distinction between the two concepts. People who come out of those days can be easily forgiven if they do not see why precision is needed, and, even if they do see it, if they are not aware that techniques of precise thought exist and are learnable. Mathematics is still considered by many to be the science of numbers rather than that of argumentation, and therefore irrelevant to the job at hand.

This discussion of the curricular history of computer science would be relevant to any branch of computer science, but is especially relevant to AI because – we AI people are proud to say – AI is as old a field as computer science itself. Any trouble that plagues computer science is bound to plague AI. And more so, since many people in AI cannot be conscious of the techniques being developed in the sister disciplines because they did not come from these disciplines. This occasionally means reinventing these techniques or poorer substitutes for them or – even more tragically – developing superior alternatives which cannot be shared because of differences in terminology.

It is my belief that computer science has already recognized the problem and efforts are under way to remedy the situation. Better textbooks are appearing. The early leaders of the field, conscious of the difficulties – brought on by the increasing demand from industry for certifiable programs – have decided that the new trends are relevant and ought to be encouraged.

This is not universally true. There are still schools whose leaders believe that programming can be taught by examples and the Association for Computing Machinery requirements are a necessary evil impeding the growth of "real programmers." Industry is getting conscious of that fact. I understand that some industries are already deciding to produce their programmers by inhouse training rather than take the risk of hiring bachelors of computer science.

These pressures have not been felt in AI until very recently. Moreover, since AI was not initially popular in the so-called "real world", the few centers of activities in AI only drew the most dedicated and the best of students – the hordes of degree-hungry career seekers with limited abilities stayed out of the area. So the weaknesses in the way research was being conducted became evident much later – if they are evident even today. The very quality of what was being done stood in the way of the realization that it should be done better. The weaknesses may be even less evident to the senior people, who came from the early days when none of us knew what needed to be done and few, if any, knew what we were doing.

Just as in the case of computer science, we are beginning to see the need for a change. And just as in computer science or any field of human endeavor undergoing change, there will be resistance to change. It is a commonly accepted fact in psychology, I believe, that the deeper is one's previous commitment to an idea, the harder it is to realize that the idea has to be changed.

AI and computer science

I guess I am arguing that AI needs to become more theoretical: new innovations have reached a plateau, because the very size and complexities of the programs that support these innovations are rendering them difficult to describe, debug, support, and maintain. The difference between a debug and an innovation is becoming harder to see: the chance for false claims for programs is increasing from a level which was never comfortably low.

It is probably obvious that when I say theoretical, I do not mean that I am demanding that somebody comes to a definitive discussion on the nature of intelligence. However, it is probably worthwhile to point this out, since I have heard some leaders in the field arguing the futility of theory by defining theory to be exactly such a discussion. What I am suggesting is that it is neither a futile nor a useless activity for an AI programmer to specify a program, to calculate its complexity and to prove its correctness. Having struggled with such activities myself, I do not underestimate the difficulty of doing this. I am merely saying that the seemingly easier task of unleashing a cleverly conceived (as opposed to well-designed) program on a problem does not necessarily advance the study of the problem.

I have made it obvious where my sympathies lie: I would like to see AI programs developed along the same lines that other software is developed. However, that does not necessarily mean that I am advocating that one writes a specification, freezes it in concrete, develops an algorithm, proves that the algorithm meets the specification, and then (and only then) proceeds to write an implementation. It seems to me that Partridge and Wilks in this volume ("Does AI have a methodology different from software engineering?") indicate that as the accepted method for software development – thus verifying my contention above that AI specialists are about as far from the developments in software engineering as most computer practitioners. The fact is that what these authors call the SPIV paradigm is only one among several approaches that are being suggested and tried out. Attempts have been made to verify programs by informed choice of test data, by statistics and – as is often the case in the field – by trial and error on the specification and proof. It is true, however, that whoever tries to pursue any of these lines, feels an obligation to define terms, and to put down some methods that can be followed by people other than the intimate friends and colleagues of the author, and that no claim is made for a program that can not be substantiated. I am sure that most of these demands would be made by anyone serious about establishing a viable AI methodology. On that basis, it may be worthwhile to discuss my reactions to Partridge and Wilks. My thesis is that what these authors call the RUDE paradigm is not so alien from acceptable software practice that an entirely new discipline needs to be built around it.

I shall not comment on the lines of development that Partridge and Wilks have suggested ("decompiling," "adequacy validation," etc.). Even the definitions of those terms are not clear to me and the chances are high that different people would place different interpretations on them. As an example, their use of the term "entropy" in defining "structured growth" seems to be entirely different from standard usage in any well-defined discipline. In what follows, I shall try to avoid the use of such terms.

Partridge and Wilks are entirely within their rights when they claim that "the set of meaningful sentences, however described, will be confronted with meaningful utterances outside it." To me, that means that no matter what program be written to understand meaningful sentences, it will be faced with a sentence which it cannot understand or understands wrongly. It is not clear to me from this that natural-language processing programs would then be capable of handling all meaningful utterances only if one stops trying to specify them. Even if we did accept that, it would not follow that if one stops demanding that the set of meaningful sentences be specified, then natural-language processing programs would be able to handle them (to claim such a deduction valid would be one of the earliest fallacies that a student of discrete mathematics in computer science would be warned against). However, it is not clear to me either (as it might be clear to SPIV protagonists – at least according to Partridge and Wilks) that no attempt be made to write and improve natural-language processing programs. Indeed, as we all know, significant gains have occurred in our understanding of natural languages and of knowledge engineering techniques because of attempts at writing such programs.

Let us, therefore, analyze how this happened. To do this, we shall imagine what might be a typical scenario of progress.

A program is written to answer questions about some data domain, using a conversational mode in natural language. After the obvious bugs are removed and the program is ready for serious testing, it answers some question in a silly manner. After some effort, the reason for this silly answer is unraveled. Probably at this point Partridge and Wilks would say that understanding has occurred and then when the reason for the silly answer is removed, one would say that debugging has taken place. In the process one may have a different (even a somewhat improved) parser, a different (perhaps more flexible) knowledge representation and some other things.

Following a SPIV terminology (and perhaps a mental set engendered by it) one could have said that when the bug was found, one realized that certain sentences would be answered in a silly manner. This would lead one to understand what kind of questions would be answered correctly. This would lead to an improved specification of the class of sentences that can be handled by the program. The class would be understood either syntactically (if the "error" was in the parser) or semantically (if the error was found in the knowledge system) or in some vague interaction of the two. One might say that in either case, one came closer to specifying, not the set of all meaningful utterances, but the power of the program. A software engineer, whichever be his school of thought, would not feel comfortable about removing the bug before understanding what the bug did to the overall performance. He would be afraid that if he changed the program just to remove the problem at hand, he would be "patching" rather than debugging the program.

A good AI programmer would behave no differently. Thus, depending on the purpose of the program, he would either warn the user about the limitations of the program or he would improve the program in such a way that he could almost visualize what the next problem sentence would be. When I say my sympathies are with SPIV, I mean that such an AI programmer should be applauded and encouraged to learn the available techniques of specification and methods of proof which would sharpen his intuition towards doing what he just did, even if he could not use the techniques to their perfection. No software engineer can use SPIV to perfection; nor can an antenna designer use Electromagnetic Theory to predict the perturbation caused by every supporting strut: he can only roughly guess the amount of deviation he can expect from the specification and decide on whether he can accept it.

The point that needs to be made is that such failure on the part of the antenna designer does not give him justification to burn his books on Electromagnetic Theory. Nor does it justify a movement to start an approach towards a new paradigm for understanding radio waves.

A practical software engineer deviates from the strict rulings of program verification because he has to, not because the rulings are bad. His clear knowledge of those rulings helps him to design his deviations in a way that he can have a good insight into what kind of risks he is taking. His art flourishes because of his science, not in spite of it.

In sum, I have argued that the U(nderstanding) and the D(ebug) of RUDE are essentially the same as the S(pecification) and the P(roof) of SPIV and a solid training in software science (with all its present imperfections) would do the AI practitioner the same good as the compiler writer.

A few words need to be said about heuristics, since there is a tendency in the AI community to claim that once a problem is known to be NP-complete, one need not make any attempt to understand or control the limitations of any program that is written to solve it efficiently "in some cases." The experience of the complexity theorists (a group of people whose efforts are not considered relevant to the study of AI, unfortunately), however, does not indicate that such a liberation from all discipline is necessary. Several careful efforts have been made to solve NP-complete problems partially. One approach has been to isolate a subclass of the NP-complete class of problems that can be solved efficiently. The other (the "heuristic" approach) has been to write programs that "satisfice" the solution, just as the AI community does. The only difference is that the "satisficing" complexity theorists often try to find out what the maximum or expected deviation from the optimum would be. I have not heard any cogent argument as to why this is undesirable in AI, any more than I am convinced that trying to specify an AI program detracts from its value. I am also very afraid that by refusing to look at AI programs as normal programs, we are often confusing debugs with patches. What is even worse, I have a fear that once an unspecified program is hailed as a breakthrough, and patch or debug on it has a tendency to be called an innovation. This proliferates publications and obfuscates issues.

11 Limitations on current AI technology

Commercial AI is now big business, but AI itself is full of fundamental, unsolved problems; so what exactly is being marketed? Whether we wish to call it AI or expert systems, what are the scope and limitations of this technology?

Hewitt argues that there are severe limitations inherent in the 'logic programming' movement, because of its close association with current expert systems technology. He sees a need to deal with "open" systems that involve inconsistent knowledge and will need "due process reasoning" for decision-making.

On a broader front, Hewitt is questioning the suitability of the symbolic-search-space paradigm (the foundational hypothesis of AI for the last thirty years) as a basis for intelligent systems. This paradigm, with its prerequisites of well-defined initial states, goal states, and state-transformation operators, is applicable to "artificial domains like chess and mathematical theorem proving. It is not very adaptable to the hurly-burly of solving problems involving interaction with the physical world."

The Dreyfus brothers also argue that current expert systems' technology (CEST) is severely limited and it is built upon a fundamentally misguided view of human expertise. They see future progress in AI only when some fundamental assumptions are abandoned (such as knowledge as a collection of context-free units – another manifestation of the general pervasiveness of the symbolic-search-space paradigm) and radically new approaches to the problem are taken, such as attempting to understand and implement, on appropriate architecture, holistic reasoning methods.

They conclude their paper with a suggestion that connectionism may be a paradigm that offers a route to AI systems that can transcend the limitations of the symbolic-search-space paradigm.

Michie picks up some of the threads of the Dreyfus brothers' argument, but he takes them off in a different direction. CEST has failed to deliver systems that can match human expertise in just those areas in which the human skill is intuitive: the human expert cannot articulate his or her skill, hence the knowledge engineer cannot codify it in a set of rules. For the

382

Dreyfus brothers, this is one indication that intuitive expertise is not symbolic-rule based, but for Michie the lesson is that CEST should be based on computer induction: intuitive expertise is codified by automatic induction over a set of instances of that expertise. But decision trees, typically the product of automatic induction, are conceptually opaque and thus not a useful embodiment of information. So Michie's suggestion is that machine induction should be developed so that it can generate "concept-structured rules from database-stored examples. This is the 'superarticulacy' phenomenon." He then proposes that the machine might coach the human expert and by so doing raise him or her to the level of a "superexpert."

In conclusion, Michie stresses the need for computer systems that are "amenable to conceptual debugging," for these are the only systems that can be regarded as safe. This last point brings us back to what may turn out to be one of the major obstacles to the development of the connectionist paradigm as a foundation for useful AI systems: distributed parallel systems are by their very nature not readily interpretable at the conceptual level.

The challenge of open systems
Carl Hewitt

Systems of interconnected and interdependent computers are qualitatively different from the relatively isolated computers of the past. Such "open systems" uncover important limitations in current approaches to artificial intelligence (AI). They require a new approach that is more like organizational designs and management than current approaches. Here we'll take a look at some of the implications and constraints imposed by open systems.

Open systems are always subject to communications and constraints from outside. They are characterized by the following properties:

Continuous change and evolution. Distributed systems are always adding new computers, users and software. As a result, systems must be able to change as the components and demands placed upon them change. Moreover, they must be able to evolve new internal components in order to accommodate the shifting work they perform. Without this capability, every system must reach the point where it can no longer expand to accommodate new users and uses.

Arm's-length relationships and decentralized decision making. In general, the computers, people, and agencies that make up open systems do not have direct access to one another's internal information. Arm's-length relationships imply that the architecture must accommodate multiple computers at different physical sites that do not have access to the internal components of others. This leads to decentralized decision making.

Perpetual inconsistency among knowledge bases. Because of privacy and discretionary concerns, different knowledge bases will contain different perspectives and conflicting beliefs. Thus, all the knowledge bases of a distributed AI system taken together will be perpetually inconsistent. Decentralization makes it impossible to update all knowledge bases simultaneously. This implies that it is not even possible to know what kinds of information are contained in all the local knowledge bases in the system at any one time. Systems must be able to operate in the presence of inconsistent and incomplete knowledge bases.

Need for negotiation among system components. In a highly distributed system, no system component directly controls the resources of another.

The various components of the system must persuade one another to provide capabilities. Consequently, a distributed AI system's architecture must support a mechanism for negotiation among components.

Inadequacy of the closed-world assumption. The closed-world assumption is that the information about the world being modeled is complete in the sense that exactly those relationships that hold among objects can be derived from the local information possessed by the system. Systems that depend on the closed-world assumption make use of the principle that they can find all existing instances of a concept by searching their local storage. At first glance it might seem that the closed-world assumption, almost universal in the AI literature, is smart because it provides a ready default answer for any query. Unfortunately, the default answers provided become less realistic as open systems increase in size and less of the information is available locally.

Continuous growth and evolution, arm's-length relationships, inconsistency among knowledge bases, decentralized decision making, and the need for negotiations are interdependent and necessary properties of the open systems.

Parallel computation in open systems

The theory of recursive functions (e.g. Turing machines) is based on a batch-processing model of computation. Output is obtained from a recursive function when it finally halts. Open systems require a theory of computation in which processing might never halt, may be required to provide output while still in operation, and can accept input from sources not anticipated when the computation began.

Asynchronous parallel computer systems make use of a two-input, two-output computing element called an arbiter. Arbiters are the fundamental hardware primitives that make parallel asynchronous computing different from sequential synchronous computing. Arbiters make decisions for which there is no logical justification (proof) because the decision cannot be predicted from knowledge of the structure of the computing system and its input. In a very fundamental sense, arbiters are not equivalent to Turing machines (Clinger, 1981). Figure 1 shows an arbiter with inputs x and y and outputs x' and y'.

An arbiter decides the order in which it receives requests. Thus, if inputs x and y are asserted at about the same time, the result will eventually be one of the possibilities shown in figure 2.

The output of an arbiter is not a logical function of its input, in the sense that it is not a simple Boolean function, because the dimension of time enters into the semantics of arbiter modules in a fundamental way. However, the *feasible* sets of outputs can be described in logic using the *subsequently* relation (see Agha, 1984):

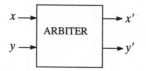

Figure 1 An arbiter with inputs x and y and outputs x' and y'

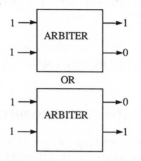

Figure 2 Given that the inputs to the arbiter are asserted almost simultaneously, the resulting output will be one of the above two cases

$(x = 1$ and $y = 1)$ *subsequently*
(or
$(x' = 0$ and $y' = 1)$
$(x' = 1$ and $y' = 0))$

Logic cannot be used to determine which particular eventuality will occur. Systems with arbiters are not equivalent to a nondeterministic Turing machine, since an arbiter can require an unbounded amount of time to make a decision (possibly while other computations are taking place). If a nondeterministic Turing machine is required to make a decision, there is a bound on the amount of time it can take and this bound is determined before it starts. Each individual choice of a nondeterministic Turing machine takes one step.

In practice, the inputs to an arbiter are analog signals that vary continuously between 0 and 1. For example, if the actual inputs to an arbiter were .97 and .96 then the output might be as shown in figure 3.

The arbiter has only digital outputs (0s or 1s) even though the input is analog. It makes a definite digital choice out of the analog quantities of time and its two inputs. Because of the continuous nature of time and the analog nature of the input, an arbiter cannot be strictly modeled as a nondeterministic-state machine.

In a parallel computation, arbiters are used repeatedly so that the number of possible outcomes grows exponentially with time. Thus, the actual operation of a parallel computer system cannot be determined logically by the inputs to the system. The indeterminacy of the arbiters used in open

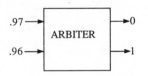

Figure 3   In practice, the inputs to an arbiter are analog signals varying between 0 and 1

computer systems results in their making decisions that cannot be proved from knowledge of structure of the computing system and its input.

Decisions justified by agreements

The electronic-banking system is a good example of an open system. You're probably familiar with it through the use of automated teller machines that enable you to withdraw cash thousands of miles from where you opened an account. Teller machines are continually being added to the system.

Decisions about which transactions to honor are justified on the basis of an agreement between the bank and its depositors. Often an agreement will provide that the bank does not have to honor a withdrawal if there are insufficient funds present in the account when the withdrawal is requested. The withdrawal would be refused even though it might be covered by subsequent deposits.

The decisions of which withdrawals not to honor cannot be deduced from complete information about the structure of the bank's computers and the input from the teller machines. Thus, the decision whether or not to honor a withdrawal is not subject to logical proof. For example, suppose Account 1 has a balance of $1,000, Account 2 has a balance of $2,000, and they share a common reserve account with a credit limit of $3,000. If two electronic withdrawals of $4,000 each are attempted at about the same time from both Account 1 and Account 2 then one of the attempts will be refused and the other one will be honored though it is impossible to deduce which one will be honored and which one refused.

The above example shows how a decision of a open system can be justified even though it does not follow from any proof. Instead, the decision is justified by an agreement to act in certain ways. We see a divergence between the theories used in the construction of the open systems and their operation. Theory informs practice: e.g. the design of the banking mechanism is based on a financial theory. However, the financial theory does not determine the actual accounts of the bank accounting system. The operation of the bank accounts is determined by the order in which asynchronous events occur inside the system. Each performance of a complicated open system is unique.

This illustrates the divergence between classic recursive-function theory and theories needed to model open systems. (For a further discussion of the mathematical semantics needed to model the behavior of open systems, see Agha, 1984; Clinger, 1981.)

Exploration versus search

Searching in problem spaces is the traditional AI framework. Problem spaces and problems have been defined as follows (see Newell, 1979):

Problem Space: A problem space consists of a set of symbolic structures (the states of the space) and a set of *operators* over the space. Each operator takes a state as input and produces a state as output, although there may be other inputs and outputs as well. The operators may be partial, i.e. not defined for all states. Sequences of operators define *paths* that thread their way through sequences of states.

Problem: A problem in a problem space consists of a set of *initial* states, a set of *goal* states, and a set of *path constraints*. The problem is to find a path through the space that starts at any initial state, passes only along paths that satisfy the path constraints, and ends at any goal state.

A good example of a problem space is that of the game of chess:

1 Initial state: chess pieces in starting position
2 Operations: legal moves
3 Goal states: checkmate, stalemate, etc.

I claim that searching through problem-solving spaces provides a narrow foundation for the analysis and synthesis of intelligent systems. The perspective must be broadened to include *exploration* that goes beyond search. An excellent perspective on some of the differences between search and exploration is provided by the means used to explore and develop the North American continent.

1. *Initial state:* There was no well-defined initial global state of the North American continent in the middle 1600s. Leif Ericson and Christoper Columbus had led some early probes, but the information was fragmentary, dispersed, and self-contradictory.

2. *Operations:* The set of operations used to explore the continent was not defined in advance. Instead, it was improvised dynamically and interactively in the course of initial probes. Furthermore, the explorers operated *in parallel* so that there is no path of states of the continent that adequately explains how it was explored. That is, the continent was not explored by finding a single path through a space of states. Exploration of the North American continent can be better modeled as a partial order of causally linked historical events than as a problem space.

3. *Goal state:* There was no set of immutable global goal states for the continent that the explorers set out to achieve. Rather, the explorers' goals evolved with the exploration methods as the exploration proceeded.

Searching problem spaces is limited mainly in its applicability to artificial domains like chess and mathematical theorem proving. It is not very adaptable to the hurly-burly of solving problems involving interaction with the physical world. Problem spaces do not provide sufficient flexibility to represent the problem-solving processes of communities because they require us to represent the problem solving of individual actors a single global state. This limitation of problem spaces is closely related to the inadequacies of the Turing machine as a model of asynchronous distributed systems. Problem solving in open systems is more analogous to the exploration of North America than the playing of games like chess.

Planner

Planner was one of the first AI programming languages to support goal oriented problem solving without an externally specified problem space. It was based on the following principles (see Hewitt, 1972):

Accessibility: Planner aims for a maximum of flexibility so that whatever knowledge is available can be incorporated into the problem-solving process even if it is fragmentary and heuristic.

Pattern-directed invocation: Procedures in Planner can be invoked by patterns of what they are supposed to accomplish. Suppose that we have a stopped sink. One way we could try to solve the problem would be to know the name of a plumber whom we could call. An alternative that is more analogous to pattern-directed invocation is to advertise the fact that we have a stopped sink and the qualifications needed to fix it. In Planner this is accomplished by making the advertisement (i.e. the pattern that represents what is desired) into a goal.

Procedural interpretation of logical statements: One basic idea behind Planner is to exploit the duality that we find between certain imperative and declarative sentences. Consider the statement (implies A B). The statement is a perfectly good declarative. In addition, it can also have certain imperative uses for Planner. It can say that we might set up a procedure that will note whether A is ever asserted and if so to consider the wisdom of asserting B in turn. Furthermore, Planner permits us to set up a procedure that will watch to see if it is ever our goal to try to deduce B and if so whether A should be made a subgoal. Exactly the same observation can be made about the contrapositive of the statement (implies A B). Statements with universal quantifiers, conjunctions, disjunctions, etc., can also have both declarative and imperative uses. Planner theorems are used as imperatives when executed and as declaratives when used as data.

Planner represented an advance over the "uniform proof procedures" of resolution theorem-proving systems then current. The design for Planner was implemented by Sussman, Winograd, and Charniak (see Hewitt, 1969; Sussman, Winograd and Charniak, 1970). Winograd used it to implement his interactive natural language program, SHRDLU, for a world with simulated toy blocks (see Winograd, 1971).

In order to understand how procedural interpretation works, consider this logical statement:

(For all x ((man x) implies (mortal x)))

The implication has two parts: the antecedent (man x) and the consequent (mortal x). It says: for every x, if x is a man, then x is mortal. Logical rules of inference permit certain deductions from the above statement. For instance, that Socrates is mortal can be derived from the premise that Socrates is a man as follows:

(Man Socrates)
———————————
(Mortal Socrates)

I proposed that logical implications like "all men are mortal" could be interpreted as procedures in a programming language. One interpretation, the *belief-invoked* interpretation (called the "antecedent interpretation" in Planner), provides that when the belief that x is a man is held, then the belief that x is mortal can be logically derived. We can express this as follows:

(*when* (belief (man x)) *do*
(believe (mortal x)))

Another interpretation, the *goal-invoked* interpretation (called the "consequent interpretation" in Planner), provides that from the goal that x is a man can be logically derived:

(*when* (goal (mortal x)) *do*
(show (man x)))

The ideas in Planner have been generalized and perfected in subsequent artificial-intelligence programming languages. However by themselves they do not address the needs of open systems.

Logic programming

Logic programming has been proposed by some as the programming paradigm for the future (Kowalski, 1980). Let's focus on limitations that are inherent in the enterprise of attempting to use logic as a programming language for dealing reliably with empirical knowledge and interacting with the physical world. The remarks in this section continue a debate that begins with the genesis of AI. I recommend that interested readers consult the appendix to Marvin Minsky's frames paper (Minsky, 1975) and the subsequent analysis of David Israel (Israel, 1984).

Logic programming must be based on logic. But what is logic? First-order logic, with its well-defined semantics and syntax, is the basis claimed by most of those who call themselves logic programmers. In part, the confidence of logic programmers is based on the fact that first-order logic augmented with set theory has proved to be a good foundation for mathematical semantics.

Omega-order logic is an extension to first-order logic that allows quantification over predicates and functions. It has advantages over first-order logic in that it includes the full lambda calculus as a sublanguage and has arbitrary powers of abstraction. When certain technical problems having to do with Russell's Paradox have been dealt with, omega-order logic may be the preferred logical language (Rudin, 1981). Therefore, we should consider it to be in the mainstream of logic programming. Experts have argued that the merits of other logics can be found in first-order logic (McCarthy, 1977a; Weyhrauch, 1980), so the analysis here is confined to first-order logic without loss of generality.

The inconsistency problem

I make the following claim, which I call the Conjecture of Inconsistency: the axiomatizations of the human knowledge of all physical systems are uniformly inconsistent in practice.

I've used the term *conjecture* because the above claim is in principle impossible to prove rigorously, easy to disprove by counterexample, and has a preponderance of evidence in its favor. The reasons for the inconsistency have to do with the dispersed asynchronous nature of human knowledge, including the following factors:

Environmental context: The physical system being axiomatized is related to various other physical systems. For example, a diseased kidney is often related to a diseased heart. Knowledge of the kidney cannot be separated from knowledge of the heart.

Spatiotemporal context: A physical system is situated in space and time. Knowledge of the physical system comprises knowledge of its history and mode of production.

Terminological context: The predicates used in the axiomatization of the properties of a physical object are always somewhat problematic in practice. For example, specifying in practice what it means for a physical table to be flat raised many problematic issues.

Evidential context: It is impossible to separate what we know about a physical object from how we came to know it. Axiomatization of the methods by which the axiomatized knowledge came to be known further enlarges the axiomatization.

The DEC System–20 is a good case in point. In the first place, observe that the DEC System–20 is an extremely simple system in comparison with, say, the human kidney. Furthermore, the DEC System–20 is an artificial human construct that was designed to be consistent with some simple requirements. Nevertheless, despite the best efforts of software engineers, the formal description (axiomatization of documentation and code) of the DEC System–20 remains inconsistent. There are inconsistencies in the documentation as well as inconsistencies between the documentation and the code. Although inconsistencies are continually being removed from the system, the experience is that more inconsistencies are always found immediately.

Suppose that we were given unlimited funding to undertake the job of making the description of the DEC System–20 consistent. We would have to control the process by which the system grows and evolves. In particular, we would have to handle all changes to the documentation and code in face of the following external requirements:

> Bugs in both the code and documentation must be fixed
> New functions must be incorporated to meet the customers' changing needs
> The system must accept changing interfaces to other systems such as peripherals and networks.

There is no way to prove that the process by which the DEC System–20 evolves will result in new releases with consistent formal descriptions. An axiomatization of the code and documentation of even a system as simple as the DEC System–20 is, in practice, inconsistent despite enormous efforts made to achieve consistency.

A second claim I make is that the axiomatizations of the human knowledge about any physical systems will forever be inconsistent. I call it the Conjecture of Perpetual Inconsistency: removing some inconsistencies from an axiomatization of the human knowledge about a physical system leaves an axiomatization which is nevertheless inconsistent.

Message-passing semantics

Consideration of the previous claim suggests that we need to examine how logic treats inconsistency. Inconsistencies have some important implications for the utility of logic programming as a foundation for intelligent systems. The logical view of inconsistent theories is clear: They are meaningless because they correspond to no possible world. The logical account of meaning is too stringent for nontrivial empirical systems because inconsistent beliefs and descriptions are not meaningless. Inconsistency is inherent in the enterprise of expressing the human knowledge of physical systems. A theory of meaning that maintains that inconsistent descriptions are meaningless is not directly applicable to problems of empirical knowledge.

In model theory, the meaning of a sentence is determined by the models that make it true (Tarski, 1944). For example, the conjunction of two sentences is true exactly when both of its conjuncts are true. Truth-theoretic semantics assumes that it is possible to give an account of truth in itself, free of interactional issues, and that the theory of meaning can be based on such a theory of truth.

Message-passing semantics takes a different perspective on the meaning of a sentence: it takes the meaning of a message to be the effect it has on the subsequent behavior of the system. In other words, the meaning of a message is determined by how it affects the recipients. Each partial meaning of a message is constructed by a recipient in terms of how it is processed (Kowalski, 1980). At a deep level, understanding always involves categorization, which is a function of interactional (rather than inherent) properties using the perspective of individual viewpoints (Lakoff and Johnson,1980). Meaning is thus fundamentally interactional. The meaning of a message is open-ended and unfolds indefinitely far into the future as other recipients process the message. According to message-passing semantics, meaning is communication-based, not logic-based.

Need for due-process reasoning

In the presence of conflicting information and contradictory beliefs, logical proof is inadequate as a reasoning mechanism. Instead we need due-process reasoning that investigates different sides of beliefs, goals, and hypotheses that arise.

Consider the following hypothesis to illustrate due-process reasoning: "Nixon was guilty of destruction of evidence in the Watergate case by erasing a portion of a tape recording." One possible approach in logic programming is to gather evidence in favor of the hypothesis and attempt to fashion the evidence into a logic proof (perhaps augmented with "certainty factors" or "default assumptions"). The other approach is to use "negation as failure" to conclude that the hypothesis is false because it cannot be proved from the available knowledge. Both of the approaches are inadequate in this case. No matter how much evidence is produced and analyzed, logical proof (either for or against Nixon's guilt) is unbalanced because it presents only one side of the case in the form of a proof. Using "negation as failure" to draw conclusions from the inability to construct such a proof is equally limited. A balanced approach requires debate between differing positions and weighing presented evidence. Debates are not structured in the same way as logical proofs.

Due-process reasoning is the process of collecting and analyzing the evidence and arguments presented by all interested parties. *Advocates* collect evidence and organize arguments in favor of the hypothesis. In parallel, *skeptics* collect evidence and organize arguments against the hypothesis. Then a debate is conducted on grounds for deciding the case in terms of *motive* and *ability*. The question of motive is whether Nixon thought he would benefit by erasing the tape. The question of ability is whether he could have erased the tape. Both advocates and skeptics *recursively* make use of due-process reasoning while investigating, organizing, and presenting their cases. The advocates and skeptics operate interdependently in collecting evidence (through discovery processes and disclosure requirements) as well as interacting by debating each others' cases in a decision-making process that is fundamentally different from logical proof.

Prolog

Advocates of logic programming initially developed a programming language called Prolog that was based on the goal-invoked procedural interpretation of implication discussed earlier in the section on Planner (Kowalski, 1974). The example discussed earlier to the effect that "In order to show that x is mortal, establish a subgoal to show that x is a man" is written in Prolog as:

mortal (x) :- man (x)

The original Prolog was a much simpler language than Planner, which was a considerable advantage in terms of pedagogy and ease of implementation. But now Prolog, like the Planner-like languages before it, has fissioned into incompatible dialects based on the procedural interpretation of logic, pattern-directed invocation, message-passing theory, and description systems (Doyle, 1980; Khan, 1984; Kowalski, 1980).

In addition to the general limitations of logic programming discussed earlier, Prolog has some weaknesses all its own. The closed world assumption is the hypothesis that the locally available knowledge is complete, i.e. if a proposition does not follow from the local knowledge base, then it is assumed to be false (Reiter, 1981). Planner could make use of the closed-world, assumption using its ability to conditionalize a plan (theorem) on the exhaustive failure to establish a goal. In fact, Winograd made strong use of the capability in SHRDLU. Influenced by Planner, Prolog went much further and adopted a very strong form of the closed-world assumption as a basic postulate of the programming language in incorporating *negation as failure*. (Relational database systems make use of a similar strong hypothesis: if an entry is not found in a relational table, then the relationship is false). The strong use of the closed-world assumption in Prolog is incompatible with the need in open systems to allow for the open-ended incremental introduction of new beliefs and objects.

Information-processing principles for the future

The term *reflection* has been much discussed in the current AI literature (Batali, 1983; Doyle, 1980; Hewitt and De Jong, 1983; Smith, 1982; Weyhrauch, 1980). It is universally conjectured that reflective problem capabilities will be important to improving machine problem-solving capabilities. However, a danger is developing that the important problems will be neglected unless reflective problem solving is taken to encompass the following *minimum* capabilities:

History of its own behavior. What did you do then?

Representation of its own information-processing procedures. How do you make decisions?

Knowledge of the relationship between its previous behavior and current procedures. What would you do differently and why?

Representation of its procedures for interacting with the external world. How do you control things?

The current state of the art in implementing reflective systems is extremely primitive. Many of the issues and questions itemized above have not yet been properly addressed.

Besides reflective problem solving, other principles should be adopted in constructing reliable systems that meet the needs of open systems.

Serendipity: It is not critical whether the system learns of a result before it can be used in a problem-solving task or after work has commenced on the task.

Pluralism: There is no central arbiter of truth in the system.

Accessibility: All knowledge of the system (including its own procedures) should be able to be applied to any problem.

Parrallelism: The system should be able to mobilize its full resources in parallel instantiations for different aspects of large-scale problems.

Due-process reasoning: The system collects and debates alternatives to decide among beliefs and goals.

Reflection in practice. Knowledge (including self-knowledge) should inform practice, and practice should modify hypotheses, beliefs and goals.

Reasonableness: The system should perform efficiently in the face of conflicting information and inconsistent beliefs.

Conclusion

In practice, the human knowledge of a physical system cannot be consistently axiomatized. Every physical system is open in the sense that it is embedded in a larger physical environment with which it interacts asynchronously. In general, open systems are not totally in control of their fate. In contrast, closed systems (like Peano arithmetic and point-set topology) are exactly characterized by rules and laws.

Proponents of logic programming have maintained that it is a suitable basis for all programming and is the programming paradigm for the future. Logic programming has some fundamental limitations that preclude its becoming a satisfactory programming methodology. It is inadequate for the needs of open systems because it is based on logical operations instead of communication primitives, and logical reasoning instead of due-process reasoning. Decisions in open systems are justified by agreements to act in certain ways. Justification by agreement stands in contrast to justification by logical proof: interaction with the physical world involves dealing with conflicting and contradictory information in a way that does not fall within the scope of decision making by logical proof. Prolog also suffers from the limitation of "negation as failure" restricting it to a closed-world assumption that is incompatible with the nature of open systems.

We need foundations for intelligent systems based on principles of commutativity. Pluralism, accessibility, reflection in practice, and due-process reasoning. Logical reasoning is a useful module in the repertoire of an intelligent system, but it is not the whole show.

Notes

Many of the ideas in this paper have been developed jointly with the members of the MIT Message Passing Semantics Group and the Trement Research Institute. I would especially like to express my appreciation to Gul Agha, Gerald Barber, Peter de Jong, Elihu M. Gerson, and Susan Leigh Star for their aid and the foundational work on which this paper builds. Jonathan Amsterdam, Mike Brady, Mike Brooks, Toni Cohen, Peter de Jong, John Kam, Henry Lieberman, John Mallery, Fanya Montalvo, Karen Prendergast, Claudia Smith, and John Teeter provided valuable comments and criticisms that helped greatly to improve on earlier drafts. Over many years I have benefited from extensive interactions with Richard Weyhrauch, who has a profound understanding of the issues discussed here.

The content of this paper comes from talks I have given at Stanford University in June 1983, at panels for IFIP–83 in Paris, at the MIT Artificial Intelligence Laboratory in November 1983, at BBN, at MIT Sloan School, and at the AAAS in New York during June 1984. Comments, criticisms, and arguments developed in these seminars have been invaluable in developing this paper. I would like to express special appreciation to Bob Moore, Nils Nilsson, Steve Hardy, Richard Waldinger and others for valuable feedback during and after the Stanford seminar, Bob Kowalski and Doug Ross at the IFIP–83 panel, Ian Komorowski at the MIT seminar, David Israel at the BBN seminar, Tom Malone and Gerald Barber at the Sloan School seminar, as well as Victor Lesser, Jerry Hobbs, and Lucy Suchman at the AAAS session. Allen Newell took the time to give me an overview of some of the aspects of his recent work on foundations in July 1984.

This paper describes research done at the MIT Artificial Intelligence Laboratory. Major support for the research reported in this paper was provided by the System Development Foundation and Wang Laboratories. Major support for other related work at the Artificial Intelligence Laboratory is provided, in part, by the Advanced Research Projects Agency of the US Department of Defense under Office of Naval Research contract N0014–80–C–0505. I would like to thank Charles Smith and Patrick H. Winston for their support and encouragement.

Towards a reconciliation of phenomenology and AI

Stuart E. Dreyfus and Hubert L. Dreyfus

The traditional account of skills

The rationalist philosophical tradition which descends from Socrates, to Plato, to Leibniz, to Kant, to conventional AI and knowledge engineering takes it for granted that understanding a domain consists in having a theory about that domain. A theory formulates the relationships between objective, context-free features (attributes, factors, data points, cues, etc.) in terms of abstract principles (covering laws, rules, programs, etc.) As this tradition develops, even everyday practice is assumed to be based on unconscious theory.

In one of his earliest dialogues, *The Euthyphro*, Plato tells us of an encounter between Socrates and Euthyphro, a religious prophet and so an expert on pious behavior. Socrates asks Euthyphro to tell him how to recognize piety: "I want to know what is characteristic of piety . . . to use as a standard whereby to judge your actions and those of other men." But instead of revealing his piety-recognizing principles, Euthyphro does just what every expert does when cornered by Socrates. He gives him examples from his field of expertise; in this case situations in the past in which men and gods have done things which everyone considers pious. Socrates persists throughout the dialogue in demanding that Euthyphro tell him his rules, but although Euthyphro claims he knows how to tell pious acts from impious ones, he cannot state the rules which generate his judgments. Socrates ran into the same problem with craftsmen, poets, and even statesmen. None could articulate the theory underlying his behavior.

Plato admired Socrates and sympathized with his problem. So he developed a partial account of what caused the difficulty. In theoretical domains such as mathematics, at least, experts had once known the rules they use but then they had forgotten them. In these domains, the rules are there functioning in the expert's mind whether he is conscious of them or not. How else could we account for the fact that he can perform the task? The role of the philosopher is to help such experts remember the principles on which they act.

396

Plato's account did not apply to everyday skills but only to theoretical domains in which there is a priori knowledge. It took another thousand years before Leibniz boldly generalized the rationalist account to all forms of intelligent activity.

> [T]he most important observations and turns of skill in all sorts of trades and professions are as yet unwritten. This fact is proved by experience when passing from theory to practice we desire to accomplish something. *Of course, we can also write up this practice, since it is at bottom just another theory more complex and particular* . . .[1]

Now, three centuries after Leibniz, knowledge engineers such as Edward Feigenbaum say with confidence that the rules the expert uses have been put in a part of their mental computers where they work automatically.

> When we learned how to tie our shoes, we had to think very hard about the steps involved . . . Now that we've tied many shoes over our lifetime, that knowledge is "compiled," to use the computing term for it; it no longer needs our conscious attention.[2] We also have a new name for what Socrates and Plato were doing: "knowledge acquisition research."[3]

But although philosophers and even the man in the street have become convinced that expertise consists in applying sophisticated heuristics to masses of facts, there are few available rules. As Feigenbaum explains:

> [A]n expert's knowledge is often ill-specified or incomplete because the expert himself doesn't always know exactly what it is he knows about his domain.[4]

So the knowledge engineer has to help him recollect what he once knew.

> [An expert's] knowledge is currently acquired in a very painstaking way; individual computer scientists work with individual experts to explicate the expert's heuristics – the problem of knowledge acquisition is the critical bottleneck in artificial intelligence.[5]

When Feigenbaum suggests to an expert the rules the expert seems to be using he gets a Euthyphro-like response: "That's true, but if you see enough patients/rocks/chip designs/instrument readings, you see that it isn't true after all."[6] And Feigenbaum comments with Socratic annoyance: "At this point, knowledge threatens to become ten thousand special cases."[7]

There are also other hints of trouble. Ever since the inception of artificial intelligence, researchers have been trying to produce artificial experts by programming the computer to follow the rules used by masters in various domains. Yet, although computers are faster and more accurate than people in applying rules, master-level performance has remained out of reach. A recent evaluation of expert systems lists only 9 as being in commercial use out of some 180 that have been developed.[8] Of all the expert systems funded by the military, according to an authority in US

Defence Advanced Projects Research Agency, only one has gone beyond the prototype stage.

The same story is repeated in every area of expertise. In each area where there are experts with years of experience, the computer can do better than the beginner, and can even exhibit useful competence, but it cannot rival the very experts whose facts and supposed heuristics it is processing with incredible speed and unerring accuracy.

A phenomenological account of skill acquisition

In the face of this impasse it is necessary, in spite of the authority and influence of Plato and 2,000 years of philosophy, for us to take a fresh look at what a skill is and what the expert acquires when he achieves expertise. One must be prepared to abandon the traditional view that a beginner starts with specific cases and, as he becomes more proficient, abstracts and interiorizes more and more sophisticated rules. It might turn out that skill acquisition moves in just the opposite direction: from abstract rules to particular cases. Since we all have many areas in which we are experts, we have the necessary data, so let's look and see how adults learn new skills.

Stage 1: novice

Normally, the instruction process begins with the instructor decomposing the task environment into context-free features which the beginner can recognize without benefit of experience. The beginner is then given rules for determining actions on the basis of these features, like a computer following a program. The beginning student wants to do a good job, but lacking any coherent sense of the overall task, he judges his performance mainly by how well he follows his learned rules. After he has acquired more than just a few rules, so much concentration is required during the exercise of his skill that his capacity to talk or listen to advice is severely limited.

For purposes of illustration, we shall consider two variations: a bodily or motor skill and an intellectual skill. The student automobile driver learns to recognize such interpretation-free features as speed (indicated by his speedometer) and distance (as estimated by a previously acquired skill). Safe following distances are defined in terms of speed; conditions that allow safe entry into traffic are defined in terms of speed and distance of oncoming traffic; timing of shifts of gear is specified in terms of speed, etc. These rules ignore context. They do not refer to traffic density or anticipated stops.

The novice chess player learns a numerical value for each type of piece regardless of its position, and the rule: "always exchange if the total value of pieces captured exceeds the value of pieces lost." He also learns that when no advantageous exchanges can be found, center control should be sought, and he is given a rule defining center squares and one for calculating extent of control. Most beginners are notoriously slow players, as they attempt to remember all these rules and their priorities.

Stage 2: advanced beginner

As the novice gains experience actually coping with real situations, he begins to note, or an instructor points out, perspicuous examples of meaningful additional components of the situation. After seeing a sufficient number of examples, the student learns to recognize them. Instructional maxims now can refer to these new *situational aspects* recognized on the basis of experience, as well as to the objectively defined *non-situational features* recognizable by the novice. The advanced beginner confronts his environment, seeks out features and aspects, and determines his actions by applying rules. He shares the novice's minimal concern with quality of performance, instead focusing on quality of rule following. The advanced beginner's performance, while improved, remains slow, uncoordinated, and laborious.

The advanced beginner driver uses (situational) engine sounds as well as (non-situational) speed in his gear-shifting rules, and observes demeanor as well as position and velocity to anticipate behavior of pedestrians or other drivers. He learns to distinguish the behavior of the distracted or drunken driver from that of the impatient but alert one. No number of words can serve the function of a few choice examples in learning this distinction. Engine sounds cannot be adequately captured by words, and no list of objective facts about a particular pedestrian enables one to predict his behavior in a crosswalk as well as can the driver who has observed many pedestrians crossing streets under a variety of conditions.

With experience, the chess beginner learns to recognize over-extended positions and how to avoid them. Similarly, he begins to recognize such situational aspects of positions as a weakened king's side or a strong pawn structure despite the lack of precise and universally valid definitional rules.

Stage 3: competence

With increasing experience, the number of features and aspects that need to be taken account becomes overwhelming. To cope with this information explosion, the performer learns, or is taught, to adopt a hierarchical view of decision-making. By first choosing a plan, goal or perspective which organizes the situation and by then examining only the small set of features and aspects that he has learned are the most important given that plan, the performer can simplify and improve his performance.

Choosing a plan, a goal, or perspective, is no simple matter for the competent performer. He has expectations about how things will turn out but he is often surprised that his expectations are not fulfilled. No wonder. Nobody gives him any rules for how to choose a perspective, so the competent performer has to make up various rules which he then adopts or discards in various situations depending on how they work out. This procedure is frustrating, however, since each rule works on some occasion and fails on others, and no set of objective features and aspects correlates strongly with these successes and failures. Nonetheless the choice is unavoidable. While the advanced beginner can get along without recognizing and using a particular situational aspect until a sufficient number of examples makes identification easy and sure, to perform competently *requires* choosing an organizing goal or perspective. Furthermore, the choice of perspective crucially affects behavior in a way that one particular aspect rarely does.

This combination of necessity and uncertainty introduces an important new type of relationship between the performer and his environment. The novice and the advanced beginner applying rules and maxims feel little or no responsibility for the outcome of their acts. If they have made no mistakes, an unfortunate outcome is viewed as the result of inadequately specified elements or rules. The competent performer, on the other hand, after wrestling with the question of a choice of perspective or goal, feels responsible for, and thus emotionally involved in, the result of his choice. An outcome that is clearly successful is deeply satisfying and leaves a vivid memory of the situation encountered as seen from the goal or perspective finally chosen. Disasters, likewise, are not easily forgotten.

Remembered whole situations differ in one important respect from remembered aspects. The mental image of an aspect is flat in the sense that no parts stand out as salient. A whole situation, on the other hand, since it is the result of a chosen plan or perspective, has a "three-dimensional" quality. Certain elements stand out as more or less important with respect to the plan, while other irrelevant elements are forgotten. Moreover, the competent performer, gripped by the situation that his decision has produced, experiences the situation not only in terms of foreground and background elements but also in terms of senses of opportunity, risk, expectation, threat, etc. As we shall soon see, if he stops reflecting on problematic situations as a detached observer, and stops thinking of himself as a computer following better and better rules, these gripping, holistic experiences become the basis of the competent performer's next advance in skill.

A competent driver beginning a trip decides, perhaps, that he is in a hurry. He then selects a route with attention to distance and time, ignores scenic beauty, and as he drives, he chooses his maneuvers with little concern for passenger comfort or for courtesy. He follows more closely than normal, enters traffic more daringly, occasionally violates a law. He feels elated when decisions work out and no police car appears, and shaken by near accidents and traffic tickets.

The class A chess player, here classed as competent, may decide after studying a position that his opponent has weakened his king's defenses so that an attack against the king is a viable goal. If the attack is chosen, features involving weaknesses in his own position created by his attack are ignored as are losses of pieces inessential to the attack. Removal of pieces defending the enemy king becomes salient. Successful plans induce euphoria and mistakes are felt in the pit of the stomach.

In both of these cases, we find a common pattern: detached planning, conscious assessment of elements that are salient with respect to the plan, and analytical rule-guided choice of action, followed by an emotionally involved experience of the outcome.

Stage 4: proficiency

Considerable experience at the level of competency sets the stage for yet further skill enhancement. Having experienced many situations, chosen plans in each, and having obtained vivid, involved demonstrations of the adequacy or inadequacy of the plan, the performer involved in the world of the skill, "notices," or "is struck by" a certain plan, goal, or perspective. No longer is the spell of involvement broken by detached conscious planning.

Since there are generally far fewer "ways of seeing" than "ways of acting," after understanding without conscious effort what is going on, the proficient performer will still have to think about what to do. During this thinking, elements that present themselves as salient are assessed and combined by rule to produce decisions about how best to manipulate the environment. The spell of involvement in the world of the activity will thus temporarily be broken.

On the basis of prior experience, a proficient driver approaching a curve on a rainy day may sense that he is traveling too fast. Then, on the basis of such salient elements as visibility, angle of road bank, criticalness of time, etc., he decides whether to take his foot off the gas or to step on the brake. (These factors would be used by the *competent* driver consciously to *decide that* he is speeding.)

The proficient chess player, who is classed a master, can recognize a large repertoire of types of positions. Recognizing almost immediately and without conscious effort the sense of a position, he sets about calculating the move that best achieves his goal. He may, for example, know that he should attack, but he must deliberate about how best to do so.

Stage 5: expertise

The proficient performer, immersed in the world of his skillful activity, *sees* what needs to be done, but *decides* how to do it. With enough experience with a variety of situations, all seen from the same perspective (with the same goal, significance, issue), but requiring different tactical decisions, the proficient performer gradually decomposes this class of situations into subclasses, each of which share the same decision, single action, or tactic. This allows an immediate intuitive response to each situation which is characteristic of expertise.

The number of classes of discriminable situations, built up on the basis of experience, must be immense. It has been estimated that a master chess player can discriminate roughly 50,000 types of positions. Automobile driving probably requires the ability to discriminate a similar number of situations. These discriminable classes of stimulae, unlike the situational elements learned by the advanced beginner, bear no names and, in fact, defy complete verbal description.

While the proficient performer must be aware of the meaning of the situation in order to decide what to do in it, the expert is only sometimes aware of the significance of the situation. In those areas of activity such as martial arts, sports such as basketball and tennis, as well as the give and take of everyday social situations, an expert has no time to deliberate. The quality of expertise then depends on how many subtly different types of situations the brain can appropriately discriminate. Each type of situation calls forth an appropriate type of response. What transparently *must* be done *is* done.

In other types of activity such as business management, sensitive press conferences, sports like golf and bowling, and tournament chess, there is time to deliberate. Deliberation occurs in either of two types of cases. In one type, the same stimulae present themselves compellingly in several different Gestalts, i.e. under several different perspectives. Here the expert must decide what to see as the current issue. More commonly, but less crucially, the issue is clear but more than one response presents itself as attractive. Here the expert must decide what to do. In both cases the expert must deliberate. He uses such techniques as counting out (in formal games) or getting more information to decide between almost equally plausible interpretations or courses of action (in the everyday world). If the expert has had sufficient experience, simply choosing whatever looks best no matter how slight the difference will normally produce high quality performance. The above types of deliberative decision, however, determine who will have the edge.

The expert chess player, classed as an international master or grandmaster, in most situations experiences a compelling sense of the issue and the best move. Excellent chess players can play at the rate of five to ten seconds a move and even faster without any serious degradation in performance. At this speed they must depend almost entirely on intuition and hardly at all on analysis and comparison of alternatives. We recently performed an experiment in which an international master, Julio Kaplan, was required rapidly to add numbers presented to him audibly at the rate of about one number per second while at the same time playing five-second-a-move chess against a slightly weaker, but master level, player. Even with his analytical mind almost completely occupied by adding numbers, Kaplan more than held his own against the master in a series of games. Deprived during most of the game[9] of the time necessary to see problems or construct plans, Kaplan still produced fluid and coordinated, long-range strategic play.

Julio is only rarely aware of making plans and having expectations at all. But here the question arises: how can the expert initiate and carry through long-range strategies without having assessed the situation, chosen a perspective, made a plan, and formed expectation about how the situation will work out? To answer this question the tradition has assumed that goal-directed action must be based on conscious or unconscious planning involving beliefs, desires, and goals. If, however, the expert responds to each situation as it comes along in a way which has proven to be appropriate in the past, his behavior will achieve the past objectives without his having to have these objectives as goals in his conscious or unconscious mind. Thus the expert is moving into the future, and although he does not consciously entertain expectations, he is set to respond to some developments rather than others. If events take a turn that is new to him, he will be startled, and, at best, fall back to competence.

Kaplan's performance seems somewhat less amazing when one realizes that a chess position is as meaningful, interesting, and important to a professional chess player as a face in a receiving line is to a professional politician. Bobby Fischer, perhaps history's greatest chess player, once said that for him "chess is life." Almost anyone can add numbers and simultaneously recognize and respond to faces, even though the face will never exactly match the same face seen previously, and politicians can recognize thousands of faces just as Julio Kaplan can recognize thousands of chess positions similar to ones previously encountered.

Herbert Simon has studied the chess master's almost instantaneous understanding of chess positions and accompanying compelling sense of the best move. While it is in principle possible, in a formal game like chess, to associate a move with each different board position, there are far too many positions for such a method to be applied in practice. To cope with this difficulty he claims that chess masters are familiar with thousands of patterns, which he calls chunks. Each chunk is a remembered description of a small group of pieces in a certain relationship to each other. The master supposedly associates an appropriate move with each chunk. Each position thus causes a small number of moves to spring to the master's mind and he chooses among these without need for rule-like calculations.[10]

There are at least two problems with Simon's speculation. Because most chess positions are comprised of several chunks, at each move more than one move would come to mind and need to be evaluated before the player would have a sense of which was best. Yet, Julio Kaplan rarely seems to require such evaluation when he plays rapidly while simultaneously adding numbers. Hence Simon's conceptualization of chess in terms of chunk recognition, while providing a theory about why moves spring to mind, still seems to fall far short of the actual phenomenon of masterful play. Furthermore, for Simon, chunks such as a standard castled king's formation are defined independently of the rest of the position. A configuration that didn't quite fit the description of a chunk, but in a real chess position played the same role as the chunk, would not count as such. But chess players can recognize the functional equivalence of configurations which don't fall under a single definition. For example, in some cases a configuration would count as a standard castled king's formation even if one pawn were advanced, but in other cases it would not.

Simon's model can easily be programmed as a standard AI production system but it cannot account for the expert's normal ability intuitively to see one clearly preferable move. An elaboration of the production rule approach could in principle solve this problem without needing a production rule for every possible board position. What would be required would be a production rule for a large number of board positions and a rule for computing similarity, so that every position could be treated as identical to the one to which it was most similar. Such a system would map all positions directly into moves. The practical drawback is that no chess player has introspective knowledge of any rules for computing similarity. As we shall see in the next section, neural net models of the brain can accomplish this mapping without being programmed with explicit rules.

The expert driver, generally without any awareness, not only knows by feel and familiarity when an action such as slowing down is required, but he knows how to perform the action without calculating and comparing alternatives. He shifts gears when appropriate with no conscious awareness of his acts. Most drivers have experienced the disconcerting breakdown that occurs when suddenly one reflects on the gear-shifting process and tries to decide what to do. Suddenly the smooth, almost automatic, sequence of actions that results from the performer's involved immersion in the world of his skill is disrupted, and the performer sees himself, just as does the competent performer, as the manipulator of a complex mechanism. He detachedly calculates his actions even more poorly than does the competent performer since he has forgotten many of the guiding rules that he knew and used when competent, and his performance suddenly becomes halting, uncertain, and even inappropriate.

It seems that a beginner makes inferences using rules and facts just like a heuristically programmed computer, but that with talent and a great deal of involved experience the beginner develops into an expert who intuitively sees what to do without applying rules.

Given our account of the five stages of skill acquisition, we can understand why the knowledge engineers from Socrates to Feigenbaum have had such trouble getting the expert to articulate the rules he is using. The expert is simply not following any rules! He is doing just what Feigenbaum feared he might be doing – discriminating thousands of special cases. This in turn explains why expert systems are never as good as experts. If one asks the experts for rules one will, in effect, force the expert to regress to the level of a beginner and state the rules he still remembers but no longer uses. If one programs these rules on a computer one can use the speed and accuracy of the computer and its ability to store and access millions of facts to outdo a human beginner using the same rules. But no amount of rules and facts can capture the knowledge an expert has when he has stored his experience of the actual outcomes of tens of thousands of situations.

On the basis of our skill model we predict that in any domain in which people exhibit holistic understanding, no system based upon heuristics will consistently do as well as experienced experts, even if they were the informants who provided the heuristic rules. There is, however, at least one expert system that is both expert and heuristic and performs as well as anyone in its field. It is the very impressive XCON developed at Digital Equipment Corporation (DEC) to check the way components of VAX computers can be combined to meet customers' needs. This, however, is not a case of intuitive expertise. Even the experienced "technical editors" who perform the job at DEC depend on heuristic-based problem solving, and take about ten minutes to work out a simple case, so it is no surprise that an expert system can rival the best experts. In domains like the above where there are no intuitive experts – loading cargo vehicles seems to be another case – one can expect expert systems to be of great value.

The connectionist model

The knowledge engineer might still say that in spite of appearances the mind/brain of the expert *must* be reasoning – making millions of rapid and accurate inferences like a computer. After all the brain is not "wonder tissue" and how else could it work? But there *are* models for what might be going on in the hardware that make no use of the sort of symbols and principles presupposed in traditional philosophy and AI. That is, they do not use symbols that correspond to recognizable features of the world and rules that represent these features' relationships.

Such models are called connectionist models and use artificial neural systems and parallel distributed processing. Specifically we have in mind the most sophisticated models which not only have a set of elements that encodes the stimulae from the real world and a set that encodes an associated response, but also have intermediate (hidden) nodes which play a role in translating the input into the output. A recent example is Hinton's network for learning concepts by means of distributed representations.[11] Hinton's network can be trained to encode relationships in a domain, which human beings conceptualize in terms of features, without the network being given the features that human beings use. Hinton produces examples of cases in which in the trained network some nodes can be interpreted as corresponding to the features that human beings pick out, although they only roughly correspond to these features. Most nodes, however, cannot be semantically interpreted at all. A feature used in a concept is either present or not. In the net, however, although certain nodes are more active when a certain feature is present in the domain, the amount of activity varies not just with the presence or absence of this feature, but is affected by the presence or absence of other features as well.

Given the state of the art in conventional AI and what connectionism can do, how might one explain how the brain produces skilled behavior? We will sketch the mechanisms underlying the first and last stages of skill acquisition.

As we have already noted, the novice uses rules and features like a conventional AI program. Obviously, this processing is performed by interconnected neurons, but the question is open which if any of the connectionist models proposed thus far can instantiate procedures which allow the appropriate level of abstraction. As far as we can see, it makes no philosophical difference how the formal operations employed by conventional AI in producing novice performance are instantiated.

While it is easy to see how conventional AI explains the feature-detecting and inference-making of the novice, and hard to see how a connectionist network would implement the required step-wise processing, when we turn to the expert, things are reversed. A connectionist account of learning by examples and recognition of similarity seems much more natural than any conventional AI account.

A neural net such as Hinton's is demonstrably capable of adjusting its connection strengths and thresholds so as to produce a desired output for each member of a specified set of inputs. (Hinton's program for learning family relationships learns 100 such input/output pairs.)

Similarity recognition, while crucial to intuitive expertise, plays no role in Hinton's concept-learning model. It could, however, easily be incorporated in a connectionist architecture. Consider the case where a massive Hinton-like network is used to map inputs representing chess positions into outputs which are representations of the issue and one or more associated moves. Any new chess position which is not identical with any previous learned input will produce some particular output. If that output is similar to the learned issue/action output which has been associated with some given input position P, one can say that the system has recognized the new input position as similar to position P. Such a net can be said to recognize similarity without using a predefined similarity measure – without asking and answering the question: "similar with respect to what?" Similarity simply means in this case whatever the net takes to be similar based on its particular past training.

Sometimes the outputs will not be interpretable as representations of any issue and move. Then the system can be said to recognize that the current input is not similar to any input to which it has been exposed. In the above way, a large enough net should be able to discriminate the approximately 50,000 different situations which a grandmaster needs to distinguish, and to respond to a new situation as similar to one of these or as outside its intuitive expertise.

Conclusion

What are the implications of all this for conventional AI? That, of course, depends on what you take to be the essential commitments of conventional AI, and also on what one means by a distributed representation. We shall attempt to distinguish three progressively non-conventional senses of distribution. Although we describe each kind of distribution abstractly, we shall also use Hinton's network for learning family relationships to illustrate what we have in mind by each type. In so doing, we shall discuss possible interpretations of Hinton's first level of hidden nodes.

Conventional AI generally takes as the features in terms of which to encode the relevant structure of a domain the sort of features which human beings can pick out and use. Thus from Newell and Simon's protocols, through frames, scripts, procedures, and productions, to recent knowledge engineering, AI has used introspection to determine what features to use. As we have seen, even in a net as simple as Hinton's, after learning a set of associations some nodes can sometimes be interpreted as simple feature detectors, i.e. as detecting the sort of features human beings use in conceptualizing a domain. This would be a case of non-distributed representation.

These everyday features (for Hinton, generation, nationality, etc.) could also be represented in a distributed way, i.e. when one of these features is present a certain *group* of nodes would always be active. However, representations can be distributed in a second, stronger sense. Single nodes or even sets of nodes need not detect the sorts of features people pick out. They could equally well detect combinations of these features. To take the simplest case: if there are two hidden nodes and three features A, B, and C, and only one of these features can be present in any given input, then if one hidden node detects the presence of either A or B, and one detects the presence of B or C, the behavior of these two will uniquely determine which feature is present. So it is not necessary that one node detect A, one detect B, and both together, say, detect C.

In Hinton's model, one node or group of nodes might, for example, detect both second generation Italians and English people on the left side of their family tree. Once one admits that the features are distributed this second way, there is no reason to believe that in large networks, the distributed features are the sort that the mind can recognize or even unconsciously use. Moreover, in the third and most extreme case, there is no reason to suppose that the features being detected are any combination of the features people ordinarily detect. In Hinton's model, it is not obvious that nationality or generation need play any role in learning to map the input information (person and relationship) into the output (another person). In this case the Hinton model could be said to be using features which are abstract and non-mental.

Hinton has picked a domain, family relationships, which is constructed by human beings precisely in terms of the features human beings normally notice, such as generation and nationality. Furthermore, though some people can be better than others in figuring out these family relationships, the domain is so small and combinatorial it does not lend itself to intuitive expertise. Hinton's paper analyzes those cases in which, for certain random initial connection strengths, some nodes can be interpreted as representing the everyday features people use. Our experience with Hinton's model shows, however, that even his model seems, for some random initial connection strengths, to learn its associations without any obvious use of these everyday features.

If in domains that people analyze in terms of everyday features the network uses other features, one would expect the situation to be even worse for interpreting nodes of neural nets that have been trained to capture intuitive expertise. For example, if it turns out that the brain processes information using distributions of the third kind in domains such as chess, then if one could train a neural net to capture the mapping of situations to issues and moves that a given player has seen, there would be no reason to believe that the individual nodes or combinations of nodes could be interpreted as detecting the sort of features that people talk about in chess, or even the 50,000 context-free chunks that Simon would like to isolate.

It seems that the above combination of phenomenology and connectionism may well be devastating to conventional AI as a *practical* endeavor. Could anything be salvaged of the cognitivist-rationalist intuition that for any domain that can be mastered, there exists a set of features and rules which explains that mastery? If the connectionist hierarchical account turns out to be correct,[12] then, given any particular domain and the experience of a particular person in that domain, there would, indeed, always exist an account of his expertise in terms of higher-order abstract features. To construct this account from the network that has learned his associations, each node one level above the input nodes could be interpreted as detecting when one of a certain set of input patterns is present. If the set of input patterns which that particular node detects is given an invented name (it almost certainly won't have a name in our vocabulary), the nodes could be interpreted as detecting the feature so named. Hence, every node one level above the input level can be characterized as a feature detector. Similarly, every node a level above these nodes can be interpreted as detecting a higher-order feature which is defined as the presence of one of a specified set of patterns among the first-level features detectors. And so on up the hierarchy.

The fact that a given expert's expertise can always be accounted for in terms of relations among a number of highly abstract features of his skill domain does not, however, preserve the rationalist intuition that these explanatory features must capture the essential structure of the domain. If the net is taught one more association of an input/output pair (where the input prior to training produces an output different from the one to be learned), the interpretation of at least some of the nodes will have to be changed. So the features which some of the nodes picked out before the last instance of training could turn out not to have been invariant structural features of the domain.[13] The traditional rationalist account of skilled behavior would in this case be shown to be mistaken. Skill would turn out to be based not on principles and features but characteristics of whole situations. The philosophical dream of rational analysis would have to be abandoned.

Notes

1 Leibniz, *Selections*, edited by Philip Wiener (New York: Scribner, 1951), p. 48 (our italics).
2 See Feigenbaum and McCorduck (1983) *The Fifth Generation*, p. 55.
3 *Ibid.*, p. 79.
4 *Ibid.*, p. 85.
5 *Ibid.*, pp. 79–80.
6 *Ibid.*, p. 82.
7 *Ibid.*, p. 82.
8 See Waterman (1986), *A Guide to Expert Systems*.
9 At a few points in the game when things do not seem obvious and deliberation of the type described above is called for, Julio sneaks in a bit of short range look-ahead. His addition slows down a fraction of a second and he sometimes makes mistakes in his addition.
10 See Simon (1979) *Models of Thought*, pp. 386–403.
11 See Hinton (1986) Learning Distributed Representations of Concepts.
12 Obviously no one thinks that the Hinton type model captures in detail what is going on in the brain. For example, the brain seems to use lateral connections with feedback at each level and neurons respond in complex ways to their neighbors. However, these considerations seem to only complicate but not to negate the philosophical issue we wish to raise.
13 As long as the behavior of each pattern-recognizing net at each point in its training must be explained in terms of some different features, there is no guarantee that the similarities picked out by a given net, in the way described in the previous section, are the ones that would produce high-quality performance across the domain. Unless the system detects as similar the class of inputs which require the same response in the real world, the system will respond to overall patterns without analysis like an expert but will not produce masterly perform-ance. Class A and expert level chess players, when playing intuitively, do not share a sense of similarity with each other, i.e. they often disagree with each

other as to whether two board positions present the same issue or require the same type of move.

Chess grandmasters, on the contrary, exhibit remarkable unanimity when evaluating a position. One can speculate that they have had so much chess experience that the number of neurons in their brain dedicated to the chess net has approached the minimum necessary for encoding their experience (or, conversely, their number of chess experiences is approaching the largest that a fixed number of neurons can correctly associate), and that therefore the abstract, higher-order, non-mental features they detect are the minimal necessary features for getting the job done. This seems to be the only remnant of the cognitivist-rationalist intuition that expertise can always be explained in terms of stable features that depend only on the domain and not on the particular set of experiences of the expert. Such abstract, higher-order features, however, would not be useful to conventional AI and would only be domain-independent relative to the size of the net of neurons dedicated to this domain.

The superarticulacy phenomenon in the context of software manufacture

Donald Michie

1 Divergent growth-curves of hardware and software

A natural inference from the tabulation shown in table 1 is that a crisis of under-production relative to need is developing in the programming industry. The inference is borne out by the rate at which programmers' salaries are rising, especially in the USA.

Table 1. *Widening gap between supply and industry requirement for programming (Dolotta, 1976)*

indicator	1955	1965	1975	1985
industry size	1	20	80	320
hardware performance for fixed cost	1	100	10 000	1 000 000
programmer productivity	1	2.0	2.7	3.6

University training of new generations of programmers is now commonly interrupted by the lure of a quick start in industry. Temptation is heightened by a further salary bonus if the student's Master's dissertation was in the branch of software technology known as knowledge engineering. This circumstance offers a convenient introduction to my theme. In knowledge engineering, where the malady is most acute, the beginnings of a remedy can today be discerned. Partial but cost-effective automation of program construction has been shown feasible via computer induction, that is to say by the inductive synthesis of rules (which are run on the machine as program modules) from examples of expert decision taking.

Knowledge engineering, like steam engineering before it, is defined by the nature of its characteristic artifact We do not, as a matter of fact, ordinarily speak of knowledge engines, but rather of expert systems. Table 2 sets forth the salient features of the old species of problem-solving computer program, table 3 outlines the new, knowledge-based species and table 4 sketches its mode of operation.

411

Table 2. *The behaviour of a conventional system is driven by the instruction sequence*

conventional algorithm-based system

- deterministic
- no redundancy ('brittle')
- no self-explanation possible
- opaque
- incremental improvement difficult

Table 3. *The behaviour of a production-rule system is driven by pattern-matches with the database*

rule-based system

| database | $\xrightarrow{\hspace{2cm}}$ $\xleftarrow{\hspace{2cm}}$ | situation–action rules |

situation: a pattern that may or may not be satisfied in the database
action: some process that possibly changes the database

Table 4. *The 'recognize-act' cycle for execution of production rules. The action may have the form of offering advice or asking a question. If the user responds by querying the action the system may explain it by displaying the sequence of rules which triggered it*

each cycle the inference engine:
    finds which rules have their situation part satisfied in the 'database';
    selects one of them to be 'fired';
    performs the action part of the selected rule (thus possibly changing the data

The following inter-linked questions will be discussed. (1) Can bodies of knowledge be automatically synthesized from expert-supplied data when the expert possessors of this knowledge cannot give an articulate account of it? (2) Can the synthetic knowledge be cast into a sufficiently human mould to put into the practitioner's hands a new kind of reference text?

2 Manufacture of factual knowledge

Synthetic knowledge is not in essence new. At the tedious level of ground-level facts, the manufacture of new knowledge has been in progress for over a century in the preparation of numerical tables. In their way these exemplify machine-aided synthesis of knowledge. In the nineteenth century, Charles Babbage played a part in developing the arts of numerical tabulation by machine. Although these arts today make massive contributions to factual knowledge, from an AI point of view one regards them as useful but not interesting. I shall consider their extension along two dimensions. First is the increase in the size of tabulations, becoming possible with the advent of cheap trillion-bit memories. I shall discuss the use that can be made of this new development, not only for numerical tabulations, but more generally for the preparation of very large dictionaries of non-numerical facts. The second dimension is concerned not with the quantity of the knowledge encoded in lookup form, but rather with the quality. Here the tabulations' questions and answers are descriptions rather than atomic individual facts. Hence a step is taken towards machine synthesis of concept-structured knowledge.

3 Possibility of manufacturing descriptions from facts

Before discussing synthetic methods, let me recall the difficulties that confront what is called 'dialogue acquisition' as a method of building an expert system. Anybody who works with experts as a source of expertise for preparing commercial knowledge bases soon becomes painfully aware, as does the expert, that the latter has a highly subjective perception of where his strengths and weaknesses lie. The expert tends to be rather modest about the things that he is good at. He is aware that he can recognize examples of key concepts. This is the skill that primarily he is hired for. To the onlooker, the speed at which a highly experienced specialist comes to correct snap decisions seems miraculous. The basis for these snap decisions is hard for the expert to formulate or codify in spite of a strong subjective impression that he is capable of this codification. In point of fact, he is not. Above a certain level of complexity of the domain, he may be almost without merit as a source of descriptions. It is becoming generally appreciated that the expert's faith in his own capacity to articulate is not well founded.

Better founded is the expert's belief that he is good at identifying the key primitives of his specialized problem domain. He can usually supply a list of primitive measurements or attributes that are relevant. An expert-supplied list typically includes not only virtually all the attributes needed to develop classifications of a domain, but very often a number of additional 'passenger' attributes. At the end of the knowledge engineering cycle these passengers are found left on one side as logically redundant. From a practical standpoint their initial presence imposes no significant handicap. Nor would it be correct to assume that the redundant attributes are not providing some kind of cognitive support for the expert, although they are not relevant to knowledge engineering as practised today.

Further, the expert knows that he is good at generating tutorial examples. Indeed, that is a key skill for which his employer normally hires him. The expert is not only supposed to perform, he is also supposed to train and to indoctrinate new recruits in his job. To the bystander, his ability to implant the right concepts in the head of the trainee by cleverly selected and sequenced tutorial examples is impressive. We may reasonably conclude that instead of building expert systems on the one competence which he does not possess, we should build on what he does possess: the ability to identify key primitives; the ability to generate good tutorial examples; and the ability to act as an oracle to recognize key examples and to assess the performance of the trainee.

So to reconstruct the intuitive decision rules of the imperfectly articulate expert, we seek to automatically generate them from examples. We can then use the expert in the style to which he is accustomed when he uses illustrative cases in training his apprentices. It is noticeable how frustrated the expert becomes when he is asked to supply satisfactory rules under the dialogue-acquisition discipline, perhaps not altogether surprising when one considers that this method demands explicit articulation of rules which, for the most part, he stores subliminally. But when he is provided with software tools suitable for the example-driven style, then he is in his element. Since the availability of the domain expert is a critical factor in knowledge engineering work, whatever will speed him up and make him feel at home is commercially advantageous. Our laboratory now routinely uses for this purpose variants of Quinlan's ID3 (Iterative Dichotomiser 3) algorithm for inductively generating decision trees (see table 5).

Table 5. *Quinlan's ID3 (Iterative Dichotomiser 3) can convert a set of expert-supplied example decisions into a machine-executable decision tree*

ID3

given: a collection of positive and negative *instances*, where each instance is the description of an object in terms of a fixed set of *attributes* or properties

produces: a decision tree for differentiating positive and negative instances

4 Opacity of decision-trees as descriptions

Although not in common use in AI, decision-trees are not difficult to connect with more classical production rule systems. On the other hand, beyond a rather trivial level of task complexity, when a decision-tree representation is shown to the expert, he does not recognize it as being part of his mental world. The example I will give is a relatively simple chess endgame, king and pawn against king. The task is the classification of positions arbitrarily selected from a space of about 80,000. In each given case is it a win for the pawn side, or is it a draw? This is a recognition that a chessmaster can perform within a second or two, and was the subject of study by Shapiro and Niblett (1982). Table 6 was generated by ID3. It runs very fast as Pascal code, and classifies correctly every member of the problem space. The result is complete, correct and efficient, but a

Table 6. *Example of a decision-tree program synthesized by application of ID3 to an exhaustive file of examples*

```
No of examples in final window = 304
No of nodes in final tree = 79
Time taken to generate rule = 113 CPU seconds
imcap
    f:psquare
        f:wkahd
            f:LOST
            t:near c 8
                f:LOST
                t:DRAWN
        t:rookpawn
            f:pmove
                f:mpl
                    f:r 6patt
                        f:dirop 56
                            f:mp 56
                                f:btop 1
                                    f:rank 56
                                        f:DRAWN
                                        t:LOST
                                    t:interfere
                                        f:plus 2
                                            f:ahead
                                                f:LOST
                                                t:DRAWN
                                            t:DRAWN
                                        t:ahead
                                            f:DRAWN
                                            t:LOST
                                t:rank 56
                                    f:rank 7
                                        f:mp 2
                                            f:diropw
                                                f:interfere
                                                    f:DRAWN
                                                    t:LOST
                                                t:LOST
                                            t:LOST
                                        t:stimt
                                            f:plus 1
                                                f:LOST
                                                t:diropb
                                                    f:DRAWN
                                                    t:LOST
                                            t:DRAWN
                                    t:LOST
                            t:LOST
                        t:LOST
                    t:stimt
                        f:LOST
                        t:DRAWN
                t:stimt
                    f:LOST
                    t:mp 1
                        f:DRAWN
                        t:LOST
            t:near c 8
                f:rp 1
                    f:near 2 p
                        f:stalemate
                            f:nearp
                                f:rp 2
                                    f:near a 8
                                        f:LOST
                                        t:DRAWN
                                    t:DRAWN
                                t:ahead
                                    f:plus 2
                                        f:LOST
                                        t:DRAWN
                                    t:DRAWN
                            t:DRAWN
                        t:DRAWN
                    t:LOST
                t:crit
                    f:DRAWN
                    t:plus 1
                        f:wkand
                            f:LOST
                            t:DRAWN
                        t:DRAWN
        t:DRAWN
```

Table 7. *Information-processing parameters of the 'brain machine' which critically exclude three forms commonly encountered in representations designed for computing machines, namely: (1) database-like, (2) algorithmic, (3) ramifying, as in the arbitrarily nested 'if-then-else' expressions corresponding to unrestricted decision trees*

(1) maximum amount of information explicitly storable by the age of 50	10^{10} bits	excludes very *shallow* representations
(2) number of mental discriminations per second during intellectual work	18	excludes very *deep* representations
(3) number of addresses which can be held in short-term memory	7	excludes very *branched* representations

failure as an expert system. To the expert, such a ramifying and formless decision-structure is opaque, unmemorizable and not mentally checkable. So however useful it may be as an embodiment of information, as an embodiment of knowledge it is not useful. A chessmaster does not recognize any meaning in it. Translation into English does not make it more transparent.

We should look at the reason why this is so. Let us concentrate attention on three numerical facts about human cognition against which annotations have been placed in table 7. Starting from the bottom, we first encounter George Miller's magical number seven, plus or minus two; the number of addresses which can be held in short-term memory. The smallness of this number excludes very branched representations. It excludes even mildly branched representations. The problem is that the significance of any attribute call (node in the decision-tree) depends on how control arrived at that particular call. Therefore to keep track of the whereabouts of control in the tree and to interpret a node's outcome branches requires an index of the tree. As background for this see a brief discussion of tree-indexing methods by Snyder (1984). Other than in very trivial cases, maintaining and processing such an index requires a bigger short-term memory than seven locations. So arbitrary decision-trees are poor models for human concepts, being in the general case unintelligible to the human, unmemorizable and impossible to execute in the head.

5 Constraints of processing power

We should now look at other numerical properties of information structures which can lock the human out, either through his being unable to execute the structure or being unable to understand it, or both. Consider the very slow calculation speed of the brain, about twenty bits per second. The estimates in table 7, characterizing as they do biological material, are subject to variations possibly as large as plus or minus a factor of two. But it is not really material whether the calculation speed is twenty or ten or forty bits per second. In modern supercomputers, calculation rates are now measured in hundreds of millions of machine instructions per second, corresponding to more than a billion bits per second. So, compared with the bit rate of computer processes, the brain as a calculator is slow. If we are to remain faithful, as we must, to human forms when practising the arts of knowledge-based programming, computationally deep representations are therefore disqualified. That is to say, representations which are processor-intensive cannot share with concept-expressions the property of being executable by the user's brain.

The exclusion of processor-intensive, or deep, representations was well-known to Claude Shannon as early as 1950. In his paper (Shannon, 1950) he satirized a belief which is still common even among professional people, namely that intellectual giants owe their performance to thinking faster than others. This view is wrong. A chess grandmaster does not calculate more than a club player. As a matter of fact he calculates somewhat less (see, for example, de Groot, 1946).

Shannon envisaged two intellectual giants whom he called Mr A and Mr B. He used this fantasy to illustrate the 'foregone conclusion' theorem of two-person games of a certain class. Such games are in principle decideable by exhaustive calculation. Mr A and Mr B sit down opposite each other and briefly survey the chessboard. Then one of three things happens: either Mr A says 'I resign' or Mr B says 'I resign' or Mr A says 'I offer a draw' and Mr B says 'I accept'.

What is wrong with this story? At twenty bits a second, there is no time for skilled decisions unless they can be assembled from ready-made patterns in memory. Heroic mental exploration of a tree of possibilities containing more than 10^{40} nodes is not an option. Any calculative sequence which cannot be fitted into the three minute average allowance in tournament chess is ruled out. In lightning chess, skill becomes yet more pattern-intensive. Opportunities for the forms of reasoning employed by the correspondence chess player do not arise at all. In spite of that, a grandmaster of world calibre playing lightning chess generates a quality of chess that is at least of international master quality, almost entirely on pattern lookup.

Even a numerical calculating prodigy, who makes his living by lightning calculations on the stage, does not calculate faster than his audience. Instead he exploits a lifetime's accumulation of pattern-indexed and cross-referenced mental catalogues of the properties of the number system and useful calculative tricks, from which he assembles a 'plan of calculation' (Hunter, 1962). These mental catalogues are not to be thought of as structureless aggregations of elementary facts, but as highly organized conceptual constructs. Once he starts executing the plan, or program as we may call it in the present context, the calculating prodigy has no more hardware to bring to bear than any member of his audience. It seems that memory is all, but it has to be *organized* not brute-force memory. The brain cannot batter down the task-complexity barrier by sheer dictionary power. To understand why not, we must refer again to table 7.

6 Constraints of memory capacity

As table 7 shows, the maximum amount of information that is explicitly storable in retrievable long-term memory by the age of fifty is about ten to the power ten bits. This can be confirmed by simple arithmetic on the typical rate of input along any channel into long-term memory. The rate is thirty bits per second (plus or minus a possible two-fold variation). There are only 32 million seconds in a year. Hence even if someone had been taking in information about chess at maximum rate and remembering it all, to memorize a tabular representation requiring ten to the ten bits would be at best marginally possible in the time. So very shallow (lookup) representations are ruled out.

Thus complex concepts cannot validly be modelled in computer memory as lookup tables. Yet economic considerations are driving the software industry in that direction. A new situation is developing from a trend in hardware capability. Processing per dollar, as is well known, has been getting cheaper. So has memory been getting cheaper. But memory has been getting cheaper faster. The result is that the economics of computing machines has been tilting, more every year, towards memory-intensive representations. Trillion-bit optical disc memories are no longer expensive. The efficiency of a given problem representation depends on the relative cost of processor to memory. We are therefore likely to find the use of new forms of representation for some applications, namely in the shape of giant stored lookup tables. The areas of application in which these will first move outside the laboratory are problem domains of high complexity. For the most part, these are the same domains which attract AI work. But the kinds of brute-force tabular solutions which will be the first to emerge have very little in common with AI representations. A harbinger of what is to come is the software system developed by Ferranti for giving effect to pilot commands in high-speed manoeuverable aircraft by appropriate responses of the head-up display. Some seventy logical states of the total system are distinguished, each setting a separate context in which an appropriate input-output function can be defined. The corresponding (states $\times$ command-patterns) matrix contains two or three thousand cells, in each of which an appropriate response pattern is entered to give a complete table-driven solution. Even in this simple case, for some purposes, such as maintaining and modifying the matrix, more concept-oriented representations of the same information would be advantageous. For a more complex case, involving tens of thousands, or millions, of cells, the tabular representation would necessarily have to be replaced or accompanied by a concept-oriented structure. The following example will illustrate in a more complex case some of the issues to be resolved before table-driven solutions can readily be transformed into concept expressions.

7 Lookup strategies embodying superhuman skill

In tasks of the highest complexity, the art of correct decision-taking is simply not accessible to human cognition. Such skills exist in principle but are not acquirable by man through any amount of unaided effort. Mr John Roycroft is one of the world's leading scholars of the chess endgame, regarded as an intellectually deeper specialism that the tournament play of the unrestricted game of chess itself. Through the combined good offices of a number of institutions Mr Roycroft became available for an eighteen-month collaborative study. He identified the endgame king and two bishops against king and knight (KBBKN) as having the desired property of inaccessibility to unaided human expertise. The problem space comprises the order of 10^8 legal positions and had wrongly been believed to be in general a draw. At Mr Roycroft's instigation Mr Kenneth Thompson of Bell Laboratories, Murray Hill, USA, computed by an exhaustive method a complete lookup table in which against every legal position was entered the information (1) whether the position is won for White or drawn and (2) if the former then which subset of moves legally available from the given position are optimal moves.

This computation provided the first in what has become a series of surprises. With the exception of a few freak positions, the KBBKN game, regarded by masters as a draw, was shown to be won by White against any defence from any starting position within the entire problem space. The worst case requires a total of 66 moves by white, which when put together with Black's 65 replies amounts to 131 'plies'. Dr Alen Shapiro subsequently augmented Thompson's work with the addition of an interactive user-interface. A player can now engage in the play of either side against a move-perfect lookup-driven opponent. This facility was reserved for the second phase of an experiment planned in four phases. In all phases we ignored the stipulation derivable from the official laws of chess that for a win to be valid in a pawnless ending it must not contain more than fifty successive non-capture moves. Figure 1 shows the frequency distribution of legal White-to-move positions plotted against distance from the goal along the optimal path. A curious feature is the presence in the distribution of two 'pinches' of which the more extreme (containing no more than 100,000 positions) occupies the interval 38–44 moves from the end, which is defined as checkmate of safe knight capture. This later 'pinch' is associated with a celebrated family of positions named after Kling and Horwitz (1851) which

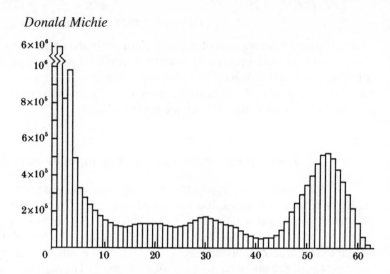

Figure 1   Depth (horizontal axis) of legal KBBKN White-to-move positions plotted against frequency (vertical axis)

has a conjectured property of 'unavoidability' according to which optimal play starting sufficiently far from the goal is obliged to pass through a member of this family, exiting via one of only four essentially different positions of the critical cluster. Figure 2 shows these four Kling and Horowitz exit positions.

Phase 1 During the first phase Mr Roycroft was not allowed access to the lookup table. His task was to see how far he could climb up this rock face, so to speak, by intensive study using his own resources. These were supplemented by the knowledge that move-perfect winning play was theoretically attainable. He had also been allowed a small piece of machine-generated knowledge to give him courage; of the thirty-two positions which are most distant from the kill he had been given one, and had also been given twelve machine-generated optimal variations leading from it to the goal. This as already stated lies sixty-six moves from each one of the thirty-two worst-case start positions.

After four months of uninterrupted study of the KBBKN game, Mr Roycroft announced the end of the first phase, in the sense that he had gained all the mastery of it that he felt was in his unaided power to gain. Testing his performance as White against the table-driven machine defence confirmed his subjective prediction that his mastery would be shown to be patchy. In two of ten test games he 'offered a draw' after much inconclusive skirmishing. The average 'path efficiency' (Doran and Michie, 1966) of his play was 38 percent.

Phase 2 Mr Roycroft was allowed free access to the database, from which he could obtain an instant answer to any factual question he cared to put. He thus had unlimited machine access to facts, but not to concepts. After all, the machine did not have these. We were in a sense testing Roycroft's brain as a device for turning facts into concepts. This phase ran for two

either side to move

number 1

number 2

number 3

number 4

Figure 2   The four known Black-to-move compulsory exits from a Kling and Horowitz position. In 1 Black loses in 39, in 2 and 3 in 38, but in 4 Black loses in 40 moves. 1, 2 and 3 occur in the computer output supplied by Ken Thompson in 1985, but 4 does not. 4 seems to occur very rarely

Table 8. *The upper ten test positions were administered to the subject (A.J.R)*
at the end of phase 1, and the lower ten at the end of phase 2 (see text)

(Path efficiency is the ratio between optimal depth and solution depth, expressed as a
percentage.)

number	WK	WB	position WB	BK	BN	optimal depth	A.J.R.'s estimate of depth	A.J.R.'s solution depth	path efficiency (%)
1	c2	d5	f2	f4	h7	54	55	68	79
2	d2	c1	g8	a8	a5	19	52	52	37
3	c1	c8	f8	a4	d8	51	—	122	42
4	b1	d6	e8	e6	h5	58	57	abandoned after 75	0
5	b2	e1	b3	e2	g1	60	54	109	55
6	c1	c3	a2	e7	a3	51	—	abandoned after 69	0
7	d2	h7	c1	h2	d7	20	18	34	59
8	c2	d2	c8	g2	h1	15	15	32	47
9	c1	a3	a4	f1	f2	17	19	53	32
10	d2	g5	e8	h8	f8	18	20	66	27
	WK	WB	WB	BK	BN				
11	c2	c1	a6	f2	b6	20	16	114	18
12	d4	g5	f3	f2	h6	16	20	111	14
13	c2	f6	h5	h2	d5	17	16	18	94
14	c2	e6	h8	b4	e1	18	19	20	90
15	d4	b2	g8	f4	d6	49	34	abandoned after 60	0
16	a1	g1	e8	g7	d2	56	40	74	76
17	a1	h7	a3	d2	h5	53	36	74	72
18	b1	c5	g4	d5	b3	60	57	abandoned after 92	0
19	c1	c8	c7	e2	g6	54	46	85	64
20	a1	c7	a4	d2	f6	59	49	68	87

months, at the end of which he felt that he had failed to use the time to
significant advantage, and remained at a loss as to how to set out the needed
facts-to-concepts conversion. Systematic tests partly confirmed Mr Roycroft's impression of lack of progress. Again two out of ten tests were failed,
but the mean efficiency stood somewhat higher, at 50 percent. Table 8
summarizes the results obtained from the two sets of tests.

Whether a professional cryptanalyst or a trained scientist placed under
identical conditions would find himself equally at a loss is not yet known.
These professions uniquely inculcate a developed craft of converting raw
facts to concepts. Until results are to hand we cannot be sure how far the
Roycroft result should be generalized.

Phase 3 Instead of interactive access to the multi-mega-store of atomic
facts, Mr Roycroft will be provided with a small number of specimen
sequences of optimal play, variations analogous to those available to him
for study during phase 1, but carefully pre-selected to represent sparsely

scattered sub-spaces in the total problem space. We have suggestive evidence that facts structured into such 'molecular' form constitute assimilable and potentially instructive material whereas even a superabundancy of individual facts does not.

Phase 4 Others associated with the project, Stephen Muggleton and Alen Shapiro, have undertaken the long-term task of building an expert system that has complete mastery, not in the purely operational sense of the present table-driven program, but as a concept-structured program which can thereby codify and explain its skill along lines already show feasible in small domains (Shapiro, 1987; Shapiro and Michie, 1986). The method is the inductive inference of concept-structured rules from database-stored examples. This is the 'superarticulacy' phenomenon.

8 Commercial uses of superarticulacy

Phase 4 aims to make it possible for Roycroft to inject the machine's tactical conceptualization of the entire task into his own head in such a way that he acquires the mental mastery for himself. The aimed-for transformation is thus:

human expert + expert system → human superexpert.

The machine system now acts as tutor, coaching the human expert interactively through the medium of annotated and structured examples.

In enquiring into anticipated commercial benefits of success with this development – always supposing that it proves susceptible to generalization to other skills including industrial – we may assess likely impact at various levels. In his lecture to the Siemens Foundation, C. Freeman (1985) characterized three levels in the following terms:

(i) Incremental innovation: This is a relatively smooth continuous process leading to steady improvement in the array of existing products and services and the way in which they are produced . . .

(ii) Radical innovations: These are discontinuous events and may lead to serious dislocations, economic perturbations and adjustments for the firms in a particular sector . . .

(iii) Technological revolutions: These are the 'creative gales of destruction'. The introduction of railways or electric power are examples of such transformations.

9 Incremental innovation: more productive programmers

Today the introduction of code generators working on the 'rules from examples' principle is beginning to affect the economics of software production in large development projects. Dr M A-Razzak and his colleagues have developed a Fortran-based inductive software tool (Hassan et al., 1985) to produce compact and reliable Fortran 77 code at rates exceeding 100 lines per man day. This is a tenfold advance on rates regarded as typical in the industry as a whole. One application, co-developed with ITT (Europe), was in computer diagnosis of faults in printed circuit boards; another with a multinational oil company involved parameter setting for batch runs of numerical routines for seismic analysis. More recently, the Rocketdyne division of Rockwell International has found similar gains in use of the same software tool to construct an expert system for assessing tests of the Space Shuttle's main engines (Asgari and Modesitt 1986).

10 Radical innovations: superarticulate programs

The foregoing are examples of quantitative augmentation of the cost effectiveness of program synthesis. Gains derive more from automation of the inductive inference component of the programming process than from any radical approach to articulacy. As with heavier-than-air flight in the nineteenth century, self-articulate software has been seen as desirable but not in general realizable. I shall review evidence that past incapacity to develop the needed self-articulacy has in certain areas of high engineering complexity brought matters to a point of industrial and military peril. I shall also support the position that this incapacity need not continue.

Instances where technology is vanquished by complexity abound in the control and operation of civil and military engineering systems. Some conspicuous examples are: (1) failure of operators to intervene when sophisticated factory automation systems have drifted beyond their ambit of effective control; (2) the Three Mile Island episode, leading to the setting up of a full-scale Presidential enquiry; (3) the NORAD military computer network which falsely signalled a Soviet nuclear attack on three separate occasions; (4) numerous near-misses at Kennedy and other busy national and international airports.

These incidents have been reviewed in a report to the European Community (Kopec and Michie, 1983). They lend emphasis to the idea that as technology advances and computers are given more responsibilities, the role of the man-machine interface becomes more critical. In contrast to past assumptions in software technology, the need has become paramount for a 'human window'. By this is meant a fully transparent conceptual interface between man and machine. On the presumption that mankind intends to be in charge of communications with machines, and not vice versa, the goal of humanizing the relationship is now more pressing than the goal of further extending the machine's brute-force capabilities.

It would seem therefore that the past research and development thrust towards stand-alone automation has headed the engineering industries in a dangerous direction. This thrust should be replaced by a new emphasis on man-machine cooperation with the human role as central. The Kopec-Michie study concluded by recommending the construction of human-transparent 'intelligent front ends' (requiring knowledge-based software systems) in the more critical application areas as a matter of urgency. For a relevant overview of knowledge-based systems the reader is referred to Alty and Coombs (1984).

General view

For certain tasks which are socially critical, stand-alone information systems should not be entrusted with operational supervision. Certification should only be granted to systems which demonstrably augment the user's understanding of his task environment. A clear distinction between 'surface' (cosmetic) and 'structural' (conceptual) causes of misunderstanding in an information system is also needed. Some tasks may be too complex for complete elimination of the latter cause of user-inscrutability to be possible. This theoretical case can be demonstrated in model domains on a laboratory scale and is, for example, under investigation in the KBBKN endgame discussed earlier. The possibility must be kept in mind as real-life tasks of ever-increasing complexity are penetrated by machine systems. In software today, the issue of 'deep' inscrutability has yet to be addressed by the profession at large.

Commitment must be to interactive man-machine systems wherever possible. Within this context the only computer-based decision structures which can be regarded as safe are those amenable to *conceptual debugging* by non-programming personnel. The combination of the required features in forms engineered to modern commercial standards has enabled expert system development to be placed on a cost-effective basis. Using various software tools clients have been able to develop applications in such exacting areas as process control in nuclear fuel enrichment, fault diagnosis in circuit boards, dimensioning computing and communications systems to customer requirements, logical and statistical analysis of real-time meteorological data, premonitory advice of fault conditions in rotating machinery, and trouble shooting in electrical equipment using chemical analyses of transformer oil samples. Central to the above commercial successes is the semi-automatic production of reliable program code which can be read and understood by the domain expert and his colleagues. This is achieved by marrying the process of top-down analysis into sub-problems, which is associated with the discipline known as structured programming, with the inductive generation from data of solutions to the individual sub-problems. In figure 3 Shapiro-Niblett 'structured-induction' partitions the domain into a procedural hierarchy of sub-domains, for each of which a separate decision tree is induced.

Table 9. *Example, using the Rulemaster system, of a user developed 'specification by examples' of a decision routine to operate during landing of the space shuttle*

MODULE: shuttle
STATE: one
ACTIONS:
    noauto   [advise "Don't use auto land"]
    auto   [advise "Use auto land"]
CONDITIONS:
    stab   [ask "stable?" "stab, xstab"] {stab xstab}
    error   [ask "errors?" "XL, LX, MM, SS"] {XL LX MM SS}
    sign   [ask "sign?" "pp, nn"] {pp nn}
    wind   [ask "winds?" "head, tail"] {head tail}
    mag   [ask "magnitude?" "L, M, S, O"] {L M S O}
    vis   [ask "visibility?" "y, n"] {y n}

EXAMPLES

stab	error	sign	wind	mag	vis		goal
—	—	—	—	—	n	=>	(auto)
xstab	—	—	—	—	y	=>	(noauto)
stab	LX	—	—	—	y	=>	(noauto)
stab	XL	—	—	—	y	=>	(noauto)
stab	MM	nn	tail	—	y	=>	(noauto)
—	—	—	—	O	y	=>	(noauto)
stab	SS	—	—	L	y	=>	(auto)
stab	SS	—	—	M	y	=>	(auto)
stab	SS	—	—	S	y	=>	(auto)
stab	MM	pp	head	L	y	=>	(auto)
stab	MM	pp	head	M	y	=>	(auto)
stab	MM	pp	tail	L	y	=>	(auto)
stab	MM	pp	tail	M	y	=>	(auto)
stab	MM	pp	head	S	y	=>	(noauto)
stab	MM	pp	tail	S	y	=>	(auto)

Structured induction

The method known as 'structured induction' (Shapiro and Niblett, 1982; Shapiro, 1987) gives the user his own 'specification by examples' language. With a personal computer-based or workstation-based facility he can (1) convert his requirement specification into a runnable prototype solution, and (2) test and modify successive trial prototypes himself, using test problems and data of his own selection.

The user, who may have been assisted in this process by a systems analyst, then uploads the files he has created, including the finalized prototype, from personal computer or workstation to main-frame. Programming staff finally convert it into a fully engineered application, for routine use via dumb terminals or after downloading into workstations of user departments.

Input consists of successive attempts by the user at a fully developed requirements specification using the examples-language provided. Table 9 shows such an 'operational spec' developed by a group of NASA engineers

Table 10. *Runnable prototype from specification shown in table 9 by application of Rulemaster's induction module*

MODULE shuttle IS

```
STATE: one
    IF (ask "visibility?" "y, n") IS
    "y": IF (ask "errors?" "XL, LX, MM, SS") IS
    "XL": (advise "Don't use auto land", goal)
    "LX": (advise "Don't use auto land", goal)
    "MM": IF (ask "stable?" "stab, xstab") IS
        "stab": IF (ask "sign?" "pp, nn") IS
            "pp": IF (ask "magnitude?" "L, M, S, O") IS
                "L": (advise "Use auto land", goal)
                "M": (advise "Use auto land", goal)
                "S": IF (asks "winds?" "head, tail") IS
                    "head": (advise "Don't use auto land", goal)
                    ELSE (advise "Use auto land", goal)
                ELSE (advise "Don't use auto land", goal)
            ELSE (advise "Don't use auto land", goal)
        ELSE (advise "Don't use auto land", goal)
    ELSE IF (ask "stable?" "stab, xstab") IS
        "stab": IF (ask "magnitude?" "L, M, S, O") IS
            "L": (advise "Use auto land", goal)
            "M": (advise "Use auto land", goal)
            "S": (advise "Use auto land", goal)
            ELSE (advise "Don't use auto land", goal)
        ELSE (advise "Don't use auto land", goal)
    ELSE (advise "Use auto land", goal)
GOAL OF shuttle
```

as a class exercise in a knowledge-programming course conducted by Radian Corporation. One of the group was Mr Roger Burke, chief designer of the Space Shuttle's auto-lander. When the monitored variable 'stable' has the value xstab during landing of the shuttle, then the condition lies outside the range of circumstances for which the auto-lander was designed and provided that the pilot has adequate seeing conditions an attempt at manual landing would be preferable. The four 'errors' relate to estimates of altitude and speed made by on-board and by ground instruments. The two values of 'sign' refer to the attitudes nose-up and nose-down, while the 'magnitude' variables refers to atmospheric turbulence with possible values low, medium, severe, and out of range. It might be thought that the first line of the examples spec embodies self-evident wisdom; if the pilot cannot see, then surely it is best to stay on auto. Since much other information is available to him from instruments, this decision is not as obvious as it might seem. More complex attribute-value combinations soon obscure the picture for the lay viewer, while remaining confidently decidable by the engineers.

Output consists of automatically generated prototype solutions presented on the screen in a user-transparent decision language. Table 10 shows the simple single-procedure prototype generated from the examples-set of

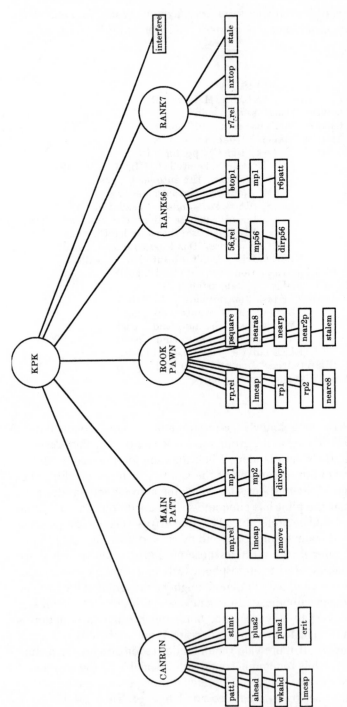

Figure 3   Hierarchical framework of a structured solution induced from sample data for the problem of table 6. The top-level solution was of the form: *if* can run *then* LOST *elseif* mainpatt *then* LOST *elseif* rookpawn *then* LOST *elseif* rank56 *then* LOST *elseif* rank7 *then* LOST *elseif* interfere *then* LOST *else* DRAWN

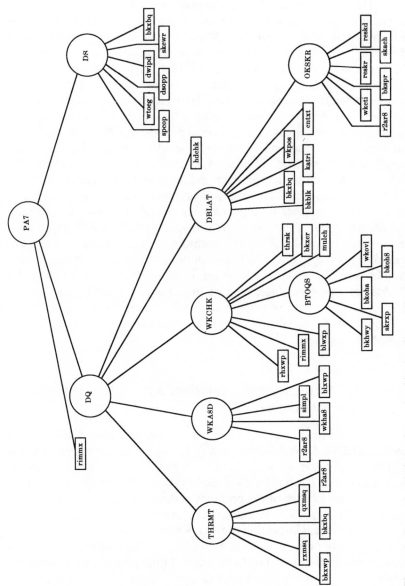

Figure 4   Procedural hierarchy evolved in the course of computer induction from expert-supplied examples of a decision rule for the ending king and pawn (on a7) against king and rook (White to move). As in figure 3 boxes denote procedural attributes whose bodies were instantiated in each case by induction of a linear (non-tested) 'if-then-else' expression

table 9. The combination of this particular procedure's small size with its near-linear structure when represented as a decision-tree results in its being intelligible to the shuttle engineers. What of more complex problems such as that of table 6 where the single-procedure approach yields a monster?

At first demonstrated by Shapiro and Niblett, structured induction, just as structured programming, performs a top-down analysis of the problem into sub-problems, leading to a procedural hierarchy as in figure 3. The difference from structured programming is that the builder of the application does not instantiate the procedure bodies with code but with operational specs of the kind shown earlier in table 9. Figure 4 shows a more complex case. As sketched in figure 5, structured induction augments the fourth-generation language approach and integrates it smoothly into existing database systems and languages. Traditional systems are strongest in selecting, retrieving, rearranging, analysing and tabulating stored instances using known rules. Rule-induction software generates new rules from user-selected instances and enables even the computer naïve user to work up complex and complete applications in prototype, ready to be translated into code, compiled and run. Moreover, by straightforward use of text files embedded at prototype stage, the resulting application can be equipped to give a readable account of itself at run time (Shapiro and Michie, 1986), thus exhibiting the superarticulacy phenomenon referred to in the title of this paper.

11 Technological revolution: automated synthesis of new knowledge

The auto-lander example is a case where a substantial degree of articulation of the desired decision-taking had already been achieved by the shuttle engineers, but not to a level from which reliable software could be hand constructed. Automatic construction was, however, possible, given only an operational spec of the problem in the form of a set of exemplary situation-action decisions. Moreover, the engineers were able directly to assess reliability from inspection of this operational spec, to test its derived decision-rule embodiment with new data, and where necessary to make modifications, to the spec, not to the code. In the process, they improved the completeness and articulacy of their own grasp of the problem, as well as generating for the first time code which they could trust. The style is superficially similar to that of decision tables, which for a time enjoyed a vogue in commercial programming. Unfortunately decision tables cannot be transformed to executable form until and unless the author meets certain restrictive conventions of completeness and irredundancy. These preclude the incremental approach which is at the heart of inductive programming, and of human problem-solving more generally.

Significant consequences may be anticipated from the importation into

domain of expert

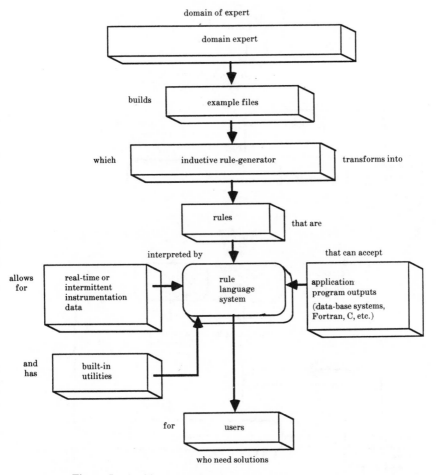

Figure 5   Architecture of an inductive expert systems generator

software manufacture of structured induction in the style illustrated in figure 6. These consequences, however, still belong to Freeman's (1985) categories (i) and (ii), and are limited to a particular sector of society, namely the software industry. The point at which the bounds of category (ii) overflow must be sought in what at first appears to be a mere side-product of knowledge engineering, namely the human-readable codifications of new knowledge which may be extracted from inductively synthesized code.

If the objectives of the KBBKN experiment, sketched earlier, are reached, then we will know that conceptualized codifications of knowledge far beyond what already exists in books or brains, constitute a practical possibility. Meanwhile, success has already been reported in two problem domains where near-complete skill, but not articulacy, already existed in human expert practitioners. It is arguable that human specialists, armed

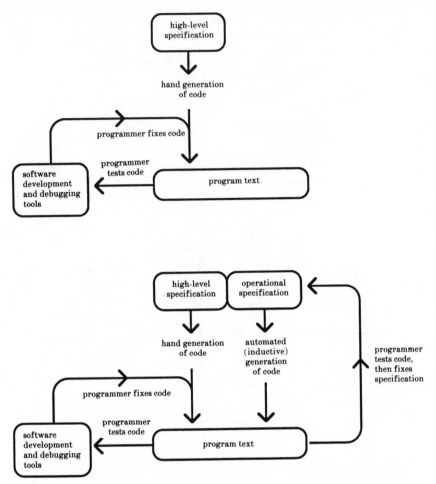

Figure 6   The upper diagram shows the customary de-bugging cycle traversed by a programmer developing an application. In the lower diagram an alternative path is provided whereby the programmer can de-bug his operational specification of what a procedure is supposed to do instead of trying to fix the code directly

only with unlimited data and their own intellectual resources, might have achieved complete codification. But historically this did not happen. One domain concerns the interpretation of electro-cardiogram records (Bratko *et al.*, 1988). The other is Shapiro's (1987) work on a subset of the chess endgame king and pawn against king and rook (KPKR). Because of personal familiarity and my own involvement, I shall take my closing illustration from this second investigation.

The size of the problem space was reduced by the restriction that the pawn (by convention White) must be a rook-pawn on the seventh rank,

White having the move and hence threatening to win by promotion. The classification of this ending into 'White has a win' against 'White does not have a win' is by no means uniformly trivial for a chess-master, who may reflect for as long as a minute before adjudicating, and very occasionally adjudicates erroneously. Shapiro's solution followed the normal top-down regime of structured programming as in figure 4, with the difference that the bodies of all the procedures were instantiated by automatic inductive inference instead of by hand coding.

To ensure the product's articulacy (or superarticulacy, since as far as could be discovered no human articulation pre-existed), each procedure body was constrained to a linear form known to be conducive to transparency. The question arises: can the inductively generated program be got to print out its own knowledge base in such a style as to yield a compact, complete and correct 'how to do it' manual for a previously uncharted and perhaps humanly unchartable problem?

Shapiro and I have published details elsewhere (Shapiro and Michie, 1986). They involve use of text files of natural-language phrases associated with the entry point and exits of each constituent module of figure 4's procedural hierarchy. A narrative-construction algorithm is also described for generating to-the-point explanations for the run-time user, of which some examples are shown in figure 7. For the requirements of another type of user, the scholar rather than the practitioner, a related procedure can be caused to generate an English language version of the complete synthetic rule-base. Such a rule-base is reproduced in Appendix A. Here we see an early product of a new form of semi-automatic manufacture where fabrication by the old hand methods is wholly infeasible. Just as the potential commercial value of the Kitty Hawk resided in the property of flight, so that of Shapiro's machine-made text resides in the property of superarticulacy. Likewise Bratko's cardiological knowledge base, almost wholly of machine authorship, represents a decisive extension of exact and articulate codification beyond the frontiers of existing medical texts.

Is it an exaggerated response to see technological revolution in laboratory demonstrations? Perhaps, but we should at the same time not lose sight of the potential lethality of the technological poison to which superarticulacy is offered as an antidote. The four cases selected in the study conducted for the European Economic Community (EEC) FAST programme were taken from what lay to hand. Other cases could have been chosen, equally illustrative of the overthrow by man-made complexity of human comprehension and control. Throughout the advanced nations a widening sector of the installed base of mechanical and electronic equipment has already become unmaintainable. Correspondingly the role played by traditional documentation – maintenance manuals, inspection guides, test procedures, codes of practice and the like – is insensibly changing from that of practical guide to that of mere compliance with legislation. Moreover, as each generation of technicians retires, for example from the engine-testing

since the BR has safe access to a file A or rank 8 (because WK can't cover both intersect points) it follows
that the potential skewer is good
from this it follows that there is a good delay due to a double attack threat
from this it follows that there is a simple delay to white's queening the pawn
from this it follows that this position is not won for white

since the BR has safe access to file A or rank 8 (because WK can't cover both intersect points)
　　when the mating square isn't attacked in some way by the promoted WP
　　and the BK is not attacked in some way by the WP
　　and the BK can't attack the WP
　　and the BR doesn't attack a mating square safely (because the WK can attack the mating square)
　　it follows that there is a good delay from a mate threat
from this it follows that there is a simple delay to white's queening the pawn
from this it follows that this position is not won for white

since the WK is overloaded
　　when the BK isn't on rank 8 in a position to aid the BR (the BK is not on rank 8)
　　and the BK isn't on file A in a position to aid the BR (the BK is not on file A)
　　and the BR can't achieve a skewer and the BK can't attack the WP
　　and the BK isn't in the BR's way
　　it follows that black can attack the queening square
from this it follows that there is a good delay due to the white king being in check
from this it follows that there is a simple delay to white's queening the pawn
from this it follows that this position is not won for white

Figure 7   Six representative KPa7KR WTM positions with machine-
generated 'comment' texts

since the BK is attacked in some way by the promoted WP
    when there is a potential skewer as opposed to a fork
    and the WK distance to intersect point is not too great
    and the kings are in normal position
    and the WK is one away from the relevant edge
    and there is no special opposition pattern present
it follows that there is not a good delayed skewer
from this it follows that this position is won for white

since the BR has safe access to file A or rank 8 (because WK can't cover both intersect points) when the WK
is on square a8
it follows that there is a good delay due to the white king being on a8
from this it follows that there is a simple delay to white's queening the pawn
from this it follows that this position is not won for white

since the BR can be captured safely
it follows that this position is won for white

This last was a trick problem posed from the floor when the work was presented to the 4th Advances in
Computer Chess Conference. If the white pawn captures the rook and promotes to queen, then the position
is not won for White because of stalemate. The proviso 'safely' in the machine response was judged sufficient
for acceptance of the comment as sound.

sheds of the aircraft industry, the new generation hangs back from absorbing their precious know-how, relating as it does to designs seen as obsolescent.

In summary, combinatorial problems, escalating beyond human comprehension, abound not only in industrial and military affairs but through modern society as a whole. The possibility of mass manufacture of usable 'how to do it' codifications is now sufficiently established. The time-scale in which these techniques may progress from laboratory to large-scale field trials remains unclear. Little imagination, however, is needed to extrapolate what I have described. This revolution, to borrow words again from Professor Freeman (1985), may in the end 'not only lead to the emergence of new leading branches of the economy and a whole range of new product groups, but also have deep-going effects on many other branches of the economy by transforming their methods of production'.

Appendix A

Machine-generated 'How to do it' text from a complete and correct rule base synthesized by machine within an expert-supplied hierarchical framework. The list of primitives given to the inductive synthesizer is given in Appendix B

Machine generated advice text for PA7, top-level rule to decide whether or not this position is won for white
this position is won for white (PA7 top-level rule) IFF
    the BR can be captured safely (rimmx)
OR none of the following is true
    a Black piece controls the queening square (bxqsq)
    OR there is a simple delay to White's queening the pawn (DQ level 2.1)
    OR the WK is in stalemate (stlmt)
    OR there is a good delayed skewer (DS level 2.2)

Machine generated advice for DQ. level 2.1 to decide whether or not there is a simple delay to White's queening the pawn
there is a simple delay to White's queening the pawn (DQ level 2.1) IFF any of the following is true
    there is a good delay from a mate threat (THRMT level 3.1)
    OR there is a good delay due to the white king being on a8 (WKA8D level 3.2)
    OR there is a good delay due to the white king being in check (WKCHK level 3.3)
    OR there is a good delay due to a double attack threat (DBLAT level 3.4)
    OR there is a good delay because of a hidden check (hdchk)

Machine generated advice text for DS. level 2.2 to decide whether or not there is a good delayed skewer

there is a good delayed skewer (DS level 2.2) IFF
> there is a special opposition pattern present (spcop)

OR all of the following are true
>> the WK is one away from the relevant edge (wtoeg)
>> AND the kings are in normal opposition (dsopp)
>> AND the WK distance to intersect point is too great (dwipd)
>> AND there is a potential skewer as opposed to a fork (skewr)
>> AND the BK is not attacked in some way by the promoted WP (bkxbq)

Machine generated advice text for THRMT. level 3.1 to decide whether or not there is a good delay from a mate threat

there is a good delay from a mate threat (THRMT level 3.1) IFF
> the BR attacks a mating square safely (rxmsq)

AND the BK can attack the WP (bkxwp)
OR none of the following is true
>> the BK is attacked in some way by the promoted WP (bkxbq)
>> OR the mating square is attacked in some way by the promoted WP (qxmsq)
>> OR the BR doesn't have safe access to file A or rank 8 (r2ar8)

Machine generated advice text for WKA8D, level 3.2 to decide whether or not there is a good delay due to the white king being on a8

there is a good delay due to the white king being on a8 (WKA8D level 3.2) IFF
> the WK is on square a8 (wkna8)

AND any of the following is true
>> the BR has safe access to file A or rank 8 (r2ar8)
>> OR B attacks the WP (BR in direction x $= -1$ only) (blxwp)
>> OR a very simple pattern applies (simpl)

Machine generated advice text for WKCHK. level 3.3 to decide whether or not there is a good delay due to the white king being in check

there is a good delay due to the white king being in check (WKCHK level 3.3) IFF all of the following are true
> the WK is in check (wknck)

AND the BR can't be captured safely (rimmx)
AND any of the following is true
>> black can attack the queening square (BTOQS level 4.2)
>> OR the BK can attack the critical square (b7) (bkxer)
>> OR the BR bears on the WP (direction x $= -1$ only) (rkxwp)
>> OR there is a skewer threat lurking (thrsk)
>> OR B can renew the check to good advantage (mulch)

Machine generated advice text for OKSKR. level 4.1 to decide whether or not the potential skewer is good
the potential skewer is good (OKSKR level 4.1) IFF any of the following is true
 the BR has safe access to file A or rank 8 (r2ar8)
 OR the WK can't control the intersect point (wketi)
 OR the BK can support the BR (bkspr)
 OR the BR alone can renew the skewer threat (reskr)
 OR the WK can be reskewered via a delayed skewer (reskd)

Machine generated advice text for BTOQS. level 4.2 to decide whether or not black can attack the queening square
black can attack the queening square (BTOQS level 4.2) IFF
 the BK isn't in the BR's way (bknwy)
AND any of the following is true
 the BR can achieve a skewer or the BK can attack the WP (skrxp)
 OR the BK is on file A in a position to aid the BR (bkona)
 OR the BK is on rank 8 in a position to aid the BR (bkon8)
 OR the WK is overloaded (wkovl)

No machine generated text for DBLAT (level 3.4) was produced because it contains a 3-valued attribute which the text-producing system cannot parse.

Appendix B

List of unique primitive attributes invoked in the text of
Appendix A
(Those marked † are specific to DBLAT and are not included above.)

is the BK in the way (bkblk)†
is the BK in the BR's way (bknwy)
is the BK on rank 8 in a position to aid the BR (bkon8)
is the BK on file A in a position to aid the BR (bkona)
can the BK support the BR (bkspr)
is the BK attacked in some way by the promoted WP (bkxbq)
can the BK attack the critical square (b7) (bkxer)
can the BK attack the WP (bkxwp)
does B attacks the WP (BR in direction x = − 1 only) (blxwp)
does one or more B piece control the queening square (bxqsq)
is the WK on an edge and not on a8 (entxt)†
are the kings in normal opposition (dsopp)
is the WK distance to intersect point too great (dwipd)
is there a good delay because there is a hidden check (hdchk)
does any king control intersect point. If so, which (katri)†
can B renew the check to good advantage (mulch)

is the mating sq attacked in some way by the promoted WP (qxmsq)
does the BR have safe access to file A or rank 8 (r2ar8)
can the WK be reskewered via a delayed skewer (reskd)
can the BR alone renew the skewer threat (reskr)
can the BR be captured safely (rimmx)
does the BR bear on the WP (direction $x = -1$ only) (rkxwp)
does the BR attack a mating square safely (rxmsq)
does a very simple pattern apply (simpl)
can the WK be skewered after one or more checks (skach)
is there a potential skewer as opposed to fork (skewr)
can the BR achieve a skewer or BK attack the WP (skrxp)
is there a special opposition pattern present (speop)
is the WK in stalemate (stlmt)
is there a skewer threat lurking (thrsk)
can the WK control the intersect point (wketi)
is the WK on square a8 (wkna8)
is the WK in check (wknck)
is the WK overloaded (wkovl)
is the WK in a potential skewer position (wkpos)†
is the WK one away from the relevant edge (wtoeg)

12 Annotated bibliography on the foundations of AI

Annotated bibliography on the foundations of AI

Imre Balogh and Brian M. Slator

Originally this bibliography was intended to fill a perceived need for a reasonably complete annotated listing of the foundational literature in AI. To do this we combed the back issues of the *AI Journal, AI Magazine*, the *SIGART Newsletter*, the *Communications of the Association for Computing Machinery*, the *International Journal of Man-Machine Studies*, the *Machine Intelligence* series, *Behavioral and Brain Sciences* and several others, as well as thumbing through piles of edited collections like *Computers and Thought, Semantic Information Processing, Representation and Understanding*, and many more; and, naturally, we asked around.

This final section contains a annotated collection of the references that we judge to have made some foundational contribution to the field of AI. In the interests of simplicity it also contains all of the references that occur in the previous chapters and the individual papers themselves.

We quickly discovered that opinion differs on what exactly constitutes "foundational" AI, as opposed to, say, papers on "classic" AI systems, ages-old treatises on the Philosophy of Mind, landmark papers in Cognitive Psychology, descriptions of special purpose AI programming languages (Lisp, Prolog, Conniver, Poplog ...), or knowledge representation schemes (KRL, FRL, SRL ...), or original applications to AI of computational mechanisms (resolution, fuzzy logic, production systems ...), the standard AI textbooks, and of course all the "classic" edited collections. Each candidate provoked some debate but, in general, we tended to look to a narrow interpretation of "foundational," which saved space. In the annotations we have tried to make explicit what it is that in our view makes the chosen references foundational.

The decision to consolidate our little bibliography with the combined references from all of the papers in this volume was based on the reasoning that this would form a fairly closed circle of foundational authors, mostly citing each other. We were wrong. For whatever reasons, the authors in this collection have cited very far afield indeed: from all of the related areas listed above, to office management, political science, and vertebrate zoology. This conflation has made our bibliography appear somewhat unfocussed – for which we offer no apology. We have tried, where possible, to give more easily accessible references from readily available sources, and for the sake of completeness, have listed as many alternatives as we were able to track down (since many papers have appeared in more than one place over the years). Those references which have been cited by papers in this volume are identified by one or more bold-faced three-character mnemonics: mappings encoded in table 1 (an alphabetized version of the table of contents).

Table 1. *Three-character codes for papers in this volume*

Code	Author(s)	Title
BOD	M. A. Boden	Has AI helped psychology?
BUN	A. Bundy	What kind of field is AI?
B&O	A. Bundy & S. Ohlsson	The nature of AI principles
CAM	J. A. Campbell	Three novelties of AI: theories, programs, and rational reconstructions
CH	B. Chandrasekaran	What kind of information processing is intelligence?
CHU	P. M. Churchland	Representation and high-speed computation in neural networks
DEN	D. C. Dennett	Evolution, error, and intentionality
DIE	E. Dietrich	Programs in the search for intelligent machines: the mistaken foundations of AI
D&D	S. E. Dreyfus & H. L. Dreyfus	Towards a reconciliation of phenomenology and AI
FOD	J. A. Fodor	Why there STILL has to be a language of thought
HEW	C. Hewitt	The challenge of open systems
MAR	D. Marr	AI: a personal view
MIC	D. Michie	The superarticulacy phenomenon in the context of software manufacture
PAR	D. Partridge	What's in an AI program?
P&W	D. Partridge & Y. Wilks	Does AI have methodology which is different from software engineering?
PRZ	T. C. Przymusinski	Non-monotonic reasoning versus logic programming: a new perspective
R&H	G. D. Ritchie & F. K. Hanna	AM: a case study in AI methodology
SIM	T. W. Simon	Artificial methodology meets philosophy
SMO	P. Smolensky	Connectionism and the foundations of AI
SPA	K. Sparck Jones	What sort of a thing is an AI experiment?
WEY	R. W. Weyhrauch	Prolegomena to a theory of mechanized formal reasoning
YW1	Y. Wilks	One small head: models and theories
YW2	Y. Wilks	Some comments on Smolensky and Fodor
WIN	T. Winograd	Thinking machines: can there be? Are we?

We wish to extend our thanks to the editors, Derek Partridge and Yorick Wilks, for enlisting us in this project, which has turned out to be a lot more work, and a lot more interesting, than we at first suspected; thanks also to all the helpful people who eased our labors, particularly at Massachusetts Institute of Technology's Media Laboratory and in the offices of Behavioral and Brain Sciences; and thanks especially to Homa Aidinejad, Dan Fass, Jeannine Sandefur, and Rita Slator, for aid, comfort, and service, above and beyond the call.

Achinstein, Peter (1965). Theoretical Models. *The British Journal for the Philosophy of Science*, 16, 62, pp. 102–120. Reference **YW1**

(1968). *Concepts of Science*. Baltimore: The Johns Hopkins Press. Reference **SIM**

Ackerman, D. (1972). Opacity in Belief Structures. *Journal of Philosophy*, 69, pp. 55–67. Reference **DEN**

Ackley, D. H., G. E. Hinton, and T. J. Sejnowski (1985). A Learning Algorithm for Boltzmann Machines. *Cognitive Science*, 9, pp. 147–169. An example of a 'learning' algorithm, which uses 'simulated annealing', applied to an important subclass of connectionist models – the Boltmann machines. Reference **SMO**

Agha, Gul (1984). Semantic Considerations in the Actor Paradigm of Concurrent Computation. *Proceedings of the NSF/SERC Seminar on Concurrency*. New York: Springer-Verlag. Reference **HEW**

Aiken, H. (1956). The Future of Automatic Computing Machinery. In *Elektronische Rechenmaschinen und Informationsverarbeitung*, pp. 32–34. Braunschweig: Vieweg. Proceedings of a symposium published in Nachrichtentechnische Fachberichte 4. Reference **DIE**

Akins, K. A. (1988). Information and Organisms: Or Why Nature Doesn't Build Epistemic Engines. Doctoral dissertation. Ann Arbor: University of Michigan. Reference **DEN**

Allman, J. M., J. F. Baker, W. T. Newsome, and S. E. Petersen (1982). Visual Topography and Function. In *Cortical Sensory Organization*, edited by C. N. Woolsey, Clifton, NJ: Humana Press. Reference **CHU**

Alty, J. L. and M. L. Coombs (1984). *Expert Systems: Concepts and Examples*. Manchester, UK: NCC Publications. Reference **MIC**

Anderson, Alan R. (ed.) (1964). *Minds and Machines*. Englewood Cliffs, NJ: Prentice-Hall [An absolute gem of a collection, covering most of the ground in the Philosophy of Mind (as regards computers), and much of the debate as it continues today; starting with a reprint of "Computing Machinery and Intelligence" by Alan Turing, and featuring articles by J. R. Lucas, Keith Gunderson, Hilary Putnam (see this bibliography), Michael Scriven, and others. Anderson notes that between 1950 and 1964 over 1,000 papers were published on the question of whether "machines" can "think."]

Anderson, D. Bruce, Thomas O. Binford, Arthur J. Thomas, Richard W. Weyrauch, and Yorick A. Wilks (1974). After Leibniz . . .: Discussions on Philosophy and Artificial Intelligence. *Stanford AI Laboratory Memo*. (AIM–229). Stanford, CA: Stanford University. [An edited transcript of discussions on the implications for AI of philosophy and other disciplines that study intelligence and knowledge.]

Anderson, D. Bruce and Patrick J. Hayes (1973). *The Logician's Folly*. Edinburgh: University of Edinburgh [Argues that theorem proving is not useful for formal mathematics or robot reasoning, and that "knowledge of how to construct a machine which can reason about and act in the real world as well as converse about itself in natural language is a necessary (but not sufficient!) condition for achieving a real artificial intelligence."]

Anderson, D. Z. (1986). Coherent Optical Eigenstate Memory. *Optics Letters*, 11, pp. 56–58. Reference **SMO**

Anderson, John R. (1981). *Cognitive Skills and Their Acquisition*. Hillsdale, NJ: Lawrence Erlbaum. Reference **SMO**

(1983). *The Architecture of Cognition*. Cambridge, MA: Harvard University Press. Reference **SMO**

Anderson, J. A. and E. Rosenfeld (eds.), *Neurocomputing: Foundations of Research*. Cambridge, MA: MIT Press

Apt, K., H. Blair, and A. Walker (1986/1988). Towards a Theory of Declarative Knowledge. In *Foundations of Deductive Databases and Logic Programming*, edited by J. Minker, pp. 89–148. Los Altos, CA: Morgan-Kaufmann. Reference **PRZ**

Apt, K. and M. H. van Emden (1982). Contributions to the Theory of Logic Programming. *Journal of the ACM*, 29, pp. 841–862. Reference **PRZ**

Arbib, Michael A. (1972). *The Metaphorical Brain: An Introduction to Cybernetics as Artificial Intelligence and Brain Theory*. New York: Wiley [A book that presents neuroanatomy and systems theory as the basis for AI. Arbib has long been a central figure in the "brain modeling" approach to AI.]

Arbib, Michael A. and S. Amari (1985). Sensorimotor Transformations in the Brain. *Journal of Theoretical Biology*, 112, pp. 123–155. Reference **CHU**

Arbib, Michael A. and David Caplan (1979). Neurolinguistics Must Be Computational. *Behavioral and Brain Sciences*, 2, 3, pp. 449–459 [Argues that neurolinguistics would benefit from using AI techniques to "model the cooperative computation underlying language processing." This means, essentially, that there is a space (for connectionism), between current neurolinguistic modeling and actual neuroanatomy.]

Asgari, D. and K. L. Modesitt (1986). *Space Shuttle Main Engine Analysis: A Case Study for Inductive Knowledge-based Systems Involving Very Large Data Bases*. Proceedings, First International Conference on Expert Database Systems South Carolina, April 1986: IEEE, pp. 65–71. Reference **MIC**

Ashby, W. R. (1956). *An Introduction to Cybernetics*. London: Chapman and Hall. Reference **DIE**

Athanasiou, Tom (1987). High-Tech Politics: The Case of Artificial Intelligence. *Socialist Review*, pp. 7–35. Reference **WIN**

Austin, J. L. (1962). *How to Do Things with Words*. Cambridge, MA: Harvard University Press. Reference **WIN**

Ballard, D. H. (1986). Cortical Connections and Parallel Processing: Structure and Function. *Behavioral and Brain Sciences*, 9, pp. 67–120. Reference **CHU** ["This paper explores the hypothesis that an important part of the cortex can be modelled as a connectionist computer that is especially suited for parallel problem solving."]

Balogh, Imre and Brian M. Slator (1990). Annotated Bibliography on the Foundations of AI. In *The Foundations of AI: A Sourcebook*, edited by Derek Partridge and Yorick Wilks, pp. 443–492. Cambridge, UK: Cambridge University Press

Balzer, R., T. E. Cheatham, and C. Green (1983). Software Technology in the 1990s: Using a New Paradigm. *IEEE Computer*, November, pp. 39–45. Reference **P&W**

Banerji, Ranan B. (1980). *Artificial Intelligence: A Theoretical Approach*. New York: North-Holland [The goal of this book is to develop a mathematical theory of problem solving in the hope that such a theory will help establish a formal theoretical basis for AI. The theory is restricted to the study of problems that have clearly defined state spaces. Games are used as a vehicle for investigating how such problems can be solved. Using the insights gained from this study, a methodology is developed for learning and automatic heuristic discovery. The main part of the book does not require a strong background in formal mathematics, but the appendix give a rigorous formal development of the theory.]

(1990). AI, Computer Science, and Education. In *The Foundations of AI: A Sourcebook*, edited by Derek Partridge and Yorick Wilks, pp. 373–379. Cambridge, UK: Cambridge University Press

Barr, A. and Edward A. Feigenbaum (1981/1982). *Handbook of Artificial Intelligence*, vols. I and II. Los Altos, CA: William Kaufman. Reference **DIE** [Volume I covers search, knowledge representation, natural language, and speech recognition. Volume II covers programming languages, expert systems, and automatic programming. See Cohen and Feigenbaum (1982), this bibliography.]

Bartoshuk, L. M. (1978). Gustatory System. In *Handbook of Behavioral Neurobiology*, Volume I, *Sensory Integration*, edited by R. B. Masterton, pp. 503–567. New York: Plenum. Reference **CHU**

Batali, J. (1983). Computational Introspection. *Massachusetts Institute of Technology AI Technical Report*. February. (AI-TR–701). Cambridge, MA: Massachusetts Institute of Technology AI Laboratory. Reference **HEW**

Becker, Joseph D. (1975). Reflections on the Formal Description of Behavior. In *Representation and Understanding*, edited by Daniel G. Bobrow and Allan Collins, pp. 83–101. New York, San Francisco, London: Academic Press [An easy-to-read discussion of the problems of describing conceptual entities from within a formal system. Becker starts with the difference between an object and a process, and touches on most of the representational issues facing AI. He concludes that formal descriptions of cognitive processes are only possible when the criteria for sufficiency are established in advance; that is, formal descriptions of behavior are more or less appropriate depending on the "level" of description, and the purposes for which they are to be used.]

Ben-Shakhar, G. (1980). Habituation of the Orienting Response to Complex Sequences of Stimuli. *Psychophysiology*, 17, 6. Reference **PAR**

Bennett, J. (1982). Large Computer Project Problems and their Causes. *Technical Report*. (No. 188). Basser Department of Computer Science, University of Sydney. Reference **P&W**

Berkeley, Edmund C. (1949). *Giant Brains, or Machines That Think*. New York: Wiley [Gives the state of the art in computing prior to 1946, with some technical details on Massachusetts Institute of Technology's Differential Analyzer, Harvard's IBM Automatic Sequence-Controlled Calculator, Bell Laboratory's General-Purpose Relay Calculator, and the Moore School's ENIAC. Attempts to reach a general audience and even includes little tutorials on physics and mathematical logic. Chapter 1 is titled "Can Machines Think?", and, since memory, arithmetic, and deciding (branching instructions), are counted as forms of "thinking," the answer is a visionary "yes." While still less than 40 years old this book is a quaint antiquity – an interesting picture of how much has happened in less than four decades.]

Bernstein, Jeremy (1981). *The Analytical Engine*. New York: William Morrow [Revised from the 1963 original, written for a general audience by the science editor of *The New Yorker*; contains a small annotated bibliography relevant to the foundations of AI.]

Bibel, W. and B. Petkoff (eds.) (1985). *AI Methodology, Systems, Applications*. Amsterdam: North-Holland [Selected papers from a 1984 conference that claimed to lay special emphasis on methodological issues in AI. The methodology section is, in fact, quite small (9 pages in 84), and sustained, general, methodological arguments are absent.]

Bidoit, N. and C. Froidevaux (1986). *Minimalism Subsumes Default Logic and Circumscription in Stratified Logic Programming*. Preprint. Reference **PRZ**

Binford, Thomas O. (1971). Visual Perception by Computer. *IEEE Conference on Systems and Control*, December. Reference **MAR**

Bobrow, Daniel G. (1975). Dimensions of Representation. In *Representation and Understanding*, edited by Daniel G. Bobrow and Allan Collins, pp. 2–33. New York, San Francisco, London: Academic Press [An excellent introduction to, and review of, the issues of knowledge representation. Also an excellent introductory essay, referring aptly and often to the later chapters, in a volume that has become a classic in AI. Bobrow's thesis is simply that there is no one, true, knowledge representation. Each scheme offers advantages, but always at a price; and the obvious move, towards multiple representations, itself carries the cost of difficult choices between alternative representations, and extra overhead to insure consistency among the various representations, when the state of the world being modelled is changed.]

(ed.) (1980). Special Issue on Nonmonotonic Logic. *Artificial Intelligence*, 13, 1. Reference **WIN**

Bobrow, Daniel G. and Patrick J. Hayes (1985). Artificial Intelligence – Where Are We?. *Artificial Intelligence*, 25, 3, pp. 375–417 [A collection of answers to foundational questions generated to celebrate the 25th volume of the AI Journal, and answered by many of the long-term practitioners in, or observers of, the field. Issues such as "What is the nature of AI?" and "Where is it going?" are met by a spectrum of answers.]

Bobrow, Daniel G., R. M. Kaplan, D. A. Norman, H. Thompson, and T. Winograd (1977). Gus, a Frame-Driven Dialog System. *Artificial Intelligence*, 8, 1. Reference **BUN**

Bobrow, Daniel G. and Mark J. Stefik (1986). Perspectives on Artificial Intelligence Programming. In *AI and Software Engineering*, edited by C. Rich and R. C. Waters, pp. 581–587. Los Altos, CA: Morgan Kaufmann [It is argued that AI programs must be easily understandable and changeable, and that a judicious mix of different programming "styles" (e.g. object-oriented or logic programming) can facilitate the achievement of these goals. Thus they argue for programming environments composed of an integrated set of alternative styles.]

Bobrow, Daniel G. and Terry Winograd (1977). KRL: Another Perspective. *Cognitive Science*, 3, pp. 29–43. Reference **R&H**

Boden, Margaret A. (1977,1987). *Artificial Intelligence and Natural Man*. New York: Basic Books [This book is still probably the best description of existing AI systems (at the time it was written, i.e. 1977), with each set into a general intellectual/philosophical context, and with the nature of the cognitive and epistemological claims made by the researchers (implicitly or explicitly) clearly set out. There is also a strong emphasis throughout on the beneficial social effects of intelligent machines. The current (and second) edition has been updated with a new chapter to cover the intervening decade.]

(1981). *Minds and Mechanisms: Philosophical Psychology and Computational Models*. Ithaca, NY: Cornell University Press [A collection of philosophical essays divided into four parts: 1) explanation and computation; 2) what we have in mind; 3) psychologists ancient and modern; 4) values and psychological theory.]

(1984). Methodological Links Between AI and Other Disciplines. In *The Mind and the Machine*, edited by S. B. Torrance, pp. 125–132. Chichester, UK: Ellis Horwood. Reprinted from *The Study of Information*, edited by F. Machlup and U. Mansfield, New York: Wiley, 1983 [Argues that there is a need for more inter-disciplinary interaction between AI and related areas like psychology, linguistics, and philosophy. Gives reasons why the social effects of AI might be re-humanizing rather than dehumanizing.]

(1984). What is Computational Psychology? *Proceedings of the Aristotelian Society*, 58, Supplement, pp. 17–35. Reference **BOD** [This paper looks at two views of computational psychology. The first is Marr's view of different levels, the other is the view offered by the connectionist movement. The conclusion is that both are useful, since each model seems to avoid the problems of the other. (See Mellor, 1984, this bibliography.)]

(1990). Has AI Helped Psychology? In *The Foundations of AI: A Sourcebook*, edited by Derek Partridge and Yorick Wilks, pp. 108–111. Cambridge, UK: Cambridge University Press

Bossu, G. and P. Siegel (1985). Saturation, Nonmonotonic Reasoning and the Closed World Assumption. *Artificial Intelligence*, 25, 1, pp. 13–63. Reference **PRZ**

Brachman, Ronald J. (1979). On the Epistemological Status of Semantic Networks. In *Associative Networks*, edited by Nicholas V. Findler, pp. 3–50. New York: Academic Press. Reprinted in *Readings in Knowledge Representation*, edited by R. J. Brachman and H. J. Levesque, pp. 191–215. Los Altos, CA: Morgan Kaufman, 1985 [Attempts to clarify what is meant by a semantic network. The history of semantic networks from Quillian (1968) onwards is traced. By examining the semantic primitives in semantic networks, five different kinds of knowledge are factored out and organized into five levels. The levels are implementational, logical, epistemological, conceptual, and linguistic. The epistemological level is argued to be a hitherto unrecognized separate level that is concerned with the structure of knowledge and hence with phenomena such as inheritance, abstraction, and the structure of descriptions. Brachman describes his own epistemological level language called KLONE.]

Braitenburg, V. (1984). *Vehicles*. Cambridge, MA: MIT Press. Reference **DEN**

Braithwaite, R. B. (1962). Models in the Empirical Sciences. *Proceedings 1960 International Congress on Logic, Methodology and Philosophy of Science*, edited by E. Nagel, P. Suppes, and A. Tarski. Stanford, CA. Reference **YW1**

Bramer, Max A. and Jadzia Cendrowska (1984). Inside an Expert System: A Rational Reconstruction of the MYCIN Consultation System. In *Artificial Intelligence: Tools and Techniques*, edited by M. Eisenstadt and T. O'Shea, pp. 453–497. New York: Harper and Row. Reference **CAM**

Bratko, I., I. Mozetic, and N. Lavrac (1988). Automatic Synthesis and Compression of Cardiological Knowledge. In *Machine Intelligence*, vol. 11, edited by J. E. Hayes, D. Michie, and J. M. Richards. Oxford University Press. Reference **MIC**

Brooks, F. P. (1975). *The Mythical Man-Month*. Reading, MA: Addison-Wesley. Reference **P&W**

Bruner, J. S. (1957). On Perceptual Readiness. *Psychological Review*, 64, pp. 123–152. Reference **CHA**

Buchanan, B. and Edward A. Feigenbaum (1978). Dendral and Meta-Dendral: Their Applications Dimension. *Artificial Intelligence*, 11, pp. 5–24. Reference **DIE**

Bundy, Alan (1980). Artificial Mathematicians: The Computational Modelling of Mathematical Reasoning. *Department of AI, Occasional Paper*. (No. 24). Edinburgh: University of Edinburgh. Reference **R&H**

(1981). Mental Models Rule OK. *Department of AI, Occasional Paper* (No. 25). Edinburgh: University of Edinburgh. Reference **BUN**

(1983). The Nature of AI: A Reply to Schank. *The AI Magazine* (Winter), 4, 4, pp. 29–31. Reference **P&W, BUN**

(1990). What Kind of Field is AI? In *The Foundations of AI: A Sourcebook*, edited by Derek Partridge and Yorick Wilks, pp. 215–222. Cambridge, UK: Cambridge University Press

Bundy, Alan and S. Ohlsson (1990). The Nature of AI Principles. In *The Foundations of AI: A Sourcebook*, edited by Derek Partridge and Yorick Wilks, pp. 135–154. Cambridge, UK: Cambridge University Press An exchange originally published in *AISB Quarterly*, vols. 46–50, 1983. Also *Department of AI, Research Paper* (No. 226). Edinburgh: University of Edinburgh

Bundy, Alan and B. Silver (1982). A Critical Survey of Rule Learning Programs. Proceedings *European Conference on AI* (ECAI–82), pp. 150–157. Reference **BOD**

Bundy, Alan, B. Silver, and D. Plummer (1984). An Analytical Comparison of Some Rule Learning Programs. *Department of AI Research Paper* (No. 215). Edinburgh: University of Edinburgh. Reference **B&O**

Burge, T. (1979). Individualism and the Mental. *Midwest Studies in Philosophy*, 4, pp. 73-121. Reference **DEN**

(1986). Individualism and Psychology. *Philosophical Review*, 95, 1, pp. 3–46. Reference **DEN**

Bylander, T. C. and Sanjay Mittal (1986). CSRL: A Language for Classificatory Problem Solving and Uncertainty Handling. *The AI Magazine*, 7, 3, pp. 66–77. Reference **CHA**

Campbell, J. A. (1979). Two Classes of Special Functions for the Phase-Integral Approximation. *Journal of Physics* A, 12, 8, pp. 1,149-1,154. Reference **CAM**

(1986). Principles of AI. In *AI: Principles and Applications*, edited by M. Yazdani, pp. 13–30. London: Chapman and Hall [Explores the possibilities of AI as a science. In particular, he examines the view that AI is a proto-science in search of a general framework of description. Heuristics and models are singled out as two necessary components of any abstract description.]

(1990). Three novelties of AI: Theories, Programs and Rational Reconstructions. In *The Foundations of AI: A Sourcebook*, edited by Derek Partridge and Yorick Wilks, pp. 237–246. Cambridge, UK: Cambridge University Press

Carnap, R. (1936-1937). Testability and Meaning. *Philosophy of Science*. Reference **YW1**

Ceruzzi, P. (1986). An Unforeseen Revolution: Computers and Expectations

1935–1985. In *Imagining Tomorrow: History, Technology, and the American Future*, edited by J. Corn. Cambridge, MA: MIT Press. Reference **DIE**

Chandra, A. and D. Harel (1985). Horn Clause Queries and Generalizations. *Journal of Logic Programming*, 1, pp. 1–15. Reference **PRZ**

Chandrasekaran, B. (1983). Towards a Taxonomy of Problem-Solving Types. *The AI Magazine*, 4, 1, pp. 9–17. Reference **CHA**

(1986a). Generic Tasks in Knowledge-Based Reasoning: High-Level Building Blocks for Expert System Design. *IEEE Expert*, Fall, pp. 23–30. Reference **CHA**

(1986b). From Numbers to Symbols to Knowledge Structures: Pattern Recognition and Artificial Intelligence Perspectives on the Classification Task. In *Pattern Recognition in Practice*, vol. II, edited by E. S. Gelsema and L. N. Kanal, pp. 547–559. Amsterdam: North-Holland. Reference **CHA**

(1987). Towards a Functional Architecture for Intelligence Based on Generic Information Processing Tasks. *Proceedings International Joint Conference on AI* (IJCAI–87), pp. 1,183–1,192. Milan, Italy. Reference **CHA**

(1990). What Kind of Information Processing is Intelligence? In *The Foundations of AI: A Sourcebook*, edited by Derek Partridge and Yorick Wilks, pp. 14–46. Cambridge, UK: Cambridge University Press

Chandrasekaran, B. and Sanjay Mittal (1983). Deep Versus Compiled Knowledge Approaches to Diagnostic Problem Solving. *International Journal of Man-Machine Studies*, 19, 5, pp. 425–436 [A discussion of the call for codification of "deep" knowledge in knowledge-based reasoning and what this seemingly desirable but elusive class of knowledge might be. Argues that it is possible to create a "diagnostic problem-solving structure" from a suitable body of knowledge, with everything needed for diagnostic reasoning "compiled" into it, that avoids combinatorial growth.]

Chao, Y. R. (1962). Models in Linguistics and Models in General. *Proceedings 1960 International Congress on Logic, Methodology, and Philosophy of Science*, edited by E. Nagel, P. Suppes, and A. Tarski. Stanford, CA. Reference **YW1**

Charniak, E. and D. McDermott (1985). *Introduction to Artificial Intelligence*. Reading, MA: Addison-Wesley. Reference **DIE**

Chisholm, R. (1957). *Perceiving: A Philosophical Study*. Ithaca, NY: Cornell University Press. Reference **DEN**

Chisholm, R. and W. Sellars (1956). Intentionality and the Mental. In *Minnesota Studies in the Philosophy of Science*, vol. I, edited by H. Feigl and M. Scriven. Minneapolis: University of Minnesota Press. Reference **DEN**

Chomsky, N. (1957). *Syntactic Structures*. The Hague: Mouton. Janua Linguarum. Reference **YW1**

(1962). Explanatory Models in Linguistics. *Proceedings 1960 International Congress on Logic, Methodology, and Philosophy of Science*, edited by E. Nagel, P. Suppes, and A. Tarski. Stanford, CA. Reference **YW1**

(1964). Current Issues in Linguistic Theory. Janua Linguarum, 7. Reference **YW1**

(1965). *Aspects of the Theory of Syntax*. Cambridge, MA: MIT Press. Reference **YW1, MAR**

(1968). *Language and Mind*. New York: Harcourt Brace Jovanovich. [A much expanded 2nd edition appeared in 1972.] Reference **YW1**

Church, A. (1936). An Unsolvable Problem of Elementary Number Theory.

American Journal of Mathematics, 58, pp. 345–363. Reprinted in *The Undecidable*, edited by M. Davis. New York: Raven Press. 1965. Reference **DIE**

Churchland, P. M. (1986a). Cognitive Neurobiology: A Computational Hypothesis for Laminar Cortex. *Biology and Philosophy*, 1, 1, pp. 25–51. Reference **CHU**

(1986b). Some Reductive Strategies in Cognitive Neurobiology. *Mind*, N.S. 95, 379, pp. 1–31. Reference **CHU**

(1990). Representation and High-Speed Computation in Neural Networks. In *The Foundations of AI: A Sourcebook*, edited by Derek Partridge and Yorick Wilks, pp. 337–359. Cambridge, UK: Cambridge University Press

Churchland, Patricia S. (1986). *Neurophilosophy: Towards a Unified Science of the Mind-Brain*. Cambridge, MA: MIT Press. Reference **CHU**

Clancey, W. J. and R. Letsinger (1984). NEOMYCIN: Reconfiguring a Rule-Based Expert System for Application to Teaching. In *Readings in Medical Artificial Intelligence*, edited by W. J. Clancey and E. H. Shortliffe, pp. 361–381. Reading, MA: Addison-Wesley. Reference **CHA**

Clark, K. L. (1978). Negation as Failure. In *Logic and Data Bases*, edited by H. Gallaire and J. Minker, pp. 293–322. New York: Plenum Press. Reference **PRZ**

Clarke, J. J. (1972). Turing Machines and the Mind-Body Problem. *The British Journal for the Philosophy of Science*, 23, 1, pp. 1–12 [Argues that the sequence of states that a Turing machine goes through is essentially different from human thought – because computer memory configurations are open to unintended alternative interpretations while thoughts are not. An argument, against the notion that machines can think, based on the assertion that machine states and brain states are fundamentally different.]

Clinger, W. D. (1981). Foundations of Actor Semantics. *Massachusetts Institute of Technology AI Technical Report*. (AI-TR–633). Cambridge, MA: Massachusetts Institute of Technology AI Laboratory. Reference **HEW**

Club of Rome (1972). *The Limits to Growth*. New York: Universe Books. Reference **WIN**

Cohen, M. S. (1986). Design of a New Medium for Volume Holographic Information Processing. *Applied Optics*, 14, pp. 2,288–2,294. Reference **SMO**

Cohen, Paul R. and Edward A. Feigenbaum (1982). *Handbook of Artificial Intelligence*, vol. III. Los Altos, CA: William Kaufman [Volume III covers cognitive modelling, inference, vision, learning and planning. See Barr and Feigenbaum (1981/1982), this bibliography.]

Colby, Kenneth M., S. Weber, and F. Hilf (1971). Artificial Paranoia. *Artificial Intelligence*, 2, pp. 1–25 (See also Kenneth M. Colby. *Artificial Paranoia: A Computer Simulation of Paranoid Processes*. New York: Pergamon Press, 1975. [PARRY was reasonably robust (never at a loss for words), but mostly got by because people would ignore erratic output as the ravings of a lunatic. The system used a simple pattern matcher and had a library of canned responses chosen on the basis of variables named "alarm" and "trust" (or similar). If the dialogue happened to wander into topics like gambling, horses or the Mafia, PARRY would launch into a pages-long paranoid diatribe.]

Colmerauer, A., H. Kanoui, P. Roussel, and R. Passero (1973). *Un Système de Communication Homme-Machine en Français*. Marseille, France: Groupe de Recherche en Intelligence Artificielle, Université d'Aix-Marseille. Reference **PRZ**

Cooley, J. M. and J. W. Tukey (1965). An Algorithm for the Machine Computation of Complex Fourier Series. *Mathematical Computing*, 19, pp. 297–301. Reference **MAR**

Cummins, Robert (1977). Programs in the Explanation of Behavior. *Philosophy of Science*, 44, pp. 269–287. Reprinted in *Scientific Knowledge*, edited by Janet A. Kourany, Belmont, CA: Wadsworth, 1987. Reference **SIM**

Cynader, M. and N. Berman (1972). Receptive Field Organization of Monkey Superior Colliculus. *Journal of Neurophysiology*, 35, pp. 187–201. Reference **CHU**

Davenport, J. (1981). *On the Integration of Algebraic Functions*. Berlin: Springer-Verlag. Reference **CAM**

Davis, M. and J. T. Schwartz (1977). Correct-program Technology/Extensibility of Verifiers – Two Papers on Program Verification. *Courant Computer Science Report* (No. 12). New York: New York University. Reference **WEY**

Davis, Philip J. and Hersh Reuben (1986). *Descartes' Dream: The World According to Mathematics*. San Diego: Harcourt Brace. Reference **WIN**

Dawkins, R. (1976). *The Selfish Gene*. Oxford: Oxford University Press. Reference **DEN**

Delbruck, M. (1986). *Mind from Matter?* Palo Alto, CA: Blackwell Scientific. Reference **DIE**

Dell, G. S. (1985). Positive Feedback in Hierarchical Connectionist Models: Applications to Language Production. *Cognitive Science*, 9, pp. 3–23. Reference **SMO**

De Groot, A. (1946). *Thought and Choice in Chess*. Paris: Mouton. Reference **MIC**

De Millo, R. A., R. J. Lipton, and A. J. Perlis (1979). Social Processes and Proofs of Theorems and Programs. *Communications of ACM*, 22, pp. 271–280. Reference **P&W**

Dennett, Daniel C. (1969). *Content and Consciousness*. London: Routledge & Kegan Paul. Reference **DEN**

   (1975). Brain Writing and Mind Reading. In *Minnesota Studies in the Philosophy of Science*, vol. 7, edited by Keith Gunderson. Minneapolis: University of Minnesota Press. Reference **CHU** [Argues that, given a language of thought, cognition must be systematic to the point that brain-state configurations can be consistently "read-out." Points out that, due to space limitations, it must be that humans generate rather than store their beliefs.]

   (1978). *Brainstorms*. Cambridge, MA: MIT Press [This book is a collection of essays through which runs Dennett's distinctive philosophical approach to mental modeling by machines. Very broadly his line is (a) that the contents of consciousness in humans is far more limited and less vital or unique than many seem to believe, and (b) that mentalist language (e.g. "intention," "belief," etc.) consists fundamentally of terms in a theoretical language that we use to explain the behavior of other people, and that it could just as well be used (and at the same philosophical level, as it were) to describe the behavior of machines. He is an anti-realist about mental terms in the application to humans and machines: they are simply functional, theoretical terms with no clear semantics, but are perfectly adequate for their (limited) purposes. He descends directly from the Vahinger "As If" school of nineteenth-century German thought.]

(1980). The Milk of Human Intentionality. Commentary on Searle, "Minds, Brains, and Programs". *Behavioral and Brain Sciences*, 3, 3, pp. 428–430. Reference **DEN**

(1982). The Myth of the Computer: An Exchange. *The New York Review of Books*, June 24, pp. 56–57 (See Searle, 1982, this bibliography.). Reference **DEN**

(1984a). *Elbow Room: Varieties of Free Will Worth Wanting.* Cambridge, MA: MIT Press. Reference **DEN**

(1984b). The Role of the Computer Metaphor in Understanding the Mind. In *Computer Culture: the Scientific, Intellectual, and Social Impact of the Computer*, edited by Heinz Pagels. Annals of the New York Academy of Sciences, 426. Reference **DEN**

(1986). The Logical Geography of Computational Approaches: A View from the East Pole. In *The Representation of Knowledge and Belief*, edited by M. Brand and R. M. Harnish. Tucson, AZ: The University of Arizona Press. Reference **CHA**

(1990). Evolution, Error and Intentionality. In *The Foundations of AI: A Sourcebook*, edited by Derek Partridge and Yorick Wilks, pp. 190–211. Cambridge, UK: Cambridge University Press [A longer version appears in "The Intentional Stance," MIT Press/Bradford Books, 1987.

(forthcoming). A Route to Intelligence: Oversimplify and Self-monitor. In *Can Intelligence be Explained?*, edited by J. Khalfa. Oxford, UK: Oxford University Press. Reference **DEN**

Dennett, Daniel C. and John Haugeland (1987). Intentionality. In *The Oxford Companion to Mind*, edited by R. L. Gregory. Oxford, UK: Oxford University Press. Reference **DEN**

Dietrich, E. (1990). Programs in the Search for Intelligent Machines: the Mistaken Foundations of AI. In *The Foundations of AI: A Sourcebook*, edited by Derek Partridge and Yorick Wilks, pp. 223–233. Cambridge, UK: Cambridge University Press

Dietrich, E. and C. Fields (1986). Creative Problem Solving Using the Wanton Inference Strategy. *Proceedings of the First Annual Rocky Mountain Conference on Artificial Intelligence* (RMCAI–86). Boulder, CO: University of Colorado/Breit International. Reference **DIE**

(1987). Solving Problems by Expanding Search Graphs: Mathematical Foundations for a Theory of Open-World Reasoning. *Computing Research Laboratory Memoranda in Computer and Cognitive Science.* (MCCS–87–88). Las Cruces, NM: New Mexico State University. Reference **DIE.**

(1988). Some Assumptions Underlying Smolensky's Treatment of Connectionism. *Behavioral and Brain Sciences*, 11, 1, pp. 29–31. Reference **YW2**

Dijkstra, E. W. (1972). The Humble Programmer. *Communications of ACM*, 15, 10, pp. 859–866. Reference **P&W**

(1976). *A Discipline of Programming.* Englewood Cliffs, NJ: Prentice-Hall. Reference **P&W**

Dolotta, T. A. (1976). *Data Processing in 1980–1985.* Chichester, UK: Wiley. Reference **MIC**

Doran, J. E. and Donald Michie (1966). Experiments with the Graph Traverser Program. *Proceedings of the Royal Society of London* A, 294, pp. 235–259. Reference **MIC**

Doyle, J. (1979). A Truth Maintenance System. *Artificial Intelligence*, 12, pp. 231–272. Reference **CHA**

(1980). A Model for Deliberation, Action, and Introspection. Massachusetts Institute of Technology AI Technical Report. (AI-TR–581). Cambridge, MA: Massachusetts Institute of Technology AI Laboratory. Reference **HEW**

Dretske, F. (1981). *Knowledge and the Flow of Information*. Cambridge, MA: MIT Press/Bradford Books. Reference **DEN** [Dretske makes the distinction between pure information and the meaning of information. He uses ideas of communication theory to show how meaning, knowledge, learning and other cognitive activities can be explained in terms of pure information.]

(1985). Machines and the Mental. In *The Proceedings and Addresses of the APA*, 1985, 59, 1. (Western Division APA Presidential Address, April 26, 1985). Reference **DEN**

(1986). Misrepresentation. In *Belief*, edited by R. Bogdan. Oxford, UK: Oxford University Press. Reference **DEN**

Dreyfus, Hubert L. (1965). Alchemy and Artificial Intelligence. *Rand Corporation Paper* (P–3244). Reference **WIN**

(1972). *What Computers Can't Do: The Limits of Artificial Intelligence*. New York: Harper & Row. Reference **SIM, WIN, CHA** [Gives a sharp criticism of current AI. Judging from the harsh reaction it received from the AI community, some of the criticisms seem to be very close to the mark. The second edition, with a new preface, which appeared in 1979, is a revision of the 1972 book in which Dreyfus argues that AI has made very little progress, especially when compared to the promises made. In the revision he claims that the "results" obtained since the first edition further support his position. He feels that intelligent behavior is dependent on the total interaction between an intelligent being and its environment, therefore computers cannot have intelligence until they have the ability for this level of interaction.]

(1979). A Framework for Misrepresenting Knowledge. In *Philosophical Perspectives in Artificial Intelligence*, edited by Martin H. Ringle, pp. 124-138. Hassocks, Sussex, UK: The Harvester Press. Also Atlantic Highlands, NJ: Humanities Press [Dreyfus claims that the Massachusetts Institute of Technology move, in the early 70's, from building intelligent machines to simulating intelligence, is of no consequence, and that the symbolic information-processing approach should give way to non-symbolic neurological research.]

(1981). From Micro-Worlds to Knowledge Representation: AI at an Impasse. In *Mind Design*, edited by John Haugeland, pp. 161–204. Cambridge, MA: MIT Press. Reprinted in *Readings in Knowledge Representation*, edited by R. J. Brachman and H. J. Levesque, pp. 71–94. Los Altos, CA: Morgan Kaufman, 1985 [A revision of the 1979 introduction to Dreyfus' book *What Computers Can't Do* (see above).]

Dreyfus, Hubert L. and Stuart E. Dreyfus (1986). *Mind Over Machine: The Power of Human Intuition and Expertise in the Era of the Computer*. New York: The Free Press. Reference **SIM, WIN** [A general assault on the conventional wisdom of expert systems technology. A five-step process of acquiring expertise is presented. In particular they claim that rule following, of the type that current expert system technology (CEST) is based upon, is characteristic of the human novice rather than the expert, except in domains where there are no intuitive human experts.

(1987/88). *Making a Mind versus Modeling the Brain: AI Again at the Crossroads*. 117, 1, pp. 15–44. Daedalus. Reference **WIN**

Dreyfus, Stuart E. and Hubert L. Dreyfus (1990). Towards a Reconciliation of Phenomenology and AI. In *The Foundations of AI: A Sourcebook*, edited by Derek Partridge and Yorick Wilks, pp. 396–410. Cambridge, UK: Cambridge University Press

Duda, R. O. and P. E. Hart (1973). *Pattern Classification and Scene Analysis*. New York: Wiley-Interscience. Reference **CHA**

Duffy, M. C. (1984). Technomorphology, Engineering Design and Technological Method. *Proceedings Annual Conference of the British Society for the Philosophy of Science*. Reference **P&W**

Eliezer, C. J. (1946). On Dirac's Theory of Quantum Electrodynamics: the Interaction of an Electron and a Radiation Field. Proc. Royal Society *A 187*, pp. 197–210. Reference **CAM**

Ernst, G. and Allen Newell (1967). Some Issues of Representation in a General Problem Solver. *Proceedings of the Spring Joint Computer Conference*, pp. 583–600. Reference **B&O**

(1969). *GPS: A Case Study in Generality and Problem Solving*. New York: Academic Press. Reference **DIE, B&O**

Etherington, D. (1986). Reasoning with Incomplete Information: Investigations of Non-Monotonic Reasoning. Doctoral dissertation. Vancouver, BC: Department of Computer Science, University of British Columbia. Reference **PRZ**

Etherington, D., R. Mercer, and R. Reiter (1985). On the Adequacy of Predicate Circumscription for Closed-World Reasoning. *Computational Intelligence*, 1, pp. 11–15. Reference **PRZ**

Evans, T. (1968). A Program for the Solution of Geometric-Analogy Intelligence Test Questions. In *Semantic Information Processing*, edited by Marvin Minsky, pp. 271–353. Cambridge, MA: MIT Press. Reference **MAR** [An early theorem-prover approach to heuristic problem solving, with aspects of generalization and concept formation, in a program called ANALOGY.]

Feferman, S. (1962). Transfinite Recursive Progressions of Axiomatic Theories. *Journal of Symbolic Logic*, 27, pp. 259–316. Reference **WEY**

Feigenbaum, Edward A. and Julian Feldman (eds.) (1963). *Computers and Thought*. New York: McGraw-Hill. Reprinted in 1981 by Robert E. Kreiger [A classic early collection of AI papers. The book contains (among other things): Turing's paper introducing the Turing Test; Samuel's foundational demonstration of machine learning; the General Problem Solver of Newell and Simon; Minsky's "Steps towards AI"; and an extensive bibliography on early AI.]

Feigenbaum, Edward A. and Pamela McCorduck (1983). *The Fifth Generation: Artificial Intelligence and Japan's Computer Challenge to the World*. Reading, MA: Addison-Wesley. Reference **WIN, D&D**

Feldman, J. A. (1981). A Connectionist Model of Visual Memory. In *Parallel Models of Associative Memory*, edited by G. E. Hinton and J. A. Anderson, pp. 49–81. Hillsdale, NJ: Lawrence Erlbaum. Reference **SMO**

(1985). Four Frames Suffice: A Provisional Model of Vision and Space. *Behavioral and Brain Sciences*, 8, pp. 265–289. Reference **SMO**

(1986). Neural Representation of Conceptual Knowledge. *Technical Report*. (No. 189). Department of Computer Science, University of Rochester. Reference **SMO**

Feldman, J. A. and D. H. Ballard (1982). Connectionist Models and Their Properties. *Cognitive Science*, 6, pp. 205–254. Reference **SMO** [Sometimes styled as a "good introduction to the field," or as a "connectionist call to arms," this paper is quite possibly the latter, but not at all the former. The early sections give an elementary and readable overview of connectionism and the typical elements and topologies of connectionist networks, but the second half gets into extremely obscure and difficult examples that somehow pivot on "Bill's blue frisbee." Since the sentences are grammatical, and the paragraphs seem to cohere, this paper keeps up the appearance of being, at least locally, quite good – while being globally otherwise. Still, this is undoubtedly one of the most heavily referenced papers in the connectionist literature.]

Feldman, J. A., D. H. Ballard, C. M. Brown, and G. S. Dell (1985). Rochester Connectionist Papers: 1979–1985. *Technical Report*. (No. 172). Department of Computer Science, University of Rochester. Reference **SMO**

Fetzer, J. H. (ed.) 1987. *Aspects of Artificial Intelligence*. Dordrecht, Holland: Kluwer

Feynman, R. P. (1962). *The Theory of Fundamental Processes*. New York: W. A. Benjamin Inc. Reference *CAM*

(1965). *The Character of Physical Law*. Cambridge, MA: MIT Press. Reference **B&O**

Fields, C. (1987). The Computer as Tool: A Critique of a Common View of the Role of Intelligent Artifacts in Society. *Social Epistemology*, 1, pp. 5–25. Reference **DIE**

Fields, C. and E. Dietrich (1987). A Stochastic Computing Architecture for Multi-Domain Problem Solving. *Center for Cybernetic Communication Research Report*. (3CR/AI–87–01). Fort Collins, CO: Colorado State University. Reference **DIE**

Filman, R. E. and Richard W. Weyrauch (1976). A FOL Primer. *Stanford AI Laboratory Memo*. (AIM–228). Stanford, CA: Stanford University. Reference **WEY**

Flores, C. Fernando (1982). Management and Communication in the Office of the Future. Doctoral dissertation. Berkeley, CA: University of California, Berkeley. Reference **WIN**

Fodor, Jerry A. (1966). Information and Association. *Notre Dame Journal of Formal Logic*, 27, 3. Reference **FOD**

(1978). Tom Swift and His Procedural Grandmother. *Cognition*, 6, pp. 229–247. Reference **R&H**, **YW2**

(1980). Methodological Solipsism Considered as a Research Strategy in Cognitive Psychology. *Behavioral and Brain Sciences*, 3, pp. 63–73. Reprinted in *Mind Design*, edited by John Haugeland, pp. 307–338. Cambridge, MA: MIT Press/Bradford Books, 1981 [Fodor argues that while both a naturalist and computational view of cognitive psychology may be desirable, only a computational model is practically possible. The formal nature of the computational model implies that there is no way to connect real world semantics to the symbols of a model, therefore we should only concentrate on the workings of the model. From this it follows that it is useful to view the methodology in cognitive psychology as a solipsist methodology (hence the title).]

(1981). *Representations*. Cambridge, MA: MIT Press/Bradford Books. Reference **DEN**, **FOD**

(1983a). Reply to Brian Loar's "Must Beliefs be Sentences," edited by P. Asquith and T. Nickels. *Proceedings of the Philosophy of Science Association for 1982.* East Lansing, MI: Michigan University Press

(1983b). *The Modularity of Mind: An Essay on Faculty Psychology.* Cambridge, MA: MIT Press/Bradford Books. Reference **CHA, BOD, DEN**

(1987). *Psychosemantics.* Cambridge, MA: MIT Press. Reference **DEN, YW2**

(1990). Why There Still has to be a Language of Thought. In *The Foundations of AI: A Sourcebook,* edited by Derek Partridge and Yorick Wilks, pp. 289–305. Cambridge, UK: Cambridge University Press. Originally in *Psychosemantics.* Cambridge, MA: MIT Press, 1987

Fodor, Jerry A. and Zenon W. Pylyshyn (1988). Connectionism and Cognitive Architecture: A Critical Analysis. *Cognition,* 28, pp. 3–71. Reference **CHA** [A scathing attack on the foundations of connectionism. The strongest of their arguments is based on the lack of compositionality in connectionist architecture: semantics is not reflected by syntactic constituents. "What is deeply wrong with Connectionist architecture is" its failure to acknowledge either syntactic or semantic structure in mental representations.]

Freeman, C. (1985). The Economics of Innovation. *IEEE Proceedings,* 132. Reference **MIC**

Gaines, B. R. (1976). Foundations of Fuzzy Reasoning. *International Journal of Man-Machine Studies,* 8, 6, pp. 623–668 [Argues that fuzzy reasoning falls between the imprecise psychological explanations of intelligence and the strict rigorous account arising from formal logic. The principal appeal of such a system, it is claimed, is as a vehicle for "natural language reasoning" – a formal system to operate over language, as found, to attempt linguistic inference (but see Haack, S. (1979). "Do We Need Fuzzy Logic?" this bibliography, for an alternative view).]

Gaines, B. R. and L. J. Kohout (1977). The Fuzzy Decade: a Bibliography of Fuzzy Systems and Closely Related Topics. *International Journal of Man-Machine Studies,* 9, 1, pp. 1–68. [A large categorized bibliography on fuzzy set theory, multi-valued logics and related subjects complete with a very useful introductory section outlining the important relationships among these conceptual disciplines.]

Gardner, Howard (1985). *The Mind's New Science: A History of the Cognitive Revolution.* New York: Basic Books. Reference **WIN** [A good history of cognitive science that concentrates on the interaction of the disciplines (such as AI) that form cognitive science.]

Gazdar, G. (1983). NLs, CFLs, and CF-PSGs. In *Automatic Natural Language Parsing,* edited by Karen Sparck Jones and Yorick Wilks. Chichester, UK: Ellis Horwood. Reference **P&W**

Gelfond, M. (1987). On Stratified Autoepistemic Theories. *Proceedings American Association of AI Conference* (AAAI–87), pp. 207–211. Seattle, WA. Reference **PRZ**

Gelfond, M. and H. Przymusinska (1986). Negation as Failure: Careful Closure Procedure. *Artificial Intelligence,* 30, pp. 273–287. Reference **PRZ**

Gelfond, M., H. Przymusinska, and T. C. Przymusinski (1986a). The Extended Closed World Assumption and its Relationship to Parallel Circumscription. *Proceedings Association for Computing Machinery SIGACT-SIGMOD Symposium on Principles of Database Systems,* pp. 133–139. Cambridge, MA. Reference **PRZ**

(1986b). On the Relationship between Circumscription and Negation as Failure. *Technical Report*. El Paso, TX: University of Texas at El Paso. Reference **PRZ** (in preparation). On the Relationship between Circumscription and Negation as Failure II. In preparation. Reference **PRZ**

Geman, S. and D. Geman (1984). Stochastic Relaxation, Gibbs Distributions, and the Bayesian Restoration of Images. *IEEE Transactions on Pattern Analysis and Machine Intelligence*, 6, pp. 721–741. Reference **SMO**

Genesereth, M. R. and Nils J. Nilsson (1987). *Logical Foundations of AI*. Los Altos, CA: Morgan Kaufmann. Reference **PRZ** [An extensive work intended to be a key reference on the fundamentals of AI from the standpoint of logic.]

Giddings, R. V. (1984). Accommodating Uncertainty in Software Design. *CACM*, 27, 5, pp. 428–435. Reference **P&W**

Goguen, J. A., J. L. Weiner, and C. Linde (1983). Reasoning and Natural Explanation. *International Journal of Man-Machine Studies*, 19, 6, pp. 521–559 [Gives a good overview of the function and purpose of reasoning in AI and other disciplines, and argues that systems must be able to both understand and generate explanations in order to be effectively intelligent.]

Gold, E. M. (1967). Language Identification in the Limit. *Information and Control*, 10, pp. 447–474. Reference **CHA, YW2**

Goldberg, Allen and Ira Pohl (1984). Is Complexity Theory of Use to AI? In *Artificial and Human Intelligence*, edited by A. Elithorn and R. Banerji, pp. 43–56. Amsterdam: Elsevier Science Publishers [From the NATO Symposium on "Artificial and Human Intelligence," Lyon, France, 1981. Argues that AI and complexity theory (the analysis of the asymptotic running times of algorithms), will increasingly interact. In particular, the undecidability of first order logic, proven by Church and Turing, will have profound theoretical bearing on AI (since AI regularly resorts to this and related formalisms).]

Goldberg, M. and D. L. Robinson (1978). Visual System: Superior Colliculus. In *Handbook of Behavioral Neurobiology*, Volume I, *Sensory Integration*, edited by R. Masterson, pp. 119–164. New York: Plenum. Reference **CHU**

Goldstein, Ira and Seymour Papert (1977). Artificial Intelligence, Language, and the Study of Knowledge. *Cognitive Science*, January, 1, 1, pp. 84–123 [Argues that "intelligence is based on the ability to use large amounts of diverse knowledge in procedural ways, rather than on the possession of a few general and uniform principles." Along the way they give a good history of thought in AI and a succinct analysis of several systems.]

Gomez, F. and B. Chandrasekaran (1981). Knowledge Organization and Distribution for Medical Diagnosis. *IEEE Transactions on Systems, Man, and Cybernetics*, SMC-11, 1, pp. 34–42. Reference **CHA**

Good, I. J. (1982). Ethical Machines. In *Machine Intelligence*, vol. 10, edited by J. Hayes, D. Michie, and Y-H Pao, pp. 555–560. Chichester, UK: Ellis Horwood [Argues that with intelligence will come rationality and a need for a philosophy of ethics. Good believes that, given examples of ethical human behavior, and relevant discussions of ethics (and Asimov's Laws of Robotics), intelligent machines will formulate a consistent general theory of ethics on their own.]

Gordon, B. (1973). Receptive Fields in Deep Layers of Cat Superior Colliculus. *Journal of Neurophysiology*, 36, pp. 157–178. Reference **CHU**

Gould, S. J. (1980) *The Panda's Thumb*, New York: Norton, Reference **DEN**

Grabiner, J. (1986). Computers and the Nature of Man: A Historian's Perspective on Controversies in Artificial Intelligence. *Bulletin of the American Mathematical Society*, 15, 2. Reference **DIE**

Gries, D. (1981). *The Science of Programming*. New York: Springer-Verlag. Reference **P&W**

Groves, P. M. and R. F. Thompson (1970). Habituation: A Dual-Process Theory. *Psychological Review*, 77, 5. Reference **PAR**

Gunderson, Keith (1964). The Imitation Game. In *Minds and Machines*, edited by Alan Ross Anderson. Englewood Cliffs, NJ: Prentice-Hall. Also in *Mentality and Machines*, K. Gunderson, 1971. New York: Doubleday/Anchor. Reprinted from *Mind*, 1964, 73, pp. 234–245. [This paper questions the validity of the "Turing test" as a test for intelligence. To illustrate the point, Gunderson introduces the near-famous "toe-stepping game" where an interrogator places one foot through an opening in a wall in order to have it either a) stepped on by a hidden human or b) dropped on by a rock. The question is whether the interrogator can tell the difference; this test seeks to answer the question, "Can rocks imitate humans?"]

(1971). *Mentality and Machines*. New York: Doubleday, Anchor Books [A humorous book that investigates the philosophical arguments for the possibility of AI, and argues that they miss the point. While Gunderson seems to doubt the merit of current AI, he points out that he is not arguing for an anti-mechanistic point of view, he only wants to point out the flaws of the "computers can think" arguments.]

Haack, Susan (1979). Do We Need Fuzzy Logic? *International Journal of Man-Machine Studies*, 11, 4, pp. 437–446 [Argues that fuzzy logic is just a variation of multi-valued logic and that the arguments in its favor (avoiding complexity when formalizing informal argument, and allowing true and false to be fuzzy predicates) do not hold in that fuzzy logic itself introduces enormous complexity. She argues further that the linguistic evidence supporting "degrees of truth" constructions is flawed.]

Habermas, Jurgen (1979). *Communication and the Evolution of Society*. (Translated by Thomas McCarthy). Boston, MA: Beacon Press. Reference **WIN**

Haining, P. (1979). *The Man Who Was Frankenstein*. London: Frederick Muller. Reference **CAM**

Hall, C. E. (1980). Artificial Intelligence and Some Questions on the Nature of Science. *Applied Mathematics, Computer Science, and Statistics Report*. (January). Johannesburg: University of the Witwatersrand [Read at the Seventh Annual Congress of the Philosophical Society of Southern Africa, 1980. Describes, with examples from research, the fundamental difference between a logic of discovery and machine learning.]

Hall, Roger P. and Dennis F. Kibler (1985). Differing Methodological Perspectives in Artificial Intelligence Research. *The AI Magazine* (Fall), 6, 3, pp. 166–178 [They explain and lay out a typology of methods used in AI research. They argue that more effective communication of the results of AI research must be based upon an explicit statement of the methodological orientation of the research.]

Hammond, Allen L. (1973). Artificial Intelligence: A Fascination with Robots or a Serious Intellectual Endeavor? *Science*, June 29 [A summary of the infamous Lighthill report of 1972, the reactions to it from the AI community, and its consequences for AI research (particularly in Britain).]

Hanks, S. and Drew McDermott (1986). Default Reasoning, Nonmonotonic Logics, and the Frame Problem. *Proceedings American Association for AI Conference* (AAAI–86), pp. 328–333. Philadelphia. Reference **PRZ**

Hassan, T., M. A-Razzak, Donald Michie, and R. Pettipher (1985). Ex-Tran 7: A Different Approach for an Expert System Generator. In *Proceedings of the Fifth International Workshop on Expert Systems and their Applications*, Palais de Congres, Avignon, France, May 13–15, 1985. Paris: Agence de l'Informatique. Reference **MIC**

Haugeland, John (1985). *Artificial Intelligence: The Very Idea.* Cambridge, MA: MIT Press. Reference **WIN** [A philosophically oriented discussion of the potential of AI. He characterizes formal systems and points out that much of AI focusses on such systems but that much of the subject matter of AI does not seem to be easily reducible to such formal systems. He characterizes Good Old-Fashioned AI (GOFAI) and states its two essential claims: (a) intelligence is due to our capacity to think about things reasonably; (b) thinking about things reasonably amounts to a faculty for internal "automatic" symbol manipulation.]

Haugeland, John (ed.) (1981). *Mind Design: Philosophy, Psychology, Artificial Intelligence.* Cambridge, MA: MIT Press/Bradford Books. Reference **DIE, DEN, WIN** [This book is intended to be a sequel to *Minds and Machines* (1964), edited by Alan R. Anderson (this bibliography), bringing up to date and augmenting the topics discussed in that book.]

Hayes, Patrick J. (1973). The Frame Problem and Related Problems on Artificial Intelligence. In *Artificial and Human Thinking*, edited by A. Elithorn and D. Jones. San Francisco: Jossey-Bass. Reprinted from *Stanford AI Project Memo*. (AIM-153). Stanford, CA: Stanford University, 1971 [Hayes discusses how the frame problem arises in AI systems, specifically in the interaction of a robot with its environment. Some partial solutions using frame rules are presented, along with a simple example.]

(1975a). Computer Programming as a Cognitive Paradigm. *Nature*, 254, pp. 563–566 [He argues for the writing of computer programs as a central activity in AI. He discusses the realization of the view that programming in AI is a form of knowledge representation, and, moreover, a form that must concern itself with how to deal with the knowledge as well as what is true.]

(1975b). Nine deadly sins. AISB European Newsletter, July, pp. 15-17. Reference **R&H**

(1977). In Defense of Logic. Proceedings *International Joint Conference on AI* (IJCAI–77), 5, pp. 559–565. Cambridge, MA [Argues that logic is useful for representing declarative knowledge while conceding its limitations as a procedural language, and in the face of inconsistency.]

(1978). Trends in Artificial Intelligence. *International Journal of Man-Machine Studies*, 10, 3, pp. 295–299 [A short survey/position paper that characterizes AI as founded on the proposition that the brain is a computer whose computations can be discovered and modelled. The division in AI, between science and engineering, is characterized by the status of programs: experiment or end-product. Since AI is centered around working programs it is bound to diverge from systems science because such systems analyses look for general properties of intelligent systems (the architecture of intelligence), while AI looks for programs (the software of intelligence); the twain, he claims, cannot meet.]

(1979a). The Naïve Physics Manifesto. In *Expert Systems in the Electronics Age*, edited by D. Michie, pp. 242–270. Edinburgh: Edinburgh University Press. Reprinted from *Working Paper* (No. 34), Geneva, Switzerland: Institut Pour Les Etudes Semantiques et Cognitives, Universite de Geneve, 1978 [Hayes' paper started a new trend in the knowledge representation of the commonsense world. The underlying claim is that the mechanisms of first-order logic can be used to represent not only the "objective" world of physics, but also the anthropocentric real world as humans encounter it. It is the commonsense knowledge of that world (i.e. of naïve, not real, physics) that is needed, in the form of representations, for computers to navigate and manipulate the world in the way we do. An example of the difference would be the way in which the anthropocentric physical world consists largely of surfaces, since we do not (in general) navigate through the mass of the earth itself. From a real physics point of view, the earth's surface, as a boundary between the atmosphere and the "solid" mass, has no significance. The contrast between real and naïve physics is discussed (before Hayes) in Anderson *et al.*, 1974 (this bibliography).]

(1979b). On the Difference Between Psychology and AI. *AISB Quarterly*, 34, July. Reference **SIM**

Hayes-Roth, F., Donald A. Waterman, and Douglas B. Lenat (1983). *Building Expert Systems*. Reading, MA: Addison-Wesley. Reference **DIE, P&W**

Hebb, D. O. (1949). *The Organization of Behavior*. New York: Wiley. Reference **SMO, CHA** [One of the first works that proposes a theory of learning in neural networks. Many learning rules used in the connectionist work are derived from the learning rule given by Hebb.]

Hempel, C. (1966). *Philosophy of Natural Science*. Englewood Cliffs, NJ: Prentice-Hall. Reference **R&H**

Hesse, M. (1965). The Explanatory Function of Metaphor. *Proceedings 1964 International Congress on Logic, Methodology and Philosophy of Science*. Amsterdam. Reference **YW1**

Hewitt, C. (1969). Planner: A Language for Proving Theorems in Robots. *Proceedings International Joint Conference on AI* (IJCAI–69), May. Washington, DC. Reference **HEW**

(1972). Description and Theoretical Analysis (Using Schemata) of Planner: A Language for Proving Theorems and Manipulating Models in a Robot. *Massachusetts Institute of Technology AI Technical Report*. April. (AI-TR–258). Cambridge, MA: Massachusetts Institute of Technology AI Laboratory. Reference **HEW**

(1977). Viewing control structures as patterns of passing messages. *Artificial Intelligence*, 8, pp. 323–364. Reference **R&H**

(1985). The Challenge of Open Systems. *BYTE*, 10, April, 4, pp. 223–242 [Reprinted in this volume.]

Hewitt, C. and P. De Jong (1983). Analyzing the Roles of Descriptions and Actions in Open Systems. *Proceedings American Association for AI Conference* (AAAI–83), August, pp. 162–167. Washington, DC. Reference **HEW**

Hinton, G. E. (1981). Shape Representation in Parallel Systems. *Proceedings International Joint Conference on AI* (IJCAI–81), pp. 1,088–1,096. Reference **BOD**

(1987). Learning Distributed Representations of Concepts. *Proceedings of the Cognitive Science Society* (CSS–9), 8. Reference **D&D**

(1988). Representing Part-Whole Hierarchies in Connectionist Networks. *Proceedings of the Cognitive Science Society* (CSS-10). Reference **YW2**.

Hinton, G. E. and John R. Anderson (eds.) (1981). *Parallel Models of Associative Memory*. Hillsdale, NJ: Lawrence Erlbaum. Reference **SMO**

Hinton, G. E., J. L. McClelland, and D. E. Rumelhart (1986). Distributed Representations. In *Parallel Distributed Processing*, Vol. I, edited by D. E. Rumelhart, J. L. McClelland, and the PDP Research Group. MIT Press/ Bradford Books. Reference **SMO**

Hinton, G. E. and T. J. Sejnowski (1983a). Optimal Perceptual Inference. *Proceedings IEEE Conference on Computer Vision and Pattern Recognition*, pp. 448–453. Reference **BOD, SMO**

(1983b). Analyzing Cooperative Computation. *Proceedings of the Cognitive Science Society* (CSS-5). Reference **SMO.**

(1986). Learning and Relearning in Boltzmann Machines. In *Parallel Distributed Processing*, Vol. I, edited by D. E. Rumelhart, J. L. McClelland, & the PDP Research Group. MIT Press/Bradford Books. Reference **SMO**

Hoare, C. A. R. (1981). The Emperor's Old Clothes. *Communications of ACM*, 24, 2, pp. 75–83. Reference **P&W**

Hofstadter, Douglas R. (1979). *Gödel, Escher, Bach: An Eternal Golden Braid*. New York: Basic Books. [An engaging book that coaxes the reader into pondering many of the fundamental issues of AI. These issues are considered from both a "formal" mathematical and a philosophical perspective. The main premise of the book is that self-referential structures hold the key to many of these problems.]

Hofstadter, Douglas R. and Daniel C. Dennett (eds.) (1981). *The Mind's I*. New York: Basic Books. Reference **DEN** [A collection of essays that attempt to characterize intelligence, and try to identify in what way intelligence differs from other information processing systems.]

Holt, Anatol (1974). Remarks made at US Advanced Research Projects Agency Principal Investigators' Conference. Los Angeles, February 6–8. (Unpublished manuscript). Reference **WIN**

Hook, Sidney (ed.) (1960). *Dimensions of Mind*. New York: New York University Press [This is a collection of papers on the "mind/body" problem that were presented at a 1959 New York University symposium on philosophy. The book has three sections: the first deals with the purely philosophical aspects of the question, the second with the implications of machine intelligence, and the last with concept formation. The section on machine intelligence reflects the optimistic view towards AI of that time.]

Horn, B. K. P. (1975). Obtaining Shape from Shading Information. In *The Psychology of Computer Vision*, edited by P. H. Winston, pp. 115–155. New York: McGraw-Hill. Reference **MAR**

Howard, Robert (1986). *Systems Design and Social Responsibility: The Political Implications of "Computer-Supported Cooperative Work."* Address delivered at the First Annual Conference on Computer-Supported Cooperative Work, Austin, TX, December. Reference **WIN**

Hubel, D. and T. Wiesel (1970). The Period of Susceptibility to the Physiological Effects of Unilateral Eye Closure in Kittens. *Journal of Physiology*, 206, pp. 419–436. Reference **DIE**

Huerta, M. F. and J. K. Harting (1984). Connectional Organization of the Superior Colliculus. *Trends in Neuroscience*, 7, 8, pp. 286–289. Reference **CHU**

464   *Imre Balogh and Brian M. Slator*

Hunter, I. M. L. (1962). An Exceptional Talent for Calculative Thinking. *British Journal of Psychology*, 53, pp. 243–258. Reference **MIC**

Israel, David J. (1984). A Short Companion to the Naïve Physics Manifesto. In *Formal Theories of the Commonsense World*, edited by J. Hobbs and R. C. Moore, pp. 427–447. Norwood, NJ: Ablex. Reference **HEW**

Jaki, Stanley (1969). *Brain, Mind, and Computers*. South Bend, IN: Gateway Editions [A very anti-AI book but some of the points raised are worth considering.]

James, E. B. and Derek Partridge (1972). Machine Intelligence: The Best of Both Worlds? *International Journal of Man-Machine Studies*, 4, 1, pp. 23–31 [An early argument for world-knowledge (for processing over ill-defined problems within the context of a changing environment). Points out that all of this peripheral yet necessary processing may mean that machine intelligence will not not be any faster, or more precise, than human intelligence.]

Jardine, N. and R. Sibson (1971). *Mathematical Taxonomy*. New York: Wiley. Reference **MAR**

Johnson-Laird, Philip N. (1977). Procedural Semantics. *Cognition*, 5, pp. 189–214. Reference **YW2**

 (1983). *Mental Models: Towards a Cognitive Science of Language, Inference and Consciousness*. Cambridge, MA: Harvard University Press [This book presents a description of human mentality, based on the idea that this can best be done in terms of mental models of the world that we construct in our minds. The book is a good overview of this approach to explaining human cognitive processing.]

Johnston, V. S., D. Partridge, and P. D. Lopez (1983). A Neural Theory of Cognitive Development. *Journal of Theoretical Biology*, 100, 3, pp. 485–509. Reference **PAR**

Josephson, J. R., B. Chandrasekaran, J. W. Smith, and M. C. Tanner (1987). A Mechanism for Forming Composite Explanatory Hypotheses. *IEEE Transactions on Systems, Man, and Cybernetics*, SMC-17. Reference **CHA**

Julesz, B. (1975). Experiments in the Visual Perception of Texture. *Scientific American*, 232, April, pp. 34–43. Reference **MAR**

Kahn, K. M. (1984). How to Implement Prolog on a LISP Machine. In *Implementations of Prolog*, edited by J. A. Campbell, pp. 117–134. New York: Wiley. Reference **HEW**

Kanaseki, T. and J. M. Sprague (1974). Anatomical Organization of the Pretectal Nuclei and Tectal Laminae in the Cat. *Journal of Comparative Neurology*, 158, pp. 319–337. Reference **CHU**

Kant, I. (1787/1963). *Critique of Pure Reason*. Translated by N. Kemp Smith. 2nd edition. New York: MacMillan. Reference **SMO**

Kleene, S. C. (1952). *Introduction to Metamathematics*. Princeton, NJ: Van Nostrand. Reference **WEY**

 (1967). *Mathematical Logic*. New York: Wiley. 398 pp. Reference **WEY**

Kling, J. and B. Horwitz (1851). *Chess Studies, or Endings of Games*. London: Skeet. Reference **MIC**

Knapman, J. (1978). A Critical Review of Winston's Learning Structural Descriptions from Examples. *AISB Quarterly*, 31, pp. 18–23. Reference **CAM**

Konishi, M. (1986). Centrally Synthesized Maps of Sensory Space. *Trends in Neuroscience*, 9, 4, pp. 163–168. Reference **CHU**

Konolige, K. (1987). On the Relation Between Default Theories and Autoepistemic Logic. *Proceedings International Joint Conference on AI* (IJCAI-87), pp. 394–401. Milan, Italy. Reference **PRZ**

Kopec, D. and Donald Michie (1983). Mismatch Between Machine Representations and Human Concepts: Dangers and Remedies. *FAST Series Report.* (No. 9). Brussels: European Community. Reference **MIC**

Kornfeld, W. A. and C. Hewitt (1981). The Scientific Community Metaphor. *IEEE Transactions on Systems, Man, and Cybernetics*, SMC-11, 1, pp. 24–33. January

Kowalski, R. A. (1974). Predicate Logic as a Programming Language. *Proceedings IFIP–74*, pp. 569–574. Reference **HEW, WEY, PRZ**

(1979). Algorithm = Logic + Control. *Communications of ACM*, 22, pp. 424–436. Reference **PRZ**

(1980). A Position Statement. In *The SIGART Special Issue on Knowledge Representation*, edited by R. Brachman and B. Smith. *SIGART Newsletter*, 70, February. Reference **HEW**

(1984). Software Engineering and Artificial Intelligence in New Generation Computing. *The SPL-Insight 1983/84 Award Lecture*. Reference **P&W**

(1986). *Database Updates in the Event Calculus*. Department of Computing, Imperial College. Reference **PRZ**

Kowalski, R. A. and M. Sergot (1986). A Logic-based Calculus of Events. *New Generation Computing*, 4, pp. 67–95. Reference **PRZ**

Kripke, S. (1982). *Wittgenstein on Rules and Private Language*. Cambridge, MA: Harvard University Press. Reference **DEN**

Kuhn, T. S. (1962). *The Structure of Scientific Revolutions*. Chicago: University of Chicago Press. Reference **DIE, P&W** [Proposes that sciences do not evolve smoothly, but as a series of "revolutions" where the science is in a state of turmoil, separated by periods of slow but steady development. Though it discusses sciences in general, much of what is said about methodological incompatibilities and conflicting paradigms can be applied to the current state of AI.]

(1970). Logic of Discovery or Psychology of Research. In *Criticism and the Growth of Knowledge*, edited by I. Lakatos and A. Musgrave, pp. 1–22. Cambridge, UK: Cambridge University Press. Reference **DIE**

Kunen, K. (1986). Negation in Logic Programming. *Journal of Logic Programming*, 3. Reference **PRZ**

Laird, John, Paul Rosenbloom, and Allen Newell (1986). *Universal Subgoaling and Chunking: The Automatic Generation and Learning of Goal Hierarchies*. Hingham, MA: Kluwer. Reference **WIN**

Laird, John E., Allen Newell, and Paul S. Rosenbloom (1987). SOAR: An architecture for General Intelligence. *Artificial Intelligence*, 33, pp. 1–64. Reference **CH**

Lakatos, I. (1976). *Proofs and Refutations: The Logic of Mathematical Discovery*. Cambridge, UK: Cambridge University Press. Reference **B&O**

Lakoff, G. and M. Johnson (1980). *Metaphors We Live By*. Chicago, IL: University of Chicago Press. Reference **HEW**

Land, E. (1977). The Retinex Theory of Color Vision. *Scientific American*, 237, 6, pp. 108–128. Reference **DIE**

Langley, P. (1980). Descriptive Discovery Processes: Experiments In Baconian Science. *Techical Report*. Pittsburgh, PA: Carnegie-Mellon University. Reference **B&O**

(1982). Language Acquisition Through Error Recovery. *Cognition and Brain Theory*, 5, pp. 211–255. Reference **B&O**

Langley, P., G. L. Bradshaw, and Herbert A. Simon (1983). Rediscovering Chemistry with the BACON System. In *Machine Learning*, edited by R. S. Michalski, J. G. Carbonell, and T. M. Mitchell, pp. 307–329. Palo Alto, CA: Tioga. Reference **DIE**

Larkin, J. H., John McDermott, D. P. Simon, and Herbert A. Simon (1980). Models of Competence in Solving Physics Problems. *Cognitive Science*, 4, 4, pp. 317–345. Reference **SMO**

Lashley, K. (1950). In Search of the Engram. In *Psychological Mechanisms in Animal Behavior*, Symposia of the Society for Experimental Biology, No. 4, pp. 454–483. New York: Academic Press. Reference **SMO**

(1985). Bureaucracy as Artificial Intelligence. In *Knowledge Representation for Decision Support Systems*, edited by L. B. Methlie and R. H. Sprague, pp. 125–132. New York: Elsevier/North-Holland. Reference **WIN**

Leibniz, Gottfried Wilhelm (1951). *Selections*, edited by Philip Wiener. New York: Scribner. (Leibniz or Leibnitz, Gottfried Wilhelm, Baron Von, 1646–1716, German philosopher and mathematician). Reference **D&D**

Lenat, Douglas B. (1976). An Artificial Intelligence Approach to Discovery in Mathematics as Heuristic Search. *Stanford AI Laboratory Memo*. (AIM–286). Stanford, CA: Department of Computer Science, Stanford University. Reference **R&H**

(1977a). Automated Theory Formation in Mathematics. *Proceedings International Joint Conference on AI* (IJCAI–77), 5, pp. 833–842. Cambridge, MA. Reference **R&H**

(1977b). The Ubiquity of Discovery. *Proceedings International Joint Conference on AI* (IJCAI–77), 5, pp. 1093–1105. Cambridge, MA. Reference **R&H**

(1979). On Automated Scientific Theory Formation: A Case Study Using the AM Program. In *Machine Intelligence*, vol. 9, edited by J. E. Hayes, D. Michie and L. I. Mikulich, pp. 251–283. Chichester, UK: Ellis Horwood. Reference **R&H**

(1982). AM: An Artificial Intelligence Approach to Discovery in Mathematics as Heuristic Search. In *Knowledge-Based Systems in Artificial Intelligence*, edited by R. Davis and D. Lenat, pp. 3–217. New York: McGraw-Hill. Reference **DIE**

(1983). Eurisko: A Program that Learns New Heuristics and Domain Concepts. The Nature of Heuristics III: Program Design and Results. *Artificial Intelligence*, 21, pp. 31–59. Reference **DIE**

Lenat, D. B., M. Prakash and M. Shepherd (1986). CYC: Using Common Sense Knowledge to Overcome Brittleness and Knowledge Acquisition Bottlenecks. *The AI Magazine*, 6, 4, pp. 65–85. Reference **WIN** [The CYC project is a long-term attempt to construct a very large knowledge base in the hope that such an encyclopaedic database will be sufficient to support commonsense reasoning in AI systems.]

Lenat, Douglas B. and John Seely Brown (1984). Why AM and Eurisko Appear to Work. *Artificial Intelligence*, 23, pp. 269–294. Reference **DIE**

Lettvin, J. Y., Humberto R. Maturana, W. S. McCulloch, and W. H. Pitts (1959). What the Frog's Eye Tells the Frog's Brain. *Proceedings of the Institute of Radio Engineers*, 47, pp. 1940–1951. Reference **DEN**

Levesque, H. J. (1984). Foundations of a Functional Approach to Knowledge

Representation. *Artificial Intelligence*, 23, 2, pp. 155–213 [Argues for a dynamic knowledge representation characterized in functional terms (what can the system produce and consume), rather than in structural terms.]

(1986). Making Believers out of Computers. *Artificial Intelligence*, 30, 1, pp. 81–109 [Levesque introduces the notion of a "vivid" knowledge base (KB). By "vivid" he means a KB that is structured in such way that much of the knowledge is in an explicit form. He argues that while such KBs would be large, database management techniques allow many forms of reasoning to become tractable, and therefore such systems should be used as the basis for many reasoning systems.]

(1987). All I know: preliminary report. Technical Report. Univ. of Toronto. Reference **PRZ**

Levitt, M. and A. Warshel (1975). Computer Simulation of Protein Folding. *Nature*, 253, pp. 694–698. Reference **MAR**

Lewis, C. H. (1978). Production System Models of Practice Effects. Doctoral dissertation. Ann Arbor, MI: University of Michigan. Reference **SMO**

Lifschitz, V. (1985a). Computing Circumscription. *Proceedings International Joint Conference on AI* (IJCAI–85), pp. 121–127. Los Angeles. Reference **PRZ**

(1985b). Closed World Data Bases and Circumscription. *Artificial Intelligence*, 27, pp. 229–235. Reference **PRZ**

(1986). On the Satisfiability of Circumscription. *Artificial Intelligence*, 28, pp. 17–27. Reference **PRZ**

(1986/1988). On the Declarative Semantics of Logic Programs with Negation. In *Foundations of Deductive Databases and Logic Programming*, edited by J. Minker, pp. 177–192. Los Altos, CA: Morgan-Kaufmann. Reference **PRZ**

Lighthill, Sir J. (1972). *Artificial Intelligence: A General Survey*. London: Science Research Council [The influential and infamous critique of AI that found, with few exceptions, little in AI worth doing (or funding).]

Lindsey, Robert K. (1973). In Defense of Ad Hoc Systems. In *Computer Models of Thought and Language*, edited by Roger C. Schank and Kenneth Mark Colby, pp. 372–395. San Francisco: W. H. Freeman [Argues for a general procedure for constructing special representations over a general representation like predicate calculus. The argument generally rests on an appeal in favor of psychologically motivated mechanisms over theorem proving.]

Liskov, B. and J. Guttag (1986). *Abstraction and Specification in Program Development*. New York: McGraw-Hill. Reference **P&W**

Llinas, R. R. (1975). The Cortex of the Cerebellum. *Scientific American*, 232, 1, pp. 56–71. Reference **CHU**

Lloyd, J. W. (1984). *Foundations of Logic Programming*. Berlin: Springer-Verlag. Reference **PRZ**

Lucas, J. R. (1964). Minds, Machines, and Gödel. In *Minds and Machines*, edited by Alan Ross Anderson, pp. 43–59. Englewood Cliffs, NJ: Prentice-Hall [This controversial paper uses Gödel's incompleteness theorem to argue that machine intelligence is not possible. In brief the argument is: since computing machines are just physical embodiments of formal systems, the theoretical limitations of such systems must apply to machines. Therefore there are true propositions that can be expressed in the language of machines but cannot be proved or derived by them. Yet we humans can see that the proposition is true. This implies that human intelligence is capable of doing things that are provably impossible for machines, so machines can never do everything humans can. The debate sparked by this paper is still going on today.]

Lycan, W. G. (1985). Tacit Belief. In *Belief*, edited by R. J. Bogdan. Oxford: Oxford University Press. Reference **CHU**

McCarthy, John (1960). Programs With Common Sense. *Mechanization of Thought Processes*, pp. 77–84. London: Her Majesty's Stationery Office. Reference **PRZ**

(1968). Programs with Common Sense. In *Semantic Information Processing*, edited by Marvin Minsky, pp. 403–418. Cambridge, MA: MIT Press. Reprinted in *Readings in Knowledge Representation*, edited by R. J. Brachman and H. J. Levesque, pp. 299–308. Los Altos, CA: Morgan Kaufman, 1985 [Proposes formal logic as a basis for intelligent machines and discusses the various problems, and proposed solutions, to the approach (including a move to second-order logic).]

(1977a). First Order Theories of Individual Concepts and Propositions. *Stanford AI Laboratory Memo*. July. Stanford, CA: Stanford University. Reprinted in *Readings in Knowledge Representation*, edited by R. J. Brachman and H. J. Levesque, pp. 523–534. Los Altos, CA: Morgan Kaufman, 1985. Reprinted in *Machine Intelligence*, vol. 9, edited by J. Hayes, D. Michie, L. I. Mikulich, pp. 129–147. Chichester, UK: Ellis Horwood, 1979. Reference **HEW**

(1977b). Epistemological Problems in Artificial Intelligence. *Proceedings International Joint Conference on AI* (IJCAI–77), 5, pp. 1038–1044. Cambridge, MA. Reprinted in *Readings in Knowledge Representation*, edited by R. J. Brachman and H. J. Levesque, pp. 23–30. Los Altos, CA: Morgan Kaufmann, 1985. Reference **PRZ** [McCarthy discusses some of the knowledge representation problems of AI. He argues that since we have no adequate way of representing many types of knowledge, computational speedups will not help us. As a proposed solution he introduces circumscription as a new form of reasoning.]

(1979). Ascribing Mental Qualities to Machines. In *Philosophical Perspectives in Artificial Intelligence*, edited by Martin H. Ringle, pp. 161–195. Hassocks, Sussex, UK: The Harvester Press. Reprinted from *Stanford AI Laboratory Memo* (AIM–326), Stanford, CA: Stanford University, 1979 [Argues that we need to ascribe mental states like belief and desire to machines simply in order to understand their behavior at a level of abstraction above that of the program itself. Points out that intelligent agents must have beliefs about their own beliefs, as well as beliefs about others' beliefs, in order to explain, or understand, either themselves or others.]

(1980). Circumscription – A Form on Non-Monotonic Reasoning. *Artificial Intelligence*, 13, 1, 2 [special issues], pp. 27–41. Reference **PRZ** [This paper provides a detailed discussion on Circumscription. Circumscription is a form of reasoning that provides a way of "jumping to conclusions." By allowing such mechanisms, formal consistency is sacrificed, in order to allow reasoning from partial information to become tractable.]

(1984). We Need Better Standards for AI Research. *The AI Magazine*, 5, 3, pp. 7–8 [Presidential Address to the American Association for Artificial Intelligence, University of Texas at Austin, August, 1984. Reprinted in this volume.]

(1986). Applications of Circumscription to Formalizing Commonsense Knowledge. *Artificial Intelligence*, 28, pp. 89–116. Reference **PRZ**

(1987). Mathematical Logic in Artificial Intelligence. Draft paper. Reference **PRZ**

McCarthy, John and Patrick J. Hayes (1969). Some Philosophical Problems from the Standpoint of Artificial Intelligence. In *Machine Intelligence*, vol. IV, edited by B. Meltzer and D. Michie, pp. 463–502. Edinburgh: Edinburgh University Press. Reference **CHA, PRZ**

McClelland, J. L. and D. E. Rumelhart (1981). An Interactive Activation Model of Context Effects in Letter Perception: Part 1. An Account of the Basic Findings. *Psychological Review*, 88, pp. 375–407. Reference **SMO**

McClelland, J. L., D. E. Rumelhart, and G. E. Hinton (1986). The Appeal of Parallel Distributed Processing. In *Parallel Distributed Processing*, vol. I, edited by D. E. Rumelhart, J. L. McClelland, and the PDP Research Group. Cambridge, MA: MIT Press/Bradford Books. Reference **CHA** [A good introduction to why neurally inspired models are enjoying a resurgence in popularity.]

McClelland, J. L., D. E. Rumelhart, and the PDP Research Group (eds.) (1986). *Parallel Distributed Processing: Explorations in the Microstructure of Cognition*. Volume II: *Psychological and Biological Models*. MIT Press/Bradford Books. Reference **SMO** [This volume focuses on how the PDP models have been used to model cognitive behavior. The papers discuss different models and their relative successes. See also Rumelhart, McClelland, and the PDP Research Group for vol. I.]

McCorduck, Pamela (1979). *Machines Who Think*. San Francisco, CA: Freeman. Reference **DIE** [Foundations of AI in the sense of who, of the prime movers in this field, was motivated to do what, when, and why.]

McCulloch, W. S. and W. H. Pitts (1943). A Logical Calculus of the Ideas Immanent in Nervous Activity. *Bulletin of Mathematical Biophysics*, 5, pp. 115–137. Reference **CHA, DIE** [This paper was the first to show that networks of "simplified neurons" can compute any boolean function. Though the behavior of neurons is now thought to be more complex, this paper is still considered to provide the formal computational foundation for many of the brain-inspired AI models.]

McDermott, Drew (1981). Artificial Intelligence Meets Natural Stupidity. In *Mind Design*, edited by John Haugeland, pp. 143–160. Cambridge, MA: MIT Press. Reprinted from *SIGART Newsletter 57*, 4–9, April, 1976. Reference **PAR, R&H, B&O, BUN**

(1982). Non-Monotonic Logic II: Non-Monotonic Modal Theories. *Journal of ACM*, 29, 1, pp. 33–57. Reference **PRZ**

(1987/to appear). A Critique of Pure Reason. *Computational Intelligence*. Reference **PRZ**

McDermott, Drew and J. Doyle (1980). Non-Monotonic Logic I. *Artificial Intelligence*, 13, pp. 41–72. Reference **PRZ**

McDermott, Drew, M. Mitchell Waldrop, Roger C. Schank, B. Chandrasekaran, and John McDermott (1985). The Dark Ages of AI: A Panel Discussion at AAAI–84. *The AI Magazine* (Fall), 6, 3, pp. 122–134 [A lively and timely discussion featuring some of the shaggier heads in AI, who caution us that: (1) expert systems and Lisp programming do not constitute "science" of AI and (2) that too many unkept promises might result in less of the research pie going to AI. Also an interesting illustration of the basic insecurity that AI has as to its status as science/engineering.]

McDermott, John (1981). R1: The Formative Years. *The AI Magazine*, 2, 2, pp. 80–119. Reference **DIE** [A review of some years of use of an AI expert system. Long-term studies of the practical application of AI systems are in short supply. This is one; it may even be unique.]

Mackenzie, A. W. (1978). Intentionality-One: Intentionality-Two. Presented at the Canadian Philosophical Association Meetings, unpublished. Reference **DEN**

Mackworth, A. (1973). Interpreting Pictures of Polyhedral Scenes. *Artificial Intelligence*, 4, pp. 121-137. Reference **BOD**

MACSYMA Group (1977). MACSYMA Reference Manual. *Massachusetts Institute of Technology AI Laboratory Technical Report*. Cambridge, MA. Reference **DIE**

March, James G. and Herbert A. Simon (1958). *Organizations*. New York: Wiley. Reference **WIN**

Marek, W. (1986). On Predicate Autoepistemic Logic. Draft paper, unpublished. University of Kentucky. Reference **PRZ**

Marr, D. A. (1974). A Note on the Computation of Binocular Disparity in a Symbolic, Low-level Visual Processor. *Massachusetts Institute of Technology AI Technical Report*. (Memo 327). Cambridge, MA: Massachusetts Institute of Technology AI Laboratory. Reference **MAR**

(1976). Early Processing of Visual Information. *Philosophical Transactions Royal Society B*, 275, pp. 483–524. Reference **MAR**

(1977a). AI: a Personal View. *Artificial Intelligence*, 9, 1, pp. 37–48. Also in Mind Design, edited by John Haugeland, pp. 129–142. Cambridge, MA: MIT Press/Bradford Books, 1981 [Reprinted in this volume.]

(1977b). Analysis of Occluding Contour. *Proceedings Royal Society of London B*, 197, 1,129, pp. 444–475. Reference **MAR**

(1982). *Vision: A Computational Investigation into the Human Representation and Processing of Visual Information*. San Francisco: Freeman. Also as *Vision*. Cambridge, MA: MIT Press, 1982. Reference **BOD, DEN**

Marr, D. A. and H. K. Nishihara (1977). Representation and Recognition of the Spatial Organization of Three Dimensional Shapes. *Proceedings Royal Society of London B*, 200, 1,140, pp. 269–294. Reference **MAR**

Marr, D. A. and T. Poggio (1976). Cooperative Computation of Stereo Disparity. *Science*, 194, pp. 283–287. Reference **MAR**

Maturana, Humberto R. (1970). Neurophysiology of Cognition. In *Cognition: A Multiple View*, edited by P. Garvin. New York: Spartan Books. Reference **DIE**

Maturana, Humberto R. and Francisco Varela (1987). *The Tree of Knowledge*. Boston, MA: Shambhala. Reference **WIN**

Mays, L. E. and D. L. Sparks (1980). Saccades Are Spatially, Not Retinocentrically, Coded. *Science*, 208, pp. 1,163–1,165. Reference **CHU**

Mellor, D. H. (1984). What is Computational Psychology. *Proceedings of the Aristotelian Society*, 58, Supplement, pp. 37–55 [Mellor argues against the existence of a computational explanation of psychology (except perhaps at the perceptual level), since, he claims, no computational model can explain how attitudes differ from beliefs, or from each other. (See Boden, 1984, this bibliography.)]

Meltzer, B. (1977). Review of "An Artificial Intelligence Approach to Discovery in Mathematics as Heuristic Search" by D. B. Lenat. *AISB Quarterly*, 27, pp. 20–23. Reference **R&H**

Meredith, M. A. and B. E. Stein (1985). Descending Efferents from the Superior Colliculus Relay Integrated Multisensory Information. *Science*, 227, 4,687, pp. 657–659. Reference **CHU**

Merzenich, M. and J. Kaas (1980). Principles of Organization of Sensory-Perceptual Systems in Mammals. *Progress in Psychobiology and Physiological Psychology*, 9, pp. 1–42. Reference **CHU**

Mey, J. (1970). Toward a Theory of Computational Linguistics. *Proceedings Association for Computational Linguistics* (ACL-70). Columbus, OH: Association for Computational Linguistics. Reference **YW1**

Michie, Donald (1974). *On Machine Intelligence*. Edinburgh: Edinburgh University Press. 2nd edition, 1986, Chichester, UK: Ellis Horwood. [A collection of essays that address some foundational issues in AI, and span over a quarter of a century.]

  (1986). The Superarticulacy Phenomenon in the Context of Software Manufacture. *Proceedings of the Royal Society of London A*, 405, pp. 185–212 [Reprinted in this volume.]

Michie, Donald and Rory Johnston (1984). *The Creative Computer*. New York: Viking. Reference **WIN**

Millar, P. H. (1971). On Defining the Intelligence of Behaviour and Machines. *Proceedings International Joint Conference on AI* (IJCAI-71), 2, pp. 279–286 [Argues against the Turing Test for not measuring the right qualities and for introducing anthropomorphism into the experiment. An analysis of machine intelligence, it is claimed, must cover not only input-output behavior, but also the mechanisms and resources selected from among those available.]

Miller, G. A., E. Galanter, and Karl H. Pribram (1960). *Plans and the Structure of Behavior*. New York: Holt, Rinehart and Winston

Miller, Laurence (1978). Has Artificial Intelligence Contributed to an Understanding of the Human Mind? A Critique of Arguments For and Against. *Cognitive Science*, 2, pp. 111–127 [Miller examines the debate around the question of whether AI research has helped psychology. He argues that the depth of the rift between the two sides of this issue (yes, has helped a great deal versus no, AI is of little value) is not caused by ordinary disagreement about a scientific theory but stems from a fundamental methodological difference. The difference centers around the role of experiments in the development of psychological theory. The critics of AI believe that experiments should only be used to verify or refute theory, but the supporters of AI believe that experiments are essential in the process of developing theory. Miller feels that until both sides of this issue understand this difference there is little hope of resolving this conflict.]

Millikan, Ruth (1984). *Language, Thought and Other Biological Categories*. Cambridge, MA: MIT Press/Bradford Books. Reference **DEN**

  (1986). Thoughts Without Laws: Cognitive Science Without Content. *Philosophical Review*, 95, pp. 47–80. Reference **DEN**

  (forthcoming). *Truth, Rules, Hoverflies, and the Kripke-Wittgenstein Paradox*. Reference **DEN**

Minker, J. (1982). On Indefinite Data Bases and the Closed World Assumption. Proceedings 6th Conference on Automated Deduction, pp. 292–308. Springer Verlag. Reference **PRZ**

Minsky, Marvin (1967). Why Programming is a Good Medium for Expressing Poorly-Understood and Sloppily Formulated Ideas. In *Design and Planning II –*

472   *Imre Balogh and Brian M. Slator*

Computers in Design and Communication, edited by Martin Krampen and Peter Seitz, pp. 117–121. New York: Hastings House [An early defense of AI against the charge that "computers can only do what they are programmed to do (and hence they can never be intelligent)." Minsky argues that, since AI means writing programs to solve ill-specified and imprecise problems, acceptable outputs will not be precisely definable; so, with heuristics, and context that changes over time, program behavior can change, even given identical input. The notion that computers are too rigid to be intelligent stems from confusion between form and content, he claims; computers are rigid in the same way that violins and typewriters are.]

(1968). Matter, Mind, and Models. In *Semantic Information Processing*, edited by Marvin Minsky, pp. 425–432. Cambridge, MA: MIT Press [An argument that intelligent agents must have, besides knowledge of the world, knowledge of themselves and a special way of thinking about themselves and their knowledge.]

(1970). Form and Content in Computer Science. *Journal of ACM*, 17, 2, pp. 197–215 [Minsky's Turing lecture in which he discusses the uneasy relationship that exists between AI and computer science. He argues for the appropriateness of AI's lack of interest in formal specifications, etc. of problems. AI, he claims, is a context-rich domain (i.e. we know a lot about certain aspects of intelligence), but as yet ill-formed (i.e. we have little grasp of useful general theories at the level of detailed specifics). This being the case, it is entirely appropriate for AI research to use techniques such as exploratory programming to explore elements of context knowledge, and so eschew attempts to start with complete and detailed specification.]

(1975). A Framework for Representing Knowledge. In *The Psychology of Computer Vision*, edited by P. H. Winston, pp. 211–280. New York: McGraw-Hill. Reprinted in *Readings in Knowledge Representation*, edited by R. J. Brachman and H. J. Levesque, pp. 245–262. Los Altos, CA: Morgan Kaufmann, 1985. Abridged version reprinted in *Mind Design*, edited by John Haugeland, pp. 95–128. Cambridge, MA: MIT Press/Bradford Books, 1981. Reprinted in *Frame Conceptions and Text Understanding*, edited by Dieter Metzing. Berlin: Walter de Gruyter, 1980. Reference **HEW, SMO, MAR, CHA, R&H, PRZ** [This is Minsky's classic "Frame" paper in which he introduces the concept of a frame as a structure that can be used to organize the parts of a knowledge base so that pertinent information (for a given situation) can be easily accessed.]

(1980). K-Lines: A Theory of Memory. *Cognitive Science*, 4, pp. 117–133. Reprinted in *Perspectives on Cognitive Science*, edited by D. A. Norman, pp. 87–103. Norwood, NJ: Ablex, 1981 [An introduction to the "Society of Mind" theory and an attempt to explain memory as a function of recreating states of mind. "K-Lines" are created when we "get an idea" or "solve a problem" and they connect the active "mental agencies" thereby providing a basis for reactivating those same when the K-Line itself is later reactivated.]

(1982). Why People Think Computers Can't. *The AI Magazine* (Fall), pp. 3–15 [Discusses the many different reasons why most people are convinced that computers will never be able to really think.]

(1986). *The Society of Mind*. New York: Simon and Schuster. Reference **WIN**

[Minsky presents a theory that intelligence can be described as a "society" of unintelligent cognitive agents. The book gives a comprehensive description of the human mind in these terms.]

Minsky, Marvin and Seymour Papert (1969). *Perceptrons: An Introduction to Computational Geometry*. Cambridge, MA: MIT Press. Reference **SMO**, **CHA**, **B&O** [This book is of historical significance, since it was the work that reputedly killed the perceptron model, and in some sense helped end the first golden age of AI research. The bulk of the book deals with the meticulous analysis of the properties of perceptrons. The conclusion that came from this analysis was that the classes of perceptrons that could be analyzed were too weak to be of use, and the classes that were powerful enough to be useful were too complex to be understandable. The additions in the 1987 edition argue that while on the surface connectionism claims to have made progress since the perceptron days, the problems that were pointed out then have not been solved, only sidestepped, and that more rigorous foundation is needed before real progress can be made. It was revised in 1972, and again in 1987 when a foreword and epilogue on connectionism was added.]

Mooney, R. D. *et al.* (1984). Dendrites of Deep Layer, Somatosensory Superior Collicular Neurons Extended Into the Superficial Layer. *Abstracts: Society for Neuroscience*, 10, part 1, p. 158. Reference **CHU**

Moor, James (1978). Three Myths of Computer Science. *The British Journal for the Philosophy of Science*, 29, 3, pp. 213–222 [The three myths are: (a) that the hardware/software distinction is meaningful – Moor claims it is not and hence Gunderson's program-receptive/resistant distinction loses force; (b) that the digital/analog distinction is meaningful – Moor claims it is not and hence Dreyfus's argument against digital simulation loses force; (c) that the model/theory distinction is not meaningful – Moor claims that it is and hence Winston's claim, that the program is the theory, is almost always false.]

Moore, Robert C. (1984). A Formal Theory of Knowledge and Action. In *Formal Theories of the Commonsense World*, edited by J. R. Hobbs and R. C. Moore, pp. 319–358. Norwood, NJ: Ablex [A description of important work on the nature of intelligent action and the knowledge required, and produced by, reasoning with such.]

(1985). Semantic Considerations on Non-monotonic Logic. *Artificial Intelligence*, 25, 1, pp. 75–94. Reference **PRZ**

Moses, J. (1967). Symbolic Integration. *Massachusetts Institute of Technology Project MAC Report*. (MAC-TR-47). Cambridge, MA: MIT Project MAC. Reference **CAM**

(1974). MACSYMA – the Fifth Year. *SIGSAM Bulletin*, 8, pp. 105–110. Reference **MAR**

Mostow, J. (1985). Response to Derek Partridge. The AI Magazine, 6, 3, pp. 51–52. Reference **P&W** [A response to the challenge that the design process in AI is not a separate precursor of the implementation process.]

Nagel, T. (1986). *The View From Nowhere*. Oxford, UK: Oxford University Press. Reference **DEN**

Naqvi, S. A. (1986). A Logic for Negation in Database Systems. *Microelectronics and Computer Corporation Technical Report*. Austin, Texas. Reference **PRZ**

National Physical Laboratory (1959). *Mechanization of Thought Processes*.

London: Her Majesty's Stationery Office [Proceedings of one of the first AI conferences. Contains several classic and still interesting papers from people like Marvin Minsky (on heuristics), John McCarthy (on logical representations), Frank Rosenblatt (on the Perceptron), Oliver Selfridge (on the Pandemoniun system), and Y. Bar-Hillel (on literature searching), as well as less well-remembered papers from people like Grace Hopper and John Backus (both on "automatic programming"). Every paper is followed by a transcription of the subsequent question-answer-debate session featuring lively, often acid, repartee.]

Nau, D. S., V. Kiemar, and L. Kanal (1982). A General Paradigm for AI Search Procedures. *Proceedings American Association for AI Conference* (AAAI–82), pp. 120–123 [Summarizes work on a General Branch and Bound formulation which includes previous formulations as special cases and provides a unified approach to understanding most heuristic search procedures developed in AI.]

Needham, R. M. (1990). Is There Anything Special About AI? In *The Foundations of AI: A Sourcebook*, edited by Derek Partridge and Yorick Wilks, pp. 269–273. Cambridge, UK: Cambridge University Press

Nelson, R. J. (1982). Artificial Intelligence, Philosophy and Existence Proofs. In *Machine Intelligence*, vol. 10, edited by J. E. Hayes, D. Michie, and Y-H Pao, pp. 541–554. Chichester, UK: Ellis Horwood [Defines "mechanism" as the philosophy that the human mind is an information-processing system and argues that, unless intentional attitudes like explanation, belief, and desire can be analyzed and manipulated by programs, "mechanism" must be considered a failure. Notes the difficulty in AI of finding criteria for judging whether some artifact, equivalent to Turing machine, can be said to "perceive," "believe," or have any other mentalistic ability. Sketches an automata construction for a theory of "expectation" arguing, in the end, that such mentalisms are indeed mechanical.]

Neurath, O. (1959). Protocol Sentences. In *Logical Positivism*, edited by A. J. Ayer. Glencoe, IL. Reference **YW1**

Newell, Allen (1973). Production Systems: Models of Control Structures. In *Visual Information Processing*, edited by W. Chase. New York: Academic Press. Reference **CHA** [Description, with examples, of a production system that "appears to be a suitable model of . . . human control"; this claim based, primarily, on a limited short-term memory capacity of seven data elements and several other metaphors of psychological plausibility.]

(1973). Artificial Intelligence and the Concept of Mind. In *Computer Models of Thought and Language*, edited by Roger C. Schank and Kenneth Mark Colby, pp. 1–60. San Francisco: W. H. Freeman [Gives a state-of-the-art review of AI at the time from three perspectives: AI as "the exploration of intellectual functions," AI as "the science of weak methods," and AI as "theoretical psychology." An engaging think piece from the "mind as information processing" school.]

(1977). On the Analysis of Human Problem Solving. *In Thinking: Readings in Cognitive Science*, edited by P. N. Johnson-Laird and P. C. Wason. Cambridge, UK: Cambridge University Press. Reference **B&O**

(1978). Harpy, Production Systems and Human Cognition. *Technical Report*. (CMU-CS-78-140). Pittsburgh, PA: Department of Computer Science, Carnegie-Mellon University. Reference **R&H**

(1979). Reasoning, Problem Solving, and Decision Processes: The Problem Space as a Fundamental Category. *Technical Report.* (CMU-CS–79–133). Pittsburgh, PA: Department of Computer Science, Carnegie-Mellon University. Reference **HEW**

(1980). Physical Symbol Systems. *Cognitive Science*, 4, pp. 135–183. Reprinted in *Perspectives on Cognitive Science*, edited by D. A. Norman, pp. 37–85. Norwood, NJ: Ablex, 1981. Reference **DIE, CHA** [A long paper that argues, in a nutshell, that human intelligence is most profitably viewed as symbol manipulation (and most profitably modeled on computers in the same way).]

(1981). The Knowledge Level. *The AI Magazine* (Summer), 2, 1, pp. 1–20 [Presidential Address to the American Association for AI Conference (AAAI–80), Stanford University, 19 August, 1980.]

(1982). The Knowledge Level. *Artificial Intelligence*, 18, pp. 87–127. Reference **WIN** [Argues that logic is an appropriate tool for analyzing the knowledge of an agent – under the assumption that knowledge is a "potential for action" independent of symbolic representation. See also Newell (1981), this bibliography.]

(1983). Intellectual Issues in the History of Artificial Intelligence. In *The Study of Information: Interdisciplinary Messages*, edited by F. Machlup and U. Mansfield. New York: John Wiley. Appeared originally as Carnegie-Mellon University Technical Report (CMU-CS–82–142) [A first-rate review, well written and easy to read. A must for anyone interested in the history of the philosophy of the science of AI.]

Newell, Allen, J. Shaw, and Herbert A. Simon (1963). Empirical Explorations with the Logic Theory Machine: A Case History in Heuristics. In *Computers and Thought*, edited by E. Feigenbaum and J. Feldman, pp. 39–70. New York: McGraw-Hill. Reference **DIE**

(1969). Report on a General Problem-Solving Program. *Proceedings of the International Conference on Information Processing.* Paris. Reference **B&O**

Newell, Allen and Herbert A. Simon (1972). *Human Problem Solving*. Englewood Cliffs, NJ: Prentice-Hall. Reference **CHA, B&O, BOD, MAR, WIN**

(1976). Computer Science as Empirical Inquiry: Symbols and Search. *Communications of ACM*, 19, 3, pp. 113–126. Reprinted in *Mind Design*, edited by John Haugeland, pp. 35–66. Cambridge, MA: MI Press/Bradford Books, 1981. Reference **DIE, WIN** [This is the text of the tenth Turing Award Lecture. It presents Newell and Simon's view of how computer science and AI can be seen as an empirical study of symbol systems.]

Newquist, Harvey P. III (1987). The Machinery of Medical Diagnosis. *AI Expert*, 2, 5, pp. 69–71. Reference **WIN**

Nilsson, Nils J. (1971). *Problem-Solving Methods in Artificial Intelligence.* New York: McGraw-Hill. Reference **DIE**

(1980). Principles of Artificial Intelligence. Palo Alto, CA: Tioga. Reference **DIE** [A complete treatment of AI viewed as a heuristic search problem in discrete, and well-defined search space, and as a set of problems described in terms of the predicate calculus.]

(to appear). Logic and Artificial Intelligence. *Proceedings Massachusetts Institute of Technology Workshop on Foundations of AI.* Reference **PRZ**

Norman, D. A. and D. E. Rumelhart (1974). *Explorations in Cognition.* San Francisco, CA: W. H. Freeman. Reference **MAR**

Ohlsson, S. (1982a). On the Automated Learning of Problem Solving Rules. *Proceedings of the Sixth European Conference on Cybernetics and Systems Research*. Vienna. Reference **B&O**

(1982b). Transfer in Procedural Learning: A Matter of Conjectures and Refutations? *Technical Report*. UPMAIL. (No. 13). Uppsala, Sweden. Reference **B&O**.

Palmer, Anthony (1984). The Limits of AI: Thought Experiments and Conceptual Investigations. In *The Mind and the Machine*, edited by S. B. Torrance. Chichester, UK: Ellis Horwood [Argues that the real question in the philosophy of mind is centered around the problem of intentionality and that that question/problem cannot be answered/solved by AI methods.]

Partridge, Derek (1984). What's in an AI Program? *Proceedings European Conference on AI* (ECAI–84), pp. 669–673 [Reprinted in this volume.]

(1986a). RUDE vs. COURTEOUS. *The AI Magazine*, 6, 4, pp. 28–29. Reference **P&W**

(1986b). *Artificial Intelligence: Applications in the Future of Software Engineering*. Chichester, UK: Ellis Horwood / Wiley. Reference **P&W, PAR**

(1987). Human Decision Making and the Symbolic Search Space Paradigm. *AI and Society*, 1, 2, pp. 103-114. Reference **DIE**

Partridge, Derek, V. S. Johnston, and P. D. Lopez (1984). Computer Programs as Theories in Biology. *Journal of Theoretical Biology*, 108, pp. 539–564. Reference **P&W, PAR, SIM, DIE**

Partridge, Derek and Yorick A. Wilks (eds.) (1989). *The Foundations of AI: A Sourcebook*. Cambridge, UK: Cambridge University Press

(1990). Does AI have a Methodology Which is Different from Software Engineering? In *The Foundations of AI: A Sourcebook*, edited by Derek Partridge and Yorick Wilks, pp. 363–372. Cambridge, UK: Cambridge University Press. Also appeared as *Computing Research Laboratory Memoranda in Computer and Cognitive Science*. (MCCS–86–53). Las Cruces, NM: New Mexico State University; and in *AI Review* (1987), 1, 2, pp. 111–120

Peacocke, Christopher (1986). Explanation in Computational Psychology: Language, Perception and Level 1.5. *Mind and Language*, 1, 2 [Level 1.5 in the title refers to a level of description of a computational psychological process that lies between level 1 (which function is computed), and level 2 (which algorithm computes the function), as distinguished in Marr (1982, reprinted in this volume).]

Pearl, J. (1985). Bayesian Networks: A Model of Self-Activated Memory for Evidential Reasoning. *Proceedings of the Cognitive Science Society* (CSS–7). Reference **SMO**

Pellionisz, A. (1984). Tensorial Aspects of the Multi-Dimension Approach to the Vestibulo-Oculomotor Reflex. In *Reviews in Oculomotor Research*, edited by A. Berthoz and E. Melvill-Jones. Elsevier. Reference **CHU**

Pellionisz, A. and R. R. Llinas (1979). Brain Modelling by Tensor Network Theory and Computer Simulation. The Cerebellum: Distributed Processor for Predictive Coordination. *Neuroscience*, 4, pp. 323–348. Reference **CHU**

(1982). Space-Time Representation in the Brain. The Cerebellum as a Predictive Space-Time Metric Tensor. *Neuroscience*, 7, pp. 2,949–2,970. Reference **CHU**

(1985). Tensor Network Theory of the Metaorganization of the functional Geometries in the Central Nervous System. *Neuroscience*, 10. Reference **CHU**

Pfaff, D. W. (ed.) (1985). *Taste, Olfaction, and the Central Nervous System*. New York: Rockefeller University Press. Reference **CHU**

Plotkin, G. (1969). A Note on Inductive Generalization. In *Machine Intelligence*, vol. 5, edited by D. Michie and B. Meltzer, pp. 153-164. Edinburgh: Edinburgh University Press. Reference **B&O**

Poggio, T. and W. Reichardt (1976). Visual Control of the Orientation Behaviour of the Fly: Towards the Underlying Neural Interactions. *Quarterly Reviews of Biophysics*, 9, pp. 377–438. Reference **MAR**

Polikarov, A. (1985). Methodological Problems and Approaches in AI. In *AI: Methodology, Systems, and Applications*, edited by W. Bibel and B. Petkoff, pp. 11–17. Amsterdam: Elsevier [The interrelation of methodology of science and AI is discussed. The conclusion is that there are reasons to expect that the "the role of AI in the specification and development of science will increase parallel with the progress of AI itself."]

Pollack, J. B. (1987). Cascaded Back-Propagation on Dynamic Connectionist Networks. *Proceedings of the Ninth Annual Conference of the Cognitive Science Society*, pp. 391–404. Seattle, WA. Reference **YW2**

(1988). Personal communication. Reference **YW2**

Popper, K. and J. Eccles (1977). *The Self and Its Brain* (Parts I and II). Berlin: Springer-International. Reference **DEN**

Prawitz, D. (1965). *Natural Deduction – A Proof Theoretic Study*. Stockholm: Almqvist and Wiksell. Reference **WEY**

Pribram, Karl H. (1971). *Languages of the Brain*. Englewood Cliffs, NJ: Prentice-Hall. Reference **YW1**

Przymusinska, H. (1987a). On the Relationship between Autoepistemic Logic and Circumscription for Stratified Deductive Databases. *Proceedings of the Association for Computing Machinery SIGART International Symposium on Methodologies for Intelligent Systems*. Knoxville, TN. Reference **PR**

(1987b). Personal communication. Reference **PRZ**

Przymusinski, T. C. (1987a). On the Declarative and Procedural Semantics of Logic Programs. *Journal of Logic Programming*. Reference **PRZ**

(1987b). An Algorithm to Compute Circumscription. *Artificial Intelligence*. Reference **PRZ**

(1987/1988). On the Declarative Semantics of Stratified Deductive Databases and Logic Programs. In *Foundations of Deductive Databases and Logic Programming*, edited by J.Minker, pp. 193–216. Los Altos, CA: Morgan-Kaufmann. Reference **PRZ**

(1990). A Review of Formal Approaches to AI. In *The Foundations of AI: A Sourcebook*, edited by Derek Partridge and Yorick Wilks, pp. 49–71. Cambridge, UK: Cambridge University Press

Puccetti, Roland (1974). Pattern Recognition in Computers and the Human Brain. *The British Journal for the Philosophy of Science*, 25, 2, pp. 137–154 [Describes two competing paradigms for pattern recognition (template matching and feature analysis), and points out that neither may turn out to be brain simulation. Visual recognition, he argues, might be a Gestalt ability that machine analysis will never solve. Cites the now famous chess-master data (incredible recall of meaningful board configurations versus merely average recall of random piece placement), to support the notion that human and machine chess playing are fundamentally different.]

Punch, W., M. C. Tanner, and J. R. Josephson (1986). Design Considerations for Peirce, High Level Language for Hypothesis Assembly. *Proceedings Expert Systems In Government Symposium*, pp. 279–281. Silver Spring, MD: IEEE Computer Society Press. Reference **CHA**

Putnam, Hilary (1960). Minds and Machines. In *Dimensions of Mind*, edited by Sidney Hook, pp. 138–164. New York: New York University Press. ["... all the issues and puzzles that make up the traditional mind-body problem . . . arise in connection with any computing system capable of answering questions about its own structure." The implication of this, he argues, is that the "mind-body problem" goes away.]

(1967). The Innateness Hypothesis and Explanatory Models in Linguistics. *Synthese*, 17, pp. 12–23

(1973). Reductionism and the Nature of Psychology. *Cognition*, 2, pp. 131–146. An abridged version is reprinted in *Mind Design*, edited by John Haugeland, pp. 205–219. Cambridge, MA: MIT Press/Bradford Books, 1981 [Putnam argues that reductionism is not compatible with psychology or other "higher" sciences (e.g. sociology). His argument is based on the fact that while these disciplines should not contradict the "lower" sciences (biology etc.), these lower sciences do not uniquely determine the phenomena of the higher sciences. That is, the lower sciences are equally compatible with hypothetical worlds that are radically different from the observed world.]

(1975). The Meaning of "Meaning," In *Mind, Language and Reality. Philosophical Papers*, 2, pp. 215–271. Cambridge, UK: Cambridge University Press. Reference **DEN**

Pylyshyn, Zenon W. (1978). Computational Models and Empirical Constraints. *Behavioral and Brain Sciences*, 1, pp. 93–127. Reference **PAR**

(1979). Complexity and the Study of Artificial and Human Intelligence. In *Philosophical Perspectives in AI*, edited by Martin Ringle, pp. 23–56. Atlantic Highlands, NJ: Humanities Press. A revised version is reprinted in *Mind Design*, edited by John Haugeland, pp. 67–94. Cambridge, MA: MIT Press/Bradford Books, 1981 [A paper that challenges the strong objection to much of AI – the Searlean objection that mimicking some function tells us nothing about the internal "structure" of the mimicked function. Pylyshyn argues that computations can be viewed as empirical hypotheses about the nature of human intelligence. He proposes a notion of "strong equivalence" of processes; a notion in which the similarities between the two processes goes beyond mere input-output equivalence and extends to similarities in the internal realization of the equivalent behaviors.]

(1984). *Computation and Cognition: Toward a Foundation for Cognitive Science*. Cambridge, MA: MIT Press/Bradford Books. Reference **WIN, CHA** [Destined to be a landmark in the cognitive science literature, this book argues that cognition as computation is more than a metaphor, and that cognitive descriptions of mental states can be mechanistically framed. The point is to discover the "functional architecture" of the mind, and the sorts of representations of symbols and rules being processed.]

Quillian, M. R. (1968). Semantic Memory. In *Semantic Information Processing*, edited by Marvin Minsky, pp. 216–270. Cambridge, MA: MIT Press. Reference **MAR** [The paper from which the notion of a semantic network as a plausible model of human memory arose.]

Ramachandran, V. S. (1985a). Apparent Motion of Subjective Surfaces. *Perception*, 14, pp. 127–134. Reference **DEN**

(1985b). Guest Editorial. *Perception*, 14, pp. 97–103. Reference **DEN**

Randell, B. (1982). *The Origins of Digital Computers*. Berlin: Springer-Verlag. Reference **DIE**

Raphael, B. (1968). SIR: Semantic Information Retrieval. In *Semantic Information Processing*, edited by Marvin Minsky. pp. 33–134. Cambridge, MA: MIT Press. Reference **MAR**

(1971). The Frame Problem in Problem-Solving Systems. In *Artificial Intelligence and Heuristic Programming*, edited by N. Findler and B. Meltzer, pp. 159–172. Edinburgh: Edinburgh University Press. Also New York: Elsevier [Describes the frame (of reference) problem as "the difficulty of creating and maintaining an appropriate informational context ... in certain problem-solving processes," and reviews the several approaches being attempted at that time.]

Reddy, M. (1979). The Conduit Metaphor. In *Metaphor and Thought*, edited by A. Ortony. Cambridge, UK: Cambridge University Press

Reggia, J., D. S. Nau, P. Wang, and Y. Peng (1985). A Formal Model of Diagnostic Inference. *Information Sciences*, 37, pp. 227–285. Reference **CHA**

Reiter, R. (1978). On Closed-World Data Bases. In *Logic and Data Bases*, edited by H. Gallaire and J. Minker, pp. 55–76. New York: Plenum Press. Reference **PRZ**

(1980). A Logic for Default Theory. *Artificial Intelligence*, 13, pp. 81–132. Reference **PRZ**

(1981). On Closed World Data Bases. In *Logic and Data Bases*. New York: Plenum Publishing. Reference **HEW**

(1982). Circumscription implies Predicate Completion (sometimes). *Proceedings America Association for AI* (AAAI-82), pp. 418–420. Reference **PRZ**

(1987). A Theory of Diagnosis from First Principles. *Artificial Intelligence*, 32, pp. 57–95. Reference **CHA**

(to appear). Nonmonotonic Reasoning. *Annual Reviews of Computer Science*. Reference **PRZ**

Rescorla, R. A. and P. C. Holland (1976). Some Behavioural Approaches to the Study of Learning. In *Neural Mechanisms of Learning and Memory*, edited by M. R. Rosenzweig and E. L. Bennett, pp. 165–192. Cambridge, MA: MIT Press. Reference **PAR**

Rich, Elaine (1983). *Artificial Intelligence*. New York: McGraw-Hill. Reference **DIE** [This is a good introduction to AI that covers most of the major areas of the field.]

Riley, M. S. and P. Smolensky (1984). A Parallel Model of (Sequential) Problem Solving. *Proceedings of the Cognitive Science Society* (CSS-6). Reference **SMO**

Ritchie, G. D. and F. K. Hanna (1984a). AM: A Case Study in AI Methodology. *Artificial Intelligence*, 23, 3, pp. 249–269. Reference **CAM** [Reprinted in this volume.]

(1984b). Retrospectives: A Note from the Editor. *Artificial Intelligence*, 23, 3, pp. 247–249. Reference **CAM**

Robinson, D. A. (1972). Eye Movements Evoked by Collicular Stimulation in the Alert Monkey. *Vision Research*, 12, pp. 1,795–1,808. Reference **CHU**

Robinson, J. A. (1965). A Machine Oriented Logic Based on the Resolution Principle. *Journal of ACM*, 12, 1, pp. 23–41. Reference **PRZ** [The paper which proved to be the theoretical foundation for the language PROLOG and transformed a logician into a celebrity in AI.]

(1968). The Generalized Resolution Principle. In *Machine Intelligence*, vol. 3, edited by D. Michie. Edinburgh: University of Edinburgh [The resolution principle is a computationally efficient proof procedure that was a necessary basis for the mechanization of the process of logical proofs. The design of efficient algorithms for resolution gave rise to the language PROLOG.]

Robinson, R. M. (1950). An Essentially Undecidable Axiom System. *Proceedings of the International Congress Mathematics*, 1, pp. 729–730. Reference **WEY**

Rosch, E. (1976). Classifications of Real-World Objects: Origins and Representations in Cognition. *Bulletin de Psychologie*, Special Annual, pp. 242–250. Reference **MAR**

Rosenblatt, Frank (1962). *Principles of Neurodynamics: Perceptrons and the Theory of Brain Mechanisms*. Washington, DC: Sparta Books. See also "The Perceptron," *Psychological Review* (1956), 65, pp. 386–407. See also National Physical Laboratory (1959), *Mechanization of Thought Processes*. London: Her Majesty's Stationery Office (this bibliography). See also *Cornell Aeronautical Laboratory* (Report 1196-G–8), 1962. Reference **CHA** [This book was intended to provide a theoretical foundation for the study of perceptrons, and as a guide for further research in the area. The book provides a detailed analysis of the simplest non-trivial configuration as an illustration of how the theory should be applied. Rosenblatt hoped that by stimulating future work on perceptrons, the more powerful configurations would prove to be analyzable and useful in the study of intelligence. Work in this area all but ceased after the publication of Minsky and Papert's book Perceptrons (1969, this bibliography), in which they pointed out the inherent limitation of this model. The more recent "connectionist" movement can trace its roots in part to this work.]

Roszak, Theodore (1986). *The Cult of Information: The Folklore of Computers and the True Art of Thinking*. New York: Pantheon. Reference **WIN**

Roussel, P. (1975). *PROLOG, Manuel de Reference et d'Utilisation*. Marseille, France: Group d'Intelligence Artificielle U.E.R. de Marseille. Reference **PRZ**

Royden, H. L. (1963). *Real Analysis*. New York: Macmillan. Reference **WEY**

Rudd, R. S. (1966). *Philosophy of Social Science*. Englewood Cliffs, NJ: Prentice-Hall. Reference **R&H**

Rudin, L. (1981). Lambda-Logic. *Technical Report*. May. (No. 4,521). Pasadena, CA: California Institute of Technology. Reference **HEW**

Rumelhart, D. E. (1975). Notes on a Schema for Stories. In *Representation and Understanding*, edited by D. G. Bobrow and A. Collins, pp. 211–236. New York, San Francisco, London: Academic Press. Reference **SMO**

(1980). Schemata: The Building Blocks of Cognition. In *Theoretical Issues in Reading Comprehension*, edited by R. Spiro, B. Bruce, and W. Brewer. Hillsdale, NJ: Lawrence Erlbaum. Reference **SMO**

Rumelhart, D. E., G. E. Hinton, and R. J. Williams (1986). Learning Internal Representations by Error Propagation. In *Parallel Distributed Processing*, vol. I, edited by D. E. Rumelhart, J. L. McClelland, and the PDP Research Group, pp. 318–362. Cambridge, MA: MIT Press/Bradford Books. Reference **SMO**, **CHU** [This paper gives a description of back-propagation, which is one of the more significant learning procedures for multi-layered connectionist networks.]

Rumelhart, D. E. and J. L. McClelland (1982). An Interactive Activation Model of Context Effects in Letter Perception. Part 2: The Contextual Enhancement Effect and Some Tests and Extensions of the Model. *Psychological Review*, 89, pp. 60–94. Reference **SMO**

(1986a). PDP Models and General Issues in Cognitive Science. In *Parallel Distributed Processing*, vol. I, edited by D. E. Rumelhart, J. L. McClelland, and the PDP Research Group. Cambridge, MA: MIT Press/Bradford Books. Reference **CHA, WIN**

(1986b). On Learning the Past Tenses of English Verbs. In *Parallel Distributed Processing*, vol. II, edited by J. L. McClelland, D. E. Rumelhart, and the PDP Research Group. Cambridge, MA: MIT Press/Bradford Books. Reference **SMO, CHA**

Rumelhart, D. E., J. L. McClelland, and The PDP Research Group (eds.) (1986). *Parallel Distributed Processing: Explorations in the Microstructure of Cognition*. Volume I: *Foundations*. Cambridge, MA: MIT Press/Bradford Books. Reference **SMO** [This volume contains papers on foundational aspects of the connectionist (PDP) models. The papers cover topics from motivational issues, and learning procedures, to formal mathematical analysis of the models. See also McClelland, Rumelhart, and the PDP Research Group for vol II.]

Rumelhart, D. E., P. Smolensky, J. L. McClelland, and G. E. Hinton (1986). Schemata and Sequential Thought Processes in Parallel Distributed Processing Models. In *Parallel Distributed Processing*, vol. II, edited by J. L. McClelland, D. E. Rumelhart, and the PDP Research Group. Cambridge, MA: MIT Press/Bradford Books. Reference **SMO, CHA**

Russell, Bertrand (1952). *A History of Western Philosophy*. New York: Simon and Schuster. Reference **WIN**

Sadri, F. (1986). *Three Recent Approaches to Temporal Reasoning*. Department of Computing, Imperial College, London. Reference **PRZ**

Sampson, Geoffrey (1975). Theory Choice in a Two-level Science. *The British Journal for the Philosophy of Science*, 26, 4, pp. 303–318. Reference **P&W** [Describes linguistics as a two-level science (level 1: the study of grammars; level 2: the study of classes of grammars). This separation, in any science, leads to the problem, and conflict, that the preferred theories at each level might be seen as incompatible. Sound familiar?]

Samuel, Arthur L. (1983). AI, Where It Has Been and Where It Is Going? *Proceedings International Joint Conference on AI* (IJCAI–83), 8, pp. 1,152–1,157 [An anecdotal diversion from one of the "grand old men" of Artificial Intelligence and computing. Samuel quickly traces the history of AI, as it happened to him, and reviews the (over-optimistic) predictions for AI that he published in 1963. He maintains that the single most fundamental issue, then as now, is basic research in machine learning; and he observes that the past twenty years have not borne anything like the fruit that he and his contemporaries had expected (and predicted). He offers a few predictions for computing in the year 2000 (pocket computers and so forth), but leaves predictions for the future of AI as "an exercise for the reader."]

Sandewall, E. J. (1971). Representing Natural Language Information in Predicate Calculus. In *Machine Intelligence*, vol. 6, edited by B. Meltzer and D. Michie, pp. 255–280. Edinburgh: Edinburgh University Press [Proposes first-order predicate calculus as a representation for natural language, and theorem-proving programs to manipulate these "meanings." Mostly glosses over the problems of logical paradox and inconsistency, time variability, and effectively translating from natural language into logic.]

(1977). Some Observations on Conceptual Programming. In *Machine Intelligence*, vol. 8, edited by E. W. Elcock and D. Michie. Chichester, UK [Proposes that programs will be better organized and understood if written in a dataflow style that does not distinguish between programs and data. Gives a good, non-standard, introduction to Lisp programming principles.]

(1979). Biological Software. *Proceedings International Joint Conference on AI* (IJCAI–79), 6, pp. 744–747 [Argues that, contrary to popular belief, AI systems should not need to appear human-like, and that it is necessary, both from the AI and the software engineering points of view, that the next level down in the AI system has quasi-biological properties, such as the ability to reproduce (self-adaptive software that creates a modified copy of itself).]

Sayre, Kenneth (1976). Cybernetics and the Philosophy of Mind. London: Routledge and Kegan Paul [As the title suggests, this is a study of the human mind from a cybernetic perspective. The premise is that by applying communication and control theory to questions of how the mind works, significant insights can be gained into the nature of intelligence.]

Schank, Roger C. (1972). Conceptual Dependency. *Cognitive Psychology*, 3, pp. 552–631

(1973). Identification of Conceptualizations Underlying Natural Language. In *Computer Models of Thought and Language*, edited by Roger C. Schank and Kenneth M. Colby, pp. 187–247. San Francisco: W. H. Freeman. Reference **MAR**

(1975a). *Conceptual Information Processing*. Amsterdam: North-Holland. Reference **DIE, MAR**

(1975b). The Primitive Acts of Conceptual Dependency. In *Theoretical Issues in Natural Language Processing*. Cambridge, MA: Association for Computational Linguistics. Reference **SIM**

(1982a). *Dynamic Memory: A Theory of Reminding and Learning in Computers and People*. New York: Cambridge University Press. Reference **CHA**

(1982b). Inference in the Conceptual Dependency Paradigm: A Personal History. In *Language, Mind, and Brain*, edited by Thomas W. Simon and Robert J. Scholes. Hillsdale, NJ: Lawrence Erlbaum. Reference **SIM**

(1983). The Current State of AI: One Man's Opinion. *The AI Magazine* (Winter/Spring), pp. 3–8. Reference **P&W**

(1986). *Explanation Patterns: Understanding Mechanically and Creatively*. Hillsdale, NJ: Lawrence Erlbaum. Reference **SIM**

(1987). What is AI Anyway? *The AI Magazine*, 8, 4, pp. 59–65 [Reprinted in this volume.]

Schank, Roger C. and R. P. Abelson (1977). Scripts, Plans, Goals and Understanding. Hillsdale, NJ: Lawrence Erlbaum. Reference **CHA**

Schiller, P. H. (1984). The Superior Colliculus and Visual Function, edited by I. Darian-Smith. *Handbook of Physiology*, vol. III, pp. 457–504. Reference **CHU**

Schiller, P. H. and J. H. Sandell (1983). Interactions Between Visually and Electrically Elicited Saccades Before and After Superior Colliculus and Frontal Eye Field Ablations in the Rhesus Monkey. *Experimental Brain Research*, 49, pp. 381–392. Reference **CHU**

Schiller, P. H. and M. Stryker (1972). Single-Unit Recording and Stimulation in

Superior Colliculus of the Alert Rhesus Monkey. *Journal of Neurophysiology*, 35, pp. 915–924. Reference **CHU**

Scott, Dana and C. Strachey (1971). Towards a Mathematical Semantics for Computer Languages, edited by J. Fox. *Proceedings of the Symposium on Computers and Automata*, pp. 19–46. Brooklyn, NY: Polytechnic Institute of Brooklyn, NY. Reference **YW2**

Searle, John R. (1980). Minds, Brains, and Programs. *Behavioral and Brain Sciences*, 3, 3, pp. 417–424. Reprinted in *Mind Design*, edited by John Haugeland, pp. 282–306. Cambridge, MA: The MIT Press, 1981. Reprinted in *The Mind's I*, edited by Douglas Hofstadter and Daniel Dennett, pp. 353–373. New York: Basic Books, 1981. Reference **SIM, DEN** [Introduces the "Chinese room experiment," where a room's walls are covered with Chinese symbols and their English counterparts; the question is – if a person is handed a Chinese message and follows a wall-lookup procedure to translate it, does that person know Chinese?]

(1982). The Myth of the Computer: An Exchange. *The New York Review of Books*, June 24, pp. 56–57. (See Dennett, 1982, this bibliography). Reference **DEN**

(1983). *Intentionality: An Essay in the Philosophy of Mind*. Cambridge, UK: Cambridge University Press. Reference **DEN**

(1984a). Panel Discussion: Has Artificial Intelligence Research Illuminated Human Thinking? In *Computer Culture: The Scientific, Intellectual, and Social Impact of the Computer*, edited by Heinz Pagels. Annals of the New York Academy of Sciences, 426. Reference **DEN**

(1984b). *Minds, Brains and Science*. Cambridge, MA: Harvard University Press. Reference **DEN** [Primarily of interest as a recent restatement of the celebrated Chinese-room experiment case against the possibility of AI as anything more than a model of some aspects of human intelligence. Searle makes his stand on the point that structure cannot be inferred from function; thus a computer that behaves intelligently does not warrant the automatic inference that human intelligence has been reproduced, whatever the Turing Test advocates might say. He takes his argument even further: he claims to demonstrate the impossibility of AI. The bones of his argument are that brains cause minds which have mental states, i.e. they have semantics; computer programs are formal, and they are purely syntactic objects; such purely syntactic objects are insufficient to generate semantics; thus programs cannot cause minds.]

Selfridge, O. (1958). Pandemonium: A Paradigm for Learning. Technical Report. (JA-1140). Cambridge, MA: MIT Press. See also National Physical Laboratory (1959). *Mechanization of Thought Processes*. London: Her Majesty's Stationery Office (this bibliography). [Presents one of the classic early parallel models for a cognitive system.]

Sembugamorthy, V. and B. Chandrasekaran (1986). Functional Representation of Devices and Compilation of Diagnostic Problem Solving Systems. In *Experience, Memory and Reasoning*, edited by J. Kolodner and C. Reisbeck, pp. 47–73. Hillsdale, NJ: Lawrence Erlbaum. Reference **CHA**

Shannon, C. (1950). Programming a Computer for Playing Chess. *Philosophical Magazine*, Series 7, 41, pp. 256–275. Reference **DIE, MIC**

Shapiro, A. D. (1987). *Structured Induction in Expert Systems*. Turing Institute Press in association with Addison-Wesley Publishing Co. Reference **MIC**

Shapiro, A. D. and Donald Michie (1986). A Self Commenting Facility for Inductively Synthesised Endgame Expertise, edited by D. Beal. *Advances in*

Computer Chess, vol. IV. Oxford: Pergamon. Reference **MIC**

Shapiro, A. D. and T. Niblett (1982). Automatic Induction of Classification Rules for a Chess Endgame, edited by M. R. B. Clarke. *Advances in Computer Chess*, vol. IV, pp. 73–91. Oxford: Pergamon. Reference **MIC**

Sharkey, N. E. and G. D. A. Brown (1986). Why AI Needs an Empirical Foundation? In *AI: Principles and Applications*, edited by M. Yazdani, pp. 267–293. London: Chapman and Hall [Argues that typical definitions of intelligence are circular or worthless since they rely on accounts of human behavior which is not well explained by computational models. Implementable explanations, they claim, must be grounded in psychological data in order to be useful.]

Sharkey, N. E. and R. Pfeifer (1984). Uncomfortable Bedfellows: Cognitive Psychology and AI. In *AI: Human Effects*, edited by M. Yazdani and A. Narayanan, pp. 163-172. Chichester, UK: Ellis Horwood [They discuss three criteria to be used to decide whether a theory is a good explanation of some cognitive function. The criteria are: demonstration of physical possibility, i.e. a running program; statement of rules of interaction between proposed mechanisms; and, the program must be shown to perform the cognitive function to be explained. They subsequently examine what underlies an AI explanation.]

Shastri, L. (1985). Evidential Reasoning in Semantic Networks: A Formal Theory and its Parallel Implementation. *Technical Report*. (TR-166). Department of Computer Science, University of Rochester. Reference **SMO**

Shepard, R. N. (1975). Form, Formation, and Transformation of Internal Representations. In *Information Processing and Cognition: The Loyola Symposium*, edited by R. Solso. Hillsdale, NJ: Lawrence Erlbaum. Reference **MAR**

Shepherdson, J. (1984). Negation as Failure: A Comparison of Clark's Completed Data Bases and Reiter's Closed World Assumption. *Journal of Logic Programming*, 1, 1, pp. 51–79. Reference **PRZ**

(1985). Negation as Failure. *Journal of Logic Programming*, 2, pp. 185–202. Reference **PRZ**

(1986). Negation in Logic Programming. Draft paper. Reference **PRZ**

Shoham, Y. (1988). *Reasoning about Change: Time and Causation from the Standpoint of Artificial Intelligence*. Cambridge, MA: Mit Press. Reference **PRZ**

Shortliffe, E. H., Axline, S. G., Buchanan, B. G., Merigan, T. C. and Cohen, N. S. (1973). An Artificial Intelligence Program to Advise Physicians Regarding Antimicrobal Therapy. *Computers and Biomedical Research*, 6, pp. 544–560. Reference **SIM**

Simon, Herbert A. (1969). *The Sciences of the Artificial*. Cambridge, MA: MIT Press [A small but stimulating collection of four essays on foundational AI issues. "The Architecture of Complexity" is reprinted here, in which Simon introduces the term "near decomposability" and argues for both the necessity of modularity of complex systems (if we are to understand them), and the probability of such modularity in natural systems.]

(1979). *Models of Thought*. New Haven and London: Yale University Press. Reference **D&D**, **WIN**

(1980). Cognitive Science: The Newest Science of the Artificial. *Cognitive Science*, 4, pp. 33–47 [Cognitive science, being the search for invariants between cognitive systems (human, mechanical, even social), is founded on symbol processing and decomposability. That intelligent systems are adaptive makes the search for invariance particularly difficult.]

(1983). Fitness Requirements for Scientific Theories. *The British Journal for the Philosophy of Science*, 34, 4, pp. 355–365 [Introduces a formalism for describing theories as languages whose expressions are composed of observations, predications over them, etc. Fitness is then judged according to criteria of well-formedness.]

(1983). Why Should Machines Learn? In *Machine Learning*, edited by R. S. Michalski, J. G. Carbonell and T. M. Mitchell, pp. 25–37. Palo Alto, CA: Tioga [Simon expresses the view that developing machine learning is a misguided endeavor.]

Simon, Thomas W. (1979). Philosophical Objections to Programs as Theories. In *Philosophical Perspectives in Artificial Intelligence*, edited by Martin H. Ringle, pp. 225–242. Atlantic Highlands, NJ: Humanities Press. Also Hassocks, Sussex, UK: The Harvester Press. Reference **SIM, P&W, DIE**

(1990). Artificial Methodology Meets Philosophy. In *The Foundations of AI: A Sourcebook*, edited by Derek Partridge and Yorick Wilks, pp. 155–164. Cambridge, UK: Cambridge University Press

Slagle, J. R. (1963). A Heuristic Program that Solves Symbolic Integration Problems in Freshman Calculus. In *Computers and Thought*, edited by E. A. Feigenbaum and J. Feldman. pp. 191–206. New York: McGraw-Hill. Reference **MAR, CAM**

Slator, Brian M., Richard H. Fowler and Imre Balogh (1989). Cognitive Systems and Cognitive Reality. *Proceedings of the 4th Annual Rocky Mountain Conference on Artificial Intelligence*. Denver, CO. pp. 199–206. [Argues that many allusions to psychological plausibility in the AI literature are weak and that these appeals should be more rigorous or left out.]

Sloman, Aaron (1971). Interactions Between Philosophy and AI: The Role of Intuition and Non-Logical Reasoning in Intelligence. *Artificial Intelligence*, 2, 3/4, pp. 209–225. Also in *Proceedings International Joint Conference on AI* (IJCAI–71), pp. 270–278. Imperial College, London [Discusses the relations between philosophy and AI as regards reasoning about time and space. Basically supports Minsky, against McCarthy and Hayes, in the debate over the proper role of formal logic in AI.]

(1978). *The Computer Revolution in Philosophy: Philosophy, Science and Models of Mind*. Hassocks, Sussex, UK: Harvester Press [Sloman looks at many traditional questions of philosophy, and investigates how computers, more specifically AI has, or can, affect the answers to these questions.]

(1978). The Methodology of AI. *AISB Quarterly*, 30, May. [An attack on the traditional symbolic search space paradigm of AI. The paradigm assumes the existence of objectively-specifiable sets of well-defined, independent alternative states as an adequate characterization of a problem. Many problems do not appear to fit comfortably into this mold. Hence the misguided nature of much of AI, based as it is (it is claimed) on false assumptions.]

(1984). The Structure of the Space of Possible Minds. In *The Mind and the Machine*, edited by S. B. Torrance. Chichester, UK: Ellis Horwood [Argues that many organisms have some quality of "mind" and that many different systems should be analyzed as an avenue to understanding the human mind.]

Smith, B. (1982). Reflection and Semantics in a Procedural Language. *Technical Report*. (LCS-TR–272). Cambridge, MA: Massachusetts Institute of Technology Laboratory for Computer Science. Reference **HEW**

Smith, D. V. *et al.* (1983). Coding of the Taste Stimuli by Hamster Brain Stem Neurons. *Journal of Neurophysiology*, 50, 2, pp. 541–558. Reference **CHU**

Smolensky, P. (1983). Schema Selection and Stochastic Inference in Modular Environments. *Proceedings American Association for AI Conference* (AAAI–83). Washington, DC. Reference **SMO**

(1984a). Harmony Theory: Thermal Parallel Models in a Computational Context. In *Harmony Theory: Problem Solving, Parallel Cognitive Models, and Thermal Physics*, edited by P. Smolensky and M. S. Riley. *Technical Report*. (No. 8404). Institute for Cognitive Science, University of California at San Diego. Reference **SMO**

(1984b). The Mathematical Role of Self-Consistency in Parallel Computation. *Proceedings of the Cognitive Science Society* (CSS–6). Reference **SMO**

(1986a). Information Processing in Dynamical Systems: Foundations of Harmony Theory. In *Parallel Distributed Processing*, vol. I, edited by D. E. Rumelhart, J. L. McClelland, and the PDP Research Group. Cambridge, MA: MIT Press/Bradford Books. Reference **SMO, DIE**

(1986b). Neural and Conceptual Interpretations of Parallel Distributed Processing Models. In *Parallel Distributed Processing*, vol. II, edited by J. L. McClelland, D. E. Rumelhart, and the PDP Research Group. Cambridge, MA: MIT Press/Bradford Books. Reference **SMO**

(1986c). Formal Modeling of Subsymbolic Processes: An Introduction to Harmony Theory. In *Advances in Cognitive Science*, edited by N. E. Sharkey, pp. 204–235. Chichester, UK: Ellis Horwood. Reference **SMO**

(1988) On the Proper Treatment of Connectionism, The Behavioral and Brain Sciences, 11, 1, pp. 1–23. Reference **SMO, CHA**. See also P. Smolensky (1987). On the Proper Treatment of Connectionism. *Technical Report*. (CU-CS-359-87). Boulder, CO: Department of Computer Science, University of Colorado at Boulder

(1990). Connectionism and the Foundations of AI. In *The Foundations of AI: A Sourcebook*, edited by Derek Partridge and Yorick Wilks, pp. 306–326. Cambridge, UK: Cambridge University Press

Snyder, J. (1984). Indexing Open-Ended Tree Structures. *BYTE*, 9, May, 5, pp. 406–408, 410–411. Reference **MIC**

Sokolov, E. N. (1963). *Perception and the Conditioned Reflex*. New York: Pergamon Press. Reference **PAR**

Solomonoff, R. J. (1957). An Inductive Inference Machine. *IRE National Convention Record*, pt. 2, pp. 56–62. Reference **CHA**

Sparck Jones, K. (1990). What Sort of Thing is an AI Experiment? In *The Foundations of AI: A Sourcebook*, edited by Derek Partridge and Yorick Wilks, pp. 274–281. Cambridge, UK: Cambridge University Press

(ed.) (1981). *Information Retrieval Experiment*. London: Butterworths. Reference **SPA**

Stanfill, Craig and David L. Waltz (1986). Toward Memory-Based Reasoning. *Communications of ACM*, 29. December [This paper suggests that future AI systems will need to use a form of reasoning that will be based on recalling events from the past that are similar to the current events. This will require memories that will be able to participate actively in problem solving, as opposed to being passive storage entities. Some models for the large parallel machines are given.]

Stefik, Mark J., J. Aikins, R. Balzer, J. Benoit, L. Birnham, F. Hayes-Roth, and E. Sacerdoti (1982). The Organization of Expert Systems, a Tutorial. *Artificial Intelligence*, 18, pp. 135-173. Reference **DIE**

Stein, B. E. (1984). Development of the Superior Colliculus and Visual Function, edited by W. M. Cowan. *Annual Review of Neuroscience*, vol. VII, pp. 95-126. Reference **CHU**

Stich, S. (1983). From Folk Psychology to Cognitive Science. Cambridge, MA: MIT Press

Suppes, P. (1960). A Comparison of the Meaning and Uses of Models in Mathematics and the Empirical Sciences. *Synthese*, 12, pp. 196-214. Reference **YW1**

Sussman, G. J. and R. M. Stallman (1975). Heuristic Techniques in Computer-aided Circuit Analysis. *IEEE Transactions on Circuits and Systems*, CAS-22, pp. 857-865. Reference **MAR**

Sussman, G. J., Terry Winograd, and E. Charniak (1970). MICRO- PLANNER Reference Manual. *Massachusetts Institute of Technology AI Technical Report*. (AI Mem 203). Cambridge, MA: Massachusetts Institute of Technology AI Laboratory. Reference **HEW**

Tarski, A. (1944). The Semantic Conception of Truth. *Philosophy and Phenomenological Research*, vol. IV, pp. 341- 375. Reference **HEW**

(1965). *Logic, Semantics and Metamathematics*. Oxford, UK: Oxford University Press. Reference **YW1**

Thorndike, L. (1923-58). *A History of Magic and Experimental Science*. 8 vols. New York: Columbia University Press. Reference **DIE**

Turing, A. M. (1936). On Computable Numbers, with an Application to the Entscheidungsproblem. *Proceedings of the London Mathematical Society*, Series 2, 42, pp. 230-265. Reprinted in *The Undecidable*, edited by M. Davis. New York: Raven Press. 1965. Reference **DIE**

(1950). Computing Machinery and Intelligence. *Mind*, N.S. 59, pp. 433-460. Reprinted in *Minds and Machines*, edited by A. R. Anderson, pp. 4-30. Englewood Cliffs, NJ: Prentice-Hall, 1964. Reprinted in *Computers and Thought*, edited by E. Feigenbaum and J. Feldman, pp. 11-35. New York: McGraw-Hill, 1963. Reference **DIE** [This is the paper that introduced the "imitation game" (Turing Test) as a way of testing to see if a machine could be considered intelligent.]

(1970). Intelligent Machinery. In *Machine Intelligence*, vol. 5, edited by B. Meltzer and D. Michie. Edinburgh: Edinburgh University Press [". . . . a previously unpublished paper . . . written as a report during [Turing's] 1947 sabbatical leave, which makes forecasts and predictions on the future of digital computers." (Quoted from Capsule Reviews of *Artificial Intelligence: Bibliographic Summaries of the Select Literature*, a Report Store Book.)]

Turkle, Sherry (1987). A New Romantic Reaction: The Computer as Precipitant of Anti-mechanistic Definitions of the Human. Paper given at conference on Humans, Animals, Machines: Boundaries and Projections, Stanford University, April. Reference **WIN**

Turner, R. (1984). *Logics for AI*. Chichester, UK: Ellis Horwood [An introductory source book that presents a spectrum of non-standard logics which may contribute to the formal foundations of AI.]

Ullman, S. (1976). On Visual Detection of Light Sources. *Biological Cybernetics*, 21, pp. 205-212. Reference **MAR**

Van Emden, M. H. and R. A. Kowalski (1976). The Semantics of Predicate Logic as a Programming Language. *Journal of ACM*, 23, 4, pp. 733–742. Reference **PRZ**

Van Gelder, A. (1986/1988). Negation as Failure Using Tight Derivations for General Logic Programs. In *Foundations of Deductive Databases and Logic Programming*, edited by J. Minker, pp. 149-176. Los Altos, CA: Morgan-Kaufmann. Reference **PRZ**

Van Gigch, John P. (1979). A Methodological Comparison of the Science, Systems, and Metasystem Paradigms. *International Journal of Man-Machine Studies*, 11, 5, pp. 651–663 [A somewhat vague discussion of the relative merits of different design methodologies for problem solving. Points up the difficulty of evaluating complex entities in the real world.]

Von Neumann, John (1958). *The Computer and the Brain*. New Haven, CT: Yale University Press ["Part of this book is in finished form and part consists of fragments that were written at the end of von Neumann's life. All of the book repays careful reading." (Bernstein, 1981.)]

Waldrop, M. Mitchell (1984). Artificial Intelligence in Parallel. *Science*, 225, pp. 608–610. Reference **SMO**

Waltz, David L. (1975). Understanding Line Drawings of Scenes with Shadows. In *The Psychology of Computer Vision*, edited by P. H. Winston, pp. 19–91. New York: McGraw-Hill. Reference **MAR**

 (1978). An English Language Question Answering System for Large Relational Database. *Communications of ACM*, 21, pp. 526–539. Reference **SMO**

Waltz, David L. and J. B. Pollack (1985). Massively Parallel Parsing: A Strongly Interactive Model of Natural Language Interpretation. *Cognitive Science*, 9, pp. 51–74. Reference **SMO**

Warren, D. (1977). Implementing PROLOG – Compiling Predicate Logic Programs. *Department of AI, Research Reports*. 1, 2. (Nos. 39, 40). Edinburgh: Edinburgh University. Reference **WEY**

Warrington, E. K. (1975). The Selective Impairment of Semantic Memory. *Quarterly Journal of Experimental Psychology*, 27, pp. 635–657. Reference **MAR**

Waterman, Donald A. (1986). *A Guide to Expert Systems*. New York, Reading, MA: Addison-Wesley. Reference **D&D, WIN**

Webber, B. L. and N. J. Nilsson (eds.) (1981). *Readings in AI*. Palo Alto, CA: Morgan Kaufmann / Tioga [Primarily a collection of papers on specific theories and implementations in AI, but some of the contributions do address the formal foundations of AI. In particular, it contains: Hayes on "The Frame Problem"; McCarthy and Hayes' classic on the epistemological and heuristic distinction in AI; McCarthy on "Circumscription"; and a complete reprint of Weyhrauch's "Prolegomena."]

Weber, Max (1968). *Economy and Society: An Outline of Interpretive Sociology*. Berkeley, CA: University of California Press. Reference **WIN**

Weizenbaum, Joseph (1965). ELIZA – a Computer Program for the Study of Natural Language Communication between Man and Machine. *Communications of ACM*, 9, pp. 36–45. Reference **MAR** [ELIZA was the first of the well-known machine dialogue programs (see also Colby, Weber, and Hilf, 1971, and Colby, 1975, this bibliography), that were once considered candidates for "passing the Turing Test." ELIZA worked by a very simple pattern-matching and slot-filling techniques so as to give the illusion of conversation, but it was of very poor quality. Often the system did no more than respond by typing "TELL ME MORE ABOUT X," where X was the last thing mentioned by the human interlocutor.]

(1976). *Computer Power and Human Reason*. San Francisco: W. H. Freeman. Reference **MAR** [In this book Weizenbaum claimed both to have been horrified by the success of his own ELIZA program and also that programs like the one he had created were socially dangerous in a capitalist economy, as, by extension, was all of AI. The book enormously exaggerates the dangers as it does the success and persuasiveness of the ELIZA program itself.]

Weyrauch, Richard W. (1980). Prolegomena to a Theory of Mechanized Formal Reasoning. *Artificial Intelligence*, 13, 1, 2, pp. 133-170. April. Reprinted in *Readings in Knowledge Representation*, edited by R. J. Brachman and H. J. Levesque, pp. 309–328. Los Altos, CA: Morgan Kaufman, 1985. Reference **HEW** [Short version reprinted in this volume.]

Wielinga, R. J. (1978). AI Programming Methodology. *Proceedings of the AI and Simulation of Behaviour/Gesellschaft fur Informatik Conference on AI*, pp. 355–374. Hamburg. Reference **PAR**

Wiener, Norbert (1948). *Cybernetics, or Control and Communication in the Animal and the Machine*. New York: Wiley. Reference **CHA, DIE**

Wilkes, Kathleen (1980). Brain States. *The British Journal for the Philosophy of Science*, 31, 2, pp. 111-129 [Argues that psychology and neuropsychology need each other and that, furthermore, they overlap. This overlap indicates that there is no meaningful psychological-physical dichotomy, and that there are lawlike principles relating mental states with brain states.]

Wilks, Yorick A. (1968). On-line Semantic Analysis of English Texts. *Mechanical Translation and Computational Linguistics*. Reference **YW1**

(1971). Decidability and Natural Language. *Mind*, N.S. 80, pp. 497–516. Reference **YW1, P&W** [The paper argues that the space of meaningful utterances cannot be determined by any decidable property in the way that the propositional calculus can, and that that fact has consequences for the modeling of human language behavior: particularly that, since it is not a decidable area, there can be no true algorithmic techniques available (as some formal linguists seem to believe), and that human language modeling must be a matter of approximation and best fit, with inevitable failures.]

(1972a). *Grammar, Meaning and the Machine Analysis of Language*. London: Routledge and Kegan Paul. Reference **YW1**

(1972b). Lakoff on Linguistics and Natural Logic. Stanford AI Project Memo. (AIM-170). Stanford, CA: Stanford University. Reference **YW1**

(1974). One Small Head – Models and Theories in Linguistics. *Foundations of Language*, 11, pp. 77–95. Reference **P&W** [Revised version reprinted in this volume.]

(1975a). Preference Semantics. In *Formal Semantics of Natural Language*, edited by E. Keenan. Cambridge, UK: Cambridge University Press. Reference **YW1**

(1975b). Putnam and Clarke and Mind and Body. *The British Journal for the Philosophy of Science*, 26, 3, pp. 213–225 [Argues that Putnam (1960, this bibliography) is wrong but for different reasons than those given by Clarke (1972, this bibliography).]

(1976). Philosophy of Language. In *Computational Semantics*, edited by Eugene Charniak and Yorick Wilks, pp. 205–233. Amsterdam: North-Holland [The chapter expounds and discusses aspects of the work of two sharply contrasting philosophers: Montague and Wittgenstein. The dimension along which they are contrasted is that of the role of formalization in the understanding of language by humans and machines. It is argued that their roles have been fundamentally malign in the case of the first and benign in the case of the second, and that the way in which the philosophy of language bears, and fails to bear, on AI can be illuminated by that contrast.]

(1976). Dreyfus's Disproofs. *The British Journal for the Philosophy of Science*, 27, 2, pp. 177–185 [A defense against the Dreyfus claim that AI has failed, by pointing to more contemporary work; and against the Dreyfus claim that AI is impossible, by pointing to a mistaken idea about the digital/analog distinction.]

(1982). Some Thoughts on Procedural Semantics. In *Strategies for Natural Language Processing*, edited by Wendy G. Lehnert and Martin H. Ringle, pp. 495–516. Hillsdale, NJ: Lawrence Erlbaum. Reference **YW2** [The chapter examines the claims that are often expressed in the phrase "procedural semantics" and asks whether they can provide a theory of the meaning or significance of AI programs. It argues that, properly construed, they can, but also argues that recent attempts to justify the notion by Woods and Johnson Laird are misguided. The function of the theory is to provide an account more adequate than that given by conventional program, or formal, semantics.]

(1984). Machines and Consciousness. In *Minds, Machines, and Evolution*, edited by Christopher Hookway. pp. 105–128. Cambridge, UK: Cambridge University Press [The paper argues that the "independent module" model of human mental processing, espoused at different times by Minsky, Fodor, *et al.*, is a less good machine model of the phenomenon of consciousness than that of "level of language" in the sense of compilation or translation of higher level languages into lower ones. That model would, it is argued, give a better account of the kinds of opacity of mechanism that mental life exhibits (and we may assume, artificial intelligences should have no less opacity than ourselves to their own processes).]

(1986). Bad Metaphors: Chomsky and Artificial Intelligence. In *Noam Chomsky: Consensus and Controversy*, edited by S. and C. Mogdil. Also as Computing Research Laboratory Memoranda in Computer and Cognitive Science. (MCCS–85–8). Las Cruces, NM: New Mexico State University. Reference **P&W**

(1990). Commentary on Smolensky and Fodor. In *The Foundations of AI: A Sourcebook*, edited by Derek Partridge and Yorick Wilks, pp. 327–336. Cambridge, UK: Cambridge University Press

(forthcoming). Reflections on Connectionism. *Journal of Experimental and Theoretical AI*. Reference **YW2**

Wimsatt, W. (1974). Complexity and Organization. In *Proceedings of Philosophy of Science Association for 1972*, edited by K. Schaffner and R. S. Cohen. Dordrecht: Reidel. Reference **DEN**

Winograd, Samuel (1976). Computing the Discrete Fourier Transform. *Proceedings National Academy Science*, 73, pp. 1,005–1,006. Reference **MAR**

Winograd, Terry (1971). Procedures as a Representation for Data in a Computer Program for Understanding Natural Language. *Massachusetts Institute of Technology Project MAC Report*. (MAC-TR-83). Cambridge, MA: Massachusetts Institute of Technology Project MAC. Reference **HEW**

(1972). Understanding Natural Language. New York: Academic Press. Reference **MAR, DIE, R&H** [Arguably the most famous and most often cited work in all of AI, or at least from the language processing contingent. Winograd showed the power of procedural semantics in a closed world. The system, SHRDLU (a printers term), is equally interesting for what it could not do as for what it could.]

(1975). Breaking the Complexity Barrier Again. *SIGPLAN Notices*, 10, 1, pp. 13–30 [Transcript of a talk which argues for AI-style program development environments as an essential aid in the management of complexity of AI systems development. A strong argument against the traditional computer science SAV (Specify-And-Verify) methodology. The second half of the paper is a transcript of the discussion that these suggestions engendered.]

(1979). Beyond Programming Languages. *Communications of ACM*, 22, 7, pp. 391–401 [He argues for a change of emphasis from the traditional computer science concern with the detailed specification of algorithms to the description of properties of the packages and objects with which we build. "Computers are not primarily used for solving well-structured mathematical problems or data processing, but instead are components in complex systems."]

(1980). What Does It Mean to Understand Language? *Cognitive Science*, 4, pp. 209–241 [A rejection of the bulk of previous AI work and a call for a framework of cognitive "interaction and commitment" based on Maturana's hermeneutic study of interpretation and biological foundations of cognition.]

(1987/88). A Language/Action Perspective on the Design of Cooperative Work. *Human-Computer Interaction* 3, 1, pp. 3–30. Reference **WIN**

(1990). Thinking Machines: Can There Be? Are We? In *The Foundations of AI: A Sourcebook*, edited by Derek Partridge and Yorick Wilks, pp. 167–189. Cambridge, UK: Cambridge University Press. Also as Center for the Study of Language and Information Report (CSLI-87-100), Stanford, CA

Winograd, Terry and C. Fernando Flores (1986). *Understanding Computers and Cognition: A New Foundation for Design*. Norwood, NJ: Ablex. Reprinted Addison-Wesley 1987. Reference **WIN, DIE**

Winston, P. H. (1977). *Artificial Intelligence*. Reading, MA: Addison-Wesley. Reference **DIE**

(1978). Learning and Reasoning by Analogy. *Communications of ACM*, 23, 12, pp. 689–703. Reference **DIE**

Woods, William A. (1975). What's in a Link: Foundations for Semantic Networks. In *Representation and Understanding*, edited by Daniel G. Bobrow and Allan Collins, pp. 35–82. New York, San Francisco, London: Academic Press. Reprinted in *Readings in Knowledge Representation*, edited by R. J. Brachman and H. J. Levesque, pp. 217–241. Los Altos, CA: Morgan Kaufmann, 1985 [One of the classic AI essays, and the first in the long series of "What's in a . . ." papers. Woods takes on the world of network knowledge representation (as it existed in the early seventies), lamenting the state of the art and rebuking the population for their slothful, unrigorous ways. He outlines exactly what semantics are (and are not), and cites examples of concepts and relations that should be formally specifiable within a system of semantics, but which the "average" network representation fails to keep straight for various reasons. A must-read paper for anyone seriously interested in representing symbolic knowledge.]

Yahya, A. and L. Henschen (1985). Deduction in Non-Horn Databases. *Journal of Automated Reasoning*, 1, 2, pp. 141–160. Reference **PRZ**

Yourdon, E. (1975). *Techniques of Program Structure and Design*. Englewood Cliffs, NJ: Prentice-Hall. Reference **P&W**

Zucker, S. W. (1976). Relaxation Labelling and the Reduction of Local Ambiguities. *Technical Report*. (TR–451). University of Maryland Computer Science. Reference **MAR**

Index of names